# THE BIRDS OF MICHIGAN

# THE BIRDS OF

*Editor: Gail A. McPeek*
*Consulting Editor: Raymond J. Adams*

*Project Coordinators:*
*Richard Schinkel, Raymond J. Adams, and Charles Nelson*

# MICHIGAN

By

**James Granlund, Gail A. McPeek, Raymond J. Adams**

Philip C. Chu, Jack Reinoehl, Charles Nelson, Richard Schinkel,
Michael Kielb, Stephen Allen and Andrea Trautman

## Original paintings by
**Cyndy Callog, John Felsing, Heiner Hertling, David Mohrhardt,
and Gijsbert van Frankenhuyzen**

*Book Sponsors:*
*Sarett Nature Center, Kalamazoo Nature Center,*
*and First of America Bank*

INDIANA UNIVERSITY PRESS  |  BLOOMINGTON & INDIANAPOLIS

The paper used in this publication meets the minimum requirements of American
National Standard for Information Sciences—Permanence of Paper for Printed
Library Materials, ANSI Z39.48-1984.
⊗™
Manufactured in Singapore

**Library of Congress Cataloging-in-Publication Data**

The Birds of Michigan / editor, Gail A. McPeek ; consulting editor,
Raymond J. Adams ; by James Granlund . . . [et al.] ; original
paintings by Cyndy Callog . . . [et al.]
     p.    cm.
Includes bibliographical references and index.
ISBN 0-253-30122-X (cloth : alk. paper)
1. Birds—Michigan.  I. McPeek, Gail A.  II. Adams, Raymond John.
III. Granlund, James, date.
QL684.M5B57  1994
598.29774—dc20                 94-8521

1  2  3  4  5    00  99  98  97  96  95  94

# CONTENTS

## SPECIES ACCOUNTS

*Birds are listed in the Species Accounts in taxonomic order*
*according to the 1983 American Ornithologists' Union Checklist and its supplements.*
*In the index they are listed alphabetically by common name.*

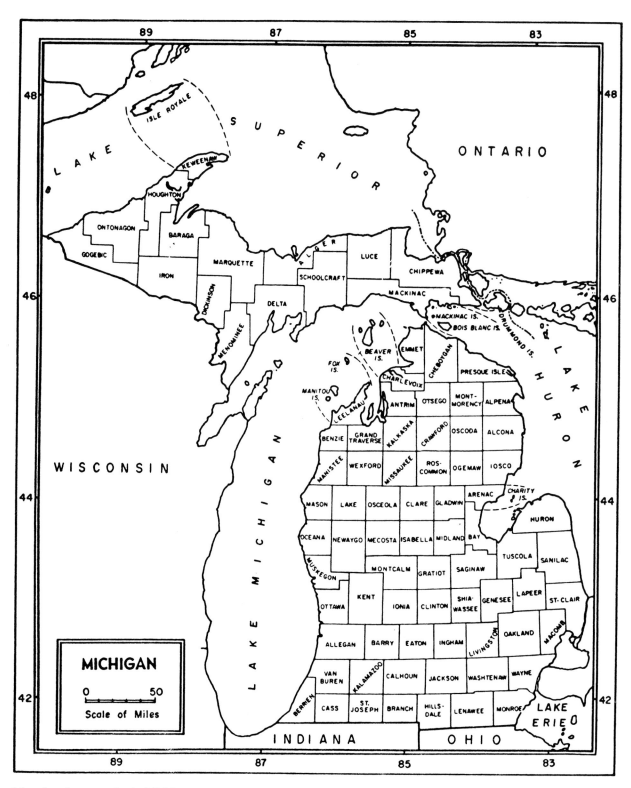

Map showing counties in Michigan
SOURCE: University of Michigan Museum of Zoology

# PREFACE

Much work goes into writing a comprehensive book about Michigan's bird life, and even more effort and expense are involved in illustrating a book with color paintings. No doubt this is why a publication of this magnitude has not been undertaken before, but such was the vision and hope of a few naturalists and long-time birders at the Sarett and Kalamazoo Nature Centers. Given the enormous popularity of bird-watching and bird art, it seemed only natural to strive to produce a book which combines the two. With Michigan's rich tradition in ornithology and natural history, such a book would truly be a masterwork.

Making this vision a reality began with a search for artists. This proved an easy task, as Michigan is home to many talented artists who specialize in paintings of birds and other wildlife. Five well-known artists were recruited to produce original color paintings for the book. Obtaining sponsors for the paintings and a special edition of prints was the next critical step. Production of such a book hinged on the funds raised through these sponsorships. The two nature centers with the help of the artists devoted nearly a year's time to finding enough sponsors to meet the necessary costs for successful completion of the project. The other major phase was the preparation of the book's text. While the artists were busy painting, a small contingent of authors were researching and writing about the avifauna of Michigan.

The text consists of an introduction and accounts for more than 400 species of birds recorded in Michigan through 1993. The individual accounts vary in length depending on the bird's status, with the more lengthy treatments reserved for resident species and shorter writings for casual and accidental visitors. The major topics discussed are status, distribution, abundance, habitat, and seasonal occurrence as well as issues of conservation and popu-

lation trends when applicable. The accounts draw on the large numbers of literary sources for Michigan, from the early writings of Walter Barrows, Norman Wood, and others to the vast quantities of published and unpublished bird records. Invaluable was *The Atlas of Breeding Birds of Michigan*, published in 1991, which served as a significant source of information for the state's nesting species.

The 115 color plates contained within the pages of this book include a total of 223 bird species known to breed in the state. Michigan's endangered and threatened species are featured separately, along with some of the more popular birds such as the Black-capped Chickadee, Eastern Bluebird, and Northern Cardinal. All other plates include two or more species, with both sexes depicted when plumages are significantly different. Most groupings are of closely related species which typically share a similar habitat. For the few instances when this was not possible, unrelated species are shown together. Also included is a special composition of three species which formerly bred in Michigan—the extinct Passenger Pigeon, the extirpated Greater Prairie-Chicken, and the Lark Sparrow.

Every effort was made to produce a book which would have broad public appeal and instill a greater appreciation of birds and bird art. People of all backgrounds, ages, and bird-watching experience will enjoy and treasure this beautiful collector's edition. Not since Wood's 1951 book has there been an all-inclusive volume about all of Michigan's birds, and none of the state's bird publications have ever featured color paintings. What began as a vision is now a reality, and one which the project sponsors, authors, and artists are proud to bring to the people of Michigan.

—Gail A. McPeek

# ACKNOWLEDGMENTS

There are many people deserving of special thanks and recognition for their involvement or assistance with the production of this book. Responsible for the initial planning, preparation, and organization of various aspects of the project were Charles Nelson and Richard Schinkel, representing the Sarett Nature Center; Raymond Adams and Willard Rose, with the Kalamazoo Nature Center; John Gallman, with Indiana University Press; and James Granlund and Gail McPeek. This book never would have come into being were it not for the efforts of these individuals.

Tremendous appreciation is extended to the artists and authors for the time devoted to their paintings and writings. The spouses and families whose lives were affected by the hours their loved ones spent on this project also deserve mention.

A special note of thanks is extended to all individuals who supported this project through their sponsorship of one or more paintings and prints. Your contribution helped make this book possible. A full listing of sponsors is included in the back of the book. We are also extremely grateful to First of America Bank and President John Schreuder for embracing our vision to bring this book to the people of Michigan. Their corporate sponsorship and contribution to the project were instrumental to its success.

Numerous staff members and volunteers of the two sponsoring nature centers provided valuable logistical support. Helping from the Sarett Nature Center was Kathy Nelson along with Dianne Braybrook, Maria Daly, Laura Jasper, Kim McFarland, Rob Pearce, Bob Rickel, and Owen Smith. Assistance at the Kalamazoo Nature Center was provided by Stephen Allen, Mary Louise Avery, Jason Briddell, April Crowley, John Eastman, Brenda Keith, Carol Stefanich, Russell Utych, April Westphal, and Doris Whyment.

The editor and consulting editor would like to acknowledge a few people who assisted with matters involving the book's text and sources of information. James Granlund and Philip Chu helped with reviews and compilation of records for many of the rarer bird species found in the state. Current information for the breeding bird survey was provided by Sam Droege and Bruce Peterjohn at the U.S. Fish and Wildlife Service, while additional data were obtained from the Service's Bird Banding Lab. Also consulted for up-to-date records regarding specific species were Joe Johnson at the Kellogg Bird Sanctuary and Glenn Belyea, John Urbain, and Thomas Weise at the Michigan Department of Natural Resources (DNR) Wildlife Division.

# INTRODUCTION

*Gail A. McPeek*

While we cannot boast as many bird species as the tropical regions of the Americas, the current Michigan bird list does include approximately 400 species, of which about 350 are present on a regular or near-regular basis. Why are we blessed with such a wonderfully diverse avifauna? The reasons are many, but much of the variety can be attributed to the influence of the Great Lakes and the latitudinal juxtaposition of Michigan in a zone where the major northern and southern vegetation types come together. The Great Lakes attract many waterfowl, large wading birds, gulls, terns, and shorebirds, including both common and rare species as well as numerous vagrants. The inclusion of northern Michigan in the boreal zone gives us residents such as the Black-backed Woodpecker, Gray Jay, Boreal Chickadee, and Red Crossbill, while deciduous communities in southern Michigan provide nesting habitat for such southerly distributed species as the White-eyed Vireo and Cerulean, Prothonotary, and Hooded Warblers. Additionally, the state's midwestern location in the United States places us in the ranges of species with eastern or western affinities.

Michigan's landscape was shaped by the glacial events of the Pleistocene, which began some 2 million years ago and ended about 10,000 to 15,000 years ago with the retreat of the last glaciers. These forces carved out the Great Lakes as well as thousands of inland lakes, ponds, rivers, and streams. They also covered much of the land with thick glacial deposits, creating a variety of landforms.

About 70 percent of the state's land mass is surrounded by water, with Lake Superior to the north, Lake Michigan to the west, and Lakes Huron and Erie to the east. This commanding presence of water has a significant influence on climate (known as the "lake effect"), affecting temperatures, the growing season, and precipitation. Landforms in the Upper Peninsula vary from mostly high-relief areas in the west (the only major region in the state where glacial activity exposed the Precambrian bedrock) to low-relief plains in the east. Well-drained loam and clay soils characterize the western region. In contrast, sandy soils typical of outwash and lake border plains prevail in the eastern region, along with poorly drained sites that give rise to peatlands and other wetlands. The divergent topography between these two regions also results in a climatic difference, with the western region having colder minimum temperatures.

The Lower Peninsula also comprises a mix of high- and low-elevation landforms. Most higher-relief areas are toward the Lake Michigan side, including bluffs and sand dunes, while extensive lake border plains dominate lands adjacent to Lakes Huron and Erie. The rich soils characterizing these latter areas, primarily from Saginaw Bay south, provided fertile farmland, but not without extensive draining. The rolling plains and loamy soils which cover much of the southern and central sections of the peninsula became the state's other major farming regions. Outwash plains with thick sand deposits constitute a large portion of the north-central Lower Peninsula, where dry conditions and periodic fires created the distinctive jack-pine plains.

The diversity of plant communities in Michigan stems from the combined influences of landforms, soils, and climate. After the last glaciers receded, the landscape was much like the present-day arctic tundra. The invasion of flora and fauna occurred rapidly, however, and according to Farrand and Eschman (1974), plant and animal communities began to take on a "modern" appearance about 7,000 years ago. Influenced by a mild climate and mostly Alfisol soils, southern hardwoods (beech, maple, oak, hickory, ash, elm) prevailed in the southern Lower Peninsula, with sections of prairie and savanna in the southwest. Also present in the region were extensive marshes and swamps. The cooler climate and mostly Spodsol soils in northern Michigan gave rise to northern hardwood and coniferous (boreal) forest types. These included maple-birch-hemlock, pine-oak, and spruce-fir or spruce-tamarack-cedar communities. In the middle of the state (around the 43rd to 44th parallels) was a transitional zone, often referred to as the "tension zone," where northern and southern plant communities merged.

Not long after the Ice Age, sometime around 10,000 years ago, American Indians arrived in Michigan. Early cultures were hunters and gatherers, while cultures practicing cultivation came much later. Indians lived on the land for thousands of years, and except for the use of fire, their impact on the landscape was minimal. The earliest Europeans reached Michigan about 1640, but these were mostly hunters and fur traders; it was not until the early 1800s that the first major wave of settlers arrived. From that point forward, Michigan's landscape would undergo a dramatic change, this time brought about by man rather than the forces of nature.

An attempt will not be made here to detail the events of logging, farming, mining, and other land uses which followed settlement, as there are numerous books on the subject. A comprehensive and interesting overview of these changes as they relate to bird communities is provided by Richard Brewer in *The Atlas of Breeding Birds of Michigan* (1991). Suffice it to say that the landscape we see today is vastly different from that of 200 years ago.

In fact, when Walter Barrows produced the state's first comprehensive book, entitled *Michigan Bird Life*, in 1912, major alterations had already occurred. Regarding logging he wrote, "Unquestionably the deforesting of the northern parts of the Lower Peninsula has made noteworthy changes in the birds of the region and such changes are still in progress and doubtless will continue, since the axe is commonly followed by fire, and that again by more or less complete reforestation or by the cultivated fields of the farmer and fruit grower." He also noted that the drainage of many of the extensive swamps and marshes "has altered in a marked degree the character of large portions of the state and has changed correspondingly the conditions under which the birds of these regions live."

Today, the landscape of the southern Lower Peninsula is primarily a mix of urban and suburban developments, large agricultural fields (mostly row crops), small woodlots, and an array of disturbed edge and old field habitats. Except for a few remnant patches, the prairies and oak savannas are gone and the vast majority of wetlands have been drained, filled, or otherwise altered. Larger tracts of second-growth forest in southern Michigan are largely limited to our game areas, parks, and other public lands.

While a large portion of northern Michigan has reverted to forest, it is of a less contiguous nature and different composition in many areas. The hot slash fires which followed lumbering killed most pine seeds in the soil, so that many regenerating forests lacked a pine component. Instead, pioneer species with wind-dispersed seeds, particularly aspen and birch, became a common forest type. Also different is the fact that most of today's forests are in an intensively managed state, whether for timber products, wildlife, recreation, or some combination of these. Another change has been the extent of farmland and other open country associated with human habitation in parts of northern Michigan, which has allowed some species to extend their ranges in the state. In some cases, grassland birds are now faring better in many northern counties compared to those in the south.

Other human-related factors which have had a profound impact (positive, negative, or both) on bird populations include bird feeding, nesting habitat provided by human structures, modernization of agriculture, the introduction of chemicals into the environment, and the introduction of nonnative species. Many of the effects of such factors on Michigan's avifauna are addressed in the individual species accounts.

The current landscape in Michigan includes a wide mix of forested and nonforested habitats. For the purposes of this book, descriptions of habitat in the species accounts closely follow those used during the Michigan Breeding Bird Atlas (1983–88), as adopted from the DNR Natural Features Inventory classification.

A brief overview of the major habitat categories is given below.

*Deciduous forest.* Dry deciduous communities are classified as either poplar–white birch, oak-hickory, or oak savanna, with the latter type being of only minor extent in the current landscape. In fact, most oak-hickory and oak savanna habitats were converted to farmland many years ago. On mesic sites, American beech, sugar maple, and a complement of southern hardwoods predominate in mild conditions, while the northern hardwood forest type of sugar maple and yellow birch (with or without beech) occurs in cooler climates. Deciduous swamp and floodplain forests characterize the lowland and riparian habitats in southern Michigan, although many of these sites have been drastically altered. Among the dominant tree species are elms, ashes, red and silver maples, swamp white oak, and sycamore.

*Coniferous forest.* Dry conifer types include pine forests and plantations, mostly red and/or jack pine. White spruce and balsam fir are the primary species in the mesic coniferous type. Considered the true boreal community, these spruce-fir forests are generally uncommon in northern Michigan and are best represented on Isle Royale. Wet coniferous forests with black spruce, tamarack, and/or white cedar are more prevalent in the state, and are most extensive in the glacial lake basins in the eastern Upper Peninsula.

*Mixed deciduous-coniferous forest.* Forests are generally classified as mixed if hardwoods and evergreens each constitute more than 25 percent of the dominant tree species. Oak-pine was a widespread forest type on dry sites prior to settlement, but such communities were mostly replaced by the aspen-birch forest type following the removal of red and white pines. Mesic to wet mixed forests primarily include northern hardwoods (birch-maple-beech) and various conifers such as hemlock, white pine, and balsam fir. Such forests are common in the northwestern Lower Peninsula and northern Upper Peninsula. Other mesic to wet mixed types include white spruce–poplar and northern hardwood–white cedar.

*Nonforested habitats.* The remainder of Michigan's habitats can be classified as nonforested. These range from shrub- and grass-dominated communities to various aquatic habitats (lakes, rivers, streams, etc.) to human environs. The shrub upland category includes a variety of early-successional habitats dominated by shrubs, briers, and saplings, such as those found in regenerating clearcuts or abandoned farmlands. Shrub wetlands occur on poorly drained sites and are typically associated with stream, lake, bog, or marsh borders. Alder, willow, dogwood, and buttonbush are among the dominant plant species. Open wetlands also occur in poorly drained areas but are characterized by mostly herbaceous vegetation. Common examples include sedge meadows, cattail marshes, and open bogs with sphagnum, blueberry, and leatherleaf.

Old field habitats are far more prevalent in today's landscape than native grasslands. Old fields are composed of weedy, mostly nonnative, plants with or without scattered shrubs and trees. Fallow or recently abandoned farm fields provide most of these common, open-country habitats. True grasslands, on the other hand, are scarce in Michigan. Prairies, which were among the first habitats to be farmed, occur in only a few remnant patches or prairie reconstructions, while dune grasses have also been severely affected by human land uses. The stump prairies left in the wake of logging and hot fires are also included in the grassland category. These areas contain various grasses, bracken fern, and the charred stumps of white pine.

The last major types of nonforested habitats are associated with human development and agriculture. Among these are orchards, pastures, hayfields, and row crops; roadsides, rights-of-way, fence-rows, and other "edge" habitats; and urban and residential areas including gardens, yards, lawns, and our many buildings and other artificial structures.

For more detailed descriptions and information on Michigan plant communities, physiographic features, and climate, readers can refer to *Michigan Trees* by Barnes and Wagner (1981); *Regional Landscape Ecosystems of Michigan* by Albert et al. (1986); *Geology of Michigan* by Dorr and Eschmann (1970); *The Climatic Atlas of Michigan* by Eichenlaub et al. (1990); and chapters 3 and 5 in *The Atlas of Breeding Birds of Michigan* (1991). Full citations for these sources are provided in the bibliography.

# SPECIES ACCOUNTS

This comprehensive volume was conceived and written with a broad audience in mind. It was our hope and intention to cover a range of topics and information in the species accounts which would appeal to the general bird enthusiast, the serious bird-watcher, and the scientific community of ornithologists, biologists, naturalists, and others. One important objective was to make the content of the accounts as specific to Michigan as possible, providing only complementary information from general sources such as field guides, encyclopedias, and life history works.

The nomenclature and order of the species accounts follow the current taxonomic classification of North American birds developed by the American Ornithologists' Union. Included are accounts for 398 species of birds which were on the official state list at the end of 1993; this list is continually changing as new birds are documented. There are also brief write-ups for 7 additional species considered "hypothetical," meaning the records do not meet the criteria for inclusion on the list. These species are designated by brackets around the common name. A full accounting of the current Michigan bird list, including documentation criteria and recent changes to the list, is provided in a separate section of the introduction.

The content of the species accounts focuses on several major subject matters. Among these are status, distribution, abundance, history, habitat, and seasonal occurrence in Michigan, along with a general description of North American (or worldwide) breeding and wintering ranges. Issues of population changes and/or conservation are addressed when appropriate. Depending on the individual species, authors had the option of discussing supplementary topics such as plumage, song, life history traits, and subspecies or forms which may occur in the state.

Direct citations within the body of the text were kept to a minimum because of the vast amounts of literature and information consulted. An overview of the many sources and references is given in the following section, and the book's bib-liography acknowledges the primary literary sources. For the more recent records of accidental and casual species gleaned from seasonal surveys or documentation forms, names of the observer(s) were not included so as not to misrepresent or wrongly omit persons involved in the sighting. It is not uncommon for first discovery and the documenting evidence to come from different observers. In some cases, the accounts recognize persons responsible for specimen or historical records and research conducted in the state.

Below is a list of terms and definitions used to describe the status of a species in the state, including frequency of occurrence. Readers will find it beneficial to become familiar with these terms.

GENERAL STATUS TERMS

*Permanent resident:* A species present in the state throughout the year.

*Summer resident:* A species that nests in the state and is present primarily in the breeding season.

*Summer visitor (or visitant):* A species that occurs primarily in the summer but does not nest in the state.

*Winter resident or visitor:* A species that occurs primarily in the winter. (The term "visitor" is generally used if occurrence is more irregular.)

*Migrant:* A species that regularly arrives or passes through in spring or fall. Some are summer or winter residents; others occur in the state only as migrants (also called transients).

*Irregular:* A species that does not occur each year and may show cyclic irruptions.

*Local:* A species of limited distribution.

RELATIVE ABUNDANCE TERMS

*Abundant:* A species found in very large numbers in suitable habitat at the correct season.

*Common:* A species found in large numbers in suitable habitat at the correct season.

*Fairly common:* A species found in moderate numbers in suitable habitat at the correct season.

*Uncommon:* A species found in small numbers in suitable habitat at the correct season.

*Rare:* A species found in very small numbers in suitable habitat at the correct season.

*Casual:* A species somewhat outside its usual range; found at widely spaced intervals in very small numbers, but with an apparent pattern of occurrence.

*Accidental:* A species outside its usual range generally found only a few times in the state (typically 1 to 5 records).

OTHER TERMS

*Hypothetical:* A species that does not satisfy the criteria for inclusion on the official state list.

*Extinct:* A species known or believed to be extinct.

*Extirpated:* A species once present in Michigan but no longer found here, although still present in other areas and may possibly occur here again.

*Exotic:* A species believed to have escaped from captivity that has not become established in a feral (wild) state.

*Introduced:* A species which has been purposely introduced and has become established in the state.

*Vagrant:* A species found out of normal range.

The seasonal terms of spring, summer, fall, and winter correspond to those periods used in the Michigan seasonal survey. The spring period is March through May, summer is June through July, fall is August through November, and winter is December through February.

When discussing distributional patterns, reference is made to various regions in the state. The *southern Lower Peninsula* is the region from the southern border north to Muskegon, Saginaw, and Huron counties. The *northern Lower Peninsula* extends from Oceana and Bay counties north to the Straits of Mackinac. The *Upper Peninsula* includes the entire northern peninsula area and Isle Royale. Other commonly used designations are southwestern Michigan (the western half of the southern Lower Peninsula); southeastern Michigan (the eastern half of the southern Lower Peninsula); the Thumb (that area which generally includes Huron, Sanilac, Tuscola, Lapeer, and St. Clair counties); the northwestern Lower Peninsula (the western counties of the northern Lower Peninsula); the northeastern Lower Peninsula (the eastern counties of the northern Lower Peninsula); the north-central Lower Peninsula (that area centered around Kalkaska, Crawford, and Oscoda counties and corresponding to the dry pine forests and jack-pine plains); the western Upper Peninsula (from Marquette County west); the eastern Upper Peninsula (from Alger County east); and the south-central Upper Peninsula (Delta, Menominee, and Dickinson counties). A map showing county names is provided in the front of the book for reference. County names are frequently used to delineate distributions and identify specific places or locations of records.

## SOURCES OF INFORMATION

We are fortunate in Michigan to have such a rich collection of natural history and ornithological writings and records. At our disposal was a wide range of sources and references allowing us to produce this comprehensive and up-to-date publication. Available records and writings through 1992 and, in many cases, through 1993 were reviewed and incorporated in the text when appropriate. With respect to accidental, casual, and rare species, emphasis was placed on documented records, with inclusion of undocumented reports in some accounts, but not all. This does not mean, however, that those records not mentioned did not occur.

The primary literary sources were *Michigan Bird Life* by Barrows (1912); *The Birds of Michigan* by Wood (1951); *A Distributional Check-list of the Birds of Michigan* by Zimmerman and Van Tyne (1959); *A Distributional Checklist of the Birds of Michigan* by Payne (1983); and *The Atlas of Breeding Birds of Michigan* by Brewer, McPeek, and Adams (1991). Both Barrows and Wood provide a thorough accounting of the various historical writings (for example, Sager 1839, Kneeland 1857, Gibbs 1879, 1885, and Swales 1903–1904), while the other three major publications deal primarily with information from the modern era, but with reference to changes in records or bird populations over time.

Along with these major state books and checklists, a large number of regional and local publications were consulted. Such sources were particularly useful for their information on timing of migration, breeding chronology, winter occurrence, and local patterns of distribution and abundance. Another extremely valuable source was the Michigan seasonal survey, initiated in 1957–58 for the purpose of publishing state bird records on a seasonal basis, including uncommon to rare sightings, noteworthy concentrations and high or low counts at a location, and early and late dates of migration and breeding. (These surveys were published in the *Jack-Pine Warbler* from 1958 to 1989 and 1991 to 1993, and beginning in 1994 in the new state journal, *Michigan Birds and Natural History*.)

Other major sources of Michigan information were the federal breeding bird surveys (1966 to present) and Audubon Christmas bird counts (including data from 1959–60 to 1992–93). The breeding bird survey is a standardized monitoring program which involves bird counts conducted on 25-mile routes located throughout the state. Similarly, the Christmas bird counts help document and monitor winter populations through an annual census conducted in a predetermined area. Data sets for both programs are housed at the Kalamazoo Nature Center. Christmas bird counts are published in *American Birds* as well as the state journal. Analyses of the breeding bird surveys were provided by the U.S. Fish and Wildlife Service Office of Migratory Bird Management.

Along with publishing thousands of Michigan bird records, the *Jack-Pine Warbler* contains hundreds of articles and notes on research, surveys, and bird sightings for the state and Great Lakes region. Valuable information was also available from a variety of other sources, mostly unpublished. Among these were records from bird-banding and migration-monitoring stations; Audubon feeder counts; DNR surveys, records, and projects (for example, the Nestbox Networker); and federal and state reports for endangered, threatened, and special concern species.

Supplementing all of these Michigan sources were many books and journals from other states and Canadian provinces (mostly in the Great Lakes and Midwestern regions), as well as ornithological journals and numerous general publications about birds (field guides, population biology and life history books, etc.).

## MICHIGAN'S BIRD LIST

Just as a birder's personal species list increases with experience and improved skill, Michigan's list of birds has grown over the years as field identification and equipment have evolved, and as more and more people have taken an interest in bird-watching. State lists around the turn of the century, such as those of Cook (1893) and Barrows (1912), included approximately 320 to 330 species. More recently, Payne's 1983 checklist contained 370 species, and by 1993 the total was approaching 400.

It is important to emphasize, however, that the changes which have occurred on these lists through the years are more than simple addition of species. As criteria and evidence for documentation have changed over time, some species have been removed from the official list while others have been added. One major difference stems from the fact that early lists were normally compiled from specimen records only, while current bird records committees also consider diagnostic photographs, banding records, tape recordings, and well-documented sight records as evidence. Museum collecting is no longer a common practice, and most current information on bird distribution and occurrence comes from field observations.

Further complicating the production of bird lists are the continual modifications in taxonomic classification, which can result in an increase or decrease in numbers through splitting or lumping of species. Other problems arise from the deterioration or loss of specimens, the absence of sufficient location data for older specimen records, and the release or escape of captive birds. This latter problem involving the question of origin is especially prevalent among certain waterfowl and gamebirds which are commonly kept in captivity.

Keeping the above information in mind, we can now turn our attention to Michigan's current bird list. A total of 398 species have been accepted by the Michigan Bird Records Committee through 1993. This list includes all species documented by a verified specimen, photograph, or banding data, and in a small number of cases, by sight record only. We also chose to provide brief accounts for 7 species (Black-bellied Whistling Duck, Barnacle Goose, Black Vulture, Crested Caracara, Willow Ptarmigan, Ivory Gull, Mountain Bluebird) which do not meet the current committee's selection criteria, but have been on lists in the past, either officially or "hypothetically." Readers should refer to the individual accounts for details regarding the reasons for their hypothetical status.

There are a number of other species that have been reported in the state which are presently not accepted by the committee. Among these are sightings which lacked physical evidence to qualify as the state's first record (for example, Yellow-billed Loon, Anhinga, Long-billed Curlew, Black Skimmer, Swainson's Warbler). Some of these species, however, have been seen by reliable observers and were carefully described. Other birds seen in the state can be classified as introduced but not established, such as the Gray Partridge, or as exotic. Species in this latter category include escaped or released captives, such as Greater Flamingo, Bar-headed Goose, Chukar, Monk Parakeet, as well as a few other waterfowl and parrot species. For more detail on these other species which have been reported in Michigan, readers can refer to Payne (1983) and other past publications, or to the reports of the Michigan Bird Records Committee.

Contained within the current Michigan list of 397 species are 233 birds which are known to have bred at least once in the state. The remainder of the list is made up of a wide variety of migrants, winter residents, and casual or accidental visitors. The list includes one extinct species, the Passenger Pigeon, a formerly abundant breeding resident in the state. Some authors suspect that the extinct Carolina Parakeet was found here as well, but there is no proof supporting such a claim. Also on the list is the nearly extinct Eskimo Curlew, which was known to occur in Michigan as a migrant many years ago. There are presently two species with the status of extirpated. The first is the Greater Prairie-Chicken, formerly a permanent resident. The second is the Lark Sparrow, considered extirpated as a breeding resident but still found in the state as a rare migrant and visitor.

A total of 19 species are considered endangered or threatened in Michigan. Among the endangered species are the Peregrine Falcon, King Rail, Piping Plover, Barn Owl, Short-eared Owl, Loggerhead Shrike, and Kirtland's Warbler. Those designated as threatened are the Common Loon, Least Bittern, Osprey, Bald Eagle, Red-shouldered Hawk, Merlin, Yellow Rail, Caspian Tern, Common Tern, Long-eared Owl, Yellow-throated Warbler, and Prairie Warbler. The Michigan DNR also maintains a list of species of special concern, which includes such birds as the American Bittern, Black-crowned Night-Heron, Northern Harrier, Spruce Grouse, Common Moorhen, Forster's Tern, Black Tern, Prothonotary Warbler, Louisiana Waterthrush, Hooded Warbler, and Western Meadowlark.

Those readers interested in the more rare and unusual records will find that 30 species have been upgraded (from hypothetical) or added to the state list since Payne's 1983 checklist, which included records through 1982: Pacific/Arctic Loon, Garganey, Mississippi Kite, Ferruginous Hawk, Prairie Falcon, Snowy Plover, Wilson's Plover, Black-necked Stilt, Mew Gull, Sandwich Tern, Arctic Tern, White-winged Dove, Rufous Hummingbird, Golden-fronted Woodpecker, Hammond's Flycatcher, Vermilion Flycatcher, Gray Kingbird, Fork-tailed Flycatcher, Clark's Nutcracker, Sage Thrasher, White/Black-backed Wagtail, Virginia Warbler, Townsend's Warbler, Painted Redstart, Western Tanager, Cassin's Sparrow, Black-throated Sparrow, Chestnut-collared Longspur, Brambling, and Gray-crowned Rosy Finch.

While the majority of these species were substantiated by physical evidence (specimen or diagnostic photograph), others were accepted based on well-documented sight records, usually with several corroborating observers, but not always. Among the important considerations for such reports are the competence of observer(s), viewing conditions, vagrancy patterns, and the degree to which the bird could be mistaken for another species. Persons observing an unusual bird at their feeder or in the field are strongly encouraged to obtain good photographs (when possible), find others to corroborate the sighting (preferably an experienced birder), and immediately report the information for documentation.

# THE BIRDS OF MICHIGAN

# RED-THROATED LOON
## (*Gavia stellata*)

The Red-throated Loon, the smallest and most widely distributed of the five loon species in the world, is an uncommon migrant and casual winter visitor to Michigan. Every spring and fall, a relatively small segment of the continent's population passes through the Great Lakes region as they travel between their summer and wintering grounds. Breeding occurs on lakes and ponds throughout the arctic tundra, and winters are spent along the Atlantic and Pacific coasts, and sporadically on the Great Lakes. This species has also been known to nest along the north shore of Lake Superior.

In Michigan, most Red-throated Loon sightings come from coastal waters during the months of April, May, September, October, and November. Occasionally, individuals are sighted on rivers and inland lakes, and in other months of the year. The sporadic winter records usually coincide with milder weather conditions. Singles have been reported on five Michigan Christmas bird counts since 1960, and in 1991–92 an extraordinary seven were seen on the Coloma count (Berrien County).

Southern Lake Michigan is one of the regular stopover spots for this aquatic bird, particularly off the shores of Berrien County, but the premier place to see Red-throated Loons is Whitefish Point, a well-known migratory hot spot on the southeastern shore of Lake Superior. Annual counts conducted by the Whitefish Point Bird Observatory typically record 200 to 300 individuals each spring and 100 to 200 in the fall, with individual flocks as large as 10. The spring flight usually peaks between 15 and 31 May, while the fall movement is more drawn out, beginning in August and lasting into November, with the bulk of the migration in September and October.

Most spring migrants are in breeding plumage, and the trademark red throat may be visible if the lighting is right or the bird is close to shore. More often, an observer must rely on body shape and flight pattern to distinguish this species from a Common Loon. In fall and winter plumage, loons are much paler, and separating the two species is more difficult. Profile is again the best distinguishing character for loons in flight. For a bird on the water, a paler gray head, extensive white throat, and slender, slightly upturned bill identify the Red-throated Loon.

Before operations began at the Whitefish Point Bird Observatory, the status of this loon in Michigan was clearly underestimated. Barrows (1912) mentions few records but said it was found only in winter, or at least from fall until spring. He did indicate that spring sightings were more frequent than fall and that it was seen every spring in St. Joseph, Berrien County. Wood

*Common Loon*
DAVID MOHRHARDT

(1951) later characterized it as a rare transient and winter visitant, as did Zimmerman and Van Tyne in 1959.

Standardized counts conducted at the Observatory have greatly improved our knowledge about Red-throated Loons in the state, including recognition of identification features in flight. There even appears to have been an increase in numbers passing Whitefish Point since counts began, but more long-term data are needed to see if this is a real trend rather than observer bias. —Gail A. McPeek

# PACIFIC / ARCTIC LOON
## (*Gavia pacifica / arctica*)

These two species (formerly classified as one) must be considered together since they are inseparable in the field and either could occur in the state accidentally. Pacific Loons nest on tundra and taiga lakes in Alaska and northern Canada to Hudson Bay, and winter primarily along the Pacific coast and rarely along the Atlantic. The Arctic Loon breeds in Eurasia (where it is called the Black-throated Diver) and is probably the least likely of the two species to reach Michigan, though it, too, has been recorded along the East Coast. Since 1983 there have been at least nine documented sight records of a Pacific / Arctic Loon in Michigan. Eight are from Whitefish Point between the dates of 12 May and 13 June, with most in the last two weeks of May. These wayward loons were spotted along the Lake Superior shoreline during migration. All were in breeding plumage, which includes a distinctive silver-gray head and black throat and chin. In flight, the combination of gray head and checkered back is usually the recognizable field mark. The ninth Michigan report is of a Pacific / Arctic Loon in breeding plumage on 6–8 October 1986 at Agate Harbor, Keweenaw County. It is possible that other individuals have gone by unidentified in autumn, when typically they are in their duller winter plumage. —Gail A. McPeek

# COMMON LOON
## (*Gavia immer*)

Of the five loon species inhabiting the northern regions of the world, the breeding range of only the Common Loon extends southward to reach the northern United States. Consequently it is the most well known of its family, not to mention one of our most popular birds, with its picture adorning mailboxes, sweatshirts, t-shirts, calendars, cards, and a plethora of other items. People's fascination with loons goes back a long way, evident in the myths and legends of Native Americans and early civilizations across the North. You can read about many of these stories in the numerous books about the Common Loon or other loon species.

Today our fascination with these aquatic birds has turned into a desire for preservation. While Common Loons still nest abundantly across Canada and Alaska and a few states, such as

Minnesota, Wisconsin, and Maine, their populations have declined or disappeared in other northern states, namely those where human densities are high and use of lakes has conflicted with the loon's needs. Michigan has thousands of lakes, and although there is no mention of approximate loon numbers in the early literature, we do know the species was common throughout the state, breeding to the southern border and slightly beyond into northern Ohio and Indiana. Declines resulting in a northward retraction of its range began around the turn of the century, such that by 1960, nesting pairs were extremely rare in the southern Lower Peninsula.

The Common Loon's current North American range does not reach as far south, and in Michigan the species has vacated all of the southern Lower Peninsula except for a few pairs each in Barry and Montcalm counties. Breeding pairs are still fairly common in northern Michigan, though numbers are certainly less than they once were, and in some areas declines are readily apparent. One such area is the eastern Upper Peninsula, where a large percentage of lakes no longer have nesting pairs, and surveys have documented a 50% drop in numbers in this region (Evers 1992).

Results of recent surveys, including the Breeding Bird Atlas, place Michigan's current loon population somewhere around 350 to possibly as high as 450 pairs, with hundreds of nonbreeders summering primarily on the Great Lakes. Isle Royale and the southwestern Upper Peninsula have the largest concentrations of nesting pairs, and birds seem to be holding their own in the more remote sections of the northern Lower Peninsula.

The loon's disappearance from nearly all of southern Michigan coincided with human population growth and encroachment of lakes, with shoreline development and recreational activities eventually driving loons away. The more recent declines in the north are associated with these same factors but also with other threats, some of which we do not yet know the full extent or impact of. These include contaminants such as mercury which accumulate in the loon's food chain, mortality in commercial fishing nets in the Great Lakes, lead poisoning from the ingestion of lead sinkers, and lake acidification. Researchers are now investigating these problems in Michigan and other parts of the range.

Common Loons occur in the state for a good part of the year, not departing until November or early December for their wintering areas, which we now know to be primarily in coastal waters (Gulf or Atlantic) around Florida owing to recoveries of some banded loons from Michigan. Arrival in spring begins in March in the south, with breeding residents reaching the northern Lower and the Upper Peninsula in April to early May. It is amazing how loons suddenly appear on the day (or day after) iceout occurs on a lake. In addition to the return of nesting pairs, there is a substantial later migration of birds bound for lakes farther north. The Whitefish Point Bird Observatory is an ideal spot to witness this event; more than 1,000 Common Loons may be seen there in a day during peak flights in early May.

April and May are a time of great activity, as loons partake in their territorial and pair-bonding rituals highlighted by chases, bill-dipping ceremonies, and haunting yodels, wails, and tremolos. Many people have probably heard loon calls on television or recordings, but there is nothing like the real experience provided by a full nighttime chorus in the heart of loon country.

Most Michigan loons are nesting by the end of May. Lake islands or bog mats are the most optimal nest sites, providing better protection from mammalian predators. If these are not available, a marshy shoreline will usually suffice. Loons are very susceptible to disturbance during incubation (26 to 31 days); this is a critical time for people to keep their distance. Two-egg clutches are typical, with the first chick hatching 12 to 24 hours before the second. Sibling rivalry can be intense, and survival of one chick is more common than two. It takes nearly all summer for the chicks to grow, and the adults often depart the lake to join other loons, leaving their young to follow later.

The Common Loon was placed on Michigan's list of threatened species in 1987, after surveys indicated the magnitude of declines in parts of the state. A comprehensive recovery plan has since been prepared, outlining important steps for loon conservation including habitat protection, monitoring, research, management, public education, and enforcement of laws. There is also an active citizens' group, the Michigan Loon Preservation Association, which has quickly grown into a major force behind preserving loons for future generations of Michigan residents to enjoy.
—Gail A. McPeek

# PIED-BILLED GREBE
## (*Podilymbus podiceps*)

The Pied-billed Grebe is a shy inhabitant of ponds, marshes, and lakes throughout Michigan. This highly aquatic bird feeds by diving underwater to catch insects and small fish. It can escape attention by swimming with only its head above water, and this is the method (along with diving) often chosen to avoid danger. In fact, few birders have ever seen this species in flight.

The most familiar of our grebes, the Pied-bill ranges throughout the Western Hemisphere, breeding from central Canada south to Argentina and Chile. It withdraws from the north in the fall as ponds and lakes freeze, wintering from the lower Great Lakes and British Columbia south. In Michigan, this species occurs in both peninsulas as a common migrant and fairly common summer resident. During the 1980s Breeding Bird Atlas project, Pied-bills were found to breed most frequently in the southwestern part of the Lower Peninsula. Small numbers also winter locally in southern Michigan.

The nesting habitat of the Pied-billed Grebe is various marshy bodies of water. Reeds or other emergent vegetation are required to provide cover for the nest, with nearby open water for feeding. The species is seen on large open lakes during migration, and in

*Pied-billed Grebe*
*American Coot*
*Common Moorhen*
Gijsbert van Frankenhuyzen

GIJSBERT-1993

the early fall, favored shallow lakes may host groups of 30 to 50 individuals. Pied-bills are seen only occasionally on the Great Lakes, and then on shallow inlets and bays, never in open water.

These grebes, clever at hiding in their marshy nesting areas, are most often detected by their loud call—a series of ten throaty "kowp" notes, slowing down at the end. This call is one of those mysterious spring marsh sounds for which it is difficult to trace the source. Outside the breeding season, this species is completely silent.

Spring arrival of the Pied-billed Grebe in southern Michigan usually commences in the latter half of March. Warm weather, which causes an early breakup of inland ice, will sometimes bring a few individuals north early, even in February, though this is the exception. Observations in Hillsdale County suggest that Pied-bills arrive, on average, about ten days after the first ice breaks up. This slight delay is necessary for the survival of a species that is helpless on land or ice, and can obtain food only from underwater. Passage of migrants continues through April, but any Pied-billed Grebe seen in the Lower Peninsula in May is probably nesting locally.

The nest is hidden in thick vegetation; the bulky structure floats in water rather than being suspended. Eggs, numbering five to seven, are laid in May, June, or sometimes as late as July. The incubation period is about three and a half weeks, and the young are able to swim shortly after hatching. The downy chicks, protectively patterned with dark lines and spots, ride on their parents' backs when small. In about six weeks the young have attained their juvenal plumage, similar to that of breeding adults but lacking the dark throat and ring about the bill.

By August these grebes are dispersing from their nesting areas and may show up at sites where they do not breed. Fall migration is very prolonged, with the greatest passage in southern Michigan from mid-September to mid-November. A few remain until right before freeze-up, and this species is always detected on 5 to 15 Christmas bird counts in the state, usually in numbers totaling one to three dozen. Overwintering is observed where power plants or other activity keeps inland lakes open for the entire season.

Walter Barrows in 1912 described this species as nesting abundantly throughout the state. It has certainly decreased in numbers to some extent since then. Many of the small ponds and marshes where it nested are now unsuitable or completely gone as a result of drainage, removal of vegetation, pollution, or a high level of disturbance. However, those who wish to observe this interesting waterbird may still locate it in every county in the state. —Jack Reinoehl

summer visitant in Michigan. It breeds mainly through the Canadian Prairie Provinces west to central Alaska, and winters on both the Atlantic and Pacific coasts.

First arriving migrants begin appearing in the southern portions of the state in mid-March and the northern portions in early April. The migration peaks by mid-April in the south and late April in the north. Most sightings are of individual birds or groups of 30 or less, but sometimes larger numbers are seen. Examples include 260 on 16–17 April 1992 at the Midland Co-generation Venture Ponds (Dow Ponds), Midland County; 190 on 2 April 1993 migrating past New Buffalo, Berrien County; and a staggering 1,000+ on 29 April 1983 on Sunday Lake, Gogebic County. Rarely birds linger into mid-June, and there are even a few records from July, such as individuals on 12 July 1976 in Muskegon County and on 29–30 July 1992 at Nayanquing Wildlife Area, Bay County.

Recent autumn migration counts in the Upper Peninsula at Whitefish Point, Chippewa County, and at Agate Harbor, Keweenaw County, indicate that first returns occur in early August, suggesting the aforementioned records in July were simply unusually early fall migrants. Regardless, most fall migrants begin appearing in early to mid-September, with the migration dragging out well into November. As in spring, most groups encountered are quite small, but occasionally larger numbers are seen. Examples include 300+ on 7 November 1987 at Tawas Point, Iosco County, and 586 on 11 September 1992 at Agate Harbor, Keweenaw County. During both spring and fall migrations, Horned Grebes are most abundant on the Great Lakes, but good numbers are also seen on larger inland lakes.

Scattered birds overwinter on the Great Lakes, appearing occasionally on open water in inland locations. During Michigan Christmas bird counts from 1970 to 1992, individuals were recorded each year, with totals ranging from 310 in 1991–92 to a low of 5 in 1973–74. In winter Horned Grebes are most abundant in northern Lake Michigan in the Leelanau County area, where as many as 92 were reported as late as 27 December in 1991.

There are no confirmed nesting records for the Horned Grebe in Michigan, although early writers indicated it bred in the St. Clair Flats and along the Detroit River. No breeding evidence was collected during the Michigan Breeding Bird Atlas; however, the Ontario atlas project did record several summer individuals in southern Ontario and postulated that some breeding may occur in the St. Clair marshes around Walpole Island. This suggests that a similar situation may exist in these difficult-to-census areas on the Michigan side. —James Granlund

# HORNED GREBE

### (*Podiceps auritus*)

Unlike the "horns" of the Great Horned Owl, those of the Horned Grebe are golden feathers that form a wide band extending from behind the eye to the nape, resembling ears more than horns. Exquisitely colored in the breeding season, this medium-sized grebe is a common migrant, rare winter resident, and casual

# RED-NECKED GREBE

### (*Podiceps grisegena*)

Recent discoveries about the migration of the Red-necked Grebe present an excellent example of how much remains to be learned about Michigan bird life. Once thought to be an uncommon but regular migrant through the state, this species has been recently documented by autumn censuses at Whitefish Point Bird Observatory to be an abundant fall migrant in eastern Lake Superior.

Counts at the Observatory in 1990, 1991, and 1992 tallied 11,025, 12,882, and 18,789 Red-necked Grebes, respectively, including a staggering 5,079 individuals on 18 August 1992. The census has revealed the migration to be not only larger than expected, but also initiated in late July, much sooner than expected. Recent counts in the Keweenaw Peninsula are finding similar results. There is not an analogous migration in the spring, although several hundred individuals have been seen in some years at Whitefish Point.

Even though quite abundant at the aforementioned locations, the Red-necked Grebe is uncommon in the rest of the state, being seen in small numbers in the northern portions of the Great Lakes on migration and casually in the southern portions of the state and at inland locations. The spring migration is initiated in late March and early April, with birds passing through well into May, and into early June in the Upper Peninsula.

Migrants begin returning by late July in the Upper Peninsula, reaching peak numbers from late August through early September. Apparently most birds must pass directly on to their wintering areas on the Atlantic coast, as few are seen in the southern portions of the state. Those that do appear in the south begin arriving in September and continue through November. Some birds attempt to overwinter, with individuals often being seen well into December. On Christmas bird counts from 1970 to 1992, 19 individuals were recorded, mainly from northern Lake Michigan.

Summering Red-necked Grebes are very rare in the state, with few published reports. There is one known breeding record, that of a nest found on 16 June 1976 in a marsh of dense cattails and sedges in Cedarville Bay in northern Lake Huron (Mackinac County). Although the original nest was abandoned, researchers were able to document renesting and the eventual hatching of three young. The family group was last observed on 28 September. Visits to the site in subsequent years did not reveal further breeding. There have been no confirmed nesting records since, indicating that Red-necked Grebes breeding in Michigan must be a very rare event. This species breeds across the Northern Hemisphere, and in North America is found from Minnesota west to the Pacific coast and north to central Alaska, with most wintering on the Atlantic and Pacific coasts. This species has been known to breed peripheral to its range as far east as New Hampshire. —James Granlund

## EARED GREBE
### (*Podiceps nigricollis*)

The "ears" of the Eared Grebe are really golden-yellow feathers located just behind the eye which are present only during the breeding season. The species name *nigricollis*, meaning "black neck," is perhaps a more useful reference, as it describes a trait that is apparent throughout the year. This handsome grebe is a rare but regular migrant and summer visitor to Michigan. Despite its presence in summer, breeding has not been confirmed within the state.

The first record of this species in Michigan was of a well-described bird on 22 November 1955 in Benton Harbor, Berrien County. The first physical evidence came ten years later when an emaciated Eared Grebe was found near Marlette, Lapeer County, on 20 January 1965. This bird later died in rehabilitation, and the specimen is housed at the University of Michigan Museum of Zoology. In the early 1970s more reports began to trickle in, and from 1979 to the present the species has been reported annually. Encounters have occurred in all months of the year, but most sightings are from early April to early November.

Without a doubt the most frequent location for this species has been the Muskegon Wastewater System, where as many as five individuals have been seen at a time. From 1979 to 1993, Eared Grebes were reported at this site every year but 1986. Many of these reports involved oversummering birds, leading many to postulate breeding at this location. Even more tantalizing were reports of birds at the Midland Cogeneration Venture Ponds (Dow Ponds), Midland County. On 27 May 1990 a pair appeared at this location and were seen frequently until 25 June, only to reappear 28 August with another individual in winter (juvenile?) plumage. While this incident is highly suggestive of breeding, it is insufficient for confirmation. Other locations where this species has been frequently recorded include the Fremont Sewage Ponds, Newaygo County, and the harbors along Lake Michigan in Berrien County.

Other Great Lakes states have had a similar experience with this species, with its being unrecorded or exceptionally rare prior to the mid-1900s and becoming increasingly regular in the 1970s and 1980s. Whether this is a function of a range expansion, a change in migration pattern, or simply better coverage and field observation techniques is difficult to ascertain. Currently this species breeds throughout the Northern Hemisphere, and here in North America, mainly from the Great Plains west to the Great Basin and south to California and Texas. It winters in the southern extreme of this range and south as far as Guatemala. —James Granlund

## WESTERN GREBE
### (*Aechmophorus occidentalis*)

The genus name *Aechmophorus* means "spear bearer," an apt description of this elegant waterbird with its blade-like bill. A species of western North America, the Western Grebe breeds from the northern Great Plains west to Washington and south to central Mexico, and winters primarily on the Pacific coast. Although this grebe is probably a casual transient to Michigan, its exact status in the state is complicated by the 1985 split of the Western Grebe complex into two species, the Western and Clark's (*A. clarkii*) Grebes. Michigan records prior to this split were not adequately documented to differentiate which new species they represented. Since the new classification, the first fully documented Western Grebe was an individual which appeared at New Buffalo, Berrien County, from 6 to 12 November 1992. The individual was examined closely by many observers, and diagnostic photographs were obtained. Likely the same bird reappeared at that location on 21 November 1993.

Prior to the New Buffalo record, there were a number of Western Grebe sightings which should now all be relegated to

H.C.Hertling

*Aechmophorus* species. Included in these records are one bird photographed at Seney National Wildlife Refuge on 15 August 1985. Although the picture clearly shows it to be an *Aechmophorus* grebe, it does not show sufficient detail to ascertain the facial pattern or the critical bill color. Other physical evidence includes a specimen at the Grand Rapids Public Museum which was said to have been collected on 17 February 1917 in Kent County. This old taxidermy mount needs to be cleaned and studied further to ascertain its true affinity; however, more troubling is the lack of an attached specimen tag, making its true origin uncertain. Among the nine published Michigan sight records, dates range from 23 April to 12 November, with Berrien County and the Muskegon Wastewater System having multiple sightings. —James Granlund

# NORTHERN GANNET
## (*Sula bassanus*)

Few seabirds reach Michigan, but one that has is the Northern Gannet, an accidental visitor from the North Atlantic. The closest populations to the Great Lakes nest on islands and cliffs around the Gulf of St. Lawrence in northeastern Canada and winter south along the Atlantic and eastern Gulf coasts. Periodically small numbers of immature gannets apparently follow the St. Lawrence River to the eastern Great Lakes, with occasional birds wandering as far as western Lake Erie and Lake St. Clair.

There are at least six conclusive records of the Northern Gannet for Michigan, all during autumn, and four of which date back more than fifty years. Specimens include an immature female obtained from Walker Lake, Livingston County, on 19 October 1911; an immature male taken at Thunder Bay, Alpena County, on 10 November 1925; an adult collected at Strawberry Island, Lake St. Clair, around 1 December 1929; and an immature captured at Birmingham, Oakland County, on 29 November 1942. Published reports regarding the specimen taken 10 November 1925 are contradictory; both Payne (1983) and Kenaga (1956) list its origin as Thunder Bay, while Zimmerman and Van Tyne (1959) and Wood (1951) give the locale as Tawas Bay. The two recent gannet reports accepted by the Michigan Bird Records Committee are of an immature observed and photographed at Port Huron on 13 October 1978, and another immature seen on 1 December 1991 on Lake Erie, Monroe County. There were a number of sightings in the eastern Great Lakes from 1980 to 1987, but none were reported in Michigan. —Raymond J. Adams

*Double-crested Cormorant*
HEINER HERTLING

# AMERICAN WHITE PELICAN
## (*Pelecanus erythrorhynchos*)

Many people associate pelicans with the ocean, but this species breeds in large colonies on lakes in the western United States and Canadian prairies. Its winter range is more coastal, with populations occurring primarily in the far Southwest, the Gulf coast states to Florida, and coastal Mexico. The American White Pelican is a casual to rare migrant and summer vagrant in Michigan, showing up on inland lakes and rivers as well as the Great Lakes. It is substantially larger than the Brown Pelican, having a body over 5 feet in length and a wingspread between 8 and 10 feet.

In Michigan, back around the turn of this century, Barrows (1912) called this pelican "little more than a straggler." Most records for that period are of specimens obtained by shooting, as laws protecting migratory birds were nonexistent. For the next seventy years or so, the occurrence of the White Pelican in Michigan followed a similar pattern (as a straggler), except that the passage of migratory bird laws afforded it protection. Then, in the late 1970s, sightings became more regular. Today, White Pelicans appear annually somewhere in the state, showing up almost anywhere there is water to fish in. Among those locations with multiple sightings are the western shores of Lake Erie, Saginaw Bay, Muskegon County, and Whitefish Point.

As the frequency of observations has changed, so too has the timing. The vast majority of the older records are from late summer and fall, whereas in recent decades, May and June have been the best months for White Pelicans. Presumably, late summer and fall reports represent post-breeding wanderers and the May–June birds are nonbreeders. Observations typically consist of singles, pairs, or small flocks of 5 to 7 birds. Groups as large as 12 have been seen near Linwood in Bay County on 22 September 1940, and at Pte. Mouillee in Monroe County in the summer of 1948. The best time to look for White Pelicans is from May through September, although individuals have been seen as early as 10 April (1949) and as late as 27 December (1948). This latter sighting occurred on a Christmas bird count.

The dramatic white plumage, contrasting black primaries and outer secondaries, and foot-long orange bill and pouch make this bird truly unmistakable. White Pelicans fly with their heads retracted, the reverse of other large white birds with black wing tips, which fly with their heads extended. Unlike the Brown Pelican, this species feeds by dipping its bill while swimming. At times, several birds will engage in a group feeding, where fish are herded into shallower water to be captured more easily. —Raymond J. Adams

# BROWN PELICAN
## (*Pelecanus occidentalis*)

The huge bill and throat pouch of these large waterbirds are universally recognized. In addition to plumage differences, the Brown Pelican's penchant for diving headfirst for its food, something the White Pelican does not do, is useful for identification at long distances. Brown Pelicans nest on marine islands from California, the Gulf coast, and North Carolina south to the northern and western coasts of South America. They inhabit saltwater most of the time, although a few wander inland north to the Great Lakes. This species is considered a casual visitor to Michigan, with at least 11 reported occurrences.

Barrows (1912) recounts three older records: a specimen from Macomb County in 1882 and two separate sightings around St. Joseph, Berrien County, in 1904. Following a hiatus of nearly fifty years, five were seen on 21 July 1950 at Grand Beach, and two were seen on 29 August 1965 at Grand Mere, both in Berrien County. The next observation, documented by a photograph, came on 13 June 1978 on Lake Macatawa, Ottawa County. Ten years later another individual was photographed on AuSable Lake, Ogemaw County. Already, there have been four records in the 1990s—perhaps a consequence of the recovery taking place on the breeding grounds since the banning of the pesticides DDT and Dieldren. In 1990, a Brown Pelican was found irregularly from 24 June to 27 July in Van Buren and Berrien counties. In 1991, a bird appeared on 26 July at Munising Bay, Alger County, and this individual or another showed up on 26 September at the St. Marys River, Chippewa County. Then on 30 April 1993 one was present at a pond along I-75 in Saginaw County. Undoubtedly, other Brown Pelicans have wandered to Michigan, but relatively few people are aware of the value in reporting such sightings. —Raymond J. Adams

# DOUBLE-CRESTED CORMORANT

(*Phalacrocorax auritus*)

The Double-crested Cormorant can best be described as a survivor, having rebounded from extirpation in the state to a current status of common summer resident and migrant and rare winter resident. In 1912, Walter Barrows characterized this species as being generally distributed in Michigan during migrations but nowhere common. He postulated that it bred within our limits, but he had no evidence to support this claim. The first confirmation of breeding occurred on 27 June 1936 when two nests were found on the Huron Islands, Marquette County, with fledged young confirmed on 10 August. By 1951, Norman Wood could add several more nesting records and characterized the species as an uncommon migrant, more common in fall than spring.

About this time, cormorant populations began to increase rapidly in Ontario, so fast that control measures were instituted to reduce suspected competition with commercial fisheries. (Studies have since proven that few game fish are eaten; most prey are small fish such as alewives, smelt, and yellow perch.) However, these measures were not required for long, as a hidden, more insidious control was already beginning to reduce cormorant numbers. This hidden factor was the pesticide DDT. As with many other avian species, DDE (a breakdown by-product of DDT) thinned the shells of cormorant eggs, resulting in almost total nest failure. By 1966, the entire Great Lakes breeding population had plummeted to 30 pairs at two inland colonies in Wisconsin. Sale and use of DDT in the United States was banned in the early 1970s, and cormorant numbers soon began to recover.

The first post-DDT nesting attempts in Michigan occurred in the summer of 1976 on Gravelly Island, off the shores of Delta County in the north end of Green Bay. Although these first 8 nests failed, 8 more were found in 1977, which produced up to four young. James Ludwig documented the growth of Michigan's nesting population from those 8 original nests in 1976 to 311 in 1981, 1,077 in 1984, and more than 2,000 in 1988—an average increase of 38% per year. This resurgence can also be seen in migration counts, which showed only scattered individuals prior to the 1970s and then a steady increase through the 1980s, reaching astounding levels such as the 8,000 to 10,000 seen in the last week of August 1992 in Green Bay, Delta County. Today, the Double-crested Cormorant is more abundant in Michigan than at any time in the past century.

This current situation may, however, be threatened by new complications surfacing from Great Lakes contaminants. Recent research has indicated that persistent chemicals, particularly PCBs, may be resulting in increased genetic disorders, such as bill crossing, as well as increased reproductive failure due to gross deformities in developing embryos. It is too early to determine what effect these new threats will have on cormorant populations.

These aquatic birds breed along the Pacific and Atlantic coasts and inland across the Great Lakes and northern Great Plains. Wintering occurs primarily along the coasts in the southern portions of the breeding range. In Michigan, spring migrants begin arriving in April to mid-May, with nesting ensuing soon after. Hatching may occur as early as 20 May and as late as 10 August. Most cormorants depart the state between August and September, with a few lingering throughout the winter where open water exists.

Double-crested Cormorants nest in colonies, often associated with gulls. Their stick nests are placed either in trees or directly on the ground. The typical clutch of three to four pale blue eggs is incubated for 25 to 29 days, with fledging occurring in another 35 to 42 days. Most breeding colonies in Michigan are adjacent to, or on islands in, the northern Great Lakes, although inland nesting has been confirmed in Dickinson County. —James Granlund

# MAGNIFICENT FRIGATEBIRD

(*Fregata magnificens*)

The passage of Hurricane Gilbert in 1988 precipitated one of the most exciting ornithological events of the 1980s. Gilbert's powerful winds carried dozens of Magnificent Frigatebirds inland into Texas, and then as the storm remnants continued north, these large seabirds appeared in numerous states including Michigan, Wisconsin, Minnesota, Illinois, and Indiana, as well as Ontario. At

*American Bittern*
*Green Heron*
GIJSBERT VAN FRANKENHUYZEN

GIJSBERT-1993

least four reports were received for Michigan waters: an immature on 28 September along the St. Clair River (across from Point Edward, Ontario); an immature on 30 September at Weko Beach, Berrien County; an adult male on 16 October at Leland, Leelanau County; and an adult on 21 October at Warren Dunes State Park, Berrien County. Unlike Wisconsin, Illinois, and Indiana, Michigan had no previous records of this species. Magnificent Frigatebirds nest on islands south of the United States in the Pacific and Atlantic oceans and the Gulf of Mexico. Individuals usually require five to seven years to reach maturity and adult plumage. A long, slender body, long forked tail, and seven-foot wing span allow these seafarers to cover long distances easily. —Raymond J. Adams

# AMERICAN BITTERN
## (*Botaurus lentiginosus*)

The American Bittern, a bird which spends much of its time in cattails, rushes, and other marshy vegetation, employs a distinctive and interesting behavior to escape detection. When alarmed, this large bird strikes a motionless pose with its bill raised skyward. The slender neck, streaked in brown, and long pointed bill cause this species to blend in and become nearly invisible while standing among tall reeds. While this behavior helps the bird to hide in a marsh, it is not adaptive in all situations. I have seen a bittern strike this pose in a damp meadow where it could be easily seen in the short grass.

This bittern is an uncommon and locally distributed summer resident in Michigan. It occurs most commonly in the northern half of the state, with the healthiest populations found in the Upper Peninsula. In most southern counties, the species is now seen infrequently owing to a decline in numbers over the past several decades. Decreasing populations have been noticed elsewhere in its breeding range. It has been placed on the endangered list in Ohio and Indiana and on the special concern list in Michigan, based on alarmingly low numbers found during the Breeding Bird Atlas.

Disturbance and destruction of wetland habitat are labeled as main causes, but other factors may be involved as well. The bird's preference for large expanses of suitable habitat is doubtless of importance. Continued surveys, research, and habitat protection are certainly needed, and one hopes that the decline will not spread northward.

The American Bittern breeds from about the middle United States to northern Canada. With nesting populations found north to the treeline, this species breeds the farthest north of any heron. Marshes, bogs, and other wetlands are the most commonly chosen habitats, though it will also nest in damp meadows. Its food includes fish, frogs, and aquatic insects, often stalked while moving along at an imperceptibly slow pace.

The spring arrival of the American Bittern occurs mostly in early April in southern Michigan, with an occasional March sighting. In the Upper Peninsula, the average arrival is in late April. Migrants heading north of Michigan pass through later in spring but are seldom detected except at strategic and closely watched migration areas, such as Whitefish Point, where transients are seen through 20 May.

Nesting gets underway in early May. The nest may be built on dry ground or over water, and is generally a platform of reeds and other aquatic vegetation. Bitterns will sometimes arch material over the nest, making it difficult to observe from above. In Michigan, egg dates range from early May to mid-July. The eggs, typically numbering five, hatch after about a month. Fledglings may be seen as late as the first part of August.

During October, American Bitterns depart the state for their wintering grounds in the coastal and southern United States and on into Mexico and Central America. Occasional stragglers are found in Michigan in November and December. One or two bitterns were regularly seen on Christmas bird counts during the 1970s but were mostly unrecorded during the 1980s, perhaps a consequence of the harsh winters of the late 1970s.

The adult American Bittern is colored rich brown above and lighter brown and more streaked below. Its white throat is framed by dark whisker marks. At a distance in flight, the species appears as an unpatterned brown bird which, except for its dark flight feathers, resembles an immature night-heron. Its vocal performance is distinctive and very memorable. In spring at any time of the day or night, this bittern may give its repeated, mechanical "oi-boink." The loud second tone is of unusual quality, at once both hollow and metallic. When one hears it at a distance, with the softer first tone often inaudible, the source of such colorful colloquial names as "stake driver" and "thunder pumper" is very plain. —Jack Reinoehl

# LEAST BITTERN
## (*Ixobrychus exilis*)

The Least Bittern is a small, secretive heron which breeds in some of the inland and coastal marshes of Michigan. Only the most persistent observer can expect to glimpse this species. The fortunate will see a dark bird, about 12 inches in size, flying low over the marsh. The most distinctive field mark is the large buffy patch on each wing which, with the small size, distinguishes this heron from all others. The bittern will disappear into dense cover on landing, generally not to be seen again.

The summer range of the Least Bittern includes most of the eastern United States, becoming extremely local in parts of the West and extending south into Mexico. In winter, populations withdraw to the southern border states from Florida to California

*Least Bittern*
Cyndy Callog

Cyndy Callog

and Mexico. This species is also a resident in Central and northern South America.

Michigan lies at the northern edge of the Least Bittern's summer range, with breeding mostly confined to the southern half of the state. North of Saginaw Bay, it is a rare breeder encountered most regularly in marshes along the Great Lakes. Although this species is found most frequently in the southern Lower Peninsula, even here it is uncommon and locally distributed and apparently not present in every county, according to the Breeding Bird Atlas data. In recent years, Pte. Mouillee in Monroe County and Nayanquing Point in Bay County are among the locales where the species has been seen most often, in part because they are favorite Michigan birding sites.

This bittern occurs in a variety of marshy habitats but shows a decided preference for extensive areas of cattails. Dense reeds or other vegetation in standing water is a necessity, and this species often moves through the marsh by clinging to the reeds rather than wading in the water. Its food includes a large variety of aquatic life, especially fish and insects, with dragonflies constituting a major portion of the diet.

The Least Bittern arrives in Michigan from early to mid-May. In Kalamazoo County the species has been seen as early as 1 May, but in the Saginaw Bay area the earliest record is 21 May. The call, several soft cooing notes, is generally the easiest way of noting its arrival. Calling is most frequent at dawn and dusk, and largely ends once nesting activities start.

The nest is constructed from twigs and grasses and suspended low over the water. Like another inhabitant of cattail marshes, the Marsh Wren, the Least Bittern builds several nests in the vicinity of its primary nest, though these others will not be used. Clutches (usually four to five eggs) are mostly laid in the first half of June, and the young are ready to leave the nest by early to mid-July.

Fall migration is thought to occur mainly in September, and by the end of the month this species has generally left the state. Stragglers are occasionally seen in October, as evidenced by a handful of records for southern Michigan. Their short four-and-a-half-month visit is more typical of small insectivorous birds than of herons.

If early writings are compared with those of today, it is readily apparent that Least Bittern populations have declined in Michigan during this century. As a consequence of the Breeding Bird Atlas, which had reports for only 102 out of 1,896 townships, this species was assigned the status of threatened in the state in 1990. Declines have not been restricted to Michigan, as it is presently regarded as endangered in Illinois and Ohio and of special concern in Indiana. Populations have fared somewhat better in the southeastern United States, where it is still common.

Loss or degradation of its preferred marsh habitat is the primary cause of such declines. Early this century, the Least Bittern was described by Barrows (1912) as abundant in proper habitat. It is telling that the location to which he refers, Chandler's Marsh north of Lansing, is now completely drained. Even in what appears to be suitable habitat, however, this species often seems to be absent or present in only small numbers. Its decline may be due to other causes as well, but these remain largely unidentified. To maintain this bittern in the state, populations should be closely monitored, and research into the cause of its decline is desirable. —Jack Reinoehl

# GREAT BLUE HERON
## (*Ardea herodias*)

The majestic Great Blue Heron is the largest bird species regularly seen by most people in the state. Standing four feet tall, with a wingspread of six and one-half feet, these birds cannot fail to be noticed. Most wetlands in Michigan are visited by this species from time to time, and the sight of these great birds returning to their breeding colonies at dusk is part of the rhythm of summer evenings.

The large size and dark colors distinguish this species from all other long-legged birds except the Sandhill Crane. Indeed, the heron is often called a "crane" colloquially. However, the heron is mostly blue-gray and flies with its neck folded, while the crane is slate-gray and flies with its neck extended. The habits of these two birds are also different. The Great Blue nests in trees and forages primarily in wetlands, whereas the Sandhill Crane nests on the ground and does much of its foraging in dry fields and meadows.

The Great Blue Heron is a fairly common summer resident throughout the state of Michigan. The full breeding range extends from central Canada and southern Alaska to Mexico, the West Indies, and the Galapagos Islands. Its winter range is from the northern United States to northern South America. This species has a white morph, the Great White Heron, which resides in southern Florida and was formerly regarded as a separate species.

To feed, these wading birds visit wetlands of many types, including ponds, lakes, streams, and mud flats. Their food is predominantly fish and amphibians but includes other types of animals, both vertebrate and invertebrate. Where food is abundant, large groups will gather. Along rivers and ponds, however, they are quite solitary and will defend their feeding area from other individuals. Great Blues are generally shy, often not noticed until surprised into flight; then the loud, harsh braying call of these normally silent birds startles the observer.

Great Blue Herons start to arrive in southern Michigan from their wintering grounds with the first warm breezes in March. Full numbers may not arrive in the Upper Peninsula until early April. This species nests in colonies in woodlands of different types. Floodplains or other low-lying areas are common sites, as are islands in the Great Lakes. Deciduous trees are typically selected in the south, while in the north coniferous trees are often used.

Nesting activity begins in April or May. The nest is a platform of sticks high in a tree; nesting colonies are usually in the largest trees in the area. Historically, colonies as large as 200 nests were known in the state. William C. Sharf's 1987 survey of 35 Great Lakes colonies found 4 containing 80 nests or more, with the largest at 125. In the summer of 1993, I counted about 80 in a

***Great Blue Heron***
GIJSBERT VAN FRANKENHUYZEN

colony in Gratiot County near the Maple River, though the size of most inland colonies seems to be 10 to 40 nests. Young are fully grown in southern Michigan by July. At this time, the colony is a remarkable sight, with the small platform nests shared by two or three lanky heron chicks. Juveniles at this age resemble adults except for their solid black cap.

This heron departs the state slowly, and numbers will remain through the winter where open water is available. As cold weather overtakes the state, individuals show much resourcefulness in finding food. I once saw a Great Blue in January standing on the nearly frozen Looking Glass River (Clinton County), fishing through a small hole in the ice.

The Michigan Great Blue Heron population has been closely monitored over the last few decades. Sharf's work revealed a 60% increase in numbers in Great Lakes colonies between 1978 and 1987. Some of this growth is attributed to losses and declines at inland colonies, with some of these birds shifting to less disturbed coastal and island sites. Despite some localized decreases, nesting was documented at 175 inland colonies during the Breeding Bird Atlas. The current outlook is generally positive, but close monitoring needs to continue because colonies are constantly under threat from development, logging, and even shooting. This species has shown great resilience in responding to the changes wrought in the environment by humans. —Jack Reinoehl

# GREAT EGRET

## (*Casmerodius albus*)

The beauty of the Great Egret led to its near-extinction early in this century. The elegant filmy nuptial plumes were very fashionable for women's hats, and since these are present only during the breeding season, the result was uncontrolled shooting of adults at nesting colonies. That this species may be seen in good numbers over most of the eastern United States today is a tribute to the efforts of the National Audubon Society in its early days and the passage of the Migratory Bird Treaty Act in 1918.

The Great Egret ranges over most of the world. It is found on every continent, being absent only in deserts, mountains, and high latitudes. In North America this long-legged wading bird breeds in coastal regions and up the Mississippi River valley to the lower Great Lakes. At present, it is a fairly common but localized summer resident in southern Michigan, seen in large numbers in the marshes around Lake Erie and in lesser but substantial numbers around Saginaw Bay. Away from the southeastern region, there are scattered small breeding populations.

The history of this species in Michigan was affected by its persecution around the close of the 19th century. At that time those seen in the state were mostly post-breeding wanderers, and with its decrease in numbers to our south it became exceedingly rare here. Protection caused quick recovery of numbers in the South, and the Great Egret began spreading its range northward. In 1929 the species was recorded in the Saginaw Bay area for the first time ever, and nesting in Michigan was first documented in the 1950s at Bay City.

In feeding, these egrets seem very tolerant in their choice of wetland. They make use of marshes and ponds, both large and small. In many areas they are a common and impressive sight as they forage in roadside ditches. Their food is aquatic life—mostly fish, frogs, and crayfish but also insects and snakes. Where stalking food in the usual manner is not possible, these herons will employ unexpected methods of feeding. On Lake Pontchartrain in Louisiana, I have seen them obtain food by swimming in or hovering above the surface of deep water.

The Michigan breeding population of Great Egrets arrives in numbers about mid-April. As with many of our early spring migrants, the date of first arrival is affected by the weather, and occasional March sightings are recorded. Spring migration regularly takes this species north of its normal range. Upper Peninsula records in spring include two sightings at Whitefish Point Bird Observatory in the last ten years and a sighting at Marquette in 1990. All these records have been within a few days of 20 May.

Nesting activities begin in late May or early June. The nest is a platform of sticks, two to three feet across. In Michigan, this species usually nests in a colony with another heron species—most often Great Blue Herons, but with Black-crowned Night-Herons at Pte. Mouillee. By August, the young are ready to leave the nest.

After nesting is complete, this species becomes a great wanderer. Egrets nesting to our south actually travel north and arrive in Michigan during July and August. At this time, individuals are often seen away from nesting areas, and the highest counts are recorded, such as the 176 at Shiawassee National Wildlife Refuge (Saginaw County) on 8 August 1991. During the months of September and October, egrets depart the state, and by November they are generally gone. Michigan's Great Egrets migrate to the southeastern United States for the winter. —Jack Reinoehl

# SNOWY EGRET

## (*Egretta thula*)

The exquisite Snowy Egret, like the Great Egret and other relatives, suffered decimation from plume hunters around the turn of this century. An adult is an exceptionally elegant bird in the spring, with its filmy aigrettes. Adult Snowys are distinguished from other white egrets and herons by their small size and black legs with bright yellow feet. Immatures, whose legs are mostly greenish, are more of an identification problem but like adults have a slender black bill and yellow lores.

The Snowy Egret is an uncommon visitor to Michigan. Its usual range includes the southern and western United States south through most of South America. In the East breeding

*Great Egret*
*Cattle Egret*
HEINER HERTLING

H.C. Hertling

occurs in the southern Mississippi Valley and extends along the Gulf and Atlantic coasts north to Long Island.

This species has recently become a regular visitor to Michigan in spring, summer, and fall. Most observations are from Monroe County and the Saginaw Bay area, but there are records from other localities around the state, including spring sightings from Chippewa (Whitefish Point), Marquette, and Houghton counties. During spring, Snowy Egrets are recorded anytime between mid-April and the end of May. Most encounters involve single birds seen at sites along the Great Lakes, and occasionally individuals are seen into the summer months. Largest numbers occur in fall in Monroe County, including 14 at Erie Marsh Preserve in late August and early September 1992. Pte. Mouillee has also hosted good numbers in fall.

Breeding in Michigan has not been definitely proved, although it is known in nearby Ohio. Nesting was verified on West Sister Island in western Lake Erie in 1983, and 8 to 10 pairs were thought to be using the island in 1987 and 1989, according to the Ohio Breeding Bird Atlas. Documentation of nesting by the Snowy Egret in Michigan is highly possible at Pte. Mouillee in the near future. Very young juveniles have been observed here in recent years, and adults were present at the Pte. Mouillee heronry from 1989 through 1991. —Jack Reinoehl

## LITTLE BLUE HERON
### (*Egretta caerulea*)

The Little Blue Heron is a rare visitor to Michigan, little seen in most parts of the state but considerably more regular in a few favored spots in the southeast. Adults in breeding plumage are slate blue with a deep purple head and neck. Immatures are small all-white herons with greenish legs; most have blue tips to the wings. In their first spring Little Blue Herons show blue patches in their white plumage. Adults and first-spring birds are readily identified, but immatures are easily confused with the immature Snowy Egret, whose legs are greenish in back and black in front. Observers should be aware that the Snowy Egret has a jet black bill with a bright yellow patch before the eye, while this species has a duller two-toned bill.

Little Blues breed from the southeastern United States to South America. Wandering individuals reach Michigan in both spring and fall. The species was first verified in the state by a specimen taken near Detroit in 1882. It was a more regular and numerous visitor here in the early part of this century. More than 160 individuals were recorded in 1930, the year of greatest abundance. Large numbers continued to be reported for a few decades, but Alice Kelley noted that the species became scarce in the Detroit area after 1969. During the 1970s and 1980s, Little Blues were quite uncommon and sporadic in spring and fall, with several reported across the state during some seasons, and then none seen for several seasons consecutively.

Of the 12 sightings published in the *Jack-Pine Warbler* between 1990 and 1992, 8 were in Monroe County, 2 in the Saginaw Bay area, and 1 each in Washtenaw and Ionia counties. The earliest spring record was in late April, with the others in mid-May. Most

Little Blues are seen in the fall season from late July through September, with a late sighting on 25 October. Birders wishing to see this species would thus maximize their chances by visiting Pte. Mouillee or the Erie Marsh Preserve in May, August, or September. —Jack Reinoehl

## TRICOLORED HERON
### (*Egretta tricolor*)

The Tricolored Heron is primarily a tropical species and a bird of coastal habitats. Its name refers to the beautiful three-color plumage of the adult, which is purplish-blue above and white below with a chestnut streak on the throat. The combination of blue plumage and white belly immediately distinguishes this medium-sized heron from all others. Immature Great Blues may appear somewhat similar in plumage, but their size is nearly twice as large.

The normal range of this species is the Gulf and Atlantic coasts north to New Jersey, so it is not surprising that the Tricolored Heron has been rarely found in Michigan. The first state record was of a bird discovered on 8 May 1965 at the Erie Gun Club in Monroe County. The rate of sightings increased over the next decade to the point that there were at least 25 records between 1975 and 1990, making this species a casual visitor. Tricolored Herons have been sighted as early as mid-April, but most are found in the latter part of May. Records indicate a few July and August appearances as well, including a high of six seen on 31 August 1988 at Holland in Ottawa County. Individuals have wandered as far north as Waugoshance Point in Emmet County and the Paradise area in Chippewa County, but the majority are seen along the southeastern coastal area of the Lower Peninsula. The large marshes along Lake Erie are the best places to look for this casual visitor to Michigan. Tricolors have been reported in spring, summer, and autumn at Pte. Mouillee, Erie Gun Club, and Erie Marsh Preserve (all Monroe County). —Jack Reinoehl

## CATTLE EGRET
### (*Bubulcus ibis*)

Before the 1870s, the Cattle Egret was restricted in range to the Eastern Hemisphere. It has since spread to North and South America and also Australia. The explosiveness of this expansion has been quite remarkable. It was first detected in South America in the 1870s and in North America, in Florida, in the 1940s. Within the next 40 years, Cattle Egrets were recorded in every state (though they did not spread naturally to Hawaii).

The expansion of this species to the Western Hemisphere during relatively recent times raises interesting questions. Why should such an expansion occur in the last 100 years when it might easily have taken place, one supposes, any time in the preceding 10,000 years? One probable factor is the more open landscape created after the widespread clearing of forests. Before settlement of the New World, any Cattle Egrets wandering to the coast from Africa would have found unbroken forest unsuitable for this open-country species.

A second factor is that many herons, the Cattle Egret included, are among the greatest wanderers in the bird world. They habitually wander after completing nesting, a behavior which brings several species of herons of the southeastern United States to Michigan. It is thus not surprising that this egret quickly became established in the Americas once the landscape was made hospitable.

The successful expansion of this species can also be attributed to its flexible nesting habitat and diet. Cattle Egrets roost and nest in various wetlands with other herons but forage most regularly in dry fields. This egret earned its name by its practice of following cattle and other large ungulates, feeding on insects disturbed by grazing activity. In this situation they feed primarily on grasshoppers. When foraging in wetter habitats, they consume aquatic invertebrates as well as fish and frogs.

The Cattle Egret has been recorded throughout the United States but is common only on the East Coast, in the lower Mississippi Valley, and in southern California. In Michigan this species occurs as both an uncommon visitor and a very rare nester. As a visitor it could occur anywhere in the state during spring, summer, or fall. Nesting, to date, has been limited to a few locations on the east side of the Lower Peninsula.

This species was first found in Michigan in the spring of 1961 at Erie Marsh in Monroe County. It was soon recorded in other locations, such as Cheboygan in 1964 and Schoolcraft County in November 1970—the first Upper Peninsula record. The number of sightings increased rapidly thereafter, and Cattle Egrets have been reported annually since the early 1970s. Since 1989, large numbers have often been seen in late summer at Pte. Mouillee. As many as 50 were counted there in late summer of 1991, and the capturing and marking of individuals verified that some of these spent part of their time with the large concentration of Cattle Egrets at Holiday Beach, Ontario.

Migrant Cattle Egrets arrive in Michigan during April, having been seen as early as 4 April in Macomb County in 1983. Many of these are wandering individuals which disappear after a few days. Since 1980, the species has been sighted in five or six counties during spring on several occasions. Nesting was first verified in 1985 at the Saginaw River Diked Disposal Island in a colony of Black-crowned Night-Herons. As with other herons, the nest is a platform built of sticks. Egg dates are in early June in the northeastern United States, and young are able to leave the nest by mid-August.

There is another influx of Cattle Egrets in the fall, and in about one year in three there is a wide dispersal through the state. A group of 15 at Whitefish Point Bird Observatory on 22 October 1992 typifies the fall wanderings of this species. Small numbers are found through November in Michigan, but the species has yet to be encountered on a Christmas bird count here.
—Jack Reinoehl

# GREEN HERON
## (*Butorides virescens*)

I remember as a young boy going fishing on a small lake in Mason County with my dad and brother. A crow-sized bird would fly up from the lakeside brush with a yelping "kee-yow." It would then fly ahead to a new spot on the shoreline, only to be flushed again on our trip around the lake. My dad called this bird a "Shite-poke." A few years later I learned from bird books that the bird was called a Green Heron.

The Green Heron is a fairly common summer resident over most of Michigan's Lower Peninsula, becoming uncommon in the northern three tiers of counties. In the Upper Peninsula, it is found with some regularity along the Wisconsin border but is rare to absent across the rest of the region. This species ranges over all continents in temperate and tropical areas, and has several forms with varying plumages. Our form, which occurs over most of the United States and south to Panama, has a dark green back and chestnut neck. It winters from the southern coastal areas of North America south through Central America.

The Green Heron is a bird of brushy wetlands such as those found along borders of lakes, ponds, and streams. It feeds on aquatic life of all sorts, including fish and frogs and also many insects. It catches food with a quick stab of its long bill, often after standing motionless in a watchful pose—a behavior common to all herons. It also employs an extraordinary method of feeding observed in this species alone, in which the bird holds an insect, feather, or other small object in its bill and feeds on fish attracted to the bait.

This heron returns from its southern wintering grounds during the last week of April or first week of May, though an early pulse of warm air often brings one or more individuals north a week or two earlier. Nesting begins in mid- to late May and continues into July. The nest is a platform of twigs much like that of other herons. It is placed in the thick cover of a tree or shrub, usually at a low elevation, and occasionally some distance from water. This species is much less social than other herons, and nesting is almost always solitary, though small colonies have been recorded.

Fall migration occurs during September, and by the end of the month nearly all have left the state. Stragglers have been noted into December, but these are extremely rare, and a Green Heron reported on a Christmas bird count in Michigan must be carefully documented to be believable. This heron was first recorded on a Michigan count in 1975, and very few have been seen since then.

The Green Heron has apparently expanded its range northward in Michigan during this century. The historic literature contains only two reports in the late 1800s from the Upper Peninsula, where it is now a regular breeder in some parts. On the other hand, its numbers in the state must have diminished since a large proportion of the state's wetlands have been drained and developed. For future residents of Michigan to have the continued pleasure of observing this species as I did in my youth, the preservation of remaining wetlands in their natural state is a necessity.
—Jack Reinoehl

GIJSBERT
1993

# BLACK-CROWNED NIGHT-HERON

*(Nycticorax nycticorax)*

The Black-crowned Night-Heron is a medium-sized, stocky heron seen mostly near the Great Lakes. Flying overhead at dusk in stately fashion, this species can be identified as a night-heron by the chunky body and broad, rounded wings. The black, gray, and white plumage of adults is striking and distinctive, but immatures and first-year birds closely resemble the immature Yellow-crowned Night-Heron, a close relative.

Black-crowns occur on all continents except Australia and Antarctica. North American birds nest over most of the United States north to southern Alberta and Manitoba. The winter range is along the East, West, and Gulf coasts south to Central America and the West Indies.

In Michigan this heron is a localized summer resident. Most of the state's population is found near Lake Erie and the Saginaw Bay area. The Breeding Bird Atlas (1983–88) also revealed nesting pairs in Alpena County, the Straits region, and Delta County. Black-crowned Night-Herons may be seen in good numbers in such locations as Pte. Mouillee in Monroe County, where a count of 32 in June 1992, consisting of both breeding adults and first-year birds, is typical. Over most of the rest of the state (except for the aforementioned sites), this heron is a rare migrant or visitor.

When seen during the day, night-herons are most often perched quietly at a roost. These may be on or near the ground in a marsh, but are more often in trees in a swampy area. Preferred foraging areas are large marshes, where this species feeds on a variety of aquatic life. The large eyes allow it to do most of its feeding at night. During the nesting season, night-herons will opportunistically feed on the eggs and young in nearby colonies of birds such as gulls and terns.

The Black-crowned Night-Heron arrives at its Michigan nesting grounds mostly during April, though it may not reach northern areas until early May. Nesting typically occurs in colonies, which are often on islands affording good protection from terrestrial predators. The nest, a platform made of sticks and reeds, is placed in a low bush or young tree. Egg laying occurs sometime between May and July, varying in response to local conditions.

This species has a tendency to wander, so occasionally a few will appear far from their nesting grounds in late summer. Departure from the state is gradual, with most individuals gone by October. Small numbers remain into December every year, and Black-crowns are always recorded on Christmas bird counts in southeastern Michigan. Usually the number found in the state is less than 10, but during the 1986–87 season 24 were found on

two counts. Away from the southeast, wintering individuals are very rare.

This heron declined in numbers in Michigan during the latter half of this century and was listed as a species of special concern in the state in the 1970s. Kenaga (1983) noted that in the 1940s and 1950s there were quite a few colonies, 200 to 500 in size, in the Saginaw Bay area. These suffered a major decline during the DDT era of the 1960s. Population surveys later showed an increase during the 1980s, but numbers were still far short of the mid-century level. W. Scharf and G. Shugart found 374 nests at six coastal sites in 1985, and numbers appear to have continued to increase since then.

Some new nesting habitat for Black-crowns has been created by dredging projects, and the present nesting colonies and foraging areas are mostly on public lands and safe from immediate development. Like other wetland inhabitants, this species remains under continual threat from degradation and pollution of its habitat, both here and on its wintering grounds. Regular surveys of populations are important to provide information not only on the health of each individual species, but also on the health of the state's wetlands in general. —Jack Reinoehl

# YELLOW-CROWNED NIGHT-HERON

*(Nyctanassa violacea)*

The Yellow-crowned Night-Heron is an inhabitant of floodplains and wooded swamps ranging across the eastern United States and south through Central America to coastal South America. Wintering is from Florida and the Gulf coast south. Regular breeding occurs north along the East Coast to southern New England and in the Mississippi Valley to southern Indiana and southern Ohio. Presently in Michigan the species is a sporadic breeder and rare spring and fall visitant. Transients and post-breeding wanderers are seen almost annually, and this night-heron has bred in southern Michigan on a few occasions.

The range and habitat of the Yellow-crowned Night-Heron are determined in large part by its preference for crustaceans. Its thick, heavy bill is an adaptation for feeding on these hard-shelled creatures. Along the coast its primary food is crabs, while at inland sites its diet consists largely of crawfish, with some insects. With its large eyes, this species is well adapted to the low light of swamp forests, and feeds at dusk and night though it is regularly active during the day as well.

The Yellow-crowned Night-Heron appeared in Michigan only recently as the result of range expansion. The first acceptable Michigan record was in 1960. First nestings were confirmed in Wayne and Monroe counties in 1971 and 1972, respectively. Nesting has since been observed only at a site in Wayne County (Westland) between 1978 and 1982, with possible nesting reported in both of these counties in 1983 and 1988. The few Michigan nestings have involved single pairs, but elsewhere in its range loose colonies have been reported.

One of the aforementioned nesting pairs was observed to arrive

*Black-crowned Night-Heron*
*Yellow-crowned Night-Heron*
GIJSBERT VAN FRANKENHUYZEN

in mid-April, with egg laying and incubation beginning soon after. The young were capable of flight by late June, although they stayed in the vicinity of the nest for another two to three weeks. In Wayne County the nesting habitat was an oak woodland next to a small swamp, while in Monroe County it was a grove of cottonwoods and aspens inside a small marsh.

Most recent sightings of the species are of spring migrants or wanderers. After fairly consistent reports in the 1970s, observations have been more irregular since 1980. Most records have been in counties bordering the Great Lakes, with Muskegon County the northern limit of sightings. In 1981, between 9 and 23 May, Yellow-crowned Night-Herons appeared in Ionia, Kalamazoo, Berrien, and Macomb counties. The next good spring was not until 1987, when this species was found in Barry, Monroe, and Muskegon counties. There were no additional spring sightings until 1993.

On 2 June 1993 I had the pleasure of watching an adult of this species at the Maple River State Game Area in southern Gratiot County. During 15 minutes of observation, it once appeared to be stalking prey among the marsh grass, but did not attempt any capture. This heron had been present at the site two weeks before I saw it. Once in a while such an individual will remain through the summer. Records from summer include four adults in Berrien County in July 1988, the largest recent concentration in the state. Fall wanderers have been seen in 5 of the last 12 years, mostly in Monroe County. This species departs the state by mid-September.

Adult Yellow-crowns with their boldly striped heads and gray bodies are unmistakable. Immatures, however, can be distinguished from the more common immature Black-crowned Night-Heron only by subtle details of structure and plumage. Wandering immatures in late summer are thus easily overlooked. The most reliable distinctions are the Yellow-crown's heavier bill and longer legs, which extend beyond the tail in flight. —Jack Reinoehl

## WHITE IBIS

### (*Eudocimus albus*)

The White Ibis resides in coastal marshes and mangrove swamps from the southern United States to South America. Occasionally, though, individuals stray north of their traditional breeding grounds after the nesting season, a behavior shared by ibises, herons, and other wading birds. Three such wanderers have made it to Michigan, qualifying the White Ibis as an accidental visitor. The first report came from Fred Rapp, a long-time birder in Kalamazoo County, who observed an adult White Ibis (unmistakable with its pink legs and long, pink, downcurved bill) feeding with a Great Egret on 1 August 1948 at a pond near Vicksburg (Adams 1979). The next record, and the only one with physical evidence (photograph) documenting this species' occurrence in the state, was of an immature bird at Harsen's Island in Macomb County, present from 19 to 26 September 1970. Immatures have a mottled brown and white plumage, but their pinkish bill and legs are distinctive. Most recently, an adult White Ibis was discovered in the company of a flock of Great Egrets on 26 September 1983 at the Shiawassee National Wildlife Refuge in Saginaw County (Francke

1984). A general increase in the vagrancy of ibis in the Midwest over the past 30 years provides hope that other White Ibis may appear in the state someday. —Raymond J. Adams

## GLOSSY IBIS

### (*Plegadis falcinellus*)

Originally a wide-ranging inhabitant of the Eastern Hemisphere, the Glossy Ibis apparently first appeared on this continent in the early 1800s. Today its breeding range includes the eastern coastal region of the United States, north to Maine and west in the Gulf to Texas, as well as the West Indies. Individuals also wander inland east to the Great Lakes, and the Glossy Ibis is an occasional transient and summer visitor to Michigan.

State records from the modern era begin with a female specimen collected 14 June 1939 from Bay County. Subsequent reports involve observations from Monroe and Tuscola counties, both on 11 May 1956. Since then, Glossy Ibis or indeterminate ibis species have shown up in at least ten different years, with the bulk of the sightings from the 1960s and from 1989 to present. The largest influx to the Great Lakes took place in 1962, when well over 60 were seen in the region, including about 30 in Michigan. While the majority were found here or in Ohio, birds also reached Indiana, Illinois, and Wisconsin that year.

Michigan Glossy Ibis reports fall neatly into spring–early summer and late summer–fall time periods, with 18 of 23 observations during the earlier period. Extreme dates are 24 April 1967 from the marshes in Monroe County and 24 November 1993 at Pte. Mouillee, also Monroe County. Most published reports are from the eastern side of the state; exceptions from the west are individuals seen in Berrien County (10 May 1993), Charlevoix County (1 May 1962), and Kalamazoo County (31 August 1989). They have also appeared at central locales, such as the Maple River State Game Area, Gratiot County, and Haehnle Sanctuary, Jackson County. Certainly if you want to see a Glossy Ibis in Michigan, your best bet is to bird the marsh systems in Monroe County beginning in May.

Glossy and White-faced Ibis are very similar in appearance, both adults and young, so it is possible that some Glossy Ibis reports refer to White-faced individuals. There are also some summer-fall records listed as indeterminate, as the bird could not be identified as to species. Since most records are from the breeding season (when plumages are most distinct) and many were at close range, it is reasonable to suggest that most observations in Michigan have indeed been Glossy Ibis, as is the case with adjacent states. —Raymond J. Adams

## WHITE-FACED IBIS

### (*Plegadis chihi*)

The White-faced Ibis, a western counterpart of the Glossy Ibis, is an accidental migrant and summer vagrant to Michigan. At present there are only three conclusive records for the state. Normally the White-faced Ibis breeds irregularly throughout the western United States, east to Minnesota and south to Texas and Mexico, with populations withdrawing southward toward the Pacific and Gulf coasts for the winter. Michigan's three records span a period of 77 years. The species was added to the state bird list in 1916 by virtue of a specimen obtained 15 October in Jackson County. It was 1969 before another White-faced Ibis was confirmed, this time through a photograph taken of a bird on 5 May at the mouth of Dowagic Creek in Cass County. Most recently, an individual seen by many birders was present on 19–20 June 1990 at Nayanquing Point in Bay County. The paucity of records in Ohio, Indiana, Wisconsin, and Ontario, as well as Michigan, suggests that this species is not prone to wander like the Glossy Ibis, and that few of the state's unidentified *Plegadis* records are White-faced individuals. For much of the year these two ibis species are nearly impossible to separate; only breeding adults can be readily differentiated. A White-faced Ibis in breeding plumage is characterized by red eyes, reddish bill and legs, and a wide strip of white feathers bordering the red facial skin and eye. —Raymond J. Adams

## WOOD STORK
### (*Mycteria americana*)

Storks are large, long-legged birds belonging to the worldwide family Ciconiidae. Of the three species present in the Western Hemisphere, only the Wood Stork (formerly Wood Ibis) ever finds its way to Michigan. This species inhabits large swamps and other wetlands from South Carolina, Florida, and the Gulf coastal states south into Middle and South America. Occasionally individuals stray northward in summer or fall, and evidently such peregrinations are more common following widespread nest failure on the breeding grounds.

There are three documented Michigan records beginning with our only specimen, an immature collected on 19 June 1910 in Monroe County. The next visit came on 31 May 1963, when an immature was spotted near Mason in Ingham County, where it remained much of the summer along Willow Creek. Confirming photographs were obtained on 31 July, and the bird was last seen on 10 August, at which time it appeared to be injured. Most recently, an adult and immature were photographed on 29 May 1975 on South Manitou Island, Leelanau County. It is important to note that Wood Storks take at least three years to reach adult plumage, and most breed for the first time in their fourth year. There has been much concern for this species in the United States as populations have suffered major declines over the past five decades. Losses of food resources and nesting habitat have been identified as the most serious problems. —Raymond J. Adams

## FULVOUS WHISTLING-DUCK
### (*Dendrocygna bicolor*)

The Fulvous Whistling-Duck, formerly Fulvous Tree Duck, is an accidental visitor to Michigan. The range of this goose-like duck extends across the southernmost Atlantic and Gulf coast states south through Mexico to Panama. It is a fairly mobile species, withdrawing to Central America for the winter. This species was first recorded in Michigan on 14 October 1962, when two birds were taken from a flock of ten at North Cape in Monroe County. These two specimens, along with another taken on 29 September 1979 on Drummond Island, are in the University of Michigan Museum of Zoology collection. One additional record is of two birds present for two weeks (and photographed) in mid-June 1974 in Bloomfield Township, Oakland County. Because the Fulvous Whistling-Duck is often kept in captivity, there is always the possibility that some of these individuals were feral. However, this species is known to wander, and there are multiple records from across the continent north to Quebec and British Columbia. Furthermore, the likelihood of ten birds escaping from captivity seems remote. —James Granlund

## [BLACK-BELLIED WHISTLING-DUCK]
### (*Dendrocygna autumnalis*)

The Black-bellied Whistling-Duck has been recorded only once in Michigan, when an individual was photographed on a pond near Kalamazoo on 25 July 1981. This was most likely a bird of captive origin since this species is not known to wander far from its southwestern breeding grounds. Two records in Minnesota were, indeed, found to be escaped birds. At the date of this writing, there is no clear pattern of vagrancy for the Black-bellied Whistling-Duck, and it is not accepted by the Michigan Bird Records Committee as a valid species in the state. —James Granlund

## TUNDRA SWAN
### (*Cygnus columbianus*)

The Tundra Swan or Whistling Swan, as it was formerly known, is a common migrant and uncommon winter visitor in Michigan. This species occurs throughout the Northern Hemisphere, nesting on lakes, ponds, and wetlands in the high arctic tundra. In North America, populations winter mainly along the middle Atlantic coast, particularly in the Chesapeake Bay region, and in the Central Valley of California in the West. Tundra Swan pass through the interior of the continent on migration, traveling in large V-shaped flocks at rather high altitudes. From a distance, the whistling notes given in flight make the flock sound like a group of children at play.

Analysis of returns from color-marked Tundra Swans indicate that birds migrating through Michigan breed from Manitoba to the Northwest Territories and winter in the mid-Atlantic states. The migration pathway between these two areas follows an angular route through the central region of the state. As a result, this species is a very common migrant in most of the Lower Peninsula but generally uncommon in the Upper Peninsula.

In spring, large numbers of Tundra Swans occur most frequently in the eastern part of the state, from Lake Erie to Saginaw Bay. Major concentrations are recorded each year in the Saginaw Bay area, with numbers of 4,000 or more not uncommon. Best locations to see these large flocks are the Fish Point area in Huron and Tuscola counties and Shiawassee National Wildlife Refuge in Saginaw County. Migrants begin arriving soon after the first warm fronts of spring push through the state. In years with early warm weather, migration may peak in early March, but best numbers are more typically found from the last week of March through the first two weeks of April. Lingering birds are recorded well into May nearly every year.

Small numbers of Tundra Swan have been recorded during summer in Michigan, but some of these reports must be attributed to injured or otherwise impaired individuals. There are, however, at least two records of immature birds—one from Seney National Wildlife Refuge, Schoolcraft County, and one from Rogers City, Presque Isle County—which were probably lingering nonbreeders.

The first fall migrants generally begin arriving in late September, although a few individuals are sometimes recorded as early as late August. The migration peaks from late October through mid- to late November. Unlike that of spring, the fall movement is spread more uniformly across the state, with good numbers recorded on both the Lake Huron and Lake Michigan coasts. High totals in Muskegon and Ottawa counties often exceed 1,000 individuals. An excellent location to view migrating Tundra Swans in late October and early November is the mouth of the St. Clair River at Port Huron. Birds commonly linger into late November, and some overwinter where open water and appropriate forage are available.

The Tundra Swan is one of three swan species which may occur in the state. Each is best distinguished by the color and shape of the bill. The adult Mute Swan has an orange bill with a black knob, noticeably different from the smooth black bill of the other two species. Separation of Tundra and Trumpeter Swans is much more difficult, requiring careful inspection of the shape and color of the bill. Most Tundra Swans, but not all, have a yellow spot on the bill just forward of the eye; this area is always black on a Trumpeter. Additionally, the Trumpeter's bill has a gradual slope to the upper mandible, reminiscent of a Canvasback, while a Tundra's bill rises at a steeper angle. —James Granlund

# TRUMPETER SWAN

## (*Cygnus buccinator*)

The exact status of the Trumpeter Swan is complicated by its brush with extinction in the last century. Heavily hunted for its pelt for the millinery trade, the species had dwindled in number by 1932 to a meager population of 26 individuals in the lower 48 states, all in Red Lakes, Montana. Then, in 1954, a sizable population of several thousand birds was discovered in Alaska.

Though the exact extent of this species' presettlement distribution is unknown, several researchers believe its breeding range went from Alaska south to central Washington, then eastward to south-central Illinois and north to James Bay. Such a range would have extended into Michigan, encompassing most of the northern and western portions of the Lower Peninsula and all of the Upper Peninsula. H. G. Lumsden (1984) further extended this range to include all of Michigan and the eastern coast of Canada. He used the availability of dietary calcium, archaeological remains of Trumpeter Swan bones, and historical accounts to draw his map.

Unfortunately there is no direct evidence to verify that Trumpeter Swans ever bred in Michigan. The best evidence to date is the accounts of Father Louis Hennepin from 1679 and M. de Lamothe de Cadillac in 1701. Both men reported swans as being numerous from late July through early October. Since neither migrant Tundra nor Trumpeter Swans would be expected this early in autumn and Tundra Swans nest far north on the tundra, speculation is that these were post-breeding Trumpeter Swans.

It may be unclear whether Trumpeters bred in Michigan, but it is certain that they occurred here on migration. One specimen was collected from St. Clair Flats on 20 November 1875 and is now preserved in the National Museum in Washington, D.C. In fact, many researchers felt that the eastern population of the Trumpeter most likely wintered along the eastern seaboard in the Chesapeake Bay area, and migration to and from the breeding grounds would have brought many through the Great Lakes region.

Today there is an active program to reestablish the Trumpeter Swan in parts of its former range. Transplants have already been successful in South Dakota and several other western states. Michigan began such a program in 1986 in the Allegan State Game Area, using Mute Swans for cross-fostering Trumpeter Swan eggs. Unfortunately, mortality from predators, thought to be mainly snapping turtles and owls, caused this effort to be abandoned. In 1990 the program shifted emphasis to releasing subadult Trumpeter Swans, raised at the Kellogg Bird Sanctuary or Detroit Zoo. Introduction sites include Seney National Wildlife Refuge, the Allegan State Game Area, and the Baker Sanctuary

*Trumpeter Swan*
HEINER HERTLING

H.C.Hertling

in Calhoun County plus a few other selected locales. The goal is to establish 200 wild Trumpeters in Michigan by the year 2000.

At the time of this writing it is too early to assess the success of this project. Already two birds have perished from ingesting lead shot picked up during foraging. This health hazard may prove to be a significant obstacle, even though lead shot is now banned. An additional four swan died from collisions with power lines, two were shot, and one hit a fence.

In the period 1989–91, three individuals known via their neck collars to be from reintroduction programs in other states were sighted in Michigan. A bird from Minnesota was seen from 3 to 14 April 1989 at Nayanquing Wildlife Area in Bay County. In the summer of 1990 an adult female from the established population in South Dakota was seen on numerous occasions near Seney National Wildlife Refuge. This marked the first truly "wild" Trumpeter Swan sighting in Michigan since the late 1800s. In 1992, an individual from the Wisconsin reintroduction program was seen at Ludington State Park in Mason County on 22–25 February.

The reintroduction program has had more promising outcomes the past few years. In 1992 a pair in Cass County hatched 2 cygnets, with 1 surviving to fledging, and a Seney pair successfully reared 2 of 4 hatched young. This was followed in 1993 by at least nine pairs in the state, with confirmed nesting again at Cass and Seney. This time the Cass pair hatched 3 young, and the five nesting pairs at Seney produced a total of 16 cygnets. While the survival rate of young has been less than desired so far, the release of an additional 30 subadults in various areas, including the Huron Manistee National Forest, bodes well for the future.
—James Granlund

# MUTE SWAN

## (*Cygnus olor*)

Revered for its graceful form and beauty, the Mute Swan has been introduced into many locations outside of its Eurasian range. In North America individuals are widely scattered, but established populations are found along the East Coast from Massachusetts to Maryland and in the western Great Lakes. The Michigan birds are thought to originate from a single pair released in East Jordan, Charlevoix County, in 1919. These birds apparently spread on their own, and some were transferred to other locales, including Oakland and Barry counties. Further introductions must have occurred to account for disjunct populations in such places as Baraga County in the western Upper Peninsula.

The Mute Swan is now a common breeding species and permanent resident in scattered locations throughout Michigan. Individuals remain within the state year-round, but in winter they withdraw to locations where open water and food are available. Some traditional wintering areas are the bay and mouth of the Boardman River in Traverse City, Muskegon Lake, the Upjohn Pond in Kalamazoo County, and the St. Clair River through the eastern end of Lake Erie. Breeding pairs are concentrated across the southern four tiers and northwestern counties in the Lower Peninsula and in the Straits of Mackinac and lower Keweenaw Bay area in the Upper Peninsula.

Mute Swans set up territories 4 to 10 acres in size which they strongly defend, ejecting other waterfowl and even people. Adults are generally paired for life, but remating has been recorded for individuals who have lost their mates. The nest site is selected in March or early April and is an elevated clump of vegetation, either one built by the swans or an existing mound such as a muskrat house. The female may lay up to eight eggs, but clutches of five are most typical. Both sexes, which are identical in appearance, share incubation, and the eggs hatch in 36 to 38 days. The cygnets take most of the summer to grow, reaching the flight stage in anywhere from 115 to 155 days.

Michigan's Mute Swan population has been increasing steadily since introduction. In the northwestern Lower Peninsula, numbers went from 47 in the middle 1940s to over 500 by 1980. The rate of increase is also accelerating, as can be seen in Christmas bird count data, which show a total of 357 swan (2.6 individuals/10 party-hours) in 1970–71 compared to 1,737 (4.3/10 party-hours) in 1991–92. Much of this increase occurred between 1985 and 1991, when the number of Mute Swan encountered doubled. There seems to be no immediate end in sight to the population growth of this species, although one eventual factor will probably be wintering habitat, particularly for swan in the northern part of the state which are already dependent on supplemental food provided by people. In some areas, the number of suitable nesting territories also seems to be limited based on the presence of unpaired nonbreeders.

The expansion of this nonnative species poses significant concerns to native wildlife. Of particular concern are its interactions with the Common Loon, a threatened Michigan species, and with the reintroduced Trumpeter Swans. The Mute Swan is very aggressive and has been known to drive off many other waterbirds, even such belligerent species as Canada Geese and birds equal its size like the Trumpeter. Reports of Mute Swan–Common Loon conflicts are being heard more frequently as the swan population grows. Wildlife managers will have to watch these situations closely in the coming years and take actions to control the exotic Mutes in areas where native species are being negatively affected.
—James Granlund

# GREATER WHITE-FRONTED GOOSE

## (*Anser albifrons*)

The Greater White-fronted Goose or Specklebelly is a rare to casual visitor to Michigan. This species has a circumpolar breeding distribution and several recognizable forms, of which

*Canada Goose*
*Mute Swan*
Gijsbert van Frankenhuyzen

three are found in North America. It is the Pacific White-fronted Goose (*A. a. frontalis*) that is most likely to occur in Michigan. This race breeds on the high tundra west of Hudson Bay through Alaska. Most of the Pacific race winters in the Central Valley of California, in Mexico, and along the coasts of Texas and Louisiana, although recently more individuals have been wintering farther north in Arkansas and Oklahoma. Also possible is the Greenland race (*A. a. flavirostris*), which nests in Greenland and migrates to the British Isles, with rare stragglers seen along the northern Atlantic coast.

The number of Greater White-fronteds in the Central Flyway has increased in recent years, and there has been a parallel increase in reports in Michigan. The largest group seen was 14 birds on 1 April 1989 in Clinton County. This species is now seen almost annually in the state, with most reports clustered in late March through April and again from late September through early December. Some have even overwintered in the past few years. White-fronted Geese are often found with large flocks of Canada Geese, so areas where Canadas congregate are the best places to search. Some of the better locations are Fish Point and the surrounding areas in Tuscola County, the Todd Farm in Allegan County, in and around the Kellogg Bird Sanctuary in Kalamazoo County, and the Muskegon Wastewater System. Observers should be aware that some domestic geese are easily mistaken for White-fronteds, especially immatures, so care should be used when identifying this species. —James Granlund

# SNOW GOOSE

## (*Chen caerulescens*)

The Snow Goose is a common spring and autumn migrant and rare winter visitor in Michigan. This species occurs in two color phases: a white phase, which is commonly referred to as the Snow Goose, and a dark phase, known as the Blue Goose. Once considered two different species, these forms were lumped into a single species in 1973 based on evidence of interbreeding.

As well as having two color phases, this species is divided into two subspecific forms: the Greater Snow Goose, which lacks a blue phase, and the Lesser Snow Goose. This latter form is the one which is commonly encountered in Michigan. There are some published records of Greaters in the state, but specimen and photographic evidence does not support the claim.

Snow Geese breed on the high arctic tundra from Wrangel Island in Siberia east to northwestern Greenland. The Greater subspecies winters mainly along the mid-Atlantic coast, whereas the Lesser has three main wintering areas. Those passing through Michigan go primarily to the Texas and Louisiana coasts. The other wintering grounds are from New Mexico to central Mexico and in the Central Valley of California. There has been a gradual change in winter distributions of both subspecies over the past few decades, with the blue form of the Lesser predominating in the east and the white form in the west. Both phases are regularly encountered in Michigan.

Snow Geese begin arriving in the state soon after the first warm

fronts, usually during late February. However, the bulk of the migration occurs during late March and early April. In spring small numbers of Snow Geese may be found statewide, whereas large concentrations are relatively rare, although numbers over 200 have been recorded. Locations which may have sizable spring flocks include Fish Point in Tuscola County and nearby areas in and around Saginaw Bay. Some Snow Geese linger into late May and even early June. The small number of summer records for Michigan may involve injured or otherwise impaired birds.

In fall, flocks begin arriving in mid-September, with main flights from mid-October through November. These migrants pass through the state in a southwesterly direction, in contrast to another large white bird, the Tundra Swan, which has a southeasterly route. Fall concentrations of Snow Geese, unlike those of spring, are often large and may exceed several hundred individuals. Excellent locations for observation include the Muskegon Wastewater System, the Allegan State Game Area, Shiawassee National Wildlife Refuge in Saginaw County, Quanicassee Wildlife Area and Fish Point in Tuscola County, and Wildfowl Bay in Huron County. During the late 1970s and middle 1980s there was a rise in Snow Goose numbers in the state. For example, the maximum seen at Muskegon surpassed 3,000 individuals. Unexplainably, numbers have been lower in more recent years, even though the continentwide population continues to increase.

Snow Geese are mostly grazers of grasses, sedges, and other plants, and increasingly, both Canada and Snow Geese are feeding on green shoots of pasture grasses and cereal grains. Therefore, any field which harbors Canada Geese on migration may also have Snow Geese. Individuals typically remain into early winter and are regularly found on Christmas bird counts, although never in high numbers. Occasionally some remain, but this species must be considered rare during winter in Michigan.

A potential identification pitfall is distinguishing between white domestic geese and white-phase Snow Geese. The latter always possesses a black "grinning" patch on its bill, a trait lacking in domestic geese, and the Snow has black wing tips; a feature rarely seen in domestics. —James Granlund

# ROSS' GOOSE

## (*Chen rossii*)

The Ross' Goose is an accidental visitant to Michigan. This small white goose with a stubby pink bill breeds on the high arctic tundra with an extremely limited range in central Canada, northwest of Hudson Bay. Wintering is mainly in the Central Valley of California, but lately this species is being recorded with increased frequency among large flocks of Lesser Snow Geese along the coasts of Texas and Louisiana and inland to Missouri and Oklahoma.

The first record for this species in Michigan was of an individual seen from 27 October through 12 November 1979 at the Todd Farm Unit of the Allegan State Game Area. Other sight records include two birds seen on 5 October 1986 at the Kellogg Bird Sanctuary in Kalamazoo County; two on 25 October 1986 at the Todd Farm; one on 27 March 1988 in Allegan County; and one to three birds seen from 15 to 21 March 1990 at Fish Point in Tuscola County. Also, one bird was taken by a hunter on 9 October 1980 at Shiawassee National Wildlife Refuge in Saginaw County, but the specimen was not preserved. As with all accidental waterfowl, the question of origin must be raised when a Ross' Goose is reported. This species is kept by aviculturists in live collections, meaning that birds seen in the wild could be escaped or released individuals. Based on migration patterns and the frequency and timing of reports, the Michigan Bird Records Committee has accepted them as being of wild origin. —James Granlund

# BRANT

## (*Branta bernicla*)

The Brant is a rare but regular migrant to Michigan. This species resembles the Canada Goose but can be distinguished by its smaller size, dark head and chest, and, in flight, the sharp demarcation between its black chest and white belly. There are three recognizable forms or races, of which the Atlantic Brant (*B. b. hrota*) is encountered here. This race migrates from its breeding grounds in Greenland and islands to the west to staging areas in James Bay, and eventually to the East Coast of the United States, where it winters. The route follows a nearly direct line over the eastern end of Lake Ontario and New York State, bringing the species close enough to Michigan to postulate its occurrence, in small numbers, on the western Great Lakes each season.

Indeed Brant are recorded almost annually between mid- and late October at Port Huron in St. Clair County. Some sightings are of several individuals, and an incredible flock of 45 was seen on 22 October 1981 at this location. This species has been recorded at scattered sites throughout the state from October through January. Although individuals have been seen at inland locales, Brant are most likely to be found in harbors or bays along the Great Lakes. In spring, the best hope for viewing Brant is at Whitefish Point in Chippewa County. Reports include 8 individuals on 1 June 1981, 12 on 2 April 1986, and singles on 4 May and 18 June 1989. Also in 1989, an individual was seen at the Tahquamenon River mouth south of Whitefish Point from 26 April to 23 May. The most unusual record is that of a Brant which appeared on 3 July 1991 and remained through 22 July in Marquette, where it spent much of its time grazing on the lawn of the Big Boy Restaurant along U.S. 41. —James Granlund

# [BARNACLE GOOSE]

## (*Branta leucopsis*)

The Barnacle Goose has been reported in Michigan on several occasions as an accidental visitor, but the origin of these individuals is questionable. First of all, this species breeds along the northeast coast of Greenland east to Novaya Zemlya and winters in the British Isles, the Netherlands, and Germany, where it is found on coastal pastures and grassy islands, rarely far from the sea. Also, like many other species of waterfowl, the Barnacle Goose is commonly kept by aviculturalists. Therefore any Barnacle Goose away from its normal range is suspect of being an escaped collection bird, while any away from the sea are also considered to be of feral origin. Based on these facts, the Michigan Bird Records Committee does not include the Barnacle Goose on its official state list.

Among the reports in Michigan are two specimens (at Central Michigan University): one from the Shiawassee State Game Area on 18 October 1973, and one from the Shiawassee National Wildlife Refuge on 25 October 1974. Photographic records include an individual at the Todd Farm, Allegan County, from late October through 1 November 1979 (with a second bird not photographed); one at the Allegan State Game Area from late October to 6 November 1983; and a bird shot in Kalamazoo County in October 1985. Additionally, there are sight records on 21 May 1965 from Naubinway, Mackinac County; in October 1976 (two birds) and on 30 March 1980 from Fish Point, Tuscola County; and on 7 March 1983 from the Muskegon Wastewater System. —James Granlund

# CANADA GOOSE

## (*Branta canadensis*)

The Canada Goose is an abundant migrant and common permanent resident in Michigan. This species originally bred across the northern portion of North America, from the high tundra south to the prairie potholes region and the Great Lakes. Today it is the world's most common goose as the result of widespread introductions.

The Canada Goose has many races or forms, of which 12 are widely recognized. Several of these have been recorded in the state, including some of the smallest races. The two forms most commonly encountered here are the migrant interior form, *B. c. interior*, and the breeding Giant form, *B. c. maxima*.

Migrant Canada Geese in Michigan typically originate from populations south and west of James Bay. They "stage" or stop over in the state on their migration to and from their breeding grounds in the north and wintering grounds in Alabama, Tennessee, Kentucky, and Illinois. Migrants begin arriving in late February and reach peak numbers by early April, rapidly disappearing by late April to early May. The reverse trip occurs from late September through December, with peak numbers in mid-November. Exactly how many of these migrants remain for the winter is complicated by the local populations of Giants which regularly stay. Canada Geese tend to congregate in large numbers in wildlife refuges or other areas with accessible grazing habitat. Among those places known to have big winter flocks are the Todd Farm in Allegan County, the Muskegon Wastewater System, Shiawassee National Wildlife Refuge in Saginaw County, and the Kellogg Bird Sanctuary in Kalamazoo County.

The exact breeding distribution of this species in presettlement Michigan is unclear because it was already absent from the state as a breeder by the middle 1800s, the result of overhunting. In the 1920s, W. K. Kellogg introduced in Calhoun County and H. M. Wallace in Livingston County the then recently rediscovered race of the Giant Canada. These programs were highly successful, and birds were soon moved to stock other locations such as the Seney National Wildlife Refuge in 1936.

Today, the Giant Canada Goose is a common breeding species throughout the state. It is versatile in its choice of nesting habitat, preferring sites with emergent wetland vegetation, especially islands in small ponds or marshes, but using a wide range of structures, even old Osprey nests and old boats. Along with a nest site, the breeding pair needs an associated upland grazing area. Because this species adapts well to human-modified environments, geese can be found nesting at golf courses, city parks, farm ponds, even roadside ditches.

The nest is often built on an elevated platform, such as a muskrat house, and consists of a hollow scrape lined with vegetation and down. Clutches average five eggs but may sometimes contain up to a dozen because of egg dumping by other females. In Michigan, laying normally begins in late March in the Lower Peninsula and mid-April in the Upper Peninsula. Incubation takes 25 to 30 days, and the goslings are reared in about 10 weeks.

Most resident Canadas migrate to the southern Lower Peninsula to winter, although in harsh winters they move farther south, some as far as Mississippi. Conversely, in mild winters thousands may remain in the state. One indication of the remarkable increase in geese is the Christmas bird count per 10 party-hour totals, which may have more than doubled since 1970; the 1992–93 count exceeded 56,000.

The population of resident Canada Geese is expected to continue increasing in the future. Already, negative confrontations between man and goose have become a growing problem in many urban and suburban communities. Attempts to control nuisance birds by removal and extended hunting seasons have seemingly had little impact, as birds move into protected areas during times of hunting. The establishment of the Giant Canada Goose, which has been one of the greatest success stories for wildlife managers, may well become one of their greatest nightmares. —James Granlund

# WOOD DUCK

(*Aix sponsa*)

As if constructed in an artist's studio, the male Wood Duck is a rich blend of vibrant colors and intricate patterns. This species is a common summer resident and migrant and a rare winter resident in Michigan. The Wood Duck is divided into eastern and western populations. The former breeds from the Gulf coast to central Texas and north to the Canadian prairies and Maritime Provinces, and winters primarily from Maryland west to Arkansas and south to the Gulf coast. The western population nests west of the Sierra Nevadas and Cascades from southern California north to Vancouver Island and east to British Columbia, and

winters mainly in the Central Valley of California.

Wood Ducks begin arriving on their Michigan breeding grounds in mid-March to early April, although mild winters may encourage an earlier return. After the nesting season, departure for the southern wintering grounds begins in early September, and most are gone by mid- to late October. Small numbers remain into December and may overwinter in the Lower Peninsula in mild years. On Michigan Christmas bird counts from 1970 to 1992, totals averaged about 30 Wood Ducks per season.

Nesting is initiated soon after spring arrival, usually by mid- to late April in the Lower Peninsula and a week or two later in the Upper Peninsula. Optimum breeding habitats include creek or river bottoms, floodplains, and other similar sites which provide mature hardwood trees with cavities for nesting, typically within a mile of water. The entrance to the cavity is usually 10 to 19 inches in diameter and located about 30 feet or more above the ground, although some are found as low as 2 feet and as high as 65 feet. Nest boxes have been widely used to supplement natural cavities, and these have been very successful.

Wood Duck clutches typically contain 12 eggs, which are laid at a rate of 1 per day. Egg dumping is common in this species, whereby several females may lay eggs into a single nest; these are sometimes not incubated and may reach clutch sizes of 40 or more. Incubation by hens lasts from 28 to 37 days.

After hatching, the hen broods the chicks for 24 hours before leading them from the nest, an exit which often requires the young to freefall 30 feet or more. The chicks are led to water, where they are cared for by the hen, fledging after 8 to 10 weeks. Well-meaning persons often find seemingly unattended ducklings, bringing them to rehabilitation centers for care. In most instances, though, these chicks are being led to water and the secretive hen is hiding nearby. The young's diet consists mainly of animal life, mostly insects, and progressively changes to plant food as they mature. Acorns are the preferred food of adults, but they will also utilize other seeds, fruit, and even waste corn.

The secretive nature of the Wood Duck alters our perception of how common this species is in Michigan. During the Breeding Bird Atlas project, it was found throughout the state, reaching its highest breeding concentrations in the southwestern portion of the Lower Peninsula. Like several other ducks, this species had a brush with extirpation from the state in the last century. Overhunting and habitat loss caused a severe reduction in populations such that by the early 1900s it was rare in Michigan. The implementation of strict hunting regulations and the later use of nest boxes to supplement natural cavities have aided in the remarkable comeback of this colorful duck. —James Granlund

*Wood Duck*
HEINER HERTLING

H.C.Hortling

H.C.Hertling

# GREEN-WINGED TEAL

## (*Anas crecca*)

The smallest and perhaps prettiest dabbling duck in Michigan, the Green-winged Teal is a common migrant and rare summer and winter resident. This diminutive duck breeds in a continuous band around the northern portion of the Northern Hemisphere. In North America, Green-winged Teal breed in Alaska, Canada, and the northern United States south to northern California, the Central Plains, and the Upper Great Lakes. This species has a very large wintering range extending as far north as Alaska and the Great Lakes and as far south as South America. The majority winter along the Atlantic coast of the Carolinas, the western Gulf coast, the Central Valley of California, and the Pacific coast of Mexico.

Green-winged Teal begin arriving in Michigan around mid-March or earlier, depending on the mildness of the winter. Migrants are common in the Lower Peninsula into mid-April and then are essentially gone by early May, although a few may linger into early June. Green-wings remain longer in the Upper Peninsula, and individuals seen after late May are either summering nonbreeders or possible breeders. In fall migrants begin returning by mid-September, with numbers peaking in mid-October and decreasing to low levels by December. In mild years some Green-winged Teal will remain through winter where there is open water and proper forage. Small numbers are regularly encountered on Christmas bird counts in the southern portion of the state.

Large marshes provide excellent habitat during migration, and numbers can build to impressive totals. The Shiawassee National Wildlife Refuge in Saginaw County provides some of the best habitat in the state, and numbers exceeding 500 individuals are often recorded each spring and autumn. Even more impressive were the 1,900 recorded on 14 September 1991 at Pte. Mouillee, Monroe County. Other good locations are Nayanquing State Game Area, Bay County, and the Erie Marsh Preserve, Monroe County.

Being on the periphery of their range, relatively few Green-winged Teal remain to nest in the state. During the Michigan Breeding Bird Atlas only 82 reports of this species were received, of which only 20 were of confirmed breeding. These confirmations were spread throughout the state, but were most common in the Upper Peninsula and Saginaw Bay area. Although specific nesting data for Michigan were unavailable in the literature, one might presume that nesting is initiated in late May to late June. Green-winged Teal select upland sites, with the nest constructed on the ground, typically within 100 feet of a pond, lake, or slough. The nest is a simple depression in the vegetation located in dense grass or other cover. Clutches average nine eggs, and incubation takes 21 to 23 days. Soon after incubation commences, the drake deserts the hen, leaving her to the task of rearing the chicks. Green-winged Teal prefer to forage on mud flats or shallowly flooded fields, where they eat seeds, mollusks, and insects.
—James Granlund

*Blue-winged Teal*
*Green-winged Teal*
HEINER HERTLING

# AMERICAN BLACK DUCK

## (*Anas rubripes*)

Resembling the more familiar female Mallard, the American Black Duck is not really black but a sooty brown. It is an uncommon permanent resident and wintering species in Michigan, found here more commonly on migration. This duck of the eastern woodlands breeds from the treeline of the Atlantic coast west to central Manitoba, south to southern Michigan, and east to coastal North Carolina. It winters from the Gulf coast of Texas and northern Florida north to southern New England and central Wisconsin. In Michigan, some individuals may remain year-round, but most are driven from their northern breeding areas by the progressing ice, to winter on the Ohio and Mississippi rivers.

Migrant Black Ducks first arrive in the state as the ice begins to melt in late January and early February, while others winter in the southern portions of the state where open water exists. This species is commonly encountered on Christmas bird counts, with annual totals averaging about 2,000 individuals in the period from 1970 to 1992. During migration large concentrations of Black Ducks may build up in appropriate habitats. Two exceptional locations are Shiawassee National Wildlife Refuge, Saginaw County, where a daily total of 2,000 is not unusual, and the Muskegon Wastewater System, Muskegon County, with totals approaching 1,500 or more.

American Black Ducks in Michigan nest in forested wetlands, shrublands, riparian habitats, and beaver impoundments. The nest is typically built on the substrate near water, although some have been found in tree cavities and other unusual locations. Nesting begins early, often in April in the south and by May farther north. A clutch normally consists of nine eggs, with incubation lasting about 27 days and fledging occurring in an additional seven to eight weeks. The Black Duck's forage includes both animal and vegetable matter, with the former being particularly important on the wintering grounds. Like many other ducks, this species has become increasingly attracted to agricultural spoilage and can often be found feeding in fields with Mallards.

The exact status of this species in Michigan prior to settlement is unclear, but it became increasingly abundant as a breeder in the middle of this century. At one time the American Black Duck was the most abundant breeding duck in the state. Since the 1950s its numbers have declined, and today it is eclipsed by the Mallard, Blue-winged Teal, and Wood Duck for that honor. During the Michigan Breeding Bird Atlas, the Black Duck was found sparingly in all counties. It was encountered most frequently in the Upper Peninsula, a result of the greater availability of suitable breeding habitat. Because of the difficulty of censusing the often remote habitats occupied by the Black Duck, the extent of its occurrence in Michigan may have been underrepresented by the Atlas.

The reasons for declines in Black Duck numbers in the last half of this century are unclear. Loss of habitat on both the wintering and breeding grounds may account for some of the decline, but not all. Other factors cited in the literature include lake acidification and its associated loss of forage, and genetic swamping by the Mallard due to hybridization. —James Granlund

## MALLARD
### (Anas platyrhynchos)

Perhaps the most recognized of all ducks, the Mallard is a common permanent resident and abundant migrant in Michigan. This prairie species has been widely introduced into new habitats across North America and currently breeds from Arctic Alaska to southern California and east to Quebec and central Pennsylvania. It additionally breeds throughout northern Eurasia and may well be its most abundant duck. In Michigan there are numerous local populations of permanent residents, of which many may be escaped domestic ducks or domestic-wild crosses. Truly wild birds tend to migrate from the state in late December to early January as the ice front approaches. Most winter on the Mississippi River and Atlantic coast, but some remain where open water and food are available.

In spring Mallards begin arriving as early as late January and early February, well before the lakes are completely free of ice. During both spring and fall migrations, resident Mallards are supplemented with large numbers of birds which breed in Canada and other Great Lakes states, and concentrations exceeding 30,000 are regularly reported in such locations as the Shiawassee National Wildlife Refuge, Saginaw County, and the Muskegon Wastewater System.

Historically, Mallards were probably present as a breeding species in the prairie areas of presettlement Michigan. In the early part of this century, like many other ducks, this species declined in numbers to the point where it was an uncommon resident. By the 1950s and 1960s populations rebounded, and today it is the most common breeding duck in Michigan. During the Breeding Bird Atlas, Mallards were found nesting in every county of the state, and breeding bird surveys show them to be most abundant in the southwestern portion of the Lower Peninsula and in the Saginaw Bay area.

Mallards use a wide variety of nesting habitats, and it appears that the most critical requirement is access to shallow water areas for feeding. The Mallard also requires a suitable nest site, but again the species shows a great deal of flexibility in its selection. Preferred sites appear to be upland areas such as dry marshes or hayfields. The nest itself is placed on the ground and is well concealed by vegetation. Egg laying begins as early as March, and the season extends into August. A typical clutch consists of nine eggs, with incubation lasting 24 to 32 days. The young fledge in an additional 55 to 60 days, a rather long period for a duck. Nearly 90% of a Mallard's diet consists of vegetable matter, including wild rice, pond weeds, and other emergent plants. They also consume a large amount of agricultural grains and during migration are often seen feeding in fields.

The great plasticity in the selection of both nesting habitat and forage ensures the Mallard a continued common existence in Michigan. Its ability to interbreed with several other duck species has become of increasing interest to biologists. Of particular concern is the amount of hybridization between the Mallard and the American Black Duck, which appears to threaten the continued existence of the latter as a species. —James Granlund

## NORTHERN PINTAIL
### (Anas acuta)

The Northern Pintail is a common migrant across Michigan but only a rare summer and winter resident. As with many ducks, its breeding distribution is circumpolar. On this continent, pintails breed from the high arctic south to central California, the central Great Plains, the Upper Great Lakes, and east to the Maritime Provinces. The wintering grounds are also expansive, covering much of the United States (coastal and interior) and extending south through Mexico to Central and South America. One of the most abundant ducks in North America, this species is much more common in the West than the East.

In Michigan pintail begin arriving as early as late February, although the migration does not peak until the middle of April. Most have departed the state by mid-May, with only small numbers oversummering as nonbreeders and even fewer pairs as breeders. The autumn migration commences in mid-September, peaks toward the end of October, and most individuals have departed by mid-December.

Small numbers of pintail overwinter in lower Michigan, where open water and forage are available. This dabbling duck is not uncommon on Christmas bird counts, with an average of 60 seen each year since 1970. There has been a slight increase in numbers over the past few winters, and a record high total of 365 was reported on the 1990–91 count.

The majority of Northern Pintails follow migratory flyways west of the Great Lakes, with smaller proportions following easterly routes. In Michigan, numbers are typically higher in spring, with flocks generally averaging less than 1,000 birds. There are some years when considerably larger groups may be encountered, as happened on 9 April 1970 when 6,000 were recorded at Shiawassee National Wildlife Refuge, Saginaw County. In contrast, the highest flock counts in fall rarely exceed 300. Major pintail concentrations in both seasons occur in large marshy wetlands such as those in the Saginaw Bay area. According to banding recoveries, most traveling through Michigan appear to nest from the western prairies of Canada to the Ontario region north of Lake

*Mallard*
*American Black Duck*
GIJSBERT VAN FRANKENHUYZEN

Superior and winter along the Atlantic coast to the Caribbean.

The Northern Pintail probably nested in the state historically, though it is unlikely that it was ever common, since Michigan is at the southernmost periphery of its breeding range. During this century nests have been found sparingly and in widely scattered locales throughout the state. In the 1980s Atlas survey, breeding for pintails was confirmed in 12 townships, nearly all of which were adjacent to the Great Lakes. This mirrors previous nesting records from large coastal marshes. One of the most often used areas is St. Clair Flats in St. Clair County. Other recent breeding spots include Pte. Mouillee in Monroe County, the Saginaw Bay area (Crow Island State Game Area, Fish Point, and Nayanquing Point), the coastal marshes of Delta County, plus sites in Emmet and Houghton counties.

One of the earliest-breeding ducks, pintail are known to initiate nesting in Michigan around the middle of April in the south, probably a week or so later in the north. Nests are a scrape on the ground in low or sparse vegetation, sometimes even on bare ground. They are normally located within 100 yards of water, although distances of a mile or more have been recorded. A typical clutch contains eight eggs, with incubation lasting about 23 days. An additional seven to eight weeks are needed for the young to mature to fledging stage.

The Northern Pintail along with other prairie ducks suffered rather severe declines during the past decade. Surveys in 1987 indicated that numbers were down 44% from their past 31-year average. Michigan has seen a similar drop in its migrant totals, as the thousands regularly recorded during spring migrations in the 1970s and early 1980s dwindled to hundreds by the latter half of the 1980s and early 1990s. Declines are attributed primarily to loss of breeding habitat farther west in the prairie pothole region, worsened by drought conditions during the period, and to loss of habitat in the Central Valley of California, where traditionally about half of the continent's pintail population wintered. Whether these declines continue will be determined by actions taken in the preservation of critical breeding, wintering, and migration areas for pintail as well as for other prairie ducks. —James Granlund

# GARGANEY

## (*Anas querquedula*)

The Garganey is accidental in Michigan, with a single sight record on 24 April 1991 near Bridgeport in Saginaw County. A member of the Old World avifauna, this teal breeds across northern Eurasia and winters from western Africa to southern Japan. Gar-

*Northern Shoveler*
*Northern Pintail*
HEINER HERTLING

ganeys generally migrate in a westerly fashion in fall and an easterly fashion in spring, and individuals often overshoot their breeding grounds, resulting in extralimital records. Since the late 1950s, Garganeys have been appearing in North America with increasing frequency. Most records, including the one for Michigan, are of the striking male with its distinctive crescent-shaped head marking. Females, on the other hand, are much more difficult to separate from their relative the Blue-winged Teal. Because of its showy plumage, the Garganey is common in private collections, thereby complicating the origin of sightings of these supposed accidental visitors. Most records, however, do occur during the normal migration for this species and in flocks of Blue-winged Teal, as was the case for Michigan. This supports the hypothesis that many of the individuals seen on this continent are true vagrants, and for this reason the Garganey was added to the official state bird list, though there is always the possibility that this bird originated from captivity and not the wild. —James Granlund

# BLUE-WINGED TEAL

## (*Anas discors*)

The Blue-winged Teal is a common breeding resident and migrant in Michigan. This species has one of the widest ranges of any duck in North America, breeding across the continent as far north as Alaska and as far south as Maryland and Arizona, with occasional breeding to Florida. It is also among the most highly migratory waterfowl, wintering in Central and South America as far south as Argentina, although most occur in Central America and the Gulf of Mexico. Substantial numbers also remain during the winter in the extreme southern reaches of the lower 48 states.

In Michigan the Blue-winged Teal is widespread and likely breeds in all counties of the state. Breeding densities reach their maximum in the southwestern Lower Peninsula and Saginaw Bay area, where open fields adjacent to marshes and small impoundments provide optimum habitat. The species is least common in areas where heavy forest predominates in the northern Lower and Upper peninsulas. On migration this teal often stages on large shallow ponds and impoundments; even flooded fields can host hundreds of migrants.

The Blue-wing's winter status, as well as its occurrence on Christmas bird counts, is difficult to assess because of misidentification with the very similar Green-winged Teal, which winters regularly in the state. True winter records are most likely of birds whose migration was impaired by injury or similar problems. Blue-winged Teal typically arrive in Michigan in late March and depart by early October. Peak migration over most of the state probably occurs in mid-April and again in late August through early September. In years when ice lingers late into spring, impressive numbers will build in the southern Lower Peninsula until they can head farther north.

Most individuals pair on the wintering grounds or during migration; as a consequence, nesting ensues soon after their arrival on the breeding grounds. Ideal breeding habitat includes open fields of bluegrass or sedges adjacent to wetlands or ponds. Hayfields are also used but are less favorable, as hens and nests are subject to injury or destruction from mowing. The Blue-wing's nest is a shallow depression on the ground, lined with grasses or cattails plus down from the female. Muskrat houses or other slightly elevated locations close to water are frequently chosen. Nests are very well concealed, making detection difficult. Incubation of the 10 eggs (average) lasts 21 to 27 days, with young fledging after about six weeks. Nest losses can be high from predators such as crows, skunks, and raccoons. Also deleterious are fluctuating water levels which flood many nests.

The Blue-winged Teal was first reported in Michigan by Sager (1839). It was likely a common breeding species in the Lower Peninsula during presettlement times and remained so into the late 1800s. Given their habitat preference, Blue-wings would certainly have been less common in the northern Lower and Upper peninsulas in that same period. By the turn of the century, populations had suffered serious declines due to both habitat loss and hunting pressures. With imposition of new harvest regulations and gradual recovery of some habitats, the Blue-wing began a comeback in the early 1930s and by the 1940s was again considered a common breeding or summering species statewide. More recent loss of habitat, particularly draining and filling of wetlands and succession of grasslands, has once again caused local declines in Michigan. The Blue-wing's fate, as well as that of many marsh species, rests in our willingness and ability to preserve wetlands. —James Granlund

## CINNAMON TEAL

### (*Anas cyanoptera*)

This westerly distributed teal is an accidental visitant to Michigan. Of the five races inhabiting the Western Hemisphere, only one nests in North America, from southern British Columbia, Alberta, and the extreme western Dakotas south to Mexico and Texas. The winter range extends from central California through Mexico to Central America. It is during migration that vagrant Cinnamon Teal occur east of their usual range.

This species was first recorded in the state in April of 1939 or 1940, when Dr. Charles Black examined a teal killed by a hunter in Saginaw County. It was not reported again until 19 April 1959, when detailed notes were taken for a bird at Zilwaukee, also in Saginaw County. Subsequent observations include a male on 9 May 1968 at Fish Point, Tuscola County; an individual on 2 May 1977 near St. Ignace, Mackinaw County; a male on 26–28 April 1982 in Macomb County; a male on 29 March 1988 at Pte. Mouillee, Monroe County; a male on 2 April 1988 in Allegan County; and a male on 12 April 1992 at Nayanquing, Bay County. The only fall record and existing specimen is from 30 September 1969 in Marcellus, Cass County.

As with other waterfowl which may be kept in collections, the origin of extralimital records must be considered. Although one can never be certain, the case for the aforementioned records being legitimate wild birds is strong. As is typical of vagrant Cinnamon Teal, those found in Michigan were associated with

Blue-winged Teal and were encountered during their normal migration period. Frank Bellrose postulated that "strays [Cinnamon Teal] become attached to flocks of Blue-winged Teal on their mutual wintering grounds and become, at least temporarily, a part of the Blue-wings' traditional migration pattern." More enlightening is the fact that in 1988, when two appeared in Michigan, several others were seen in the Great Lakes and even farther east. —James Granlund

## NORTHERN SHOVELER

### (*Anas clypeata*)

The large spatulate bill is the most conspicuous feature of this duck, which is a common migrant in Michigan, but only a rare winter and summer resident. The Northern Shoveler is cosmopolitan in distribution, found widely in both the Northern and Southern hemispheres. In North America, breeding populations occur primarily west of the Great Lakes, with greatest densities in the northern prairie pothole region. Marshes and lagoons in the southern United States, Mexico, and Central America constitute the main wintering grounds. Banding and migration data indicate that most Northern Shovelers passing through Michigan probably breed in the Canadian prairies and winter along the central Atlantic coast.

Excluding the small numbers which stay the winter in Michigan, first arrival of northbound migrant shovelers is usually in mid- to late March, with numbers peaking during April and mostly departed by late May. This species is rarely encountered in large flocks in spring; instead gatherings of 5 to 20 shovelers are typical. Some individuals will linger through the summer in Michigan, but very few breed.

In the fall, a few transients may be seen in late August, but the main flight commences in September and peaks around the middle of October. This is the season when larger flocks approaching several hundred shovelers are found in coastal marshes and sewage lagoons, with the Muskegon Wastewater System being a particularly prime location. This is also a good time to watch this duck use its uniquely shaped bill to feed on microscopic plankton and various macroscopic animal life, such as water beetles, water boatmen, and midge and caddisfly larvae. The southbound migration gradually tapers off through November, with very few individuals remaining through the winter at locations where open water and food remain available.

The Northern Shoveler is one of the rarest winter ducks in Michigan, recorded in most years but only in small numbers.

*Gadwall*
*American Wigeon*
HEINER HERTLING

Christmas bird count totals since 1970 have averaged about 10 shovelers per year, although there has been a gradual trend of increasing numbers since 1990, with a high total of 60 on the 1991–92 count.

Although we know that the Northern Shoveler was present in Michigan historically because of its inclusion on A. Sager's 1839 list, its exact status during this time is unclear. Breeding confirmations for this species have apparently always been rare, a fact most attributable to its westerly distribution. Known breeding locales include the marshes of Saginaw Bay, Lake St. Clair and Lake Erie, Seney National Wildlife Refuge in Schoolcraft County, Houghton Lake marshes in Roscommon County, and various sewage lagoons around the state. The first published breeding record appears to be from Fish Point, Tuscola County, where an adult female and two downy young were collected on 19 June 1936. Interestingly, one of the three confirmed breedings during the recent statewide Breeding Bird Atlas was from the same location. The two others were at Pte. Mouillee, Monroe County, and the Wakefield Sewage Ponds, Gogebic County.

Shovelers typically locate their nest within 75 to 200 feet of water, usually a pond. Upland sites with grasses less than 12 inches high are preferred. The ground nest is lined with grass and then down. Nesting in the state is probably initiated sometime during May. Females lay an average of nine eggs, which are incubated for 28 days. The hen and her brood remain together for 36 to 66 days.

While there seems to be a slight increase in the occurrence of the Northern Shoveler in the state over the past decade, it remains both a rare breeding and winter resident. Only during the migration period, particularly fall, can it be labeled as common. Most breeding has occurred in association with the large marsh complexes at wildlife refuges or sewage ponds. There certainly appears to be ample habitat to support more breeding pairs, but since Michigan is situated at the periphery of its range, the Northern Shoveler will most likely remain one of our rarer breeding ducks.
—James Granlund

# GADWALL

## (Anas strepera)

The Gadwall is a common migrant, rare summer resident, and rare winter resident in Michigan. This rather plain, grayish-brown dabbling duck occurs throughout the Northern Hemisphere, and in North America breeds predominantly in the West from Alaska to California and Colorado and east across the northern Great Plains to Minnesota. Recently it has expanded this range in the Great Lakes region and beyond. In winter Gadwalls are found mainly on the Gulf coast of the United States (especially Louisiana) and Mexico, with lesser numbers scattered about coastal and inland sites from California to the Chesapeake and north to the Great Lakes.

In Michigan, Gadwall begin arriving toward the end of March, peak in numbers in mid-April, and are mostly gone by mid- to late May. A small number of birds remain through the summer, very few of which breed. Fall migration commences in mid-

September but does not reach its peak until the middle of November. Most have departed the state by mid-December, though some may linger through the winter where water remains open, such as in Prairie Ronde Township in Kalamazoo County. Numbers on Michigan Christmas bird counts during the late December–early January period average about 300, but many of these move on as the water freezes.

Most of the migrants to Michigan appear to originate from the western Great Plains population and winter in the Chesapeake Bay area. Large congregations are infrequent during migration, and high totals at any one site rarely exceed 50 individuals in spring and 200 in fall. Inland ponds, lakes, and marshes are the aquatic habitats frequented by this duck.

For some unexplained reason the Gadwall has extended its breeding range into the East over the past several decades. This expansion has included Michigan, with the first confirmed breeding record documented in 1950 on Black River Island, Alpena County. Since then scattered nestings have been recorded throughout the state. During the 1980s Atlas, Gadwall were reported in 20 townships with breeding confirmed in seven locations, all in counties adjacent to the Great Lakes and two from islands, Drummond and the Beaver Island group. The most inland breeding locale was the Muskegon Wastewater System.

Gadwalls nest in upland sites within 100 yards of water. The nest is built on the ground in dense vegetation, and a typical clutch contains 10 eggs. Hens incubate the eggs for about 26 days and tend to the hatchlings until they reach fledging age, around seven weeks. The onset of breeding is rather late compared to other ducks, with most nests initiated in mid- to late May. This late start may explain the unusually high success rate of 68% documented for this species elsewhere in its range. Typical forage consists mainly of vegetative parts of submerged plants.

The Gadwall was probably present as a transient in Michigan during presettlement times, as it was listed as early as 1839 by A. Sager. Barrows (1912) considered it to be a rare duck here, but believed it probably nested in the state even though he had no direct evidence. Wood (1951), on the other hand, described the species as an uncommon transient. Payne (1983) then upgraded its status to common transient and uncommon summer resident. Interestingly, these modifications in description mirror well the change in status which has taken place in the heart of its range. The Gadwall is known for its long-term cycles of abundance and scarcity. For example, populations underwent a downturn near the beginning of the century but have been increasing rapidly since about the 1950s, which may account for the aforementioned range shift. In neighboring Ontario this species has gone from breeding obscurity to sizable local populations. Only time will tell if the same will be true for Michigan. —James Granlund

# EURASIAN WIGEON

## (Anas penelope)

The Eurasian Wigeon is a casual visitor to Michigan. A relative of the American Wigeon, this species resides in the Old World but is

a regular wanderer to both coasts of North America, more frequently to the Pacific. Banding returns indicate that birds showing up on the Atlantic coast originate from Iceland, whereas Pacific coast visitors most likely come from the Kamchatka Peninsula. The origin of inland records is more problematic since this handsome duck is often kept in aviculturalists' collections. However, nearly all of the 55 reports of Eurasian Wigeons published in the *Jack-Pine Warbler* since 1960 fall within the normal migration period of the American Wigeon (mid-March to mid-April and mid-August to mid-December), with which the Eurasian usually occurs. This suggests that the Eurasian Wigeons seen in Michigan are mostly wild vagrants rather than escaped birds. There is one specimen for the state, providing official documentation of its occurrence. This was a bird taken from Erie Marsh in Monroe County on 25 October 1936, housed at the Carnegie Museum. —James Granlund

# AMERICAN WIGEON

## (*Anas americana*)

The American Wigeon or Baldpate is a common migrant and rare winter and summer resident in Michigan. As with many ducks, the female is a plain-colored bird while the breeding male is distinctively marked, especially on the head, which has a white crown and shiny green side bands in this species. The American Wigeon breeds from Alaska across most of Canada to James Bay and south into the United States to northern California, Nevada, the Dakotas, and Minnesota. The primary wintering areas are in the Central Valley of California, coastal Louisiana, and the Texas Panhandle, with lesser numbers along the Atlantic coast, in Florida and some of the Caribbean Islands, along other parts of the Gulf coast, and south through Mexico into Central America.

Spring migrants begin arriving in Michigan in the first half of March, with the peak occurring during the middle of April. Most wigeon have departed for more northerly nesting grounds by late May to early June, leaving behind a small number of over-summering nonbreeders and breeding pairs. The return of autumn migrants commences in late August and early September, with peak numbers occurring in mid-October. Most of these southbound individuals are gone by late November, although some linger through December, and a few may select to stay the winter where appropriate food and open water exists. On Michigan Christmas bird counts for the 1970–91 period, the average number of American Wigeon reported per year was 85.

During the spring migration, this duck is rarely seen in very large concentrations, with totals below 200 individuals usual at any one locale. Such is not the case in the fall season, when gatherings are much larger, oftentimes approaching 500 and even 1,000 birds. Most impressive was the report of 3,000 American Wigeon on 28 September 1991 at the Erie Marsh Preserve, Monroe County. Other locations where observers regularly find large fall flocks are the Muskegon Wastewater System, the entire Saginaw Bay area, and the Shiawassee National Wildlife Refuge in Saginaw

County. Most of the migrants passing through Michigan apparently winter along the Atlantic coast.

It is difficult to interpret the historical status of the American Wigeon in the state. Barrows (1912) called it rare in Michigan and doubted that it ever nested or wintered here. Yet in 1938, this species was confirmed breeding at Seney National Wildlife Refuge, Schoolcraft County, and since then it has been found breeding sporadically throughout the state. During the 1980s Breeding Bird Atlas it was noted in suitable habitat in 34 townships, with documented breeding in three counties: Houghton, Chippewa, and Saginaw. In Houghton and Chippewa counties broods were found on sewage ponds, while in Saginaw breeding was confirmed at the Shiawassee National Wildlife Refuge.

Typically this species prefers to nest on an upland site, with the distance from water varying from a few yards to more than 400. The nest is a depression in the ground, situated in a clump of concealing vegetative cover. Clutches of eight to nine eggs are usual, with incubation requiring about 23 days and young fledgling in an additional seven weeks. Wigeon primarily eat aquatic weeds, grazing upon their leafy parts, stems, and seeds. They have also been observed eating agricultural wastage and can be found on migration in farm fields feeding among Mallards and Canada Geese.

Like several other species of ducks, the American Wigeon has expanded its range eastward over the past half-century, a change which is clearly evident by its increased presence in Michigan. What has caused this expansion remains a mystery, although one must suspect loss of habitat in its traditional breeding areas to our west and the creation of new habitats (e.g., sewage ponds) in the east as having a major role. Today the American Wigeon remains a rare breeding species in the state, though ample habitat appears to exist to allow for further increase and a larger population. —James Granlund

# CANVASBACK

## (*Aythya valisineria*)

This handsome duck with the chestnut-red head and sloping profile is a common migrant and winter resident in the state, but only a rare summer resident. Michigan lies at the southeastern periphery of the Canvasback's breeding range, which extends from Alaska and western Canada to extreme northern California, Nebraska, central Manitoba, and Minnesota. The main wintering areas are along the Atlantic and Pacific coasts, with high concentrations in the Chesapeake and San Francisco bays. Lesser numbers winter in the southern and eastern Great Lakes, on scattered inland waters elsewhere in the United States, along the Gulf coast, and in Mexico.

In Michigan, most migrating Canvasbacks begin arriving in mid-March and have departed by early May. A small number linger into early June, and a few remain all summer, with breeding rarely reported. Autumn migrants are generally first noted around the middle of October, with numbers peaking through November. By early December, Canvasbacks have va-

GIJSBERT-1992

cated most of the state except for the southeast, where flocks become concentrated on the St. Clair and Detroit rivers and western Lake Erie and remain until permanent ice formation drives them to wintering areas on the East Coast. Based on recoveries of banded individuals, it appears that most transients in Michigan nest in the Canadian Prairie Provinces.

During mild winters, large numbers of Canvasback will stay all season along the coast of southeastern Michigan. Between late autumn and early spring, more Canvasback are seen here than at any other location in the state, with totals in some places exceeding 10,000 individuals and even approaching 20,000. Among the prime spots to witness these masses are Anchor Bay, St. Clair County; Metrobeach, Macomb County; Belle Isle, Wayne County; and Pte. Mouillee, Monroe County. Since 1980, totals reported on Michigan Christmas bird counts have averaged about 10,000 to 15,000 individuals, ranging from a low of 3,872 in 1981–82 to an exceptionally high total of 43,147 in 1991–92.

The Canvasback was likely an abundant migrant in Michigan historically, particularly from southern Lake Huron to western Lake Erie—an area which was once a vast wetland. Even into the middle 1800s, the species was apparently abundant in this region, as it was extensively harvested by market hunters. By the turn of the century, however, this and many other ducks had declined precipitously, likely from hunting pressure and loss of habitat. With the institution of harvesting seasons and bag limits, populations recovered in the early part of the 1900s, only to incur serious declines decades later as habitat further deteriorated.

Today the Canvasback is still a common migrant here, but the numbers are no doubt lower than those of decades ago, since populations continentwide are known to be much reduced. Its breeding status historically remains unclear because of a lack of evidence. Payne (1983) lists a record of breeding in the Portage Marsh, Delta County, when a female with small downy young was observed on 18 July 1955. More recently breeding was documented via brood sightings at two additional sites, the Muskegon Wastewater System and Pte. Mouillee.

Canvasbacks nest in an array of habitats including marshes, ponds, and sloughs. Although much variation exists among sites, the nest is typically located in cattails or similar cover over water 6 to 24 inches in depth. In the heart of their breeding range, nesting begins in May, and the 7 to 12 eggs hatch in 25 days. Animal foods are the choice of hens and broods, but for much of the rest of the year, Canvasbacks are primarily vegetarians and show an appetite for wild celery. The abundance of this plant in southeastern Michigan explains the large concentrations here during migration and winter.

Canvasback populations have declined seriously over the past 30 years, to the point that a moratorium on hunting this species has been imposed. Declines are attributed primarily to loss of breeding habitat in the western prairies, but degradation of winter and migration habitats must also have an effect. Of particular concern in Michigan is the loss of forage, particularly wild celery, in the staging and wintering areas in the southeastern Lower Peninsula. Pollution from waste oil and other chemicals as well as changes in topography of the rivers has greatly reduced the wild celery supply, according to state biologists. Continuing damage to the habitat may further harm this already stressed species. —James Granlund

## REDHEAD

### (*Aythya americana*)

Both the male Redhead and the male Canvasback have red heads, but the long, sloping bill of the latter species easily separates the two in the field. In Michigan, the Redhead is a common migrant, uncommon winter resident, and generally rare and local summer resident. Its main breeding grounds are the prairies and parklands in the north-central region of the North American continent, with scattered populations elsewhere, west to northern California and east to the Great Lakes. In winter Redheads stay primarily along the Gulf and Atlantic coasts north to the Chesapeake Bay and along both coasts of Mexico. Proportionally small numbers overwinter at inland locations across the continent, including the lower Great Lakes.

Migrants begin arriving in Michigan soon after the ice recedes in late February, with numbers peaking from late March to early April and most individuals departed by mid-May. Small numbers remain through the summer in the larger marshes in the state, but relatively few pairs breed. Autumn migrants begin returning in late August, with numbers building through October and peaking in November.

In the fall large congregations of Redheads stage in the Straits of Mackinac, remaining until inclement weather and ice drive them farther south. Another major staging area extends from the St. Clair Flats area south through the western end of Lake Erie, and substantial numbers linger here, either for the entire winter or until ice forces them out. Concentrations of 1,000 or more are commonly noted in the St. Clair area and an incredible 10,000 were reported there in 1988. Other good concentration points are Pte. Mouillee (Monroe County), Belle Isle (Wayne County), and Metrobeach (Macomb County). Elsewhere in the state Redheads are casual in winter but do remain where open water and forage are available. On Michigan Christmas bird counts since 1970, yearly totals have averaged about 2,000 individuals, with a high of over 12,000 in 1988–89.

Undoubtedly the Redhead was a common migrant in Michigan prior to settlement, most likely staging in the vast marshes of the southeastern Lower Peninsula. Even through the turn of this century it was a common game bird. As with many other ducks, though, populations must have experienced declines as breeding habitat in the northern prairie lands disappeared. Although numbers are reduced, the Redhead is still a common migrant in the state at present.

This diving duck has always been a rare nesting species in

*Canvasback*
*Redhead*
Gijsbert van Frankenhuyzen

Michigan, with early records coming from the St. Clair Flats and Saginaw Bay areas. Breeding was confirmed in nine townships, including Gogebic, Schoolcraft, Bay, Tuscola, St. Clair, and Monroe counties, during the 1980s Breeding Bird Atlas. This may underrepresent the actual numbers of pairs, since the Redhead's habit of nesting in large marshes makes censusing difficult. Based on the various records, nesting occurs most frequently in the St. Clair Flats and Saginaw Bay, although it also is a regular breeder at the Seney National Wildlife Refuge in the Upper Peninsula. In 1992, an unusually large number of Redheads stayed the summer at Pte. Mouillee, with a minimum of six broods detected.

As mentioned, this species prefers large marshes for breeding, with nests placed in thick, emergent vegetation directly over the water. A typical clutch averages 11 eggs, with incubation lasting 24 days and hens tending to broods for up to eight weeks. Egg dumping into other nests is a regular habit of hens, and as a result, clutches with 19 to 39 eggs are not uncommon. The Redhead is primarily a vegetarian, feeding on aquatic weeds and other submerged plants but switching to animal life when preferred forage is scarce.

Like most other wildlife that rely on wetlands, Redhead populations are threatened from loss of breeding habitat. Of greater concern in Michigan is the loss of migration habitat, as thousands of Redheads rely on the wild celery and other aquatic foods in the coastal waters of the southeastern Lower Peninsula. Degradation of water quality and the alteration of marshes have seriously depleted these food stocks. Unless these trends are stemmed, the Redhead may become not only a rare breeder in the state, but a rare species period. —James Granlund

# RING-NECKED DUCK

## (*Aythya collaris*)

The chestnut neck collar for which this duck is named is visible only under ideal conditions; however, the ring on its bill is quite obvious. This species is a common migrant and uncommon summer and winter resident in Michigan. Ring-necked Ducks breed in the boreal forests from central Canada east to the Atlantic coast and south to the northern tier of states. They winter mainly along the Atlantic and Gulf coasts from Massachusetts south to northern Central America.

Migrant Ring-necks begin arriving in Michigan soon after the ice retreats from the lakes, normally in late February or early March, with numbers peaking in mid-April. Most migrants have left the southern portions of the state by late April, although some may linger through the summer. Breeding birds in the northern portions of the state initiate nesting in May and continue through June. Fall migrants begin returning in late August, with numbers peaking by late October and most individuals gone by early December.

Where adequate open water and forage are available, this species will overwinter in small numbers. Although not numerous, the Ring-necked Duck is recorded annually on Christmas bird counts, with numbers from 1970 to 1992 averaging less than 40 individuals per year and a high count of 177 in 1987–88. On mi-

gration, large numbers may build up on large, shallow inland lakes. Totals exceeding 2,500 individuals have been recorded at locations such as the Shiawassee National Wildlife Refuge, Saginaw County.

The Ring-necked Duck must certainly have been a migrant to Michigan in presettlement times, but whether it bred within our limits is unknown. According to Walter Barrows (1912), it did not nest within the state; he further indicated it was an uncommon to rare migrant. In 1928 M. Pirnie discovered several broods of this species at Munuscong Bay in Chippewa County, and by the late 1930s several other breeding records were obtained from the eastern and central Upper Peninsula. By 1959 nesting also had been reported sparingly in the northern Lower Peninsula. Most interesting were breeding records from 1971 to 1974 in Kalamazoo County, far south of the traditional range for this species. For unexplained reasons this disjunct population disappeared and has not bred at this location since.

During the recent Breeding Bird Atlas, the Ring-necked Duck was confirmed breeding in 37 townships: 27 in the Upper Peninsula, 9 in the northern Lower, and only 1 in the southern Lower Peninsula (St. Clair Flats). The northern Lower Peninsula pairs were concentrated in the marshes from southern Otsego through Roscommon counties. Upper Peninsula records were spread uniformly through those counties with extensive boreal forests.

The Ring-neck's preferred breeding habitat includes small lakes, bogs, and sedge-dominated wetlands within boreal forests. The nest is often built on islets of floating marsh plants or in clumps of marsh vegetation, particularly sedges, sweet gale, and leatherleaf. A typical clutch consists of nine eggs, with incubation averaging 26 days and fledging occurring in an additional seven to eight weeks. This species typically feeds in waters less than six feet deep, shallower than most other diving ducks, taking both vegetation and animal life. On migration they show a fondness for wild rice and other seeds.

The Ring-necked Duck has certainly expanded its breeding range in Michigan since the 1930s, as it has in the eastern portion of North America as a whole. Today it seems limited within the state to areas of boreal-type vegetation. —James Granlund

# TUFTED DUCK

## (*Aythya fuligula*)

There is a single documented record of a Tufted Duck in Michigan, that of a male collected by a hunter in October 1973, on Whitmore Lake near the Livingston–Washtenaw County line. This specimen was examined and photographed at the University

*Ruddy Duck*
*Ring-necked Duck*
GIJSBERT VAN FRANKENHUYZEN

GIJSBERT - 1993

of Michigan Museum of Zoology, but even though identification was verified, the origin of the individual remains uncertain. This Old World duck breeds across the entire northern portion of Eurasia, south to about the 50th parallel. It is a long-distance migrant and no stranger to North America, being recorded with some regularity, particularly on the West Coast. But it is also a showy bird and popular among aviculturalists; thus the dilemma of origin plagues this species as it does so many other waterfowl vagrants. In addition to the one specimen, there are two records of Tufted Duck hybrids, the first being described as a Tufted–Ring-necked Duck cross found on Campau Bay in Macomb County on 2 April 1978, and the other a Tufted Duck–scaup hybrid seen from 10 January to 28 February 1989 at Belle Isle in Wayne County. —James Granlund

## GREATER SCAUP

### (Aythya marila)

"Great means green" is a good way to remember the color of the Greater Scaup's head, although this field mark is generally not very useful in separating the two scaup species. The Greater Scaup is a common migrant, uncommon winter resident, and rare summer visitant to Michigan. This species is nearly Holarctic in distribution, breeding in the high arctic from Iceland east through Eurasia and North America to the western shore of Hudson Bay. On this continent it winters along both coasts and inland on the Great Lakes.

Migrant Greater Scaup begin arriving in the state in early to mid-March, with the bulk of the migration occurring in mid- to late April. Most individuals are gone by mid-May, although some nonbreeders may linger and in some cases remain through the summer. The fall migration commences in early to mid-September, with the migration peaking in October. Numbers of Greater Scaup may become quite high on larger lakes and particularly in the southeastern portion of the state along the Detroit and St. Clair rivers. Areas known for their large concentrations include Ecorse and Belle Isle, both in Wayne County, Metrobeach in Macomb County, and the St. Clair River in St. Clair County.

Greater Scaup may overwinter in sizable numbers, particularly in the aforementioned locations if sufficient forage and open water remain, although small numbers may be found on lakes statewide. On Michigan Christmas bird counts, large numbers have been reported in some years; the highest total during the 1970–92 period was 1,253 in 1988–89. Nearly half of those were seen on the Anchor Bay count at the northern end of Lake St. Clair. More typical totals per year in the same period averaged around 500 individuals.

The historical status of the Greater Scaup in Michigan is confused by the difficulty in distinguishing this species from the very similar Lesser Scaup. Early authors such as Walter Barrows (1912) asserted that it was not possible to do so in the field and very difficult in the hand; therefore their accounts typically lumped the two species together. Today, better optics and field identification criteria allow observers to separate the two species under good

conditions, although many still forgo the task. Based on current information, it is quite reasonable to assume that the Greater Scaup has always been a common migrant on the Great Lakes, and less common inland. Today many observers take this distribution to an extreme, assuming flocks of scaup on the Great Lakes are Greaters and those inland are Lessers. There simply is not enough evidence to corroborate this notion. Based on data from census points such as Whitefish Point, both Lesser and Greater Scaup are common on the Great Lakes, and observers must use care in determining which variety they are encountering.

There is a single questionable breeding record for this species from the St. Clair Flats in 1879. The record states that a nest, eggs, and female were collected from this locality; however, none of the specimens are extant. Based on the breeding range of the Greater Scaup and the similarity of its nest and eggs to those of the Redhead, a known breeder at that location, the validity of this record is doubtful. —James Granlund

## LESSER SCAUP

### (Aythya affinis)

The Lesser Scaup or Bluebill is a common migrant, uncommon winter resident, and rare summer visitant to Michigan. This species breeds from central Alaska east to Hudson Bay and south to the central Great Plains and northern California. Populations winter along both coasts and in central Mexico, but more than half winter in the lakes and coastal marshes of Louisiana.

Lesser Scaup begin arriving in the state in late February, soon after the ice has left the lakes, and the migration reaches a peak in mid-April. Most migrants have departed by mid-May, but some lingering nonbreeders may remain through the summer. Autumn migrants begin returning to the state in early September, but the bulk of migration does not commence until mid- to late October. During both spring and fall migration, large numbers may be found inland and on the Great Lakes. Examples of inland locations include Austin Lake, Kalamazoo County, and the Dow Ponds, Midland County, both of which have had spring concentrations exceeding 1,100 individuals. Coastal locations which draw large numbers of this species include Pte. Mouillee, Monroe County, and Metrobeach, Macomb County.

Most Lesser Scaup depart from inland locations by early December or as lakes "ice in," but individuals remain longer on the Great Lakes, and particularly on the Detroit and St. Clair rivers in the southeastern Lower Peninsula. Some invariably remain through the winter where open water and food are available. On Michigan Christmas bird counts, the Lesser Scaup is less common than the Greater Scaup, the former averaging slightly more than 140 individuals annually in the period from 1970 to 1992.

As with the Greater Scaup, the exact status of the Lesser Scaup in Michigan is complicated by the difficulty in distinguishing between these two very similar species. It must certainly have been an abundant migrant in Michigan in presettlement times. Early writers such as Walter Barrows (1912) commented that it occurred in large rafts on migration and was a favorite game species. Barrows also mentioned that it was thought to breed in the St. Clair Flats, and Zimmerman and Van Tyne (1959) indicated that it bred in Mason County, although neither assertion is backed by corroborative evidence. There is but one confirmed breeding record for Lesser Scaup in Michigan—from Dickinson County on 20 May 1941. Today the species is still very common and is often the most abundant duck seen on migration on the Great Lakes or on large inland lakes.

Considering the number of summering Lesser Scaup and the proximity of Michigan to its primary breeding range, it is a mystery why it is not found nesting more regularly. There is an isolated breeding population of this species in Ontario, to the east of Michigan, and it is an occasional breeder in Wisconsin to the west. It may simply be a situation of detection, though this seems doubtful, particularly in the context of the breeding confirmations for other ducks gathered in recent years. —James Granlund

## COMMON EIDER
### (*Somateria mollissima*)

Although this species has been reported ten times in Michigan since 1969, the only documentation to verify its occurrence is one confirmed sighting (documented by a photograph) of a female on 20 April 1978 at Port Huron, St. Clair County. The problem lies in the difficult challenge of separating female and young male Common Eiders from King Eiders. Wood (1951) felt the evidence for the few historic reports was wholly unsatisfactory, and as far as more recent records are concerned, examination by the Michigan Bird Records Committee of photographs said to be Common Eiders often are of Kings. Similar situations have occurred in neighboring states, making the status of this species on the Great Lakes a murky issue. —James Granlund

## KING EIDER
### (*Somateria spectabilis*)

The King Eider is a casual migrant and winter visitor to Michigan. Individuals which show up in the Great Lakes have strayed far from their usual range. This large, bulky duck breeds in the northern polar regions of the world and winters in ice-free waters of the northern Atlantic and Pacific coasts south to Massachusetts and the state of Washington.

The King Eider's historical status in Michigan is unclear because of the ambiguity of most early records. Barrows (1912) mentions several specimens, none of which are extant, along with a few observations which lack corroboration. Wood (1951) was of the opinion that there were only two fully verified records through the early 1940s: an immature female taken on Gun Lake, Barry County, in November 1911, and one found dead at Union Pier, Berrien County, on 11 November 1936.

Since 1950, King Eiders have been reported with some regularity and with better documentation, including both specimens and photographs. Nearly all records involve immature males or females and either one or two individuals, the exception being a flock of 20 seen in migration on 1 December 1979 at Port Huron, St. Clair County. The majority of observations have occurred between November and February, and Christmas bird counts since 1970 include a total of 14 reports. Autumn migration counts recently initiated by the Whitefish Point Bird Observatory have recorded several King Eiders in early October, suggesting the species may arrive earlier on Lake Superior. Locations with multiple records include the Edison Power Plant at Sault Ste. Marie and Whitefish Point, both in Chippewa County; the mouth of the St. Clair River at Port Huron; and the piers at Muskegon, Holland, St. Joseph, and New Buffalo, all along southern Lake Michigan.

Records for the King Eider seem to come in groups, with sightings of late clustered in the years 1976, 1977, 1987, and 1989, whereas in other years there are no reports. The most extraordinary record to date is that of a male molting into breeding plumage at the Saginaw River Dike Disposal project on 17 June 1981. There have been rumors that this species may even summer in the deep, open waters of the Great Lakes. Considering its ability to dive to great depths, this seems feasible, although it has yet to be corroborated. —James Granlund

## HARLEQUIN DUCK
### (*Histrionicus histrionicus*)

The Harlequin Duck is a rare migrant and winter visitor in Michigan, occasionally wandering from its normal range along the northern rocky coasts of the Atlantic and Pacific oceans and adjacent inland rivers. This small sea duck breeds from Baffin Island east in northern Canada and south to Iceland, and from central Siberia east through much of Alaska and south to California and Wyoming.

The historic status of the Harlequin Duck in Michigan is curious, to say the least. The first specimens documenting its occurrence were taken on 7 February 1962 in Port Huron (St. Clair County) and 18 February 1962 in Kent County, followed by two others on 31 December 1965 in Saugatuck (Allegan County) and 6 October 1971 in St. Clair County (Payne 1983). Wisconsin, however, has numerous records dating back to the early part of this century, including a group of eight on 21 December 1921 at Milwaukee. It seems incomprehensible that this species would have been seen numerous times on the west side of Lake Michigan and not on the east.

From 1970 to the present, one or more Harlequin Ducks have been encountered in the state annually. Most reports occurred between late October and March, including 16 observations from state Christmas bird counts. At Whitefish Point individuals have been sighted as early as 21 August and as late as 24 May. Observations are mostly of immature males or females and typically involve a single individual, though as many as three have been seen at one site. Perhaps the most curious record of late is that of an adult male seen on the early date of 11 August 1991 at Rogers City.

Nearly all Harlequin reports have occurred along the Great

Lakes. Exceptions include the aforementioned specimen from Kent County, and sightings at the Fremont Sewage Ponds (Newaygo County) on 16 October 1984 and on the Kalamazoo River (Kalamazoo County) from mid-January through 7 April 1977. Locations in the state with multiple records include Whitefish Point and the Edison Power Plant, Sault Ste. Marie (both Chippewa County), Rogers City (Presque Isle County), Alpena (Alpena County), Port Huron (St. Clair County), Muskegon (Muskegon County), Holland (Ottawa County), South Haven (Van Buren County), and St. Joseph, Stevensville, and New Buffalo (all Berrien County). There tend to be more records from the Lake Michigan harbors, but this species is likely to appear at any rock jetty from November through March. —James Granlund

# OLDSQUAW

## (*Clangula hyemalis*)

The Oldsquaw or Long-tailed Duck, as it is called in Europe, is an uncommon to abundant migrant and winter resident in Michigan. This species occurs throughout the Northern Hemisphere, with breeding confined to the higher latitudes of the tundra. It winters along both coasts of North America and in the Great Lakes basin, being much less common on interior lakes and streams.

The Oldsquaw was first recorded in the state by Sager (1839), and the various historical references indicate that its status has remained constant through the years. It occurs annually on the Great Lakes in migration and winter, attaining its greatest abundance on Lake Superior and the northern reaches of Lakes Huron and Michigan. In some years flocks of hundreds, even thousands, are encountered. Oldsquaw are much less common on inland waters, but individuals are seen in most years on large lakes such as Houghton Lake in the northern Lower Peninsula. They are even encountered on small streams in years when most larger inland bodies of water are frozen. Oldsquaw are only rarely observed in the southern Great Lakes; one site at which one or more are seen nearly every year is Port Huron in St. Clair County.

Published information for Michigan indicates that Oldsquaw generally arrive in late October and depart in April or May. Standardized censuses at the Whitefish Point Bird Observatory provide a more detailed accounting for Lake Superior, with first arrival in early October and numbers peaking from late October to early November. In spring the peak flight at Whitefish Point occurs in mid-May, with individuals remaining into early June. In recent years there have been some unsubstantiated reports by fishermen of Oldsquaw summering well offshore in Lake Michigan.

This duck is renowned for its diving abilities, with individual dives of over 150 feet recorded. Oldsquaw feed on a wide variety of food, but a study by R. S. Ellarson (1956) in Lake Michigan found that amphipods—a close relative to shrimp—constitute a major part of their diet. Although able to dive to great depths, they often forage in water no deeper than 25 feet. Food preference and foraging habits often take this species well away from shore, suggesting that wintering populations are underestimated by shorebound observers. Totals from Michigan Christmas bird counts over the past several years ranged from 17 to 418, even the latter of which may be hundreds less than actual numbers present. Summing up counts for the entire Great Lakes region, Frank Bellrose (1980) reported a total of nearly 20,000 Oldsquaw in 1966–67.

Pair formation begins on the wintering grounds, and by early spring many male-female pairs can be observed. The courtship display involves a "bill-toss" and "rear-end" display accompanied by the male's loud musical yodeling, given both in flight and on the water. The distinctive drake with its bold black and white pattern and long tail is unlikely to be confused with any other duck occurring in Michigan. The female is plainer and could be confused with a female Harlequin Duck, which also lacks prominent field marks. The best identifying feature is the Oldsquaw's gleaming white sides. In flight this species has a very pot-bellied appearance, with pointed wings flapping in rapid motion. Oldsquaw often fly in single file and dive immediately upon landing. —James Granlund

# BLACK SCOTER

## (*Melanitta nigra*)

The Black Scoter, also known as the American or Common Scoter, is an uncommon fall migrant, rare spring migrant, and casual winter visitor in Michigan. The male of this species is completely black except for a large orange knob at the base of the bill, a feature which gave rise to the nickname Butterbill. Females and first-year males are dark brown with a contrasting pale face and throat. Among the three species of scoters, this is the smallest and least abundant.

The breeding range of the Black Scoter is not thoroughly known. It has a Holarctic distribution, and the North American subspecies (*M. n. americana*) is thought to breed from eastern Siberia through Alaska and irregularly in Newfoundland. The more familiar winter range includes most of the Pacific and Atlantic coasts of North America. Routes between breeding and wintering grounds are primarily coastal, which is why this species is an uncommon to rare migrant in the Great Lakes.

In spring, transient Black Scoters begin arriving in Michigan in April and have mostly departed by late May. Unusual is a record of four individuals on 25 June 1983 in Ottawa County. The fall migration commences in September, with the earliest known record on 10 September 1990 at the Whitefish Point Bird Observatory, Chippewa County. The majority of sightings occur from mid-October through December, with individuals lingering into January and very rarely overwintering. In 1990, for example, a single bird was observed throughout the winter in coastal waters at St. Joseph, Berrien County. On Michigan Christmas bird counts from 1970 to 1993, the total number of Black Scoters was only 35, with many years having no reports.

Most sightings of this stocky diving duck come from Great Lakes waters, though observations on large inland lakes are not uncommon. For example, Black Scoters have been seen several times on Gull Lake, Kalamazoo County. Coastal locations where this species occurs annually include the Whitefish Point Bird Observatory, Port Huron in St. Clair County, Muskegon State Park, and St. Joseph and New Buffalo in Berrien County. Sightings of multiple individuals occur with regularity; the largest reported group is 130 on 17 October 1982 at Port Huron.

Of the three scoter species, the Black is the least common in Michigan. In the standardized waterbird counts conducted at the Whitefish Point Bird Observatory, this species constitutes less than 1% of the scoters encountered in the spring and about 5% of the scoters in the fall. Statewide, Black Scoters are far more numerous in fall than spring. Again, using Whitefish Point data, the average number encountered in the spring is 5 individuals, with a maximum seasonal count of only 16, while the fall average to date is 135 with a maximum of 159. —James Granlund

## SURF SCOTER

### (*Melanitta perspicillata*)

The Surf Scoter is an uncommon migrant and rare winter visitor in Michigan. This sea duck nests near water in tundra and boreal forest habitats from Alaska east through Canada to Labrador. Winters are spent along the Pacific coast from the Aleutian Islands south to California, and along the Atlantic coast from Maine through Virginia and in some years south to Georgia. A relatively small proportion of the overall population passes inland through the Great Lakes during travels to and from the coast.

Surf Scoters begin arriving in Michigan in mid-April, with the migration peaking in mid- to late May. Some individuals linger into early June, the latest dates being singles on 6 June 1970 at Grand Haven, Ottawa County, and 7 June 1990 at Whitefish Point, Chippewa County. In fall, migrants begin reaching Michigan in September, with numbers peaking in early to mid-October. The earliest fall arrival date on record is of an individual on 17 September 1991 at Whitefish Point. A few will stay into December and even January, leaving only when the ice drives them from lakes. Although they are not seen every year, 16 Surf Scoters were detected on Michigan Christmas bird counts from 1970 to 1993.

Most reports of this species come from Great Lakes coastal sites, though inland records on larger lakes are not uncommon. Two such lakes with multiple sightings include Gull Lake, Kalamazoo County, and Baw Beese Lake, Hillsdale County. Among the many coastal locations where the Surf Scoter is frequently observed are Whitefish Point, Thunder Bay (Alpena County), Port Huron (St. Clair County), Metrobeach (Macomb County), and the piers along southern Lake Michigan from Muskegon south through Berrien County. Most encounters are of singles to flocks of less than 10, though sometimes larger numbers are seen, such as the 205 on 2 October 1990 at Whitefish Point. Females and immature birds make up the bulk of the sightings, with the more distinctive adult males seen less frequently. The male Surf Scoter has all-black plumage like the other two scoters, but the head has two white patches, one on the crown and one on the nape, and the bill is a bright orange (distinguishable from the orange knob on the bill of the Black Scoter).

The status of the Surf Scoter in Michigan appears to have changed little over time, as Barrows (1912) also described it as an uncommon migrant and not rare on larger inland lakes and Lake Michigan in winter. Of the three scoter species, the Surf Scoter is more numerous than the Black but not as abundant as the White-winged. In the annual waterbird census conducted by the Whitefish Point Bird Observatory, Surf Scoters make up about 2% of the scoter totals in spring and 24% in fall. The autumn flight far exceeds that of spring, with numbers averaging around 600 in fall versus only 25 in spring. —James Granlund

## WHITE-WINGED SCOTER

### (*Melanitta fusca*)

The White-winged Scoter is an uncommon to common migrant and winter resident in Michigan. This is and has always been the most abundant scoter found in the state, both on the Great Lakes and inland. It is also the easiest of the three scoters to identify in flight because of the white secondaries which appear as a conspicuous white patch on the trailing edge of the wings of an otherwise mostly black duck. For a bird on the water, the folded wings have a small white patch which may or may not be visible.

Known as the Velvet Scoter in Eurasia, this species occurs throughout the Northern Hemisphere. The North American subspecies (*M. f. deglandi*) breeds from Alaska through most of western and central Canada and as far east as western Hudson Bay. As with other scoters, the wintering range includes both coasts of the continent, from the Aleutian Islands to Baja on the Pacific side and from Newfoundland to Georgia on the Atlantic. A variable number winter on the Great Lakes, though proportions are small compared to either coast.

The first White-winged Scoters begin arriving in Michigan in late April, with the migration peaking in mid- to late May and a few individuals lingering into early June. The latest published date comes from a record of two dead birds found on 18 June 1974 on the beach of Beaver Island in northern Lake Michigan. The autumn migration usually begins in early October, with numbers peaking by the end of the month into early November in the south. A few individuals arriving in September is not uncommon, but records on 16 August 1986 at Grand Marais, Alger County, and 16 August 1990 at Whitefish Point, Chippewa County, are very early. The possibility that these birds oversummered on the Great Lakes seems high.

White-winged Scoters remain in good numbers into December, with individuals and small flocks overwintering on the Great Lakes. On Michigan Christmas bird counts, just over 400 individuals were recorded from 1970 to 1993. During this period this species was recorded every year, with totals ranging from 1 to 63.

Most records of this sea duck come from the Great Lakes, and yet individuals are also commonly encountered on large inland lakes. Observations tend to be of singles or small flocks (less than 25 birds), especially those on inland waters. At prime coastal sites, though, large numbers are often encountered when the migration is at its peak. Examples include 1,200 on 20 May 1972 at Thunder Bay, Alpena County, and 1,774 recorded on 1 May 1980 at Whitefish Point. Without a doubt this latter site is the single best locale in the state to observe White-winged Scoters, with large strings of migrants seen in May and October. In the annual waterbird cen-

suses conducted by the Whitefish Point Bird Observatory, the White-winged Scoter accounts for 94% of all scoters encountered in spring and 47% of those in fall. Unlike the other two scoter species, the White-winged is equally abundant during the two seasons, averaging 1,251 individuals in spring and 1,218 in fall.
—James Granlund

## COMMON GOLDENEYE
### (*Bucephala clangula*)

In Michigan the Common Goldeneye occurs as a common migrant and winter resident and an uncommon summer resident in the north. This species resides around the northern regions of the world, with the North American subspecies (*B. c. americana*) breeding in coniferous forest habitats throughout Canada and Alaska, with smaller numbers in northern New England, the northern Great Lakes, North Dakota, and Montana. By far the main wintering area for Common Goldeneye is the northern Pacific coast from the Aleutians to British Columbia. Lesser numbers winter farther south along the Pacific, on the Atlantic and Gulf coasts, and on inland open waters primarily across the northern states.

Migrant Common Goldeneyes begin joining the winter resident population in the state as early as late February, and their northward flights continue from late March into April. Data from the Whitefish Point Bird Observatory show that the migration in northern Michigan peaks in mid- to late April. Nearly all have departed the southern counties by mid-April, though some individuals may linger into June, and a few may even oversummer on southern lakes. Small numbers of returning birds arrive in September, but the bulk of the migration begins in October and reaches its peak from late October to early November.

Thousands of Common Goldeneye remain through the winter in Michigan where open water exists. This species is frequently seen on the Great Lakes as well as on inland lakes, rivers, and even streams with only small patches of open water. On Michigan Christmas bird counts since 1970, annual totals are typically in the 4,000 to 5,000 range with a high of 6,800 on the 1988–89 count. The Common Goldeneye is our fourth most abundant wintering duck, trailing only the Mallard, Canvasback, and Common Merganser, yet it is perhaps the most widespread of the group because it is found on a diverse array of water bodies.

On migration and in winter, this duck is most often seen in small to moderate numbers, but large flocks are sometimes encountered. Examples include a flock of 1,000 recorded on 21 January 1979 at Ecorse, Wayne County, and a gathering of 1,184 on 2 November 1989 at Whitefish Point, Chippewa County.

Considering the writings by Barrows (1912) and Wood (1951), it seems that the Common Goldeneye's migrant and wintering status has changed little over the past hundred years. Whether or not its breeding status in the state has changed is more difficult to discern. Barrows lists only one breeding record from Neebish Island, Chippewa County, while Wood listed several records extending from Roscommon and Wexford counties northward into the eastern Upper Peninsula.

During the 1980s Breeding Bird Atlas, reports came from 67 townships, mostly in the Upper Peninsula, with breeding confirmed on Isle Royale and in Dickinson, Delta, Luce, Chippewa, Mackinac, Cheboygan (Bois Blanc Island), and Roscommon counties. Except for local concentrations on Isle Royale and in Luce and Mackinac counties, this species is an uncommon to rare nesting duck in the state. Despite the intensive effort during the Atlas, even these data probably underrepresent the actual occurrence because of the remoteness of its habitat; certainly there is more to be learned about this species' breeding population in Michigan. Frank Bellrose (1980) asserted that possibly 4,000 Common Goldeneyes were breeding through the Upper Peninsula of Michigan and south along Lake Huron through Presque Isle County.

The Common Goldeneye nests in natural cavities and nest boxes (same as those for Wood Ducks) near lakes and streams in boreal forest habitats. Nesting data for the state are meager, but egg laying is probably complete by early May. An average clutch ranges from 8 to 10 eggs, with incubation lasting about 30 days. June is the best time to look for hens with their broods. The family stays together for about eight weeks until the young fledge. Animal foods, mainly aquatic insects, crustaceans, and mollusks, constitute the bulk of the diet, with plants making up about 25%.
—James Granlund

## BARROW'S GOLDENEYE
### (*Bucephala islandica*)

The Barrow's Goldeneye is a casual or perhaps accidental migrant and winter visitor in Michigan. The exact status and frequency of occurrence is difficult to discern because of the complexities of separating this species from the similar Common Goldeneye, which occurs regularly in the state at all times of the year.

The breeding range of the Barrow's Goldeneye includes two widely separated eastern and western populations, the former occurring from the northeastern coast of Labrador to Iceland and the latter from Alaska south to the mountains of central California and southern Wyoming. Winter ranges are along the Atlantic coast near the breeding areas and within the mouth of the St. Lawrence Seaway, and along the Pacific from the Aleutians to central California. The western birds also winter on rivers and other open waters in their mountainous breeding areas. Although there are no recognized subspecies or races, there are subtle differences in bill and body coloration which may allow for separation of the two populations in the field.

Historically there are few records for this species in the state.

*Common Goldeneye*
*Red-breasted Merganser*
HEINER HERTLING

H.C.Hertling

Norman Wood (1951) listed two possible records, one of which was a specimen (1907), the location of which is presently unknown. On 7 November 1946 a Barrow's Goldeneye was collected on Gun Lake, Barry County, with a photograph on file and the pharynx (windpipe) preserved at the University of Michigan Museum of Zoology. Also on file at the museum is a photograph of an adult male observed at Kensington Metropark, Oakland County, on 28 March 1986. Lastly, there are photographs documenting a male which has returned to Elk Rapids, Antrim County, for the winters of 1989–92.

Beyond these physically documented occurrences, there are 27 sight records from the 1940s to the present. Four of these were adult males, and the remainder either were not sexed or were identified as females or immatures. All 27 fell within the period from November to May, with the majority during the winter between December and February. There are five sightings offshore from Marquette, another five along the coast of Port Huron (St. Clair County), and two from Sault Ste. Marie (Chippewa County). A majority of the records, especially those from earlier decades, lack written documentation or physical evidence. One record which was well documented was that of a female on 7–10 November 1991 at Port Huron, likely of the eastern population.

The separation of an adult male Barrow's from a Common Goldeneye is not difficult; unfortunately, separating females and immatures is no trivial matter and may actually be impossible in some circumstances. The real pitfall in the identification is reliance on bill color. In early field guides the all-yellow bill of the female Barrow's Goldeneye was touted as a good field mark. Today we know the character of a nearly all-yellow bill is also shared by many Common Goldeneye females. Considering this, it is highly likely that some, and perhaps many, of the undocumented records of female Barrow's Goldeneyes in Michigan were actually yellow-billed Commons. In all reality the only safe field mark is the shape of the head and bill—peaked forehead and small bill in Barrow's compared to a sloping forehead and large bill in Common—but even this is difficult to use in many circumstances. Any encounter of a Barrow's Goldeneye in Michigan should be carefully documented or photographed. —James Granlund

# BUFFLEHEAD

## (*Bucephala albeola*)

The boldly marked Bufflehead is one of the smallest ducks encountered in Michigan. The male is easily recognized by its purplish head with a conspicuous white patch, while the female is plainer but can also be recognized by a white spot behind the eye. In flight, both are identified by the white panels fore and aft on the wing.

The Bufflehead is a common migrant, uncommon winter resident, and rare summer visitor in the state. It breeds across a vast area of northern North America, but within this range its distribution is generally sparse. Most breeding occurs in western Canada and Alaska, with smaller numbers south to northern California and northwestern Minnesota and east to Quebec.

Main wintering areas are on the Pacific coast from the Aleutian Islands to Puget Sound, the Atlantic coast from Maine to North Carolina, and the Gulf coast from Florida to Texas. Good numbers also winter on inland streams and lakes, including the Great Lakes.

The first spring transients begin arriving in Michigan in early March, with the migration peaking in mid- to late April. Most Bufflehead have departed by early May, although some tend to linger into June, and a few may even oversummer in the Upper Peninsula or, on extremely rare occasions, in the Lower Peninsula. While pairs have been noted in summer, there is no conclusive evidence that this species has ever bred in Michigan. Robert Payne (1983) describes a report of breeding in Baraga County in 1959 as unsubstantiated.

Fall migrants begin arriving in the state in late September or early October, with the numbers peaking in late October and early November. Many Bufflehead continue on to coastal or southern wintering areas, but good numbers usually remain through the winter where open water and forage are available. Like its relative the Common Goldeneye, this species frequents small rivers and springs as well as larger bodies of water during winter. On Michigan Christmas bird counts since 1970, yearly totals were typically in the range of 400 to 600 Bufflehead. The highest total to date came on the 1991–92 count, with 1,901 individuals.

During migration and winter, Bufflehead are rarely seen in large flocks, with maximum numbers reported at some locales of between 100 and 200 individuals. More typical are flocks of 10 to 50 birds often associated with Common Goldeneye. An exceptional spot to view migrating Bufflehead is the Whitefish Point Bird Observatory from late October to early November. In 1989, a single daily total of 2,116 individuals was recorded there. Prime winter locations are areas with open water adjacent to the Great Lakes, such as Port Sheldon in Ottawa County, or on the Great Lakes themselves.

Based on writings by Walter Barrows (1912) and Norman Wood (1951), the Bufflehead's status appears to have remained fairly constant over the years. Barrows conjectured that this species may have bred within the state, although he had no direct evidence. This seems reasonable considering the proximity of Michigan to its breeding range, and that Wisconsin has a breeding confirmation from the 1800s. The Upper Peninsula, with its rare but regular summer sightings, seems the most likely region if nesting does occur. This duck nests in tree cavities, often flicker holes, so finding one is probably quite difficult. If any do occasionally breed here, one is more likely to observe a hen and her brood than to locate a nest. Perhaps through diligent effort by Michigan birders, Walter Barrows's prediction can be realized sometime in the future. —James Granlund

*Hooded Merganser*
*Common Merganser*
HEINER HERTLING

H.C. Hertling

# HOODED MERGANSER

## (*Lophodytes cucullatus*)

The Hooded Merganser is a common migrant, uncommon summer resident, and rare winter resident in Michigan. The smallest of the three mergansers, this species inhabits wooded ponds, lakes, and rivers throughout the state, though it occurs much more frequently in the northern regions. Whereas the other two species have worldwide distributions, the Hooded Merganser is exclusive to North America. There are two main breeding areas: one in the East from lower Canada to Louisiana and Georgia, with most breeding in the Upper Midwest east to New York and Ontario, and the second in the West from southern Alaska and Alberta to Idaho and northern California. Most winter on fresh water in the Pacific coastal states and in the Gulf and Atlantic coastal states north to New England.

Hooded Mergansers begin arriving in Michigan in March and early April, with the spring migration peaking by mid-April. Those which are transients have mostly passed through the state by early May, although a few may linger in southern Michigan into early June. Returning fall migrants begin arriving in mid-October, with numbers peaking around the middle of November and most individuals departed by mid-December. Small numbers overwinter where open water and food are available. Hooded Merganser totals have averaged 90 to 100 birds on Michigan Christmas bird counts since 1970, making it the rarest of the three mergansers in winter. The highest total to date was in 1990–91, with 312 recorded.

During migration when Hooded Mergansers are most common in the state, they are often encountered on shallow inland lakes and marshes in small flocks averaging less than 100 individuals. Exceptional were the 500+ seen on 24 November 1987 on Hudson Lake, Lenawee County, and the 230 found on 24 November 1990 on Thorn Lake, Jackson County. Of the three merganser species, the Hooded is the least likely to be seen on the Great Lakes. This is best demonstrated by migration data at Whitefish Point Bird Observatory, where thousands of Common and Red-breasted Mergansers are recorded but the Hooded is rarely seen, and in some years is not recorded at all.

Based on early writings, it appears that the Hooded Merganser was a common, if not abundant, breeding species in presettlement times. Around the end of the 1800s, the population in Michigan declined because of the pressures of hunting and habitat loss, and by the early part of this century, it was considered an uncommon if not rare breeder. Recently, trends suggest that the Hooded Merganser has been making a recovery thanks to years of hunting restrictions and regrowth of woodlands along inland riparian areas. During the 1980s Michigan Breeding Bird Atlas, the species was found breeding uncommonly in the Lower Peninsula as far south as Oakland and Allegan counties and in greater abundance across the Upper Peninsula, particularly in the eastern portion.

The Hooded Merganser has fairly specific nesting requirements, selecting tree cavities in river bottom habitats, swamps, beaver ponds, or along heavily wooded streams. The other important component is clear, clean water, providing an ample supply of fish and aquatic invertebrates, which make up about equal portions of the diet. Like the Wood Duck, the Hooded Merganser will use artificial cavities in proper habitat for nesting, and boxes can help supplement the supply of natural tree hollows. Studies have documented a strong homing ability in this species, with pairs regularly returning to the same nesting area and often the same cavity as the previous year.

Breeding in Michigan is initiated in late April to early May in the north. Clutches are fairly large, averaging 11 eggs, which are incubated by the hen for about 33 days. The young depart the nest cavity within 24 hours and remain together in the care of the female for up to 10 weeks. Broods are much easier to find than the nests themselves, and one of the best locales in the state to observe Hooded Mergansers throughout the breeding season is Seney National Wildlife Refuge, Schoolcraft County, where the many managed shallow pools and beaver ponds are ideal habitat for this species. —James Granlund

# COMMON MERGANSER

## (*Mergus merganser*)

The Common Merganser is an abundant migrant and winter resident and a generally uncommon breeding bird in Michigan. This large, elongated duck breeds throughout the Northern Hemisphere in association with the boreal and montane forest zones. The North American subspecies (*M. m. americanus*) breeds from Alaska across most of Canada and south to Maine and the northern Great Lakes, and extending farther south in the western mountain ranges to central California and Colorado. Its winter range is also extensive, encompassing much of the lower 48 states to the Northern Highlands of Mexico.

Migrant Common Mergansers begin arriving in Michigan in late February or early March, with numbers peaking in early to mid-April. Most continue on to their northern breeding grounds, but a fair number stay and nest along the Great Lakes and inland lakes and rivers in the northern half of the state. The fall migration extends from late September in the Upper Peninsula through November in the southern Lower Peninsula. The trailing lines of migrating mergansers, flying low over the water, are a common sight at various vantage points along the Great Lakes. During the fall season, separating the basic-plumaged Common and Red-breasted Mergansers can be difficult, particularly in flight, and observers should use caution when identifying the two.

While many pass through the region to areas farther south, thousands of Common Mergansers overwinter on the Great Lakes and adjacent open waters. Christmas bird counts provide a good measure of the magnitude of the winter population. For the period 1970–93, numbers typically ranged between 5,000 and 25,000, with a high count of 35,226 in 1992–93 and a low of 1,301 in 1976–77. Large concentrations can be encountered at such locations as the Karn Plant, Bay County, where an estimated 20,000 were counted on 18 January 1991, or the Shiawassee National Wildlife Refuge, Saginaw County, where counts approaching 20,000 were made in December 1987. Other good concentration points are near Ecorse in Wayne County and Lake Muskegon.

The status of the Common Merganser has probably not changed appreciably since historic times. Barrows (1912) characterized it as "not being uncommon" on migration and reported breeding from Saginaw Bay northward through the Upper Peninsula. He also called it one of the commonest wintering ducks on Lake Michigan. These descriptions fit well with its current status. During the recent Michigan Breeding Bird Atlas, the Common Merganser was confirmed breeding in 23 counties from Huron north through the Upper Peninsula. It was found to be generally uncommon in the northern Lower Peninsula, except for the Grand Traverse Bay area and Leelanau County, and the Thunder Bay area, Alpena County, where it was locally common. One apparent difference from earlier years is its near-absence as a breeder in Saginaw Bay. In the Upper Peninsula this duck is a common breeder, being fairly evenly distributed from east to west, and nesting pairs are especially numerous on Isle Royale.

The Common Merganser normally nests in tree cavities and therefore tends to breed along secluded wooded streams or lakes. In other situations, females will choose a site on the ground or on a rocky shelf, allowing them to nest along the Great Lakes. Nesting begins early, usually late April or early May. A typical clutch contains 9 to 12 eggs, which take about 30 days to hatch. The hen and brood remain together for an extended period, usually 10 weeks. Nests are extremely difficult to locate, but observers visiting suitable habitat in June have a good chance of finding family groups.

The thin, serrated bill is unique to the mergansers—a design specific to catching fish, their primary prey. On bays and river mouths of the Great Lakes, analysis of Common Merganser stomachs found that forage fish (shiners, minnows, suckers, etc.) made up about 50% of the items taken, with the remainder being yellow perch, unidentified fish, and crayfish. The availability of fish plays a major role in selection of breeding, migration, and wintering sites for this species. —James Granlund

# RED-BREASTED MERGANSER

## (*Mergus serrator*)

Like the two other mergansers, the Red-breasted can be found in Michigan throughout the year. It is an abundant migrant in the state and an uncommon winter and summer resident. This species breeds throughout the Northern Hemisphere. In North America it occurs in the tundra and boreal forest zones, from Alaska to Labrador and south to British Columbia, Alberta, the northern Great Lakes, and Maine. Winters are spent primarily along the Pacific, Atlantic, and Gulf coasts, with lesser numbers on the Great Lakes.

Spring migrants begin arriving in Michigan in March, with the movement peaking in mid-April in the south and from late April to early May in the north. Most Red-breasted Mergansers continue north, but small numbers remain and breed in the northern third of the state. Fall migration commences in September, with numbers peaking from mid-October through November. Extremely large concentrations may be seen at this time, such as the 20,000 reported on 27 October 1991 offshore from Au Gres, Iosco County.

Unlike the Common Merganser, most Red-breasted Mergansers depart the state for the coast by mid-December. On Michigan Christmas bird counts over the past few decades, numbers of Red-breasteds varied from the low hundreds to a high of 5,509 on the 1971–72 count. By January this species becomes rather scarce, although it is regularly encountered along the Lake Michigan shoreline south of Ottawa County and is sometimes seen at other locales, even as far north as Sault Ste. Marie, Chippewa County.

As a breeding resident, the Red-breasted Merganser may have declined slightly since historic times, its distribution withdrawing farther north. Barrows (1912) indicated that the species had nearly the same range as the Common Merganser, breeding from Saginaw Bay northward through the Upper Peninsula. The Michigan Breeding Bird Atlas conducted in the 1980s gave a similar picture but with the breeding population mainly confined to the Upper Peninsula and only sporadic occurrence in the northern Lower Peninsula south to Roscommon County. Atlas data further indicate that breeding is concentrated along the Great Lakes and their islands.

The Red-breasted Merganser usually nests on the ground near a treefall, shrub, or other dense vegetation. Rarely, nesting takes place in a tree cavity as with the other two North American merganser species. A typical clutch averages about eight eggs, which are incubated for 30 days. The ducklings remain in the care of the hen for eight to nine weeks. Fish are the primary prey of the Red-breasted Merganser at all times of the year.

Early authors have indicated that the status of the Red-breasted and Common Mergansers was confused by the difficulty of separating females and immatures in the field. At Whitefish Point Bird Observatory, where standard waterbird censuses are conducted, the Red-breasted is about ten times more abundant in spring than the Common Merganser. In fall the disparity is even greater, with the former being as much as thirty times more abundant. This pattern seems to hold at many sites during migration. In winter, however, the trend is reversed, and the Common Merganser far outnumbers the Red-breasted, particularly on inland waters. In summer the two seem relatively equal in numbers across the state, with Red-breasteds more common at coastal sites and Common Mergansers more numerous on lakes and rivers. —James Granlund

# RUDDY DUCK

## (*Oxyura jamaicensis*)

The Ruddy Duck is another waterfowl species which is common in the state during spring and fall migration, but rare in summer and winter. The North American race (*O. j. rubida*) breeds from northwest Canada to California and the southern Rockies, and east to western Ontario and Minnesota, with sporadic nesting farther east to Maine. Within this range, the northern prairies support the largest concentrations of breeding Ruddies. Wintering occurs in scattered locales along the Pacific, Atlantic, and Gulf coasts to Central America, and at inland locations along the Mississippi River.

Spring and autumn are the best times to observe this chunky, stiff-tailed duck in Michigan, especially in the south, where it is considerably more abundant than in the north. Impressive flocks with totals exceeding 1,000 Ruddies are not uncommon in suitable habitat. Examples include 2,200 reported on 18 April 1981 at Lake Erie Metropark in Wayne County; 2,500 on 20 October 1989 at the Fremont Sewage Ponds in Newaygo County; and nearly 4,000 on 8 October 1987 at the Muskegon Wastewater System. This species favors large inland lakes, marshes, and coastal areas bordering deeper waters of the other Great Lakes. It is most common along the marshes at the western end of Lake Erie.

Spring transients begin arriving in late March, with the migration peaking around the second and third weeks of April. Most Ruddy Ducks are through the state by late May, except for those which choose to linger on some of the state's large marshes and sewage lagoons. Nesting, however, is very rare and irregular. Fall migrants first appear in September, with numbers peaking in early to mid-October. Most Ruddy Ducks depart the state by the middle of December.

This species is generally rare in winter, but there are years when large numbers linger well into December and overwinter where open water and food are available. This variability is evident on Michigan Christmas bird counts, where since 1970 totals have ranged from 1 in 1970–71 to 735 in 1975–76, with the second highest being 205 in 1976–77. More typical are counts in the 10 to 40 range, which is a more realistic assessment of its abundance in early winter in the state. In both high years the majority of Ruddies were tallied on the Rockwood count, which includes the Lake Erie marshes. Why so many more remained during those two years is unknown.

The Ruddy Duck generally has the same status today as it did at the time of settlement. Walter Barrows (1912) described it as "coming from the north in great numbers," indicating that it was a common migrant. It may have been a rare breeder, as there is a report of an egg collected on 15 June 1880 from St. Clair Flats. Unfortunately this evidence is no longer extant. By the 1940s, numbers of Ruddy Ducks must have declined, as Norman Wood (1951) called this species a "very uncommon transient" and much reduced from its former numbers, yet he gives no explanation for the apparent decline. Hunting was probably not a factor; this species is not a favorite of sportsmen because it prefers to dive rather than fly to escape danger.

Records from recent decades clearly show that the Ruddy Duck is again a common migrant in the state, with large numbers encountered in both spring and fall. There is also documentation to confirm its rare breeding status. Richard Wolinski (1973) summarized breeding records from Dickinson County on 14 June 1949, Bay County on 20 June 1961, the Maple River State Game Area in Gratiot County on 19 July 1962, and Nayanquing Point Wildlife Area in Bay County on 31 July 1971. Subsequent breeding has been confirmed at the Muskegon Wastewater System (1 September 1973), Pte. Mouillee in Monroe County (July 1978, 22 July 1990), and Fish Point in Tuscola County (Breeding Bird Atlas, 1983–88). The profusion of sightings of summering Ruddy Ducks suggests that they may breed more regularly than we realize, though certainly in small numbers.

This duck nests in emergent vegetation of large and small marshes, the nest being a bulky basket-like structure anchored to the vegetation slightly above the water. Based on records at similar latitudes to Michigan, nesting here probably begins in late May or the first part of June. A typical clutch consists of eight eggs, with incubation lasting 23 to 25 days. The brood remains in the care of the female for six or seven weeks; and unlike the males of many other duck species, the Ruddy male shares in the parental duties. Foods of this species include many aquatic plants and their seeds as well as some animal life. —James Granlund

## [BLACK VULTURE]
### (Coragyps atratus)

The Black Vulture is a widespread resident from southern Indiana and southern Ohio through the southern United States, Mexico, Central America, and South America. It appears casually north to Wisconsin, Ontario, and Quebec, and is an accidental vagrant to Michigan with three reports to date. The first came on 8 April 1972 at the Sarett Nature Center, Berrien County, when a bird identification class saw a Black Vulture soaring overhead (with Turkey Vultures and an Osprey nearby for comparison). The next sighting was on 26 May 1974, when a group of Audubon members on a field trip observed an individual in the company of a Turkey Vulture and a Red-shouldered Hawk at Good Harbor Bay, Leelanau County (Carpenter 1975). The third occurrence took place in the Upper Peninsula, on 7 July 1984 south of Whitefish Point, Chippewa County.

As with a small number of other species, there is no physical evidence to corroborate the Black Vulture's presence on the state list, and its status remains hypothetical. Extralimital records are usually during the spring or post-breeding periods. Michigan is due for another Black Vulture sighting, and hopefully it can be captured on camera. Keys to identification are its all-black plumage, relatively short tail, and large white patches near the end of the wings. —Raymond J. Adams

## TURKEY VULTURE
### (Cathartes aura)

North America's premier scavenger, the Turkey Vulture is a common summer resident in the Lower Peninsula of Michigan, and an uncommon summer resident in the Upper Peninsula. From mid-March until mid-October, these large, dark birds with a six-foot wing span can be seen soaring over fields throughout

*Turkey Vulture*
*Northern Harrier*
HEINER HERTLING

H.G. Hertling

the state, sometimes gathering into kettles of 30 to 50 birds.

The Turkey Vulture is found throughout the United States, reaching its northern limits in southern Canada and extending south into Mexico, Central America, and the southernmost regions of South America. It is common to abundant throughout its range. Much of the North American population passes through Mexico and Panama on the way to the species' southerly wintering grounds. Peak flights in late October and early November at Panama City sometimes number over 175,000 a day, with more than 1,100,000 passing during the fall.

Turkey Vultures are creatures of open areas bordering woodlands which are used for nesting. The southern two-thirds of the Lower Peninsula forms the stronghold of their distribution in Michigan, although small numbers nest at scattered locations throughout the northern Lower and the Upper Peninsulas. While this vulture is most commonly seen soaring over open fields, it is also regularly found at local roosts, where up to 50 or more individuals will spend the night.

The spring vulture migration in Michigan begins in early March and extends into early May. Migratory flocks or kettles of vultures are a common sight in southern Michigan. Numbers dwindle as you proceed north in the state, although small groups are still a common sight at the Straits of Mackinac. At Whitefish Point in the Upper Peninsula, near the northern limit of its North American range, the Turkey Vulture is an uncommon migrant, averaging 99 birds a year during 1988–92.

In the fall large numbers of vultures migrate through the state. Greatest numbers are usually seen in Monroe County. Virtually the entire Turkey Vulture population from Ontario passes over the Detroit River mouth into southern Michigan on their way farther south. The peak is between 5 and 20 October, when 10,000 to 16,000 vultures pass through the area, with single daily highs of 2,000 to 3,000.

The nests of Turkey Vultures are isolated and aromatic. Hollow trees, stumps, logs, and abandoned buildings make up the array of typical nest sites. For 16 Michigan nest records that I have examined, the average clutch size was two eggs. These nests with eggs were observed between 25 April and 6 June, with nestlings present between 19 June and 7 July. There have been several recent nestings near Manchester in Washtenaw County in a stall in an abandoned barn, where two young were raised for three consecutive years.

A child's drawing of a bird in the sky closely resembles a Turkey Vulture. In flight the bird holds its wings in a dihedral, thus resembling the letter V. Additionally, since the birds have a very low weight relative to their large wing area, they have a very tippy flight, rocking back and forth as they soar overhead. The Turkey Vulture is your basic black and white bird. All of its plumage, with the exception of the white flight feathers below, is dark. The featherless head, an adaptation to carrion feeding, is red in adults and black in juveniles.

Both the range expansion and population growth of the Turkey Vulture are well documented. Barrows (1912) found it confined to the southern counties of Michigan; 40 years later Wood (1951) considered it common in the southern two-thirds of the Lower Peninsula; and 30 years later Payne (1983) listed it as common throughout the Lower Peninsula, and uncommon and increasing in the Upper Peninsula. I wonder what role the great number of road-killed animals has played in this growth and expansion. Obviously the final chapter on the range and status of the Turkey Vulture is not yet written. Currently the population appears to still be growing, since more vultures are seen annually across the state. —Michael Kielb

# OSPREY
## (*Pandion haliaetus*)

No raptor in North America is more strongly tied to its aquatic environment for feeding than the Osprey. Their spectacular plunge dives are a familiar sight in areas where these large fish-eating birds spend the summer. As a migrant and summer resident in Michigan, the Osprey is an uncommon species.

The Osprey is one of the most widely distributed birds in the world. It is found on all of the continents, with the exception of Antarctica, as either a breeding or a wintering species. In North America there are approximately 8,000 pairs in the lower 48 states, with about 500 pairs in the Great Lakes region. Additionally, there are about 12,000 pairs in Canada and Alaska (Johnsgard 1990). The Michigan population is currently estimated at 220 pairs (T. Weise, pers. comm.), about two-thirds of which are located in the Upper Peninsula, with nearly all of the remainder in the northern Lower Peninsula.

While Michigan's Osprey population appears to be healthy today, it has not always been so. Since Osprey feed exclusively on fish, they are particularly susceptible to pesticides and other chemicals which are concentrated through the food chain into fish. As a result of the introduction and indiscriminate use of DDT in the middle 1900s, the Osprey population in Michigan plummeted. It was not until the 1980s that the concentration of DDT began to decrease in the environment and in the nesting birds themselves.

The spring migration of this raptor peaks in mid- to late April, with nesting birds present in the northern Lower Peninsula by late April. At Whitefish Point the average number of migrant Osprey recorded during 1988–92 was 156. In the spring of 1992, 164 were tallied at the tip of the Keweenaw Peninsula. In the fall greatest numbers occur from 4 to 22 September, and during the 1988–92 period an average of 120 passed from southern Ontario into southern Michigan. Their wintering grounds extend from the southern United States to southern South America.

Osprey build large stick nests, often in dead trees close to or standing in water. These nests can reach four to six feet across and up to ten feet in height, although three to four feet is more typical. There are usually two or three eggs laid at two- to three-day

*Osprey*
Heiner Hertling

intervals, with incubation starting with the first egg. During the early part of the nesting cycle when the female is on eggs or with small young, the male does all of the fishing. Additionally, Osprey are the most colonial of North America's diurnal raptors. The nests may be quite close to each other; I have visited swamps and lakes where you can look out and see four to six nests within less than a mile.

Nesting success can be improved (and pairs increased) in areas with few natural sites available through the erection of man-made nest platforms. An excellent area to observe the positive effects of human intervention is around Houghton Lake (Roscommon County). In the Dead Stream Swamp and Michelsen's Landing area, there are numerous man-made platforms, and many are occupied annually by Osprey. However, randomly erecting nest platforms in areas where there are no Osprey does not appear to induce pairs to take up residence. There must be a population nearby to supply birds for the new nesting area.

Osprey are identified by their overall whitish plumage, with dark facial mask and dark wrist patches on the underwing. It was previously believed that males and females could be reasonably well separated and identified in the field by the darkness of their breast band. This has proved to be an unreliable trait. Head-on in flight, the Osprey presents a profile resembling the letter M with the two legs splayed out, more of an inverted W.

Osprey hover while hunting at a height of 30 to 50 feet. When a fish is located they fold their wings and dive, plunging into the water feet-first and becoming completely submerged, a technique quite unlike the fishing style of the Bald Eagle. Upon resurfacing the bird shakes the water from its head and shoulders and with a lumbering takeoff regains flight, sometimes with a fish in its talons. I have always been amazed at how often Osprey miss their target.

According to Sergej Postupalsky, writing in *The Atlas of Breeding Birds of Michigan* (1991), the number of nesting Osprey in the state doubled between 1977 and 1988, and the population is still increasing. Nonetheless, it remains a threatened species in Michigan and is protected under the Endangered Species Act. Pairs continue to be vulnerable to habitat degradation, including loss of nesting trees, and they still face the threat of new pesticides and other chemicals which are concentrated in fish. —Michael Kielb

# AMERICAN SWALLOW-TAILED KITE

(*Elanoides forficatus*)

This attractive and graceful raptor is an accidental visitor to the Great Lakes states. The only Michigan record from the modern era is a bird spotted by four observers in Irving Township, Barry County, on 8 August 1992. The written documentation clearly describes an American Swallow-tailed Kite with the diagnostic white and black plumage and long, black, forked tail. This vagrant was far from its current breeding range, which extends from South Carolina to Louisiana in the United States and south through Central and South America. This kite's range has not always been

so restricted; at the time of European settlement, it nested in variable abundance in the prairies of Ohio and Indiana north into Wisconsin and Minnesota. Writing in *The Atlas of Breeding Birds of Michigan* (1991), Richard Brewer suggested that this kite "might have nested in the larger prairies or grassy marshes of southern Michigan." During the 1800s, declines were evident across the Midwest, and in the late 1800s there was a spate of records in Michigan, including reports of specimens which no longer exist. Barrows (1912) mentions one killed in Washtenaw County (15 September 1880), a pair shot in Monroe County (19 June 1882), a specimen from the Detroit area (1878 or 1881), and one from Kalamazoo County in 1897 plus other undocumented reports. The last known record prior to the modern era was an immature collected on 4 October 1924 in Washtenaw County. —Raymond J. Adams

# MISSISSIPPI KITE

(*Ictinia mississippiensis*)

W. Barrows (1912) listed the Mississippi Kite in *Michigan Bird Life* based on the premise that a specimen had been procured in Cass County many years before. At that time the nearest breeding population was in southern Illinois. The species declined from the northern portion of its range around 1900, and it was 1981 before another individual appeared in the state. Today, the Mississippi Kite is an accidental spring visitor to Michigan with seven reports, including two with photographic documentation.

The first modern-day record came on 24 May 1981 at Whitefish Point, Chippewa County. Another sighting at this locale on 31 May 1988 marked the state's fifth recent record. Photographs were taken of individuals at the Muskegon State Game Area from 25 to 27 May 1986 and at Midland on 22–23 May 1988. Additional sight records are from 30 April 1984 at the Kalamazoo Nature Center, 4 May 1990 in Mackinac County, and 11 May 1993 at Warren Dunes State Park, Berrien County.

The recent increase in Michigan observations corresponds to a northern expansion of this species' breeding range and an increase in extralimital records. Currently, Mississippi Kites nest in parts of the southeastern and south-central United States west to Arizona and north along the Mississippi River to southern Illinois and Kentucky. These buoyant, graceful fliers leave the States to winter in South America. Michigan observers should look for this kite from 30 April to 31 May, and be aware that summer records are also possible. Adult Mississippi Kites are dark gray above and lighter below with a pale gray head. Their long, flared tail is dark above and below, and the white secondaries appear as a wing

*Bald Eagle*
HEINER HERTLING

H.C. Hertling

patch in flight. Most of the Michigan records have been of first-summer birds, which are similar to adults but show a juvenile-like banded tail and streaked underwing. —Raymond J. Adams

# BALD EAGLE

## (*Haliaeetus leucocephalus*)

The Bald Eagle is an uncommon permanent resident of Michigan, with its nesting stronghold in the northern Lower and Upper peninsulas. Individuals overwinter in the state as far north as open water allows for access to fish, their primary food source, or in areas where there are substantial numbers of dead deer or other larger mammals to scavenge.

The North American representative of the worldwide genus *Haliaeetus* (fish-eagles), the Bald Eagle nests or has nested along most major waterways and large bodies of water in the United States and Canada, as far south as Florida in the East and Baja California and Mexico in the West. The total world population of Bald Eagles was estimated at 70,000 to 80,000 birds in 1982 (Stalmaster 1987).

While nesting pairs are fairly widely distributed across their range, in winter eagles are found in large, localized congregations. Numbering into the thousands, these winter roosts and feeding areas are important to the survival of the Bald Eagle. The Mississippi River and its major tributaries in the Midwest are one such major wintering area, supporting several thousand birds. Sites along coastal Washington and Alaska (where 40,000 or more overwinter) host even greater numbers of eagles, which feed on winter-spawning salmon.

Migration of Bald Eagles in Michigan is difficult to assess, since numbers are quite small in relation to other migrating diurnal raptors, and since migrants are often difficult to separate from residents. Spring movements appear to peak in March in the south and in mid-April in the Upper Peninsula, with an average of 85 recorded annually at Whitefish Point between 1988 and 1992. Larger numbers are seen in the Keweenaw Peninsula in the western Upper Peninsula, where 254 were reported in the spring of 1992. In the fall, sightings of migrant eagles are fewer and generally scattered throughout the state. At Erie Metropark in Monroe County the species is a regular, though somewhat rare, fall migrant.

Although the Bald Eagle nests as far south as Monroe County in Michigan, the bulk of the breeding population resides in the upper third of the Lower Peninsula and the Upper Peninsula, especially in those counties near the western boundary with Wisconsin. With an estimated population of 250 pairs in 1993 (T. Weise, pers. comm.), the number of Bald Eagles has grown steadily during the last 15 years, a recovery from the DDT era. As recently as 1982 the count was only 96 pairs (Stalmaster 1987), although that was the sixth-largest breeding population among the lower 48 states.

The aerial courtship of Bald Eagles is both complex and elaborate. Stalmaster (1987) has divided their courtship into four basic components: vocal display, chase display, undulating or roller-coaster flight, and the grand finale, the cartwheel display—an aerial extravaganza. During this climax, the pair will fly together to great heights, lock talons, and tumble downward, separating just before reaching the ground. Throughout the courtship process, the birds are also building a nest or adding sticks to refurbish an old nest. Finally egg laying starts, and the two (rarely one or three) eggs are laid over two to four days. As with all raptors, incubation begins after the first egg is laid, resulting in asynchronous hatching.

An adult Bald Eagle is an unforgettable sight with its stark white head, neck, and tail feathers contrasting with its chocolate-brown body plumage. Adults lack any white in their wings, unlike all subadult eagles, which may have extensive amounts of white in their underwing linings. It takes an eagle four to five years to reach adult plumage.

Since the early 1980s there has been a dramatic increase in the number of Bald Eagle pairs nesting in Michigan. This increase has been seen at both inland sites, along rivers and larger inland lakes, and along the Great Lakes shoreline. While this appears at first to be an entirely successful situation, there are warning signs of problems with the Great Lakes pairs. These birds are experiencing below-average productivity, including reduced numbers of hatchlings and fledglings, failure to lay eggs, or laying of infertile eggs, all of which may indicate significant changes in water quality and health of the prey base in the Great Lakes, specifically in regards to contaminants. The threatened status for the Bald Eagle still holds in Michigan, as does the need for continued monitoring and research. —Michael Kielb

# NORTHERN HARRIER

## (*Circus cyaneus*)

The Northern Harrier, once called the Marsh Hawk, is an uncommon summer resident and migrant throughout the state. These hawks inhabit marshes, fields, and large forest clearings, and are most often seen quartering slowly over these open spaces searching for small mammalian prey. They often glide with their wings in a slight dihedral above their bodies and their white rumps highly visible.

The Northern Harrier has a circumpolar distribution; in Eurasia it is known as the Hen Harrier. In North America it nests from the Arctic Circle to southern California and Mexico, withdrawing from northern regions in winter and ranging as far south as Central and South America. Once common throughout its range, the harrier has undergone a severe population decline in many areas. This reduction in numbers is directly related to losses in wetlands, grasslands, and prairies, and a decrease in acreage of uncultivated fields.

The distribution of harriers in Michigan is strongly tied to availability of suitable grassy habitats. With the exception of large forest openings and large fields in the Upper Peninsula and parts of the northern Lower Peninsula, much of the habitat required by this raptor has been disappearing from the state, matched by a similar decline in numbers of harriers. Old fields and hayfields are among the more frequently occupied habitats at present. One hundred years ago the harrier was one of our most common hawks; today it is on the list of species of special concern because of the severe drop in numbers. Only through protection of current marshlands and grasslands and management to increase these habitats elsewhere can the declining trend be stopped and perhaps reversed.

After arriving on their breeding territories, Michigan's Northern Harriers begin courtship displays, usually in early April. Of the 29 nest records I examined in the literature, an average of four eggs were laid, with full clutches present between 17 April and 21 June. All of the nests were placed on the ground, either in fallow fields or on hummocks in marshes, and had nestlings between 5 June and 24 July.

The spring migration of harriers in Michigan begins in March and peaks around late April, although migrants are still seen in small numbers in early May. At Whitefish Point, where this species is a common transient, an average of 300 harriers were recorded during the 1988–92 period. In the fall the first migrants, all immatures, begin to appear in late August, with an increase noticed in mid-September and the bulk of the migrants passing through during October and early November. From 1988 to 1992, an annual average of 1,087 harriers migrated from southern Ontario into southern Michigan. An amazing flight was recorded on 31 October 1993, when more than 250 were observed at nearby Holiday Beach in Ontario, following the passage of a cold front.

Not all harriers vacate the state for the winter. Small numbers are seen annually, mostly in the southeastern Lower Peninsula. Tallies from Christmas bird counts between 1980 and 1990 ranged from a low of 39 to a high of 109.

This hawk has a flat-faced appearance, with a facial disk similar to that of an owl. This facial design is believed to aid in their hearing, allowing them to hunt in lower light levels than most diurnal birds of prey. Harriers are one of the few raptor species in which sexes of adults can be identified in the field. Adult males, dubbed "gray ghosts," are unmistakable with their white underparts and gray upperparts with black-tipped wings. Adult females, in contrast, are streaky brown below and brown above. Immatures are colored similarly to females except that their breast and upper belly are an unstreaked orange. —Michael Kielb

# SHARP-SHINNED HAWK

## (*Accipiter striatus*)

The Sharp-shinned Hawk is the smallest of the three accipiters found in Michigan. This species can be separated from the similar Cooper's Hawk by its smaller size and noticeably squared or notched tail. Although the Sharp-shin is a very common migrant at sites with migratory concentrations of raptors, it is otherwise uncommon in the state. As a breeding species it is primarily confined to the northern two-thirds. Small numbers of Sharp-shins are recorded on Christmas bird counts in southern Michigan, but the majority of the population withdraws to warmer climates for the winter.

This species breeds throughout most of North America, from the treeline in Alaska and Canada to the southern United States, although it is scarce in the Southeast and Central Plains. Nesting is associated with boreal and montane forests, either conifer or a conifer-hardwood mix. Its greater familiarity as a migrant does not apply only to Michigan but is true across much of its range. Populations vacate the more northerly parts of the range, wintering from the southern United States into Mexico and Central America.

Migrant Sharp-shinned Hawks are common throughout Michigan during much of April. The five-year average at Whitefish Point from 1988 to 1992 was 9,031, with peak flights occurring during periods with southerly winds in mid- to late April and extending into early May.

Sharp-shinned Hawks begin setting up territories shortly after arriving from their wintering areas. Of the 19 nest records I reviewed for Michigan, 11 nests were placed in spruces, with the remainder in hemlocks and tamaracks. Clutches, with an average of four eggs, were laid between 17 April and 10 June, with nestlings present between 26 June and 8 August.

The southbound migration commences in mid-August and extends through October. From 1988 to 1992, an average of 14,782 Sharp-shins migrated through southern Ontario into Michigan in the fall. The early portion of this flight is composed almost entirely of immature birds, and counts for this five-year period indicate a steady decline in numbers recorded during this early flight. While this decrease may seem insignificant for such a common migrant, when viewed in the light of the population crash evident along the East Coast migratory routes, it may signal the start of a large-scale decline. During the last 16 years at Cape May, New Jersey, an average of 33,357 Sharp-shinned Hawks were observed, but this includes the peak years in the early 1980s when 40,000 to 60,000 birds were tallied annually. By the late 1980s these numbers had declined by more than 50%, and in 1992 only 8,207 birds were recorded, 25% of the 16-year average.

This downward trend is apparent not only in the East but throughout much of the Sharp-shin's range in North America. The extent and causes of this decline are not easily explained, and there probably are several contributing factors. First, the general decline of small passerine species, which make up the bulk of their prey, may be affecting Sharp-shin populations. Second, some have wondered what effect acid rain plays in this scenario. Boreal trees are particularly susceptible to the negative effects of acidification, resulting eventually in their death. Together, these factors may be reducing food resources and nesting habitat. Pesticides are a third possible factor. DDT, while banned in the Northern Hemisphere, is still widely used in the tropics, where Sharp-shins and their prey are exposed to its toxic effects during winter.

Considering this recent information, the Sharp-shinned Hawk should be a species of concern to bird-watchers. Although it is still common at present, the alarming rate of decrease apparent over much of North America warrants attention. Populations migrating through and nesting in the Great Lakes region should be closely monitored and studied, with suitable habitat protected for the species' benefit. —Michael Kielb

H.C.Hertling

# COOPER'S HAWK

### (*Accipiter cooperii*)

The Cooper's Hawk is the mid-sized accipiter occurring in Michigan. Once called the Chicken Hawk for its habit of dining on free-range chickens, the Cooper's is an uncommon year-round resident in the southern Lower Peninsula, and a rare summer resident in the remainder of the state. This is the most commonly encountered accipiter in the southern counties, with the exception of a brief period in April and September during the migration of the Sharp-shinned Hawk.

The Cooper's Hawk is a generally uncommon resident throughout its North American range, which includes all of the United States, southern Canada, and northern Mexico. It is an inhabitant of deciduous and coniferous woodlands. In southern Michigan hardwoods dominated by oak and hickory are preferred, although coniferous woodlots are also used if available. Their territories frequently include large woodland openings. Birds are the predominant prey of the Cooper's Hawk, although it is becoming apparent that mammals make up a greater portion of its diet than previously believed.

Fairly large numbers of migrants travel through the state in the fall. The peak passage in southeastern Michigan is during early to mid-October, when more than 100 individuals a day can move from Ontario into Monroe County. Spring migrants are noted in southern Michigan starting in March. The Cooper's Hawk is an uncommon migrant at Whitefish Point (at the northern edge of its range), averaging 86 birds over the spring seasons from 1988 to 1992. Here the main flight occurs in late April and early May.

Cooper's Hawks begin courtship in March, followed by nest building. Commonly there will be two or three nests in a territory, each used for one or two seasons before the pair switch to another nest. For 40 nest records which I examined in the literature, clutches averaged three eggs, with full clutches between 4 April and 4 June. The noisy nestlings can help give away the location of a nest, and records show they are generally found between 16 June and 17 July. Nests are typically located near the forest canopy; the average height for the 40 records was 43 feet, with 50% of the nests in oak and American beech, and 20% in pines. The nest is made of deciduous sticks and large twigs and is conspicuously lined with conifer limbs.

The identification of the Cooper's Hawk in the field presents a difficult situation for most bird-watchers. There are, however, several criteria which can be used to separate this species from the similar Sharp-shinned Hawk. The Cooper's is a larger, longer-bodied bird with a distinctively long, rounded, white-tipped tail. Additionally, when gliding, the Cooper's Hawk

*Sharp-shinned Hawk*
*Cooper's Hawk*
HEINER HERTLING

extends its head and neck so that they protrude well beyond the bend of the wing. These criteria apply equally to both adult and immature birds.

The status of the Cooper's Hawk changed notably in the 1950s, when the population in Michigan and the eastern United States underwent a precipitous decline. A combination of shooting as a pest species, toxins such as DDT, and reduction of habitat led to this decline. By the 1970s it was evident that this was a species of special concern in North America. Since then, however, populations have stabilized and started to slowly increase during the 1980s—the result of education about predators, banning of DDT, and maturation of woodlands. Throughout the 1960s and '70s there were fewer than 2 pairs per township in Washtenaw County, with many townships having none. As of 1993 this number had dramatically increased to 8 to 10 pairs in some townships. Currently the status of the Cooper's Hawk in Michigan appears to be healthy, viable, and on the increase. —Michael Kielb

# NORTHERN GOSHAWK

### (*Accipiter gentilis*)

The powerful and striking Northern Goshawk has been described as "a magnificent but bloodthirsty bird" (Barrows 1912), "the worst offenders among the commoner hawks" (Roberts 1932), and "the most dreaded of the *Accipiter* tribe" (Bent 1937). With such descriptions from ornithologists, it is easy to understand why this species has been persecuted for so many years by its human neighbors. This large accipiter is an uncommon permanent resident in Michigan, which is in the southern portion of its North American range.

The Northern Goshawk has a circumpolar distribution, nesting across Europe, Asia, and North America. Throughout its range it is a rare to uncommon resident of extensive tracts of hardwood or mixed hardwood-conifer forests. The goshawk hunts in the lower canopy of forests as well as taking prey off the forest floor. The stout tarsi of this species attest to its ability to snatch large prey from the ground. Grouse, rabbits, and hares make up a large portion of the goshawk's diet. Interestingly, as the cycles of their prey wax and wane, so do populations of this raptor. The greatest portion of their prey base has a 10-year population cycle, which in turn leads to a 10-year cycle in numbers of goshawks.

The breeding range for the Northern Goshawk in Michigan encompasses the northern half of the Lower Peninsula and the entire Upper Peninsula, although several nesting pairs have recently been located as far south as Kalamazoo and Lapeer counties. In winter there are often scattered reports of goshawks throughout the state, with immature-plumaged birds dominating the southern sightings. The exception occurs during years of major invasions of goshawks from farther north, roughly every ten years. In these winters, there are about equal numbers of adult and immature birds encountered.

Small numbers of goshawks migrate through Michigan during both spring and fall. In March and April they are uncommon migrants at Whitefish Point, where an average of 71 birds were sighted between 1988 and 1992. Typically starting in mid-October,

a small number (average 35, 1988–92) migrate from southern Ontario into southern Michigan, with peak numbers occurring in early November. In contrast to the migration in Michigan, counts from Hawk Ridge at Duluth, Minnesota (average 841, 1988–92), give a better indication of the magnitude of the irruptive 10-year cycle. Here, 5,152 goshawks were observed in 1972, 5,819 in 1982, and 2,292 in 1992, mostly during October and November.

The earliest of the nesting accipiters, the goshawk begins its courtship and nest building in March. For 30 Michigan nest records I examined, an average of three eggs were laid, with complete clutches between 12 April and 10 May. Nestlings were present between 14 May and 6 July. The average nest height was 38 feet, and selected tree species were aspen and birch (67%) or beech. The Northern Goshawk is well known as a defiant and aggressive defender of its nest, eggs, and nestlings.

The adult goshawk is readily identified by its dark blue-black head, with contrasting white eye stripes, dark steel-blue back, and light gray underparts. The rounded tail is proportionately shorter than that of the Cooper's Hawk. In overall flight shape it is similar to a greatly enlarged Sharp-shinned Hawk. Immature plumage is light brown, and the contrasting eye stripe is still present. The breast is boldly streaked, fading into the belly.

The goshawk has never been a common species in Michigan. Barrows in 1912 stated that it probably nested in the state regularly but in small numbers, and Wood in 1951 considered it rare with its status little known. Thirty years later Payne (1983) remarked that it was an uncommon transient and a winter visitant, and that there were nest records from 10 Upper Peninsula and 17 Lower Peninsula counties. *The Atlas of Breeding Birds of Michigan* presents the most recent and complete nesting-season "snapshot" of the goshawk in Michigan, where it is now fairly widespread in large tracts of woods throughout the northern three-quarters of the state. There are current concerns for the state population in regards to its nesting habitat—northern mature hardwood and mixed hardwood-conifer forests dominated by aspen, poplar, and birch. These woods are most often clearcut by the timber industry, thus disrupting local populations and/or pairs. If this practice continues unabated, the future of the goshawk in the state will remain as tenuous as it has appeared to be during the last hundred years. —Michael Kielb

# RED-SHOULDERED HAWK

## (*Buteo lineatus*)

The Red-shouldered Hawk, the least common of Michigan's resident buteos, is probably also the most stunning in appearance.

*Broad-winged Hawk*
*Northern Goshawk*
GIJSBERT VAN FRANKENHUYZEN

This bird of prey is an uncommon summer resident in the northern third of the Lower Peninsula, while elsewhere in the state it is an uncommon to rare summer resident. Most Red-shouldered Hawks retreat from Michigan in the winter, although a small number of sightings in the southern third of the state are evident from examination of Christmas bird count records.

Throughout much of the eastern United States, the Red-shouldered Hawk is a common permanent resident; only at the northern periphery of its range is the species migratory. This is most evident in southern Ontario and Monroe County, Michigan, where the majority of the Canadian population (approximately 1,200 birds) funnels through en route to their wintering areas in the south-central United States.

The Red-shouldered Hawk is a denizen of moist, mature deciduous woods. Forested floodplains and river bottoms are excellent examples of what is considered to be typical habitat. It is also evident from the Craigheads' studies in Superior Township, Washtenaw County, that closed-canopy woodlands are suitable. Similar mature woods dominated by beech and sugar maple in the northern Lower Peninsula are the primary habitat used today.

In the fall large numbers of Red-shouldered Hawks pass through Monroe County headed south from their breeding grounds in Ontario. The peak flights occur in late October, typically between 15 and 30 October, when 250 to 400 birds may exit Canada on a single day. The spring period is less clear since the only site where diurnal raptor migration is regularly monitored in spring is Whitefish Point, which lies beyond the range of most Red-shoulders in Michigan. During the 1988–92 period, an average of 32 birds were sighted at Whitefish Point. Spring migration is best quantified just south of the Michigan border at the Ottawa National Wildlife Refuge in Ohio. Here large numbers of Red-shouldered Hawks migrate in late March and early April, with peak flights approaching or exceeding 200 birds per day.

Red-shouldered Hawks begin nesting in late March and early April. For a series of 116 Michigan nest records that I have reviewed, an average of three eggs were laid, with complete clutches between 3 April and 23 May. Nestlings were present as early as 12 May and as late as 5 August. Nests were placed at an average height of 51 feet, and American beech accounted for 33% of the nest sites, followed by oak (26%) and American elm (9%).

The beautiful Red-shouldered Hawk is easily identified. Overhead the tail and wing pattern are distinctive—the tail is banded and the wings show a light-colored crescent at the base of the outer primaries. Perched birds are best identified by viewing the upperwing pattern, reddish-brown shoulder color, and numerous white flecks in the flight feathers. Adult body plumage is warm reddish in the breast, fading to a paler reddish-pink in the belly, while immatures are streaky brown.

In the past 50 years the status of the Red-shouldered Hawk has changed dramatically in Michigan. Norman Wood (1951) referred to this species as a common summer resident in the southern third of Michigan, whereas today it is rare in this region. In Superior Township the Craigheads found more than 19 pairs nesting in the 1940s, but by the 1980s there were none. This situation is typical of what has happened in southern Michigan. During the 1980s Breeding Bird Atlas, this species was found in only 12% of the southern Lower Peninsula townships, with a mere seven con-

GIJSBERT- 1993

firmed nestings. The toxic effects of DDT, changes in woods including the clearing of much of the older, closed-canopy growth, and the invasion of the Red-tailed Hawk into these newly cleared areas spelled the demise of the Red-shoulder. As of 1993, the Red-shouldered Hawk has not reestablished itself in these areas.

The stronghold for this species in Michigan is now in the northern Lower Peninsula, where extensive beech-maple-aspen woods are available for nesting. The Red-shouldered Hawk was listed as threatened in the state in 1986, and its future status in the southern counties remains unclear, although the population in the north appears to be viable and stable. —Michael Kielb

# BROAD-WINGED HAWK

## (*Buteo platypterus*)

The Broad-winged Hawk is the smallest of the buteos that occur in Michigan. It is a widespread, common summer resident in the Upper Peninsula, where it inhabits hardwood and mixed forests. In the Lower Peninsula it is a common to uncommon summer resident in the upper third, and generally rare and irregularly distributed in the southern two-thirds. The entire population retreats to South America for the winter.

The Broad-winged Hawk is one of the most abundant buteos breeding in the eastern United States. This becomes evident when migration data are examined. In the fall, daily high counts of 100,000 to 200,000 birds are tallied in southern Texas. Farther south at Panama City, seasonal counts of over 800,000 in late October and early November give an indication of the number of birds exiting North America in search of their South American wintering grounds.

In Michigan the distribution of the Broad-winged Hawk is delineated by the distribution of large tracts of hardwood and mixed hardwood-conifer forests, especially those dominated by aspen, beech, and birch. As a result of these habitat needs, the Broad-wing is most commonly seen during the nesting season in northern Michigan, although small, local populations occur in the more forested areas of southern Michigan.

This long-distance migrant is the most common buteo during both spring and fall migrations, even though it occurs in the shortest window of time. In the fall large numbers of Broad-wings are seen in the vicinity of Erie Metropark in Monroe County. Greatest movements occur on days with northerly winds and clear skies following the first cold front, usually after 10 September; thus peak numbers are seen between 12 and 17 September. The magnitude of migration through this area is staggering, with daily totals of 30,000 to 40,000 birds not uncommon,

*Red-shouldered Hawk*

GIJSBERT VAN FRANKENHUYZEN

and seasonal totals numbering 50,000 to 60,000. In the spring the greatest numbers are seen in late April and early May. At Whitefish Point and Keweenaw Peninsula in the Upper Peninsula and on the Lake Michigan coast of Berrien County, late April days with southern winds can produce flights numbering into the thousands. During the 1988–92 period, an average of 4,620 were observed at Whitefish Point, and in 1992, 7,498 were counted at the tip of the Keweenaw Peninsula.

Broad-winged Hawks are surprisingly fast at establishing territories, building nests, and setting up their familial responsibilities upon arrival, primarily in late April and early May. I have found that by 28 April some birds in southern Michigan were already sitting on full clutches, which averaged three eggs. Throughout the Great Lakes region, especially in the north, nests with eggs were found until 4 July. Nestling dates in the area range from 3 June to 26 July. The average nest height for seven Michigan nests was 42 feet, slightly higher than for all Great Lakes nests, which averaged 32 feet. Most of the nests were in aspen and American beech.

The population of Broad-winged Hawks in Michigan is large and stable, with the exception of the southern third of the Lower Peninsula, where the number of nesting birds appears low, although on the rise. In recent years breeding pairs have become established in Washtenaw, Wayne, and Oakland counties, where nesting now occurs on a regular basis. This increase is probably due to the maturation of hardwood woodlots, making available more habitat for nesting.

The smallish Broad-winged Hawk is best identified in flight by its strongly banded tail and very light underwing coloration, fringed throughout the flight feathers by a trailing edge of black. The body plumage of the adult is a solid brick-red in the breast, becoming distinctly barred in the upper belly and fading to white in the lower belly. The juvenile is streaky brown with similar tail and wing patterns to the adult. —Michael Kielb

# SWAINSON'S HAWK

## (*Buteo swainsoni*)

This hawk is a wide-ranging, open-country buteo, nearly the size of a Red-tail but with long, narrow wings and paler wing linings contrasting with dark primaries underneath. The Swainson's Hawk resides in western North America from Alaska to Mexico, and mostly migrates to South America for the winter. Migrants typically travel in large single-species flocks, although individuals can be found in the company of Broad-winged Hawks, another long-distance migrant.

The historical status of the Swainson's Hawk in Michigan is subject to debate. A century ago, hawk identification was not as well understood, and confusion existed over the separation of some buteo plumages. Barrows (1912) noted only two unquestionable records; some other reported specimens were no longer available for examination, while others were misidentified. Sight records were given little credence even through the 1950s, when Zimmerman and Van Tyne (1959) listed only four specimens from museum collections. Whether the Swainson's Hawk was more than an occasional migrant is unclear.

With the improvement of hawk identification guides and consistent coverage of migration points, a better picture of Swainson's Hawk occurrence has emerged. Today this species is a casual but nearly regular transient through the state, as birds have been seen most years since 1975, with a maximum of eight in 1990. Most observations emanate from the Upper Peninsula, primarily at the Whitefish Point Bird Observatory in Chippewa County. Spring reports in the state outnumber those in fall at least four to one. This hawk seldom appears before 19 April and has been seen as late as 29 May. Exceptionally early dates include 26 March 1991 in Eaton County and 3 April 1984 and 1987, both at Whitefish Point. Additionally, there is one summer report on 11 June 1988 from Alpena County. Fall dates are widely spread but embrace the period 6 September through 2 November.

The Michigan status of the Swainson's Hawk coincides with data from adjacent states. It is a rare spring and fall migrant in Wisconsin, a casual migrant in Indiana, and accidental in Ohio. The closest nesting population of this raptor is in northwestern Illinois. —Raymond J. Adams

# RED-TAILED HAWK
## (*Buteo jamaicensis*)

The Red-tailed Hawk is the familiar large, soaring hawk seen throughout the state of Michigan. It is a common permanent resident in the southern half of the state, becoming somewhat less common in the north, where it is nonetheless an easily observed species. In winter the state's population is augmented by migrants from more northerly areas. This ubiquitous buteo occurs throughout North America, with breeding populations in every state of the United States and every country from Canada in North America to Panama in Central America.

The Red-tailed Hawk is an inhabitant of mixed open fields (for hunting) and scattered woods (for nesting). The size of the woods utilized by the Red-tail is quite variable, and its tolerance of humans and ability to use smaller woodlots has allowed it to proliferate even in areas of high human occupation. The southern half of the Lower Peninsula, with its large number of farms and one- to ten-acre woodlots, offers the perfect habitat, and it is in this area that the species has its greatest nesting density in the state. In the northern half of the Lower Peninsula, with more continuous forests and fewer large open areas, there is a decrease in Red-tail numbers, and in the Upper Peninsula even fewer are resident. Here, the smaller Broad-winged Hawk is the most common buteo.

Spring migration is evident from late March in southern Michigan until early June in the Upper Peninsula, with numerous Red-tails returning from wintering grounds in the south-central United States. At Whitefish Point large numbers migrate in April and early May, with the peak coming during the passage of warm fronts with southerly winds. During the 1988–92 period an average of 994 were sighted at this locale.

In the fall, large numbers of Red-tailed Hawks migrate through Michigan, with greatest concentrations observed in the southeastern region. Starting in late August, small numbers of juvenile Red-tails migrate into Monroe County from Ontario; this trickle of migrants numbers in the thousands by late October and early November, when adults dominate the flight. During this period 1,000 to 1,500 or more may pass in a single day; the largest flight of Red-tails in North America was documented on 10 November 1980, when 2,724 migrated from Ontario into Michigan.

Territorial displays, courtship flights, and nest building signal the onset of the breeding season. These activities may occur as early as February in the southern Lower Peninsula. The large stick nest of the Red-tail is conspicuous and most easily located in February and March, when adults are refurbishing old nests. Examining 111 Michigan nest records, I found that the average number of eggs was two, and full clutches were present between 26 March and 26 June, with nestlings present between 29 April and 26 June. The average nest height was 51 feet, and the nest was most often placed in an oak (52%), American elm, or American beech (29% combined). In the northern Lower Peninsula and the Upper Peninsula, conifers are used for nesting, but to a lesser extent than hardwoods.

The Red-tailed Hawk is one of the most familiar and easily recognized hawks in Michigan. It is frequently seen along highways and country lanes as it perches in trees and atop telephone poles, or soars overhead searching fields for small rodents—the main component of its diet. The brick-red tail is an excellent field mark for adults; juveniles, however, lack the red and have an indistinctly banded tail. The glowing white breast is evident in both adult and juvenile birds. The presence of a very dark belly band usually indicates a juvenile, while adults have a highly variable belly band. Additionally, there are other variations in plumage seen on rare occasions, including albinistic individuals. At Whitefish Point in the Upper Peninsula, a small number of dark-morph Red-tails with chocolate-brown body plumage and wing linings are seen each spring, mostly in late April and early May. —Michael Kielb

# FERRUGINOUS HAWK
## (*Buteo regalis*)

A casual migrant and accidental winter visitant to Michigan, the Ferruginous Hawk was first reported for our state in the 1970s. Besides photographs, there is ample documentation to justify its inclusion on the state bird list. This elegant hawk is one of the largest and most powerful buteos in North America, appearing almost eagle-like at a distance with its large head and long wings. During the breeding season, it can be found in the western United States north to the Canadian Prairie Provinces, with wintering mostly in the southwestern states and Mexico.

*American Kestrel*
*Red-tailed Hawk*
Gijsbert van Frankenhuyzen

GIJSBERT - 1992

There have been at least 12 separate Michigan reports since 1973, 7 of which have solid documentation. Three of these were from the winter period, beginning with an adult Ferruginous Hawk seen on 9 January 1977 in Cooper Township, Kalamazoo County. The next winter sighting was of an immature bird discovered at the Allegan State Game Area on 25 December 1989. This bird was viewed by many observers, as it remained until at least 27 January 1990. The following year, the same individual or another immature bird was again present at this locale and was sighted sporadically from 7 November 1990 through 11 February 1991.

The other reports of Ferruginous Hawks have been during times of migration, all from the spring season except one. Those which are well documented include a light phase immature on 25 April 1985 at Whitefish Point, Chippewa County; a light phase adult on 11 May 1990 also at Whitefish Point; a light phase adult on 1 May 1992 at Port Crescent State Park, Huron County; and a light phase immature on 9 November 1991 at Trenton, Wayne County. Of the remaining five reports, some or all may have been Ferruginous Hawks, but the information is inconclusive. These latter sightings all occurred within the spring migration window of 14 April to 30 May.

As you have probably surmised by this writing, identification of this hawk is not simple. There are three different color phases plus substantial plumage changes from immature to adult birds. Of the various plumages, the light phase adult is probably the most distinctive; these birds show rufous on the back and upper-wing coverts with a large white patch on the primaries, and are mostly white below (with some rufous flecking), with rufous leg-gings and a whitish to rufous-tinged tail. —Raymond J. Adams

# ROUGH-LEGGED HAWK

### (*Buteo lagopus*)

The Rough-legged Hawk has a circumpolar breeding distribution, which in North America includes the far regions of Canada and Alaska. As winter approaches, birds vacate the tundra, migrating to southern Canada and the northern and middle United States. This stunning winter visitor from the North has a highly variable status in Michigan. Approximately every three to four years, Rough-legged Hawks are common migrants at hawk concentration points, and are fairly common winter residents in open habitats statewide. This cycle is caused by natural fluctuations in prey species, primarily lemmings and voles, on their breeding grounds. During noninvasion years, the species is present in Michigan but in lesser numbers.

Rough-legged Hawks are denizens of open country including grasslands, cultivated and uncultivated fields, marshes, and dikes. These areas offer the best hunting grounds for small mammalian prey. Arrival in the fall generally occurs in October and November, with some individuals appearing in the Upper Peninsula as early as September, particularly in major irruption years. In Monroe County, peak numbers exiting Ontario occur between 23 October and 15 November, with an average annual fall tally of 190 Rough-legs during the 1988–92 period.

The variability of numbers wintering within our borders is evident in Christmas bird count data. Totals since 1970 range from a low of 30 in 1984–85 to a high of 278 in 1989–90. Generally, if harsh weather hits early in winter and snow cover is significant across the state, most Rough-legs will continue farther south, and numbers seen here are small. The reverse is true if relatively mild conditions persist prior to and during the late December–early January count period. Largest concentrations are found in areas with the greatest amounts of farmland, marsh-land, and fallow fields. The Saginaw Bay and Thumb regions, Lake Erie and Lake St. Clair marshes, and Allegan and Muskegon counties are among the more reliable places to encounter this hawk in winter.

Rough-legs returning north pass through southern Michigan in March and April, and on through the Upper Peninsula from mid-April to mid-May. As a spring migrant at Whitefish Point, the species is most common from 13 April to 12 May, with peak numbers typically occurring during the first ten days of this period. On exceptional migration days, up to and exceeding 100 birds will be recorded here. From 1988 to 1992, the annual average at the point was 693, with a high of 1,224 in the spring of 1990. Occasional individuals linger into early June, and a few have even been recorded later in the Upper Peninsula.

In all plumages, the Rough-legged Hawk is quickly separated from other buteos by the wide white subterminal tail band. Additionally, the underwing pattern is quite striking, showing bold markings on both the wing linings and flight feathers plus a prominent dark wrist patch. Complicating identification is the occurrence of dark and light color morphs (or phases). In the dark morph all of the body and wing linings are a dark chocolate brown, eliminating most of the above field marks. The tail and flight pattern are thus critical in distinguishing these birds. In contrast to other buteos, the wings are typically held slightly above the body and are slightly bent at the wrist. Unlike most hawks in flight, Rough-legs can be identified as to age and sex with experience and careful observation, and birders should consult good raptor field guides for more detailed descriptions. —Michael Kielb

# GOLDEN EAGLE

### (*Aquila chrysaetos*)

The Golden Eagle is one of the most dynamic hunters among the diurnal raptors, preying upon ducks, geese, grouse, and rabbits. With a worldwide breeding distribution in northern mountainous and hilly regions, its North American stronghold is in the Rocky Mountains from Canada south to Arizona and New Mexico. A small relict population exists in the Appalachians and northern New England in the eastern United States, and in northern Ontario and Quebec in Canada.

The Golden Eagle is an uncommon spring and fall migrant in Michigan, seen most regularly at points along the Great Lakes shorelines and occasionally at inland sites such as the jack-pine plains in the northern Lower Peninsula. Additionally, this eagle is a casual winter visitor, as small numbers may occur in locations with large concentrations of Canada Geese and ducks. The Allegan State Game Area and Thorn Lake in Jackson County are two sites in southern Michigan where this species has been found most often during late fall and winter in recent years. One to three birds have been encountered on Christmas bird counts in about half of the winters since 1980.

As a spring migrant at Whitefish Point, Golden Eagles are seen in greatest numbers in late March and early April. The average number sighted during the 1988–92 period was 34, with a peak count of 50 in 1992. During fall migration, highest numbers are recorded during the last week of October and the first week of November, when 10 or more a day may be sighted near Erie Metropark, Wayne County, or Pte. Mouillee, Monroe County. Between 1988 and 1992, an annual average of 65 Golden Eagles migrated from southern Ontario into southern Michigan. A regionally significant number of 24 was recorded at Holiday Beach, Ontario, on 10 November 1991, all headed toward Michigan.

At first many bird-watchers are confused by the various plumages of the Golden Eagle versus the Bald Eagle. Careful observation and practice should eliminate these difficulties. Adult Golden Eagles are a rich dark brown with no white; a lighter golden-colored nape is visible under ideal conditions. Immature birds have a wide white tail band and white patches at the base of their flight feathers, unlike immature or subadult Bald Eagles, on which the outer tail feathers show some brown and there are variable amounts of white in the wing linings. Additional differences are seen in the flight profiles of the two species, which can be critical in proper identification at a distance. Bald Eagles soar and glide on very flat wings, whereas Golden Eagles keep their wings in a slight to fairly exaggerated dihedral, resembling a Turkey Vulture but without its "tippy" flight. —Michael Kielb

# [CRESTED CARACARA]

## (*Caracara plancus*)

This large-headed, long-necked bird of prey inhabits open country and brushland in a discontinuous range in the extreme southern United States (mostly Texas and Florida), Mexico, Central America, and much of South America. On 3 September 1977 at the Muskegon Dunes State Park, a Crested Caracara was observed and carefully described by three observers. However, because this species is not known for vagrancy, this sighting and records from Oregon, Ontario, Pennsylvania, New Jersey, and North Carolina (AOU 1983) are thought to involve birds which escaped from captivity. —Raymond J. Adams

# AMERICAN KESTREL

## (*Falco sparverius*)

The diminutive and colorful American Kestrel is a common summer resident throughout Michigan. Once known as the Sparrow Hawk, this small falcon is a familiar sight along roadsides where it perches on telephone poles, utility wires, and the tops of trees, scanning fields for small rodents and grasshoppers. As winter approaches, kestrels withdraw from the northern portions of Michigan, and the population in the southern third of the state is augmented by numerous wintering birds from outside the area.

Kestrels are ubiquitous in the New World, occurring from Canada and Alaska in the far north to Argentina and Chile in South America. Throughout their range they are common to uncommon residents and abundant migrants at many North American coastal sites, including the Great Lakes shorelines. Breeding commonly in every county in Michigan, including Isle Royale, the kestrel has the most even distribution of any raptor in the state. Extensive forests limit the species somewhat in the northern regions, but kestrels manage to find suitable places to live wherever there are forest openings with access to dead trees for nest sites.

Tree cavities at woodland fringes adjacent to forest openings or fields are used for nesting by this falcon. Additionally, pairs readily accept man-made nest boxes in areas where natural cavities are not available. These boxes are typically placed on poles at a height of 10 to 15 feet, facing into open fields. Residents and travelers in the state will notice numerous boxes along the highways in the northern Lower Peninsula and eastern Upper Peninsula.

The kestrel's breeding season commences in spring, with egg laying sometime in April in the southern counties, and in May farther north. The female lays three to five eggs at daily intervals, although eggs are sometimes laid on alternate days. An average of three to four fledglings are commonly seen in farmlands and near forest openings in July and early August.

In addition to our substantial resident population, large numbers of kestrels migrate through Michigan in spring and fall. In the spring, such movements are particularly evident at the Whitefish Point Bird Observatory in the northeastern Upper Peninsula, where an average of 437 were tallied per year from 1988 to 1992. In the fall, an even larger passage of kestrels occurs through Monroe County in the southeast corner as birds make their way around the western end of Lake Erie. Hawk counts indicate that peak flights are bimodal, with an early concentration in mid-September and a second peak about three weeks later in early October. An average of 4,518 kestrels were recorded annually during the 1988–92 period.

With its small size and attractive plumage, the American Kestrel hardly looks threatening to any possible prey species, but this is certainly not the case. These versatile hunters consume numerous small rodents and a great number of grasshoppers and other invertebrates during the summer, switching to a diet almost entirely of rodents in the winter. As they hunt from an open perch, males are readily distinguished from females by their bluish wings, brick-red back, and mostly unmarked tail. Females are a warm brick-red overall, with fine barring on the tail.

Various data sources for Michigan suggest that kestrel populations are generally stable and are not threatened by either development or habitat loss, except perhaps on a local level, especially in the more densely populated southern counties. Breeding bird surveys for the state even identified a small increase in numbers from the mid-1960s to the mid-1980s. The greatest limitation or threat to this species may be the elimination of large dead trees which supply cavities of sufficient size for nesting. Because of the kestrel's strong association with agricultural lands, particularly in southern Michigan, pesticide applications are also a concern for maintaining healthy populations. —Michael Kielb

# MERLIN

## (*Falco columbarius*)

The Merlin is one of the rarest of Michigan's nesting diurnal raptors. Small numbers nest in the boreal forests of the Upper Peninsula, and there are few summer and breeding records for the northernmost counties of the Lower Peninsula. The habitat preferred by this falcon is open coniferous woods, often spruce-dominated and close to lakeshores or inland lakes.

Within its circumpolar distribution, the Merlin is an uncommon nester in most regions, but can be locally common, as is the case in the urban populations of Thunder Bay, Ontario, as well as Saskatoon and Edmonton in western Canada. Scattered across the boreal forests of North America, the Merlin sparsely fills its habitat, with Michigan located at the southern periphery of its nesting range.

Greatest numbers of transient Merlins are reported in the fall at East Coast hawk watches, especially Cape May, New Jersey, where 100+ individuals a day pass in early October and a yearly average of 1,403 were seen from 1988 to 1992. Merlins winter as far south as Mexico and Central America and are a common migrant along the Gulf coast of Mexico on their spring passage north.

The fall Merlin migration in Michigan peaks in mid- to late September and is dominated by immature and female birds. The movement from Ontario into southern Michigan (concentrated along the Lake Erie shoreline) typically numbers from 60 to 90 birds, a far cry from the thousands that migrate along the East Coast. The spring migration in the state is best observed at Whitefish Point, where Merlins pass from late April to mid-May. An annual average of 67 were recorded at Whitefish Point from 1988 to 1992. It is not uncommon at this time of year to encounter Merlins hunting the beach at dawn, where they make short forays from snags of driftwood or survey posts to catch passerines in passage.

Male Merlins establish territories soon after returning from their southern wintering areas. As females pass through, the males attempt to entice them with gifts of passerines, presented prior to or just after copulation. The female may then choose to stay and seek out a nest site, most often an old crow nest in a spruce, or she may press on in search of a better nesting situation. Territorial and courtship displays are typically seen in late April through late May. Nests with young are usually found from the middle of June into early July, with fledglings present throughout July. I have observed numerous copulations and nestings in late April in Chippewa County, and have discovered a female feeding two fledglings on 13 July at the mouth of the Tahquamenon River, Chippewa County.

This falcon is sexually dimorphic in coloration—the male is dark steel blue across the upper wings and back, and the female is chocolate brown. Most people are surprised to learn that the Merlin is roughly the size of an American Kestrel; it is not a very large falcon, although it does act large. In flight it can easily be confused with a kestrel, and observers should consult field guides to learn the several characteristics which differentiate the two.

Michigan's Merlin population is quite small, probably 30 to 50 pairs scattered across the Upper Peninsula, not counting the stronghold on Isle Royale where there were an estimated 9 pairs in 1988. While this entire state population seems small, it is probably a historical high (or nearly so), is stable, and has increased during the 1980s. —Michael Kielb

# PEREGRINE FALCON

## (*Falco peregrinus*)

The Peregrine Falcon is a rare reestablished resident and uncommon migrant in Michigan. This majestic bird of prey nests on all continents except Antarctica. In North America there are breeding populations scattered throughout the Canadian and Alaskan Arctic, along both the Atlantic and Pacific coasts, through the Rockies south into Mexico, in the Appalachians, and in the Great Lakes. In the eastern United States most current nesting is a direct result of the Peregrine Falcon reintroduction program. Starting in the 1970s, over 3,000 birds were released throughout the United States. More than 400 have been released in the Great Lakes region, including over 100 in Michigan. Most recent estimates show that there are about 3,000 pairs of Peregrines in North America, the majority in Canada and Alaska.

Peregrines are cliff-nesting birds and will reuse nest sites repeatedly for many years. There are examples in Europe of prime sites in continual use by a succession of pairs for 300 years! There are historical records of a small tree-nesting population in the Great Lakes region, but they have been gone for well over 100 years.

Peregrine Falcons of wild origin last nested in Michigan in 1957 (Berger and Mueller 1969). As a result of reintroductions, which involve the release of young, captively reared birds (known as hacking), Peregrines are now nesting on man-made "cliffs" in Detroit (beginning in 1989) and at several natural sites in the Upper Peninsula and on Isle Royale. The other city release site, Grand Rapids, has not yet seen the permanent establishment of a nesting pair. Reintroduction goals in Michigan were to attain 10 pairs by the year 2000; it seems that this goal should be achieved well before that date.

Northern populations of Peregrines are highly migratory, some traveling as far south as Chile and Argentina. The timing of their movements closely follows the peak migrations of passerines and other small birds. In Michigan, Peregrine Falcons are a rare to uncommon migrant. During spring migration at Whitefish Point,

*Merlin*
HEINER HERTLING

H.C.Hertling

counts averaged 23 Peregrines per year from 1988 to 1992, and 39 were seen during the Keweenaw Peninsula hawk watch in 1992.

A good site to observe migrating Peregrines in fall is along the coast of Monroe County, where birds enter from southern Ontario. For the 1988–92 period, a season average of 36 were recorded, with the peak flight between 2 and 9 October. The Great Lakes migration is minuscule when compared to that of sites such as Padre Island, Texas, where hundreds migrate, or Cape May, New Jersey, where the fall average during the same five-year period was 610. I was fortunate enough to be there on 3 October 1989 when 157 were tallied, more than I had seen in 13 years in the Midwest.

Peregrines are large falcons, dwarfing the Merlin and American Kestrel, the two other species which regularly occur in Michigan. Adults are steel-blue gray on the head, back, and upper wing, and are pale with fine barring below. Immatures are chocolate brown above and streaky brown below. In all plumages this species shows a dark hood and mustache. In flight Peregrines are strong and powerful; their impressive dives at prey, during which they achieve speeds of over 100 miles per-hour, are well known and spectacular to watch.

The culprit of the Peregrine's demise in the 1940s, '50s, and '60s was DDT. The accumulation of this toxin in the birds' bodies caused severe egg-shell thinning and reproductive failure. By the early 1960s, not a single pair of nesting Peregrines could be found east of the Mississippi. The banning of DDT use in the early 1970s set the stage for recovery and the success of an intensive reintroduction program. It appears that with current reintroduction efforts and protection, the population of this endangered Michigan bird will continue to grow until it reaches some maximum number of pairs which the habitat can support. Critical to this occurring, however, are the continued close monitoring of nesting pairs and protection of their habitat. —Michael Kielb

# GYRFALCON

## (*Falco rusticolus*)

For well over a century there were only two Michigan reports of Gyrfalcons—a secondhand reference from the 1800s and a specimen collected at Sault St. Marie on 21 January 1932. The saga of the Gyrfalcon in the state really begins in 1967 with the discovery of a gray phase bird on 16 March at St. Joseph, Berrien County. From 1967 through 1993 there were more than 50 reports, although some of these were apparently the same individual present in multiple years. Such a dramatic change in occurrence seems improbable, but this increase is similar to those noted elsewhere in the Great Lakes. In the 1980s the Gyrfalcon was present

*Peregrine Falcon*
Heiner Hertling

in Michigan almost every winter, and today it is a rare winter resident and casual spring and fall migrant.

This falcon reaches the state in late October or November after breeding in the arctic tundra. The earliest fall arrival date is 17 October 1982 at the Muskegon Wastewater System. Exceptional is a report from 23 August 1989 in the Upper Peninsula, where observers saw an apparent white phase Gyrfalcon near the hack site of a Peregrine Falcon. The northward migration takes place from late February to mid-April. Stragglers have been seen as late as 14 May 1983 at Whitefish Point, Chippewa County, and 29 May 1982 in Houghton County.

The best place to find a Gyrfalcon in the state is Sault Ste. Marie, Chippewa County, where 40% of the observations originate and where up to four birds have been present during the same winter season. At the "Soo" these powerful falcons put on quite a display as they pursue Common Goldeneye, Common Mergansers, and other waterfowl along the St. Marys River, or Sharp-tailed Grouse at inland locations. Elsewhere in the state, Rock Doves are also a staple item. Larger than a Peregrine Falcon, the Gyrfalcon has a somewhat slower but more powerful wingbeat and tends to depend less on a stoop when it captures prey.

Another 20% of Michigan observations originate from Whitefish Point—the best place to search for this species during migration, especially in spring. Most of the remainder of the state reports (approximately 30%) are from the Lower Peninsula, with about one-third of these from Muskegon County. A total of seven Gyrfalcons have been reported on 6 of the past 34 Christmas bird counts.

This species has three color phases (gray, dark, and white), all of which have been confirmed in Michigan. Color phase is not always mentioned in observational details, but where it is indicated, the gray phase predominates. White phase birds should be identified with caution since albino Red-tailed Hawks have caused confusion on more than one occasion. —Raymond J. Adams

# PRAIRIE FALCON

## (*Falco mexicanus*)

Only occasionally reaching east of the Mississippi, this falcon breeds throughout the dry, open mountainous country in the western United States and southwestern Canada. It is an accidental visitor to Michigan with three records to date. Similar in size to a Peregrine, the Prairie Falcon is recognized by its pale brown back, thin mustache, and dark wing linings, which are conspicuous in flight. The first state record and only spring report was a brief sighting at the Whitefish Point Bird Observatory, Chippewa County, on 3 May 1982. The bird flew swiftly out over Lake Superior heading toward Canada. On 5 November of that same year, an injured Prairie Falcon was found near Hubbardson in Clinton County, and was transported to the Veterinary Clinic at Michigan State University, where it was rehabilitated and released. The only Prairie Falcon observed by many Michigan birders was an individual found on 16 August 1987 at the Battle Creek Airport. During its stay through 19 August, this bird was observed hunting over open grassy fields and perching on the ground. Ironically, I had just returned from a trip to California, where I had been searching for Prairie Falcons in the Rocky Mountain foothills; imagine my surprise to see one less than 20 miles from home. —Raymond J. Adams

# RING-NECKED PHEASANT

## (*Phasianus colchicus*)

The Ring-necked Pheasant is a species which has been widely introduced around the world. Its native lands are in Asia, but many centuries ago this tasty bird was added to Europe's avifauna by the Greeks and Romans. The Ring-necked Pheasant was first transplanted to our continent in the 1880s, and its adaptability to open country, particularly farmlands, brought widespread success. It was not long before this species was established throughout much of the United States and southern Canada.

The first Michigan release occurred in 1895, at the Henry Harrington farm near Holland. The Department of Conservation then began a program of introduction in 1918, and hunting was allowed as early as 1925. Ring-necks flourished in habitats provided by small farms, pastures, and other cleared lands. Their abundance is evident in the record harvest figure of 1.4 million birds in 1944. Numbers then dropped sharply after a series of hard winters but recovered in the 1950s, with harvests returning to the 1 million mark.

From the mid-1960s to the mid-1980s, Ring-neck populations declined significantly, with large reductions evident in breeding bird surveys, DNR "crowing" routes, and harvest totals. While the severe winters of the late 1970s took their toll, this long-term decline has been more a product of land-use changes associated with agriculture. Row-crop monocultures, fencerow removal, fall plowing, fewer fallow fields, and chemical applications have affected food resources and cover for nesting, shelter, and escape from predators. Wetland drainage has also had an impact by eliminating important overwintering habitat.

Ring-necks congregate in areas of high-quality cover during fall and winter. Flocks are typically segregated, with males in one, females in another, and younger birds subordinate to their elders. As spring approaches, the birds disperse and males lay claim to breeding territories. This is a time of great activity marked by frequent crowing, mating rituals, and aggressive encounters between neighboring males. Pheasants are polygamous breeders, and males will fight for possession of females.

Nesting begins in late April or early May, but the entire season often extends into July and even early August as a result of persistent renesting. Incubating hens and their ground nests are susceptible to disturbance, adverse weather, and a wide range of predators. Those placed in hayfields, an attractive cover type, are frequently destroyed during mowing. Nests in old fields, brushy edges, and marshy areas tend to be more productive.

June and July are common months for brood sightings, and families can often be seen feeding on back country roads and picking up grit to aid in their digestion. Pheasants have a varied diet much like that of quail, grouse, and turkeys. Food items include insects, seeds, grains, and fruit.

Although numbers are not what they used to be, the Ring-necked Pheasant is still common in southern Michigan, and populations have made some gains over the past five years (1988–93). The big agricultural counties still have the highest densities, and numbers tend to be larger in the east because of lesser amounts of snow. Winter conditions play a determining role in pheasant distribution, and north of Muskegon, Gladwin, and Bay counties, the species is uncommon and sparsely distributed. In the Upper Peninsula, only southern Menominee County has had a sustaining population over the years.

In an effort to supplement Michigan's Ring-neck population, the DNR initiated a program in 1985 to introduce the Sichuan Pheasant, a subspecies native to China. With its preference for nesting in brushier habitats, biologists hope that the Sichuan will fare better in the current landscape. Releases have been ongoing since 1987, and to date, the Sichuan does appear to be taking hold in many areas across the southern Lower Peninsula as well as in southern Menominee and Dickinson counties (Upper Peninsula). Populations of both subspecies have been increasing since the late 1980s (G. Belyea, pers. comm.), and biologists are documenting high natural production by Sichuans plus interbreeding with Ring-necks. (Male Sichuans lack a white neck ring; otherwise the two subspecies are similar in appearance.) Time will tell if this program will prove successful. In the meantime, there is a greater need for efforts directed toward habitat improvement, such as those of the citizens' group Pheasants Forever. —Gail A. McPeek

# SPRUCE GROUSE

## (*Dendragapus canadensis*)

The Spruce Grouse is a local and generally uncommon permanent resident in northern Michigan. Its haunts are the continent's boreal forests, specifically those of spruce and pine. Its range starts at the edge of the tundra and extends south through Canada to the northern Rockies, the Upper Great Lakes, and the mountains of northern New England. Spruce Grouse in Michigan are of the Canada race (*D. c. canace*).

We do not have the volumes of information on this species that we do for relatives such as the Ruffed Grouse. For Michigan, much of what we know comes from studies by Dr. William Robinson in a place known as the Yellow Dog Plains in Marquette County. His book *Fool Hen* (1980) is a wonderful account of Spruce Grouse life. "Fool hen" is the nickname given to this bird by pioneers and woodsmen because of its seemingly foolish behavior, which often allowed them to get close enough to kill it

*Northern Bobwhite*
*Ring-necked Pheasant*
GIJSBERT VAN FRANKENHUYZEN

GIJSBERT-1992

with a stick. Whether you consider this tame, trusting, or stupid, its docile nature thrills bird-watchers.

The male Spruce Grouse is a handsome bird. Its dusky gray-brown plumage is boldly marked with velvety, black-tipped feathers and an orange-banded tail. Above each eye is a comb of red skin which is prominently displayed during courtship and territorial activities. Females are a softer blend of grays and browns, matching their surroundings.

Males lay claim to their territories in the fall, then renew their display rituals in the spring to attract females. The April–May mating season is the best time to search for Spruce Grouse, which are otherwise quiet, sedentary, and inconspicuous. After mating, the female nests in her own territory. Nests are virtually impossible to find; they are hidden from above by an overhanging spruce or pine branch, and the incubating female almost never flushes. Those who have studied this bird or have happened upon a nest tell stories of petting the hen and lifting her to count the eggs.

Hatching occurs around the height of blackfly season, typically the latter part of June. Insects are essential for growing chicks. The fruits, flowers, buds, and leaves of plants such as blueberry are also part of the summer diet. Perched on a log or stump, the hen keeps a close watch on her brood as they move about the underbrush. The young seem to know instinctively how to forage, and the female's primary role is protecting them from predators and cold, wet weather. The chicks grow quickly and within a week are able to fly short distances.

Come fall, the young disperse to find their own territories. This is also the time when the digestive system of the Spruce Grouse adjusts to a diet of spruce and pine needles. It is hard to imagine a bird subsisting largely on evergreens, but that is exactly what this grouse does. For much of the year, but particularly during the colder months, conifer needles and buds are its principal foods. The powdery, sulfur droppings resulting from this peculiar diet provide good evidence of active territories. Another special adaptation is its burrowing into snow (a good insulator) for nighttime roosting.

At one time, Spruce Grouse were quite common throughout the vast coniferous forests which dominated the northern two-thirds of the state. They may have even occurred in some southern locales, as did other boreal critters such as the porcupine and lynx. This changed when settlement and widespread logging altered the forest regime. Spruce Grouse became less common and their distribution more restricted. Hunting was banned in 1914, because of declines in numbers.

Current distribution follows the "islands" of jack-pine and spruce habitat scattered about Michigan's northern counties. The most frequent sightings come from the eastern Upper Peninsula, where it remains fairly common. Occurrence is more sparing in the west, with the Yellow Dog Plains one of the few regular spots. Outside the Upper Peninsula, Spruce Grouse are mostly limited to the jack-pine plains in parts of Crawford, Oscoda, and Ogemaw counties. Here, populations are benefiting from habitat management for the endangered Kirtland's Warbler. The Spruce Grouse was added to the state list of special concern birds in 1990, as a result of the low numbers found during the Breeding Bird Atlas and the risk to this species if any more habitat is lost.

An early spring visit to the eastern Upper Peninsula is your best bet when searching for Spruce Grouse. Reliable sites in Chippewa County include the Whitefish Point–Tahquamenon area and suitable habitat in the vicinity of Rudyard, Raco, Strongs, and Trout and Betchler lakes. The Seney area in Schoolcraft County and Two-hearted River in Luce County are also good areas. —Gail A. McPeek

## [WILLOW PTARMIGAN]

### (*Lagopus lagopus*)

This tundra bird may have been an irregular winter visitor to extreme northern Michigan many years ago, but the evidence is inconclusive as there are no known specimens for the state, only sight records. Consequently, the Willow Ptarmigan is presently listed as a hypothetical species. Barrows (1912) tells of reports fitting this ptarmigan's description from early lumber camps and a missionary on Keweenaw Point in the 1800s. Earlier writers also mentioned its occurrence at this locale and Sault Ste. Marie. Barrows was therefore satisfied that this species did occur irregularly on the Keweenaw Peninsula and probably at other points along the Lake Superior shoreline. The last unsubstantiated sightings, given in Zimmerman and Van Tyne (1959), are from December 1921 and the winter of 1930–31 at the same site in Gogebic County. Willow Ptarmigans are known to wander south of their arctic home, and specimens are on record for both Wisconsin and Minnesota. A reported attempt to introduce Willow Ptarmigans to Michigan's Upper Peninsula in the 1950s was unsuccessful. —Gail A. McPeek

## RUFFED GROUSE

### (*Bonasa umbellus*)

The Ruffed Grouse is the most familiar and most common of the three remaining grouse species found in Michigan. It occurs throughout the Upper and Lower peninsulas with the exception of Isle Royale, the urban southeast, and those parts of the state dominated by agriculture. One of the country's most popular game birds, the Ruffed Grouse has been the subject of many studies concerning its life history, habitat choices, and population cycles, and much work has been done right here in Michigan.

For a permanent resident with a sedentary nature, the Ruffed Grouse has an impressively large North American range. It lives in forested habitats from Alaska and northern Canada to the

*Ruffed Grouse*
*Spruce Grouse*
HEINER HERTLING

H.C. Hertling

Carolinas and southern Appalachians in the East and to Wyoming, Utah, and California in the West. Add to this several central states such as Missouri and Indiana, where populations have been successfully reestablished, and its current distribution probably approaches that of a century ago. This species has two color phases, a red phase which is more prevalent in the hardwoods of the south and a gray phase in the mixed and conifer forests of the north.

Although a variety of forest types are represented within its range, the Ruffed Grouse is not a bird of broad habitat tolerance. Its requirements are actually rather narrow, particularly when it comes to forest structure. This species uses early successional stages (typically between 10 and 30 or 40 years of age), and blocks of regenerating stands interspersed with mature forest and occasional openings of brush and herbaceous vegetation provide the ideal combination to satisfy grouse needs for all seasons. Work by L. Fisher (1939) identified poplar (including aspen), birch, maple, alder, dogwood, cherry, wild strawberry, and hawthorn as important in Michigan.

You cannot talk about this bird without mentioning aspen (quaking and big tooth), the major early successional species in forests where grouse live. In fact, the range of the Ruffed Grouse corresponds closely to that of quaking aspen, which happens to be the most widely distributed deciduous forest tree on the continent. Regenerating aspen provide the desired forest structure, not to mention an abundant food resource in the form of buds, catkins (flowers), and leaves.

Like many forest wildlife, Ruffed Grouse experienced declines following settlement and the widespread clearing of timber. Numbers dropped low enough in Michigan that market shooting was made illegal in 1894. The downward trend reversed itself when regenerating forests provided new habitat. Aspen-birch emerged as the dominant forest type in the state, covering some 5 million acres of land by 1935. This acreage has since decreased (to about 3.4 million in 1980) through natural succession, but aspen-birch remains a major forest community in northern Michigan because of commercial timber harvest and the continuous supply of regenerating stands.

In recent decades, southern Michigan has seen an increase in grouse, reflected in the numbers of harvested birds, which have nearly tripled since 1959. Such increases are attributed to releases and increases in second-growth woodlands, mostly maple-beech. In the northern regions of the state, however, populations have generally declined of late, as some forested lands have matured beyond the age of prime suitability.

Ruffed Grouse are best recognized by their drumming—the male's unique way of communicating his presence. While standing on a log, rock, or other elevated structure, the male beats his wings against the air, producing a deep, thumping sound which carries through the forest. Drumming can be heard on and off throughout the year and is used to advertise territories and attract females. Male grouse are promiscuous and will mate with several females in a season.

Males increase the frequency of their drumming in early spring, primarily around the early morning and evening hours. Once a female is drawn to the site, the two engage in a courtship ritual which includes fanning tails and extended ruffs, those long feathers about the neck from which it gets its name. After mating, the female goes off on her own, builds a nest, incubates the eggs (usually 9–12), and cares for the brood. Most females in Michigan are on eggs in May. The nest is a scrape in the ground, lined with dry leaves and pine needles. Placement at the base of a tree or log gives the nest protection on one side.

The female and her brood are a close-knit family, and although chicks are capable of flight at 10 days of age, the brood remains together well into the fall. Insects are an important dietary need when chicks are young. If you happen upon a brood you're sure to know it, because the female instinctively performs a display of frenzied activity, making herself conspicuous while the chicks run and hide.

The Ruffed Grouse is a hardy species and weathers the cold season fine as long as there is adequate food and cover. Berries and seeds from a variety of trees, shrubs, and herbaceous plants are the main foods in fall and winter. Aspen flower buds from older age-class stands (50+ years) are especially important. If you, too, are cold-hardy, this can be a good time to observe grouse as they perch in a bare aspen tree to feast on buds. —Gail A. McPeek

# GREATER PRAIRIE-CHICKEN

## (*Tympanuchus cupido*)

The Greater Prairie-Chicken is no longer a member of Michigan's avifauna. It was extirpated from the state sometime in the early 1980s, when the last two remnant flocks disappeared from the north-central Lower Peninsula. At present, Wisconsin, Minnesota, and southern Illinois harbor the closest populations to Michigan.

At one time this prairie inhabitant had a widespread distribution that stretched across the Plains and Midwest to parts of the East, where it was known as the Heath Hen. Now, the eastern subspecies is long gone and the Greater Prairie-Chicken survives in much-reduced numbers in a continually shrinking range in the middle United States. Biologists surmise that if local populations become more and more isolated, extinction is a probable outcome.

We can trace the ups and downs of this grouse in the literature, from its increases in the middle 1800s to its demise a little more than a hundred years later. Before settlers came to Michigan, the prairie-chicken was believed to be locally common but restricted to the prairies and oak openings of the southwest. As the land was settled and the vast forests cleared, it expanded its range both naturally and with the aid of relocation efforts. The growing supply of farm fields, pastures, and other grassland habitats offered many new places to live.

The period of prosperity for this species proved to be short-lived. A growing human population and land-use changes,

*Lark Sparrow*
*Passenger Pigeon*
*Greater Prairie-Chicken*
HEINER HERTLING

H.C.Hertling

combined with the tastiness of prairie-chickens and the ease with which they are killed, were already causing noticeable declines in southern Michigan in the late 1800s and early 1900s. Isolated flocks held on in some marshlands until the early 1940s, when the species disappeared completely from southern Michigan. Some suspect that, along with habitat changes, the Ring-necked Pheasant, considered competitively superior to the prairie-chicken, may have contributed to declines by the 1920s and 1930s.

While losses were occurring in the south, populations were increasing in the north, and for a time in the 1920s to the 1940s, the species was a local resident across much of the northern Lower and the Upper Peninsula. Like its cousin the Sharp-tailed Grouse, the prairie-chicken occupied the large tracts of burned and cut-over lands left in the wake of the lumbering era. In a 1941 survey, 106 booming grounds were located in some 17 counties, nearly all of which were in northern Michigan. It is hard to imagine that 40 years later, all of these flocks would be gone.

Evidently, numbers dropped quite dramatically after the early 1940s, as the landscape once again changed (hunting was already banned) and birds were reduced to "habitat islands." By 1960, the state's population was reduced to flocks in Chippewa County (eastern Upper Peninsula) and fewer than 10 counties in the northern Lower Peninsula. Twenty years later, all that remained were two flocks—one near the town of Marion in Osceola County and the other on the National Guard Artillery Range around the Otsego–Crawford County line. When no birds were seen at their traditional display grounds in 1982, the worst was feared, and lack of observations in subsequent years confirmed their extirpation.

In the end these remnant flocks had become so small and isolated that the populations could not maintain themselves. Had more attention been paid during the declining years, the Greater Prairie-Chicken might have been saved through habitat preservation and management, as was done in Wisconsin. Sadly, we must now travel elsewhere if we want to see this unique prairie bird and witness its striking courtship dance, with neck "pinnae" erect like horns and neck sacs distended like two big oranges. —Gail A. McPeek

# SHARP-TAILED GROUSE

(*Tympanuchus phasianellus*)

The Sharp-tailed Grouse is a nonmigratory resident of our continent's steppe habitats, including a variety of grassland communities, savannas, and sagebrush plains. These habitats are found primarily in the central and western regions of the country, and the Sharp-tail's distribution follows accordingly. Its range extends from Alaska and northern Canada to New Mexico, the Central Plains, and the western Great Lakes. Michigan lies at the periphery, where this grouse is a local resident of grasslands, shrubby plains, and open bogs scattered across the north, mostly in the Upper Peninsula.

The Sharp-tail has an interesting history in Michigan. Settlement of lands to the west cleared the way for many nonforest wildlife to extend their ranges eastward. Historical records indicate that this bird apparently colonized the state in the late 1800s, beginning with Isle Royale. Norman A. Wood from the University of Michigan collected the first specimen during expeditions to the island in 1904–1905. This isolated population likely originated from Ontario, which lies 13 miles to the north across Lake Superior. Then, in the 1920s, Sharp-tails made their way into the western Upper Peninsula from neighboring Wisconsin, an influx that was encouraged by the widespread and frequent fires of the lumbering era. The species' rather rapid spread across the state's northern region was aided by numerous introductions, including releases on Drummond and Beaver islands.

For about the next 30 years the Sharp-tail fared well in northern Michigan, finding suitable habitat in the large tracts of cleared land and boggy areas. Writings from the middle 1900s describe a locally common bird in the Upper Peninsula and north-central counties of the Lower Peninsula. By the 1960s and '70s, however, conditions were again changing, this time in the other direction. Between fire suppression and forest regeneration, optimal habitat was slowly being depleted, and Sharp-tail numbers declined.

Its current status is that of a more sparsely distributed, less common species. Populations in the northern Lower Peninsula have largely been reduced to two locales, the Grayling area in Crawford County and the Fletcher area at the Missaukee–Kalkaska County border. In the Upper Peninsula, flocks are common in parts of Chippewa, Mackinac, Schoolcraft, Alger, Delta, Marquette, Houghton, and Ontonagon counties. The extensive hay and grasslands south of Sault Ste. Marie support the greatest numbers. Management practices directed toward maintaining large grassland and savanna-like habitat have helped secure populations in some of the other areas. There is limited harvesting of this grouse in the Upper Peninsula, mostly on private lands.

The Sharp-tail has a much more social nature than the Ruffed or Spruce Grouse, with the flock being the basic social unit. Within an occupied area there is one traditional site where males gather in the spring to establish their position in the flock and attract females for mating. These male flocks are called "leks," and the sites are known as "dancing" or "booming" grounds. Leks can vary in size from a few males to a dozen or more.

Cocks may begin dancing as early as March, while fields are still covered with snow, but the most regular and intense advertising occurs in April and May, just before sunup. The dance involves bobbing and strutting while giving loud cooing and cackling calls which can be heard up to a mile away. During displays, males inflate the sacs of purple skin on the sides of their necks. Females may visit more than one lek before selecting a male, and cocks which achieve higher dominance in the flock are likely to attract more than one female.

After mating, the hen alone nests and raises the young. The

*Upland Sandpiper*
*Sharp-tailed Grouse*
HEINER HERTLING

H.C.Hertling

nest is a simple shallow depression hidden in tall grasses or brushy vegetation. Most hens are on eggs by the end of May, and a 21-day incubation results in broods by late June or early July. The hen and chicks forage in shrub-grass or open woodland, remaining in the summer habitat but away from male flocks and display grounds. Insects are important early in life; after that, the birds switch over to a mostly vegetarian diet of leaves, buds, and flowers as well as grains.

Fall is a time of post-breeding dispersal and a shift by flocks to areas which provide more cover. In October, Sharp-tails have been seen flying along the beach at Whitefish Point (J. Granlund, pers. comm.). Winter habitat often includes bogs, cutover lands, open woodlands with conifers, and croplands. Conifers or other dense cover are usual roosting sites, but Sharp-tails will also burrow in deep snow for the night. Overall flock movement throughout the year tends not to exceed a mile or two from the communal booming grounds.

If you can weather the cold and snow, the winter months are among the best time to observe Sharp-tails in northern Michigan. Flocks are regularly found between December and March in the fields south of Sault Ste. Marie, some as large as 30 or more birds. Winter bird excursions led by the Whitefish Point Bird Observatory offer a great opportunity to see this species. These excursions, along with the recent establishment of some new Christmas bird counts in the Upper Peninsula, are providing better annual information to help monitor Sharp-tail populations. —Gail A. McPeek

# WILD TURKEY

## (*Meleagris gallopavo*)

The Wild Turkey has regained its common permanent status in Michigan thanks to ambitious restoration efforts on its behalf. While it may never return to the abundance of presettlement times, this large, long-legged fowl is once again a regular forest resident in many parts of the state. Every year more people are experiencing turkeys in the wild, not just in the supermarket.

When 16th-century explorers found this superior table bird in the Americas, some were taken back to Europe and domesticated. Many years later, as settlers journeyed to the New World, this domestic version was brought along. Those left to roam often reverted back to the wild and mixed with native populations.

The Wild Turkey we know today is not the same bird of pre-Columbian times. Many Indian tribes thought it stupid and cowardly, and the pioneers regarded it as tame and easily killed. After decades of heavy persecution, the wild ancestral form became extremely wary and adopted the elusive habits now associated with turkeys and valued by sportsmen.

By 1900 this once-plentiful bird, which nearly became our national symbol, had vanished from most of the country as a result of overhunting and habitat loss. Michigan's presettlement population has been estimated at 94,000, and up until the 1870s it was still fairly common. Numbers apparently plummeted thereafter, and by 1890 turkeys were extremely rare. The last state record was in 1897.

Passage of conservation laws in the 1930s saved the turkey from complete extinction, and restoration began immediately using the remaining wild flocks (no doubt with some domestic genes). By the 1950s, stocking programs were underway in some 30 states. Michigan's first success came in 1954 in the Allegan State Forest, and within a few years flocks were established there as well as in Lake, Newaygo, Ogemaw, Roscommon, Gladwin, Clare, and Alcona counties. Natural increases and continued stocking efforts have resulted in a population estimated at 77,000 in 1992–93 (J. Urbain, pers. comm.).

The turkey's modern distribution in the state is quite different from that historically. Its former range centered on the oak- and chestnut-dominated woodlands of the southern counties, north to Bay and Isabella. The current landscape is vastly different, and the more extensive forests containing mast-producing trees occur in the northern Lower Peninsula. This region now contains the bulk of the turkey population. This species is even doing well as far north as the south-central Upper Peninsula, where hardwoods are prevalent and snow cover averages less than at similar latitudes elsewhere. Although it is a fairly hardy bird, supplemental feeding appears to be important to overwinter survival in parts of northern Michigan, particularly during severe winters when substantial mortality of turkeys has been reported.

The turkey has proven to be a very adaptable species. Biologists originally believed that large continuous tracts (10,000–15,000 acres) of primarily oak-dominated forest were a must for turkey survival. We now know that a mixture of forest and open lands can be sufficient. In recent years, the DNR has obtained birds adapted to woodland-farm areas for release in parts of southern Michigan, mostly on public lands. These, too, have been successful, and turkeys are now established in scattered locales across the region. Flocks are making use of farmlands for corn, grains, and insects, and are even becoming frequent diners at bird feeders in rural areas.

Turkeys are a gregarious sort, and much of their life is spent in flocks. Hens and their young make up brood flocks; gobblers mostly hang out in bachelor flocks; and first-year males, or jakes, consort in their own flocks. During autumn and winter, these units may utilize the same areas, but each flock maintains its separate identity.

Warmer temperatures in April bring the start of the breeding season in Michigan. Tom turkeys spend the next few weeks strutting and courting females. The males' display includes puffed feathers, drooping wings, and fanning of their gorgeous tails. The height of the gobbling season is mid- to late April, with most activity occurring in the early morning hours and again at dusk, before birds go to roost.

Turkeys are polygamous breeders, and mature toms will have small harems of females. Hens visit the gobbler until egg laying is complete, usually by mid-May. Nests are a simple depression in

*Wild Turkey*
HEINER HERTLING

H.C. Hertling

the litter but are well concealed by a fallen treetop, low-hanging branch, or other dense cover. Clutches average a dozen eggs, and incubation lasts about 28 days. Come mid-summer, brood flocks can be seen foraging for insects, berries, and leaves in forest clearings or adjacent fields. Insects are especially important for young turkeys, also known as poults. Acorns, beechnuts, hickory nuts, and other mast become the main foods in fall and winter.

Knowing the whereabouts of display grounds and foraging areas in the state greatly improves your chances of observing this wild bird. Avid turkey enthusiasts learn to recognize such signs as the long scratch marks in the litter and a gobbler's j-shaped droppings. Turkey calling has become an art form in itself, and there are a variety of box calls, diaphragms, and other devices available. —Gail A. McPeek

# NORTHERN BOBWHITE

## (*Colinus virginianus*)

This small, plump quail inhabits rural areas in Michigan, mostly in the south. Despite its preference for open country, the Northern Bobwhite is a relatively inconspicuous bird, spending much of its life on the ground in brush, weeds, or other concealing cover. Probably its most familiar trait is the clear, whistled song which seems to say its name. One of the best opportunities to see this attractive, reddish-brown bird comes when males proclaim their breeding territories, whistling "bob-WHITE" from a fencepost or other elevated perch.

The bobwhite is a year-round resident throughout its range, which includes the eastern and central United States north to southern New England and the Great Lakes and south to Mexico, with local, mostly introduced, populations farther west to Colorado and Washington. Populations in the south are generally stable, whereas those in the north fluctuate rather dramatically depending on the severity of the winter. Harsh winters spur widespread mortality and declines, and more mild winters allow populations to flourish.

Places where open woodland, brush, and farmland come together make for the best quail habitat. Grassy or weedy fields and cropland provide nesting cover and food, while fencerows and dense brush provide escape cover and places to roost. This is a bird that can thrive in agricultural areas provided there is adequate cover for nesting and shelter from enemies and adverse weather.

The nest is a hollow in the ground, well concealed in dense grasses or weeds. Finding one usually happens by accident; you practically have to step on an incubating quail before it flushes. Both sexes participate in nest sitting and brood rearing. Like other gallinaceous birds, bobwhite have large clutches averaging 14 to 16 eggs. May and June are the primary nesting months in Michigan, but second attempts may result in nests all through the summer. Broods are mostly seen in July and August.

By the end of the summer, families often join with one another, forming flocks of 20 to 30 quail or more. Then, as winter approaches, the "fall shuffle" occurs as family units dissolve and the birds regroup into slightly smaller flocks or coveys of 10 to 15 quail. These cohesive flocks stay together through the winter, and entire coveys may be lost during times of extreme cold and deep snow when quail are most susceptible to starvation and predation.

In Michigan, bobwhite are mostly limited to the southern Lower Peninsula, and within this region are most common in the central and eastern counties north to Saginaw Bay. This pattern stems from differences in winter weather and particularly snow cover, which is greater in the southwest. Quail are much more likely to survive the winter season in the southeast and south-central areas of the state than those farther west. This species has always been scarce in areas subject to lake-effect snow.

Bobwhite are also found locally in rural areas in the northern Lower Peninsula and even a few locales in the Upper Peninsula. In these regions, quail typically last for one or a few years until a severe winter brings about their extermination. Then, during milder years, as populations increase in the south, individuals again make their way northward. Bobwhite are a popular game bird and friend of the farmer, and local introductions have aided their continued existence in colder climes. Such releases make it difficult to determine the extent of their "natural" range. The quails' diet, which includes many crop-damaging insects and noxious weed seeds, makes them beneficial to have around.

Bobwhite flourished in the East following settlement and conversion of forests to farmland and pastureland. Their heyday in Michigan came in the 1800s and early 1900s, prior to the emergence of industrialized farming. Since about the middle 1900s, trends toward larger and less diverse farms, fewer pastures, and the removal of fencerows and other brushy cover around fields have had a negative impact on quail habitat. When the severe winters of the late 1970s hit, numbers plummeted, and quail hunting was suspended from 1979 until 1987. Perhaps losses would not have been as great had there been more adequate dense cover in rural areas.

Populations have shown some signs of a slow recovery from this crash, but bobwhite numbers in southwestern Michigan are still less than 20% of pre-storm levels, and statewide, quail populations are down significantly from the 1960s. These declines are evident in long-term data sets from both the DNR "whistling" routes and breeding bird surveys. Christmas bird count data are also particularly telling, as numbers seen have continued to drop even though participant effort has increased. —Gail A. McPeek

*Yellow Rail*
DAVID MOHRHARDT

# YELLOW RAIL

## (*Coturnicops noveboracensis*)

If you want to see a Yellow Rail in Michigan, your opportunities are quite limited. This small brown and yellow bird is among the rarest of our breeding rails, and even though it is a regular summer resident and transient, its distribution is extremely local. Your best bet is Seney National Wildlife Refuge, where this species has been a consistent breeder and migrant for many years.

The Yellow Rail is renowned for its local occurrence throughout its breeding range. Its distribution is northern, extending across central and eastern Canada and the northernmost regions of the Great Lakes and New England. The southern boundary of this summer range includes northern Michigan. Individuals which nest here likely winter in the Gulf Coast states.

The Yellow Rail is a highly secretive bird and one which is easily overlooked. As with other rails, the key is knowing its call and its habitat. The male's territorial song is a series of clicks, a sound easily imitated by tapping together two stones or two quarters. Optimal time to hear this call is after midnight during the May to early July breeding period.

You might think that a rail of only seven inches could nest just about anywhere, but such is not the case. This tiny bird is very particular about its marsh habitat, choosing large open bogs or wet meadows consisting mostly of a tall, matforming sedge, *Carex lasiocarpa*. The Yellow Rail is relatively scarce in Michigan because these kinds of marshes are rare. At Seney, fluctuating water levels and periodic fires maintain dense, grassy marshes and provide consistent breeding sites. Without these forces, succession renders such habitats unsuitable in a few years.

State records for the Yellow Rail are relatively meager, particularly for the breeding season. Most summer records come from the eastern Upper Peninsula, and the only confirmed nests are from Chippewa and Schoolcraft counties. In recent years, observations in the Upper Peninsula have been limited to the Seney Refuge in Schoolcraft County. A 1991 survey located 30 territorial birds at this locale.

One likely site supporting breeding pairs is the Houghton Lake Wildlife Area (Roscommon County), in the north-central Lower Peninsula. Nesting has yet to be confirmed here, but territorial individuals have been present most summers since the late 1980s. Breeding season reports at a Gladwin County marsh may represent another locale.

Information on Yellow Rail migration in the state is also minimal, but records cover a greater number of counties compared to summer, including many in southern Michigan. Spring migration generally occurs from the latter half of April to about the middle of May, and the fall migration in September and October.

This species would probably be encountered more often in migration if more people spent time visiting sedge habitats, particularly in spring when the species is more vocal. Yellow Rails have been encountered on a regular basis in Benzie County and the Waterloo Recreation Area (Jackson-Washtenaw counties) by birders who do just that. During migration, Yellow Rails may also appear in open, grassy habitats, even a suburban lawn. They travel at night, and a tired rail may stop in some unexpected places come morning.

The Yellow Rail was probably more common historically than is evident in the literature. There were very few records until the early 1930s, when Lawrence Walkinshaw made a concerted effort to locate rails in the eastern Upper Peninsula and found 64 Yellow Rails. Aided by the keen senses of a springer spaniel, he and F. C.

Gillett found the state's first nest in Munuscong Bay in June of 1934. Yellow Rails were locally abundant in the marshes of Munuscong that summer. On return visits in 1935, no Yellow Rails were found, and Walkinshaw suspected that the higher water levels may have rendered the marsh unsuitable that year.

Records from the current era are probably a close representation of Yellow Rail occurrence in the state. Certainly some are missed because of the remote nature of the species' habitat and its silence during daylight hours. On the other hand, the number of people actively bird-watching and conducting avian surveys in the wilds of northern Michigan has increased tremendously. Following the Breeding Bird Atlas survey, in which it was found in only six townships, the Yellow Rail was assigned a threatened status in the state. Habitat alterations in only one or two locations could mean extirpation of this species from Michigan. An intensive nocturnal censusing effort of appropriate habitats during the breeding season is greatly needed.

Owing to its rarity, the Yellow Rail is a popular species on the "wish lists" of many bird-watchers. For your benefit and, more important, for the rail's, participating in a tour with a qualified guide is strongly suggested. Both the Seney Refuge and the Whitefish Point Bird Observatory have successful tour programs which provide the opportunity to hear and possibly see this threatened species. —Gail A. McPeek

# BLACK RAIL
## (*Laterallus jamaicensis*)

With only two fully documented records and a handful of other sightings, the Black Rail is classified as an accidental species in Michigan. This tiny, dark-colored rail, comparable in size to a sparrow, is so elusive and inconspicuous that very little is known about its distribution and status. The Black Rail is found most regularly in the salt marshes and other grassy wetlands of the Pacific, Gulf, and Atlantic coasts, north to southern California in the West and New York in the East. There are occasional occurrences in the Midwest, mostly in a band from Colorado to Indiana, and historic accounts indicate sporadic breeding in this region, but all nest records are prior to 1900. This shy rail is incredibly difficult to census and may be more common than we realize. However, there has been a noticeable drop in the number of reports in the midwestern states over the past 50 years, with its disappearance from some parts coming, most likely, at the expense of wetland drainage.

The first possible record for Michigan (which Barrows thought

*King Rail*
DAVID MOHRHARDT

was "hardly conclusive") was of a dead bird reported from Ann Arbor on 4 June 1880, in which the specimen spoiled. The next observation, which also lacked full documentation, was of two Black Rails at Three Rivers in St. Joseph County on 22 May 1949. The first fully documented report is of an immature female collected on 12 September 1951 at Portage Lake in Jackson County (Payne 1983). The following three reports were sight records only: a bird touched and almost caught on 1 September 1953 in Livingston County, one seen in Lansing on 20 May 1967, and one from Kalamazoo on 10 August 1974. Most recently, a male was discovered on 12 June 1988 at the Hofma Nature Preserve in Ottawa County, a relatively large marsh complex comprising sedges, emergent vegetation, shrubs, and mud flats. This individual stayed for about a month, giving many birders the opportunity to hear and see their first Black Rail. —Gail A. McPeek

# KING RAIL
## (*Rallus elegans*)

Formerly an uncommon but regular summer resident and migrant in Michigan, the King Rail is now a species with an uncertain future. Populations of this chicken-size rail have declined markedly in the Midwest, warranting its listing as endangered in several states, including our own in 1987. The current population in Michigan is estimated at a meager 5 to 10 breeding pairs, perhaps fewer.

Although never as common as the smaller Virginia Rail and Sora, the King Rail was at one time clearly more numerous and more widespread in the southern Lower Peninsula than it is today. Records from the early and middle 1900s show that it was a common bird in the Lake Erie and Lake St. Clair marshes. It was also regularly seen in and around the Saginaw Bay marshlands, as well as in various interior sites north to Kent and Bay counties. In Ingham County, for example, Walter Barrows described the King Rail as "fairly abundant around the neighborhood of the Agricultural College" (now Michigan State University). Except for the record of an adult with young in 1988, King Rails have not been recorded in Ingham County or most other traditional inland sites for many years.

The destruction, drainage, fragmentation, and pollution of the large coastal and inland marshes have left little suitable habitat for this species. Since 1980, most observations have come from Pte. Mouillee and the Erie Gun Club (Monroe County), St. Clair Flats, and Crow Island and Nayanquing (Bay County), all in the southeast. Other locales with spring and/or breeding-season records include the Mt. Clemens sewage ponds (Macomb County), Sterling State Park (Monroe County), Waterloo State Recreation Area (Jackson County), Muskegon Causeway, and Warren Dunes State Park (Berrien County).

In 1986, an extensive field survey led by Mary Rabe and conducted during the breeding season (mid-May to July) located 26 King Rails, with 17 in St. Clair Flats. More recently, however, searches here have come up empty, and none have been seen at Crow Island since the habitat was altered sometime around 1987–88. There have also been no recent reports at the Erie Gun Club, and the status at Nayanquing is uncertain. Presently, only

Pte. Mouillee appears to have a breeding population of a few pairs, with possibilities at Waterloo Recreation Area, where one or two birds have been detected in four of the last five years (up to 1992).

The summer range of the King Rail covers much of the eastern United States, from the Atlantic coast to the Great Plains and from the Gulf coast to the Great Lakes. Winters are spent in Florida, the lower Mississippi Valley, and along the Gulf and Atlantic coasts. Some birds may remain farther north, especially during mild years. There are occasional winter records in Michigan, but these, too, have become less frequent, another sign of their dwindling population. A King Rail found at Asylum Lake on the 1975–76 Kalamazoo Christmas bird count is the most recent winter record.

The spring migration brings King Rails back to southern Michigan in the latter part of April and early May. Occasional overflights are apparent in the scattered May sightings as far north as Emmet County in the Lower Peninsula and Marquette County in the Upper Peninsula. These overflights have even resulted in two northern breeding records: an adult with young found on 1 June 1970, along the Boardman River near Traverse City, and a failed nesting attempt near Alpena in 1976.

The majority of nest records for the state are from the latter half of May, with brood sightings in June. Nests are built in shallow water among sedges, cattails, or other marsh vegetation. This round, platform-like structure often includes a ramp and a concealing canopy woven out of the surrounding grasses or reeds.

The fact that this is our largest rail does not make it any easier to find. Wetlands are not the most accessible of habitats, and like many marsh dwellers, the King Rail is seldom seen or flushed from its protective cover. Its blend of cinnamon-brown feathers makes for excellent camouflage. Because of the King Rail's tendency to forage in extremely shallow waters or dry areas, you may be able to catch a glimpse of one right along the marsh edge, or even in a nearby upland field. Best means for detection are its deep grunting and repetitive "kicking" calls, given almost exclusively at dusk or dawn early in the breeding season. Observers should be aware that Virginia Rails make a similar call and will respond to playback recordings of a King Rail.

Little is known about the fall departure of this nocturnal migrant. It appears to leave the state relatively early, with most individuals gone by late September or early October. In the Erie marshes around Toledo, just south of Michigan, the main flight was typically recorded around 30 August, with some birds remaining into late September. This was back in the King Rail's heyday, before the extensive Lake Erie marshes were drained for the sake of progress. —Gail A. McPeek

*Sora*
*Virginia Rail*
DAVID MOHRHARDT

# VIRGINIA RAIL

## (*Rallus limicola*)

The Virginia Rail is one of the more common rails in Michigan. It is a regular breeding resident and migrant, having a somewhat scattered distribution dictated by the availability of suitable wetland habitats in the state. Our knowledge about the distribution and status of this elusive marshbird improved tremendously as a result of the Breeding Bird Atlas. During this extensive survey, Virginia Rails were found in 18% of the townships in the southern Lower Peninsula, 9% in the northern Lower, and 5% in the Upper Peninsula. The fact that this species is more sparsely distributed in the north was expected, but the low occurrence across southern Michigan was of concern, indicating declines in the population.

Earlier this century, the Virginia Rail was considered common, even abundant, in many southern counties. While it remains locally common in certain areas, there are numerous locales in which long-term observations have verified decreases in numbers, particularly during the last few decades. As with many wetland inhabitants, the degradation of inland and coastal marshlands has had a profound impact on the Virginia Rail to the extent that it can no longer be found in many areas. A 1989 countywide census in Kalamazoo turned up 142 Virginias, a number that may seem high until you realize these were encountered at 38 of the more than 90 sites visited.

The breeding range of the Virginia Rail covers much of the northern United States and portions of southern Canada. Add to this its large winter range along the Pacific, Gulf, and southern Atlantic coasts, and you have one of the more widely distributed rails in North America. This species lives in a wide array of wetland habitats, from small swales and marshy borders of lakes, ponds, and streams to large freshwater and saltwater marshes. Like the larger King Rail, this smaller rail is partial to wetland edges where clumps of vegetation intersperse with open water. It typically forages in the shallows, using its long curved bill to probe for various aquatic insects, snails, and other small prey.

Were you able to catch more than a fleeting glimpse of a Virginia Rail, which tends to be even shyer than the Sora, its multicolored plumage might surprise you. The rusty breast, olive-brown back, black-and-white-striped flanks, gray cheeks, and red bill make for quite an attractive bird. This mix of colors also makes for an effective disguise amidst the cattails, sedges, and other plant life in its environment. Unfortunately, this small rail would much rather stay hidden in its protective cover than venture out into the open for our viewing pleasure.

Like other members of the Rallidae family, the Virginia has many marvelous adaptations for marsh living. Its cryptic plumage is one. Others include long toes, short wings, and a laterally compressed body, all of which enhance its maneuverability whether it is walking across floating vegetation or slipping between stems of cattails and rushes. This species would much rather run to safety than fly. When it does flush, sudden bursts of flight carry it a short distance before it drops back out of sight into the thickness of the marsh.

Rails are relatively early nesters, and the Virginia commences breeding soon after it returns, sometime between mid-April and mid-May. Early mornings and evenings in May are the best times to visit a marsh and listen for its metallic clicking and pig-like grunting calls, thereby confirming occupancy. The Virginia Rail builds a saucer-shaped nest of cattails, grasses, and other materials, and the nest itself is often woven into the surrounding vegetation. Clutches may contain as many as 13 eggs, but 8 to 10 are more normal. Incubation takes nearly three weeks, and hatching occurs in June.

Rail chicks are precocial, meaning they are feathered and mobile soon after hatching. One of my fondest birding memories involved the lucky discovery of a family of Virginia Rails. On a June morning, during a return trip to a marsh where I had heard numerous rails earlier that spring, something small and black caught my attention. There, in a small opening in the cattails, was a small downy-black chick with long gangly legs. Seconds later it was joined by two more fuzzy chicks and an adult Virginia Rail. Needless to say, I took advantage of my good fortune and watched the family for nearly a half-hour before they wandered from sight. The adult spent much of its time poking and picking at a tiny fish, trying to get the chicks to eat, but they seemed much more interested in doing their own exploring. One chick continually wandered away from the group only to scurry back to the safety of its parent a minute later.

The departure of Virginia Rails in the fall goes virtually unnoticed because of the lack of vocal activity. Records show that most individuals leave during September or the first part of October. A few stragglers remain for the winter, particularly in years of mild temperatures going into the season. Christmas bird counters usually find at least one Virginia Rail and sometimes several. This species was recorded on 24 Christmas bird counts between 1960 and 1992, with maximums of six observed in the winters of 1961–62 and 1973–74. —Gail A. McPeek

# SORA

## (*Porzana carolina*)

This is another one of those "heard more often than seen" birds. Marsh inhabitants seem to have this reputation, and the Sora is no exception. If you visit a cattail marsh or other similar wetland during early morning or evening hours in May, you will have difficulty seeing this secretive rail, but chances are good of hearing one. Its calls are loud and distinctive. One is a clear two-syllable whistle which, with a little imagination, sounds like its name, "so-ra." Another is a high rolling whinny, and when one bird whinnies it usually sets off the other Soras in the marsh.

The Sora is a common migrant and summer resident in Michigan. This mostly brown, quail-sized rail can best be distinguished by its gray neck and breast, black face, and bright yellow bill. It is generally more common in the southern half of the state, though there are numerous locales in northern Michigan where it is also fairly abundant. Like its cousin the Virginia Rail, the Sora has a scattered and irregular distribution following that of suitable wetland habitats in the state.

The Sora is often described as the commonest of our North American rails. Its breeding range extends from the lower half of Canada south to central California and Arizona in the West, Kansas in the Plains, southern Ohio in the Midwest, and Maryland in the East. Winters are spent in the Southwest, along the Gulf coast, and along the Atlantic coast from Virginia to Florida. Rice fields and salt marshes as well as freshwater marshes are used during winter.

Almost any kind of wetland suits this rail, although extensive marshes of cattails, sedges, and other emergent vegetation are definitely favored. Marshy ponds, bogs, fens, wet meadows, and even some roadside ditches or sloughs are inhabitable as far as the Sora is concerned. There is considerable overlap in habitat use by this species and the Virginia Rail. Both breed in similar wetland communities, though more often than not the Sora is the more abundant of the two. Their nests are so much alike that they can be positively identified only when eggs are present, the Sora's being a richer buff color and more spotted than the Virginia's.

The one main factor separating the Sora's niche is its tendency toward wetter sites, being more likely to nest where water is 6 to 10 inches deep. Differences in physical appearance also give us clues as to why these two rails are able to coexist. Most obvious is the Sora's shorter, thicker bill, and when you look at its feeding habits you find that it consumes a large number of seeds of bulrush, sedges, and other marsh plants. In addition to its stouter bill, the Sora has a plumper body shape than the Virginia, a feature more suited for the deeper parts of the marsh where swimming is often necessary.

Most Soras arrive from the wintering grounds during the latter half of April in southern Michigan and by the first half of May in the north. Early warm weather may trigger a few earlier migrants, as was the case with a bird found on 21 March in Kalamazoo County. The birds get right down to business, and breeding is usually underway within two weeks of their arrival. May is the primary nesting time for Soras in Michigan. Most young hatch by the end of May in the southern counties and by the middle to latter part of June in the Upper Peninsula.

Fall migration occurs during September and October, with very few observations of Soras after this time. Average departure time from Berrien County is 26 September. There are only a handful of late fall and winter records, including reports of singles on six Christmas bird counts since 1960.

There are many marshes throughout the state where the Sora is a locally common species. The extensive wetlands at Seney National Wildlife Refuge and the numerous drainages in the far western counties are among the good places to find this rail in the Upper Peninsula. In the Lower Peninsula, it is common in some coastal areas, such as around Saginaw Bay, and inland in such counties as Berrien, Van Buren, Kalamazoo, Ingham, Oakland, and Roscommon. During a 1989 wetland survey in Kalamazoo County, observers found 166 Soras in 36 locations.

Although common in these and other locales, the Sora, like several other wetland birds, has declined in many areas where formerly it was common, particularly in southeastern Michigan. Loss of marsh habitat due to human land-use practices has taken its toll on local populations. Rails generally respond well to taped playbacks of their calls, and many participants in the 1980s Breeding Bird Atlas survey employed this technique to locate Soras.

It was from this effort that we came to realize the extent to which this species had declined or disappeared from a number of sites.

Many of the marshes where the Sora remains common are within state game areas, recreation areas, or other public lands. Even though this opportunistic species will use small patches of marsh, the extensive wetland habitats available in these areas have become important to maintaining healthy, sustainable numbers of breeding Soras in Michigan. —Gail A. McPeek

# PURPLE GALLINULE
## (Porphyrula martinica)

This glossy, blue-green rail is an accidental visitor to Michigan. A relative of the Common Moorhen, the Purple Gallinule inhabits marshes in the southeastern United States and Central and South America. The nearest breeding populations are found in western Tennessee and the coastal Carolinas, but its propensity to wander has led to numerous records in the East, including several in Michigan. The first fully documented record for the state was an individual found dead at Grand Marais, Alger County, on 10 May 1964. (Barrows describes a few reports from the late 1800s, none of which he considered satisfactory.) Other valid records are: a specimen from Flint Township, Genesee County, 29 May 1965; a well-documented sighting from Maple River State Game Area, Gratiot County, 2–4 May 1969; a male found dead in Macomb County on 22 June 1973; and a dead bird at Mackinaw City, Cheboygan County, on 19 April 1983. There is one additional report of an ill bird (which later died) in Dickinson County on 2 May 1973, but there is question as to whether it was in Michigan or across the border in Wisconsin. —Gail A. McPeek

# COMMON MOORHEN
## (Gallinula chloropus)

The Common Moorhen is an uncommon to locally common summer resident and migrant in Michigan, with a distribution confined to the Lower Peninsula. It is more numerous and widespread in the southern half of this region, north to Saginaw Bay and Muskegon.

The Common Moorhen was formerly known as the Common Gallinule in this country, but its name was changed to match that of its counterpart in the Old World. Breeding in North America occurs from southeastern Canada through the eastern United States to coastal Mexico, and locally in the Southwest. The winter range generally follows the southern Atlantic and Gulf coasts to Central and South America, with isolated populations also in California, Arizona, and Texas.

Like its rail and coot relatives, the moorhen is a marsh inhabitant. It can be found in both large and small freshwater marshes as well as the marshy edges of ponds, lakes, rivers, and canals. You could say that its taste in habitat lies between that of rails and coots, with moorhens spending less time in the reeds compared to rails and less time in open water relative to coots. Optimal conditions are a combination of dense, emergent vegetation and fairly deep (1–3 feet), open water.

Nests are like those of other rails—a platform of plant stems and other debris anchored to the surrounding vegetation. Males have an interesting habit of building several nests in their breeding territory. These "extra" platforms are used as roosting sites by the female and newly hatched young. Clutches often contain 9 to 12 eggs, but rarely do that many chicks survive through the summer. I remember watching a family of moorhens who made regular early morning forays on my lawn. They began with a large brood of eight, but one by one this number dwindled to four within a few weeks.

As the chicks matured, they went from a downy-black plumage to a grayish-brown, and as their legs grew longer, they began to take on a distinctive chicken-like appearance. Once moorhens reach adulthood, they are mostly brown with a slate-black head and neck. Their most conspicuous feature is the bright red bill extending to a large red shield on the bird's forehead.

As is typical of most rails, the moorhen's elusive nature and remote habitat make it difficult to find. Listening for their repetitive, high-pitched calls is the best means of detection, and you can sometimes elicit calls using taped recordings, though the similar-sounding coots may also respond. Individuals are most vocal during the breeding season, around the hours of dawn and dusk. However, they tend to be most visible later in the summer, after nesting has ended.

Moorhens typically migrate back to Michigan in the latter part of April or early May. Some may return earlier, especially if warm temperatures result in an early spring thaw. The earliest Kalamazoo County record is 28 March. Nesting occurs in May, June, and sometimes July, with a 21-day incubation, and broods are seen from late June until well into August. In the better-suited marshes, usually those which are extensive and undisturbed, moorhens tend to nest in loose colonies.

The bulk of the fall migration takes place during September and early October. Occasionally a few stragglers are found into November, and in the early 1970s a moorhen was discovered in a Saginaw County marsh frozen to some vegetation but still alive. In 1992, an individual was spotted on 27 November in the far northern Upper Peninsula (Houghton County), which is highly unusual. Also extreme were the three seen on the 1973–74 Christmas bird count and one in 1989–90.

Years ago, both the moorhen and the coot were commonly referred to as "mudhen," a nickname which, according to Walter Barrows, confounds some of the records from the 1800s and early 1900s. Barrows was confident, however, that the moorhen occurred in suitable places throughout the Lower Peninsula and that it was most abundant in the southern half.

Today we see a similar distribution in the state, but in lower numbers and fewer locations because of the loss of suitable habitat. Areas where it remains locally common include Saginaw Bay, St. Clair Flats, Pte. Mouillee, and the wetland complexes in Allegan and Muskegon counties, although birders have noted declines at some of these sites as well. Most occurrences in the north are in the Houghton Lake Wildlife Area, Roscommon County, and a few scattered locales along Lake Michigan north to Benzie County.

During the Breeding Bird Atlas, the Common Moorhen was reported from only 13% of the townships in the southern Lower Peninsula and was notably absent or scarce in numerous areas where formerly it was common. Further surveys in Kalamazoo County (1989) after the Atlas turned up only 37 adults in 12 of the more than 90 sites visited. Because of findings such as these, the moorhen was added to Michigan's list of special concern species in 1991. The current distribution reaffirms the importance of public lands where marshes are maintained for the benefit of waterfowl and other wildlife. Continued protection as well as restoration of wetland habitats is essential for all our rails, the moorhen included. —Gail A. McPeek

# AMERICAN COOT
## (*Fulica americana*)

This plump, slate-gray coot can be found in Michigan during all seasons of the year, but it is most abundant in the spring and autumn months. During these times of migration, congregations of coots are a familiar sight on our lakes, bays, rivers, and marshes. In the breeding season its occurrence is more irregular and spotty, like that of other rails. The American Coot is a locally common nester in southern Michigan, becoming uncommon to rare in the north.

The coot looks and behaves more like a duck than a member of the rail family. It is an excellent swimmer and a good diver, with large, lobed feet similar to but not completely webbed like those of a duck. When it is swimming, its head bobs back and forth in a chicken-like fashion, and when it takes wing, its feet "patter" across the water's surface until it becomes airborne. The coot's calls are also fowl-like and include various clucks, cackles, and grunting sounds.

As with many waterfowl, the heart of the American Coot's nesting range lies west of the Great Lakes in the prairie pothole region of the northern Plains. Its breeding range is quite extensive, covering much of North America south to Costa Rica. Its wintering range is also large and includes the southern portion of its breeding range to northern South America.

This species uses a variety of lakes, ponds, and marshes for nesting. It prefers areas of fairly deep, open water with emergent vegetation on the periphery. Except for the requirement of more open water, its breeding habitat is much like that of the Common Moorhen. Coots widen their habitat selection during migration and winter, using saltwater bays and inlets in addition to bodies of fresh water.

Coots return to Michigan beginning in March. Their north-

*Sandhill Crane*
GIJSBERT VAN FRANKENHUYZEN

GIJSBERT-1993

ward advance depends on the spring thaw and the availability of open water. Migration continues into May, but whatever the time of their arrival, nest building is often delayed until the marsh vegetation has grown enough to provide concealing cover. State records indicate that nesting occurs primarily in June and early July. There is an exceptionally late breeding record of small downy young on 14 August 1973 in Delta County of the Upper Peninsula.

The coot's nest is a mound of plant stems and debris, usually floating on the water but anchored to the surrounding emergent vegetation. Clutches are large, with an average of 8 to 12 eggs. Those having more than 12 eggs are often the result of two females laying in the same nest.

Coots gather in large flocks in the fall, often mingling with southward-bound ducks. The migration can be rather drawn out, generally beginning in September and lasting through November. Flocks ranging from a few hundred to several thousand coots can be seen on various inland and coastal waters across the Lower Peninsula. Places known for their concentrations of migrating ducks are great locations to see coots. Among these are Saginaw Bay, Lake St. Clair, and Lake Erie in the east and the lower reaches of the Kalamazoo and Muskegon rivers in the west. The large sewage lagoons of the Muskegon Wastewater System are also popular with coots and other waterbirds, not to mention bird-watchers. Hundreds of head-bobbing coots make for quite a comical sight.

Not all coots vacate Michigan for warmer waters. They are uncommon winter residents in the southern counties. How many remain depends on the severity of autumn and early winter weather and the formation of ice on lakes. Milder temperatures mean more open water, giving us more ducks, coots, and other waterbirds. The mild winter of 1975–76 resulted in a record tally of more than 2,500 coots on the state Christmas bird counts.

Although never a very common breeder in Michigan, the coot was formerly more numerous and widespread than it is today. Declines have been documented in many locales where wetlands have been destroyed or disrupted by human activities. These decreases have been particularly evident in some of the inland southern counties. As with other marsh birds, remaining strongholds are mainly in state and federal refuges and game areas where wetlands have been protected and maintained. Places such as the Shiawassee National Wildlife Refuge, Pte. Mouillee State Game Area, and Allegan State Game Area still support good numbers of breeding coots. —Gail A. McPeek

# SANDHILL CRANE

## (*Grus canadensis*)

Michigan has birds of all sizes, and the Sandhill Crane is one of the tallest. Standing at a height of three to four feet, this long-legged, long-necked bird is a virtual giant relative to most birds in the marsh. From a distance, amidst cattails and other tall plants, its large size is less apparent, but at close range, when it is standing in a harvested field or flying overhead, one can appreciate its enormity.

The Sandhill Crane is a common summer resident and migrant in Michigan. Its distribution is not uniform, however.

Breeding populations are concentrated in two main areas: the eastern Upper Peninsula, and the south-central counties of the Lower Peninsula. Chippewa, Mackinac, Luce, Schoolcraft, and Alger counties form the core summer range in the north. The region's leatherleaf-sphagnum bogs and other peaty wetlands, like the vast sedge marshes at Seney, are the primary nesting sites. Cranes are found sparingly throughout the rest of northern Michigan, but as the population continues to grow, further expansion into the western Upper Peninsula and northern Lower Peninsula seems likely.

In the south, cranes are most common in a band that extends from Livingston and Washtenaw to Barry and Kalamazoo counties. Waterloo Township in Jackson County has one of the highest nesting densities of Sandhills in North America. Large, deep wetlands are preferred nesting habitat in this region, but pairs are also using shallow marshes, sedge meadows, and openings in shrub swamps.

Less than a hundred years ago, the Sandhill Crane was on the brink of extinction in Michigan. Heavy hunting pressure combined with the drainage of wetlands had reduced the state's population to only a few dozen pairs by the early 1900s. Numbers were so low that Walter Barrows (1912) forecast their extirpation from the state. Fortunately, this prediction did not come true. The 1918 Migratory Bird Treaty Act, which included a prohibition on the hunting of cranes, came in the nick of time.

When Lawrence Walkinshaw searched the Lower Peninsula for cranes in 1944, he estimated a population of only 27 to 35 pairs. Recovery was slow at first, with 43 pairs in 1954; then numbers increased more rapidly, to 157 pairs in 1973 and 642 pairs by the mid-1980s. This miraculous comeback is a demonstration of resilience, adaptation, and conservation. While large, undisturbed marshes are favored nesting habitat, pairs are also accepting smaller and more fragmented wetlands, even those affected by human encroachment. Strides made in wetlands protection have also benefited this species, though, unfortunately, degradation of some marshes has continued. In 1992, modifications to a drain in Oceana County destroyed Walkinshaw's Marsh, home to several pairs of cranes.

Avian history reveals that cranes are ancient birds. The Sandhill Crane we see today was present some 9 million years ago, and its ancestors date back 40 to 60 million years. The Sandhill is one of 15 species of cranes in the world. Its distribution stretches from Siberia and Alaska east to the Hudson Bay and south to Cuba and Mexico. Included in this range are three northern, migratory subspecies and three tropical, nonmigratory subspecies. We have the Greater Sandhill (*G. c. tabida*), a subspecies whose summer range extends westward and northward from the Great Lakes. Through banding data we know that Michigan Sandhills winter in the Gulf states, particularly in Florida, where they share habitat with the nonmigratory Florida subspecies.

Cranes begin their return to Michigan in mid- to late February. Most are back in southern counties by late March and in the Upper Peninsula by mid-April. Since families remain intact through the winter, immature cranes accompany their parents when they return to the breeding grounds. Once adults get down to the business of nesting, the previous year's offspring are forced from the territory. These younger birds come together, forming small flocks which, over time, will give rise to mated pairs.

Cranes partake in some rather elaborate mating dances, leaping into the air with wings extended and feet thrown forward. Pairs also perform a synchronized duet of trumpet-like sounds which can be heard a mile or more away. A dawn chorus of dueting cranes reverberating through the marsh is a sound everyone should experience at least once in life.

Cranes are early breeders, and the first warm spell often stimulates nest building. Eggs are laid in April or May, with hatching a month later. According to Walkinshaw, who has studied cranes in Michigan for decades, two eggs are the norm, with only one young usually surviving to fledging at three months of age. After hatching, they are again more conspicuous, frequenting drier areas of the marsh or upland fields to feed on a variety of foods but particularly insects for their young.

As fall approaches, cranes gather in large flocks at traditional locales. The Phyllis Haehnle (Jackson County) and Bernard Baker (Calhoun County) sanctuaries in southern Michigan are regular staging areas, as is the popular Jasper-Pulaski Game Preserve in northern Indiana, where cranes can be seen by the thousands. Numbers usually peak at these sites in late October and early November. Immatures can be identified by their brownish plumage and feathered crowns, while adults are mostly gray with bare red crowns. Cranes typically leave Michigan by December, but over the past few years small numbers have overwintered in Jackson County, and Sandhills are being reported with increasing frequency on both Michigan and Indiana Christmas bird counts.

If you want to learn more about these fascinating birds, Michigan's own Lawrence Walkinshaw, a world authority on cranes, has written two superb books: *The Sandhill Cranes* (Bloomfield Hills: Cranbrook Institute of Science, 1949) and *Cranes of the World* (New York: Winchester Press, 1973). —Gail A. McPeek

# BLACK-BELLIED PLOVER

## (*Pluvialis squatarola*)

The Black-bellied Plover is an uncommon spring and fall migrant and a rare summer visitor to Michigan. This medium-sized shorebird is striking in its breeding plumage with a velvety black face, breast, and belly, and upperparts mottled in black, white, and silver. Only during the spring migration, as they pass through on their way to the arctic, will you find them in this spectacular dress.

The Black-bellied Plover has a Holarctic breeding distribution. In North America it nests on the high arctic tundra from Alaska east to Baffin Island, and winters along the coasts as far north as Washington and New England and south to southern South America. Michigan birders can look forward to this bird's arrival beginning in late April and early May, with numbers peaking from mid- to late May. Nearly all migrants are through by early June, although some, presumed to be nonbreeding second-year birds, may linger throughout the summer where appropriate habitat exists.

Fall migrants begin passage through Michigan in mid-August, and numbers typically peak from mid-September through early October. Rarely an individual or two lingers into December. One such straggler was present until 18 December 1983, constituting the only Michigan Christmas bird count record for this species.

Historic writings describe the Black-bellied Plover as regular along the Great Lakes shores and less common inland, a distribution similar to what we find today. There are few records of high numbers for this species, and nearly all are in spring from the west end of Lake Erie or in the Saginaw Bay area. Examples include 500 on 21 May 1965 at Erie Marsh and 400 on 18 May 1989 at Pte. Mouillee, both in Monroe County; 300 on 17 May 1967 at Fish Point in Tuscola County; and 200 on 3 May 1958 at Zilwaukee in Saginaw County.

The best habitats in which to search for this plover are mud flats, grassy wetlands, sod farms, and newly plowed fields. During the fall migration it is easy to confuse juvenile Black-bellied Plovers with the similar juvenile American Golden-Plover. Both species can be bright in color in their first basic plumage. The best field mark is the black axillaries or "armpits" of the Black-bellied, and with some practice, the shape and size of the bill can be used to separate these two plovers. —James Granlund

# AMERICAN GOLDEN-PLOVER

## (*Pluvialis dominica*)

The American Golden-Plover is an uncommon migrant and rare summer visitor in Michigan. In 1993 the two forms of the Lesser Golden-Plover were split into two species, the American Golden-Plover (*P. dominica*) and Pacific Golden-Plover (*P. fulva*). The latter winters in the South Pacific and is an unlikely stray to Michigan; however, because of the very recent nature of the split, insufficient data are available to support this claim. Current specimens and other information indicate it is the American Golden-Plover which passes through Michigan on its long journey between its nesting and wintering grounds.

In spring Golden-Plovers begin arriving in the state in early to mid-April, with migration peaking in the first half of May. Unlike its cousin the Black-bellied Plover, this species is usually gone by 21 May. On occasion individuals oversummer here, clouding the issue of when the first fall migrants arrive. These summer visitors are presumably second-year nonbreeders. The first true fall migrating adults probably begin arriving in August, with juveniles coming a month or so later. There seems to be no well-defined peak, but September through mid-October have the most reports. Rarely, a few individuals linger into late November.

Unlike many other shorebirds, the American Golden-Plover frequents the interior of the state as much as the coasts, especially in the fall. This is probably because of its preference for short grassy fields rather than coastal flats or intermittent wet areas. Sod farms are ideal, and those operated by the Amish, who disdain the use of pesticides and other chemical agents, appear well suited to migrating plovers as they most likely provide a greater variety and abundance of prey. Farms in the south-central portion of the state (e.g., Clinton, Gratiot, and Hillsdale counties) seem particularly productive. For example, 200 individuals were seen on 11 May 1988 on a sod farm in Hillsdale County. This species also frequents the regular shorebird locations, such as the Muskegon Wastewater System and Erie Marsh and Pte. Mouillee in Monroe County, where good numbers have been seen in both spring and fall.

This species was probably more abundant in historical times, as Walter Barrows (1912) refers to flocks numbering in the thousands in the fall season. He also indicated that it was hunted and considered excellent table fare, which might partially explain the drop in numbers. By 1951, Norman Wood wrote that this shorebird had declined and was rare in locations where it once was considered abundant. The considerable loss of short grassy habitat due to human land-use changes no doubt played a role.

Today the American Golden-Plover is by no means abundant, but neither is it rare in certain locales. This handsome bird with the golden-spangled back is seen with regularity in numbers that sometimes reach several hundred. One can only imagine what a spectacle a flock of several thousand must have been. —James Granlund

# SNOWY PLOVER
## (*Charadrius alexandrinus*)

The Snowy Plover is an accidental visitant to Michigan with only one documented record, that of an individual photographed on 17 April 1992 near the north pier at the mouth of the Kalamazoo River in Allegan County. There is one additional published record from 23 May 1986 at Escanaba in Delta County, but the documentation was found to be inconclusive by the Michigan Bird Records Committee. This tiny plover, which is somewhat similar in appearance to the Piping Plover, is Holarctic in distribution, with six recognized races. The North American race breeds along the Gulf and Pacific coasts and locally in Nevada, interior California, and the Plains. It winters along both coasts, throughout the Caribbean, and along the Pacific coast of South America. The Snowy Plover is currently threatened on its breeding grounds because of the loss of sandy beaches and tidal flats, its preferred habitat. —James Granlund

# WILSON'S PLOVER
## (*Charadrius wilsonia*)

The first and only Michigan record for Wilson's Plover was a bird found on 1 May 1993 at Tawas Point, Iosco County. The individual remained at this locale through 7 May, and was photographed and seen by many birders. The presence of an incomplete or muted black breast band suggested the individual was an immature male. The Wilson's Plover breeds on beaches along the Atlantic coast from Maryland to northern South America, and along the Pacific from Baja California to Peru. In winter it withdraws from the northern parts of its breeding range to the tropics. The limited occurrence of this plover in the United States makes it an unlikely stray in Michigan. However, individuals have shown some propensity to wander, and it has been reported from several other Great Lakes states. —James Granlund

# SEMIPALMATED PLOVER
## (*Charadrius semipalmatus*)

The Semipalmated Plover is a common migrant and rare summer visitor to Michigan. In spring, breeding-plumaged birds are easy to recognize with their bold black neck and forehead bands and bright orange legs; however, in late summer and fall these distinctive markings are gone, making identification more challenging.

This species has a widespread breeding range which stretches from Alaska and British Columbia east across the arctic tundra to the Labrador Peninsula. It winters on the Atlantic coast from South Carolina south to the tip of South America and north along the Pacific coast to California. Very rarely, the first spring transients make it to Michigan in early April. More typically they appear in the beginning of May, with the migration peaking from mid- to late May and numbers diminishing rapidly by early June. Mud flats and wet sandy areas are preferred foraging habitats. Some individuals, presumably nonbreeding second-year birds, may oversummer where proper habitat exists.

Since adults begin departing the breeding grounds in early July, it is likely that the first returning migrants reach Michigan quite early, in mid- to late July. Juveniles do not begin appearing for about another month, in mid-August. As with many shorebirds, the fall migration is quite drawn out, with no real discernible peak, although numbers typically reach their maximum in August and diminish drastically by mid-September. Some individuals may still be seen in October, and on very rare occasions as late as mid-November.

The Semipalmated Plover is typically found as singles or in small flocks of 10 or less, and it often occurs with various other sandpiper species at both coastal and inland locales. Occasionally, however, large numbers accumulate where there are extensive areas of suitable habitat. Good examples of such occurrences include 350 seen on 19 May 1989 at Pte. Mouillee in Monroe County, and 125 seen on 25 May 1988 at the Nayanquing Wildlife Area in Bay County.

The status of the Semipalmated Plover in Michigan seems to have changed little in the past one hundred years. Both Walter Barrows (1912) and Norman Wood (1951) categorized the bird as a common migrant, though their descriptions do give the impression of a somewhat more abundant species, as in the photographic records of 500 individuals on 21 and 23 May 1937 in Calhoun County. —James Granlund

*Piping Plover*
DAVID MOHRHARDT

# PIPING PLOVER
### (*Charadrius melodus*)

Once a fairly common breeding bird along Michigan's coast, the Piping Plover is now an endangered species, being a very rare breeder and migrant. This species has two recognized subspecies: *C. m. melodus*, which breeds along the northern Atlantic coast from Quebec to Virginia, and *C. m. circumcinctus*, the interior subspecies which breeds in the northern Great Lakes basin and northern Great Plains from the Canadian Prairie Provinces south to Nebraska. The breeding population of the coastal subspecies has been somewhat stable, while the interior population has suffered severe declines.

Piping Plovers winter along the coast from Texas to the mid-Atlantic states. The return of breeding individuals to Michigan occurs from late April to early May, while a few migrants may be seen as late as early June. Nesting occurs from May through July, with most individuals departing the state by mid-August, although migrants have been detected as late as November. Piping Plovers are more likely to be encountered on the beaches of the Great Lakes than inland, with very few sightings away from their breeding areas.

Both Walter Barrows (1912) and Norman Wood (1951) listed the Piping Plover as an uncommon breeding species on the sandy beaches of the Great Lakes in Michigan, nesting as far south as Berrien and Monroe and as far north as Alger and Luce counties. It has been estimated that the total population once ranged from 155 to 215 pairs. Increased human activity on beaches and possibly the expansion of predators such as gulls, raccoons, and ravens caused numbers to plummet by the 1960s. By 1979 the Michigan population had dropped to 31 pairs, and by 1992 to only 16 pairs. Additionally, the plover's range has withdrawn to the northern portion of the state, with pairs in 1992 found in Leelanau, Emmet, Cheboygan, Mackinac, Chippewa, and Alger counties and only one pair found on the islands of Lake Michigan, a long-time stronghold for the species. Equally disturbing has been the poor productivity of late, with the 16 pairs in 1992 producing only 13 chicks. These alarming declines prompted the U.S. Fish and Wildlife Service to add the Piping Plover to the Federal Endangered Species list in 1991.

Currently the recovery plan has the optimistic goal of establishing 100 breeding pairs in Michigan. Accomplishing this plan calls for protection of breeding habitat through exclusion of human activity, particularly that of recreational vehicles and pets, and protection of nests from predators. Unfortunately, little is known about the impact of habitat changes in the wintering areas on the population or about the rate at which new pairs can be recruited from elsewhere in their range. Many managers are understandably pessimistic about the Piping Plover's recovery in the Great Lakes basin.

Males are extremely site-faithful, often nesting within a few feet of the previous year's nest. Piping Plovers do not mate for life, however, and males often breed with different females even when the previous year's mate is present. Young also return to the same general vicinity in which they hatched, but may breed several miles from the natal site. True to its name, the Piping Plover uses melodic whistled calls in combination with flight displays during courtship.

Nests are placed directly on the beach, about midway between the water's edge and a barrier dune. An important component of the site selection is an appropriate foraging area near the beach, usually a small marsh located behind the barrier dune. The nest is a simple scrape in the sand, with pebbles added to help conceal the eggs. A typical clutch contains four eggs, which are incubated for 28 days. Peak hatching in Michigan occurs in early July. Prior to hatching, many nests are lost to predators and weather, and failed pairs may attempt to renest as many as three times. After hatching, the precocial young require about 30 to 35 days to reach flight stage. During this prolonged flightless period, the young are extremely vulnerable to predators. —James Granlund

# KILLDEER
### (*Charadrius vociferus*)

The ability of the Killdeer to nest in close proximity to man, together with its loud, self-proclaiming call, makes it our most familiar "shorebird." This brown and white plover with the two black breast bands is a common breeding resident and migrant in Michigan and an occasional winter resident.

The Killdeer breeds throughout much of North America, from the edge of the tundra all the way to Central America and the West Indies. It winters along the Atlantic and Pacific coasts from New York and British Columbia to northern South America and in the interior from the Ohio River Valley through Middle America. There is an additional sedentary race in coastal Peru and Colombia.

This species begins arriving in Michigan in late February and early March, depending on weather conditions. It is not uncommon to see Killdeer roaming around snow-covered fields during this time of the year. The migration peaks in early to mid-April, and the birds tend not to concentrate in spring, though occasionally flocks of 100 or more may form. Breeding commences soon after pairs return, and typical egg dates for the state range from early April through July. Exceptional was a nest found on 20 November 1982 in Muskegon which had four young on 22 November.

Killdeer prefer open habitats for breeding, including beaches, margins of wetlands, old fields, lawns, gravel parking lots, even flat rooftops. This versatility has certainly worked in their favor, allowing populations to spread throughout eastern North America as the land was cleared. Although present in Michigan in presettlement times, Killdeer must have increased in numbers and expanded their range as the state was settled. By the early 1900s,

*Spotted Sandpiper*
*Killdeer*
DAVID MOHRHARDT

Walter Barrows (1912) and others characterized the species as common wherever appropriate habitat existed. Since then, Killdeer have been familiar breeders throughout Michigan, being a bit more abundant in the southern portion of the state than in the north.

Breeding bird survey data from the 1966–1991 period indicate that the adaptable Killdeer has continued to increase in Michigan and in many regions of the continent. These increases are likely due to the availability of even more habitat as suburban sprawl has provided new open areas.

Killdeer nesting habitat is quite variable. It seems the only major requirement for the nest site is a dry open area with some sparse cover for the nest itself, as well as more substantial cover for concealment if the adults are disturbed. There is also a need for nearby standing water for foraging habitat. The nest is a simple scrape lined with stones or small pieces of vegetation. A typical clutch consists of four eggs, and incubation averages 25 days. The precocial young are able to run about and forage within hours of hatching, but they remain with their parents for about 30 days. Adults protect the young using a broken-wing display to lead off predators. Double broods are common, as are renestings if first nests are destroyed.

After breeding is complete, individuals gather into large flocks in suitable damp habitats such as sod farms and mud flats. Some congregations reach considerable size; examples include 530 on 22 August 1990 on a sod farm in Wayne County, and 420 on 1 October 1972 in similar habitat in Ottawa County. Most Killdeer depart the state by late October, though some linger regularly into December, and a few are able to overwinter in such areas as sewage ponds where habitat is kept open by warm water.

On Michigan Christmas bird counts, Killdeer are encountered nearly every year, but usually in small numbers. Between 1959–60 and 1992–93, the highest total came in the mild winter of 1987–88, when an amazing 83 individuals were found by participants. The next highest total was 52 in 1975–76. —James Granlund

# BLACK-NECKED STILT

## (*Himantopus mexicanus*)

The Black-necked Stilt is an accidental visitor to Michigan with only one confirmed sighting (verified by a photograph), of a single bird discovered 13 June 1988 near Oscoda in Iosco County. There is also a sight record of two individuals on 6–13 June 1980 at Shiawassee National Wildlife Refuge in Saginaw County; however, the documentation was unequivocal. Stilt taxonomy is still being worked out, but the recognized North American form breeds locally in wetlands along the Gulf, Pacific, and Atlantic coasts, as far north as Oregon and Delaware and south to Chile and Argentina. It also nests in scattered interior locales in the central and western United States as well as much of northern South America. Stilts winter along the coasts through Middle America to northern South America. This sleek black and white bird on pink stilt-like legs has shown an increased propensity to wander in recent years, and its reoccurrence in Michigan is likely. —James Granlund

# AMERICAN AVOCET

## (*Recurvirostra americana*)

The American Avocet is a rare but regular visitor to Michigan. The summer range of this elegant, long-legged shorebird includes much of the Central Plains and West, from Saskatchewan and Washington to Texas and southern California. The closest breeding population to Michigan occurs in western Minnesota. The winter range is more widespread and includes the Pacific coast from California to Guatemala, the southern Atlantic coast, and the Gulf coast to Mexico. Avocets migrating to and from these more easterly locales are the likely source of Michigan's visitors.

Although Walter Barrows listed this species for Michigan at the turn of the century, none of the specimens he refers to can be found. The first fully documented record did not come until 8 September 1957, when an individual was seen in Monroe County, and a specimen was taken from the same location on 22 September. Since this first record, the American Avocet has been observed here on a regular basis.

Between 1970 and 1992 a total of 230 avocets were reported. These observations span the dates of 14 April to 2 November and mostly involve single birds or groups of less than 10. Exceptional were reports of 26 individuals on 27 April 1986 and 30 on 28 April 1987 at the Erie Marsh Preserve in Monroe County. Data show that peak spring movements generally occur from the third week of April to the second week of May, and fall sightings are most pronounced from the first week of July through August. Most spring transients appear for a day or less, while avocets which turn up toward late summer often stay for considerable lengths of time.

There are no discernible migration cycles or patterns in the state, with numbers varying from year to year. The highest annual total to date is the 52 avocets recorded in 1987. Nearly all American Avocets seen in Michigan occur in Great Lakes coastal habitats, either beaches or marshes. Berrien and Monroe counties and the Saginaw Bay area account for the bulk of the records. Particularly reliable locations include Pte. Mouillee and Erie Marsh Preserve in Monroe County, and St. Joseph and New Buffalo in Berrien County. Inland records are exceptionally rare. —James Granlund

# GREATER YELLOWLEGS

## (*Tringa melanoleuca*)

The Greater Yellowlegs is a common migrant and rare summer visitor to Michigan. This large yellow-legged shorebird breeds in wetlands and muskeg from southwestern Alaska east through the Canadian boreal zone to Labrador and Newfoundland. It winters along the Pacific coast from Oregon to Chile and the Atlantic coast from New York to Argentina.

Spring migrants may begin arriving in Michigan as early as mid-March, with one exceptional record in late February. The main flight occurs from mid-April through the third week of

May. Most spring observations are of singles or small flocks, but good numbers may build where proper habitat exists. Examples include 75 Greater Yellowlegs seen on 28 April 1985 at Coopersville Sewage Ponds in Ottawa County, and 72 on 18 April 1991 at Shiawassee National Wildlife Refuge in Saginaw County.

The fall migration is more difficult to ascertain, since apparently a few individuals oversummer in the state. The first migrant adults probably begin returning in early July, with juveniles coming two to three weeks later. Numbers of fall transients gradually build in appropriate habitat, and fair-sized concentrations can be observed well into October. Examples include 150 on 26 August 1979 in Monroe County and 100 on 5 August 1989 at Nayanquing Wildlife Area in Bay County. Most individuals have departed by November, although stragglers may be encountered as late as early December.

Like many shorebirds, the Greater Yellowlegs prefers wet meadows, mud flats, and other marshy areas. Its long legs allow it to forage well out in the water, where it dines on small fish, other vertebrates, and invertebrates. This species occurs with equal frequency inland and along coasts, and can often be found in rather small wet areas which harbor few other shorebirds. Although nearly identical in appearance to the Lesser Yellowlegs, this one stands about three inches taller. The best discriminating field marks in addition to size are the slightly upturned bill and the greater length of the bill relative to the width of the head. —James Granlund

# LESSER YELLOWLEGS

## (*Tringa flavipes*)

The Lesser Yellowlegs is a common migrant and rare summer visitor in Michigan. This species breeds from eastern Alaska across the Canadian tundra and boreal forest to eastern James Bay. Winters are spent along the Atlantic and Pacific coasts from North Carolina and southern California to Argentina and Chile, and in the interior of Mexico through South America.

The first spring migrants begin arriving in Michigan in late March, with the bulk passing through in late April and early May. On migration the Lesser Yellowlegs is more abundant in the state than its larger counterpart, the Greater Yellowlegs. Sizable flocks are often encountered in the spring. Examples include counts of 200 reported on 6 May 1974 in Houghton County, 4 May 1983 in Lenawee County, and 28 April 1985 in Ottawa County, and a most impressive 460 on 5 May 1991 at Erie Marsh in Monroe County.

Lesser Yellowlegs are typically found on mud flats, wet fields, and other marshy habitats and may be encountered with equal frequency at inland and coastal sites, although the largest concentrations are usually coastal. Some individuals may oversummer where appropriate habitat exists, making it difficult to discern the commencement of the fall migration. It is likely that the first returning adults appear in late June or early July, with juveniles arriving two to three weeks later. In 1982, an impressive flock of 800 early arrivals was reported on 25 June at the Shiawassee National Wildlife Refuge in Saginaw County.

Like many shorebirds, Lesser Yellowlegs may linger during their southbound migration, and numbers may build to impressive totals. Examples include 1,400 on 16 July 1989 and 930 on 19 August 1991 at Pte. Mouillee in Monroe County. Most Lesser Yellowlegs have departed the state by mid-October, though occasionally some are seen as late as mid-November. Individuals seen later than this are typically Greater Yellowlegs.

In *The Atlas of Breeding Birds of Michigan* (1991) a Lesser Yellowlegs was reported at Sleeper Lake in Luce County in the summers of 1987 and 1988. Observers described territorial and agitated behaviors, suggesting the possibility of nesting. The boreal habitat at this site is appropriate, but no nests or other evidence of breeding was reported. Based on its current breeding range, the Lesser Yellowlegs seems an unlikely candidate as a Michigan breeder. Nonetheless, there are historical nesting records for this species in Wisconsin, so nesting in the Upper Peninsula is not out of the question, and observers should be mindful of the possibility. —James Granlund

# SOLITARY SANDPIPER

## (*Tringa solitaria*)

The Solitary Sandpiper is a common migrant in Michigan, frequenting wetlands and coastal areas in spring and fall. It is occasionally observed in summer, but these are considered to be nonbreeders, although nesting in our remote northern parts is not out of the question. In summer and autumn, this small shorebird's white eye ring helps distinguish it from the similar-looking Spotted Sandpiper.

The Solitary's breeding range lies north of the Great Lakes, extending from central Alaska to central British Columbia and east through central Ontario to Labrador. The first spring migrants may arrive in Michigan in late March; however, mid-April is the more usual commencement time, with peak numbers in early to mid-May. Solitaries continue to appear well into June, and it is likely that some are still heading north while others are already beginning to return south. This makes it very difficult to discern when one migration begins and the other ends. To make things worse, some individuals may oversummer where appropriate habitat exists. In general, records indicate that the first fall migrants appear in late June, with the migration mostly complete by early October. Occasional birds linger into late October while November sightings are exceptional.

Sizable flocks of this species are seldom seen on either migration. Exceptions include 30 Solitaries reported on 6 August 1983 in Ontonagon County and 21 on 3 August 1991 in Washtenaw County. Like other *Tringa* species, the Solitary Sandpiper is found on the margins of mud flats, in wet meadows, or in other marshy habitats. It often uses small wet areas, even puddles, which probably accounts for the lack of large concentrations. It is regularly found at both coastal and inland locations and, unlike many other shorebird species, is often more numerous at inland sites than those at or adjacent to the Great Lakes.

The presence of individuals in summer raises the possibility of nesting within our borders. This species has bred at least twice in northern Minnesota in habitats quite similar to those found over much of the Upper Peninsula. In 1992 a pair of Solitary Sandpipers oversummered at Seney National Wildlife Refuge and demonstrated territorial behavior. Although no nest or other direct evidence of breeding was found, this observation is certainly suggestive of casual nesting in some remote parts of the Upper Peninsula. It is also possible that these were simply second-year nonbreeders.

Part of the difficulty of confirming nesting is that the species is solitary and uses abandoned nests of other species such as the Common Grackle. Therefore, unlike other shorebirds which breed in Michigan, this one nests in trees. This habit kept ornithologists from finding the first nest of a Solitary Sandpiper until 1903. —James Granlund

# WILLET

## (*Catoptrophorus semipalmatus*)

The Willet's self-proclaiming call, "will-will-willet," is seldom heard on Michigan's beaches. Although this distinctly patterned bird is rare in Michigan, it does occur each year in small numbers. The beaches at St. Joseph, Benton Harbor, Grand Mere, and New Buffalo, all in Berrien County, rank among the best places in the state to look for this large brown shorebird. Other good locations include the Muskegon Wastewater System, Pte. Mouillee and Erie Marsh in Monroe County, and Whitefish Point in the eastern Upper Peninsula.

In a review of records from 1970 to 1992, the earliest spring date for a Willet was 16 April 1988. The bulk of the migration through the state occurs from the last week of April to the last week of May, with a discernible peak from 8 to 15 May. Scattered sightings in early June probably represent oversummering birds. Fall migration commences the last week of June and continues through the second week of September, with a minor peak in the first week of July. There are a few records of Willets in October and November; the latest was 15–16 November 1970. Observations almost always involve a single bird or groups of 5 or less. Some exceptions are 27 Willets on 1 July 1983 and 22 on 3 July 1970, both in Berrien County.

There are two distinct races of this species, with little overlap in their ranges except on parts of their wintering grounds. The eastern form (*C. s. semipalmatus*) breeds along the Atlantic coast from Nova Scotia to the West Indies and winters along the southern Atlantic and Gulf coasts and the West Indies to northern South America. The western form (*C. s. inornatus*) breeds from the Canadian prairies south to Colorado and winters mainly along the Pacific coast from southern California to Peru, although some go to the Gulf coast. Specimens indicate that the western form visits Michigan, although it seems possible that the eastern form could also occur here.

Both Walter Barrows (1912) and Norman Wood (1951) report a distribution for the Willet similar to that of today. Barrows even indicated that it formerly bred throughout the southern Great Lakes region, but there is no direct evidence to support this claim. —James Granlund

# SPOTTED SANDPIPER

## (*Actitis macularia*)

The fluttering flight, teetering walk, and boldly spotted belly make this one of the most easily recognized shorebirds. The Spotted Sandpiper is a common migrant and summer resident in Michigan, being found on the margins of lakes, streams, or other wetlands.

Spotted Sandpipers are widely distributed, breeding from Alaska east to Newfoundland and south to southern California, central Texas, and Maryland. They winter mainly along both coasts of Middle America, in the West Indies, and south throughout South America to Bolivia and northern Argentina. Small numbers remain in the states and winter along the Gulf, southern Atlantic, and Pacific coasts.

The first spring migrants begin arriving in Michigan in mid-April, but the main migration occurs in the latter half of the month and peaks in early May. Breeding begins by mid-May in the southern part of the state and two to three weeks later in the Upper Peninsula. The commencement of the fall migration is difficult to determine, since the first migrants are arriving when late nesters are still on territory. In general, the first migrants arrive in early July, with numbers peaking in the last two weeks of the month. Most individuals have departed by October, although a few may linger, and on one occasion a tardy bird was detected on 29 November 1984 in Muskegon County.

In spring, Spotted Sandpipers are normally encountered in small groups, whereas in fall, large flocks may build in appropriate habitats. Examples of high totals include 105 on 14 July 1979 and 82 on 19 July 1981 at the Muskegon Wastewater System. More remarkable, however, is a spring record from Berrien County, where 400 migrating Spotted Sandpipers were seen along the Lake Michigan shoreline on 14 May 1978.

On each of the early Michigan bird lists, the Spotted Sandpiper is described as a common breeding species and migrant, a status it retains to this day. Current information shows its distribution to be fairly uniform throughout the state, but it occurs more frequently in counties with more wetlands or other suitable habitat. This sandpiper prefers nesting in open areas near the margins of streams, lakes, ponds, and even temporary wet areas. The nest is normally located well away from the water's edge in thick cover, and is a simple depression in the ground, sometimes lined with grass. Eggs are normally laid from mid-May through June, with four being a typical clutch. The chicks hatch in about 21 days, becoming independent in an additional 18 to 21 days.

Females have one or several mates during the season. Each female establishes a territory and actively competes for males, attracting them with vocalizations while chasing other females from the territory using aerial flights and pecking. In the case of a monogamous pair, both parents share the incubation, whereas in polyandrous matings the female leaves the first clutch in the male's care while she mates with another. Typically, the polyandrous female will share parental responsibilities with the last male with which she mates. Some females may mate as many as four times in rapid succession, resulting in four broods in a single season.

As with many other species which depend on wetlands for breeding, there is concern for Spotted Sandpiper populations due to loss of habitat. Fortunately, this bird uses such a wide range of habitats that even disturbed or otherwise less than optimal wet areas are used for breeding, and this fact should allow the Spotted Sandpiper to remain a common species in Michigan. —James Granlund

# UPLAND SANDPIPER

## (*Bartramia longicauda*)

The term "shorebird" hardly seems appropriate for this species, which spends a good part of its time in upland fields rather than on the beach or shoreline. In Michigan, the Upland Sandpiper is an uncommon migrant and a common to rare breeder, depending on your location. Its breeding range extends from the tundra of Alaska south to Oregon, the south-central Plains states, and Virginia, and eastward through Ontario to Labrador. Winters are spent far to the south in southern Brazil, Paraguay, Uruguay, and Argentina—an area known as the Pampas.

Upland Sandpipers begin arriving in Michigan in early to mid-April, with the majority of the breeding individuals on territory by late April or early May. Migrants continue to pass through the state throughout May and early June in the north. Returning migrants as well as post-breeding individuals gather together by late July, and most depart during August, with occasional stragglers remaining into late September. This species is seldom encountered in large flocks on migration, although numbers of post-breeding birds may build to sizable levels such as the 74 seen on 24 July 1972 in Ottawa County. These larger concentrations are typically associated with sod farms or similar grassy habitats. Unlike most other shorebirds, Upland Sandpipers are rarely seen on mud flats or coastlines.

The Upland Sandpiper uses a wide variety of grassland habitats. In the heart of its breeding area, short-grass prairies are preferred, while pastures, hayfields, dry or wet meadows, old fields, and other short-grass equivalents are commonly used throughout its range. Nesting is usually initiated in the first half of May. Courtship includes a spectacular flight in which the male rises nearly out of sight and sings a haunting song consisting of four whistled notes. Males also sing a drawn-out, two-note whistle from a fencepost or other prominent perch in advertisement of their territories.

The nest is placed on the ground and concealed with overhanging tufts of grass. This species typically breeds in loose colonies, with nests placed in fairly close proximity, ranging from 1.5 to 15 acres per nest. Clutches usually contain four eggs, which are incubated for about 24 days by both sexes. A trait of all shorebirds, the young are precocial and able to forage for themselves and follow their parents at birth. Both adults and young feed on insects and have a particular taste for larvae of beetles and lepidopterans.

The Upland Sandpiper was likely present on the southern prairies of presettlement Michigan, but the extent of its population at that time is uncertain. As forests were cleared and replaced with agricultural fields and pastureland, this species expanded its range and became more common in the state. By the middle to late 1800s Upland Sandpipers must have been rather abundant, since they became a popular market species as the Passenger Pigeon declined. By the early part of this century, ornithologists such as Barrows (1912) indicated that the once-abundant Bartram's Sandpiper (former common name) was becoming increasingly scarce within the state. Like many species of the era, it benefited from the protection laws for migratory birds passed between 1916 and 1918, and the steady decline was abated. In 1951, Wood characterized the Upland Sandpiper as a fairly common breeder in the southern third of the Lower Peninsula, being less common but widely distributed across the northern third. There were no nesting records for the Upper Peninsula at the time, although birds present during and after the breeding season were suggestive of the possibility.

The 1980s Breeding Bird Atlas indicated a northward shift in the Upland Sandpiper's distribution in Michigan, with breeding pairs spread throughout much of the state but greatest numbers present in the northern Lower Peninsula, and even a fair number scattered across the Upper Peninsula. This species is now uncommon to scarce in the southern portion of the state, being nearly absent from the southernmost tier and south-central counties. The decline in the south over the past 50 years is attributed to changes in agricultural practices, urban and suburban sprawl, and maturation of old fields. The increased presence in the north indicates a shift in availability of suitable habitat and may be facilitated by the slow maturation of stump fields left by heavy logging activity as well as retention of older agricultural practices.

Upland Sandpiper populations are being threatened on both the nesting and wintering grounds. This species' need for grasslands—one of the most endangered habitats in the country—puts it in peril, as does pesticide use and modern agriculture. Of even greater concern is the rapid development of its wintering habitat in South America. As happened to our prairies in the 1800s, the Pampas are under heavy pressure from agricultural demands. The overall impact of this habitat loss on the Upland Sandpiper and associated wintering species is yet unknown. Whether future generations of Michigan bird enthusiasts will enjoy the haunting spring song of this species may be in the hands of conservationists and governments half a world away. —James Granlund

# ESKIMO CURLEW

## (*Numenius borealis*)

Little is known about the status of the Eskimo Curlew in Michigan. Its occurrence is substantiated by a specimen taken on 28 October 1879 near Kalamazoo. Its exact status is lost to the bird's near-extinction; it is possible that this species was regularly seen in the state on migration, but how often will never be known. Barrows (1912) commented that the species was a common market bird in Detroit, although he did not indicate the source of birds. By the late 1800s market hunting throughout its range had decimated this once-plentiful bird, and by 1910 authors of the time were already writing its extinction obituary. Since then there have been sporadic sightings in North America, with the last confirmed record in 1972. Encouraging reports from the South American wintering grounds in 1993 offer a glimmer of hope that a few may still remain. Historically, the Eskimo Curlew probably bred in the northern Yukon and Northwest Territories and perhaps in Alaska, and wintered mainly from southern Brazil to Argentina. —James Granlund

# WHIMBREL

## (*Numenius phaeopus*)

The distinctive Whimbrel with its long, decurved bill and bold head stripe is an uncommon migrant to Michigan. This shorebird is Holarctic in distribution, breeding sporadically throughout the tundras of the Northern Hemisphere. There are four recognized subspecies, with the North American race (*N. p. hudsonicus*) occurring in two breeding populations—one in Alaska and the adjacent Canadian provinces and the other along the western and southern edges of Hudson Bay. Most likely it is individuals of this latter population which pass through Michigan en route to and from the wintering grounds in the southern coastal states and as far south as Chile and Brazil.

Perhaps more than any other shorebird migration in Michigan, the Whimbrel's spring flight comes en masse and in a very compressed period. In typical years the migration occurs during the last two weeks of May, and large flocks may be encountered statewide within a few days. In 1988, for example, 650 were seen on 22 May at Pte. Mouillee, Monroe County, and three days later (25 May) 700 were seen at the Whitefish Point Bird Observatory, Chippewa County. These two locations are in the extreme southeast and northeast corners of the state. In some years the spring migration may be more drawn out, with individuals arriving rarely as early as late April and others lingering into early June.

In spring Whimbrels are noticeably more common along Michigan's eastern Great Lakes shorelines, being uncommon to rare along the western shoreline and rare to accidental inland. Perhaps the best spots to see this species are Pte. Mouillee and Whitefish Point Bird Observatory, with Memorial Day weekend being particularly dependable at this latter locale as large flocks in their "V" formations or long lines can be seen and heard winging north.

The first returning fall migrants begin arriving in Michigan in mid-July. During this season, Whimbrels are encountered in smaller numbers, often as singles in any given spot. Their migration occurs on a wider front in fall, and individuals are as likely to be found on the Lake Michigan coastline as on the other Great Lakes. Most fall records occur from mid-July through early September, with rare stragglers remaining to the end of the month. Whimbrels are seen most often on beaches of the Great Lakes, but like many shorebirds, they also frequent mud flats as they stop to rest and feed during their long journey. —James Granlund

# HUDSONIAN GODWIT

## (*Limosa haemastica*)

The Hudsonian Godwit, a large, long-billed shorebird, is an uncommon spring and fall migrant in Michigan. This species has a phenomenally long journey between its arctic breeding grounds in Alaska, the western Northwest Territories, and northeastern Manitoba and its wintering grounds in southern South America, primarily along the Argentina coast. First spring migrants appear in Michigan in the second week of May, with the bulk in transit during the last two weeks of May and early June. Southbound individuals begin arriving in July, but most sightings occur in August and September. Migrants are usually seen for only a day or less, though occasionally some may linger for a week or more in suitable habitat. Except for a handful of records of birds staying into November, nearly all Hudsonian Godwits depart the state by early October.

Most reports of this species are of single birds, although flocks as large as 10 have been encountered on occasion. Examples include 10 on 20 May 1982 at Whitefish Point Bird Observatory, Chippewa County, 10 on 8 May 1983 at the Muskegon Wastewater System, 10 on 19 September 1978 at the Erie Marsh Preserve, Monroe County, and 11 on 1 September 1980 at Mentha in Van Buren County. These sites plus the Saginaw Bay area are among the best spots to observe this shorebird.

There is a wide disparity in the occurrence of this species in Michigan from year to year. The Hudsonian Godwit is practically absent from the state in some years, such as in 1991, when no individuals were reported in the spring and only 4 were seen in fall. In other years it is seen in fairly good numbers, such as in 1982 when 29 were reported. Observations tend to be fairly uniform across the state, but there is a greater chance of finding this species along the Great Lakes coasts than at inland sites. This species, like many other shorebirds, frequents mud flats as well as beaches during its migration.

Today the Hudsonian Godwit is seen each year in Michigan, but such was not the case in historical times. Wood (1951) could list but four definitive records for the species going back to the 1800s, and considered it a rare transient. A similar situation existed in Wisconsin, with the species being extremely rare in the past but more regular in recent decades. Whether this situation represents a true change in status in the Great Lakes region or is a result of better field identification and coverage is debatable. —James Granlund

# MARBLED GODWIT

## (*Limosa fedoa*)

The Marbled Godwit's name is derived from the bold, mottled pattern of the alternate (breeding) plumage. Although it loses this distinctive plumage in autumn and winter, the extremely long, slightly upturned bill and massive size (16–20 inches) make this species stand out from all other Michigan shorebirds at any time.

The Marbled Godwit is a rare migrant and summer visitant to the state. Breeding occurs in the northern Great Plains from central Alberta to western Ontario and south to Montana and Minnesota. From here it travels to wintering areas along the Pacific coast from California to Mexico and irregularly south to Chile, with smaller numbers flying to the Atlantic and Gulf coasts from Virginia to Mexico and Guatemala.

The first confirmed Michigan record of a Marbled Godwit is of two specimens taken on 1 August 1882 from the Detroit River, Wayne County. There were few reports from the time of this account until 1950, but in recent decades it has been seen with regularity. In the period 1970–92, Marbled Godwits were recorded annually, with a total of 69 published reports. Of these, 37 occurred during May, with the majority in the second and third weeks. The remaining observations were spread out evenly from June to September. The earliest spring record of the period was 19 April 1975 at Whitefish Point, Chippewa County, while the latest fall report was of an individual at the Karn Plant, Bay County, until 6 October 1971.

Most reports of Marbled Godwits involve 1 to 3 individuals; exceptional were the 15 seen on 8 May 1976 and 11 on 6 May 1989, both at Pte. Mouillee, Monroe County. Only 6 of the 69 records in the 1970–92 period were from inland locations, the remainder being along the Great Lakes shorelines. Most observations were made in the coastal marshes of Lake Erie, with Pte. Mouillee and Erie Marsh Preserve accounting for the bulk of the records. Other prime spots include the marshes of Saginaw Bay and the beaches of Berrien County and Whitefish Point. Individuals seen on Great Lakes beaches usually make brief appearances, whereas those found in marshes often linger for up to several weeks. At the marshes of the Karn Plant, for example, individuals remained from 12 September to 6 October 1971 and from 8 to 20 September 1989. —James Granlund

## RUDDY TURNSTONE

### (*Arenaria interpres*)

The bold black, white, and chestnut plumage of the spring Ruddy Turnstone is perhaps the most colorful of any Michigan shorebird. This species is most often seen along the Great Lakes as an uncommon spring and fall migrant. Holarctic in distribution, the Ruddy Turnstone breeds along the coastal plains and lowlands of the Arctic Ocean throughout the Northern Hemisphere. In the Western Hemisphere, populations winter along the Atlantic and Pacific coasts from southern New England to central Argentina and from southern Oregon to central Chile.

In spring the first arriving Ruddy Turnstones are seen in early May; however, the bulk of the migrants pass through during the last two weeks of May and the first week of June. Most encounters involve small groups of fewer than 10 birds intermingled with other shorebirds. Occasionally larger concentrations are seen, such as 77 on 26 May 1990 at Whitefish Point Bird Observatory, Chippewa County, and an astounding flock of 320 on 2 June 1989 at Pte. Mouillee, Monroe County. Nearly all northbound migrants have departed the state by the second week of June,

although one individual lingered as late as 22 June 1988 at Whitefish Point.

The first returning birds arrive as early as the second week in July, with the migration drawn out well into October. The latest report published in the seasonal survey is of an individual on 1 November 1965 in Marquette. Ruddy Turnstones are definitely less common during the fall period relative to spring, and reports rarely exceed 10 individuals at any one locale. This status seems to have changed little from earlier days, as Wood (1951) described this species as a "transient (chiefly coastal), uncommon in spring and rare in fall."

During both seasons, turnstones are much more common along the Great Lakes, with inland occurrences rare. They are especially partial to cobblestone beaches such as those at Whitefish Point and Waugoshance Point, Emmet County. Migrants can also be seen using mud flats or sandbars in coastal marshy habitats as well as on breakwalls or other rocky structures. True to its name, this species forages by probing under rocks, shells, and other debris in search of invertebrate prey.

The spring plumage of the Ruddy Turnstone is unlikely to be confused with that of any other shorebird, while its dull fall plumage is less diagnostic. Regardless, its plump shape and general appearance are distinctive enough that it is doubtful it could be confused with any other species besides its close cousin, the Black Turnstone (*A. melanocephala*), an unlikely visitor here based on its almost exclusive western range. Amazingly, though, a Black Turnstone did show up in Wisconsin on 22 May 1971, proving that anything is possible when it comes to birds. —James Granlund

## RED KNOT

### (*Calidris canutus*)

According to Coues (1903), the Red Knot was "named for King Canute by Linnaeus, who accepted the dubious tradition that connected this bird with a story of the Danish king Knut, Cnut, Canut, etc." The dubious tradition to which Coues refers is a story in which Canute commanded the tide not to rise. How that story is connected to a shorebird has been variously interpreted: Choate (1985) indicated that the connection is simply the waterline, where knots can be found; Terres (1980) suggested that by running along the waterline, knots appear to be trying to hold the tide back.

Red Knots breed in the high arctic of North America and Eurasia. North American knots nest in Greenland, on islands in the Canadian Arctic, and on scattered mainland outposts in Alaska and the Northwest Territories.

Knots from Greenland and northern islands in the Canadian Arctic winter in western Europe, while those from more southerly Nearctic locations winter in the New World. Most of the latter travel to the coasts of southern South America, but small numbers remain north to New England on the Atlantic coast and California on the Pacific coast.

In Michigan the Red Knot is an uncommon migrant in both the spring and fall, occurring on sandy beaches, mud flats, or, more rarely, among shoreline rocks. Large flocks are most likely to be encountered during the spring on the east side of the state. Good locations to try for spring flocks are the Pte. Mouillee State Game Area in Monroe County, Tawas Point State Park in Iosco County, and Whitefish Point in Chippewa County.

The spring passage for this species occurs within a comparatively narrow window: the earliest spring migrant is from 15 May, while the latest is from 15 June. The migration peaks during the May portion of this window, with most high counts numbering less than 30 birds. The highest total by far is 72 in Monroe County on 23 May 1989.

In fall, adult Red Knots are found only casually in Michigan. Consequently, although adults reappear in late July or August (early date: 21 July), the species occurs only irregularly until three or four weeks later, when juveniles begin arriving (early date: 18 August). Peak fall numbers are generally recorded in September and typically do not exceed 10 individuals; the highest fall count, 40 in Ontonagon County on 20 October 1984, is an exception to both of these generalizations. Indeed, the total of 40 individuals is late not only for a high count but also for a migrant knot in Michigan: the year's last knots are usually reported in the second or third weeks of October, and the latest knot observation on record is from 21 October. —Philip C. Chu

# SANDERLING

## (*Calidris alba*)

Sanderlings breed in the high arctic and winter from the northern temperate regions to the southern tips of the southern continents. In the Western Hemisphere nesting occurs on Greenland, on islands in the Canadian Arctic, and at several mainland sites in the Northwest Territories and Alaska. Wintering occurs along the coast from Alaska and New England to southern South America.

In Michigan the Sanderling is a fairly common spring migrant, an accidental summer visitor, and a common fall migrant. It frequents sandy beaches and exposed sand flats, and though mud substrates are used, they do not appear to be favored. Indeed, extensive areas of exposed mud often have only one or two Sanderlings, even when thousands of other shorebirds are present.

The spring's first Sanderling may appear as early as 28 April, though in most years it does not appear until the second week of May. Numbers build to a peak in the last few days of May or the first few days of June, with the maximum spring count being 100+ on 27 May 1990 in Huron County. After the peak there is a rapid decline in numbers, and the latest date for a likely northbound migrant is 12 June. There are, however, two records from late June in Berrien County; these may represent birds attempting to summer at the foot of Lake Michigan.

Southbound adults typically appear in the second or third week of July (early date: 13 July), and juveniles appear five or six weeks later (early date: 20 August). High numbers may be encountered any time between mid-July and early October, but totals exceeding 100 are unusual. The highest count on record, from Berrien County on 21 July 1973, is 250 birds.

In many years the last Sanderlings are recorded during November. Birds linger into December only rarely, and there are but two January records, the latest being 12 January.

In basic plumage, the Sanderling is white below and pale gray above, with a bold white wing stripe and white sides to the rump. It thus resembles a basic-plumaged Red Phalarope, and the two species can be confused, especially in flight. Sanderlings differ in that they possess a blackish carpal bar and lack the phalarope's dark eye patch.

In alternate plumage, Sanderlings have variably colored feather edges that make some birds look rufous while others look orange, blonde, or whitish. Blonde birds have probably been mistaken for Baird's Sandpiper; however, Sanderlings are larger, with a more truncate (less tapered) body and a proportionately longer, heavier bill. In flight, their wing bar is much more conspicuous. —Philip C. Chu

# SEMIPALMATED SANDPIPER

## (*Calidris pusilla*)

The Semipalmated Sandpiper is Michigan's most common small sandpiper. Separation of this species from the other small sandpipers, while not trivial, is usually straightforward in alternate and juvenal plumages. In basic plumage it can be more difficult, particularly with respect to the Western Sandpiper. Indeed, basic-plumaged Semipalmated and Western Sandpipers are similar enough that most or all of them should be reported as Western/Semipalmateds, not as one species or the other.

Semipalmated Sandpipers nest on the tundra from Labrador in the East to Alaska's Seward Peninsula in the West. Most migrate east of the Rockies to wintering grounds along the Atlantic and Pacific coasts of South America; smaller numbers winter in the West Indies and south Florida.

In Michigan, the Semipalmated Sandpiper is a common spring and fall migrant. It may also be an accidental summer visitor. Individuals can be found on rock breakwalls, sandy beaches, and the mud margins of sewage ponds, but by far the largest concentrations occur on bare mud flats and in the open shallow-water areas that adjoin them.

Typical arrival dates for this species range from the last week of April through the first week of May; however, there are several earlier records, the earliest being 31 March. The reliability of March and early April records is hard to evaluate, as some or all of them may pertain to birds in basic plumage for which confident separation from the Western Sandpiper is difficult at best.

The spring flight for Semipalmateds peaks in the last ten days of May or the first few days of June, as evidenced by the maximum count of 1,600 on 2 June 1989 in Monroe County. The flight then slows rapidly, and while counts of about 100 birds may be recorded as late as 10 June, they are the exception rather than the rule.

A few birds, presumably late spring migrants, trickle through as late as 16 June. However, there are three records between 20 and 24 June that could represent either late migrants or birds summering locally. All three are from the northern Lower Peninsula or the Upper Peninsula.

Fall-migrant adults appear as early as 13 July, with juveniles often arriving 18 to 25 days later (early date: 6 August). The migration is heavy between the fourth week of July and the fourth week of August, and concentrations approaching 1,000 individuals are possible in favored areas. The highest fall total recorded is 1,100 on 6 August 1989 in Monroe County.

By late September the migration slows to a crawl. Singles and small groups continue to be reported through October into November, with the latest report being 29 November. As with the early spring reports, October and November sightings are open to question because of the potential for confusion with Western Sandpipers. Nonetheless, Semipalmateds can occur in November: there is a 6 November juvenile from Tuscola County (University of Michigan Museum of Zoology) that is identifiable by both plumage features and measurements. —Philip C. Chu

## WESTERN SANDPIPER

### (*Calidris mauri*)

Western Sandpipers breed on coastal tundra in Alaska and northeastern Siberia. They winter along the shore from Washington to Peru in the West and from New Jersey to Surinam in the East. Movements between breeding and wintering areas are heaviest along the Pacific coast but occur eastward to the eastern seaboard, particularly in fall.

In Michigan, the Western Sandpiper is a casual to rare transient in spring and an uncommon transient in fall. It can be found in the same habitats as the Semipalmated Sandpiper— sandy beaches, rock jetties, and especially shallow-water areas with a mud substrate. Indeed, Westerns are often in the company of Semipalmateds, and the best strategy for finding them is to search carefully through aggregations of the latter.

Western Sandpipers have been reported once or twice per spring in almost every year since 1975. Observations span the period between 4 May and 13 June, with most being clustered in the second half of May. The majority of reports involve single birds, but 10 were claimed from Macomb County on 10 May 1981.

Westerns are encountered with much greater regularity in the fall. Adults have been recorded as early as 2 July, but are not usually observed until the second half of that month; juveniles have been recorded as early as 14 August. As in spring, most reports involve single birds, but 10 or more individuals have been tallied on several occasions between late July and the first week of October. The high count of 25 is from 16 August 1984 in Ontonagon County.

Late dates for fall-migrant Westerns are difficult to determine with confidence; some of these may pertain to birds in basic plumage, which are nearly identical in appearance to basic-plumaged Semipalmated Sandpipers. Correctly or incorrectly, a few Westerns have been identified in late October and November, with the latest being 22 November.

Western Sandpipers are often separated from other small sandpipers on the basis of their long, droop-tipped bills, and particularly long-billed individuals can resemble miniature Dunlin. However, among many of the small sandpipers, bill length varies with sex as well as with species: females have a longer bill than males. One consequence is that short-billed male Westerns often overlap with long-billed female Semipalmated Sandpipers.

In both alternate and juvenal plumages, a number of criteria exist for separating Westerns and Semipalmateds. These criteria are particularly well described and illustrated in Veit and Jonsson (1984). However, in basic plumage the two are extremely similar, and most if not all observations of basic-plumaged birds should be reported as Western/Semipalmated Sandpipers, not as one or the other. —Philip C. Chu

## LEAST SANDPIPER

### (*Calidris minutilla*)

True to its name, the Least Sandpiper is the smallest of the sandpipers. Leasts nest across the North American interior from Labrador to James Bay, and from James Bay west to Alaska. They winter from coastal Washington, central Texas, and coastal Delaware to southern Brazil. In Michigan, this species is a common spring and fall transient. It can be found on sandy beaches or gravel dikes and in open, shallow-water areas; however, it seems to prefer mud that is near sedges and other marsh vegetation.

In many years, Leasts are not recorded until the end of April or the beginning of May. Occasionally, however, they may be recorded much earlier, and there are two March records, the earliest from 12 March. During the first 25 days of May, the spring flight is heavy, with a maximum of 250 on 5 May 1991 in Monroe County. By the end of the month it has been reduced to a trickle; a few birds linger as late as 13 June.

Adult Leasts are among the earliest-returning shorebirds, with the first southbound birds being observed between the end of June and mid-July (early date: 27 June). Peak numbers are found shortly thereafter, between mid-July and mid-August. The maximum count recorded to date is 800 on 13 July 1991 in Monroe County.

Juvenile Leasts often arrive near the end of the fourth week in July, about a month behind adults. One year, an exceptionally early juvenile was observed on 18 July. Shortly after juveniles appear, the numbers of Leasts begin to decline, and by late September most sites host only a few individuals. Nonetheless, occasional birds continue to straggle through, and there are even two December records, the latest being 18 December.

Although Leasts are unique among Michigan's small sandpipers in having yellow or green (as opposed to black) legs, they are sometimes confused with the more abundant Semipalmated Sandpiper. The two species are separable, even at long distances, by overall coloration of the upperparts—dusky brown (alternate-plumaged adults) or rufous (juveniles) in Least, buffy gray (adults in alternate plumage and juveniles) in Semipalmated. In addition, adult Leasts are heavily streaked on the central foreneck and upper breast; most Semipalmated Sandpipers are only lightly marked there. —Philip C. Chu

# WHITE-RUMPED SANDPIPER

(*Calidris fuscicollis*)

As the only small sandpiper with a white rump, this species is aptly named. White-rumped Sandpipers breed from Baffin Island and northwestern Hudson Bay to northern Alaska; they winter in South America, principally from southern Brazil to Tierra del Fuego. The path between their breeding and wintering grounds is an elliptical one: the largest spring movements are north across the interior, while the largest fall movements are southeast toward the Maritime Provinces. On reaching the Maritimes, many White-rumps are thought to take an oversea route directly to the Caribbean.

In Michigan, most shorebirds whose fall migration is shifted to the east (for example, Western and Buff-breasted Sandpipers, Long-billed Dowitcher) are more abundant in the fall than in spring. However, the opposite is true for the White-rumped Sandpiper, which is a fairly common transient in spring but uncommon in fall. It is probably also a casual summer visitor. A possible explanation for the spring-fall discrepancy is that the transoceanic route used by White-rumps in fall is farther from the western Great Lakes than the interior route used in spring.

White-rumped Sandpipers are comparatively late spring migrants. The earliest arrival date on record is 22 April, the next-earliest is 5 May, and in most springs the species is first reported between 10 and 20 May. The movement peaks in the last week of May and the first week of June, but even at the height of the migration, single-site counts of more than 10 individuals are unusual. Noteworthy is the maximum count of 80 observed on 1 June 1989 in Monroe County.

A few birds linger in the southern Lower Peninsula as late as 22 June. Farther north, birds may remain even later: at Torch Lake in Houghton County, seven White-rumps were recorded on 23 June 1986, decreasing to five on 27 June and one on 1 July. Five additional records exist for the period between 7 and 14 July, all of them from Muskegon County north; some or all of these may refer to summering nonbreeders.

Adult White-rumps can reappear as early as 28 July, and (though relevant data are few) juveniles can appear as early as 29 August. Fall observations are usually of single birds or small groups of two to four individuals, with the largest totals being recorded during the last third of August. The maximum fall count recorded to date is 26 birds on 23 August 1990 in Saginaw County. Observations continue into the second half of October or early November, and there is one record from 19 November.

The White-rumped Sandpiper can be observed in a variety of habitats, including sandy beaches, sewage pond margins, and rock dikes. However, it seems to prefer mud substrates, and the largest counts are obtained in areas with extensive mud flats.
—Philip C. Chu

# BAIRD'S SANDPIPER

(*Calidris bairdii*)

When discussing the Baird's Sandpiper—named for the influential 19th-century naturalist Spencer F. Baird (Mearns and Mearns 1992)—many field guides emphasize the scaly appearance of its back. This emphasis is misleading, since the species appears scaly–backed only in juvenal plumage, and most other juvenile sandpipers look scaly-backed as well. Better cues are the Baird's long-bodied appearance in conjunction with its buff-colored face, foreneck, and breast.

The Baird's Sandpiper breeds from the Alaskan interior east across the Northwest Territories to Baffin Island, and winters throughout South America from Ecuador and Paraguay south. Migration from the wintering to breeding grounds is primarily through the Plains states and Prairie Provinces, whereas the return flight is across a broader front, with juveniles occurring west to the Pacific coast and east to the Atlantic coast.

In Michigan the Baird's Sandpiper is a casual spring migrant, and perhaps an accidental summer visitor as well. In fall it is a fairly common migrant along Lake Michigan and the Lake Superior shore of the eastern Upper Peninsula, and an uncommon transient on Lakes Huron and Erie. Birds can be found on extensive mud flats, at sod farms, and along sandy beaches.

Spring Baird's Sandpipers have been reported in about two-thirds of the years since the late 1950s. The earliest spring report is 1 May and the latest is 8 June, but most fall between 11 May and 5 June, with the largest numbers being reported after mid-May. The highest number claimed is 60 on 29 May 1958 in Mackinac County, a total that is an order of magnitude greater than the 1 to 6 individuals that are usually reported at any one time.

Most experienced shorebird observers suspect that these spring data are unreliable, and agree that Peterjohn's (1989) assessment for neighboring Ohio is appropriate for Michigan as well: "status [of Baird's Sandpiper] as a spring migrant has been obscured by numerous misidentifications. . . . Whenever a spring Baird's Sandpiper is encountered it should be thoroughly documented and photographed to help establish the spring status."

The Baird's has also been reported from 23 June and 5 July. If correct identifications are involved, the June record could refer to a late spring migrant and the July record to an early fall migrant. However, one or both records could also refer to birds summering locally.

In most years a few adult Baird's Sandpipers appear in Michigan during the last two-thirds of July. As adults are rare, most observers do not encounter the species until juvenile birds arrive in the second half of August (early date: 15 August). Peak numbers occur between the last week of August and the middle of September, when totals of 20 to 35 individuals may be recorded at favored sites. The highest fall total is 62 on 24 August 1981 in Muskegon County.

After mid-September numbers decline, and by October most Baird's are seen singly, though groups of about 10 have been recorded as late as the beginning of November. A few individuals sometimes linger into December, and the latest Michigan record is from 19 December.

The state's single best location for this species has been the

Muskegon Wastewater System. However, in 1993, concrete slabs that lined the facility's holding lagoons were replaced with rock filler, a change that will make the lagoon edges less attractive to shorebirds. —Philip C. Chu

## PECTORAL SANDPIPER
### (*Calidris melanotos*)

The Pectoral Sandpiper breeds on the tundra from Hudson Bay to Alaska. It also breeds on the Siberian tundra, but most Siberian Pectorals return to the New World to winter with their North American counterparts. Wintering occurs from Peru and Brazil to southern Argentina.

In Michigan, the Pectoral Sandpiper is a common migrant in both spring and fall. It is found in a variety of habitats, from wet lawns to sandy beaches to small mud areas in the midst of cattail stands. Impressive numbers may occur where extensive mud flats are available.

Pectorals can arrive as early as 10 March, but more often arrive in the last ten days of March or the first half of April. Numbers increase rapidly, and peak totals are recorded during the second and third weeks of April, an example being the 1,000 reported on 10 April 1986 in Tuscola County. However, counts in the hundreds are possible any time before the middle of May. By late May the passage has slowed to a trickle, with a few birds lingering into early June; the latest spring record is 14 June.

Early southbound migrants are usually recorded during the first three weeks of July; a single report from 30 June is the earliest on record. By mid-July several hundred individuals may accumulate at favored sites and, with the help of an influx of juveniles that begins six to eight weeks after the adults arrive (early date: 19 August), numbers may remain high into September. The highest fall total reported to date is 780 in Monroe County on 19 August 1991.

Numbers start to decrease during September, and in many years the latest Pectoral is recorded between 10 and 30 November. However, several December records exist, the latest being from Berrien County on 21–22 December 1987.

The Pectoral Sandpiper has prominent streaking on the neck that resembles a bib because it ends abruptly on the breast. However, the species is not named for its streaked bib. Instead, it is named for a pendulous sac beneath the skin of the male's foreneck and breast (Choate 1985); inflation of the sac area is associated with the production of resonant booming or hooting sounds during courtship (Pitelka 1959).

Male Pectorals average about 10% larger than females. This size difference may account for the surprising range of shorebird species with which Pectorals can be confused. Perhaps the most interesting source of confusion is the Sharp-tailed Sandpiper (*Calidris acuminata*), an Asian species that has not occurred in Michigan but has recently been recorded in Indiana, Iowa, Ohio, and southern Ontario. —Philip C. Chu

## PURPLE SANDPIPER
### (*Calidris maritima*)

The Purple Sandpiper breeds at high latitudes on both sides of the Atlantic. In the New World it breeds in Greenland and on islands in the Canadian Arctic; most New World breeders spend the winter along the shore from Newfoundland to North Carolina.

In Michigan, the species is an accidental spring migrant, rare fall migrant, and accidental winter visitor. It is associated almost exclusively with breakwalls, being found either on the breakwalls themselves or along the waterline at the breakwall base.

The state has only two spring records for the Purple Sandpiper, one on 22 May 1976 in Cheboygan County and the other on 23 April 1983 in Muskegon County. However, since the late 1960s there have been an average of two fall records each year, with a maximum of seven. In fall, the species has been reliably recorded as early as 10 October, and there is one earlier sighting, a report of uncertain validity from 7–8 September. Nevertheless, the great majority of fall records are concentrated between 25 October and 7 December. Most of these involve only one or two individuals; the maximum number reported is four on 24 November 1966 in Muskegon County.

Occasionally a Purple Sandpiper lingers into late December, and in four different years birds were recorded in the state between 1 and 8 January. Whether such early-winter birds represent tardy fall migrants or individuals attempting to overwinter is unclear. However, successful wintering may occur, as suggested by the single bird recorded on 28 February 1983 in Muskegon County.

Good locations to try for Purple Sandpipers are the breakwalls at the mouth of the Galien River in Berrien County, the mouth of Lake Macatawa in Ottawa County, and the mouth of Lake Muskegon in Muskegon County. However, at the correct time of year any jetty or rock-lined lakeshore dike might host this species.

Observers should note that the Purple Sandpiper is not the only shorebird to occur on jetties in the late fall and early winter; Dunlin may do so as well. Indeed, in basic plumage—the plumage usually seen in Michigan—the Purple Sandpiper bears a superficial resemblance to a Dunlin, being gray above and white below, with a droop-tipped bill. Therefore, a gray shorebird on a breakwall in the late fall or early winter cannot automatically be assumed to be a Purple Sandpiper. —Philip C. Chu

## DUNLIN
### (*Calidris alpina*)

The word "Dunlin" is a shortened version of "dunling," for "the little dark (dun-colored) one" (Choate 1985). The Dunlin is found north of the equator year-round in both the Old and New worlds. In the New World it has two breeding areas, one confined largely to Alaska and the other stretching from Victoria Island to James Bay in the central Canadian Arctic. Wintering occurs on or near the coast from New England to northern Mexico in the East, and from Alaska to Baja California in the West.

In Michigan, the Dunlin is a common spring and fall migrant and casual summer visitor. It can be abundant at sites with extensive mud flats, but also appears on sandy beaches, at rock jetties, and along the margins of sewage ponds.

Dunlin appear in Michigan as early as 9 March, though arrival dates in April are more typical. The migration peaks in the second half of May, with a maximum of 7,000 recorded on 18 May 1989 in Monroe County; however, single-site counts in excess of 1,000 birds may be tallied any time between the first week in May and the first week in June. After the first week in June, numbers decline quickly, and the last northbound migrants are observed in the middle of the month.

There is one report of a Dunlin nest in Michigan (Oldfield 1891), but the absence of other nest records south of the Hudson Bay lowlands suggests that the report is in error. However, one or two Dunlin can sometimes be found on Michigan shores between mid-June and mid-July. These birds may be summering one-year-olds, as judged by their basic or incomplete alternate plumage.

The occasional presence of a few Dunlin in mid-summer makes it difficult to determine when the earliest southbound migrants arrive. Two observations suggest that they arrive in late July or early August. First, reports of more than five Dunlin are nonexistent in the last half of June and most of July, while there is a report of 17 from 30 July; and second, the species is encountered with increasing regularity in August. Indeed, during August it is not uncommon to find one or two alternate-plumaged Dunlin in areas hosting large numbers of shorebirds.

Dunlin numbers remain low through mid-September, with counts of 20 or more individuals being unusual. Subsequently the fall passage builds, supplemented by juveniles that arrive as early as 14 September, and the heaviest movements occur between the third week of October and the first week of November. During this period, hundreds of birds may be observed at a single location. The maximum count on record is 2,250 on 28 October 1968 in Berrien County.

By the fourth week of November, most Dunlin have departed the state, though counts in excess of 100 are still possible. In many years a few birds linger into December, and one very late migrant was reported on 1 January. —Philip C. Chu

# CURLEW SANDPIPER

## (*Calidris ferruginea*)

The Curlew Sandpiper is an Old World species that is recorded regularly in North America, particularly along the Atlantic coast. In Michigan it is an accidental spring migrant and a casual or accidental fall migrant. The state's first Curlew Sandpiper was recorded on 5–8 May 1975 in Monroe County. Since then two additional spring birds have been documented, one on 19–22 May 1984 in Ottawa County and the other on 10 May 1992 in Monroe County. Five autumn records exist, all of them from Monroe County's Pte. Mouillee State Game Area: singles on 21–23 August 1988, 16 July–14 August 1989, 4–7 September 1990, 20 July–6 August 1991, and 15–23 August 1992. Because the autumn records

are from one location in consecutive years, they are sometimes thought to pertain to a single individual. All of Michigan's Curlew Sandpipers either were in the species' chestnut-red alternate plumage or showed large patches of reddish feathers on the underparts. —Philip C. Chu

# STILT SANDPIPER

## (*Calidris himantopus*)

Wood (1951) considered the Stilt Sandpiper to be a rare fall migrant in Michigan, with no verified spring records. However, Kelley (1968) noted an increase in fall reports during the mid-1960s that she attributed to both increased field work and the improved field skills of observers. By the mid-1980s the species was being reported in the state every spring, and it is now considered a rare spring and fairly common fall migrant here.

The Stilt Sandpiper is often found in the same areas favored by dowitchers—unvegetated mud flats covered by one to two inches of water. It also uses a dowitcher-like, up-and-down "sewing machine" motion when probing for food. Otherwise, however, it bears little resemblance to a dowitcher, having the long neck and legs of a yellowlegs and the dumpy body and droop-tipped bill of a Dunlin.

In Michigan, northbound Stilt Sandpipers have been recorded between 8 April and 1 June. The great majority of observations are from May, and the species is recorded most frequently between the 15th and 26th of that month. During the spring movement, single-site counts of more than two birds are unusual, and the maximum recorded to date is eight on 28 April 1972 in Berrien County.

Southbound adults appear as early as 30 June, though return dates in the first ten days of July are more typical. Juveniles appear three to five weeks later (early date: 27 July). Numbers are high by the fourth week in July and can remain elevated into the middle of September, with typical peak counts involving 20 to 60 individuals.

An astonishing 211 Stilt Sandpipers were tallied in Ontonagon County on 16 August 1983. This count, the maximum single-site total on record, was obtained during regular surveys of the White Pine Copper Company tailings basins. Such exceptionally large aggregations are apparently not a freak occurrence, since 113 were recorded from the same location a year later. Regular shorebird censuses at this site would be of considerable interest, but are unlikely because the area is closed to public use.

The year's last Stilt Sandpiper is usually recorded during the second half of September or the first week of October. However, there are two later reports, one from 18 October and the other from 26 October.

Stilt Sandpipers breed on the tundra from Alaska to James Bay. Most of them winter in South America, but there are additional wintering areas in southern California, southern Texas, and southern Florida. —Philip C. Chu

# BUFF-BREASTED SANDPIPER

*( Tryngites subruficollis )*

Buff-breasted Sandpipers breed from Point Barrow, Alaska, to Devon Island in the central Canadian Arctic. Wintering occurs thousands of miles south in Paraguay, Uruguay, and Argentina. Most Buff-breasts migrating between these areas follow a route through the Plains states and Prairie Provinces, but in autumn small numbers move farther east, reaching the Atlantic seaboard.

Prior to the 1950s, only eight Michigan records for the Buff-breasted Sandpiper were recognized (Wood 1951). However, the species has been annual in fall since 1964, and is now considered a rare fall and accidental spring migrant in the state. There are only three spring records: 14 on 16 May 1974 in Chippewa County, 1 on 18 May 1979 in Newaygo County, and 2 on 11 April 1981 in Ingham County.

Most fall records of this sandpiper come from one of two time intervals. There are a small number of reports between 23 July and 5 August, and a much larger number between 14 August and 23 October. Birds observed during the first interval may be adults, while those observed during the second interval may be juveniles. Data pertinent to this scenario are lacking, though personal observations suggest that by early September, most (if not all) Michigan Buff-breasts are juveniles.

Buff-breasted Sandpipers are usually encountered singly or in small groups of fewer than 4 individuals. However, considerably larger groups are occasionally observed. The highest total recorded is 32 from Ontonagon County on 23 August 1983. This count, made at the White Pine Copper Company tailings basins, was followed a year later by a same-location total of 25. Unfortunately, the White Pine site, which holds the distinction of Michigan's highest counts not only for Buff-breasted but also for Stilt Sandpiper, is closed to public use.

Although high numbers of Buff-breasted Sandpipers may be recorded any time in the last third of August or the first two-thirds of September, the species is most plentiful between 1 and 10 September. Thereafter numbers start to decline, and by the end of September most are gone; there are only four later records, the latest being from 23 October.

Buff-breasted Sandpipers seem to prefer drier situations than most other shorebirds, and are more likely to be found on gravel dikes and sod farms. They will utilize sandy beaches and mud flats, but when on mud they are often found in drier areas on which new vegetation is growing. In recent years the best site for this species has been the Halmich Sod Farm in southeast Clinton County; however, access to that site is presently restricted. Other good locations to try are the Pte. Mouillee State Game Area in Monroe County, the Muskegon Wastewater System in Muskegon County, and Whitefish Point in Chippewa County. —Philip C. Chu

# RUFF

*( Philomachus pugnax )*

The Ruff is a Eurasian shorebird named for the spectacular ruff of shaggy neck feathers shown by breeding males. It occurs regularly along the Pacific and Atlantic coasts of North America, and has occurred widely throughout the North American interior as well. In Michigan, it was first documented in 1959 and is now considered a casual migrant. Northbound individuals have been observed in the state 17 times between 29 March and 7 June, most of them during the last two-thirds of April and the first two-thirds of May. Southbound birds have been recorded 14 times between 26 June and 18 October, the majority between the last few days of July and the first few days of September. Occurrence was annual from 1971 through 1976 and 1988 through 1992; conversely, from 1983 through 1987 the species was reported only once. The maximum number of records in a year is 4. Michigan Ruffs have been observed in a variety of habitats, including mud flats, sewage ponds, and flooded fields. Some were in the company of yellowlegs, an association that may result from similar preferences for wet areas with a mud substrate. —Philip C. Chu

# SHORT-BILLED DOWITCHER

*( Limnodromus griseus )*

The Short-billed Dowitcher is snipe-like in shape with a heavy body, short legs, and a long, straight bill. Even its name refers to its snipe-like appearance: Coues (1903) states that "dowitcher" is a modified form of "Deutscher or Duitsch, meaning 'Dutch' or 'German' Snipe, as distinguished from the 'English' [or Common] Snipe."

There are three races of Short-billed Dowitcher: *L. g. griseus*, which breeds in Labrador and Quebec; *L. g. hendersoni*, which breeds from Manitoba to interior British Columbia; and *L. g. caurinus*, which breeds along the Alaskan coast. Wintering occurs along the Atlantic and Gulf coasts from Delaware to Brazil, and along the Pacific coast from Oregon to Peru. Only *hendersoni* is known to occur in Michigan; Wood (1951) lists a series of *griseus* specimens from the state, but subsequent examination revealed many of these to be *hendersoni*, and the rest to be indeterminate.

In Michigan the Short-billed Dowitcher is a fairly common spring migrant, casual summer visitor, and common fall migrant. It favors mud flats covered by a thin layer of water but can also occur on sandy beaches and in stands of marsh vegetation.

In most years Short-bills arrive in the last week of April or the first week of May, though individuals identified only as "dowitcher species" have been recorded as early as 23 March. Numbers peak in the second and third weeks of May, with groups of 70 or less being typical at any one locale; the largest spring total on record is 450 on 13 April 1978 in Berrien County. By the fourth week in May the passage is diminishing, and the last stragglers move through during the first week in June.

A few records of Short-bills or undifferentiated "dowitcher species" exist for the period between 5 and 25 June. Some of these may pertain to summering one-year-olds, as indicated by the basic or incomplete alternate plumage of the birds involved.

The fall passage of Short-billed Dowitchers usually begins during the last few days of June. Returning adults accumulate quickly, with a peak in mid-July, and if suitable habitat exists, impressive concentrations may develop. One particularly suitable site in Monroe County produced the state's highest Short-bill count, an aggregation of 1,300 birds on 13 July 1991. Juveniles arrive four to eight weeks after adults, with an early date of 4 August. With the influx of juveniles, counts in the hundreds remain possible into early September.

Visual separation of the Short-billed Dowitcher from its close relative the Long-billed Dowitcher is very difficult in basic plumage, the plumage that predominates as the fall season progresses. For this reason, reliable Short-bill reports are lacking after the end of September, even though the dowitcher passage continues for at least another month. Excluding a December Long-bill specimen, the latest dowitcher record is from 4 November. —Philip C. Chu

eral weeks earlier. In practical terms, this means that any August dowitcher with faded red underparts and scattered gray mantle feathers is worth a closer look; it may be a Long-bill. For the same reason, any early September dowitcher in basic plumage should be given further scrutiny.

The few data available suggest that juvenile Long-bills arrive as early as 12 September. Juvenal plumage is the easiest plumage in which to separate the two dowitcher species; excellent identification information on this and other dowitcher plumages is available in Wilds and Newlon (1983) and Paulson (1993).

By October, most of the dowitchers observed in Michigan may be Long-bills. This assertion is hard to evaluate, since the majority of these later migrants are in basic plumage, and basic-plumaged birds are very difficult to identify unless they vocalize. However, Long-bills have been identified by call as late as 28 October, and there is a single specimen collected on 5 December.

Like Short-billed Dowitchers, Long-bills favor open, shallow-water areas with a mud substrate. They are often found standing in water up to their bellies, probing repeatedly with the "sewing-machine" action that characterizes both dowitcher species. —Philip C. Chu

## LONG-BILLED DOWITCHER
### (*Limnodromus scolopaceus*)

Long-billed and Short-billed Dowitchers were originally considered to be different forms of the same species. However, variation in the latter was poorly understood, and consequently the appearance and distribution of both forms were unclear. It was Pitelka's (1950) careful analysis of specimens that yielded a clear picture of geographic variation in the dowitchers and led to recognition of the Long-billed form as a separate species.

Long-billed Dowitchers breed on the tundra in Siberia, Alaska, and northwestern Canada. They winter from southern Mexico to Virginia, central Texas, southern Arizona, and Washington State. In Michigan the species is a casual spring and fairly common fall migrant. This seasonal difference in status is a result of the different routes taken by northbound and southbound birds. In spring, most Long-bills follow a route that is west of the Mississippi River, whereas in fall the migration has a more easterly component, with birds occurring regularly to the Great Lakes and Atlantic coast.

In Michigan, spring reports for Long-billed Dowitchers are spread across the period between 16 April and 23 May. However, it is unusual to have more than two reports in a spring, and in some springs none are observed. Most reports involve single individuals, the most notable exception being a flock of six on 12 May 1990 in Bay County.

The first fall adults arrive between 21 July and about 15 August. A handful of earlier records, the earliest from 28 June, have been published but are of uncertain validity. Groups of 10 to 25 birds may be observed any time between late August and late October, and the highest single-site count on record is 38 on 6 September 1989 in Monroe County.

Fall adult Long-bills are often duller than their Short-billed counterparts, and seem to start the molt into basic plumage sev-

## COMMON SNIPE
### (*Gallinago gallinago*)

The Common Snipe belongs to a group of about 15 very similar species with chunky bodies, short legs, a disproportionately long bill, and cryptic brown plumages. It breeds in a broad band across the entire Northern Hemisphere. In the New World, nesting occurs from the northern edge of the boreal forest south to Arizona, the southern Great Lakes, and New Jersey. Wintering occurs from the Canadian border to northern South America.

The Common Snipe is a fairly common migrant and rare winter resident throughout Michigan. It is also a summer resident, common in the Upper Peninsula and northern Lower Peninsula but decreasing in abundance southward.

In the Lower Peninsula, snipe arrive as early as 4 March, with first arrivals in the last half of March being more common. The heaviest spring movements begin shortly thereafter, extending from the last week in March to the last week in April. In the Upper Peninsula the species arrives as early as 24 March, and the few data available suggest that the spring movement is most pronounced between the second week of April and the end of May.

The Michigan Breeding Bird Atlas recorded Common Snipe in about one-fourth of all townships in the Upper Peninsula; records came from every Upper Peninsula county and Isle Royale. In the

*Common Snipe*
*American Woodcock*
HEINER HERTLING

H.C.Hertling

Lower Peninsula, snipe were found with similar frequency but were less evenly distributed. Areas with few or no breeding snipe included the southernmost tier of counties and the east side of Michigan's Thumb.

In the southern Lower Peninsula, nests with eggs have been found between late April and the third week of May. Incubation typically lasts 18 to 20 days, and fledging requires about three weeks, so the earliest chicks probably hatch in mid-May and fledge in the first part of June. For the Upper Peninsula, Wood (1951) describes young that hatched on 1 June and a female that was collected on 3 July with an egg in its oviduct. Whether these Upper Peninsula data are representative is unclear.

Timing of the fall snipe movement in the Upper Peninsula is poorly known. However, unpublished flushing records compiled by the Michigan DNR suggest that the movement begins to wane in the middle of October. A few individuals remain into November, and there is a record from 20 November that might be attributed to a late migrant. In the southern Lower Peninsula, the heaviest migration occurs between early August and the end of October; a group of 13 birds from St. Clair County on 3 December probably represents very late migrants.

Small numbers of Common Snipe are found on Michigan Christmas bird counts every year, with an average of about 11 individuals statewide. Most of these are not reported subsequently, and it is unclear whether they remain or eventually move south; however, successful wintering is occasionally documented. Wintering birds have been recorded from locations as diverse as Oakland, Grand Traverse, and Marquette counties.

Snipe nest primarily in peatlands, which are poorly drained, organic-soil habitats like sedge marshes and alder swamps. However, they breed not only in extensive marshes and swamps but also in small marshy pockets along ponds and streams. Such pockets are particularly important in southern breeding areas.

Outside of the breeding season, snipe may appear in any damp area with a covering of herbaceous vegetation, including old-field puddles, mud margins of cattail stands, and even wet lawns. Occasionally large numbers may collect: high counts are 200+ on 17 April 1979 in Benzie County and 100 on 29 September 1976 in Newaygo County. However, such assemblages are unusual for this shorebird, and most snipe are seen individually or in small groups. —Philip C. Chu

# AMERICAN WOODCOCK

## (*Scolopax minor*)

The American Woodcock is a shorebird that inhabits woodland. There are as many as six woodcock species worldwide, and like their close relatives the snipe they are chunky, short-legged birds with a long, straight bill and cryptic brown plumages. However, while snipe have longitudinal striping on the crown, woodcocks have broad transverse bars there.

The American Woodcock nests from Newfoundland west to the north shore of Lake Superior and south to the Gulf states. Wintering occurs from Virginia and Missouri to the Gulf of Mexico. In Michigan the species is a fairly common, though in-

conspicuous, transient and summer resident. It is also a casual winter visitor.

The earliest record of spring-migrant woodcocks is that of a large group seen on 11 February in Ingham County. There are other late February reports from the Lower Peninsula, but in most years the species is not recorded there until the first half of March. Birds do not arrive in the Upper Peninsula for another few weeks, the earliest being recorded on 24 March in Chippewa County.

Breeding activity commences shortly after arrival. Most Lower Peninsula nests are recorded between the second week in April and the end of May, while all published Upper Peninsula nest records are from the latter month. Woodcocks incubate for about 21 days, and their chicks require between two and three weeks to fledge.

Wood (1951) characterized the American Woodcock as a fairly common summer resident that was less abundant in the Upper Peninsula. Similarly, during the 1980s Breeding Bird Atlas, woodcocks were reported in almost 60% of the townships in the northern Lower Peninsula, with the species being less widely distributed elsewhere. Although the Atlas provided a fairly good indication of its status and general occurrence, A. Ammann cautioned that the data probably underrepresent woodcock distribution (*The Atlas of Breeding Birds of Michigan* 1991). Such underrepresentation might result from the species' cryptic appearance, unobtrusive behavior, and early breeding season.

Woodcock nests may be found in a variety of habitats, including old fields, pine plantations, alder thickets, and young hardwood stands. Most nests are within a few hundred yards of the opening that the male uses as its display grounds. Working in the northern Lower Peninsula, Bourgeois (1977) found that hens usually move their newly hatched broods to habitats that are more densely vegetated and poorly drained than the nest site was, and solitary birds frequent habitats that are even more densely vegetated (Rabe 1977).

Fall migration of woodcocks in Michigan is heaviest in September and October. A few remain in the Upper Peninsula until early November, with the latest being recorded on the 15th of that month. In the southern Lower Peninsula, sizable numbers occasionally linger through the first third of November, and an individual on 29 November may represent one of the last southbound migrants. The highest total recorded to date is 82 on 14 September 1932 in Monroe County.

In some years one or a few American Woodcocks are recorded during the Christmas bird count period, with observations from such diverse locations as Kent, Grand Traverse, and Marquette counties. Whether such records represent late-lingering migrants or individuals attempting to overwinter is unclear; two records exist from late January, so it seems likely that occasional wintering does occur. —Philip C. Chu

# WILSON'S PHALAROPE

## (*Phalaropus tricolor*)

This slender shorebird breeds around shallow ponds and marshes in the Great Plains, from central Canada south to New Mexico and east to Minnesota, with sporadic nesting as far as Ontario. In Michigan the Wilson's Phalarope is an uncommon migrant and a rare, irregular summer resident. On very infrequent occasions, summering individuals have been found nesting in the state.

Rarely, the first spring transients arrive in the middle of April, but the average arrival time is the first week of May. The main spring migration flight occurs during mid-May, with most gone by early June. Those seen through June or in early July are summering birds and may even be breeders. The return trip from their nesting grounds begins in late July, and numbers peak around the middle of August. Some are still present into early September, but these, too, are mostly gone a week or two later. There are a few late records from October. Winters are spent in South America, though small numbers occasionally remain as far north as southern Texas and California.

In the spring season Wilson's Phalaropes tend to migrate through rapidly, and while pairs are commonly seen, flocks are rare. In late summer and fall, transients are more prone to lingering, and small concentrations may occur in proper habitat, such as the Lake Huron, Saginaw Bay, and Lake Erie marshes, and the sewage ponds and lagoons around the state. Examples include 20 Wilson's Phalaropes on 18 August 1989 at Pte. Mouillee and 23 on 4 September 1990 at Erie Marsh Preserve, both in Monroe County.

This species was first recorded in the state in 1857, but there was no evidence that it bred here. The first confirmed breeding came in 1929 in Jackson County. This was followed by several nestings in the 1930s, especially in the Saginaw Bay area, but by the 1940s the Wilson's Phalarope once again became absent as a breeding species. Scattered summer observations and potential breedings resumed in the 1960s and 1980s, with concentrations again around Saginaw Bay. There were a handful of confirmed nestings, the latest in 1981 at both the Shiawassee National Wildlife Refuge (Saginaw County) and Pte. Mouillee.

Females are polyandrous in this and the two other phalarope species. They are the more colorful of the sexes and select and defend males from other females using threat postures or overt chases. The bond between mates is consummated by both vocalizations and aerial chases, and this display can sometimes be seen during migration.

Based on the few state records, nesting probably occurs between mid-June and mid-July. The phalarope's nest is a scrape on the ground near the margin of a lake, pond, or marsh. Typical clutches contain four eggs, although some as large as eight have been found, suggesting some nest sharing or parasitism. After egg laying is complete, the female abandons the male, leaving him to incubate and raise the young while she seeks out another mate.

It is not clear why the Wilson's Phalarope does not nest more frequently in the state. The Great Lakes are at the periphery of its range, but ample habitat exists, numerous birds are seen on migration, and it is a regular breeder in neighboring Ontario. Perhaps it does breed more often than reported, though it certainly is one of the rarest breeders in Michigan. —James Granlund

# RED-NECKED PHALAROPE
## (*Phalaropus lobatus*)

The Red-necked or Northern Phalarope is an uncommon migrant in Michigan. Its breeding distribution is Holarctic, extending over the far northern latitudes of North America and Eurasia. Those which breed on this continent winter off the coast of Peru and rarely to Chile.

Spring migrants begin arriving in Michigan in mid-May and continue passing through the state until early to mid-June. Returning fall migrants are seen from about the middle of August to late September, although some individuals casually linger into late October. Large concentrations of this species are rarely encountered in the state, but in some years small flocks may occur. Examples include 15 on 21 September 1980 at Muskegon Wastewater System and 14 on 4 September 1990 at Erie Marsh in Monroe County.

Unlike many shorebirds, this species is as likely to be found swimming in the water as foraging on a mud flat or along the edge. Their habit of whirling in the water to disturb food from the bottom is a useful characteristic to help identify this species; however, the Wilson's Phalarope also occasionally displays this behavior. Red-necked Phalaropes frequent both inland and coastal habitats and can be found on sewage lagoons, large lakes, and even the Great Lakes. Locations which are particularly good for finding this species include Pte. Mouillee and Erie Marsh in Monroe County, the Muskegon Wastewater System, and the Dow Chemical Ponds in Midland County. —James Granlund

# RED PHALAROPE
## (*Phalaropus fulicaria*)

A nearly annual but rare visitant to the state, the Red Phalarope was first recorded here on 24 October 1888, when an individual was collected in Monroe County. For many decades there were only a scattering of subsequent observations, but since the 1970s this shorebird has been reported with some regularity. At present, it can best be characterized as a rare fall migrant and an accidental spring visitor.

From 1970 to 1992, the Red Phalarope was found 41 times in the state, with sightings in 17 of the 23 years and multiple reports in 1978, 1988, and 1991. A breakdown of these records shows that 2 were in May, 7 in September, 18 in October, 11 in November, and 3 in December. The spring sightings were of singles: one on 23–24 May 1973 in Kalamazoo County, and one on 30 May 1984 at the Muskegon Wastewater System. The earliest fall record is 10 September 1989 at Pte. Mouillee in Monroe County, the latest 29 December 1987 at New Buffalo in Berrien County. Most records fall between late September and mid-November and are of singles, although as many as four have been reported on several occasions. Three of the four December observations came on Christmas bird counts (Monroe County 1987–88, Berrien County 1987–88, 1991–92).

This species has a Holarctic breeding distribution, nesting on the high tundra of the arctic slope. Most migration occurs along the Pacific and Atlantic coasts, which explains its rarity in Michigan. Wintering in the Western Hemisphere occurs mostly in Pacific waters off the coast of South America. Considering its preference for large bodies of water, it is quite possible that this species occurs somewhat more regularly and in greater numbers on the Great Lakes away from the shore and visibility of observers. In fact, many sightings involve individuals migrating along the lakeshore on windy days, which may push them close to land.

The Red Phalarope is also found on mud flats with other shorebirds, and swimming in sewage treatment ponds. Locations which have been particularly productive for this species include the mouth of the St. Clair River at Port Huron, Pte. Mouillee, the Muskegon Wastewater System, and the piers and jetties along Lake Michigan from Manistee to Berrien County.

Complicating the identification of this species are the similar winter-plumaged Red-necked Phalarope and Sanderling. The Red-neck can be separated by bill size and shape and the general pattern of gray on the back. Separating Red Phalarope from Sanderling is an easy matter with a standing bird, but in flight these two look very much the same, and great care should be taken when attempting to identify flyby birds. —James Granlund

# POMARINE JAEGER

## (*Stercorarius pomarinus*)

The distinctive twisted ends of the central rectrices, which are so useful in identifying the Pomarine Jaeger on the ocean, are a rare sight on the immature birds typically seen in Michigan. The Pomarine is the largest of the three jaeger species. It breeds on the arctic tundra throughout the Northern Hemisphere and winters on the open oceans to the equator and less commonly farther south. It is a rare but perhaps regular migrant to the Great Lakes; however, complexities in identifying jaegers make its exact status difficult to discern.

The first fully documented record for Michigan was of a bird taken on 7 January 1941 off Granite Point, north of Marquette. The next record came 32 years later, when a bird was carefully documented at Erie Marsh, Monroe County, on 1–2 December 1973. Subsequently there have been 22 published records, of which 7 came from Port Huron, St. Clair County, 10 from Whitefish Point, Chippewa County, 4 from Berrien County, and 1 from Monroe County. Most of these records (15 of 22) occurred in the 1988–92 period. This increase in sightings may be due to the advent of a comprehensive fall survey at Whitefish Point Bird Observatory and a rise in the level of sophistication in the identification of jaegers.

The majority of the Whitefish records have occurred in September, while most of the records from the southern part of the state are from late October through November. This suggests that Pomarines reach the northern Great Lakes in August and September, remaining over open water until stormy weather pushes them farther south and eventually from the Great Lakes, although much is still to be learned about the occurrence and abundance of this species on the Great Lakes.

Nearly all the Pomarines observed in Michigan are either immatures or juveniles, making identification extremely difficult. Although characteristics such as flight pattern, size, and overall structure are useful in separating this species from other jaegers, great care must be taken to note all salient plumage characters, a subject well beyond this brief account. —James Granlund

# PARASITIC JAEGER

## (*Stercorarius parasiticus*)

The Parasitic Jaeger is named for its habit of stealing food from other birds, a behavior shared by all three jaeger species. The Parasitic Jaeger, or Arctic Skua as it is known in Europe, breeds on the high arctic tundra of the Northern Hemisphere and winters on the open oceans of both hemispheres. It is a rare but regular migrant to the Great Lakes.

The first definitive record of this jaeger in Michigan was of a bird taken on 28 September 1897 on Otter Lake, Lapeer County. Early historical accounts of the Parasitic, as well as other jaegers, are clouded by the difficulty of field identification. Norman Wood (1951) omitted all sight records in his volume "because positive identification in the field is difficult." The advent of the Michigan Bird Survey allowed the publication of such sightings, and the earliest records were of an individual from 23 September to 18 November 1945 at North Cape, Monroe County, and another the following year on 18 October 1946 at Port Huron, St. Clair County. There was not another record until 1962, when a bird was seen on 5 August on the Stonington Peninsula, Delta County, and in the same year seven were reported in autumn from Berrien County. This was not entirely surprising, since Parasitics were regularly being reported from Michigan City, Indiana, at the foot of Lake Michigan, throughout the 1950s. Between 1962 and 1970, nearly all jaeger reports came in October from Berrien County. By the 1980s, waterbird watches at several locations, including Whitefish Point, Chippewa County, and Port Huron, began to indicate that jaegers were more common on the Great Lakes than once thought, and of those that could be identified, most were Parasitic.

Today we know that Parasitic Jaegers are rare but regular migrants to Michigan, being most common in the fall. The only location where they have been dependably seen in the spring is Whitefish Point Bird Observatory. Nearly all records are from the last two weeks of May and are of single birds, although groups as large as three have been seen. There is one summer record of a bird on 4 July 1961 at Sterling State Park, Monroe County.

Of the 126 Parasitic Jaegers reported since 1945, 112 have been sighted in the fall, the majority from September to November. Of the 21 records in September, 19 have been from Whitefish Point. Many of the October records have come from the Lake Michigan shoreline, particularly from St. Joseph and New Buffalo in Berrien County, while most of the November records have come from Port Huron. Most encounters are of single birds or small groups of less than 5. Two exceptional sightings from Port Huron include 19 on 11 November 1984 and 12 on 14 October 1981.

The true abundance of Parasitic Jaegers is difficult to assess, as many jaegers seen along the Great Lakes are left unidentified as to species, though most are probably Parasitics. Additionally, one can only wonder how many of these pelagic birds stay too far from shore to be seen. Regardless, there is no greater thrill to a Michigan birder than to see an elegant Parasitic Jaeger beating past Whitefish Point on its way to the ocean. —James Granlund

## LONG-TAILED JAEGER

### (*Stercorarius longicaudus*)

The long central tail streamers of the Long-tailed Jaeger are truly remarkable; however, they are in themselves not a safe field mark to identify this species (because they are not always present). The best character on an adult is the contrast between the dark secondaries and gray back, while the identification of a juvenile or subadult is extremely difficult.

The Long-tailed Jaeger is Holarctic in distribution, breeding on the arctic tundra and wintering on the Pacific and Atlantic oceans nearly to Antarctica. Its wanderings to Michigan are documented by three specimens, one each from North Cape, Monroe County, on 21 September 1963; Keweenaw Bay, Baraga County, on 17 August 1965; and a juvenile from Whitefish Point, Chippewa County, on 19 September 1989. In addition there are three photographs: an adult on 16–19 September 1965 in St. Joseph, Berrien County; a subadult at Nayanquing Point, Bay County, on 16 August 1981; and a subadult on Drummond Island, Chippewa County, on 27 June 1985. There are also seven documented reports of adult birds in the period 1984–93, all of them from Whitefish Point Bird Observatory. Three of these are spring records, ranging in date from 11 May to 7 June, with four in fall, ranging from 5 to 19 September.

Of the three jaeger species, the Long-tailed is certainly the rarest in Michigan. Yet it is possible that the species is more common than reported. Many of the jaegers on the Great Lakes are subadults or juveniles and are left unidentified as to species; certainly the bulk of these are Parasitics, but some are likely to be Long-tails. Perhaps as jaeger identification becomes refined, we will get a better picture of the Long-tail's status. —James Granlund

## LAUGHING GULL

### (*Larus atricilla*)

Laughing Gulls are largely coastal in occurrence. In the East colonies exist from Nova Scotia to south Texas, throughout the West Indies, and south to the Caribbean coast of South America. Wintering birds occupy the same areas, but north only to Virginia. In the West there are colonies in the Gulf of California, and birds winter along the Pacific coast from southern Mexico to Peru.

The Laughing Gull was not recorded in Michigan until 1962 (Medley 1964); however, published records exist for every year since then except 1977. In Berrien County, the species is a rare spring migrant, casual summer visitor, and casual fall migrant. Elsewhere in the state it is casual in spring and accidental in fall and winter. At any time of year the great majority of records involve single individuals, with the remainder involving groups of two or three.

The earliest spring record for the Laughing Gull is 8 April, three weeks ahead of the next-earliest record (29 April). The spring movement continues through May into mid-June, with the species being recorded most frequently in the second half of May.

Laughing Gull records between mid-June and the end of September are restricted to the Lake Michigan shore of Berrien County. The species is encountered most regularly during the early part of this period, from the middle of June through the middle of July. Some of the June birds may be tardy spring migrants, and the August and September birds may be early fall migrants. However, with summer and early fall records being restricted to Berrien County, it is also reasonable to suggest that many or most Laughing Gulls observed during the summer and early fall are summering birds wandering about the foot of Lake Michigan.

Between 1 October and 15 December, Laughing Gulls have been found not only in the southwest part of the state but also in the southeast. The reappearance of birds away from Berrien County is suggestive of fall migration rather than local wandering.

Finally, there is one record of a Laughing Gull from 8 February 1986 in Ottawa County. This record may pertain to a bird attempting to overwinter. There is only one other February record of a Laughing Gull on the Great Lakes, from Ohio's Lake Erie shoreline (Peterjohn 1987).

Not surprisingly, Michigan has no breeding records for the Laughing Gull. However, an unmated female nested every year from 1984 through 1987 in an Ohio Ring-billed Gull colony (Tramer and Campbell 1986; Peterjohn 1989). Similarly, mixed Laughing Gull–Ring-billed Gull pairs were recorded during the late 1980s in Wisconsin (T. Erdman, pers. comm.). Such pairings may account for two Michigan records of adult birds thought to represent hybrid Laughing x Ring-billed Gulls: one on 4 June 1972 in Charlevoix County (University of Michigan Museum of Zoology) and another on 23 August 1992 in Monroe County.

Laughing Gulls are best found by searching through gull flocks at the St. Joseph and New Buffalo beaches in Berrien County. Searches are more likely to be effective if they are conducted in the early morning or on rainy or foggy days, when beachwalkers, dogs, and sunbathers are not present. For whatever reason, Laughing Gulls seem particularly likely to move from site to site, and so are more likely than other gull species to depart an area if disturbed. —Philip C. Chu

## FRANKLIN'S GULL

### (*Larus pipixcan*)

The Franklin's Gull was named for the explorer John Franklin, who led two British expeditions into Arctic Canada and Alaska (Mearns and Mearns 1992). It is the only gull species to grow a new set of flight feathers every spring as well as every fall. It is also one of two gull species whose primary breeding and wintering areas are on opposite sides of the equator.

The Franklin's Gull breeds in prairie marshes from western Minnesota and Iowa to northern Montana and eastern Alberta. Additional isolated breeding outposts exist south and west to Wyoming and California. The species winters mainly along the Pacific coast of South America.

In Michigan, the Franklin's Gull is an uncommon migrant and summer visitor on the Berrien County shore of Lake Michigan; it may also be an accidental winter visitor there. Along the state's other Great Lakes shores it is rare on migration and casual in summer. Occurrences away from the immediate lakeshore are unusual.

There are three early records for the Franklin's Gull: on 27 February in Berrien County, 11 March in Delta County, and 31 March in Berrien County. The individual from 27 February might have wintered on southern Lake Michigan; there is precedent for this species wintering on the southern Great Lakes (Petersen 1964). However, the individual from 11 March was probably moving northward (given especially its far north location), and the individual from 31 March may have been doing the same.

Excepting these three early records, spring-migrant Franklin's Gulls occur between 16 April and about 15 June. During this period the species is most often observed in the last ten days of May. Almost all observations are of single birds, but small groups of two to four have been recorded on several occasions.

The species occurs occasionally between 20 June and 20 August. What these occurrences represent is unclear. Some of the June birds may be late spring migrants, while some of those in July and August may be early fall migrants or individuals dispersing from breeding areas to the west. However, some may also be summering locally. Birds in first alternate plumage are the most likely candidates for summering nonbreeders.

The number of sightings increases between the beginning of September and the third week of November, suggesting that the main fall passage of Franklin's Gulls occurs during that period. Most fall reports are of single birds, and any group in excess of 10 individuals is exceptional. These numbers notwithstanding, the maximum count is an astonishing 228 on 10 November 1977 in Berrien County. This total has been questioned because it is an order of magnitude larger than any other Michigan count; however, similar sightings exist at other locations in the central Midwest, such as 600 on 6 November 1948 near Indianapolis, Indiana (Mumford and Keller 1984).

On occasion individuals of this species are reported through the third week in December, and there is a very late record from 10 January. Some of these records, particularly the latest ones, may pertain to birds attempting to overwinter.

The best search strategy for the Franklin's Gull is to scan the gull flocks loafing on the beaches at New Buffalo and St. Joseph in Berrien County. Searches are more successful when conducted during times when human disturbance is at a minimum, such as the first hour or two after sunrise. —Philip C. Chu

# LITTLE GULL
## (*Larus minutus*)

The Little Gull is an Old World species whose initial occurrence in North America was documented in 1887 (Dutcher 1888). Since then the species has been observed in most states and provinces, with reports being concentrated in the coastal Northeast and around the Great Lakes. A nest was discovered near Toronto in 1962 (Scott 1963), and breeding has subsequently been confirmed at a small number of sites in the Great Lakes region and Hudson Bay lowlands.

In Michigan the Little Gull was first recorded in 1965 (Fisher et al. 1966). Since 1971 it has been annual in the state, and the species is presently a rare migrant and casual summer visitor here. Individuals are usually observed along sandy lakeshores, except in late fall when they may also be found at river mouths and the warm-water outfalls from power plants. Inland occurrences are almost unknown.

Spring-transient Little Gulls have been recorded in Michigan as early as 11 April, but most pass through in May. Some of the few birds observed during June (late date: 22 June) may be moving north as well. Regardless of how these early-summer individuals are treated, the species has averaged about two northbound migrants per year since 1977.

Occasionally one of the birds appearing in late May or June lingers on Michigan shores for a period of weeks or months. These summer lingerers are supplemented by a small influx that begins in mid-July and continues through August and most of September. What this influx represents is unclear, since it is largely restricted to Berrien County, at the south end of Lake Michigan.

In late September Little Gulls appear at a much wider range of locations, signaling the beginning of the main fall passage. The passage peaks between about 20 October and 20 November, then declines to a trickle by the middle of December, the two latest records being from 23 December and 13 January. The species has averaged six southbound individuals per year since 1977, three per year at the foot of Lake Huron alone (D. Rupert, unpublished data).

Although Little Gulls are not known to nest in Michigan at present, nesting was documented in Delta County from 1976 through 1980 (Tessen 1976; Payne 1983). The Michigan nest records followed a series of nesting attempts along the Wisconsin shoreline of Green Bay (Erdman 1976; Robbins 1991), less than 100 miles south of the Delta County site.

Most Little Gull records pertain to single individuals, with the occasional group of 2 or 3. The only larger total was that of 17 birds during June and July of 1975 at the Pte. Mouillee State Game Area in Monroe County. The species associates with Bonaparte's Gulls on migration, though wandering individuals in the summer and early fall are often with Ring-billed Gulls. —Philip C. Chu

# COMMON BLACK-HEADED GULL

## (Larus ridibundus)

The Common Black-headed Gull is a Eurasian species that occurs regularly in the coastal Northeast. It has been annual in Ohio since 1978 (Peterjohn 1989), but remains an accidental migrant and summer visitor in Michigan. There are two acceptably documented spring records for the state, an adult on 2 June 1966 in Iosco County and a bird of unspecified age on 20 May 1987 in Berrien County. In addition, one well-documented summer record exists, a bird in first alternate plumage on 22–29 June 1991 in Monroe County. The remaining acceptable Michigan records pertain to single adults in the late fall or early winter: 24–25 November 1976, 15–29 November 1977, and 6 November–2 December 1978, all in Monroe County; 12 December 1981 in Bay County; 2–3 January 1982 in St. Clair County; and 4–5 December 1983 in Wayne County. The Monroe County sightings from 1977 and 1978 were at the same Erie Township site as undocumented singles in 1975 and 1979, and may pertain to a single individual. —Philip C. Chu

# BONAPARTE'S GULL

## (Larus philadelphia)

The Bonaparte's Gull, named for Napoleon Bonaparte's nephew Charles (Mearns and Mearns 1992), is the North American representative of a group of small hooded gull species. It breeds from Alaska across interior Canada to James Bay. Wintering is primarily coastal, from Maine and Washington to northern Mexico, but also occurs on the Great Lakes, especially Lakes Ontario and Erie. The species is an abundant migrant, uncommon summer visitor, and rare winter visitor on Michigan shores; inland it is a fairly common migrant.

In the Lower Peninsula, the spring's first Bonaparte's Gulls usually arrive between late March and mid-April (early date: 12 March). The passage increases rapidly, and single-site counts in the last third of April or first half of May may yield several thousand individuals. The most noteworthy spring count is that of 4,000 on 21 April 1968 in Berrien County. After mid-May the migration slackens, and the last northbound birds are recorded in the last week of May or the first week of June.

Along the Lake Superior shore of the eastern Upper Peninsula, the Bonaparte's Gull has been recorded as early as 30 April. In Chippewa County the heaviest movement occurs between 10 and 20 May, and late dates for spring migrants are typically at the end of May or the beginning of June.

By mid-June favored locations hold only one or two birds; usually these are one-year-olds. However, when suitable habitat is abundant, the number of summering birds may be much larger. In 1989, for example, water levels were drawn down in a Monroe County impoundment that occupied approximately one square mile; the dry flats that resulted drew hundreds of subadult Bonaparte's Gulls during June and July, with a peak of 790 on 30 June.

In July, often the middle or latter part of the month, adults and juveniles appear, signaling the arrival of birds from breeding areas to the north and northwest. Numbers remain comparatively low through August and September, and maximums in the tens are typical. Much larger movements occur in October and November. Along the southern Lake Michigan beaches, peak counts of hundreds or thousands of individuals occur between mid-October and mid-November. Peak counts in the Saginaw Bay area and western Lake Erie occur slightly later, between late October and the end of November, and favored sites can accumulate noisy, swirling concentrations in excess of 5,000 birds. The most impressive concentration on record is 10,000 on 31 October 1991 in Bay County.

By mid-December the late fall concentrations have usually dissipated; the notable exception is Lake Erie, where single sites can retain several thousand birds into the last ten days of December. In some years a few linger on the southern lakes into mid-January; more rarely, individuals are recorded in late January or February. A single bird reported on 3 February 1991 in Charlevoix County was unusual, because of both the mid-winter date and the far north location.

The Bonaparte's Gull can be recorded at any shoreline site, along inland lakes and rivers, and occasionally in agricultural fields with Ring-billed Gulls. Summering birds appear to favor sandy beaches and dry flats near water, while the large aggregations of late fall are found around river mouths and the hot-water outfalls from lakeshore power plants. —Philip C. Chu

# HEERMANN'S GULL

## (Larus heermanni)

The Heermann's Gull is a striking species from the Pacific coast of North America. Remarkably, it is an accidental fall migrant in Michigan; however, the likelihood is high that all three Michigan records pertain to a single lost individual. On 26 August 1979, a Heermann's Gull in second-fall plumage was discovered at Metrobeach Metropark in Macomb County. It remained there until at least 12 December. About two months later a Heermann's appeared at Lorain, Ohio (Pogacnik 1980), and remained for four weeks (Kleen 1980). During the autumn of 1980, an individual of this species was again located at Metrobeach. The individual, thought to be in its third fall, stayed from 24 October into early December. Shortly after its departure, a Heermann's reappeared at Lorain and spent the winter there (Peterjohn 1989). Finally, on 12 October 1981, a Heermann's Gull was found at Metrobeach for the third consecutive fall; this bird, an adult, was present until 1 November. However, the species was not observed at Lorain during the following winter; nor was it observed at Metrobeach in any subsequent fall. —Philip C. Chu

# MEW GULL

## (*Larus canus*)

The Mew Gull consists of four forms breeding across Eurasia and western North America. The North American race, *L. c. brachyrhynchus*, breeds across the interior from Alaska to Hudson Bay, and south along the Pacific coast to Vancouver Island. Wintering occurs mostly along the Pacific coast from Alaska to Mexico. In Michigan the Mew Gull is an accidental fall migrant and winter visitor. The state has four acceptably documented records: an individual in second basic plumage on 4–6 December 1987 in Berrien County; one in first basic plumage on 23–29 October 1988 in Iosco County; and single adults in basic plumage on 1 January 1993 in Berrien County and 24–28 January 1993 in Ottawa County. Plumage descriptions submitted by observers suggest that the two subadults belonged to the North American race, but do not allow the two adults to be identified as to subspecies. —Philip C. Chu

# RING-BILLED GULL

## (*Larus delawarensis*)

The Ring-billed Gull is Michigan's most familiar gull species. Along the shores of the Great Lakes it is an abundant migrant and summer resident; it is also a fairly common winter resident in the south, with abundance decreasing northwards. Inland the species is less predictable, but impressive local concentrations may form at landfills and in newly plowed fields.

In the late 1800s, authors such as Langille (1884) and Butler (1898) reported breeding colonies of Ring-billed Gulls on islands in the Great Lakes. Others considered the species to be a migrant only, and Ludwig (1943) was unable to find any Great Lakes nesting records for the years between 1906 and 1926.

In 1926 a small colony was discovered on an island in Lake Huron off the coast of Mackinac County. Subsequently other colonies were located, and by 1940 the number of breeding pairs in Lakes Huron and Michigan had increased to an estimated 20,000. These populations remained stable for the next 20 years. Then, between 1960 and 1967, the number of breeding pairs in the two lakes quintupled (Ludwig 1974). Low water levels were associated with this dramatic increase, the low water presumably exposing new areas for nesting. A similar expansion was observed in the other Great Lakes. For example, only one Lake Erie colony was known through the mid-1960s, but by 1984 ten colonies and more than 60,000 pairs had been located (Blokpoel and Tessier 1986).

Ring-billed Gulls breed not only around the Great Lakes but also across the northern plains, in a triangular area stretching between eastern Manitoba, northern Saskatchewan, and northeastern California. They winter on the Great Lakes, along the Mississippi and Ohio rivers, and along both coasts from southern Canada to southern Mexico.

In Berrien County in the southwestern Lower Peninsula, wintering birds are augmented by spring arrivals near the beginning of March, and in the Lansing area there are Ring-bill records between the second week in March and the middle of May. In the Upper Peninsula individuals appear at Whitefish Point in Chippewa County as early as 16 March, and the movement there is heaviest between mid-April and the end of May.

Ring-billed Gulls breed along all of Michigan's Great Lakes shores; however, most colonies are located in Lake Huron and northern Lake Michigan. A small number of inland colonies exist as well, with birds nesting along the dikes of man-made impoundments. Not infrequently Michigan colonies are large, with 1,000 to 5,000 pairs; the largest one contained 60,000 individuals, though more than half of these may have been chicks.

Breeding takes place over an extended period. For example, nests have been recorded on 7 May in Bay County, 24 June in Wayne County, and 4 July in Alpena County. Eggs hatch after 24 to 26 days, and the chicks fledge five to six weeks later.

During the summer, some nonbreeding individuals are also found along Michigan shores; most of these are subadults. In late June hundreds may be observed at favored locations, the highest count being 975 on 20 June 1992 in Berrien County.

According to Southern (1974), Ring-bills begin to disperse from their Great Lakes colonies in late July or early August. An influx into the southern lakes follows, and by October a shift toward Lake Erie is underway. This shift culminates in November, with western Lake Erie hosting "the largest Ring-billed Gull concentration . . . anywhere in North America," according to Southern. Massive aggregations of tens of thousands of individuals occur along the Monroe County shore, and the largest single-site concentration is 48,250+ on 21 November 1987.

In mild winters more than 10,000 birds may remain through the end of December at some Monroe County sites. More often, an exodus from western Lake Erie commences in late November, and by mid-January counts are typically in the tens or hundreds. Elsewhere in the state numbers are smaller still. A remarkably high total, especially for the northern Lower Peninsula, was the 1,500 recorded in Leelanau County on 12 January 1992. —Philip C. Chu

# CALIFORNIA GULL

## (*Larus californicus*)

The California Gull breeds across the interior West and winters along the Pacific coast. In Michigan it is an accidental migrant. There are two acceptably documented spring records, both of single adult birds: one on 26 April 1984 in Kalamazoo County, and the other on 30 April 1993 in Berrien County. In addition, six acceptable autumn records exist: a first-fall bird on 11 August 1948

*Ring-billed Gull*
*Herring Gull*
GIJSBERT VAN FRANKENHUYZEN

GIJSBERT
1993

in Iosco County; an adult in basic plumage on 20 December 1982 in St. Clair County, and another on 13 December 1983 in Monroe County; a first-fall bird on 17 October 1987 in Alger County; one in second basic plumage on 11 November 1988 in Berrien County; and a final first-fall bird on 16 September 1990, also in Berrien County.

First-year California and Herring Gulls are similar in appearance, while second-year Californias can be approximated by first-year Ring-billed Gulls. Field marks for young Californias exist, but should be employed with caution as they are largely overwhelmed by variation in the other two species. —Philip C. Chu

# HERRING GULL

## (*Larus argentatus*)

The Herring Gull is a widespread species breeding in North America, Eurasia, and North Africa. North American populations nest across the continent from the arctic coast to the Great Lakes, New England, and coastal North Carolina. They winter on the Great Lakes, along the Mississippi and Ohio rivers, and along both coasts from the Maritime Provinces and Alaska to Central America.

The species is an abundant migrant, summer resident, and winter resident along Michigan shores. Its occurrence even five miles inland is much less predictable. However, impressive numbers may gather at favored inland sites, including landfills and the St. Clair, Detroit, and Saginaw rivers. Not infrequently a few are found in plowed fields in the midst of aggregations of Ring-billed Gulls.

Herring Gull colonies are more evenly distributed across the Great Lakes than are colonies of the Ring-billed Gull, Michigan's other commonly breeding gull species. Both nest in Lake Huron, northern Lake Michigan, and western Lake Erie; however, Herrings also nest at numerous locations along the Lake Superior shore of the Upper Peninsula, an area that is practically devoid of breeding Ring-bills. As with the latter species, a few Herring Gulls nest inland along the dikes of man-made impoundments, in Muskegon, Missaukee, and Midland counties, for example.

Colonies as large as 5,000 pairs have been recorded in the state, but most have fewer than 300. The colonies are usually located on islands, and Ludwig (1962) suggested that breeding success is possible on almost any island that is predator-free: he found nests in habitats ranging from gravel bars to island cedar forests.

Incubation lasts between 28 and 30 days, and chicks fledge after an additional 35 to 40 days. Published data on the progression of breeding in Michigan colonies indicate that eggs are laid throughout May, with chicks hatching during June and fledging in July and early August.

The banding studies of Smith (1959) and Southern (1968) suggest that juvenile Herring Gulls disperse from their Great Lakes natal areas in the late summer or early fall; dispersal is in all directions but often shows an eastward component. Roughly two-thirds of the first-year birds remain on the Great Lakes to winter, but the rest begin moving south between November and January, eventually concentrating along the western Gulf coast.

Older birds do not move as far, and Smith (1959) found that most of them winter on or near the shores of the Great Lakes.

By November, numbers are peaking in most locations, including those in the Upper Peninsula, and counts exceeding 1,000 individuals are common. Some years see massive aggregations of more than 10,000 individuals develop, the most noteworthy example being that of 39,000+ on 21 November 1987 in Monroe County. The two best locations for this phenomenon are probably western Lake Erie and the Saginaw River in Bay City.

The large concentrations of November may persist into January, but usually begin to dissipate in December. However, the species remains fairly common to abundant along the shores of the Great Lakes, including Lake Superior. Even when the lakes are frozen near shore, tens or hundreds of individuals can be seen offshore along the ice edge, and a change in local ice conditions can result in the sudden appearance of thousands of birds near shore.

As the ice melts, any concentrations disappear as the birds presumably move north. The rate of northward movement is related to the rate at which the water opens, and movements through the St. Marys River into Lake Superior have been recorded as early as late February.

Finally, comparatively small numbers of nonbreeding Herring Gulls summer along Michigan shorelines. Most of these are sub-adults, and more than 100 may gather, usually in the company of summering Ring-billed Gulls. —Philip C. Chu

# THAYER'S GULL

## (*Larus thayeri*)

The Thayer's Gull has a checkered taxonomic history. The American Ornithologists' Union (AOU) treats it as a distinct species, but it has also been treated as a pale-winged race of the Herring Gull (Dwight 1917) and a dark-winged race of the Iceland Gull (Salomonsen 1950). Unfortunately, the AOU's treatment is based on a study (Smith 1966) that is coming under heavy fire (Gaston and Decker 1985; B. Knudsen in Barlow 1987; Snell 1989), and further changes in taxonomy may be forthcoming.

The Thayer's Gull breeds in the high Canadian Arctic from western Baffin Island to Banks Island. It winters along the Pacific coast from Alaska to northern Mexico, and sparingly east across the interior of the continent. The species was first reported for Michigan in 1977, and is now considered a rare migrant and winter resident in the state.

The Thayer's Gull has been recorded as early as 4 October, though first arrivals in the last ten days of October or the first ten days of November are more typical. Peak numbers occur from November to early January, when the large gull concentrations of late fall and early winter are present. However, even then it is unusual to record more than one per site; the highest total reported is three on 2–19 January 1992 in Bay County.

Numbers decrease in early to mid-January, concurrent with the breakup of the late fall–early winter gull concentrations. In March, however, the species stages a small influx, ending with a trickle of birds in April and May. The latest Lower Peninsula record is

21 April, and the latest Upper Peninsula record is 27 May.

The Thayer's Gull is almost always encountered along the shores of the Great Lakes or at near-lake sites that host large numbers of gulls. One of these sites, the Muskegon Wastewater System in Muskegon County, is the state's most reliable location for this species. There and elsewhere, the best way to find a Thayer's is to find a large group of Herring Gulls and sort patiently through it.

Thayer's Gull identification requires considerable care and a thorough knowledge of gull plumages, and observers are urged not to treat it more casually than is warranted. Useful discussions of identification are provided by Gosselin and David (1975) and Zimmer (1990, 1991). —Philip C. Chu

# ICELAND GULL

## (*Larus glaucoides*)

The Iceland Gull is a north Atlantic species with two races. *L. g. glaucoides* nests along the Greenland coast and winters primarily in Greenland, Iceland, and northern Europe, while *L. g. kumlieni* nests on eastern Baffin Island and winters primarily along the Atlantic coast of North America from Newfoundland to Virginia. Adults of the two races often differ in wingtip coloration: in *glaucoides* the primaries are whitish and unmarked, while in typical *kumlieni* they have restricted amounts of black or gray. However, the primary markings of *kumlieni* are variable, and may be reduced or absent. For a lavishly illustrated treatment of the variation in putative *kumlieni*, see Zimmer (1991).

In Michigan, the Iceland Gull is a rare migrant and winter resident. Many or most Michigan adults have dark markings in the wingtips and so are clearly referable to the race *kumlieni*. In a few, however the wingtips appear unmarked, making racial diagnosis impossible.

Iceland Gulls appear in Michigan as early as 8 November, with most arriving between the last ten days of November and the end of December. There is an additional report from the unusually early date of 17 September; however, validity of this report is difficult to assess, given the absence of documentation and the lack of other credible September records in the western Great Lakes.

Numbers are greatest between the last third of December and the first two-thirds of February. Even then, most reports are of single individuals, with an occasional group of two or three. The maximum single-site count is six on 24 December 1991–26 January 1992 in Bay County.

In many years the species is recorded into April, and in a few it is recorded into May, the latest spring report being 22 May. Some of the April and May sightings may pertain to misidentified individuals of more abundant species. For example, a white-winged gull in Berrien County during May 1991 proved to be a Ring-bill that was either abnormally pigmented or exceptionally faded (personal observations).

Iceland Gulls occur along Michigan's Great Lakes shores. They are almost unknown inland, except at a few near-lake sites where large numbers of gulls concentrate. The species is most effectively sought by finding large aggregations of gulls and working patiently through them. Two of the best spots to try this are the Muskegon Wastewater System in Muskegon County and the Saginaw River in Bay City. —Philip C. Chu

# LESSER BLACK-BACKED GULL

## (*Larus fuscus*)

The Lesser Black-backed Gull is a European species that was first reported in North America in 1934 (Edwards 1935). Since then it has been recorded in most states and provinces, with the majority of observations coming from the Midwest, the eastern seaboard, and the Gulf coast. Widespread occurrence in the western Great Lakes was initiated with first state records for Ohio in 1977 (Kleen 1977), Michigan in 1979 (McWhirter 1979), Illinois in 1980 (Kleen 1980), and Minnesota in 1984 (Eckert 1984).

In Michigan the species has occurred annually since 1986, and is appearing with increasing frequency. It is presently a rare fall migrant and a casual or accidental winter visitor in the state, and is also casual in spring and summer. All records pertain to one or two individuals found with Ring-billed or Herring Gulls.

Northbound Lesser Black-backs have been recorded between 3 March and 29 May, with an average of about two per spring since 1986; among these is the state's first Upper Peninsula sighting, on 29 May 1991 in Chippewa County. Spring migrants are most frequently encountered between the last ten days of March and the first ten days of May.

In 1988 an individual in third alternate plumage spent the summer in Berrien County. This initial summering bird was followed by six or seven others, most of them subadults as well. Such individuals appear as early as 15 June and as late as 22 August, and are known only from the Berrien lakeshore.

Presumed southbound birds have been recorded between 9 September and 16 January, with an average of about three per year since 1986. Five September reports exist, but four of them pertain to a single adult seen in consecutive falls at Bay City State Park in Bay County. If that individual is ignored, the earliest fall record is from 28 September, and the next earliest is from 9 November.

Most southbound migrants occur in November, December, and the first half of January. Observations are from all parts of the state but are concentrated in the Saginaw Bay area, southern Lake Huron, and western Lake Erie. Birds staying into January may be attempting to overwinter; however, overwintering has been documented in only two instances, on 28 December 1988–3 February 1989 in Bay County and 30 January 1993 in Wayne County.

A minimum of three subspecies are recognized for the Lesser Black-backed Gull: *L. f. graellsii*, *L. f. fuscus*, and *L. f. intermedius*. Of these, *fuscus* has been reported several times in North America, for example by Tessen (1985), but only *graellsii* has been collected here (American Ornithologists' Union, unpublished ms.). —Philip C. Chu

# GLAUCOUS GULL
## (*Larus hyperboreus*)

The Glaucous Gull breeds near arctic shores in both the Old and New worlds, wintering along northern coasts and in smaller numbers to the interior. In North America, breeding occurs from Labrador to western Alaska. Wintering occurs on the Atlantic coast from Labrador to Florida, and on the Pacific coast from the Bering Sea to California. In the interior the species winters south to the Gulf states.

Barrows (1912) was unable to find a convincing Glaucous Gull record for Michigan, but stated that "it undoubtedly occurs regularly during the colder half of the year." Subsequent field work has proven this statement correct, and the species is now considered an uncommon migrant, uncommon winter resident, and accidental summer visitor in Michigan.

In fall, Glaucous Gulls have been observed as early as 16 September, but in most years they are not recorded until the last two-thirds of October. By mid-November they are widespread throughout the state in small groups of four or fewer birds.

Numbers build slowly during the winter, and between the second half of January and the end of February, favored locations can hold as many as 8 individuals. However, at the local level, the pattern of occurrence may differ. For example, since the mid-1980s the large late fall–early winter gull concentrations near the Saginaw River mouth have yielded several counts of 20+ Glaucous Gulls, the most impressive being that of 75 on 4 January 1992. These high totals return to more normal levels as inshore waters freeze and the large gull concentrations dissipate. Curiously, the species is nearly absent from the large gull concentrations of late fall and early winter on western Lake Erie.

Glaucous Gulls are routinely observed in the second half of April or the first half of May, with a late date of 2 June. All records from 20 May or later are from the Upper Peninsula or northern Lower Peninsula. Most spring birds are seen singly, but small groups of 2 to 6 individuals are occasionally encountered, and the highest count that is not easily attributed to a lingering concentration from late winter is 10 on 19 April 1969 in Berrien County.

Glaucous Gulls have been recorded four times during the summer. One of these appeared in mid-June and was recorded through mid-August; the others were observed during the first two-thirds of July. Those for which plumage details are known were subadults.

In Michigan, Glaucous Gulls are typically found along the Great Lakes shores, and are usually associated with other gulls. They occur inland less frequently; such occurrences seem to require both a landfill at which the gulls can forage and a large body of water on which they can roost for the night. —Philip C. Chu

# GREAT BLACK-BACKED GULL
## (*Larus marinus*)

The Great Black-backed Gull is largely restricted to the north Atlantic shores of Europe and North America. In North America it has undergone a well-documented range extension down the Atlantic coast. Nesting was restricted to the Maritime Provinces as recently as the 1920s (Drury 1973), but subsequent southward expansion led to breeding records from Massachusetts in 1931 (Eaton 1931), Long Island in 1959 (Post and Restivo 1961), and North Carolina in 1973 (Potter et al. 1980).

The species has extended its range not only south but also west, establishing itself on the Great Lakes. Reports from most of the lakes existed by the turn of the century, but the first generally accepted Michigan record did not occur until 1928 in Monroe County, on the western shore of Lake Erie. By 1950 Great Black-backs were annual there, occurring between late November and late February in very small numbers.

The species is now a common migrant, fairly common winter resident, and uncommon summer visitor on western Lake Erie. Numbers there begin to build in late August and early September, with the greatest concentrations developing between the end of November and the end of December. Peak counts are in the hundreds, and the maximum recorded to date is 1,135 on 21 November 1987. In January numbers decline, and while they sometimes increase again during February, the aggregations that result are not as large as those in the early winter. By mid-April most individuals are gone from Michigan waters, and in June and July even favored sites rarely hold more than three birds.

Expansion into Lake Huron followed the pattern shown in Lake Erie: after an initial record in 1954, the species became increasingly regular in the late fall and winter, then began occurring at other times of year. It is now a fairly common migrant and winter resident and a rare summer visitor in southern Lake Huron. Abundance decreases northwards, though birds occur regularly to the Straits region.

The first Lake Michigan record, like the first record from Lake Huron, was in 1954. However, numbers on Lake Michigan have remained low, and single-day counts of more than two birds are unusual. The species occurs uncommonly from late November to mid-May and is rare or casual at other times of year.

Great Black-backs were finally recorded on Lake Superior in 1971, and are now found uncommonly in spring and casually in fall and early winter. In Chippewa County birds are observed between mid-April and late May, most of them within a few days of 1 May. They have also been recorded between late August and late December.

Despite prodigious increases in the number of Great Black-backs wintering on Lakes Ontario, Erie, and Huron, the species is only a casual breeder in the Great Lakes region. A paltry seven breeding locations were identified between the mid-1970s and mid-1980s, one on Lake Huron and the rest on Lake Ontario (Cadman et al. 1987, Andrle and Carroll 1988). Of these, only one had as many as four nests. Breeding was first recorded in Michigan in 1990, when a single nest was found on an island in Lake Huron off the coast of Mackinac County, and in 1992 four nests were found on another Lake Huron island, this one off Arenac County.

Great Black-backs frequent the shores of the Great Lakes, and are also found along the St. Clair, Detroit, and lower Saginaw rivers. At other inland locations they are casual, except in the southeast where inland occurrence is uncommon. The 15 in Washtenaw County on 20 January 1967 is an inland count without parallel. —Philip C. Chu

## BLACK-LEGGED KITTIWAKE
### (*Rissa tridactyla*)

Black-legged Kittiwakes are named for one of their common calls, variously rendered as "kitti-wa-ak," "kaka-we-ek," and so forth. They breed on northern coasts in both the Old and New worlds, dispersing to winter in the north Atlantic and north Pacific oceans. North American kittiwakes nest in two disjunct regions: from Nova Scotia and Greenland west to islands in the central Canadian Arctic, and along the coast of Alaska. Birds from Canada and Greenland winter as far south as North Carolina, while Alaskan birds winter as far south as Baja California.

Wood (1951) found no Michigan kittiwake record entirely satisfactory. However, in 1957 one was shot by hunters in Muskegon County, confirming the species' presence in the state (Zimmerman 1959). Kittiwakes are now known to be accidental spring migrants and rare fall migrants in Michigan, except at the south end of Lake Huron, where they are uncommon in fall. The species may also be an accidental summer visitor.

There are only three spring records for the Black-legged Kittiwake: singles on 28 May 1983, 5 June 1990, and 13 April 1991 in Chippewa County. One of these was in adult plumage, while a second was not; plumage of the third is unknown.

In addition to the spring records, there is a single summer report, of a bird on 30 July 1977 in Leelanau County. This report, if correct, is exceptional; it would be the only record from the Great Lakes region between 11 June and 11 August. Note, however, that a 7 July report exists from the upper St. Lawrence River (Goodwin 1976).

Black-legged Kittiwakes are annual in the autumn and early winter. Southbound birds have been observed between 19 September and 16 January, but most occur between mid-October and mid-December, with a peak during the first three weeks of November. First-fall birds dominate this movement, outnumbering adults by twenty to one (D. Rupert, unpublished data). However, adults are less distinctive in appearance, and so are more likely to be undercounted.

At most Great Lakes locations an autumn total of 5 kittiwakes would be considered good. However, at the south end of Lake Huron, where the lake funnels into the St. Clair River, 17 years of observations have yielded an average of 15 kittiwakes per fall (D. Rupert, unpublished data). The maximum number recorded in a day is 15 on 11 November 1984.

Kittiwakes are pelagic when not breeding. As a result, the best strategy for encountering one is to go to the lakeshore when there are strong onshore winds, pick a good vantage point, and spend several hours scanning the birds that are moving over the lake. Ideal conditions at the south end of Lake Huron are northeast gales, but any north or northwest wind that exceeds about 20 miles per hour could pay dividends as well. —Philip C. Chu

## SABINE'S GULL
### (*Xema sabini*)

The Sabine's Gull breeds along the arctic rim of North America and Eurasia, wintering primarily in the tropical Atlantic and Pacific oceans. In Michigan it is a casual fall migrant, and there is also one spring record of a dead bird found on 28 April 1983 in Berrien County (Smith 1983). All but three of the state's records pertain to birds in juvenal plumage. Southbound individuals have been recorded between 25 August and 11 January, with the vast majority passing through the state between 11 September and 13 November. However, the species is less than annual in occurrence, and when it does occur, the number reported statewide is usually 3 or fewer. The highest single-site total for one day is 5 on 25 September 1980 at the south end of Lake Huron (D. Rupert, unpublished data), and the highest statewide total for one year is 23 in the fall of 1991, 19 of them at Whitefish Point in Chippewa County. —Philip C. Chu

## [IVORY GULL]
### (*Pagophila eburnea*)

The Ivory Gull spends the year among Arctic Ocean ice, but in winter small numbers move south, penetrating casually to New Jersey, British Columbia, and the Great Lakes. The species has been reported four times in Michigan: a bird in first basic plumage on 12 January 1949 in Wayne County; one of unspecified age on 15 March 1963 in Berrien County; an adult on 31 December 1973 in Ottawa County; and an individual in first basic plumage on 21 December 1974 in Monroe County. The Berrien County record is undocumented and thus cannot be reviewed, but documentation for the other three was reviewed by the Michigan Bird Records Committee and judged to be unacceptable. Whether these records are correct or not, it seems likely that the Ivory Gull will appear in the state in future years, since thoroughly documented individuals have been recorded in Ohio, Illinois, Wisconsin, and Minnesota as early as 2 December and as late as 7 March. —Philip C. Chu

GIUSBERT—1993

# CASPIAN TERN

## (*Sterna caspia*)

Caspian Terns breed discontinuously across North America, Eurasia, Africa, and Australia. In North America there are colonies along the Atlantic coast, the Gulf of Mexico, and the Gulf of California, with inland colonies scattered across the Great Lakes region, the Prairie Provinces, and the western states. Wintering is coastal, from North Carolina to Venezuela in the East and from California to southern Mexico in the West.

Along Michigan shores the Caspian Tern is a fairly common migrant and summer resident. The number of pairs nesting in the state has increased over the last three decades, concurrent with a threefold increase in the Great Lakes population as a whole. Inland the species is an uncommon to rare migrant: for example, Kielb et al. (1992) report only eight records for Washtenaw County between 1987 and 1992.

In the Lower Peninsula, the spring movement of Caspian Terns is usually initiated during the first half of April, 5 April being the earliest arrival date on record. The movement is heaviest during the last ten days of April and the first ten days of May. Even then, however, it is unusual to observe more than 40 individuals at any one location, and if counts from known nesting areas are excluded, the highest single-site total is 140 on 24 April 1992 in Iosco County. By mid-May there is a decline in numbers, and at the end of the month the last spring migrants are passing through the southern part of the state.

Birds arrive in the Upper Peninsula as early as 18 April, and are usually present by the end of the month. Along Chippewa County's Lake Superior shore, the passage continues as late as 7 June.

Barrows (1912) indicated that Caspian Tern colonies have been known from the Beaver Island group (Charlevoix County) and islands near the tip of the Garden Peninsula (Delta County) since the 1800s. Colonies at these traditional Lake Michigan locations have occasionally been supplemented by others in Saginaw Bay and in Grand Traverse, Presque Isle, and Alpena counties, with the Saginaw Bay colony sites being occupied more regularly than the others. Writing in *The Atlas of Breeding Birds of Michigan* (1991), Ludwig suggested that nesting at such auxiliary locations is particularly likely during periods of low water in the Great Lakes.

Nests are located on level, open areas and are nearly always on islands. Eggs are typically laid in the first half of June but may be laid as much as a month earlier (Scharf 1983). Incubation lasts about three weeks, and fledging requires an additional 30 to 35 days.

During June and early July, Caspian Terns are sometimes observed far from any known nesting colonies. The best locations for such summering individuals are the Berrien County beaches and western Lake Erie marshes. For example, at the Pte. Mouillee State Game Area in Monroe County, one to four individuals can be seen throughout the early summer.

By mid-July Caspians are reappearing at most shoreline locations. Numbers peak in August or early September, with single-site totals of 15 to 40 birds being typical. However, larger totals are possible, the most noteworthy being that of 75 on 16 August 1970 in Monroe County. During the second half of September the fall passage slows, and by mid-October it is unusual to see aggregations of more than 5 or 6 birds. The species has been recorded as late as 28 October in the Upper Peninsula and 3 November in the Lower Peninsula.

With its large size (similar to that of a Ring-billed Gull) and massive red bill, the Caspian Tern is unmistakable. However, observers should be aware that a similar species, the Royal Tern (*Sterna maxima*), has recently been recorded from the shores of Illinois, Wisconsin, and Ontario. —Philip C. Chu

# SANDWICH TERN

## (*Sterna sandvicensis*)

The Sandwich Tern is found in both the Old and New worlds. In the New World it breeds along the coast from Virginia to Argentina; wintering is coastal as well, from Florida to Argentina in the East and Mexico to Peru in the West. This species is an accidental summer visitor to Michigan, with only one documented sight record.

Until recently, the only Great Lakes record for the Sandwich Tern was a 19th-century specimen from Ontario (Morden and Saunders 1883). However, during the late 1980s the species was recorded on the Great Lakes in four consecutive years. On 10 June 1986 an adult was discovered along the Lake Superior waterfront in Minnesota (Kienholz and Backstrom 1986). On 31 July 1987 another adult was observed, this time on the Lake Michigan shore in Berrien County. In 1988 single adults were recorded in southern Ontario on 24 April, 17 May, and 14–25 June (Coady 1988). Finally, on 26 April 1989 an adult was found on a Lake Michigan beach in Illinois (Binford 1993). L. Binford and others have suggested that all of these records pertain to a single individual that "wandered through the Great Lakes . . . adding itself to . . . state lists." —Philip C. Chu

# COMMON TERN

## (*Sterna hirundo*)

Common Terns breed in a broad belt across the Northern Hemisphere and winter from the southern portions of their breeding range to South America, Africa, and Australia. Populations in the New World nest from Labrador, James Bay, and northern Alberta to North Carolina, Vermont, the Great Lakes, and Montana. Wintering is coastal, from Florida to Argentina in the East and California to Peru in the West.

*Caspian Tern*
GIJSBERT VAN FRANKENHUYZEN

Appropriately, the Common Tern is a common migrant along Michigan's Great Lakes shorelines, while inland it is uncommon. The species is also a local summer resident. In *The Atlas of Breeding Birds of Michigan* (1991), W. Scharf indicated that the number of nests in Michigan waters decreased by 67% between 1960 and 1985, but Ludwig (1962) showed that such year-to-year comparisons can be misleading with respect to population trends. In any case, both Scharf and Ludwig recognized that expanding Ring-billed Gull populations pose a threat to nesting Common Terns, since the gulls may exclude terns from suitable nesting areas.

Common Terns arrive at least as early as 15 April in the Lower Peninsula and 20 April in the Upper Peninsula. Three earlier reports of uncertain validity exist, including a very early one from 16 March. The passage is heaviest during the first three weeks of May, with typical high counts of 50–200 and a single-site maximum of 1,000 on 16 May 1963 in Berrien County. By the end of the month, numbers of migrants are decreasing rapidly, though a few continue to trickle through during the first ten days of June.

Most of the state's breeding colonies are clustered in several regions: the Detroit River, northern Lake St. Clair, Saginaw Bay, the periphery of the eastern Upper Peninsula, and Little Bay de Noc. In addition, there are noteworthy inland colonies in Wayne and Midland counties. The colonies themselves are almost always located on unvegetated parts of islands, and many have been found on simple sand or gravel bars.

Colonies of up to 2,000 pairs have been documented in Michigan; however, Ludwig (1962) found that the number of nests at any one site is prone to extreme fluctuation. He suggested that the fluctuation is at least partially explained by routine changes in lake levels, which affect the size and availability of low-elevation reef and shoal sites.

Michigan nests are typically started between mid- and late May (Scharf et al. 1978), though initial failure may result in renesting attempts in which eggs are laid as late as 10 August (Ludwig 1962). Incubation requires three weeks, and fledging another 25 or 26 days.

A few nonbreeding Common Terns may be found summering along the state's shorelines, especially in Berrien and Monroe counties. In July, nonbreeders are joined by migrants and birds dispersing from the colonies, resulting in an increase in numbers. The increase culminates in the second half of August and the first half of September, with aggregations of hundreds or thousands of birds. The most impressive count on record is that of 8,000 on 5 September 1968 in Berrien County.

By late September numbers are decreasing. The latest Upper Peninsula record is from 3 October and the latest Lower Peninsula record is from 3 December, though there is an 18 December

record of uncertain reliability. Most of the Lower Peninsula's late records are from Monroe County, at the western end of Lake Erie. —Philip C. Chu

## ARCTIC TERN
### (*Sterna paradisaea*)

The Arctic Tern breeds from north temperate to high arctic regions in both North America and Eurasia, wintering at the opposite end of the world in high southern latitudes. In Michigan it is an accidental summer visitor and casual fall migrant. Acceptably documented summer records are: an adult in alternate plumage on 9 June 1981 in Bay County and another on 5 July 1982 in Monroe County; an adult in transition from alternate to basic plumage on 30 June 1989 in Monroe County; a bird in first basic plumage on 14–15 July 1990 in Monroe County; and an alternate-plumaged adult on 10 July 1992 in Berrien County. Convincingly documented fall records, all pertaining to single first-fall birds, are: 19 October 1989 in Chippewa County; 5 November 1991 in Chippewa County; 9–20 November 1991 in Bay County; 23–24 September 1992 in Chippewa County; and 6 November 1993 in Berrien County. Observers looking for the Arctic Tern in Michigan should be aware that many of its best-known field marks (gray underparts, all-red bill, short legs) are shared with the Common Tern, at least under certain conditions. Interested readers are urged to consult Kaufman (1990) or Hume (1993). —Philip C. Chu

## FORSTER'S TERN
### (*Sterna forsteri*)

Unlike the other terns that occur regularly in Michigan, the Forster's Tern is confined to the Western Hemisphere. It breeds in the Great Lakes region, at scattered locations across the Plains and interior West, along the Atlantic coast from Massachusetts to North Carolina, and along the Gulf coast from Louisiana to Mexico. Wintering occurs along the Atlantic and Gulf coasts from Virginia to southern Mexico and along the Pacific coast from California to Guatemala.

Wood (1951) described the Forster's Tern as a rare migrant and summer visitor in Michigan. However, he also conceded that, "since it is easily confused in the field with Common Tern . . . [it] is probably more common . . . than the few records indicate." Whether because of advances in field identification or because of a real increase in abundance, the species is now considered to be a common transient and local summer resident on the shores of the southern Lower Peninsula, with abundance decreasing northwards. Inland it is an uncommon migrant.

In the Lower Peninsula, the earliest spring date for a Forster's Tern is 25 March, but early dates in the first half of April are more usual. Numbers peak between late April and mid-May. Most spring counts involve 50 or fewer birds, and the highest total re-

*Common Tern*
GIJSBERT VAN FRANKENHUYZEN

corded to date is 250 on 15 May 1993 in Iosco County. By late May the spring movement is largely concluded, though a few individuals continue to straggle through in early June.

Little information exists regarding spring occurrence in the Upper Peninsula. The species is regular in the Straits region and along the St. Marys River. Elsewhere, however, its status is unclear, and there are only two records from the Lake Superior shore of Chippewa County, on 29 May and 2 June.

The Forster's Tern nests colonially in marshes. The nests themselves are typically placed on floating mats of dead vegetation, though receding water levels may leave the vegetation mat (and thus the nest) resting on mud (Scharf and Shugart 1984). Breeding has been recorded from the Straits region, Saginaw Bay, Lake St. Clair, and western Lake Erie; the largest colony in any of these areas comprised 240 nests (Scharf and Shugart 1984).

Data on the timing of nest initiation in Michigan are few, but suggest that clutches are completed between the second or third week in May and the second or third week in June. Incubation lasts about 24 days, and fledging probably requires an additional three to four weeks.

In the southern Lower Peninsula the species begins to accumulate at shoreline locations away from nesting areas between late June and mid-July. Numbers are highest in August and the first half of September, then decline into mid-November. Along the Lake Superior shore of Chippewa County, the species has been reported sparingly between 16 August and 3 October.

On western Lake Erie the fall aggregations are larger than elsewhere in the state, with a single-site maximum of 1,300 on 9 September 1990 in Monroe County. In addition, numbers there remain elevated for a longer time, and can exceed 100 into November. The latest Monroe County individuals are generally gone by the end of November, but two birds were recorded in December, the latest being 26 December. As there are no January or February records, such December birds probably represent very late migrants.

The Forster's and the Common Tern are similar in appearance. In adult alternate plumage the Forster's has white (rather than gray) underparts, and in basic plumage it has a white or gray (rather than black) nape. However, the situation is complicated by feather wear, molt, and age-related variation. For a thorough treatment of the identification of these two species, see Kaufman (1990) or Wilds (1993). —Philip C. Chu

# LEAST TERN

## (*Sterna antillarum*)

The Least Tern is one of several tiny tern species, each with a white forehead and pale bill. It is the only one found in North America, breeding on the Atlantic, Gulf, and Pacific coasts, along major river systems in the interior, and throughout the West Indies. The species winters along the Caribbean coast of South America and along the Pacific coast from Mexico to Peru.

Least Terns are casual summer visitors in Michigan. There are six acceptably documented records for the state: an adult in alternate plumage on 10 July 1943 in Monroe County; an adult on 4

June 1970 in Berrien County; a first-fall bird on 17–21 August 1986 in Monroe County; two adults, one in alternate plumage and the other transitional, on 29 July 1989 in Monroe County; a juvenile on 1 September 1989 in Monroe County; and an alternate-plumaged adult on 6 June 1992 in Iosco County. Most of these were encountered on bare mud or sand flats with other terns. —Philip C. Chu

# BLACK TERN

## (*Chlidonias niger*)

The Black Tern breeds in North America, eastern Europe, and western Asia. New World populations nest from the St. Lawrence River, James Bay, and northern Alberta to Indiana, Missouri, and the Great Basin states, moving to the coasts of northern South America for the winter. In Michigan this species is a fairly common migrant and local summer resident along the shores of the Great Lakes. It is also fairly common inland in extensive marshes with a mix of emergent vegetation and open water.

In the Lower Peninsula, Black Terns have been reported as early as 17 April, though they usually do not appear until the last week of April or the first week of May. The passage builds to a peak in the second and third weeks of May, but even then most observations of migrants involve single birds or small groups of 2 to 10 individuals. The earliest Upper Peninsula arrival date is 3 May. The species is a regular migrant along the north shore of Lake Michigan but is casual along Lake Superior, and there are only three spring records from the Lake Superior shore in Chippewa County, the earliest on 24 May and the latest on 13 June.

Black Terns breed commonly at some inland locations, most notably the extensive marshes associated with Higgins and Houghton lakes in Roscommon County. Other important breeding areas include Lake St. Clair, Saginaw Bay, the Straits region, and the river marshes of Muskegon, Ottawa, and Allegan counties. Marshes favored for nesting have a mix of heavy reed-beds alongside areas of open water, and large marshes are preferred when available.

The nests themselves are often located on floating mats of vegetation. The distance between nests is variable; Cuthbert (1954) found them to be at least ten yards apart in his Cheboygan County study site, an arrangement that he termed "loosely colonial." Most of the state's colonies have fewer than 30 pairs, with the largest one on record comprising 200 pairs.

Egg laying occurs in Michigan between late May and late July, and incubation lasts for three weeks. The young may fledge as early as 19 days after hatching (Dunn 1979), though Cuthbert

*Forster's Tern*
*Black Tern*
GIJSBERT VAN FRANKENHUYZEN

(1954) felt that the flying age was about 25 days in his Cheboygan County birds.

In the first half of July, the number of Black Terns increases along the shores of the Great Lakes. Numbers build to a peak in late July or early August, and under exceptional conditions impressive concentrations may develop, most notably that of 1,200 on 4 August 1991 in Monroe County. Hundreds may linger into early September at favored locations, but thereafter the movement wanes rapidly, and there are only two October records, the latest being from 5 October.

The Black Tern is declining as a breeder in Michigan. According to Adams et al. (1988), the decline has been particularly noticeable at inland locations. Decreasing numbers were also documented by Einsweiler (1988) in Cheboygan County and by the Michigan Breeding Bird Atlas in the southeastern part of the state. Likely causes of this decline are alteration and fragmentation of the state's wetlands.

With its black head, neck, and underparts, the Black Tern cannot be mistaken for any other Michigan tern. However, interested observers should familiarize themselves with the White-winged Tern (*Chlidonias leucopterus*), an Old World species that has occurred in Wisconsin, Indiana, and southeastern Ontario, and whose eventual occurrence in Michigan seems likely. —Philip C. Chu

# DOVEKIE
## (*Alle alle*)

There are two Michigan records of this petite, highly pelagic alcid. Both are substantiated by specimens housed in the University of Michigan Museum of Zoology. The oldest specimen is an immature female collected on 30 November 1881 on the Detroit River, Wayne County. The other is a female collected on 14 November 1939 on Stuart Lake near Marshall, Calhoun County. An unlikely visitor to Michigan, this species breeds along cliffs in the Arctic Circle, being most common in the North Atlantic. It withdraws from its breeding grounds to winter in the open ocean and is infrequently observed from shore. However, large storms may bring hundreds of these small birds inland, which may explain the two Michigan records as well as those in adjacent Great Lakes states. —James Granlund

# THICK-BILLED MURRE
## (*Uria lomvia*)

Based on the breeding and wintering ranges of the Thick-billed Murre, few could have predicted that this species would invade Lakes Ontario and Erie in 1896, 1907, and 1950. These invasions were documented in Michigan by specimens taken on 26 December 1896 near Gibraltar, Wayne County, on 7 December 1907 from the Detroit River, Wayne County, and on 29 November 1950 in Royal Oak, Oakland County. Sight reports from the 1896 and 1907

invasions indicate that literally "hundreds" of Thick-billed Murres arrived in the eastern Great Lakes, with scores of specimens taken in surrounding states. All of the birds collected were emaciated and had empty stomachs, pointing to an inability for these vagrants to find appropriate feeding conditions on the Great Lakes. What caused these major incursions remains a mystery to this day. Even more intriguing is whether they will happen again in the future. The Thick-billed or Brunnich's Murre breeds on cliffs throughout the arctic regions of the Northern Hemisphere and winters in North America on the ocean, from its breeding range south to the mid-Atlantic states and British Columbia in the Pacific. —James Granlund

# ANCIENT MURRELET
## (*Synthliboramphus antiquus*)

There are a surprising number of records for this small western alcid in the western Great Lakes region, including six in Minnesota, five in Wisconsin, and three in Michigan. The first Michigan record was of a beach-washed specimen found on 7 July 1965 along the Lake Michigan shoreline, four miles north of Lake Macatawa Channel in Ottawa County. The specimen was preserved at Hope College but was later discarded. The second record came on 25 November 1989, when an individual was discovered swimming in the waters off Whitefish Point, Chippewa County. The bird remained along the shoreline for several hours, being photographed and seen by several observers. It was spotted briefly the following morning but then disappeared. This species appeared again at this location on 1 November 1993, with a fly-by individual observed on that date. Inexplicably, the three Michigan records were of birds on the Great Lakes, while all the Wisconsin and Minnesota reports are from inland lakes. The Ancient Murrelet breeds in the North Pacific from Japan through the Aleutian Islands of Alaska and south to British Columbia. It winters offshore of its breeding range and as far south as Baja California. This species is known to wander, especially in autumn, and has been recorded several times in the eastern United States. —James Granlund

# ROCK DOVE
## (*Columba livia*)

The Rock Dove or pigeon is a common permanent resident of cities, towns, and farmlands in Michigan and throughout North

*Rock Dove*
*Mourning Dove*
GIJSBERT VAN FRANKENHUYZEN

GIJSBERT - 1993

America. This semidomesticated bird, originally native to the Old World, has been widely introduced to all continents except Antarctica. Introductions to North America began in the early seventeenth century, and the Rock Dove's current distribution includes southern Alaska, southern Canada, the entire United States, Mexico, and the West Indies.

Everyone is familiar with the pigeon. These plump, small-headed birds flourish around settled areas, nesting and roosting on buildings and bridges and foraging on city sidewalks, in parks, and around farms. Feelings toward these birds are generally mixed; there are many who enjoy feeding pigeons in the park, and there are many others who find them a nuisance and health hazard. Eradication programs in an attempt to reduce populations have had little effect.

The name Rock Dove refers to the rocky cliffs used for nesting by its wild ancestor. Remnant populations still utilize such habitats in remote coastal mountain ranges in northern Europe and the Balkans. For feral Rock Doves, any dark sheltered site located fairly high above ground is satisfactory, and the ledges, nooks, and crannies of human architecture offer a nearly infinite supply. Commonly used structures include building ledges, window sills, bridge beams, barns, and grain elevators. Occasionally, there are reports in this continent of pigeons reverting to natural nesting sites.

Rock Doves are sedentary, social birds, with pairs forming life-long bonds, living out their lives in the same area, and groups of pairs nesting and foraging together. Part of the pair-bonding ritual is mate feeding or "billing," in which the female's bill is placed inside the male's and the two bob their heads up and down. During this process the female receives regurgitated food from her mate. Nests are a simple collection of twigs and grasses gathered mostly by the male and presented to the female.

Most nesting in Michigan occurs from late winter to early fall, with two to three broods raised. Some pigeons in southern Michigan are able to breed year-round. Two eggs are the norm, and for the first few days after hatching the young are fed regurgitated food, known as pigeon's milk, before being started on a more substantial diet of insects, fruit, and seeds.

It should surprise no one to learn that Rock Doves are most numerous and widespread in the southern half of the state, where they were reported in 91% of the region's townships during the Breeding Bird Atlas. Distribution becomes patchy north of Bay and Muskegon counties, with birds locally common around cities and rural communities but absent from large areas dominated by forest habitats. By the time you reach the Upper Peninsula, Rock Doves are generally scarce. Most reports during the Atlas were clustered in the "Soo" area and in the south-central counties (Delta, Menominee, and Dickinson), with a lesser concentration in and around northern Houghton County.

We have little to no information on population trends or expansion for this species since it was excluded from most literature, primarily because its establishment predated most writings and because it was a feral rather than wild bird. The breeding bird surveys initiated in the mid-1960s were the first real source of data on Rock Doves. Michigan surveys from 1966 to 1985 indicated an increase in numbers, but one which was not statistically significant. Upward trends were, however, significant for the Great Lakes and eastern regions as a whole.

More recently, Christmas bird counts have also begun keeping track of Rock Doves, starting in Michigan with the winter of 1973–74. Numbers increased considerably in the first few years, but more observer effort (party-hours) and the addition of new counts account for this difference. During the 1980s, annual totals ranged from 10,606 (1983–84) to 19,411 (1988–89), and a slight increase was evident in both total numbers and numbers per party-hour between the first five years and second five years of the decade. —Gail A. McPeek

## BAND-TAILED PIGEON
### (*Columba fasciata*)

An accidental visitor to Michigan and the East, this pigeon regularly occupies a discontinuous range in western North America, breeding along the coast from British Columbia to Baja California and inland from Utah and Colorado south through Mexico to Central and South America. Michigan's only record is of a single, tailless Band-tailed Pigeon present from 24 December 1967 through at least 22 January 1968 at a bird feeder in Niles, Berrien County. It was suspected that the passage of a storm on its wintering grounds in the Southwest led to this vagrant's appearance. Photographs were taken, and even without a tail, the purplish head and breast, white collar, and iridescent greenish nape were diagnostic. Its apparent shyness was noted on several occasions, although this behavioral trait (more typical of wild birds) does not eliminate the possibility of a captive escape. There are records from other midwestern and eastern states and provinces (Minnesota, Indiana, Ontario, New Hampshire, and Maine among others), but some of these may also have been escaped birds. —Raymond J. Adams

## WHITE-WINGED DOVE
### (*Zenaida asiatica*)

The White-winged Dove is a resident of the southwestern United States, Mexico, and Central and South America, but wanderings from its usual range have resulted in records as far north as British Columbia, Minnesota, Ontario, and New York. There are two Michigan records of this accidental visitor, both from the Upper Peninsula. The first came on 10 May 1986, when a White-winged Dove was found at the Whitefish Point Bird Observatory (Evers 1989). Several other people also had the opportunity to observe this individual. The second sighting was at Copper Harbor in the Keweenaw Peninsula on 13 June 1987. This bird was seen at close range for ten minutes. The large white wing patches and short, rounded tail bordered in white make this species easy to distinguish from the familiar Mourning Dove. Currently there are no photographs or specimens of the White-winged Dove for Michigan. —Raymond J. Adams

# MOURNING DOVE

## (*Zenaida macroura*)

The Mourning Dove is one of a number of open-country birds which benefited immensely from settlement and the conversion of forests to farms and fields. This adaptable species breeds throughout the United States, north into southern Canada (casually in Alaska) and south to Mexico and Panama. Its winter range is similar except for a large withdrawal in populations from the northern edge.

Other than dense woodlands, which it avoids, the Mourning Dove finds a home in most habitats across Michigan, from open woods, evergreen plantations, and orchards to suburban yards, farmland, hedgerows, and roadside trees. Few species are as abundant, especially in the southern half of the state, and the dove's mournful "cooing" is one of the most familiar and frequently heard bird sounds of the predawn hours.

It comes as no surprise that the dove's summer and winter status in Michigan have changed appreciably over the past one hundred years. Around the turn of the century, this species was already an abundant breeding resident in the south, but north of the Saginaw and Grand valleys it was rare. By the 1950s, Mourning Doves had become locally common in the northern Lower Peninsula, and although there were scattered reports in the Upper Peninsula for a number of years, Zimmerman and Van Tyne (1959) commented on the lack of nesting evidence for the region.

Looking at the dove's distribution today, it is clear that populations continued their northward increase over the past few decades. Presently, the species is a common breeding bird throughout the Lower Peninsula and locally common farther north. Mourning Doves were reported in 35% of the Upper Peninsula townships during the 1980s Breeding Bird Atlas, with greatest concentrations in the south-central and easternmost counties and confirmations of breeding in seven counties.

The Mourning Dove's winter status has also changed, partly in its occurrence northward but more so in the overall numbers which overwinter in the south. In the early to middle 1900s, the species was a common winter resident in the southern two to three tiers of counties, and rare and local northward. Today, most doves still vacate our northern lands, but there has been some increase in those remaining around cities and farm buildings. It is not uncommon, for example, for a few hundred to winter in the Traverse City, Alpena, or Iron Mountain areas.

By far the biggest change in winter status has occurred in the size of the resident population, primarily in southern Michigan. Numbers encountered on Christmas bird counts have increased dramatically over the past three decades. During the 1960s, the average count per 10 party-hours was 19 doves, with annual totals ranging from 1,000 to 3,500. Contrast this with the 1980s, when the average per 10 party-hours was 56 doves (a threefold increase) and totals varied anywhere from 12,000 to approximately 30,000. Contributing to this increase is the greater food supply provided by bird feeders, grains left in fields after harvest, and cattle feedlots.

Even those Mourning Doves which migrate from Michigan for the winter reside here for about two-thirds of the year. This species is one of the first to arrive in spring, with the main flight from late March to early April in the south, and from late April to early May in the north. Small aggregations begin forming in late July, but the fall migration generally does not commence until mid-September and continues into early November in the southern Lower Peninsula. Flock size builds through August, commonly reaching 50 to 100 birds by the time of departure.

The nesting season for the Mourning Dove extends from March to October, with two or three broods common and some pairs occasionally raising four. The bond between males and females is strong, and mated pairs often remain together the entire year. Sexes share the two-week incubation, and when the young first hatch they are fed "pigeon milk" secreted by the parents before receiving more substantial items such as worms, insects, and seeds.

Anyone who has found a Mourning Dove nest was probably astonished by the seemingly flimsy construction of this simple twig platform. The two to (rarely) three plain white eggs are often visible through the bottom of the nest, which is typically located on a horizontal branch 10 to 25 feet above ground. Studies in Michigan and elsewhere have found evergreens to be the overwhelming nest-site choice. Thickets and vine tangles are also used, and sometimes pairs will opt for an abandoned robin, grackle, or other bird nest rather than build their own. —Gail A. McPeek

# PASSENGER PIGEON

## (*Ectopistes migratorius*)

When the last captive Passenger Pigeon (named Martha Washington) died at the Cincinnati Zoo in 1914, it marked the end of a species whose population once numbered in the billions. This was a bird touted to be the most abundant on earth, so abundant it was believed to be indestructible. Even John James Audubon believed the large-scale market killings were having no apparent effect. Then, in less than one hundred years, the masses of pigeons were gone.

The Passenger Pigeon formerly lived in the vast hardwood forests of eastern and central North America. Breeding occurred in the northern regions, from Hudson Bay south to Kansas and Kentucky, while wintering occurred primarily in the southern states. The colonies in which this species lived and traveled were of incredible size. One autumn day in Kentucky in 1813, Audubon watched a continuous stream of pigeons fill the sky from noon until sunset and figured he had seen more than one billion birds. Alexander Wilson, another well-known ornithologist of that time, observed a breeding colony in 1806, also in Kentucky, which stretched 40 miles long and from 1 to 3 miles wide and had an estimated 2,230,272,000 pigeons.

Before the lumbering and widespread killing, Michigan's hardwood forests hosted several massive breeding colonies which relocated from one year to the next, depending on supplies of mast, especially beechnuts and acorns. Thousands to millions of pigeons would appear in March and April and take up residency in the vast woodlands. The influx of birds was so large, it was said to have blackened the sky for hours. By the time nesting was underway in May, a single colony typically covered 20 to 40 square miles. Writings by W. B. Mershon (1907) and W. Barrows (1912) provide telling details about the location and size of some Michigan colonies in the 1870s and 1880s, including ones in Oceana, Charlevoix, Kalkaska, Emmet, and Benzie counties. The largest on record was near Petoskey (Emmet County) in 1878, in an area estimated at 150,000 acres and up to 100 nests per tree.

More astonishing than the existence of such enormous colonies are the stories about the slaughter of pigeons for food. Market hunting was widely practiced in those days, and thousands of people descended upon breeding colonies, shooting adults and collecting young pigeons, known as squab, by shaking the nest trees or chopping them down. From the 1878 Petoskey colony, an estimated 1.5 million birds (12,500 per day) were shipped by railway or boat to markets in Chicago, Detroit, and other cities.

Netting and baiting techniques, including the use of "stool pigeons," were also used on breeding and wintering grounds as well as during migration. Massive numbers of pigeons could easily be drawn to an area for killing. People even gathered on hilltops to knock migrating pigeons from the sky with poles, oars, or other weapons.

With the combined effects of decades of uncontrolled slaughter and removal of hardwood forests, Passenger Pigeon numbers plummeted. The flocks of millions vanished, first from one region, then the next, and by the late 1880s the species' survival was clearly in jeopardy. According to Barrows, Michigan's 1878 game laws protected pigeons on their nesting grounds, but there was no enforcement. Too late was the state legislature's 1897 prohibition of the killing of any Passenger Pigeons. The last Michigan nestings, which were among the last ever recorded for the species, were in 1886 (Missaukee County), 1888 (Wexford, Emmet, and Iron counties), and possibly 1896 (Otsego County).

Efforts to establish captive breeding populations were never successful, though a number of people tried, which is how the last-known Passenger Pigeon came to be at the Cincinnati Zoo. Thus occurred the extinction of one of the world's most abundant birds. All that remains of this colorful, long-tailed pigeon are specimens, pictures, and writings which tell both a fascinating and a sorrowful story. —Gail A. McPeek

# COMMON GROUND-DOVE

## (*Columbina passerina*)

This small, plump dove with rufous wings and a short blackish tail is an accidental visitor to Michigan. There are three records for the state, all from the fall season. The first occurred on 5 September 1966, when a Common Ground-Dove was netted and photographed on the Presque Isle County side of Long Lake. This bird, which is now in the collection at the University of Michigan Museum of Zoology, was erroneously listed for Alpena County by Payne (1983). The second state report was of an individual present in Marquette from 29 September to 1 October 1972. Most recently, good written documentation was provided

for a Common Ground-Dove found on 25 October 1991 at Whitefish Point, Chippewa County. This species is far from home when it wanders anywhere in the North. Its normal range extends from the extreme southern United States to South America. It is frequently found in human-associated habitats, such as farms, gardens, orchards, towns, and roadsides, and its general tameness around people suggests that out-of-range sightings might be escaped birds. Nonetheless, the number of sightings from the Upper Midwest and Great Lakes states, along with the pattern of fall vagrancy, implies that the large majority of Common Ground-Dove records are normal wild occurrences. —Raymond J. Adams

# BLACK-BILLED CUCKOO

## (*Coccyzus erythropthalmus*)

Often the only evidence of the presence of this secretive species is the staccato "cu-cu-cu" of its redundant song. It is probably a more common bird than most people realize. The Black-billed Cuckoo breeds from southern Saskatchewan east to the Canadian Maritimes, south to South Carolina, and west to southeastern Wyoming, with wintering primarily in northwestern South America.

In Michigan, this species breeds in small numbers throughout the state, being more common than its counterpart, the Yellow-billed Cuckoo, especially in the northern Lower and Upper peninsulas. However, in some years both species can be rather abundant, particularly in areas with caterpillar infestations. Cuckoos show a strong dietary preference for hairy caterpillars, such as tent worms, and the irruptive nature of these pests may account for the similar pattern seen in the occurrence of these birds.

Migrants typically arrive in the state in early May, although some may rarely appear in late April. Breeding primarily occurs from mid-May through June, but nesting has been noted as late as September in some years. Most individuals depart the state by mid-September, with some lingering as late as mid-October.

Black-billed Cuckoos breed in upland shrub and woodland habitats, typically in drier sites than those preferred by the Yellow-billed Cuckoo, although the two do sometimes breed in the same locations. The well-concealed nest of the Black-billed Cuckoo is placed in a deciduous or conifer tree, usually at an average height of six feet. The nest is notorious for its flimsy construction, yet it is sturdier than that of its close cousin. It is built of small twigs which are loosely woven together and then lined with catkins, dry pine needles, and similar material. A typical clutch consists of two to three greenish-blue eggs, which are incubated by both sexes for

*Black-billed Cuckoo*
*Yellow-billed Cuckoo*
JOHN FELSING

10 to 13 days. The young fledge in an additional 7 to 9 days. An interesting characteristic is that the parents routinely leave the eggshells in the nest after the young have hatched.

Like its Eurasian namesake, which belongs to a different genus, the Black-billed Cuckoo will, on occasion, lay its eggs in the nests of other birds. This nest parasitism is most often documented between the two cuckoo species; however, the Black-billed has also been found parasitizing other birds, including the Chipping Sparrow, Yellow Warbler, Northern Cardinal, and Wood Thrush. The Eurasian cuckoos are such specialists at this activity that they no longer even build nests. The only Michigan counterpart which goes to this extreme is the Brown-headed Cowbird.

The exact status and habits of the Black-billed Cuckoo are difficult to ascertain because of its retiring nature. For example, several observers have noted that the species seems to be absent from an area during the "prime" nesting season, only to be found there later in some numbers. It is unclear whether this is a case of true immigration into the area at a later date or simply the lack of detection earlier. In addition, comments in the Michigan seasonal surveys typically indicate that Black-bills are scarce most seasons but common during caterpillar outbreaks. Whether this is a result of birds actually massing in an infested area or simply becoming more visible while foraging in the open is difficult to tell. One thing that is clear is that we still have much to learn about this species. —James Granlund

# YELLOW-BILLED CUCKOO

(*Coccyzus americanus*)

Although the yellow bill of the Yellow-billed Cuckoo is a diagnostic field mark to separate it from its close relative the Black-billed Cuckoo, it is not always easy to see and is not present on young birds. To confound the situation, the two cuckoos have calls which are nearly impossible to distinguish. Luckily, there are some other means of differentiation we can use. Primarily the adult Yellow-bill's tail has a bold black and white pattern which is much different from the gray and white pattern of the Black-bill. This character is obvious even in flight. Additionally, the Yellow-billed Cuckoo has a great deal of rufous coloring in the primaries, something which is much reduced in its cousin. Also diagnostic is the Yellow-bill's song, which ends in a series of "ceow" or "kowlp" notes. Lastly, if you get really close you can see that this species has a yellow eye ring, whereas the Black-bill's is red.

The Yellow-billed Cuckoo has a much broader breeding range than its more northern counterpart, being found from Central America north to central California and diagonally east through the Great Lakes states to Maine. It winters in South America as far south as central Argentina and Uruguay. This cuckoo breeds throughout most of Michigan (except Isle Royale), being most abundant in the southern three tiers of counties and very rare once you reach the Upper Peninsula. It is the less common of the two cuckoos within the state. Determining the Yellow-bill's exact status is difficult because of its retiring habits and the complications with separating the two species in the field.

Spring migrants typically arrive in the first two weeks of May, although some may appear as early as the last week of April. The breeding season is protracted, with nest records as early as mid-May and as late as September. Birds begin departing in September, with only scattered individuals remaining into October. Exceptional was a bird discovered on 8 November 1980 in Kalamazoo County. It is rare to encounter more than one or two individuals in summer or on migration, but on occasion, small groups of Yellow-billed Cuckoos may be found foraging on caterpillars. An excellent example is the record of a group of 35 observed on 5 July 1974 feasting on tent caterpillars near the Muskegon River in Roscommon County.

The occurrence of both cuckoo species within the state appears to be cyclical in nature. Several researchers have asserted that these cycles are tied to outbreaks of certain furry (hairy) caterpillars, and there is some evidence adding credence to these claims. For example, in 1979 both cuckoos reached all-time highs on the Kalamazoo County breeding bird survey routes, a year in which there was a major outbreak of forest tent caterpillars in the county. In addition, there are numerous accounts in the Michigan seasonal surveys indicating increased numbers of cuckoos and corresponding caterpillar infestations, including those of the gypsy moth. The question remains as to whether these outbreaks actually attract more birds or concentrate those birds already present in the area, allowing for a greater degree of detection.

Yellow-billed Cuckoos prefer denser, shrubbier habitats than their black-billed cousins, often being found in marshy areas and along waterways nesting in willows or similar vegetation. However, they will also nest in drier areas and in the same habitat as the Black-billed Cuckoo. The nest is a very flimsy structure made of loosely woven sticks and twigs and then lined with catkins, pine needles, and other fibers. It is often so loosely constructed that the eggs can be seen through the bottom of the nest. Clutches contain three to four faint greenish-blue eggs, slightly larger and paler than those of the Black-bill. Incubation and nestling periods are similar for the two species. —James Granlund

# GROOVE-BILLED ANI

(*Crotophaga sulcirostris*)

This member of the cuckoo family is one of two ani species which occur in the United States. Of the two, the Groove-billed Ani is most known for vagrancy in the Midwest. There are at least seven reports for Michigan, all between 10 October and 14 November, making this species an accidental fall visitor. Six observations are from southwestern counties, including the first state record, of an individual found dead on 14 November 1951 in Allegan Township,

*Barn Owl*
David Mohrhardt

Allegan County, now a specimen at the University of Michigan Museum of Zoology. Other reports for the southwestern region are of individuals discovered on 3–4 November 1968 (photo) in Berrien Springs, Berrien County; on 20–24 October 1973 and on 27 October 1983 at the Sarett Nature Center, Berrien County; on 8–9 October 1975 (photo) in Parchment, Kalamazoo County; and on 5 October 1976 (photo) in Allendale, Ottawa County. Remaining state records include a bird collected on 12 October 1978 in Rogers City, Presque Isle County, plus an undocumented ani sighting on 1 October 1992 from Bruce Crossing in the Upper Peninsula.

The birds discovered in Allendale and Bruce Crossing were originally thought to be Smooth-billed Anis; the two species are nearly identical in appearance, and identification is further complicated by the near lack of grooves in the beaks of some Groove-billed Anis. The breeding range of this species extends from southern Texas and western Louisiana through Middle America and into South America. These birds are relatively weak fliers, and concern has been expressed that anis reaching our area may have done so by human assistance. While some birds may be escapees, the remarkable consistency in time of appearance within the Great Lakes region suggests otherwise. —Raymond J. Adams

# BARN OWL
## (*Tyto alba*)

One of two endangered owl species in Michigan, the Barn Owl appears to be nearly extirpated from the state as a breeding resident. This "monkey-faced" owl is found in temperate and tropical climates worldwide, with its North American range extending south of a line from southwestern British Columbia and southern Idaho through the lower Great Lakes region to New York and southern Vermont. While never common or widespread in Michigan, the Barn Owl was a regular, local resident in the southern third of the state during the early to middle 1900s. According to Zimmerman and Van Tyne (1959), there are historic breeding records for 15 counties north to Tuscola (1954) and Saginaw (1956).

The decline of this open-country owl began sometime in the mid-1900s. Several factors probably contributed, including the emergence of modern farming practices which decreased the availability of suitable grasslands. Row crops and other intensively managed lands are not adequate substitutes for the lightly grazed pastures, infrequently mowed hayfields, wet meadows, and native prairies required by the Barn Owl for hunting. Increased predation by Great Horned Owls, mortality from auto collisions, and several harsh winters in the past several decades are also mentioned as contributing causes.

In an effort to determine the Barn Owl's status and distribution in the 1970s, DNR biologist John Lerg contacted farmers through an agricultural newsletter. Respondents described the "barnie" as fairly common during the 1930s but indicated a drastic decline thereafter. During the 1970s, nests were confirmed in Berrien, St. Clair, Tuscola, and Monroe counties. The last strong-hold was in Monroe County, where pairs were primarily using erected boxes for nesting. A reported 17 young were raised by four pairs in 1975, with 6 young fledged from three pairs in 1978. The population apparently diminished over the next two to three years, with a single pair present until 1983.

There have been a scattering of records on a nearly annual basis since 1983. Among those documented are a bird found dead in a barn in Alcona County on 18 May 1983; one found injured in Midland County on 14 December 1986; another deceased bird recovered from a barn in St. Joseph County on 15 March 1987; and an individual which got caught in some wire in Delta County on 25 November 1992 (photograph). There are also some fairly recent unverified reports from southwestern Michigan in the fall and from Monroe County in both the summer and fall periods.

The Barn Owl is a medium-sized, "earless" owl with a distinctive white heart-shaped face and a mix of gold, brown, and gray feathers on its back. It is exclusively nocturnal, seeking refuge in tree hollows, barns, or other structures during the day and hunting at night. Laboratory experiments have demonstrated this bird's ability to successfully capture its prey, primarily voles, shrews, and mice, in total darkness.

Prior to European settlement, nesting sites for the Barn Owl were limited to natural tree cavities, holes in earthen banks, and cliffside crevices. The clearing of the continent's forests and the supply of nest sites provided by barns, church steeples, and other man-made structures were a great benefit to this owl, allowing populations to flourish in the 1800s and much of the 1900s. Pairs have the ability to nest year-round in warmer climates, with breeding in Michigan formerly reported from February to October. Clutches range from two to eight eggs, with an enormous difference in size between the first and last hatched young.

The future for the Barn Owl in Michigan is uncertain, to say the least. Its highly nocturnal lifestyle makes determination of its status exceedingly difficult. If any pairs are still nesting here, they do so on an extremely rare and irregular basis. Opportunities for recolonization are hampered by regionwide declines which limit the pool of dispersing birds. Barn Owls are also listed as endangered in neighboring Ohio and Indiana. There are currently no plans to reintroduce this species, as programs in other states have been unsuccessful, with released birds suffering high mortality. At this point we can only work to improve the quality of grassland habitats, an essential management need for many Michigan birds, in hopes that the Barn Owl may return. Observations of this species should be reported immediately to the DNR Endangered Species office. —Stephen Allen and Andrea Trautman

*Great Horned Owl*
*Eastern Screech-Owl*
GIJSBERT VAN FRANKENHUYZEN

GIUSBERT-1992

# EASTERN SCREECH-OWL

## (*Otus asio*)

This small tufted owl is a common permanent resident in the southern half of the state, becoming uncommon to rare in the northern Lower Peninsula. Nesting has been documented north to Montmorency and Antrim counties, and as of 1993 the only confirmed Upper Peninsula record is that of an individual found dead in a garage in Delta County on 15 March 1989. Michigan lies at the northern fringe of the Eastern Screech-Owl's range, which includes all states east of the Rocky Mountains, extending into southern Maine and portions of extreme southeastern Canada.

The presence of these owls is not readily determined. Their strict nocturnal habits make them an elusive subject. They do respond fairly well to a tape-recorded call, and this behavior has been utilized to more effectively survey populations throughout their range. Efforts to locate this and other owl species on the Audubon Christmas bird counts were intensified in the winter of 1973–74. Since then an average of 251 Screech-Owls per year have been reported, with totals ranging from a low of 151 on the 1978–79 count to a high of 420 in 1991–92.

Preferred habitat of the Screech-Owl is deciduous woodland with a sufficient supply of nesting and roosting cavities and adjacent fields for hunting. Suitable areas include wooded riparian habitat, farm woodlots, park-like stands or groves of trees, as well as our more wooded suburbs and urban parks. Large contiguous tracts of forest are generally avoided. Additionally, these birds seem to shun coniferous woods, which tend to lack suitable cavities. Where coverage of townships was good during the recent Breeding Bird Atlas survey, as in the southeastern and southwestern counties, Screech-Owls were frequently encountered.

Breeding in Michigan begins in early spring, with egg laying in April or May. Clutches can range in size from one to eight eggs, but the average is four to five in the Great Lakes region. Nesting cavities include natural tree hollows, abandoned woodpecker holes, and nest boxes located in appropriate habitat. The female does most or all of the egg sitting, but oftentimes the pair can be found roosting together in the nest cavity during the day. Parents will defend nestlings with surprising intensity when threatened. Fledging occurs mostly during June, but adults spend another one to two months providing for the young as they learn to hunt. When autumn approaches, those immatures which have survived will disperse to seek out their own territory. Except for these times of dispersal, Screech-Owls are highly sedentary birds.

Small mammals, birds, numerous insects, and a variety of other vertebrates and invertebrates make up the diet of the Screech-Owl. They will even venture into shallow water after small fish or crayfish. A behavior which has proven detrimental to this species is its habit of hunting near roadways, as many of these small owls are injured or killed by automobiles each year.

The "screech" in Screech-Owl came from one of the variety of sounds that this little owl makes. A "wake you from your sleep" screech is very seldom heard. The more common call is a wavering whistle/trill which is used during mating and territorial activities. The frequency of calling increases during the spring season, as the male and female conduct a duet of whistling trills, with the male taking the lower pitch. A Screech-Owl must be cautious when revealing itself, since it can become food for a passing Great Horned or Barred Owl.

This is Michigan's only small owl with ear tufts. It averages seven to ten inches in size. Females are slightly larger than males, although the difference is not nearly as pronounced as in the Great Horned Owl. An interesting feature of the Eastern Screech-Owl is the existence of two color morphologies (also called color phases). In Michigan, the gray morph appears to be about four times more frequent than the red morph. —Stephen Allen and Andrea Trautman

# GREAT HORNED OWL

## (*Bubo virginianus*)

The familiar evening call of the Great Horned Owl or "Hoot Owl" verifies its abundance in Michigan, despite the fact that it is rarely seen because of its nocturnal habits. A permanent resident throughout the state, this owl is common in the Lower Peninsula, with greatest numbers in the southern half, and generally uncommon in the Upper Peninsula, although still present in every county. No other owl is as widely distributed in the state, or in the Western Hemisphere, where it is found from the Arctic Circle to the tip of South America. A larger, paler subspecies (*B. v. subarcticus*) from the North is known to winter in the Upper Peninsula, as small numbers have been captured and banded at the Whitefish Point Bird Observatory during return flights in spring.

Deciduous and coniferous woodlands adjacent to openings provide suitable nesting and foraging habitat for this adaptable owl. Settlement and human influences on the landscape have added to the availability of Great Horned Owl habitat over the years by fragmenting the contiguous forests with open country. This species has even been observed in wooded urban parks, such as Kleinstuck Preserve, located in the city limits of Kalamazoo. Writings during this century indicate a definite increase in Great Horned Owls. Unfortunately, we have little in the way of concrete data to measure such an increase, since owls are not well represented in breeding bird surveys, and surveys and owling efforts on Christmas bird counts did not improve until 1973–74.

Great Horned Owls use old nests of large birds, most often those of Red-tailed Hawks but also Ospreys, Bald Eagles, American Crows, and Great Blue Herons, or they choose tree cavities or hollowed tops of trees. The nest is taken as is and may be selected as early as September or October, with the pair defending it until nesting begins. Breeding gets underway in the dead of winter, typically late January or February in southern Michigan and a few weeks to a month later in the north. The female does most if not all of the incubation, and must often sit through snowstorms and other severe weather. Clutches contain two eggs, or occasionally three, and the young vary in size and age depending on the timing of egg laying. Typically, the oldest and youngest owlets are several days to a week apart. Most fledging occurs in late April or during May, but the young remain in the parents' territory throughout the summer, receiving food and learning to hunt.

Like all owls, the Great Horned has superb vision. Even more acute is its hearing, with its enormous and asymmetrical ear cavities. These tremendous sensory capabilities combine with its large and powerful talons to capture a diversity of prey, including cottontail rabbit or snowshoe hare, both considered favorite items. Studies have found that northern Great Horned Owl populations fluctuate as hare numbers go up and down, and that major southward migrations coincide with down years in the hare's cycle. Other dietary items include voles, mice, skunks, and other small to medium-sized mammals, plus ducks, hawks, game birds, and other owls. Small house pets may also fall victim to a hungry Great Horned Owl.

The appearance of this owl makes it difficult to confuse with any other in Michigan. It is the only large owl with ear tufts, which extend outward from its head and are the source of another common nickname, "Cat Owl." Plumage is mostly brown with black barring and mottled whites, tans, and grays. Birds show a distinctive white throat which often extends down the belly, forming a V-shaped bib. The average size of a Great Horned is 22 inches, the weight is slightly more than four pounds, and the wing span is about four and a half feet. Sexes are identical in plumage, but females are larger than males by as much as seven inches, a pound in weight, and more than a foot in wing span. An angry glaring expression and glowing yellow eyes fit its status as the fiercest and most aggressive of the North American owls. —Stephen Allen and Andrea Trautman

## SNOWY OWL

### (Nyctea scandiaca)

The Snowy Owl is among the most recognized birds to visit our state in winter. These large white tuftless owls are found most regularly along the Great Lakes shorelines or in wide open spaces inland, including farmlands, marshlands, and airports—habitats most like their tundra home. They may even appear in some unlikely places, sitting atop a light pole in a suburban mall parking lot or on a city building.

The Snowy Owl is a denizen of the world's arctic tundra, with nesting in North America limited to extreme northern Alaska and Canada. Wintering occurs from the breeding grounds south to the northern tier of states and sporadically to California, Texas, and the Gulf states. In Michigan, the Snowy Owl is a regular winter visitor, but numbers vary considerably from year to year as southward movements are irregular and irruptive.

Snowy Owls begin arriving in Michigan in October or November, although individuals occasionally reach the Upper Peninsula sooner, especially during invasion years. At the Whitefish Point Bird Observatory, Snowies have been recorded as early as 1 and 13 September. Departure from the state generally occurs in late March and April, with stragglers seen into May. These late records typically follow major influxes and are most regular in the eastern Upper Peninsula. There are also occasional summer sightings in the state, which tend to involve injured or sick birds. Following the invasion of 1986–87, two Snowies were sighted on 4 July 1987: one in Holland (Allegan-Ottawa counties) and one in Mackinac

County. The former individual was later found dead in September, presumably hit by a car.

Seasonal surveys and other state records indicate that in most years, numbers of Snowies fall in the one to three dozen range, while large influxes occur every four to five years. The most recent invasion came during the winter of 1991–92, when more than 100 Snowy Owls were reported from over half of Michigan's 83 counties. These large influxes correspond to years when food supplies on the tundra (primarily lemmings) are severely limited, causing a mass exodus from the region. An incredible coast-to-coast invasion often described in the literature occurred in 1945–46, when more than 1,000 were reportedly shot in Michigan alone, either for trophies or as pests suspected of taking game animals. Such killing we now know is unfounded as well as illegal. The Snowy Owl diet consists primarily of small rodents. In an analysis of 40 regurgitated pellets from Snowies in the Traverse City area, researcher T. Allan found the main prey to be meadow voles (66%) and white-footed mice (18%).

It is likely that the majority of Snowy Owls seen in Michigan are young of the year, which are known to disperse a much greater distance from the breeding grounds than adults. Immatures have a much browner appearance due to dark bars and spots on their white feathers. Adult females are also a mottled white and brown; only the adult male birds achieve the nearly all-white plumage for which this bird is named. —Stephen Allen and Andrea Trautman

## NORTHERN HAWK OWL

### (Surnia ulula)

The Northern Hawk Owl is a rare and irregular winter visitor to Michigan. This boreal inhabitant breeds in northern climates around the world, and its North American range extends from the treeline in Alaska and Canada south to northern Minnesota and the St. Lawrence River in the East. For the most part this species is a permanent resident, but in years of depleted food resources, many leave the breeding grounds to winter in southern Canada and the northern tier of states.

Hawk Owls are not reported in Michigan every year, but during years when they do wander this far south, the first birds are generally noted in the latter part of October or November. The most reliable place to see this owl is in the Sault Ste. Marie area in Chippewa County. In a typical winter, numbers seen in the state range from one to a half-dozen birds, but during major invasion years numbers may be much higher. Hawk Owl invasions also reportedly follow a three-to-five-year cycle, but this pattern is not always evident in Michigan records, as influxes do not always reach our state.

The biggest invasion ever recorded in Michigan occurred in 1991–92, when an estimated 23 Hawk Owls wintered in eastern Chippewa County, with 15 around the "Soo." Other counties with reports were Mackinac and Schoolcraft, also in the Upper Peninsula, and Charlevoix and Gladwin in the northern Lower Peninsula. Historical records show that during past invasions, primarily in the early 1900s, this winter visitor was seen south to

Kalamazoo and St. Clair counties. No reports have occurred this far south in more than 50 years, and in fact, very few are seen south of the Straits.

Fortunately for bird enthusiasts, the Hawk Owl is primarily a daytime hunter, offering good looks for the hardy winter observer. This species is usually found perched atop a small tree, a snag, or a utility wire. These lookouts provide a vantage point to search open fields for voles, mice, and the occasional unattentive bird. The Hawk Owl is a medium-sized, heavily patterned owl with a long tail which is frequently cocked when perched. Both its appearance and its flight are decidedly hawk-like.

When these owls do visit northern Michigan, they generally depart by March or April, with some lingering into May. Following the 1991–92 influx, seven were recorded at Whitefish Point from 23 April to 9 May 1992, and another was seen in eastern Chippewa County until 12 May. One Hawk Owl even remained on Sugar Island (east of the "Soo") into July, and may very well have stayed the summer. In Minnesota, summering and nesting have been noted after major invasion years, and this would not be impossible for Michigan. Although there is no modern-day evidence of nesting that we know of, there is one confirmed breeding record for the state from 1905. According to Barrows (1912), a partially downy young was taken on 4 August of that year on Isle Royale, and an adult Hawk Owl was seen in the vicinity. —Stephen Allen and Andrea Trautman

# BURROWING OWL

## (*Athene cunicularia*)

The Burrowing Owl is an accidental visitor to Michigan, first documented in the state in 1949 when a specimen was taken on 2 May from Houghton County in the Upper Peninsula. Thompson (1982) cites three more records: a bird seen on 26 June 1965 in Kalamazoo County, a Burrowing Owl which was shot in May 1966 in Oakland County, and one observed on 24 April 1979 in Houghton County, about 15 miles away from the site of the first specimen. There has since been one additional occurrence in the state—a bird found on 7 June 1986 in a building in St. Joseph, Berrien County, which was taken to the Sarett Nature Center for examination and then released. The Burrowing Owl resides in desert and open grasslands in the western half of the continent, with a disjunct population in Florida. Northern populations are migratory, with vagrancy most noted in spring as birds return to their breeding grounds. This owl is like no other in appearance, primarily because of its long legs, which are used for digging out abandoned rodent burrows for nesting. —Stephen Allen and Andrea Trautman

# BARRED OWL

## (*Strix varia*)

An uncommon to common permanent resident in Michigan, the Barred Owl inhabits mature coniferous and deciduous forests across both peninsulas. This nocturnal raptor is found throughout the eastern United States and across the southern and central portions of Canada to British Columbia, Washington, Oregon, and northern California. It is closely related to the Spotted Owl (*Strix occidentalis*), a threatened species found in the ancient forests in the Pacific Northwest.

Within Michigan, the Barred Owl is generally widespread except for the urban and agricultural areas, which have little acceptable habitat and correspondingly few or no birds. Populations are highest where more extensive tracts of mature forest persist, primarily in the northern regions of the state or along river bottoms in the south. Both upland and lowland habitats are suitable, and studies have found that the average home range is approximately 700 acres. Not all territories need to be this large, but small fragmented woodlots suitable for Great Horned and Screech-Owls are not used by the Barred Owl.

Considered common at the turn of the century, the Barred Owl has declined in population as a result of the clearing of Michigan's old-growth forests. When Barrows (1912) wrote, he considered this to be the commonest large owl in the state, not the Great Horned Owl as is true today. It seems that Barred Owl numbers have rebounded somewhat since the low period of the middle 1900s, as regenerating forest matured and persecution of raptors abated. Maintaining large contiguous tracts of mature woodlands which provide a supply of older trees for nesting cavities is important to Barred Owl conservation. Placement of artificial boxes can also be a beneficial management tool where natural cavities are in short supply.

Common nesting sites of this owl are natural cavities, formed where a large limb has broken off and the heartwood has rotted away, or hollows in the top of a broken tree stub. Abandoned hawk or crow nests are also used. Very little is done to prepare the nest site, and the two to three white eggs are usually laid directly on the bottom of the cavity. Records for Michigan indicate that most egg laying occurs in March and April, with young fledging during June. Should the first attempt fail, Barred Owls are likely to lay a replacement clutch. Additionally, pairs demonstrate a strong attachment to the same nest year after year.

Most Barred Owls are year-round residents throughout their range, but there is evidence of a wintertime influx of Canadian birds into Michigan's Upper Peninsula, documented by observations and spring banding data at the Whitefish Point Bird

*Barred Owl*
*Northern Saw-whet Owl*
GIJSBERT VAN FRANKENHUYZEN

GIJSBERT—1993

Observatory. The peak period for passing northbound individuals is the last ten days of April, with the highest capture totaling 38 in 1984.

Distinctively mottled with shades of browns, grays, and whites, this large, round-headed, tuftless owl is the only Michigan owl with dark eyes; all others have yellow irises. It flies with a lumbering, easygoing motion, but can move quickly when pursued by a mob of jays, blackbirds, or crows. The Barred Owl diet includes many small mammals supplemented with opportunistic catches of birds as large as a grouse, reptiles, amphibians, and fish.

Next to the Screech and Great Horned Owls, the Barred is the most frequently seen resident owl in the state. Still, its numbers are low compared to these other two species. This owl's signature call is often described by the phrase, "Who cooks for you, who cooks for you-all?" It also produces a wide variety of other hoots, whistles, and grumbles, often ending with a prolonged descending note. Unlike most owls, which restrict their calling to evening and nighttime hours, the Barred Owl will call during the day, most likely an overcast one, which has prompted some to label it the "Rain Owl." —Stephen Allen and Andrea Trautman

# GREAT GRAY OWL

## (*Strix nebulosa*)

Often referred to as the "ghost of the north," the Great Gray Owl is a rare and local winter visitor to Michigan's Upper Peninsula, occurring only on very infrequent occasions in the Lower Peninsula. This retiring, often elusive owl inhabits northern conifer and subalpine forests around the world. In North America, its range encompasses much of Alaska and Canada east to Ontario, while breeding in the lower 48 states is confined to the northern Rockies and northeastern Minnesota. Its breeding status in Michigan remains unclear. Birds do oversummer in the Upper Peninsula on occasion, and there is one documented report of fledglings on Neebish Island (Chippewa County) in 1981. However, no active nest has ever been found in the state.

The number of Great Gray Owls visiting Michigan varies considerably from one year to the next. Years with one or no sightings contrast with irruption years when several dozen or more are seen. These invasions of Great Grays generally occur at three-to-five-year intervals, as large numbers withdraw from their usual range in response to "crashes" in prey populations, primarily voles, mice, and shrews. Species which undergo such periodic large movements are considered nomadic as opposed to migratory. The most recent and biggest invasion ever recorded in Michigan occurred in the winter of 1991–92, when an estimated 60 Great Grays were present in the eastern Upper Peninsula, doubling the previous high total.

These regal owls make their most regular appearances in the eastern Upper Peninsula, particularly around the Sault Ste. Marie area and on nearby Sugar and Neebish islands. Time of first arrivals is variable, with individuals sighted in October and even September in some years, or not seen until November or December in other years. The length of stay in winter is also unpredictable. Generally, Great Grays tend to arrive earlier and remain longer during invasion years, with departure occurring between March and May. At the Whitefish Point Bird Observatory, northbound birds are seen fairly regularly, with those springs following invasions yielding the highest totals, as in 1984 and 1992. Banding and observation data indicate that passage at Whitefish Point occurs primarily in May.

A look back through the Michigan records shows a scattering of observations from the central and western counties of the Upper Peninsula in addition to the numerous accounts in the east. There are also sporadic reports from the Lower Peninsula, including sightings from Emmet, Manistee, Roscommon, Huron, and Ingham counties since 1970. Nearly all of the historic records originate from birds shot for specimens or trophies. Such practices are now rare, although several were shot illegally during the winter incursions in 1983–84 and 1991–92.

In conjunction with the 1991–92 invasion, researchers banded 38 Great Grays and placed radio transmitters on 2 birds in the Whitefish area in an effort to learn more about their movements and winter behavior. To their surprise, one of the radio-tagged birds stayed all summer in a dense spruce forest adjacent to the mouth of the Tahquamenon River. This event marked the most recent indication of oversummering by a Great Gray in the state. The first documented summer occurrence was of a bird photographed in Emmet County on 2 June 1979. This was followed by summer records on Neebish Island each year from 1979 to 1982, with breeding in July 1981; at Trout Lake, Mackinac County, in 1982; and from Bois Blanc Island, Mackinac County, in 1984. Special platforms were erected in the Whitefish Point–Paradise area in 1990, but as yet none have been used for nesting.

The Great Gray is the largest of all owls in body size and wing span, yet it is a featherweight in comparison to the heavier Great Horned and Snowy Owls. Having had the chance to hold and band one, I was at once struck by how light the bird is and how dense its feathers are. The sight of a Great Gray perched atop a snow-shrouded spruce is something to remember, and it is no wonder this owl is highly sought by bird-watchers. Mottled gray, brown, and white plumage, a large tuftless head with circular facial disk markings, piercing yellow eyes, and a white "bow tie" are among its distinctive, memorable features. —Stephen Allen and Andrea Trautman

# LONG-EARED OWL

## (*Asio otus*)

The Long-eared Owl, a rare and local resident in Michigan, was recently accorded the status of threatened based on the scarcity of

*Great Gray Owl*
HEINER HERTLING

GIUSBERT-1993

records obtained during the 1980s Breeding Bird Atlas. While it was never a common bird in the state, historical data and writings indicate that it formerly nested in larger numbers and in more locales than it does today. This is a highly elusive owl, and surveys and research are greatly needed to document its true status in the state.

The Long-eared Owl is found throughout much of North America, being more widely distributed in the western half of the continent than in the east. Its breeding range generally encompasses the lower half of Canada west to eastern British Columbia and south to southern California, northern Texas, Missouri, and Virginia. The wintering range is similar, but with populations withdrawing from most of Canada and the southern limits extending to Mexico and the Gulf states. This species also has an extensive Eurasian distribution.

Breeding habitat of the Long-eared Owl includes mixed and coniferous woodlands with adjacent open areas for foraging. During the winter months adequate roost sites, usually dense conifers in either naturally occurring stands or plantations, are an important requirement. Studies conducted in Michigan show that both large upland and wetland openings are common foraging sites. Hunting is done exclusively during the nighttime hours, with birds quartering low over the ground in search of voles and other small rodents, which make up the bulk of their diet.

Abandoned nests, usually those of a crow or hawk, are typical nesting sites of the Long-eared Owl. These nests may be in deciduous or coniferous trees, although the latter are clearly favored. All five of the nests discovered during the Atlas survey were located in conifers. Territories are usually established in late winter, with the four to six glossy white eggs laid sometime between mid-March and mid-May. The male's territorial call, a series of low-pitched "hoo" notes, may be heard during this period. Where Long-eared Owls are permanent residents, individuals mostly remain on their territories throughout the year and use the same nesting area in consecutive years.

Based on the limited current information, breeding Long-eared Owls are mostly found in the southern two-thirds of the Lower Peninsula. In the past ten years, nesting has been confirmed in Van Buren, St. Clair, Clinton, Ionia, Isabella, and Oscoda counties. It is unknown if the lack of reports in the northern portions of the state reflects a real distributional difference or a detection difference due to the more remote nature of habitats. The lack of documented nests for Michigan as a whole concurs with results from other atlas projects published thus far, reinforcing the secretive and highly nocturnal habits of the Long-eared Owl.

The concealment abilities of this owl are commented on frequently by natural history writers. The superb cryptic coloration of light and dark browns helps conceal the bird in its wooded surroundings. Additionally, this owl will take on an elongated pose,

*Long-eared Owl*
Gijsbert van Frankenhuyzen

extending its long ear tufts so as to almost become part of the branch on which it is sitting. Keeping these characteristics in mind can help in searching for these owls in potential daytime roosting areas.

Along with our resident population of Long-eared Owls, birds from farther north migrate here in search of appropriate winter roosting areas. In fact, it is during the winter months that more Long-ears are reported in the state. Seasonal survey records include a fair number of winter records, mostly from Midland County south. Examples of some larger totals include 16 in Monroe County in 1970–71, 9 in Berrien County in 1971–72, and as many as 11 in Wayne County during late February 1986. Totals on Christmas bird counts since 1970 have ranged from a low of 1 to a high of 16 Long-eared Owls.

The most reliable location to observe this species is the Whitefish Point Bird Observatory, where an incredible 142 Long-eared Owls were captured in 1981. Long-term banding data indicate that the peak flight occurs during mid- to late April. Good numbers are also observed on clear nights during the two hours after sunset, as migrants leave their daytime roosts in the jack pines to continue on their northward journey. In 1991 a record high of 147 Long-eared Owls were detected on these "evening flight" counts, with a maximum of 26 seen on 23 April. —Stephen Allen and Andrea Trautman

# SHORT-EARED OWL
## (*Asio flammeus*)

The state-endangered Short-eared Owl is among the rarest nesting owls in Michigan. Fewer than five breeding pairs have been located in the past five to ten years, and with suitable habitat more limited, the outlook for this grassland and marshland owl is not optimistic. Most remaining open lands are now in an intensively managed state, which greatly affects the supply of small rodent prey and proper nesting cover for Short-eared Owls. Similar population decreases have been noted in other regions, leading to its listing as endangered in Illinois and Pennsylvania, threatened in Minnesota, and of special concern in Indiana and Ohio.

The Short-eared Owl has a cosmopolitan distribution encompassing all continents except Australia and Antarctica. In North America, breeding occurs throughout Alaska and Canada, with local nesting south to California, Kansas, Ohio, and New Jersey. Populations withdraw from the north, wintering across most of the United States. Michigan is situated within the southern and northern fringes of these two ranges, respectively. Currently, the Short-eared Owl is an exceedingly rare breeding bird and an uncommon migrant and winter resident in the state.

Breeding during the past ten years has been documented only in Chippewa County in the eastern Upper Peninsula. Much of this region has extensive grasslands, wet meadows, and open marshes, considered to be textbook Short-eared Owl habitat. Other recent summer and potential breeding records are from Gratiot and Isabella counties in the central Lower Peninsula and Lapeer, Tuscola, and St. Clair counties in the Thumb. In the early to mid-1900s nesting was documented in seven southern Lower

Peninsula counties, with eggs found in late April and nests with young or fledglings recorded in May and June.

The Short-eared Owl has always been more common in Michigan during the spring, fall, and winter seasons. Spring reports indicate that migrants move through the state primarily in March and April. Most sightings at any one location involve 1 or 2 birds, but occasionally sizable groups are noted. Recent examples include 13 on 3 March and 15 on 10 March 1990 in Lenawee County, and 31 on 31 March 1991 in Mason County. This latter count was part of an extraordinary report of 150 Short-ears which moved through the area between 28 March and 27 April.

The fall migration occurs during October and November, with occasional sightings in September. Eleven separate observations were reported in the seasonal survey in 1991. These came from widespread locations, including two at Whitefish Point, one each on 13 October and 3 November; two in Hillsdale County on 22 October; one in Bay County on 6 November; two in Mason County on 11 November; and one in Allegan County on 29 November.

Most winter observations of Short-eared Owls occur in counties south of the Muskegon–Bay County line. Rarely, individuals are found farther north, such as the 3 seen in Grand Traverse County in 1970–71 and 2 birds found on Christmas Day in Mason County in 1980. This species is encountered in small numbers on the Christmas bird counts, with annual totals since 1960 varying from 1 individual in several years to a high of 24 in 1975–76. During winter, Short-ears tend to congregate in communal roosts where large open areas provide ample hunting grounds. For example, during the winter of 1991–92, up to 16 owls were observed in a pine tree for over two weeks in February in the Coopersville area, Ottawa County. A total of eight counties had reports of Short-eared Owls that winter.

As in summer, small rodents are the primary prey of this owl during the winter months. In 1957, S. A. Reed examined regurgitated pellets from a large roost in Shiawassee County documented to have 32 birds on 14 February. His results found meadow voles and deer mice to be the predominant food items, with small birds being the only other prey mentioned as interesting to these owls. More diurnal than its long-eared cousin, the Short-eared Owl is commonly seen during the hours of dusk and dawn hunting over open fields or perched on a fencepost or haystack. —Stephen Allen and Andrea Trautman

# BOREAL OWL

## (*Aegolius funereus*)

This small owl of the northern boreal forest is an irregular winter visitor to Michigan, found primarily in the Upper Peninsula. Occurrence in the Lower Peninsula is extremely rare, and usually only in years that correspond with the largest invasions. As with other northern raptors which rely on small rodents, this owl's population experiences periodic southward irruptions every three to five years when prey populations on the breeding grounds are at a low point in their cycle.

Known as Tengmalm's Owl in Eurasia, this species has a circumpolar distribution in association with northern coniferous forests and muskeg communities. In North America it was previously referred to as the Richardson's Owl or Arctic Saw-whet Owl, the latter name derived from its close relations with the Northern Saw-whet Owl but with a range which extends into the arctic region. The Boreal Owl's distribution is, in fact, much more restricted to northern latitudes, encompassing most of Alaska and Canada but reaching south only to Colorado and northeastern Minnesota. Wintering occurs mostly within this range and irregularly south to the northern tier of states.

The Boreal Owl is a highly nocturnal and elusive bird. Compared to Snowy, Great Gray, and Hawk Owls, our other winter visitors, your chances of seeing this species perched in the open or coursing over a field are slim to none. It spends the day roosting in a concealing tree, usually a conifer, or in a cavity. Its Eskimo name Tuckwelinguk, meaning "the blind one," refers to the ease with which this tame owl can be approached in daylight, providing you can locate one. Black-bordered facial disks, a finely white-spotted forehead, and a yellowish bill distinguish the Boreal Owl from its slightly smaller cousin, the Saw-whet.

The limited number of fall records indicate that Boreal Owls generally arrive in Michigan beginning in October. During the recent invasion (1991–92) which involved several species of northern owls, researchers at the Whitefish Point Bird Observatory captured 20 Boreals between 15 and 21 October 1991, with a peak of 11 on 20 October. Winter sightings are extremely rare and irregular, and most reports listed in the seasonal surveys originate from recoveries of dead owls. Examples include an individual found in Mackinac County on 4 February 1958, a road kill in Presque Isle County on 8 March 1976, one in Oakland County during the winter of 1977–78, and two road kills from Emmet County in 1987–88. It is unknown how many Boreal Owls go undetected for every one that is found. During the 1991–92 invasion, four wintering birds were discovered: three in the "Soo" area (including Sugar Island) and one in Wayne County, only the second modern-day record for the southern Lower Peninsula.

Our best information on Boreal Owls comes from the long-term data collected at the Whitefish Point Bird Observatory during spring migration, as birds return to their northern nesting areas. The spring flight, monitored by nighttime banding, usually occurs during the last three weeks of April and the first two weeks of May. Year-to-year fluctuations in numbers can be dramatic, from a low of 1 bird captured in 1990 to highs of 163 in 1988 and 117 in 1992. The large totals in 1988 and again in 1992 corroborate the four-to-five-year irruption cycle of the Boreal Owl. Observatory data also show that the same migration route may be used, as an adult captured and banded in April 1988 was subsequently

*Short-eared Owl*
Gijsbert van Frankenhuyzen

GIJSBERT– 1993

recaptured in May 1992. Clearly, Whitefish Point is the place to go to see this secretive owl in Michigan, with the next invasion anticipated in 1996 or 1997.

The elusive nature of this strictly nocturnal owl has made documentation of its status difficult in Michigan. As far as we know, this species has not nested in the state, although the Upper Peninsula and Isle Royale are not far from its breeding range. Nesting has been documented in northern Minnesota only within the past 15 years, so the possibility of a Boreal Owl breeding in Michigan does exist, particularly in the eastern Upper Peninsula following an invasion year. —Stephen Allen and Andrea Trautman

## NORTHERN SAW-WHET OWL

*(Aegolius acadicus)*

The smallest of our Michigan owls, the Northern Saw-whet is an uncommon and locally distributed summer and winter resident. Determination of the exact status of this bird is exceedingly difficult because of its highly nocturnal and secretive nature. During the recent Breeding Bird Atlas, it was recorded in only 53 townships (about 3% of all townships in the state), with half of these in the Upper Peninsula. Yet when a concerted effort of nighttime censusing was made using tape-recorded calls, one observer located at least 18 territorial Saw-whet Owls during April and May in an area of Chippewa County.

Found exclusively in North America, this owl breeds in boreal and montane forests in southern Alaska, southern Canada, most of the western United States, and south to Illinois, West Virginia, and New England in the East. While some birds winter in the northern parts of the range, a substantial segment of the population migrates southward, wintering over most of the northern and central United States.

Winter populations of Saw-whet Owls in Michigan include both residents and an influx of migrants from farther north. Thick brushy tangles or dense conifers, such as cedar, are favored roosting sites. Birds typically use the same roost for days at a time, so once an individual is discovered, many observers can be treated to a look at this tiny owl. The rarity and reclusiveness of the Saw-whet are reflected in Christmas bird count totals, where only one to four have been reported in six of the past seven years.

Nocturnal netting and banding research at the Whitefish Point Bird Observatory in the northeastern Upper Peninsula documents fall migration from late August through October. This seasonal movement was demonstrated by the capture of an immature bird in Delta County in October 1991 and its recapture at Whitefish Point in April 1992. In just the past few years, there have been hundreds of Saw-whets captured at banding stations near Green Bay, Wisconsin, during the fall and early winter months, reinforcing the point that there is still much to learn about this species.

Records for the state indicate that the return flight north commences in March in southern Michigan and continues through April and into May in the Upper Peninsula. Numbers of spring migrants at Whitefish Point usually peak during the second two weeks of April, with the highest single capture of 12 birds occurring on each of two consecutive evenings, 21 and 22 April, in 1991. The average number of Saw-whets banded over the past seven spring seasons was 48, with a high of 75 in 1987. A few individuals are occasionally found into May and even early June in southern Michigan; these may represent late migrants or potential breeders.

Inhabiting moist coniferous or deciduous woods during the breeding season, this owl most often chooses abandoned cavities of the larger woodpeckers for nesting. A likely nest-site provider is the Northern Flicker. Based on limited information, nesting probably occurs in April or May, although a Tuscola County nest which fledged five young in May 1990 suggests a possible earlier start in the south. Clutches contain four to seven eggs laid at intervals of 1 to 3 days. Incubation, presumably performed solely by the female, is estimated at 21 to 28 days, with both adults caring for the owlets until they fledge at about five weeks of age. Investigations are underway by R. Bateson and researchers at the Whitefish Point Bird Observatory into the acceptance of nest boxes by the Saw-whet and possibly its cousin, the Boreal Owl.

Recent reports of confirmed or probable breeding of Saw-whets have come from widely scattered counties, mostly in the northern regions of the state. It is reasonable to suspect that this owl nests locally in all Upper Peninsula counties and on Isle Royale. The same may be true for the northernmost tiers of Lower Peninsula counties, but records are simply too scant to make any determination. Nesting has been documented several times in Alpena County, with two young fledging from a 1982 nest on 17 June. Other reported breeding confirmations have come from Benzie and Roscommon counties in the north and from Kalamazoo and Tuscola counties in the southern lower Peninsula.

The pint-sized Saw-whet feeds on small mammals, including bats, plus insects and the occasional songbird. A voracious eater, this species can consume up to twice its weight in one evening. When hunting, it must also be on the lookout or it may fall prey to one of the larger Michigan owls. Calls of the Saw-whet range from a metallic clinking, somewhat like an anvil ringing in groups of four, to the namesake call reminiscent of an old lumber saw being sharpened. This latter call is given exclusively during the nesting season. A characteristic which surely helps hide this owl is a ventriloquist-like ability to "throw its call," leading nighttime birders on some long and frustrating searches. —Stephen Allen and Andrea Trautman

## COMMON NIGHTHAWK

*(Chordeiles minor)*

The Common Nighthawk is a common summer resident in Michigan, found in our cities, towns, fields, and open woodlands.

*Chimney Swift*
*Common Nighthawk*
GIJSBERT VAN FRANKENHUYZEN

GIUSBERT—1993

It is perhaps best known for its erratic evening flights around city lights, as it captures insects on the wing. Actually, the name "nighthawk" is a misnomer, for it is neither a hawk nor exclusively nocturnal. This species belongs, instead, to the nightjar or goatsucker family and is largely crepuscular, concentrating most of its activity in the hours around dawn and dusk. The conspicuous white bars across its long pointed wings and a loud nasal "bzzzt," reminiscent of a woodcock's call, help separate the nighthawk from our other common goatsucker, the Whip-poor-will.

During the breeding season, the Common Nighthawk ranges over most of the United States and Canada, except for the high arctic and extreme Southwest. Winters are spent in the tropics of Central and South America. The nighthawk's Michigan distribution includes all counties with populations associated with open spaces which provide safe nesting locations. The flat roofs of city buildings have become especially popular sites. Other selected areas are forest clearings, fallow fields, gravel outcroppings, abandoned parking lots, and beaches.

Common Nighthawks begin arriving in Michigan during the first week of May, reaching the Upper Peninsula by the third and fourth weeks of May. Occasionally, migrants are noted the last few days of April, but reports on 14 April from Washtenaw County (southern Michigan) and Whitefish Point (Upper Peninsula) are unusually early. The nighthawk's stay is relatively brief, with fall migration commencing in August and usually complete by mid- to late September. Large flocks have been recorded during peak flights, such as the nearly 1,500 seen at Oak Park in Oakland County on 30 August 1982 and an estimated 1,000 counted on 8 September 1974 in Berrien County. A few stragglers are seen in the southern counties into October, with late dates of 29 October in Kalamazoo and 30 October in the Detroit area.

The aerial courtship display of the nighthawk is a spectacular sight. The male circles and hovers over the female, rising to considerable heights, and then dives toward the ground, producing a loud hollow "boom" or "quiver" with the primary feathers of its wings. The male may then land and advertise to the female by spreading his tail and flashing his white throat, all the while rocking and calling. This display is repeated through much of the night and each night of the mating season, which begins in late May to early June with nesting thereafter. Barrows (1912) noted that eggs are rarely laid before the first week of June.

The nest of the Common Nighthawk is nothing more than a slight depression in the soil or substrate. On rooftops, eggs are laid directly on the surface. The birds rely on their cryptic plumage to conceal the nest. The two white eggs with olive markings are incubated by the female for 19 days. A short time after hatching, the young are able to move around the ground or roof to take cover from the elements or predators, with fledging occurring in about three weeks. When adults have young to feed, it is not uncommon to observe them hunting during the day. Diurnal foraging is also common during the early spring period.

As in the past, the Common Nighthawk can still be considered locally common throughout the state. However, long-term data for Michigan and the Midwest as a whole indicate a decline in populations over the past several decades. Land-use changes in both forested and agricultural areas may be one factor contributing to the decline, primarily by limiting safe nesting places. The suppression of fire, which formerly kept many lands open, has probably reduced habitat in northern Michigan, as has the regrowth of forests in many areas. Increases in pesticide use to control flying insects are also frequently given as a probable cause. If we do not want these declining trends to continue, we need to take a closer look at the nighthawk's food resources and specific habitat requirements. —Dick Schinkel

## CHUCK-WILL'S-WIDOW

### (*Caprimulgus carolinensis*)

This large nightjar was, for a brief period, a casual migrant and summer resident in the state, with a decline in its occurrence since the early 1980s. Historically the Chuck-will's-widow summered in the southeastern and south-central United States and wintered from the extreme southern states to Colombia. The 1960s saw an increase in extralimital records at the northern edge of its nesting grounds, and these overflights precipitated a fairly dramatic range expansion in both the Northeast and the Midwest during the 1970s and early 1980s. Previously, the northern edge in the Midwest carried only to southern Indiana and southern Illinois. By 1980, as a result of this "leapfrog" dispersal, its range encompassed parts of northern Indiana, Iowa, the southern edges of Minnesota, Wisconsin, Michigan, and Ontario plus additional states in the Northeast.

The chronology for appearance of the Chuck-will's-widow was similar from state to state. In Michigan the first known occurrence came from Charleston Township, Kalamazoo County, when a bird was present for about a week in late May 1963. Nearly ten years later an individual appeared at Rose Lake, Clinton County, in August 1972. This was followed by a concentration of records from 1976 through 1982, beginning with the discovery of two individuals (presumably a pair) in Richland Township, Kalamazoo County, in the summer of 1976. During this period one or more territorial males were present each year in Kalamazoo County, with at least four territorial males at two sites in 1979 and 1980. Arrival dates for Chuck-will's-widows in the county ranged from 30 April to 19 May, and a few remained as long as 8 September. No effort was made to confirm nesting out of concern for the birds.

Along with these Kalamazoo observations, the species made appearances in Van Buren, Monroe, and Shiawassee counties between 1979 and 1982. Following 1983 reports for Barry and Hillsdale counties and a brief 1984 visit by a bird in Jackson County, verifiable records of this species have been nonexistent. It seems the Chuck-will's-widow has disappeared from Michigan as quickly as it came. Only time will tell if this bird will make a return to Michigan. —Raymond J. Adams

*Ruby-throated Hummingbird*
*Whip-poor-will*
CYNDY CALLOG

Cyndy Callog

# WHIP-POOR-WILL

## (*Caprimulgus vociferus*)

The Whip-poor-will is Michigan's other common nightjar, found in woodlands over much of the state but with an irregular, generally sparse distribution in the south. This nocturnal bird is best known by its loud "whip-poor-will" call, given in the evening and pre-dawn hours, and sometimes throughout the night. The Whip-poor-will can be easily separated from the more common nighthawk by its rounded tail and wings, absence of white wing bars, and black chin patch.

The Whip-poor-will breeds throughout most of the eastern United States west to the Great Plains, north to extreme southern Canada, and south to northern Georgia and Arkansas. A separate population breeds in Arizona and New Mexico southward into Mexico. Wintering occurs primarily in Central America, with small numbers staying in Florida and along the southeastern coastal region.

The Whip-poor-will is a bird of forest and forest edge habitats. The composition of the forest seems to be less important than its physical make-up. Preference is given to deciduous or mixed stands with a relatively open understory and little thick undergrowth. Dry to mesic conditions are chosen most frequently, but wet forests are also utilized. In Michigan these habitats are most plentiful in the northern Lower Peninsula, a region where Whip-poor-wills are still quite common. They are also fairly widespread in the eastern and central Upper Peninsula, becoming rare to absent in the western end. In the southern Lower Peninsula, breeding populations are less common and primarily confined to areas where large forested tracts persist, mostly on public lands, such as state game areas and parks, and along Lake Michigan.

Individual birds have been recorded in Michigan in early to mid-April (even 20 March in Kalamazoo County), but the peak spring migration of Whip-poor-wills begins in late April and early May. They are normally silent upon arrival, but it is not long before their distinctive calls can be heard, although periods of cold weather may delay the start of these nighttime serenades. The fall migration occurs primarily during September, sometimes continuing into mid-October in the south. Rarely are Whip-poor-wills seen in large numbers, but on 14 September 1988 as many as 100 were counted in two hours at Port Sheldon, Ottawa County.

Nesting begins in earnest in late May and continues through June. Courtship activity begins with calling by a territorial male. When a female lands nearby, the male performs a series of bobbing and weaving displays while the female "chuckles" and fans her tail and wings. Moonlit nights, during which males are most vocal, offer the best opportunities to observe these mating rituals, as well as the birds' nighttime foraging skills as they snatch flying insects from the air.

No nest is built by the Whip-poor-will. Instead the two whitish eggs with brown spots are laid on the ground among dead leaves, usually where they are hidden by some overhanging vegetation. The female's mottled brown plumage provides superb camouflage. The eggs hatch in about three weeks, and the semiprecocial chicks are on their own in another three weeks. The female cares for the family by herself.

Prior to the early 1800s, the Whip-poor-will and Common Nighthawk were thought to be the same species with different song versions. This illustrates the similarities of the two and the fact that the Whip-poor-will is frequently heard but rarely seen. With some luck, you may happen upon a Whip-poor-will during the day sitting on a horizontal limb, fencepost, power line, or on the ground.

There is no doubt that this mysterious nocturnal bird has declined in Michigan over much of the past century because of the loss of woodland habitat. Both Wood (1951) and Zimmerman and Van Tyne (1959) considered it less common than formerly. Its absence is especially evident in many parts of southern Michigan where the altered landscape has become inhospitable. Reforestation has likely improved habitat availability in some regions of the state, but elsewhere continued fragmentation of wooded areas has done just the opposite. —Dick Schinkel

# CHIMNEY SWIFT

## (*Chaetura pelagica*)

The easiest way to describe the Chimney Swift is as a short cigar with wings. Flying with rapid wing beats, this small, dark bird is a familiar sight around our cities, towns, and neighborhoods because of its habit of nesting in chimneys. The breeding range of this swift encompasses the entire eastern United States from Texas north into southern Canada. A long-distance migrant, this species is known to winter only in Peru, Chile, and Brazil.

Historically limited to nesting in hollow trees, caves, and protected rock faces, the Chimney Swift has adapted to various man-made structures. These include chimneys, silos, shafts, barns, garages, and other buildings. Given its use of these structures, one would expect to see a concentration of swifts in populated areas. This is true in the Lower Peninsula as greatest densities are found in the urban and suburban centers of the south, with birds becoming more sparsely distributed in the north. However, the species is also common and widespread in the Upper Peninsula, where comparatively few people live. This indicates that hollow trees and other natural sites are still being widely utilized. Breeding bird surveys show that swift populations are holding steady and in some areas are probably increasing in response to urban and suburban sprawl.

The first Chimney Swifts arrive in Michigan during the middle of April, with migration beginning in earnest by the first week of May. The earliest published spring record is 5 April 1981 in the Detroit area. During mid-May, when numbers are at their peak, observers have reported large flocks going to roost, such as the estimated 1,000 recorded entering a large chimney in Holland, Ottawa County. The return flight south typically gets underway in late August, with numbers building in September and the last migrants mostly gone by early October. As in spring, sizable flocks can be seen in fall. In 1978, a mass of 1,000 were counted in ten minutes on 5 October at Sterling State Park. A straggler found in Ann Arbor on 2 November 1987 is the latest known date.

Nesting begins in early June, when the four to five pure white eggs are laid in a small nest of sticks glued together with saliva and attached to the wall of a chimney or other surface. Both sexes share incubation, which takes about three weeks. Most of the time Chimney Swifts nest in colonies, even if there are only two or three pairs. It is also common for pairs to have the help of nonbreeders in the colony, in feeding the young and possibly with incubation. The altricial young may take more than four weeks to fledge, but at two to three weeks of age the nestlings begin to climb about the nest area using their long, sharp claws. As the young grow, they become increasingly active and noisy, as people who have a Chimney Swift nesting in their chimney can attest. You can follow the young's movements by the sounds they make, and it is also quite apparent by the silence as to when they have fledged.

Except when roosting, Chimney Swifts spend most of their lives in the air. Very rarely do you see these birds sitting still; they even fetch the twigs used to build their nests by swooping down and picking them up in their beaks or breaking them off a tree with their feet. Like most birds that feed on the wing, when the weather is fair swifts forage high in the air, whereas overcast conditions force them to feed closer to the ground. Since insect life tends to be more abundant in aquatic habitats, you can frequently find swifts feeding over lakes and streams, most often at dawn and dusk. —Dick Schinkel

# WHITE-THROATED SWIFT

## (*Aeronautes saxatalis*)

The White-throated Swift belongs on the Michigan bird list by virtue of a male specimen obtained at Hillsdale College in August 1926, when a bird was captured alive in a laboratory building on campus. There have been two other reports for the state, one of which was mentioned in Payne's distributional checklist (1983), but the descriptions are incomplete and not definitive even though the circumstances are plausible. This accidental visitant has not been recorded elsewhere in the Great Lakes. White-throated Swifts reside in the western part of the continent, breeding in the mountainous country from southern British Columbia south through the western United States to Central America. —Raymond J. Adams

# RUBY-THROATED HUMMINGBIRD

## (*Archilochus colubris*)

Of the more than 20 hummingbird species in North America, only the Ruby-throat is regularly found in the eastern half. Its breeding range extends into the lower parts of southern and central Canada and includes all of the eastern states south to Florida and Texas. Weighing less than a penny, the Ruby-throated Hummingbird is the smallest of our Michigan birds. Its plumage is a shiny metallic green above with white below. Only the adult males have the bright iridescent red throat.

*The Atlas of Breeding Birds of Michigan* indicates that the Ruby-throat is "well distributed throughout the state, breeding with almost equal frequency in each of the state's three major regions." Greater numbers are typically recorded in populated areas of the southern Lower Peninsula, although it is difficult to discern if this is a real pattern of abundance or the result of more observers and more hummingbird feeders which improve its detectability.

The habitat requirements of this tiny bird are fairly simple, being either a deciduous or mixed forest which can be open or fairly dense. Breeding also occurs in woodland edges, orchards, and parks and residential areas with large shade trees. Numerous authors indicate a preference for areas near water. It has been speculated that one reason for this association is to make use of willow down found near lakes and streams for nest lining. Because of this species' frequent selection of woods in aquatic areas, it has become popular for riverside and lakeside cottages to sport hummingbird feeders.

Spring arrival to Michigan usually begins in the last week of April, although a few records exist for a week or two earlier. Migration is heaviest in May, with birds reaching the Upper Peninsula by mid-May. Bird-watchers at Tawas Point in Iosco County tallied 100 hummers on 18–19 May 1989. Some studies suggest that the time of migration is somewhat related to that of the Yellow-bellied Sapsucker, with hummingbirds arriving after sapsuckers, taking advantage of the newly-flowing sapwells.

Courtship begins as soon as both sexes have arrived at the breeding territory, but nesting may not occur until later in summer. The male performs a diving, U-shaped flight in front of the female, hovering briefly at each tip of the "U." The female eventually joins the male in a face-off flight up and down, usually ending with copulation on the ground. After mating, the male plays no further role in the nesting cycle and often goes off to mate with other females.

Females build a tiny nest of lichens, bark and plant fibers, and spider webs, lining it with soft plant down. They often settle in the same territory in subsequent years, building a new nest or possibly refurbishing an old one. Nests are usually placed on a branch which angles slightly downward near or over water, at average heights of 10 to 20 feet. The two eggs are incubated for about 14 days. The young are fed a diet of insect protein and nectar and apparently fledge in about 16 to 20 days, although the timing may be longer or shorter depending on food supplies. Most nesting occurs in June and July, and occasionally into August. A nest discovered on 20 August 1970 in St. Clair County still contained young not yet ready to fledge.

Many homeowners landscape their yards to provide habitat attractive to hummingbirds. A wide variety of red and orange tubular flowers can be planted to bloom continuously throughout the spring and summer. Once birds are frequenting these flowers, they can be drawn to a feeder with a 20–25% solution of sugar water. Food coloring or honey is not recommended in these solutions. At feeders these little birds can be very feisty and territorial, allowing only one dominant bird to feed at a time. Occasionally while two birds are chasing each other, an interloper will sneak in and feed.

Fall migration begins in August and is usually complete by early October, with a few stragglers noted later. Observers in

Berrien County recorded more than 700 Ruby-throats on 28 August 1975. The hummingbird is an amazingly strong flier for its small size, traveling considerable distances over land and water, even crossing the Gulf of Mexico to reach its wintering grounds. Most winter from central Mexico to Costa Rica, although a few remain stateside along the Gulf coast. —Dick Schinkel

## RUFOUS HUMMINGBIRD

(*Selasphorus rufus*)

Several of Michigan's most unusual birds have been discovered in people's yards. Such is the case for the Rufous Hummingbird, a species which breeds in the Pacific Northwest. The Kalamazoo Nature Center received a letter describing a possible Rufous Hummingbird on 9 October 1974 in St. Joseph County. Unfortunately, this correspondence lacked the detailed plumage description demanded by bird record committees. The next report, a sighting from Niles, Berrien County, on 17 May 1981, was questioned by Payne (1983) because it did not match the timing of Rufous Hummingbird records elsewhere in the eastern United States.

Physical evidence for this species in Michigan was finally obtained in 1988, when two males were documented by photographs (Hull et al. 1989). The first was seen at a hummingbird feeder from 8 to 11 August in Rabbit Bay, Houghton County. The second male showed up on 25 September in Ogemaw County and was seen through 22 October before it disappeared.

A third *Selasphorus* hummingbird was present in 1988; this one appeared on 7 September at a feeder in the Shoreham area of St. Joseph, Berrien County. It was mid-November before word got out, but fortunately the individual remained through 9 December and was seen by many. This adult female was either a Rufous or Allen's Hummingbird. Separation of females and immatures of these two species is exceedingly difficult in the field. Of the two, the Rufous is the more frequent vagrant in the eastern United States. —Raymond J. Adams

## BELTED KINGFISHER

(*Ceryle alcyon*)

The Belted Kingfisher is Michigan's only representative of this mostly tropical family (Alcedinidae) of big-headed birds. A stocky build, bushy crest, and long, dagger-like bill give this species a top-heavy appearance, especially in proportion to its stubby legs and small feet. One thing is for sure, this bird is not like any other member of our avifauna, making identification easy. I suspect such a design must be good for fishing, something it does with great skill and success.

The Belted Kingfisher is a common inhabitant of our continent's inland and coastal waterways, from the southern states north to upper Canada and Alaska. Residency is largely permanent along the Atlantic and Pacific coasts and in the interior southern United States, while populations elsewhere migrate to places of open water, from the southern Great Lakes to northern South America. Most kingfishers vacate Michigan before the onset of winter, but some remain where conditions allow. Christmas bird counts from the past two decades report numbers in the range of 100 to 170 in most years, though they vary considerably with the extent of cold weather prior to the counts.

As the ice disappears from our lakes and rivers, kingfishers reappear. Arrival in southern Michigan begins in March and continues through April farther north. Between their loud, clattering rattle and their use of conspicuous perches, it is virtually impossible not to notice their return. Males arrive first and lay claim to a territory and an earthen bank in which to nest. The suitability of nest sites will be the criterion by which females choose mates when they return a week or two later. Females can be distinguished from males by a rust-colored band across the belly, which occurs below the blue-gray breast band seen in both sexes.

Considering the kingfisher's appearance, the nest site it chooses is most unusual. Digging and burrowing are not activities for which this bird seems suited, and yet that is exactly what it does. Using their powerful bills, the male and female take turns carving out a burrow in an exposed bank, excavating as much as a foot per day and completing a tunnel of three to six feet in about a week's time. Although it is difficult to witness their inside digging, the streams of dirt propelled from the hole by their feet signal tunneling in progress.

A chamber is made at the end of the burrow for the five to eight eggs, which are incubated by both sexes. Nesting is usually underway in April or May, with young fledging in June or July. The young stick close to their parents and stay in protected places for the first week or two. Juveniles resemble adults except for their brownish breast band.

Finding a proper site for nesting is not easy, and the availability of sites can limit kingfisher populations. Steep banks devoid of vegetation are preferred, and the soil cannot be too loose or too firm. A pair may start several tunnels before finding the right spot. Sites to choose from include naturally eroded banks along water courses and those created by human actions at sand and gravel operations, landfills, ditches, and bridge or road cutouts. When searching for a kingfisher burrow, look along the upper portions of a bank, as holes are usually located one to two feet from the top. Sites used by nesting Bank Swallows are also good places to check.

Kingfishers do not always find suitable banks in their feeding territory, and some nests may be a mile or more from their place of forage. Well over half of the pairs I have found in southwestern Michigan were nesting in areas away from water, in man-made banks in road cuts or gravel pits. While such sites are adequate, they are limiting and vulnerable to disturbance from human ac-

*Bank Swallow*
*Northern Rough-winged Swallow*
*Belted Kingfisher*
JOHN FELSING

tivity, and nest destruction or desertion is a common occurrence. I have observed several pairs nesting in what seemed to be abandoned or inactive road cuttings, only to return some weeks later to find the bank collapsed or cut deeper by a bulldozer.

Despite such hazards and limited nesting places, the Belted Kingfisher is a common and widely distributed breeding bird owing to our state's abundance of lakes, rivers, and streams. The only area where they are notably scarce or absent is in the highly urbanized southeast. Toward the end of the summer, once nesting has concluded, this species can be found at almost any body of water which supports fish, even small farm ponds and roadside ditches. Outside the breeding season, kingfishers are mostly solitary, and each individual maintains its own feeding territory.

This bird is, of course, primarily a fish-eater, although a small percentage of its diet consists of such items as crayfish, salamanders, insects, and sometimes even mice. Hunting is done from a perch, often a snag or dead limb, or by hovering in a manner similar to a tern. Shallow and clear waters are favored over those which are deep or murky. When a meal is spotted, the bird plunges headfirst into the water, grabbing the prey in its bill. Some items are consumed immediately, while others are taken back to a perch for last-minute adjustment before swallowing. If the fish is large or hard to handle, the kingfisher pounds it against the perch until it is adequately subdued. This behavior can elicit very interesting observations. I vividly remember watching one bird for several hours because it was continually catching fish which required this additional handling. On a few occasions, the prey was dropped during its beating, though it was usually retrieved again from the water below. This individual had obviously found a prime fishing hole, and I was treated to a great display of king-fishing. —Gail A. McPeek

# RED-HEADED WOODPECKER

(*Melanerpes erythrocephalus*)

The Red-headed Woodpecker belongs to a unique family of birds whose specialized body parts make them superb tree climbers and wood excavators. Among the woodpecker species found here, this is one of the easiest to recognize, with its brilliant red head, sharply contrasting black and white body, and conspicuous white wing patches. Many woodpeckers have red crowns or other reddish markings, but no others have an entire red hood like this bird.

This colorful woodpecker occurs in Michigan as a fairly common summer resident and uncommon permanent resident. During the breeding season it is widely distributed over most of the state, except the Upper Peninsula, where it occurs only locally. Winter occurrence is irregular and limited mostly to the southern counties. The Red-head's entire range includes the eastern two-thirds of the continent from the Rockies to the Atlantic and from southern Canada to the Gulf coast. Those in the southern states are year-round residents, but here in the north they are mostly migratory.

The Red-headed Woodpecker likes open country with scattered woodlands or groves of mature trees, especially oaks and hicko-

ries. Parks, orchards, pastures, golf courses, and rural roadsides are all good places to find Red-heads. Although this species lives in these human-modified environs, it is still most common in the natural oak savannas and open oak woodlands, habitats which have declined with the suppression of fire. To experience this woodpecker in its natural setting, you should travel to areas with remnants of these prime habitats, like those in the Allegan and Muskegon state forests.

Breeding time for this species is May to July. Anyone who has spent time watching this species knows of its aggressive temperament. In areas where they are common, individuals engage in frequent conflicts and territorial chases. Their harsh, rattling calls travel·far through their open country habitats. An avid flycatcher, this woodpecker can also regularly be seen leaving elevated perches to pursue winged insects in spring and summer.

All woodpeckers nest in self-made tree cavities. Some species choose live trees, while others prefer dead trees or snags. The Red-head likes the latter, building its holes in well-weathered trees which typically have broken trunks or branches, missing bark, and a few old holes. They also excavate cavities in telephone poles. This can be an ill-fated choice if the poles have been treated with creosote because eggs exposed to this chemical usually fail to hatch.

When young Red-heads emerge from their nesting holes, in June or early July, they do not resemble their colorful parents. Instead they are grayish-brown with a gray head. They do, however, have the white wing patches to identify them as Red-head offspring. Young birds begin to molt in their red heads in late winter. Both males and females are red-headed; in fact, this is the only woodpecker species in Michigan in which the sexes have identical plumages.

The main spring migration and return of Red-headed Woodpeckers to Michigan takes place in late April and early May. The reverse trip south occurs mainly in September and October. In some years, large numbers can be seen migrating along the lakeshores, particularly on the Lake Michigan side where oak woodlands and orchards border the lake. In the east, big movements can be seen at a few locales, such as Tawas Point in Iosco County.

Some Red-headed Woodpeckers overwinter in Michigan; the number depends on the supply of acorns, beechnuts, and other mast crops produced that fall. When supplies are good, Red-heads are regular winter residents, mostly in southern Michigan, relying on fall caches for much of their food. This irregular winter presence is documented in state Christmas bird counts, with several hundred found some years, only a few dozen in others.

Unfortunately, this beautiful woodpecker is not as common as it used to be in Michigan. It is doubtful that Walter Barrows would now describe it as "one of our best known woodpeckers" and "abundant in many places" as he did in 1912. Declines were

*Red-headed Woodpecker*
*Red-bellied Woodpecker*
DAVID MOHRHARDT

evident by the 1940s, especially in some southeastern counties, and today Downies, Northern Flickers, and Red-bellieds are the more well known species.

A series of changes has resulted in fluctuating numbers over much of the bird's range in the last one hundred years. Most of the natural oak woodlands and savannas have been replaced by farmland, urban and suburban developments, or woods of aspen or pine. In addition, the cutting of overmature trees has reduced nesting sites. The widespread loss of elms to Dutch elm disease helped the supply of nesting trees in the 1950s and 1960s, but since then, population declines through the 1970s and 1980s have approached 75%. Competition with the persistent and abundant starling has also played a role in Red-headed Woodpecker population changes, as has their use of tree-lined roadsides, where their low-flying habits make them prone to vehicle mortality. —Gail A. McPeek

# GOLDEN-FRONTED WOODPECKER

## (*Melanerpes aurifrons*)

A close relative of the Red-bellied Woodpecker, this species is restricted to Oklahoma, Texas, and Mexico. It is not known to have wandering tendencies, so it was a pleasant surprise when an individual appeared at a feeder in Cheboygan County on 20 November 1974. Diagnostic photographs were obtained documenting it as a Golden-fronted Woodpecker, and the fact that it remained until 2 December allowed many observers the opportunity to see this accidental visitor. The record was initially rejected in Payne's 1983 checklist, but the Bird Records Committee was able to locate additional color photographs which provided a much clearer picture, making its identity unquestionable. This remains the only Michigan report of this woodpecker to date. —Gail A. McPeek

# RED-BELLIED WOODPECKER

## (*Melanerpes carolinus*)

This medium-sized woodpecker with the zebra back has become considerably more common in Michigan in recent decades. Back in the early to mid-1900s, the range of the Red-bellied Woodpecker ended around the middle of the state, but now it occurs throughout the Lower Peninsula, though it is still uncommon in most northern counties. During field work for the Breeding Bird Atlas

*Yellow-bellied Sapsucker*
*Black-backed Woodpecker*
JOHN FELSING

in the 1980s, nesting was confirmed as far north as Benzie, Grand Traverse, and Oscoda counties. There are even casual summer observations in the Upper Peninsula, unheard of 50 years ago, and Red-bellieds now make annual appearances at Whitefish Point.

This change in status is part of a gradual increase and expansion of its range northward, due to a number of contributing factors. Among these are growing Red-bellied populations to the South, forest regeneration in parts of the Lower Peninsula, increases in winter bird-feeding, and the generally above-average winter temperatures during several decades (1920–1960). At present, this species can best be described as a fairly common to common permanent resident in the southern two-thirds of Michigan and rare to uncommon in the northern third.

Christmas bird counts in Michigan and across the North confirm a steady rise in population of Red-bellieds. In fact, winter sightings in the North are more regular and often precede summer records as wanderings in search of food bring them to residential areas. Many people have been pleasantly surprised to see this boldly patterned woodpecker appear at their bird feeder for the first time.

Perhaps the Red-headed Woodpecker was named first, because that also would have been a fitting name for this red-capped bird. Instead, its name describes a faint tinge of red on the belly which is seldom visible unless the bird is in hand. Distinctive features are its horizontally striped black and white back, white belly, and bright red cap. The sexes differ slightly in appearance, with males having the larger red cap covering both crown and nape.

Red-bellied Woodpeckers live in a variety of deciduous and mixed woodlands, both mature and second-growth. During the breeding season they are most common in floodplain forests, swamps, and other moist woodlands where dead trees are usually in good supply. Southwest Michigan boasts the greatest numbers of Red-bellieds as a result of the proliferation of these habitats in the region.

Although they are regular breeders in the southeast, loss and fragmentation of nesting habitat has resulted in noticeable decreases in numbers for this species in areas of extensive development and agriculture. European Starlings also have a profound impact on Red-bellied Woodpeckers, which are frequently run out of their cavities by this overbearing, nonnative species. They fare much better where substantial woodland remains and starling competition is less.

Northward in the state, this species has become more regular on the west side where hardwood forests prevail. The drier and more coniferous woodlands on the northeast side are less hospitable. After the breeding season, Red-bellieds are more flexible in habitat use and can be found more frequently in wooded suburbs, parks, and orchards.

Red-bellied Woodpeckers usually select dead trees or dead limbs in live trees for their cavities. They seem to have a preference for softwood trees such as basswood, maple, elm, and poplar. They also seem to like trees situated near woodland openings or edges. I discovered my first nest completely by accident while hiking in one of our state parks. After rounding a curve on a path that bordered a small opening, I suddenly found myself being showered with wood chips. There, about 20 feet up, was a Red-bellied Woodpecker intently carving out its nesting cavity, indifferent to my presence just below.

Like many of our woodpeckers, Red-bellieds begin their breeding season early. Their loud, harsh "churrs" are a conspicuous and welcome sound in the cold, quiet months of February and March. Nesting is underway by the latter half of April or early May, and the young hatch in May or June. Once incubation has begun, vocalizations diminish and the birds are a little harder to find.

Come June or early July, young Red-bellieds emerge from their cavities. Like all woodpeckers, the young are born naked and require several weeks to develop. Woodpeckers tend to have a high rate of successful nests compared to most other passerines. Their cavities give eggs and young more protection from predators and adverse weather than the open nests of most other birds.

Pairs separate after the breeding season but usually keep adjacent territories, each with a store of food and a roosting hole. Like the Red-headed Woodpecker and others in the genus *Melanerpes*, Red-bellieds cache acorns, nuts, and other food to help them through the winter. One year I found the pantry of our neighborhood Red-belly in a tree hole in our backyard. The hole was filled with hundreds of sunflower seeds, most of which came from my bird feeder. Given the stash this one bird had, I am inclined to agree with the hypothesis that bird feeders improve survival and allow this species to winter farther north. —Gail A. McPeek

# YELLOW-BELLIED SAPSUCKER

## (*Sphyrapicus varius*)

The sapsucker is a common summer resident and migrant in Michigan. Prior to moving to the state, I had seen many trees marked with this woodpecker's tell-tale sapwells, but was not that familiar with the bird itself. This quickly changed as my field work for the Breeding Bird Atlas afforded many opportunities to observe sapsuckers in the northern woods of Michigan.

The Yellow-bellied Sapsucker is associated with northern and montane forests throughout its summer range, which extends across Canada south to the Great Lakes, New England, and the Appalachian Mountains. In Michigan, it is most common in the northern hardwood and mixed forests where it finds an abundant supply of birches, maples, aspen, spruce, and other "sappy" trees to support its sugar habit. I never failed to find a sapsucker or two when conducting bird surveys in woods consisting of these tree species. This habitat association results in a breeding range which primarily extends north of the state's middle. Yellow-bellied Sapsuckers are common and widely distributed throughout most of the Upper and northern Lower peninsulas. Within these regions, they tend to occur more frequently toward the western half of the Upper Peninsula and the northeastern portion of the Lower Peninsula.

Sapsuckers are extremely rare breeders in southern Michigan, though apparently this was not always the case. Records from the latter part of the 1800s indicate regular nesting in several southern counties. This preceded the large-scale clearing of forests and virtual elimination of suitable sapsucker habitat in the region. More recently, observers for the Atlas found limited breeding evidence for sapsuckers in Allegan, Montcalm, Tuscola, and a few other southern counties. These observations may be the first signs of a gradual return to parts of southern Michigan, a response to forest regrowth in some areas.

During spring and fall migrations the sapsucker is widespread and occurs in wooded habitats throughout the state, including orchards, parks, and residential areas. It travels the farthest of our woodpeckers, leaving northern breeding grounds for warmer climates and woodlands where the sap continues to flow. It winters primarily in the southeastern United States west to Texas and south to Central America. Some remain farther north, and the sapsucker is considered a rare to casual winter resident in southern Michigan. The maximum total to date on state Christmas bird counts is 29. Those that do stay tend to be seen in orchards, cemeteries, or parks, and at feeders.

Spring migration coincides with the renewed running of sap in sugar maples and other tree species. Arrival in Michigan occurs from late March through April, and concentrations of migrant sapsuckers can be seen along the lakeshores. Breeders usually take up residence in the same territory as the year before. Thin-barked trees are preferred for excavation of their nesting cavities. Aspen trees infected with false tinder fungus are a common choice. They also seem to like their nest trees close to a lake or stream.

Breeding occurs in May and June, and the five to six young fledge the nest by the middle of July. Like most other woodpeckers, the juveniles are extremely vocal, and their relentless "mewing" calls make them relatively easy to find. Families often stay around the nesting territories and their sap sources for much of the summer. The fall migration begins at the end of August in the north, reaching southern Michigan in late September and peaking in October.

This mottled black and white woodpecker gets its name from the yellowish cast of its belly feathers and its rather peculiar habit of drinking tree sap. A great variety of trees and vines are tapped for their sweet sap. Birch trees are an especially important source in Michigan, with a sap consisting of 20 to 30% sugar. Sapsuckers gain access to sap flows by drilling small squarish pits in the tree bark.

This specialized foraging technique does more than just provide sap to drink. Sapsuckers also eat the exposed inner bark and cambium and the many insects attracted to the sap flow. Other insects are obtained by flycatching, and various berries and nuts supplement their diet. In addition to numerous insects, many other animals have learned to take advantage of the secreting sap. Among these users are hummingbirds, squirrels, chipmunks, porcupines, and bats. —Gail A. McPeek

*Hairy Woodpecker*
*Downy Woodpecker*
JOHN FELSING

# DOWNY WOODPECKER

## (*Picoides pubescens*)

The Downy is one of our most familiar woodpeckers. It occurs throughout the state and is a common permanent resident in every county. This is one of the woodpecker species regularly found around residential areas, especially during winter when they frequent feeders stocked with suet and sunflower.

At just six inches in size, the Downy is the smallest woodpecker in North America. It is a widely distributed species occurring over most of the United States and Canada north to Alaska. The Downy is a resident throughout its range, with birds in the northernmost regions being partly migratory depending on food resources and winter severity. Unique adaptations allow the Downy and many of its relatives to live year-round in more northerly latitudes. Roosting cavities provide warmth and shelter, and their tree-foraging skills enable them to extract dormant insects from bark and wood.

Downy Woodpeckers live in a wide variety of forests and woodlands, including more open situations like those found in orchards, parks, roadside edges, and residential areas. Almost any wooded habitat is suitable provided there is an adequate supply of trees for excavating their nesting and roosting cavities. Dead wood is preferred by these small, stubby-billed woodpeckers. They seem especially partial to broken tree stubs or the undersides of dead limbs.

Downy nest trees average 8 inches in diameter (at breast height), which is several inches less than that required by larger woodpecker species. The Downy's use of smaller trees has proven to be an important advantage now that second-growth woodlands and younger-age trees have replaced mature forests and larger shade trees over much of the landscape. Also, the 1 ¼-inch entrance hole is too small for the starling, a serious contender for cavities of several other woodpecker species.

The Downy's range overlaps closely with that of the Hairy Woodpecker, but rather than competing, their differences in size and foraging and nesting habits allow them to coexist. They regularly occur together in mature woodlands, and both species are about equally common across the more heavily forested regions in the northern parts of the state. The Downy, with its ability to also live in smaller and more open woodlands, is more numerous and widespread in southern Michigan. Also, populations in the state underwent a significant increase from 1966 to 1991 with a peak in numbers in the middle 1980s, according to the breeding bird surveys.

Downies consume eggs, larvae, pupae, and adults of many insect varieties. The proficiency with which woodpeckers find and extract prey is fascinating. Insects on or near the surface are often obtained by probing or prying off pieces of bark. Apparently, woodpeckers are able to detect slight sounds made by moving prey under bark or in wood. Their frequent tapping may elicit movement or cue them to a hollow tunnel of a burrowing insect. They then use their chisel-like bills to gain access to the tunnel and their long tongues to extract the prey from its refuge.

The breeding season for the Downy begins in midwinter, with pairs and territories usually established during February and March. Courtship and territorial activities can often be witnessed around feeders. Displays include head weaving, bill pointing, and erecting of the head feathers which accentuates the male's red crest.

As the weather warms and the nesting season approaches, Downies retire to quieter, more wooded areas. Cavities are excavated in April or May, and nesting occurs during May and June. Incubation of the four- or five-egg clutch takes 12 days. By midsummer juveniles can be seen and heard, following their parents from tree to tree begging for food. Even though fledglings resemble the adults, their behaviors clearly identify them as juveniles. The young often have a reddish crown instead of the red nape patch of adult males. In two to three weeks, the juveniles are independent and disperse from the area.

Breeding pairs separate by the end of the summer, but both birds remain in the area as long as there is sufficient food. In some areas, however, the Downies seen in winter may not be the same individuals of summer because of local movements or southward migrations. Little is known about these movements, but in October 1992 a major flight was recorded at the Whitefish Point Bird Observatory, with 232 individuals on 25 October ( J. Granlund, pers. comm.).

During fall and winter, you frequently find a Downy or two mixed in with a flock of chickadees, nuthatches, titmice, creepers, and other species. It is suspected that this banding together improves foraging opportunities and predator detection. What better strategy than feeding with a flock of noisy chickadees who always seem to know when a hawk or other predator is nearby. —Gail A. McPeek

# HAIRY WOODPECKER

## (*Picoides villosus*)

The Hairy Woodpecker, like its lookalike cousin the Downy, is a common permanent resident in Michigan. Both of these woodpeckers have similar black and white plumages and can occur together in the same forested habitats. This creates some confusion, but with a little experience and knowledge of certain characteristics, you can learn to tell who's who.

Visually, the Hairy is about two inches larger, has a longer, stouter bill, and lacks black spots on its white outermost tail feathers. Vocally, the bigger Hairy gives the louder call, a sharp-sounding "peek" as opposed to the Downy's duller, softer "pik." The two also differ in personality. The Hairy Woodpecker has a shy and retiring nature, often dodging behind trees or flying away when approached. My many attempts to photograph them have mostly ended in frustration as they constantly retreated to the opposite side of the trunk or managed to stay one tree ahead of me.

The Hairy Woodpecker is found throughout the forested regions of North America. Its range extends north to the arctic treeline and south to Florida, the Bahamas, and the mountains of Panama. Here in Michigan, it occurs wherever there are deciduous, coniferous, or mixed forests of sufficient size. No doubt its numbers declined in areas where forests were cleared during settlement. This species is not as flexible in habitat use as its smaller cousin. It needs larger-sized woodlands with larger trees to satisfy its territory and nesting requirements. Forests typically need to reach 50 to 100 years of age (depending on the tree species) before they have an adequate supply of cavity trees.

Today, this woodpecker is a common resident in the northern regions of the state and in the southwestern counties. The lack of mature wooded areas in much of south-central and southeastern Michigan limits its occurrence in these regions. Results of the Breeding Bird Atlas show it to be an uncommon breeder in those southern counties where the landscape is dominated by farmland and urban and suburban developments. In these areas, public lands provide essential habitat for forest birds such as the Hairy Woodpecker.

For nesting, this species prefers live trees with heartrot. It is believed that they are able to detect rotting wood from sound wood by their tapping. Several sites are often tried before a suitable one is found. Most woodpeckers, the Hairy included, build a new cavity each year. This leaves a generous supply of vacant holes which are used by a wide diversity of wildlife for shelter, nesting, and roosting. In areas where woodpeckers have declined or disappeared, many other animals are faced with a shortage of homes.

Hairies are generally solitary prior to the breeding season. Come midwinter, pairs and breeding territories are established, and their fidelity to an area often results in the same mated pair in consecutive years. The nesting cavity is usually complete by April, and the all-white eggs, usually four, are laid in April or early May. Once breeding begins, Hairies are quiet and reclusive. Incubation lasts 12 days, and the young remain in the nest about four weeks. Finding and observing Hairies becomes easier from mid-June through July, when adults and their noisy fledglings are actively foraging about the forest.

During fall and winter, Hairy Woodpeckers may wander into orchards and wooded residential areas to find food. Like Downies, they come to feeders for suet. In 1992, Hairies were reported on 64% of the Michigan feeder counts, most consistently at feeders in the north. In comparison, Downies were recorded on 92% of the counts. Likewise, Christmas bird counts reveal differences in abundance, with total numbers of Hairies only one-third to one-fourth those of Downies.

The increased visibility from feeder visits can give the impression that the Hairy Woodpecker is more common in winter. Some individuals from farther north may come into the state during this period, but there seems to be no real definable movement for this nonmigratory species, and no evidence to suggest that they actually are more common in winter. The Whitefish Point Bird Observatory has recorded some movements in October, but it is unclear if these stem from dispersal or migration.

The Hairy Woodpecker and many of its relatives play an important role in the health of our forests by consuming large quantities of injurious insects. They keep numbers of bark-boring beetles and other insects in check, helping to prevent massive outbreaks. Management practices that fail to provide habitat for woodpeckers, particularly an ample supply of snags and large trees for nesting, are not going to have the benefits provided by these natural biological control agents. —Gail A. McPeek

# THREE-TOED WOODPECKER
## (*Picoides tridactylus*)

The Three-toed Woodpecker has generally been a casual resident and winter visitant in Michigan, though recently its occurrence has been largely accidental. This is a true boreal species with a circumpolar distribution encompassing North America, Europe, and Asia. The Upper Great Lakes and extreme northern New England make up the southern border of its range in the eastern United States. Farther west this woodpecker is more wide-ranging, occurring in the higher mountains south to Arizona and New Mexico.

Forests composed of spruce, fir, tamarack, and other northern conifers are home to this woodpecker. Preference is given to bogs, swamps, burned areas, or other boreal communities with a supply of standing dead trees for nesting and foraging. This species is adept at flaking bark from trees to uncover beetle grubs and other insect morsels. It also occasionally feeds on sap, visiting the pits of sapsuckers or drilling its own.

The rarity of this species in Michigan is apparent in the state's ornithological literature. There is also ambiguity in a few records along with some probable misidentifications, mostly with young Yellow-bellied Sapsuckers. Although it was first listed by Kneeland in 1857, Walter Barrows catalogued it as hypothetical in 1912, stating that there were no authenticated records. He must have been unaware of the specimen collected from Iron County on 29 November 1910. Robert Payne (1983) lists four other specimens housed at the University of Michigan Museum of Zoology. Chronologically, these are 18 October 1920 from the Huron Mountains, Marquette County; December 1920 from Gogebic County; 4 October 1929 from Isle Royale; and 1 March 1963 from Sugar Island, Chippewa County.

Beginning in the early 1960s, several irruptive movements brought more Three-toed Woodpeckers into the Upper Great Lakes region, and there was some apparent increase in sightings in Michigan. Records published in the *Jack-Pine Warbler* indicate an influx of birds into the Upper Peninsula in 1963–65 and in some other years through much of the 1970s and early 1980s. These irruptions are highly irregular events and probably depend on food resources (affected by fire dynamics) and population size in the north. Based on the scattering of state records during these irruptions as well as those of neighbors such as Wisconsin, Minnesota, and Ontario, southward movements occur primarily between September and November and the return trip north between February and April.

Since 1985, fall and winter observations have been extremely scarce. After several years of no published reports, one Three-toed Woodpecker was spotted on 24 September 1992 near Trout Lake, and another was seen later that fall, on 26 October, at the Whitefish Point Bird Observatory. This latter sighting coincided with an incredible migration of Downies and Hairies (J. Granlund, pers. comm.).

The Three-toed Woodpecker is even more rare in the summer. There have been only a handful of summer observations, with one confirmed breeding, and no nests found. The documented breeding came on 9 August 1953, when an adult male feeding a young bird was reported in eastern Baraga County. Other counties with breeding season records are Chippewa, Luce, and Marquette in the Upper Peninsula and Cheboygan, Emmet, and Benzie in the northern Lower. The latter two observations came during the Breeding Bird Atlas—an individual seen at Wilderness State Park (5 July 1986) and a male and female at Sleeping Bear Dunes (4 July 1988).

As the name implies, the Three-toed Woodpecker has three toes, all of which face front, instead of the family's more common four-toe configuration of two front and two back. It shares this trait with the Black-backed Woodpecker, a cousin and boreal inhabitant also found in Michigan. The much rarer Three-toed has a more northern distribution, though there are many areas where its range overlaps with the Black-backed. These two bear close resemblance to each other; even the males of both species have a golden crown patch. The Three-toed's most identifying mark is its horizontal barring or "ladderback." Like many birds of the far north, the Three-toed Woodpecker is reputed to be quite tame. However, its typically silent nature and wilderness existence make finding one exceedingly difficult, and no doubt some individuals go undetected. —Gail A. McPeek

# BLACK-BACKED WOODPECKER

## (*Picoides arcticus*)

Although similar in appearance to its three-toed relative *P. tridactylus*, this species is readily distinguished by its solid black back. It is also the more numerous of the two and the one you are most likely to find in northern Michigan. The Black-backed Woodpecker can best be characterized as an uncommon but regular resident inhabiting the coniferous forests of the Upper Peninsula and the northernmost counties of the Lower Peninsula.

The range of this species corresponds to the boreal or arctic region of North America; hence its former name, the Arctic Three-toed Woodpecker. This range extends south into the United States in three main areas: the northern Great Lakes, northern New England, and the mountains of the Pacific Northwest. Here in Michigan, the Black-back tends to be locally distributed because of our location along the edge of this boreal zone.

Being a rather inconspicuous bird and one that lives in remote forest habitats, the Black-backed Woodpecker is a challenge to find. For many birders, it has become one of the more sought-after species in Michigan. The Whitefish Point area is an excellent place to see this species, particularly in late May and October. Once it is found, its rather tame nature often allows for observation at close range, and I have heard many birders recount stories of individuals foraging in the same tree for several hours. Not having spent much time in boreal habitats, I consider myself lucky to have seen two Black-backed Woodpeckers. Both observations involved relatively brief glimpses of females making their way from tree to tree. One, in particular, seemed rather nervous

and wary of my presence, suggesting that a nest may have been nearby.

Your best chance of finding this bird is to visit coniferous habitats where snags are numerous. Prime areas include tamarack-black spruce bogs, cedar swamps, or jack-pine woodlands which have recently burned. Factors such as fire, logging, beaver activity, and insect infestation are important determinants of this species' occurrence. The Black-backed Woodpecker depends heavily on trees killed or injured by disturbances. In fact, three-fourths of its diet is composed of larvae of wood-boring beetles which attack these trees.

It is this association with a particular food resource which results in its localized and dynamic distribution. Birds will move into an area following a fire or other disturbance, take advantage of the plentiful food, then move on as the supply diminishes over time. Small breeding colonies may form, especially in large burned-over areas. This happened recently near Rapid River in the Upper Peninsula following a 1988 forest fire. More than 25 Black-backed Woodpeckers were observed in the area, and nesting was documented in 1989 and 1990. The Seney Refuge has had a local concentration since the large fire in 1976. Likewise, the burned jack-pine plains of Mack Lake (Oscoda County) and other areas managed for the Kirtland's Warbler support a small resident population.

Field work for the Breeding Bird Atlas provided the first accurate picture of this woodpecker's distribution in northern Michigan. It occurs on Isle Royale and in every Upper Peninsula county, but in widely scattered locales. The Seney and Tahquamenon areas are among the more well known sites for Black-backs. Distribution in the northern Lower Peninsula is even more spotty, with individuals mostly found in and around Oscoda and Crawford counties.

State nesting records for this elusive woodpecker are few and far between. Nearly all of the Upper Peninsula counties now have at least one confirmed breeding. The first nest record did not come until 15 June 1941, when a nest with young was found in the Cusino area in Schoolcraft County. May and June appear to be the primary breeding months. Black-backs like to chip off bark around the cavity entrance, leaving a large area of bare wood. This is a diagnostic feature providing, of course, you first find a nest tree. Preference seems to be given to conifers located near water or other openings, including bogs, beaver ponds, lakes, or forest clearings.

The Black-backed Woodpecker is a permanent resident throughout its range, but irregular post-breeding irruptions do occur, most likely in response to food availability. Such movements are probably most pronounced following summers of high breeding success when overcrowding forces some birds to journey south of their usual range. These records mostly occur in the

*Pileated Woodpecker*
*Northern Flicker*
HEINER HERTLING

H.C. Hertling

October–February period, and individuals have been seen as far south as Kalamazoo and Monroe counties. Scattered observations in the southern Lower Peninsula were somewhat regular in the late 1800s and first half of the 1900s. In the past few decades, however, such wanderings have been scarce to nonexistent. The latest winter reports for southern Michigan came in the middle 1970s from St. Clair County, Detroit, and Pte. Mouillee. —Gail A. McPeek

# NORTHERN FLICKER

## (*Colaptes auratus*)

The Northern Flicker is the most abundant woodpecker in Michigan. Walter Barrows described it as such back in 1912, and it retains this distinction today. During the breeding and migration seasons, this species is common throughout the state. In winter its distribution is largely restricted to the southern Lower Peninsula, being somewhat common in the west but uncommon in the east.

This widely distributed North American woodpecker has three distinct races or forms. The Yellow-shafted race occurs in the East and is the one seen here in Michigan. The Red-shafted and Gilded Flickers occur in the West and Southwest, respectively. They were once considered separate species, but their classification was changed as more was learned about their habits and studies found that they often interbreed where their ranges come together.

Compared to most members of its family, the flicker is rather atypical. It is as much a ground-dwelling bird as it is an arboreal one, and its bill is less chisel-like, having a thinner, slightly curved shape. Both of these traits are adaptations for feeding on insects on the ground, especially ants, which are the mainstay of its diet in spring and summer.

The flicker is also quite different in appearance from other woodpeckers. Instead of a basic black and white plumage, it is a soft blend of browns and tans with bold black spots and black barring. Yellow wing and tail shafts and a scarlet crescent on the back of its head add even more color. More often than not, however, identification of this bird is made at a distance, either by its loud, repetitive calls or by its conspicuous white rump patch which catches your eye when it flushes from the roadside or flies across an open field in a graceful, undulating motion that is characteristic of woodpeckers.

Flickers can live in almost any habitat, providing there are adequate dead trees for nesting. Open woodland, forest edge, fields with scattered trees, orchards, farmland, suburbs, and parks are all used by this species. With such flexibility and adaptability, flickers have fared well in the highly human-modified landscape, although our practice of cutting dead and dying trees reduces nesting sites. Leaving some large trees and snags in clearcuts, fields, woodlots, and other habitats can make all the difference for flickers and many other cavity nesters.

This is one of the few woodpeckers that reuse holes and sometimes nest in boxes. If you can keep starlings out, you may be able to attract flickers to a properly constructed nesting box. Were it not for the starling, flickers would be even more common around rural and suburban areas.

Flickers return to Michigan in full force at the tail end of March and in the first half of April. They travel in large, loose flocks, arriving with the first warm fronts and coinciding with the renewed activity of ants, spiders, and beetles. There is a pronounced spring migration throughout the Great Lakes region, and large numbers of flickers can be seen along shorelines and at concentration areas such as Whitefish Point in the eastern Upper Peninsula.

Many people find this bird to be a welcome sign of spring; that is, until one takes to banging on the rain gutter at the crack of dawn. Flickers, along with some of their relatives, have discovered that metal objects and natural wood siding have excellent resonating qualities. They quickly adopt these surfaces as drumming posts to advertise their breeding territories. This persistent pounding wanes in a few weeks and usually ceases once nesting is underway. Till then, you might as well wake up with the flickers and enjoy the early morning bird activity around your yard.

Nesting takes place during May and June. Their six- to eight-egg clutch is the largest among the woodpeckers breeding in Michigan. The young fledge between the latter part of June and the middle of July, looking very much like their parents.

Fall migration occurs in September and the first half of October, but not all individuals vacate the state. They are not as common as permanent residents like the Downy and Hairy, but several hundred flickers are recorded annually on Christmas bird counts. The highest total to date was 502 in 1989–90.

Those that do overwinter are vulnerable to severe weather. Following the harsh winters of 1976–77 and 1977–78, there were widely noticeable declines in Michigan and elsewhere, according to data from the federal breeding bird survey. Numbers have held relatively stable since then. —Gail A. McPeek

# PILEATED WOODPECKER

## (*Dryocopus pileatus*)

The Pileated Woodpecker is a denizen of the larger, older forests in Michigan. Throughout its range in the eastern United States, Canada, and the Pacific Northwest, this big, red-crested bird lives in extensive tracts of mature dense forest—an association which has made it an important indicator of old-growth communities. Its present-day distribution in the state is primarily a northern one because of this forest affinity.

The Pileated's history in Michigan has been one of downs and ups. Its numbers and distribution were greatly affected by the widespread clearing of land during settlement. As the vast forests disappeared, so did the Pileated. When Barrows compiled *Michigan Bird Life* in 1912, the "Logcock," as it was known then, was already rare in the southern Lower Peninsula. Declines continued, and by the middle 1900s, this species was uncommon in the northern two-thirds of the state and rare to absent in the southern third.

In recent decades this forest bird has regained some of its lost ground. Signs of recovery were first apparent in the late 1950s and 1960s. A gradual but steady increase is documented by the state breeding bird survey routes from 1966 to the present, and results of the Breeding Bird Atlas in the 1980s show the Pileated to be common again in northern Michigan and uncommon in parts of the southwest. Evidence of breeding in 85 southern townships, mostly in western counties, represents a substantial recovery in this region, while it is still largely absent from the southeast because of insufficient forest habitat. A positive increasing trend in numbers is also evident on Michigan Christmas bird counts, especially through the 1980s and reaching new highs in the early 1990s (totals of 70 or more per year).

The Pileated Woodpecker has been increasing over much of its range, including other Great Lakes states. This comeback is attributed to forest regeneration, a seemingly greater tolerance of people and their activities, and its acceptance of second-growth woodlands provided they have an adequate supply of large trees. I discovered several nesting pairs in southwestern Michigan in areas once thought to be unsuitable, including some of our more wooded parks and suburbs. In some parts of its range, the Pileated is even considered a pest species now, as it weakens telephone poles with its excavations.

At 16 to 19 inches, this is the largest woodpecker found in Michigan and, with the supposed extinction of the Ivory-billed, the largest in the United States. Its large size, black body, broad white underwings, and flaming red crest make identification easy. The Pileated is heard more often than seen, and both its loud call (a repeating "wuk-wuk-wuk") and its deep, hollow drumming carry far through the dense forests. Long-distance communication is essential for a bird whose territory frequently covers a mile or more.

Pileated Woodpeckers are permanent residents throughout most of their range, and pairs typically maintain the same territory from year to year. There are a surprisingly small number of nest records published for Michigan. This is probably a result, in part, of the wildness of this bird's forest habitat and its behavior around the nest. For a large, loud woodpecker, the Pileated is extremely quiet and cautious in the vicinity of its nest tree, not wanting to reveal its location. Drumming, calling, and courting behaviors commence in January and February, marking the beginning of the breeding season.

Nests are probably initiated in late April in the southern counties, and sometime in May farther north. It takes nearly three weeks for the four-egg clutch to hatch. The young fledge the nest cavity in June or early July, and families stay together through much of the summer. Come fall, juveniles disperse to find their own food and their own territories. It is not uncommon to see Pileateds moving along the Great Lakes shorelines in northern Michigan during the spring and fall seasons.

The Pileated Woodpecker has been the subject of numerous studies to characterize its forest habitat. Large trees and high snag densities are critical components, and around the Great Lakes, forests typically must reach 80 to 100 years or older to provide enough large trees and snags to satisfy its nesting and feeding requirements. This species forages extensively on snags, stumps, and logs, working its powerful bill like a chisel to hack away large splinters in the rotting wood and expose insect prey, especially boring beetles and ants. The signs are unmistakable; no other woodpecker leaves behind such deep rectangular holes and piles of bark and debris. —Gail A. McPeek

# OLIVE-SIDED FLYCATCHER

*(Contopus borealis)*

The Olive-sided Flycatcher is a fairly common migrant in Michigan but a generally uncommon summer resident, found in open coniferous woodlands in the north. It is cousin to the more familiar Eastern Wood-Pewee, a flycatcher of slightly smaller size and prominent wing bars. Identifying features of this species are its proportionately large head and small tail, white rump tufts and dark olive sides which flank a white belly, creating a "vested" appearance. As is typical of most flycatchers, audible detection often precedes visual detection, and the Olive-sided's three-syllable whistle of "quick-three-beers!" is an easy one to recognize.

The preferential breeding habitats of this flycatcher are boreal and montane evergreen forests. This results in a distribution skewed toward the continents's northern and western regions. In the West, the extensive mountain ranges and cool coastal forests provide suitable nesting areas as far south as California and the southern Rockies. Distribution in the eastern United States is more limited, ending around middle Michigan and New England, with a few local populations in the high elevations of the Appalachians.

The Olive-sided is one of our lesser-known flycatchers on account of its northern affinity and occupation of some of the more secluded habitats in the state. Were it not for the published observations of Lawrence Walkinshaw and data collected during the Breeding Bird Atlas in the 1980s, there would be little to write about. We do know that this species is a regular breeder in all 15 Upper Peninsula counties, and that it also nests locally in some parts of the northern Lower Peninsula, south to Iosco County on the east side and Benzie, and possibly Manistee, in the west.

Look and listen for the Olive-sided in wet conifer woodlands with an abundance of spruce—a habitat characteristic of bogs, beaver floodings, and borders of northern streams and lakes. These are the areas most frequently harboring this flycatcher, which likes to sit in the open, perched on a dead branch or snag. From here it gets a good view of flying insects and is amenable to observation as it sits, waits, and sallies after prey.

Bogs and other similar, spruce-dominated habitats are not the only places to find Olive-sided Flycatchers. Greatest concentrations in the northern Lower Peninsula occur in the dry jack-pine plains in and around Crawford and Oscoda counties. It seems the cutting and burning activities carried out for the Kirtland's Warbler have also benefited this bird. The Olive-sided's diet includes bark and wood-boring beetles, and just as woodpeckers and other bark-foraging birds can be drawn to burned areas for the larvae of these insects, this and other flycatchers come to feed on the flying adults.

The breeding season is primarily June and July. There are only a handful of actual nest records for the state. Norman Wood lists two in his 1951 writing: a nest with one young found 9 July 1928 near Burt Lake, Cheboygan County, and a nest on 8 June 1934 near Munuscong Bay, Chippewa County. Larry Walkinshaw located a nest in a sphagnum-spruce bog in Schoolcraft County in 1954, which contained three eggs on 25 June and had two young on 2 July. In an article about this species, Walkinshaw describes being scolded by a pair and watching one of the birds, presumably the female, return to the same black spruce several times. This led to his discovery of the nest, which was made of dead spruce twigs placed upon a live branch away from the trunk and 14 feet above ground.

The Olive-sided Flycatcher is a late spring/early fall migrant. This is the time when you can see this species in southern Michigan, especially in counties along the lakeshores where numbers seem to concentrate. Published data show the bulk of northbound migrants are reported after 15 May. A few may arrive in the first half of the month, and the earliest date on record is 26 April, from Kalamazoo County. Migration often extends into the first or second week of June, which can throw off unknowing observers in southern Michigan where it is not a breeding resident.

The return trip is underway by the end of summer and peaks from late August to early September. Olive-sideds seen 26 July 1987 in Huron County and 27 July 1988 in Washtenaw County were getting a head start, perhaps because their nests ended in failure or they bred earlier than usual. Stragglers after mid-September are rare, and an 8 October Kalamazoo record is considered very late even though for many other bird species, the migration is just peaking. Such an early departure is most likely necessary to make it to its other home—the Andean and other mountain forests in northern South America. —Gail A. McPeek

# EASTERN WOOD-PEWEE

## (*Contopus virens*)

This is one of several small, olive-gray flycatchers found in Michigan, discernible from the Eastern Phoebe by its double wing bars and shorter tail, and from the *Empidonax* species by its lack of an eye ring. If you cannot see the bird among the foliage, as is often the case for woodland flycatchers, then song is your best clue. The male's melancholy songs of "pee-a-wee" and "pee-wee" are among the easiest to recognize. Some mistake its two-syllable song for that of the phoebe, but the two are readily separable with a little practice.

As you can probably infer from its name, the Eastern Wood-Pewee lives in wooded habitats and has an eastern distribution. Its breeding range extends from the Atlantic coast to the Plains and the Gulf coast to southeastern Canada. The other half of the country is occupied by its sister species, the Western Wood-Pewee (*Contopus sordidulus*), which is identical in appearance but different in voice. There is almost no overlap in their ranges, and there are no known instances of cross-breeding.

The Eastern Wood-Pewee is a common migrant and summer resident in both peninsulas of Michigan. You should be able to find this species almost anywhere you go, except for the most urbanized areas in the south and pure conifer stands in the north, which it shies away from. Most other wooded situations are agreeable, including forests and forest edge, farm woodlots, and shade trees in parks, in cemeteries, and along rural roadsides.

According to breeding bird surveys in the state, pewees are generally more abundant in the northern and southwestern regions of the Lower Peninsula where deciduous and mixed forests

are most prevalent. That is not to say they are not common elsewhere, just found in lower densities. While they are adaptable to many situations, with a pair or two residing in almost any wooded parcel, studies have shown that mature forests with well-developed canopies support the greatest numbers. Such habitats offer plenty of foraging and nesting opportunities.

Pewees like to forage from exposed perches just below the forest crown layer. Like many flycatchers, they employ a sit-and-wait strategy, taking insects on the wing as they fly by. The subcanopy also provides their favored nesting site—a horizontal limb covered with lichens—upon which the female makes a shallow cup nest. The outside of the nest is craftily covered with lichens so that it looks to be a part of the limb. This disguise, plus the fact that these nests are usually 20 to 30 feet above ground, makes them exceedingly difficult to find. I have seen two nests, one which was discovered through patient observation of a pair and one by pure luck when my eye caught sight of a tail sticking out from a limb about 20 feet overhead.

Pewees are among the later returnees to the breeding grounds, waiting until there are good supplies of flying insects. First reports in Michigan are typically between 5 and 10 May, with migration peaking during the third and fourth weeks. This species is known for its consistent arrival time from year to year, and while a handful of late April reports are valid, others are questionable and are probably attributable to the Eastern Phoebe, a regular early spring migrant.

The pewee's breeding season begins the last week of May and extends into July and sometimes August. Incubation of the three-egg clutch takes 12 to 13 days, with another 15 to 18 days required for growth and development of the hatchlings. Nests found well into July could be second attempts or second broods. Late published records include a nest with young on 3 August and adults feeding fledglings on 1 September, both in southeastern Michigan.

The lack of song in fall makes for a quiet and barely noticed departure. Migration commences in August, and pewees have vacated the Upper Peninsula by the first week of September and are generally through the rest of the state by the third week. Twenty years of banding at the Kalamazoo Nature Center identify the first ten days of September as the average peak movement through the southwest region. An occasional straggler is seen into early October, and a bird on 21 October 1979 in Livingston County is extreme.

Like most other flycatchers, Eastern Wood-Pewees are long-distance migrants—their other "home" being in northern South America and southern Central America. Studies in Amazonia and other tropical regions have found that their arrival in October coincides with peaking insect populations brought on by the rainy season; and that males and females each hold their own

*Olive-sided Flycatcher*
*Alder Flycatcher*
*Yellow-bellied Flycatcher*
JOHN FELSING

territories, with both sexes regularly singing a shorter derivative of the "pee-wee" song.

Unlike some other Neotropical migrants, the Eastern Wood-Pewee has fared well and has not experienced declines in the last 10 to 20 years. Its numbers have increased significantly in Michigan from 1966 to 1991, according to data from breeding bird surveys. This increase is most likely a response to the regrowth of both small and large woodlands in many parts of the state.
—Gail A. McPeek

# YELLOW-BELLIED FLYCATCHER

## (*Empidonax flaviventris*)

The Yellow-bellied Flycatcher is a fairly common migrant throughout the state and a local summer resident in the Upper Peninsula, yet is unfamiliar to many bird-watchers. This is probably the easiest of the eastern *Empidonax* to identify by sight because of the yellowish wash on its belly which extends to the throat. However, several factors contribute to its lack of recognition, including elusive behaviors, time of migration, and remoteness of breeding habitat, all of which contribute to substantial underreporting.

This is one of the latest-breeding species to return to Michigan each spring and one of the earliest to leave in late summer and early fall. The extensive foliage on trees hampers observation during both of these passages. Additionally, migrant Yellow-bellies are often quiet and spend most of their time sitting. Voice also contributes to their anonymity, as their songs and calls are quite similar to those of other flycatchers. Inexperienced birders can easily mistake the soft, whistled "per-wee" of the Yellow-bellied Flycatcher for an Eastern Wood-Pewee song. Even experienced birders have trouble at times distinguishing between the Yellow-bellied's "che-lek" and the drier "che-bek" of the Least Flycatcher.

The spring period usually offers the best opportunities to see this species in most parts of the state. A range of habitats are used, including second-growth woodlands and woodland edges, borders of streams and other wetlands, and forests with clearings. Frequently, these areas contain a mix of conifer and deciduous trees. In southern Michigan, observers should begin searching about the middle of May, while the fourth week is more suitable for northern sites, such as Whitefish Point. Yellow-bellied Flycatchers have been found as early as 6 May in Kalamazoo County, and the migration often lasts into early June, even in the Lower Peninsula.

This flycatcher is a summer resident over much of Canada and the northern United States from North Dakota east. In Michigan, breeding is largely confined to the Upper Peninsula and Isle Royale. Occasional birds are noted in summer in the northern Lower Peninsula, some of which are late migrants. Breeding has been documented in Cheboygan County, and males have been present on territory in Crawford County. During the Breeding Bird Atlas, Yellow-bellies were encountered in 119 townships, all but one in the Upper Peninsula. Records indicate concentrations of breeding pairs in Gogebic, Iron, Baraga, and Marquette coun-

ties in the western half, and Schoolcraft, Luce, and Chippewa counties in the east. The Great Tahquamenon Swamp runs through this latter region and harbors a locally common population of Yellow-bellied Flycatchers.

Much of what we know about the breeding habits of the Yellow-bellied Flycatcher comes from the noteworthy contributions of Lawrence Walkinshaw, one of the few people who made an effort to investigate the often inhospitable bogs and swamps scattered throughout the Upper Peninsula. As birds reach their northern breeding grounds, they settle in bogs dominated by black spruce, tamarack, and white cedar. Nests are located in the more open areas of the bog, in sphagnum moss on the ground or sometimes on or under stumps or root masses. Females lay a single clutch beginning in the middle of June. The seven Michigan nests described in the literature all contained four eggs, although three or five may be present.

Once juveniles have fledged and are on their own, adults begin their southward migration, usually during the last two weeks of July. Unlike most songbirds, these adults do not molt until they reach the wintering grounds in Central America. Occasionally, immature Yellow-bellied Flycatchers reach southern Michigan as early as the first week of August. Peak fall migration, at least in the south, extends from 20 August to about 10 September, with a few birds straggling through later in the month.

Long-term databases provide some information on the relative abundance of this flycatcher during migration. Results of annual spring surveys in Kleinstuck Preserve in Kalamazoo indicate that an average of 24 individuals pass through the preserve per year, although numbers fluctuate widely. In 1984, for example, a high of 102 Yellow-bellieds were counted, while only 7 were detected in each of three different years. In the fall season, approximately 14 birds per year are banded at the Kalamazoo Nature Center; and at the Whitefish Point Bird Observatory, 10 Yellow-bellied Flycatchers were captured in 1990, 25 in 1991, and none in 1992.
—Raymond J. Adams

# ACADIAN FLYCATCHER

## (*Empidonax virescens*)

This flycatcher is the southernmost *Empidonax* of the eastern United States, breeding from southern Minnesota through eastern Texas and from southern New York through Florida. In Michigan, it is a common migrant and summer resident in the southern one-third of the state, and occurs sporadically as a resident north to Oceana, Mason, Newaygo, Isabella, and Huron counties. As a migrant it has been encountered casually north to Grand Traverse and Menominee counties.

As with other *Empidonax* flycatchers, identification in the field is exceedingly difficult without the benefit of voice. The Acadian's song is described variously as an explosive "pit-see" or "wick-up." The similarities among this group are amazing, and even in the hand, they are difficult to tell apart. Identification generally depends on such details as relative length of primary feathers, width of bill, and even color of the mouth.

The Acadian Flycatcher is an inhabitant of rich riparian,

swamp, and mesic forests, preferring mature stands with large trees and a closed canopy. It is also partial to ravines with or without streams. In Michigan, good numbers are found in such areas as the majestic beech-maple forest at Warren Woods State Park and the beech-maple-hemlock forests found near Lake Michigan.

The Breeding Bird Atlas project in the 1980s and subsequent avian studies in Allegan, Kalamazoo, and Berrien counties in the 1990s have greatly enhanced our understanding of Acadian Flycatcher distribution patterns. This species is clearly most abundant where large tracts of mature contiguous forest persist, and the loss of such habitats in southeastern Michigan corresponds with the Acadian's relative scarcity in this corner of the state. Typically, the remaining concentrations of breeding pairs are associated with the larger wooded habitats found on public lands. In southwestern Michigan, the species achieves its highest densities along the riparian corridors of the Galien River in Berrien County, where 103 territories were detected in 1992. Along the Kalamazoo River, it occurs in modest numbers (26 in 1992) and becomes relatively scarce where the riparian corridor is narrow. In Allegan County, Acadians were largely absent from the dry upland woods in the state game area, and instead were concentrated in the mature floodplain forests along the Kalamazoo River and Swan Creek.

Most of the *Empidonax* flycatchers are late migrants, and the Acadian is no exception. Thirty years of records in Berrien County indicate an average arrival time of 12 May, with most birds returning in the last two weeks of the month. First arrival dates in Kalamazoo and Calhoun counties are roughly three to four days behind that of Berrien. Upon arrival, males set up territories and begin advertising for a mate.

Our excellent knowledge of the Acadian Flycatcher's breeding biology comes from the studies of Lawrence Walkinshaw in the late 1950s and early 1960s (Walkinshaw 1966). Nesting commences in late May or, more typically, in early June. The nest is built in a fork near the end of a long downward-sloping branch. It pendant cup is nowhere near as neat as the attractive structure of the Red-eyed Vireo, a common coinhabitant in forests selected by Acadians. Nests reported in the literature averaged slightly over 13 feet above ground, with a range of approximately 3 to 55 feet. The female builds the nest and incubates the eggs (usually three) for about 14 days. The young fledge in another 13 to 15 days. Walkinshaw documented numerous second clutches in July.

The southward flight to wintering areas in southern Central America and northern South America begins soon after breeding ends. Adults depart in August or early September after completing their post-breeding molt. Prior to migration, observers may note a brief recrudescence of song by males. Few if any Acadians are left in the state by mid-September. Rarely, a straggler has been reported into early October.

Information on population trends in Michigan is not available, as the habitats where Acadians reside are not adequately sampled by breeding bird survey routes. Alternative census methods need to be instituted for this and other species dependent on deep mature woods, particularly those in lowland situations. This flycatcher is considered an area-sensitive bird, and is susceptible to increased Brown-headed Cowbird parasitism and predation known to be associated with smaller woodlots. For this reason,

management efforts in southern Michigan should focus on preserving large tracts of contiguous mature forest, especially in riparian zones. —Raymond J. Adams

# ALDER FLYCATCHER
## (*Empidonax alnorum*)

One of our lesser-known *Empidonax*, the Alder Flycatcher is a fairly common transient and breeding species in the northern half of the state, becoming uncommon in the south. Among the factors limiting recognition are its nondistinct plumage, its occurrence in habitats less frequented by bird-watchers, and the lateness of spring migration. During the summer this species ranges across Alaska, Canada, and the northeastern United States south in the Appalachians to western Maryland. The winter range is not so well known but is thought to include Central America and northern South America.

In the field, the Alder Flycatcher appears identical to the Willow Flycatcher and is also visually similar to the Acadian. Even with birds in the hand, separating these species is difficult as a result of broadly overlapping characteristics. In fact, the most reliable way to differentiate between the Alder and Willow Flycatchers is by voice. While the traditional rendering of the Alder song is "fee-bee-oh," I have never heard one sound this way; the translation "rrree-beea," with the accent on the second syllable, gets my vote.

Alder Flycatchers are among the latest spring migrants, seldom arriving in the state before the middle of May. Scattered reports from early May are rarely documented and should be viewed with caution. To find this species in migration, observers should search during the early morning hours in the last two weeks of May and the first week of June. In southern Michigan, the peak period is from 20 to 30 May.

Although the distribution of this flycatcher is statewide, highest densities are found in the Upper Peninsula, particularly in the eastern counties and the far western end. It is also fairly common in the northern Lower Peninsula, and in both of these northern regions the Alder predominates whereas the Willow Flycatcher is uncommon and irregularly distributed. The Alder Flycatcher occupies various damp, brushy habitats in the north, including shrubby swamps, streamside thickets of alder and willow, bog edges, and wet meadows. As you move progressively south in the state, it tends to be more limited to wetter, more densely vegetated sites. In the central and southern portions of the Lower Peninsula, Alder and Willow Flycatchers become territorial neighbors, and in the southern counties it is exceptional to find Alders at sites where you are unable to find Willows as well.

The extent of nesting in southern Michigan is clouded by the late passage of spring migrants, not to mention identification problems. Many of the summer reports of Alders in this region come from the first two weeks of June, a time when lingering transients might still be present. Nesting commences in June and extends into July, with replacement clutches after early failures. Nests with their three to four eggs are usually located one to three feet up in buttonbush, alder, willow, dogwood, or other shrubs. These loosely constructed nests often have fibers hanging from them.

As summer progresses, singing by Alder Flycatchers declines and is mostly confined to early morning. Their secretive nature makes it difficult to determine when the southward migration occurs. Banding records provide some indication as to dates of movement for Alders and Willows; however, the measurements critical to separate these two species are seldom taken. Instead, they are usually lumped together as Traill's Flycatchers when the identity is not known. It is reasonable to assume that most Alders migrate during the last week of August and the first two weeks of September. —Raymond J. Adams

# WILLOW FLYCATCHER

### (*Empidonax traillii*)

While you are bird-watching on a late May morning, a small fly-catcher calls from a clump of dogwood at the edge of a fog-shrouded marsh. As it looks nearly identical to other small flycatchers in the book, you puzzle over its identity. Suddenly it vocalizes again, a strong two-part buzzy song accented on the first syllable, sounding like "fitz-bew." Definitely a Willow Flycatcher, you think to yourself, noting it dutifully on your checklist. A migrant and summer resident in Michigan, this species is common in the southern Lower Peninsula, uncommon and locally distributed in the northern Lower Peninsula, and extremely rare in the Upper Peninsula. Elsewhere in the United States, it occurs from coast to coast, but generally excluding the southern tier of states.

Willow, Alder, and Traill's Flycatcher are three different names for two species, so similar in appearance that for many years they were considered subspecies. In 1973 the two forms were given separate identities, with the more northern species named Alder, and the more southern species designated as Willow. The two can be distinguished only by voice in the field and by careful measurements in the hand. Traill's Flycatcher refers to birds from this complex which have not been identified as to species.

Although the Willow and Alder Flycatchers occur in similar shrub-dominated communities, the former selects a broader range of habitats and tends to be in drier situations if both are present. One of my earliest experiences with this species involved a pasture area adjacent to a narrow marsh. Willow Flycatchers were nesting in the shrubby hawthorns in the hillside pasture as well as in the gray dogwood growing in the marsh below. Writing in *The Atlas of Breeding Birds of Michigan* (1991), Payne noted that Willows tend to use more open shrubby habitats than their near relative. During the Atlas habitat survey, Willow Flycatchers were reported in shrub wetland 70% of the time, in old fields 15%, and in shrub upland 6%.

This species returns to southern Michigan beginning around the middle of May, with average arrival dates between 13 and 17 May in Berrien, Calhoun, and Kalamazoo counties. Earliest reported dates range from 3 to 6 May. Nest building generally does not begin until the first few days of June, with most egg laying taking place around the middle of June for the normal first clutch.

This flycatcher is single-brooded, but females will renest if failure occurs early in the cycle. Clutches contain three to four eggs, with four the most frequent size.

According to Walkinshaw (1966), who studied the breeding biology of the Traill's Flycatcher, nest placement averages a little more than four feet above ground, a typical height for species using shrubs. The Willow's nest contains substantial cottony material and is somewhat similar in placement and shape to nests of the American Goldfinch and Yellow Warbler. Compared to an Alder Flycatcher, the Willow builds a neater, more compact nest.

Because of replacement clutches, nests with young can be found into August. Meanwhile other birds have begun their southward migration, which continues into September and concludes by the end of the month. The winter range remains fairly ambiguous owing to the difficulties of identifying this species in the absence of song. Terborgh (1989) lists northern South America as its principal wintering grounds, and some have been reported in lower Central America. —Raymond J. Adams

# LEAST FLYCATCHER

### (*Empidonax minimus*)

This common migrant and summer resident is the earliest of the *Empidonax* flycatchers to return to Michigan in spring. Birds are typically first reported in late April and early May, often arriving on the first strong southerly winds. Passage takes roughly three weeks, with peak numbers observed in the second week of May in the south and about 10 days later in the north. Timing of migration is fairly consistent, such that the earliest spring date of 19 April is only 11 days prior to the average arrival.

As its name implies, the Least Flycatcher is the smallest of the eastern *Empidonax*. Although it is difficult to identify by sight alone, the combination of small size, gray-olive upperparts, short thin bill, and bold eye ring makes it possible to recognize many individuals. Fortunately, males sing often during spring migration, their emphatic "che-bek" helping to identify the bird.

This flycatcher has an extensive breeding range covering much of Canada and the northern United States, excluding the far west. Nesting pairs are found throughout Michigan from Monroe County to Isle Royale, but in very different numbers as you move around the state. Breeding Bird Atlas results and relative abundance data from breeding bird surveys provide a fairly complete picture of its distribution. In areas which are intensively farmed or have large metropolitan centers, the species is decidedly uncommon. The Detroit area, sections of the Thumb, and the lake border plains around Saginaw Bay are good examples. In some of

*Eastern Wood-Pewee*
*Least Flycatcher*
*Willow Flycatcher*
*Acadian Flycatcher*
JOHN FELSING

these areas, a notable decline in Least Flycatchers has occurred in the past 40 years.

Northward in Michigan, Leasts are encountered more frequently and in larger numbers. Breeding bird survey routes show a clear pattern of greater densities in the northeastern Lower Peninsula and far western Upper Peninsula. Long-term, these data also indicate no significant upward or downward trend in the statewide population since the middle 1960s.

The substantial distribution of the Least Flycatcher in Michigan ties in with the wide range of wooded habitats deemed suitable. One of the types commonly selected is stream and river borders, which attract small "colonies" of breeding pairs. Other frequently used habitats include mature deciduous forests with open mid-stories, forest edge and recently lumbered woods, aspen and aspen-birch stands, and even mixed deciduous-coniferous woodlands. There are many seeming contradictions in habitat choice because of this flexibility. Walkinshaw (1966) found Leasts to prefer drier sites in Muskegon and Calhoun counties, while in other areas, mesic to wet communities are favored. In Kalamazoo County, the species has inhabited two different sites for more than 25 years: one a mature beech-maple forest and the other mostly immature damp woods. At both of these locales, multiple pairs of Least and Acadian Flycatchers have persisted side by side in apparent mutually exclusive territories.

Extensive work by Walkinshaw indicates that nest building begins in mid- to late May in southern Michigan, and eggs are present from late May (in some years) to early July, with later nest dates being replacement clutches. Farther north at Douglas Lake, Cheboygan County, nesting has been observed into early August. Nests are usually in upright crotches of small trees or on horizontal branches well below the canopy. Incubation takes 13 to 15 days, with young fledging in about 15 days.

As with Yellow-bellied Flycatchers, adult Leasts leave for their winter homes in Mexico and Central America shortly after the young are independent, typically in late July and early August. Immatures depart in August, with peak movements toward the end of the month in the southern part of the state. Migration continues into September, rarely October. Exceptional were birds present on 21 October 1977 and 18–19 November 1982. At these late dates, great care should be given to the identity of any *Empidonax*.

The Least is easily the most abundant migrant among those species within its genus. During spring and fall, it utilizes an even wider array of habitats than in summer. City parks, orchards, willow and dogwood thickets, and brushy fields are a few additional sites in which to look for this tiny flycatcher.
—Raymond J. Adams

## HAMMOND'S FLYCATCHER
### (*Empidonax hammondii*)

Field identification of *Empidonax* flycatchers is difficult at best, and the Hammond's Flycatcher is one of the most challenging to confirm visually. A breeding resident of the western states and western Canada, this species can easily be confused with the

Dusky, Gray, and Least Flycatchers, among others. A routine check of the Kalamazoo Nature Center mist nets on 24 October 1990 produced a small *Empidonax* whose characteristics were unlike those of any of the usual flycatchers of the eastern United States. The grayish throat, thin bill, and wing measurements led the banders to suspect it was a Hammond's, and examination of the bird at the University of Michigan Museum of Zoology and at the University of California Museum of Zoology confirmed this identification. This specimen is the only Michigan record of this accidental visitor and one of the few in the eastern United States.
—Raymond J. Adams

## EASTERN PHOEBE
### (*Sayornis phoebe*)

The Eastern Phoebe is a common migrant and summer resident in Michigan, found in all areas of the state except for the most urbanized and intensively farmed. A medium-sized flycatcher, this species is widely recognized, not for its plain appearance but for such familiar traits as its habitual tail bobbing, emphatic "phoebe" song, and fondness for nesting on a wide assortment of human-made structures.

Of the three phoebe species in North America, this one has the largest distribution. Its breeding range includes the eastern two-thirds of the United States and Canada west to the Rocky Mountains and south to the northern limits of the Gulf states. For winter, birds migrate south but stay within the continent from the mid-Atlantic states to Florida, the Gulf states, Texas, and Mexico.

The timing of migration for this hardy species is atypical among flycatchers. It returns early, has an extended stay allowing for two broods, and is the last to depart in autumn. Average arrival time in southern Michigan is late March, although individuals have been reported earlier. Sightings such as the one on 14 February at the Kalamazoo Nature Center may have been a phoebe which stayed the winter. Arrival in the Upper Peninsula generally occurs in the first week of April, but here, too, there are exceptions, including records on 7 March in Marquette and late February in Sault Ste. Marie (also possible overwintering birds).

Michigan weather can still be quite cold and snowy when phoebes return, but their association with streamside habitats allows them to find some insects. They also eat berries and other wild fruits, even an occasional small fish from the shallows. This early migration does have its trade-offs, and spring storms like the blizzard of 3 April 1982 can take a toll on phoebe populations.

Upon their return, Eastern Phoebes settle in a variety of open woodland habitats, almost always in the vicinity of fresh running

*Eastern Phoebe*
*Great Crested Flycatcher*
JOHN FELSING

water with a suitable nesting site nearby. Males arrive first, followed a week or two later by females. This species exhibits a high degree of site faithfulness, often occupying the same territory and even the same nest in consecutive years. Phoebes require some kind of sheltered ledge or vertical surface on which to attach their nest of mud and grass. Originally, nesting was limited to natural sites, namely rocky ravines, cliffs, caves, and upturned roots of fallen trees, but with settlement came a plethora of new sites, including bridges, culverts, wells, and barns or other outbuildings.

Our information on the nesting habits and breeding chronology of the Eastern Phoebe in Michigan is fairly extensive thanks to numerous observations and bridge inventories. Studies in the Lansing area and Macomb County indicate that territories tend to be well dispersed, and neither found two active nests under the same bridge. Alice Kelley reported an early active nest on 19 April 1981 for southeastern Michigan, and in Macomb County, 12 nests were in the incubation stage by 1 May, with the first nestlings hatched on 12 May. During a three-year study in Kalamazoo County, nesting peaked between 30 April and 15 May and again from 4 to 19 June.

Literature for Michigan and other parts of the country gives conflicting evidence for nest parasitism by cowbirds, suggesting considerable local and/or regional variation. Long-term records from the University of Michigan Biological Station in Pellston contain no incidences of parasitism, while studies in Macomb and Kalamazoo counties reported low rates of 12% and 11%, respectively. Nests under bridges tend to experience less parasitism.

Fall migration begins in August in the north and extends well into late October in the southern Lower Peninsula. It is not uncommon for observers in southern counties to report phoebes into November, and there are even rare occurrences of individuals remaining through December and perhaps overwintering. Since the 1959–60 Christmas bird count, there have been six years in which one or two individuals were seen.

Unseasonably harsh winters or cold springs in the South are known to periodically decimate phoebe populations. Numerous authors cite weather as a major factor in the downward trend in the mid-1900s. More recently, the severe winters in the late 1970s had a negative effect on numbers returning to Michigan to breed. These losses were reflected on the state breeding bird surveys in the years which followed. Since 1982, numbers have increased significantly and now approach those of the years before the crash.

There is no doubt that phoebes flourished and increased with settlement. Barrows (1912) called the species abundant and generally distributed in Michigan, though somewhat less abundant in the northernmost Lower Peninsula and the Upper Peninsula. Results of the Breeding Bird Atlas indicate a similar status but with a slight shift in abundance; the pattern is now toward larger densities in the northern Lower Peninsula as urbanization and modern architecture predominant in the south have had an adverse impact on the suitability of bridges and other human structures as phoebe nesting habitat. —Gail A. McPeek

# SAY'S PHOEBE
## (*Sayornis saya*)

In writing about the Say's Phoebe in 1912, Walter Barrows remarked, "The color of this bird is so unlike that of any other flycatcher that it can be hardly be mistaken." He was referring primarily to the cinnamon belly and undertail coverts so distinctive of the adult plumage. Consequently, Barrows had confidence in the Reverend Charles Fox's report of a specimen taken in Owosso (Shiawassee County) in July of 1853, but unfortunately the published list by Fox had been lost. The first fully documented record of this species in Michigan did not come until more than a century later. Sometime during the 1960s, extralimital records of this western resident became more frequent in the Midwest. Michigan's first report occurred on 2 May 1974 along the Sturgeon River in Houghton County (Sloan 1975). Several additional reports have been recorded since. Physical confirmation includes photographs of an individual at Whitefish Point, Chippewa County, in April 1978, as well as photographs of a Say's Phoebe at Tawas Point, Iosco County, on 5 May 1990. Other well-documented sightings are of singles on 2 May 1975 in Muskegon County, in May 1977 in Houghton County, and on 11 May 1991 in Emmet County. All of the modern-day Michigan records are from spring; however, some other midwestern states also have reports from autumn and, rarely, winter. —Raymond J. Adams

# VERMILION FLYCATCHER
## (*Pyrocephalus rubinus*)

Without a photograph or specimen and in the absence of reports from experienced birders, Michigan's two Vermilion Flycatcher reports should be viewed with caution. However, the striking appearance of this small flycatcher, with its brilliant red crest and underparts and dark dorsal surface, lends credence to these observations. This species is usually associated with wooded areas near water in an expansive range from the southwestern United States through Central and South America to Argentina. Vagrants to the Great Lakes region have come during the spring or fall migration periods. The first Michigan sighting occurred on 8 October 1944 on Mackinac Island (Zimmerman and Van Tyne 1959). Several island residents observed this bird and provided a convincing report. Years later, on 12 November 1972, a sparrow-sized flaming red bird with dark brownish-black plumage on the back of its head and back was reported in Macomb County. This individual was seen sallying for insects in typical flycatcher manner. —Raymond J. Adams

# GREAT CRESTED FLYCATCHER

## (*Myiarchus crinitus*)

This large, long-tailed flycatcher has an ashy gray throat, lemon yellow belly, and cinnamon-edged wing and tail feathers. Together these features provide easy recognition and make it one of the more colorful flycatchers in the East. Its "great crest" is only a sometimes obvious trait, evident during times of agitation or excitement when it erects the feathers on its crown as many flycatcher species do.

The Great Crested Flycatcher is a common summer resident in Michigan and throughout the eastern United States. Its breeding range extends from the Atlantic to the prairies and reaches slightly north into southern Canada. The western part of the United States is occupied by three relatives of similar appearance: the Ash-throated, Brown-crested, and Dusky-capped Flycatchers.

For about two-thirds of the year, the Great Crested lives well south of us in southern Florida, Mexico, and Central America. Migration to and from Michigan occurs mostly in the months of May and August–September. Average date of first arrival in Berrien County is 2 May, but a few late-April sightings in the southern counties are normal. However, a 5 April record for Kalamazoo is exceptional, as is a 25 April returnee to the Upper Peninsula, reported at the Whitefish Point Bird Observatory. In autumn, southbound migrants are sometimes still observed in October, although lingering is not something flycatchers are prone to do because of their mostly insect diet.

This species is a denizen of open and semi-open woodlands, preferring deciduous or mixed stands to coniferous. Frequently occupied habitats include forest edges and clearings, orchards and parks, or other open country with large trees. It likes a high canopy for foraging, but the most important requirement is a cavity for nesting. Rather than build an open nest like other eastern flycatchers, the Great Crested uses a natural tree hollow, old woodpecker hole, or birdhouse. This nesting parameter has a profound influence on its breeding distribution and abundance, since the availability of suitable cavities varies widely from place to place. Riparian woods and swamps are among those places which typically offer a good supply.

Nest sites can be in the main trunks or limbs of trees and at a range of heights, commonly 10 to 25 feet above ground. Cavity dimensions are probably the more relevant criterion, since Great Crested Flycatchers average 8 to 9 inches in size. When a nesting box is provided, recommendations call for a depth of at least 10 inches and an entrance hole diameter of 2 inches.

Breeding in Michigan is generally underway by late May. Although Great Crested Flycatchers do not make their own cavities, pairs may spend up to two weeks making a nest within the hole using a conglomeration of leaves, bark shreds, sticks, plant stems, string, cellophane, and the trademark snakeskin. Clutches average five to six eggs, which are incubated by the female for 13 to 15 days. About two weeks later the young fledge the cavity, ready to learn the art of flycatching.

As you might suspect, this species consumes an array of insects, including many larger varieties not taken by smaller woodland flycatchers. Moths, butterflies, dragonflies, grasshoppers, bees, flies, and mosquitoes are all part of the diet. The action of their broad, flat bill makes a sharp snapping sound. They will also hover and snatch caterpillars, spiders, and other prey from the foliage.

It is apparent from the literature that this species has become more abundant in the state, especially in the north. Early accounts describe it as rare or uncommon in the Upper Peninsula and absent from Keweenaw Point and Isle Royale. This is no longer the case, as breeding pairs are now regular throughout the entire region. Nearly 70% of the Upper Peninsula townships were found to have Great Crested Flycatchers during the Breeding Bird Atlas.

Lumbering, which created openings and clearings in the more extensive tracts of forest, probably contributed to this northward increase. So, too, did the regrowth of woods in previously cut areas in both peninsulas. The greater hardwood component in the north may also be a factor, and, as Richard Brewer speculated in *The Atlas of Breeding Birds of Michigan*, the warmer climate of the 1915–55 period may have played a role.

The Great Crested Flycatcher is best located by its loud voice, which carries for a considerable distance and has a recognizable hoarse quality to it. Among the more common repertoires are a ringing "whit-whit-whit-whit," a rolling "prrr-eet," and an emphatic "wheep." Learn these sounds and you will have no problem tracking down this common Michigan bird. —Gail A. McPeek

# WESTERN KINGBIRD

## (*Tyrannus verticalis*)

Were it not for the opening of the landscape by settlers immigrating west during the 1800s, this bird would not have been able to extend its breeding range beyond the boundaries of the plains and prairies. Early writings tell of an eastern expansion which took place around the turn of the century, and by the 1930s, Western Kingbirds were showing up in such states as Minnesota, Illinois, Indiana, Ohio, and Michigan. Small numbers of migrants, vagrants, and breeders now regularly occur east of the Mississippi River, although the bulk of the population still occurs in the Plains and the West.

The first two Michigan records of this gray and yellow kingbird came from the Upper Peninsula: one in Marquette County on 1 June 1925, and one in Luce County on 11 August 1928 (Wood 1951). The following decade had several Lower Peninsula observations, including a 30 June 1937 report of a nest with three young in Barry County (Bazuin 1938).

Scattered reports, all between May and October, have continued ever since, giving the Western Kingbird a status of rare migrant and casual summer resident in Michigan. According to Robert Payne, about 30 sightings were recorded through 1981, and published records post-1981 indicate another 30–35 occurrences through 1993. Most individuals are migrants which have strayed from their usual range during travels to and from their breeding grounds. Nearly every spring between 20 and 31 May, a Western Kingbird is seen in the Whitefish Point area—a well-known concentration spot for migrating birds in the region. This has been the most consistent locale for an appearance by this species in

the state. A 9 May sighting at Whitefish is our earliest spring record.

September is the other month when a Western Kingbird or two are most likely to be seen in Michigan. In the last decade, autumn reports have come from Houghton County (twice), the Keweenaw Golf Course, and Whitefish Point in the Upper Peninsula; and from Ann Arbor, Muskegon State Park, High Island (captured and banded), and a sewage treatment facility in Saginaw County in the Lower Peninsula. The earliest date was 30 August in Keweenaw, and the latest was 21 October in Ann Arbor; all others were from September. It seems that every fall some Western Kingbirds head east and reach the Atlantic coast before turning south. This is a roundabout way to get to Central America and Mexico, where they spend the winter.

Summer occurrences in Michigan are more erratic, with breeding confirmed in only a few instances. Nearly 30 years lapsed before the second nest was found, this one in a walnut tree in Kalamazoo County in July 1960. This site was again occupied by presumably the same pair in 1961, and the next few summers which followed. Things got interesting in July 1964, when two adult Western Kingbirds and four young were seen, and not far away, observers discovered another brood of three young being fed by what appeared to be a hybrid marriage of a Western and Eastern Kingbird.

Years passed again with only a few sporadic summer observations. Then on 1 July 1984, a pair was discovered in Baraga County. It was not until 8 July 1988 that another nest was located in the state, this time in an old windmill tower in Isabella County (near Winn). This nest was being tended to by a Western Kingbird, presumed to be a female, with occasional visits by an Eastern Kingbird, most likely a male (J. Reinoehl, pers. comm.). About a week later, the three nestlings were found on the ground; it seems a mite infestation induced an early exit. Only one young survived and was transported to the Kalamazoo Nature Center. Characteristics of both species were evident in the juvenile feathers, but by the end of the summer its plumage mostly resembled that of a Western Kingbird (J. Granlund, pers. comm.).

The adult female continued to return to this rural spot in Isabella for the next several years, apparently mating with an Eastern Kingbird each time. The nest was in an apple tree in 1989, and then back in the windmill tower in 1990. This use of human structures, as well as trees, is regularly reported throughout its range. Nesting by a Western Kingbird also occurred in 1992 at this Isabella County site. Other 1992 summer sightings came from South Haven (Van Buren County), Tawas Point (Iosco County), and Delta County.

Like its eastern cousin, the Western Kingbird breeds in open country and is a conspicuous feature perched atop poles, wires, and fenceposts across the Plains. Croplands, ranches, golf courses,

and parks have all become suitable options along with the remnant prairies, savannas, and other natural grasslands. —Gail A. McPeek

## EASTERN KINGBIRD

(*Tyrannus tyrannus*)

The Eastern Kingbird is a conspicuous open-country bird and one of our best-known flycatchers. Throughout the state it is either a common or abundant summer resident, living in fields, pastures, orchards, and woodland edges and along roadsides and the borders of lakes, ponds, and wetlands. The common features of these varied habitats are scrubby trees for nesting, plenty of flying insects, and open spaces in which to pursue them. This bird is an expert when it comes to aerial hawking.

Kingbirds are among the pool of later spring migrants. Any returnees prior to 1 May are considered early, and records on 2 April 1982 in southeast Michigan (Monroe County) and 4 April 1988 in the Upper Peninsula (Marquette County) are highly unusual. Peak migration comes during the second and third weeks of May, when flocks of 100 or more are sometimes seen along the Great Lakes. Males precede females by a few days, and individuals tend to settle in the same area throughout their lives.

You cannot miss the return of this species to Michigan. In addition to occurring in mostly open habitats, the kingbird has a temperament which keeps it in nearly perpetual motion, whether hawking for insects, defending a territory, or pursuing a mate. Accompanying these activities are constant emissions of harsh notes and stuttering calls. Chases and aggressive encounters between territorial males and between mates are frequent, and since the sexes look alike, you often do not know which kind of encounter you are witnessing.

This bird has been the subject of numerous studies, from its diet and nesting to the zealous defense of its territory. If you have ever seen a small bird in relentless pursuit of a hawk or crow as it moves across an open field, you can bet it was an Eastern Kingbird. This species is "king" in its territory, and most any large bird or mammal entering its domain is likely to come under attack. The kingbird seems fearless as it dives after the trespasser, striking it in the back and sometimes plucking a few feathers.

What seems most peculiar about this behavior is that, more often than not, the intruder is flying high overhead, posing no threat to the kingbird or its nest. It is as if the bird recognizes a territory that extends far into the air. The benefit of these attacks is uncertain, but research has found that this aggressive defense around the nest tree itself does contribute to a relatively high nesting success. Not only is the kingbird good at keeping enemies away, but it also will not tolerate cowbird eggs in its nest.

The breeding season begins in the latter part of May, and by early June most pairs in the state are nesting. Kingbird nests are fairly easy to find. Look for them in scraggly trees in old fields, orchards, or pastures, along rural roadsides, or near open water. Placement is usually out on a limb away from the trunk and at mid-height in the tree or shrub. Occasionally nests are in unusual locations, such as atop a telephone pole or fencepost, or in a tree

*Eastern Kingbird*
*Western Kingbird*
JOHN FELSING

hollow, sometimes even in a snag over water. During studies of birds using the logged and burned jack-pine plains in northern Michigan, where this species also finds a home, Ben Pinkowski located four nests in the hollowed tops of fire-charred stubs.

The female kingbird makes the bulky, rather unkempt nest and has charge until hatching. She behaves quite aggressively toward her mate during building and incubation, not letting him too close to the nest. Later, the male will join in the feeding of the young. It takes a little more than a month for the three to five eggs to hatch and the young to vacate the nest, though they continue to rely on their parents for several weeks more.

Toward the end of the summer, kingbirds congregate in groups for the fall migration, and birds dot the wires from the Upper Peninsula to the southern state line. Departure occurs in August and September; rarely do individuals linger into October. A 16 October sighting in the Garden Peninsula, Delta County, and a 25 October record for Kalamazoo are extremely late.

Eastern Kingbird is a bit of a misnomer. While it is the main *Tyrannus* of the East, its distribution is by no means limited to this region. Breeding occurs in the eastern, central, and northwestern parts of the United States, as well as in most of Canada. The other seven months of the year are spent in northern South America. Here this species lives a different existence, roaming the Amazonian rainforest in large, nonterritorial flocks and feeding mostly on fruits rather than insects.

In the period from 1982 to 1992, breeding bird surveys for the state detected a significant drop in kingbird numbers. It is still one of Michigan's more common birds, but what this decline means and what has caused it is unknown. This trend could reflect the successional advancement of habitats along roadways, which survey routes typically follow. There is also the possibility of reduced productivity and/or mortality from pesticides or the series of drought years in the 1980s. Or perhaps we are seeing the first effects of tropical deforestation, which has been accelerating in the Amazonian basin. Until more evidence is in, we can only speculate and watch trends in the future. —Gail A. McPeek

# GRAY KINGBIRD

## (*Tyrannus dominicensis*)

The Gray Kingbird, a paler, larger-billed relative of the Eastern Kingbird, breeds in southern Florida and along the coast from South Carolina to Louisiana, south to northern South America. On rare occasions, vagrants have been discovered north to Massachusetts and Ontario. While the coastal nature of its distribution makes it an unlikely candidate to reach our parts, many Michigan birders were rewarded with a view of this flycatcher during a brief visit from 14 to 18 October 1984 in Oceana County. The bird spent much of its time hawking insects along adjacent drainage ditches and flying into a shrubby field across the road to feed on berries of Virginia creeper. —Raymond J. Adams

# SCISSOR-TAILED FLYCATCHER

## (*Tyrannus forficatus*)

"Beautiful," "graceful," and "sublime" are terms which describe this casual migrant and summer visitor to Michigan. My first encounter with a Scissor-tailed Flycatcher occurred along U.S. 2 in the Upper Peninsula; there, perched on a wire, was an exquisite bird, more than a foot in length, with long, black-tipped outer tail feathers and a body that was light gray above, white below, and soft salmon-pink on the sides. A regular breeding resident of the southern Great Plains states, the Scissor-tailed Flycatcher is found in open to semi-open country and is frequently seen on wires, fences, or other exposed perches. It migrates a relatively short distance, wintering primarily from Mexico to Panama. This species exhibits a tendency to wander from its usual range, and strays have been recorded throughout much of North America.

It was 1962 before Michigan had a documented Scissor-tailed Flycatcher report. That spring, birds were found on 14 May near Leland, Leelanau County, and from 31 May to 2 June south of Saginaw. Observations on 3 May 1965 at Seney National Wildlife Refuge, Schoolcraft County, and 24 October 1969 at Marquette were the only other reports of that decade. In the 1970s a bird was photographed on 11 June 1973 at Bette Gris, Keweenaw County, and another was present on 18 May 1975 in Franklin Township, Delta County. The 1980s brought at least 11 more reports, including occurrences every year from 1980 through 1987, and sightings in 1991 and 1993 indicate that this pattern of vagrancy continues. Michigan records extend from 3 May to 31 October and come from 15 different counties. There are at least 8 reports from May, 6 from June and July, and 5 from October. All observations have involved singles except for the two seen at Whitefish Point, Chippewa County, on 20 October 1986. —Raymond J. Adams

# FORK-TAILED FLYCATCHER

## (*Tyrannus savana*)

This extremely long-tailed flycatcher is native to Mexico, Central America, and South America, where it inhabits open country, usually savannas and marshes. Those which breed in southern South America migrate north to Trinidad, Tobago, and the Lesser Antilles for the winter (our summer), and on rare occasions, individuals wander into the United States. There is only one documented record of this accidental visitor in Michigan—a specimen at the University of Michigan Museum of Zoology ob-

*Horned Lark*
*Barn Swallow*
*Cliff Swallow*
David Mohrhardt

tained after the bird was hit by a vehicle in Alger County on 20 October 1983. Walter Barrows (1912) tells of s supposed specimen of a Fork-tailed Flycatcher observed by Dr. Maurice Gibbs in 1882 in A. B. Covert's collection, which apparently came from Lenawee County in July 1879. However, Barrows could not trace the specimen and considered this record unsubstantiated. Other records for the Great Lakes region include two in Wisconsin and one each in Ontario and Minnesota. —Raymond J. Adams

## HORNED LARK

### (*Eremophila alpestris*)

Although the Horned Lark is common during much of the year in Michigan, the snow-covered fields during our late winter months provide the best opportunity to observe this ground-dwelling bird. One can regularly find small, and sometimes huge, flocks gathered in desolate farm fields, feeding on leftover grains. Against the white background, these mostly brown birds are clearly more conspicuous relative to other seasons, when they blend in with the exposed soil and vegetative cover of their habitat. If you get a close view, you can see the distinctive black face and bib markings and the black feather "horns" for which they are named.

Large open fields are the preferred habitat of the Horned Lark. Today, these are typically man-made situations including row crops, hayfields, sparsely vegetated grass or weed fields, golf courses, and airports—basically any area where the soil is exposed. Such open lands provide both foraging and nesting habitat for this species. Foods are obtained from the ground, with seeds and waste grains consumed during winter, and insects and spiders added to the diet in spring and summer. Larks are often attracted to fields where fresh manure has been scattered, picking out seeds deposited by the farmer's spreader.

The Horned Lark finds suitable breeding habitat throughout most of North America, and is considered a year-round resident in southernmost Canada, all of the lower 48 states (except the extreme Southeast), and Mexico. A segment of the population migrates to and nests across Canada and Alaska, including the tundra region. In Michigan, this species is a common and widespread breeder in the Lower Peninsula, but rare and local in the Upper Peninsula, where habitat is very limited. In this region, isolated nesting populations are found in the south-central counties and in eastern Chippewa County south of Sault Ste. Marie. Greatest numbers of nesting Horned Larks are found in the southern two to three tiers of counties and the Thumb region.

During winter, distribution retracts mostly to the central and southern counties. Annual Christmas bird counts provide an index to the variability in the winter population, with totals since 1970 ranging between lows of 600 to 700 birds and highs around 5,000. Lowest numbers correspond to harsh winters with below-average temperatures and extensive snow cover by late December when counts begin. In contrast, mild early winter weather and little snow allow more larks to remain.

It is not known if the Horned Larks seen in the winter months are the same as those which breed here. Banding data indicate that some Horned Larks from Michigan migrate to the southern and southeastern United States, while others probably remain. Certainly some percentage of our winter birds are visitors from the North. Because of this year-round presence, it is difficult to determine exact migration schedules for this species.

The Horned Lark is a very early nester, as males begin their defense of territories as early as late February. Courtship begins in March and includes a fascinating flight display. The male stands on a small mound of dirt, flies into the air, sometimes to heights of up to 800 feet, sings "pit-wit, wee-pit, pit-wee, wee-pit," and then dives back toward earth, pulling up just before hitting the ground.

The nest is a simple depression in the soil, usually lined with grasses and occasional feathers, plant down, and hair, and some are circled with stones. Nesting starts in March and continues through June or July, with many pairs having two broods. Fledglings from first nests can be seen as early as April. First nests are often less vulnerable to predation, since many animals are not active yet. Probably the biggest obstacle for these first clutches is spring snowstorms. For second nests, plowing activities probably cause many losses in addition to predation. With the Horned Lark's preference for large areas of exposed soil, a farmer's unplanted fields can provide the "perfect" habitat. However, once they are planted and growing, the area is no longer suitable. For this reason late spring–early summer nests are often found in freshly cut hayfields or uncultivated fields.

The Horned Lark is a bird which benefited from settlement and clearing and cultivation of the land. The spread of agriculture created thousands of acres of new habitat during the late 1800s and early 1900s. In recent decades surveys indicate a slight drop in numbers, most likely due to reduction in overall acreage of farm and pasturelands as well as changes in agricultural practices. —Charles Nelson

## PURPLE MARTIN

### (*Progne subis*)

A graceful and acrobatic flier, the Purple Martin is a delight to watch as it swoops and dives over lakes and fields, snatching insects on the wing. This bird's larger size and the male's glossy purple plumage above and below distinguish it from other swallows. The female is duller with a pale belly and grayish breast and throat. A forked tail, though not as pronounced as the Barn Swallow's, is also a good identifying feature.

The breeding range of the Purple Martin includes much of North America, except for the mountainous areas of the West and

*Purple Martin*
*Tree Swallow*
CYNDY CALLOG

Cyndy Callog

the boreal and tundra regions of Canada. In Michigan this species is a fairly common summer resident over most of the state, with populations concentrated along the Great Lakes and around inland bodies of water, less so in areas with extensive open fields. Martins are generally more widespread and numerous in the southern Lower Peninsula, with numbers gradually decreasing northward where lands are more forested. Nesting colonies become uncommon and local once you reach the northern Upper Peninsula and are absent from Keweenaw Point and Isle Royale.

After wintering in South America, male martins are the first to return in spring, with some individuals reaching southern Michigan in late March or early April. These early arrivers or "scouts" search for suitable breeding territories and nesting sites, often selecting the same area as the year before. The rest of the martins, both females and younger males, begin arriving in force during the second and third weeks of April, and more northern residents can still be seen in migration into May.

Across the northern parts of the breeding range, populations are vulnerable to cold snaps and inclement weather in March and April. Prolonged periods of rain or snow and the resulting lack of flying insects can decimate entire colonies. Such was the case in 1982, when an early April blizzard caused widespread mortality of martins across the eastern United States.

Purple Martins, like other insect-eating birds, are also susceptible to pesticides. Martin landlords have reported finding whole colonies dead or dying in their yards or nesting boxes for no apparent reason. Foraging in areas where pesticides were recently applied for mosquito or other insect control is suspected as the probable cause in many of these situations.

At one time Purple Martins were limited to nesting in tree cavities, but they have long since adapted to an assortment of human-supplied boxes with multiple apartments or hollowed-out gourds, first used by Native Americans. The Purple Martin Conservation Association, a citizens' group formed to promote the conservation of this species, educates people on proper techniques for building, erecting, and maintaining martin houses. These houses should be set in open or semi-open grassy areas, preferably with water nearby. Wet meadows, grassy river valleys, and lakeshores are among the better locales. Generally, rural settings are more suited because they tend to have more open foraging habitat and less competition with House Sparrows and European Starlings, which readily use martin complexes.

Males are first to claim residence in the martin house, defending one or more holes. Then when the females arrive, they choose a suitable compartment and mate. Nesting activity typically starts in the first week of May in the Lower Peninsula and a week or two later in the Upper Peninsula.

By summer's end, martins gather in large flocks for their migration south. The main flight occurs during the latter half of August. At this time, flocks of several hundred can be seen resting on telephone wires, and even larger groups containing thousands of martins are reported migrating along the Great Lakes shorelines. Most have departed the state by early to mid-September, with an occasional straggler observed into October.

For reasons we do not fully understand, there has been a protracted decline of Purple Martins in the state and other regions of the continent from 1966 to 1991. The reduction in numbers approaches 80% in some southwestern counties. Following the massive mortality suffered in 1982, many states added this species to their "special concern" lists. Although martins remain common over much of Michigan, careful monitoring of their populations is warranted. —Charles Nelson

## TREE SWALLOW
### (*Tachycineta bicolor*)

The Tree Swallow is one of our most familiar and abundant swallows. These birds are a welcome sight to many each spring, occupying nest boxes provided by people and devouring large quantities of insect pests. A common summer resident throughout the state, this species is easily identified, particularly the males with their iridescent greenish-blue plumage above contrasting with white below. Females are similar but with duller grayish-green upperparts.

The summer range of the Tree Shallow includes most of North America except for large sections of the Central Plains and the far southeastern and southwestern states. Lakes, ponds, marshes, and wet meadows are all favorable habitats, providing both foraging and nesting sites. Pastures and fields far from water are also acceptable as long as suitable nesting sites can be found. This swallow requires cavities for its nest and will utilize holes in trees or fenceposts as well as artificial sites such as roof eaves and boxes.

The Tree Swallow has long been an abundant breeding resident in Michigan, but before the introduction of nest boxes, numbers in the southern third were notably smaller. Now, with greater nesting opportunities, its distribution is more uniform throughout the state, and as the number of available boxes has increased, so, too, have Tree Swallow populations. Only in the most urbanized or intensively farmed areas of the southeast is this species uncommon, owing to a lack of suitable habitat and competition for nesting sites with House Sparrows and European Starlings. Over much of the Upper Peninsula, including Isle Royale, most nesting occurs in natural cavities rather than boxes.

The Tree Swallow is one of the first swallows to return each spring. It arrives in southern Michigan between late March and mid-April, reaching the Upper Peninsula a couple of weeks later. When insects cannot be found, birds will turn to berries, but periods of prolonged cold weather can be extremely detrimental to those that have returned. Tree Swallows which have succumbed to these late cold snaps have been found, sometimes a half-dozen or more, frozen in the bottom of a single box where they were roosting. According to the Michigan seasonal survey, such an event occurred in 1982, with observers reporting that most birds which returned prior to the series of wintery April storms perished.

Nesting in Michigan takes place in May and June, with some pairs starting as early as April. Below-average temperatures during the breeding season can also have an impact on Tree Swallow populations by affecting their productivity. Data from the Michigan Nestbox Network in 1992, a year when June temperatures averaged four to five degrees below normal, documented a fledging success rate of only 54% for 1,900 nests with eggs. Compare this with a success rate of 76% recorded in 1991, a year when

June temperatures were slightly above normal. Cold June weather kills off a substantial supply of insects needed by nesting swallows to fuel their increased metabolism as well as feed their young.

After a cavity or box has been selected, a nest of straw and grass is typically built by the female, although the male may help gather materials. Once complete, the nest is usually lined with a few feathers, almost always white ones. Wanting to observe firsthand the Tree Swallow's fascination for white feathers, I set out a handful of white chicken feathers on the ground in clear view of an occupied box. Within minutes, a bird was snatching up the feathers and taking them back to the nest. I have even heard stories of swallows picking feathers from an outstretched hand.

Tree Swallows raise only one brood of four to six young per season. Being strong fliers, they have almost no post-fledgling period. Once the immature birds leave the nest, they do not return and within three days are on their own. Huge flocks of Tree Swallows start to form in July but remain in the state into October, making this the latest of the swallows to depart. Migratory flocks numbering up to 10,000 members have been recorded in the state. One excellent location to observe these massive fall congregations is the Muskegon Wastewater System. By November most Tree Swallows have left for their wintering range in the southern coastal states, Mexico, and Central America. —Charles Nelson

# NORTHERN ROUGH-WINGED SWALLOW

## (*Stelgidopteryx serripennis*)

This swallow is a common migrant and summer resident throughout both peninsulas of Michigan (excluding Isle Royale), but is found most frequently and in greatest numbers in the southern half of the state. It is commonly seen swooping low over rivers, lakes, marshes, and fields, catching and consuming flying insects. This species often associates with the smaller Bank Swallow, and while canoeing down rivers such as the Pere Marquette one can search among large flocks of darting Bank Swallows and usually find the less common Rough-wing. Look for a slightly larger swallow with a faint dusky-brown upper breast and whitish throat rather than the well-defined dark breast band and white throat of the Bank Swallow.

The Rough-winged Swallow has an extensive breeding range, which includes parts of extreme southern Canada, the United States, Mexico, and Central America. In winter it withdraws farther south, from Florida and the Gulf coast to Panama. Suitable habitat consists of open areas for foraging and either natural or man-made sites for nesting. Natural sites are usually burrows in eroded banks along streams, rivers, and lakes. Among the numerous man-made sites are steep walls of gravel pits, rock faces, or banks along railroad and highway cuts, bridges, and drain pipes.

The Rough-winged, which is the least common of our swallows, usually arrives in small numbers starting in early April in the southern Lower Peninsula and in the latter part of the month farther north. As the insect supply increases, so too do the numbers of returning Rough-wings. By early May, flocks may consist of 150 individuals.

Upon their return, pairs form and search for a suitable burrow in which to construct a nest. Rarely do they make their own burrow; more often they choose an old burrow of a Bank Swallow or Belted Kingfisher, or occupy an artificial cavity. Rough-winged Swallows typically nest singly or in small groups, unlike Bank Swallows which breed in large colonies.

The nest within the burrow or cavity is constructed of grasses, weeds, rootlets, and sometimes twigs. This species is single-brooded, and clutches average six to seven eggs. Incubation by the female takes 12 to 16 days, and fledging occurs between late June and early July, when the young are about 20 days old. Families remain intact through the summer and join others, resulting in flocks of up to 200 or more individuals by August. Departure from northern Michigan begins as early as late July, and the migration through the state is mostly complete by the middle of September. Most unusual is a record of an individual which lingered at a sewage treatment facility in Berrien County through 16 December 1987.

The Rough-winged Swallow, like some of its relatives, has been the benefactor of the addition of human structures and influence of land-use practices on the environment. The increase in the supply of nesting sites has allowed this bird to become more plentiful in southern Michigan and to expand its range northward. Breeding bird survey data indicate a significant increase in populations of Rough-wings in the Great Lakes region since 1966. —Charles Nelson

# BANK SWALLOW

## (*Riparia riparia*)

Another of our common swallows, this one is identified by its brown back, white belly and throat, and a distinctive brown band across its breast. It is the smallest of the North American swallows and has a breeding range that encompasses most temperate regions of the world. With such a widespread distribution, the Bank Swallow is readily found in all sections of Michigan except for Isle Royale. This species is a common summer resident and migrant throughout both peninsulas, but occurs in its greatest numbers in the southern counties, especially in the western corner.

Observers should look for this swallow over lakes, ponds, rivers, and open grassy fields. As it catches insects on the fly, watch for an erratic, zig-zag flight pattern that is more fluttery than that of other swallows. You can also listen for its twittering notes and a gritty "speed-zeet, speed-zeet" call, which is distinguishable from a similar call of the Rough-winged Swallow.

During the breeding season, these birds will form nesting colonies which vary from a few couples to 300 to 400 pairs. They nest in burrows constructed in steep banks that are cut away either by the force of water or by human activity. With a preponderance of excellent habitat, Michigan plays host to a relatively large and stable population of Bank Swallows along its many rivers and suitable shorelines of the Great Lakes.

While conducting birding classes I have found that some bluffs along lower Lake Michigan have the correct geologic history to be especially popular with Bank Swallow colonies. This species must find just the right mixture of glacial moraine and sand in order to make the perfect burrow. Pure sand dunes are too fragile to support nesting tunnels, and hard clay cliffs are simply too dense for digging. A compromise is needed, so they seek out mixtures of soft dune sand and harder glacial material. One such site is located on the cliffs of Camp Warren, north of St. Joseph in Berrien County. Large colonies of Bank Swallows have been nesting here longer than the 20 years I have been in the area to observe them.

This swallow returns to the southern and central Lower Peninsula in mid- to late April and reaches the more northern areas of the state in early to mid-May. Nest excavation begins soon after arrival and is usually complete by the end of May. Both sexes dig, making a burrow straight into the vertical bank using their beaks to chisel and their feet to kick the dirt out behind them. The depth of the burrow depends on the substrate texture, ranging from 16 inches to 5 feet long. In the back of the excavation, the pair build a flimsy nest of plant materials and feathers.

Laying of the four to five white eggs occurs in May or June, with occasional renesting into July. Incubation takes about 15 days, and fledging occurs when the chicks are about 20 days old. It is quite a sight to see an entire cliff come alive with young swallows popping in and out of their holes while relentlessly chattering for food.

During mid-July and August, Bank Swallows begin to congregate into their fall migration flocks. Northern and inland populations will gather by the end of August and travel down river valleys and coastlines by the thousands. Birds along southern Lake Michigan occasionally remain in the area until late September. Bank Swallows spend the winter months in Central and South America, sometimes as far south as northern Chile.

Before European settlement, Bank Swallow colonies were limited to natural nesting situations such as those occurring in riparian and dune habitats. With settlement and the advent of gravel pits, construction projects, and highway embankments, many new nesting sites were made available, allowing this species to become more widespread. There are even reports of swallows burrowing into sawdust piles. These dynamic situations cause colonies to relocate quite regularly, as dump trucks and bulldozers can easily destroy nesting banks. This makes it difficult to accurately determine inland population trends. Providing that people do not disturb suitable lakeshore sites and colonies, Michigan will continue to offer the Bank Swallow vital breeding habitat.
—Charles Nelson

# CLIFF SWALLOW

## (*Hirundo pyrrhonota*)

Once a species that nested on cliffs or other rough vertical surfaces, the Cliff Swallow now uses human structures almost exclusively for its gourd-shaped mud nests. In fact, there are no recent records in the Michigan literature of a Cliff Swallow using a cliff for nesting purposes. It seems to have adapted so well to human-made structures that it prefers these to natural surfaces.

Typical sites for attachment of their nests include old unpainted barns, cement silos, and bridges.

The distribution of this common summer resident is strongly influenced by its nesting and foraging needs. Along with suitable surfaces for nest attachment, the Cliff Swallow requires large open fields or bodies of water to satisfy its diet of flying insects. The combination of old barns and large grassy fields and lakes is abundant in the northern regions of the state. Consequently, this species is widely distributed and occurs in generous numbers in the Upper and northern Lower peninsulas. Suitable habitat is more limiting in the south, and Cliff Swallows tend to be locally common in some counties but rare in others.

Although this species shares many traits with its relatives, the Cliff Swallow has a look all its own. Distinguishing features on its head include a cream-colored crescent just above the beak, a bluish-black crown, a black throat, and rufous cheeks. Other key characteristics are its orange rump patch and a square tail, which is very unswallow-like. This swallow's body measures only 5 to 6 inches in length, but its wing span approaches 12 inches. These proportions make it a swift and agile flier, and it can be fascinating to watch as it plucks insects from mid-air at speeds of 10 to 25 miles per hour.

During the breeding season, Cliff Swallows are found throughout much of North America from Alaska to Mexico, but excluding the southeastern United States. Their winter range is far to the south, mainly from Brazil to Argentina. This is the famed swallow species which returns so predictably every spring to the Capistrano mission in San Juan, California.

The song of the Cliff Swallow, an unmusical "creak," can first be heard in southern Michigan around the middle of April as birds return to breed. Individuals begin reaching the Upper Peninsula in late April, and by the middle of May most of the nesting population will be on hand. Flocks from the north head southward in August, with the main migration through the southern counties during the first half of September. Occasionally, a few stragglers are reported into early October.

Cliff Swallows live in colonies ranging from a few pairs to more than 1,000 members. Adults gather mud with their beaks to mold their unique nests. Construction may last from 5 to 14 days, with the additional finishing touch of grass lining and a few feathers. Egg laying may start as early as mid-May or extend into July depending on conditions, disturbances, and the need for renesting. Many nests may simply fall from the vertical surface because of poor adhesion.

Although this species benefited from human structures and clearing of the land, the introduction of the House Sparrow from Europe in the late 1800s spelled disaster for the Cliff Swallow. The House Sparrow became an aggressive usurper of its nest as well as a destroyer of its eggs and young. Declines in Cliff Swallow populations were noted over much of southern Michigan in the decades following the introduction.

Another influencing factor on numbers and distribution in southern Michigan is the changes occurring to human structures over time. Old barns and silos are being replaced, often with materials which lack the rough surface needed for nest attachment. In southwest Michigan, an old bridge and a wooden barn each housed a small colony of Cliff Swallows for many years. I often took students and bird-watchers to these sites because they provided excellent viewing opportunities. Progress has now done away with these structures; a new steel bridge and metal pole barn replaced the old, and the swallows have long since moved elsewhere. —Charles Nelson

## BARN SWALLOW
### (*Hirundo rustica*)

The Barn Swallow, with its propensity for nesting in barns and other human structures, is one of the best-known birds in Michigan, as well as throughout much of the world. This species is the most widely distributed swallow, breeding in Eurasia and in North America, from Alaska to Mexico and from the Pacific to the Atlantic. It is easily distinguished from other swallows by its deeply forked tail, iridescent blue-black back, reddish-brown forehead and throat, and cinnamon breast.

Barn Swallows first return from their tropical wintering grounds in early spring, beginning with arrival in southern Michigan around the middle of April (average of 13 April in Berrien County), and reaching the central and northern regions between mid-April and the first part of May. Rarely, an individual may appear in late March, as was the case with a report on 23 March in Kalamazoo County.

This species is a common summer resident in both peninsulas, although it is generally more numerous in the southern half of the state, where nesting structures and foraging habitats are in greater supply. It is by far our most abundant swallow, reported on state breeding bird survey routes in numbers nearly twice those of the second most common species, the Tree Swallow. Abundance drops as one heads north into areas with less cultivated or other open lands. Densities are typically lowest in the Upper Peninsula, but even here in this northernmost region, Barn Swallows occur in all counties, including Isle Royale.

Suitable Barn Swallow habitat consists of almost any large open area, such as agricultural lands, pastures, upland fields, water bodies, and rural residential areas. Its distribution is especially tied to the availability of farmlands because of the nesting and foraging habitat they provide. Relying on a diet of various flying insects, grasshoppers, crickets, and leafhoppers, the Barn Swallow can be found gliding and diving in beautiful loops over these open lands, sometimes even following a farmer's tractor to snatch up prey disturbed by the plow. With its hearty appetite for insects, this species is a welcome guest around farmlands. Unfortunately for the swallows, this relationship can have its drawbacks if foraging occurs in fields where pesticides have been applied.

The Barn Swallow is named for its habit of nesting in barns, but it is by no means limited to them and has been known to nest under bridges, eaves, boat docks, or other similar human structures, as well as natural ledges provided by cliffs and caves. One of the more unusual nests I have seen was in a friend's garage on top of the electric door opener.

The nest may be placed on a horizontal surface, in which case it is called a statant nest. Otherwise it is attached to the side of a vertical surface and is known as an adherent nest. In either case, the base is made of mud or clay, and grass or straw is used to form a cup, which is then lined with hair or feathers. Barn Swallows may nest in single pairs, small groups, or large colonies. In Michigan, colonies with as many as 40 nests have been reported.

Barn Swallows typically have two broods per season, with clutches consisting of four to six eggs. Laying of first clutches generally starts in mid-May in lower Michigan and slightly later for pairs farther north. Second nests are usually found in early to mid-July. Incubation takes two weeks, and the young fledge in about three weeks' time. After the young can fly, they often remain around the nest site for a few days, even roosting in the nest at night. This is a behavior not seen in most bird species.

As summer draws to a close, migratory flocks begin to form. Swallows tend to migrate relatively early because of their insect diet, and the Barn Swallow is no exception. Most migrate during August and early September, and by the latter part of the month almost all have left the state on their long journey to lower Central and northern South America. It is highly unusual to have any individuals linger past early October, but twice (1975 and 1983) this swallow has been seen on Christmas bird counts in southern Michigan. The earlier record of six Barn Swallows lacked documentation, but the December 1983 report at a sewage treatment facility in Berrien County was confirmed. —Charles Nelson

## GRAY JAY
### (*Perisoreus canadensis*)

Historic records and tales of the Gray Jay come mostly from the trappers, hunters, lumberjacks, and miners who lived and worked in the wilds of northern Michigan during the 1800s. They were well acquainted with this bold jay which raided camps for food, snatching bacon and beans directly from their plates and tearing meat from carcasses of deer, moose, or other game. These antics earned it such nicknames as Camp Robber, Venison Bird, and Meat Hawk. Such stories and experiences are less common today, though tame individuals are found around some residences and parks in the Upper Peninsula.

The Gray Jay is a bird of boreal and montane woods found across Canada and Alaska, south in the West to California and the southern Rockies and in the east to northern New England and the northern Great Lakes. Of the three recognized subspecies, only *P. c. canadensis* (formerly Canada Jay) occurs in Michigan. For the most part these jays are permanent residents, with only the occasional irruption bringing individuals south of the usual range. Wintering Gray Jays have been recorded south to Nebraska, Pennsylvania, and Connecticut.

The Gray Jay's Michigan distribution is not as extensive today as it was one hundred years ago—a change evidently linked to the widespread logging of the virgin forests in the north. Until the turn of the century, this species was considered common in suitable places in the Upper and northern Lower peninsulas, south to Wexford, Roscommon, and Ogemaw counties. Maurice Gibbs (1879) even commented on its occasional winter visits to the southern boundary of the state. By the mid-1900s, its range had

retracted northward to include only the Upper Peninsula, and according to Zimmerman and Van Tyne (1959) there had been no summer records in the Lower Peninsula since 1915.

The current distribution of the Gray Jay, as documented by the Breeding Bird Atlas, remains limited to the Upper Peninsula, where it is a local resident, common in areas of suitable habitat such as western Chippewa County, the Seney area (Schoolcraft County), the western region from Marquette to Gogebic counties, and on Isle Royale, where it is especially common. Spruce forests are among the more favored habitats, along with spruce-tamarack bogs and cedar swamps, and to a lesser extent jack-pine plains. Writing in *The Atlas of Breeding Birds of Michigan*, D. Evers made note of the bird's association with riverine habitats lined with spruce, and scattered openings provided by beaver meadows or peatlands.

Nest records for the Gray Jay in Michigan are relatively few in number because of the remoteness of their habitat and the early onset of breeding, typically in February and March. Published reports include nests with eggs on 6 March, 28 March, and 22 April; nests with young on 30 April; and adults with juveniles seen between May and mid-July. Spruce or fir trees are commonly chosen, with nests generally located 6 to 10 feet above ground. Eggs (usually 3 to 4) hatch in about 17 days, and the juveniles, wearing a sooty-gray plumage, fledge in another 15 days.

Essential to this early nesting cycle are the food caches accumulated by Gray Jays the previous summer and fall. Food items include a variety of insects, insect eggs, and fruit, and surpluses are stored by forming a morsel of food into a bolus, coating it with a sticky saliva, and then adhering it to conifer needles, branches, or bark crevices. These caches, often scattered over a large area, are used during winter and through the following breeding season.

Fall is a time not only of caching, but also of some migration or wanderings. In most years these movements are generally small and probably associated with natural dispersal. Occasionally, though, larger influxes or irruptions of jays from farther north are evident in Michigan, and it is during these years that individuals may appear outside their usual range. Historical records indicate that such irruptions once brought birds farther south than today, as Gray Jays are now rarely encountered south of the Straits.

Recent autumn-winter irruptions occurred in 1975–76 and 1986–87. In the former, there were at least two sightings in the Lower Peninsula (26 October, Presque Isle County, and December, Ann Arbor), with 26 Gray Jays reported on the 1975–76 Christmas bird counts. This invasion was especially apparent the following spring (1976), when more than 100 Gray Jays were reported at Whitefish Point on 26 May. More recently, in 1986–87, 38 were observed on the Christmas bird counts and 50 were seen at Whitefish Point in spring. —Gail A. McPeek

*Winter Wren*
*Gray Jay*
*Boreal Chickadee*
David Mohrhardt

# BLUE JAY
## (*Cyanocitta cristata*)

This large crested blue-feathered bird needs no introduction. It is one of the most abundant and widely distributed species in Michigan, and one of the most boisterous. No matter where you live or travel in the state, the piercing calls and fervid activity of the Blue Jay are common. How can you not notice a bird whose regular affairs include mobbing raptors, dive-bombing cats and squirrels, and commandeering feeders to gorge on sunflower seeds and cracked corn?

Just how common is the Blue Jay in Michigan? During the recent statewide Breeding Bird Atlas, it made the top ten list of most frequently reported species, joining the ranks of such other notables as the American Robin, Song Sparrow, and Black-capped Chickadee. This gregarious corvid is also one of the more abundant winter residents, with Christmas bird count totals ranging from 8,000 to 14,000 in recent years, and reports from 95% of the Michigan Audubon bird feeder surveys. Even more impressive are the enormous flocks seen along Michigan's lakeshores during the spring and fall months. When the jay migration is in full swing, meticulous observers have recorded more than 10,000 in a single day.

The Blue Jay's range encompasses the eastern two-thirds of the United States and southern Canada west to Alberta, the Plains states, and eastern New Mexico. This species is considered a permanent resident of Michigan, but as we have learned through banding efforts, part of the winter population is different from that of summer. The jays at your feeder in winter may be local birds or northern migrants, and the young born in your area are probably wintering somewhere south, in states such as Kentucky, Tennessee, or Missouri. It is the withdrawal of northern jay populations which results in the massive migrations seen in Michigan.

If you have not witnessed this spectacular happening along our state's lakeshores, it is a sight worth seeing. The spring migration starts in mid- to late April in the south and continues well into June. Along the Berrien County coastline of Lake Michigan, numbers generally peak between late April and mid-May. The maximum total reported was 20,000 on 1 May 1972. At Whitefish Point in the Upper Peninsula, peak flights occur between mid-May and early June. These are two of the most reliable and rewarding locales for jay migration. At the Whitefish Point Bird Observatory, the Blue Jay concentrations are also attractive to the migrating Peregrines, Merlins, and Sharp-shinned Hawks.

Migratory jays tend to be more dispersed in the fall, though in some years numbers equal those of spring. In 1974, for example, an estimated 10,000 jays moved through Berrien County on 27 September. Records from here and other lakeshore points, such as Muskegon State Park, indicate a peak during late September and early October in the south.

For Blue Jays that stay in Michigan year-round, the fall and winter months are spent in foraging flocks, which disband as spring approaches. Older jays pair first, usually in March or April, and are quietly mate feeding and nest building while the younger generation is off consorting in noisy courtship flocks consisting of a female and several males trying to win her attention. Don't be fooled by the making of partial "dummy" nests during pair bonding; the actual nest comes later in spring, with egg laying in May or June. Families remain together for one to two months as parents tend to their clamorous juveniles.

Although we regularly see jays around our neighborhoods and parks, this species is first and foremost a forest inhabitant. Highest breeding densities are typically associated with mature woods dominated by oak, beech, pine, and other mast-producing trees. Desirable nesting sites and foods are plentiful here. Acorns, in particular, are an important dietary item and are hoarded by the thousands during the late summer and autumn months. During bumper-crop years, these provisions allow many more jays to remain farther north for the winter.

Of course, we know from daily experience that residency is by no means limited to forested habitats. The opportunistic Blue Jay is also right at home in small woodlots and semi-wooded situations such as those provided by roadside edges, old fields, orchards, and our landscaped suburbs, golf courses, and cemeteries. Ornamental plantings, especially dense conifers, are frequently chosen for nesting, and any of these habitats have ample food to satisfy the jay's omnivorous diet of seeds, fruits, and insects, with some amphibians, fish, mice, birds, and bird eggs.

Adaptable qualities have enabled this already common bird to become even more abundant. Forest regeneration and maturation have also contributed, especially to the increases in the northern counties, where it was considered uncommon earlier this century. Since at least 1966, when the standardized breeding bird surveys began, Blue Jay populations have been on the rise in Michigan and throughout much of their range, which is expanding steadily to the northwest. —Gail A. McPeek

## CLARK'S NUTCRACKER
### (Nucifraga columbiana)

There is one documented record of this western species in the state, giving it the status of accidental visitor. On 16 December 1978, a Clark's Nutcracker was found during a Christmas bird count at Whitefish Point in Chippewa County. Distinctive were its long bill, grayish body, black wings with prominent white secondary patches, and short tail comprising black central and white outer feathers. Although no picture was obtained, the written documentation left no doubt as to the bird's identity. The Clark's Nutcracker is a noisy, gregarious member of the Corvid family, which inhabits juniper and pine forests in the mountains of the West. This species is known to sporadically wander to lower elevations and occasionally reach the Midwest. —Raymond J. Adams

## BLACK-BILLED MAGPIE
### (Pica pica)

A relative of crows and jays, the Black-billed Magpie inhabits parts of Alaska, western Canada, and much of the western United States as well as Eurasia. Its occurrence in Michigan is accidental, as its North American breeding range extends only as far east as western Ontario and northwestern Minnesota. Historically, this species has had an irregular pattern of occurrence in the state. The first specimen was taken in southern Michigan by A. Sager in 1837 or 1838. Barrows (1912) refers to other sightings in the 1800s, primarily from the western Upper Peninsula.

Modern records originate with a specimen collected on 6 December 1955 in Ann Arbor, Washtenaw County. Including this specimen there have been at least 10 records from 1955 to the present, 5 from the Upper Peninsula and 5 from the Lower Peninsula. All observations fall between the dates of 1 October and 28 April except for a report at Grand Mere, Berrien County, on 26 June 1977—a date that does not fit the usual pattern of occurrence in the Midwest. The other sightings are from the following dates and locations: 1–12 October 1959, Oakland County; 14–21 February 1960, Iosco County; 3 October 1967, Alger County; 28 April 1972, Chippewa County; 20 October 1973, Berrien County; 28 January–2 February 1975, Schoolcraft County; 9 March 1975, Chippewa County; and October 1976, Isle Royale. National breeding bird surveys show a decline in magpie populations since 1966, which may explain the lack of recent sightings for Michigan.

There is seldom concern over the accuracy of reports since the magpie's black and white plumage, showy white wing patches, and long black tail make it easy to identify. There is, however, the possibility that a report could be of an escaped rather than wild bird, since this species is sometimes kept in captivity. As recently as 1985 a Black-billed Magpie in Gladwin County drew birders, including myself, from around the state before a local newspaper article revealed it was an escapee. —Raymond J. Adams

## AMERICAN CROW
### (Corvus brachyrhynchos)

Adaptable and intelligent, the American Crow is an abundant North American bird, breeding from coast to coast and from northern Canada to Florida, Texas, and northern Mexico. Only in parts of the arid Southwest is it rare or absent. Some are migratory, withdrawing from much of Canada and the extreme

*Common Raven*
*American Crow*
*Blue Jay*
HEINER HERTLING

H. C. Hertling

northern parts of the United States for the winter months. Neither the Fish Crow, Northwestern Crow, nor Mexican Crow has such an extensive range, nor are they found in Michigan.

The American Crow lives in open and wooded habitats, using the former for foraging and the latter for nesting, and its populations have thrived in the mixed landscape of farm, field, and forest created by settlement and human land use. Given how abundant the crow is today, it is hard to fathom its being absent from the state historically. Such was apparently the case, however, according to archaeological evidence and the earliest writings. First listed for Michigan in 1853, it proceeded rapidly in its occupation of the state, with large flocks already present in Detroit in 1858, and expansion into the Upper Peninsula underway. By the turn of the century, this species was a common to abundant summer resident and migrant.

During the 1900s, we have seen a further change in the crow's status, this time involving its winter residency. At the time Barrows wrote in 1912, nearly all crows departed the state and congregated in large roosts near the Ohio River. Then, beginning in the 1940s, flocks numbering in the hundreds to thousands were reported in the southern Lower Peninsula. Although flocks have not been as large in recent decades, the crow is a common winter resident in the south and a rare winter bird north into the Upper Peninsula. Foods provided by agricultural waste, landfills, and roadkills have likely played a major role in allowing more crows to winter farther north.

Christmas bird counts provide good documentation of over-wintering crows in Michigan. Following a record high of 17,351 in 1959–60 (and an incredible 206 per 10 party-hours), a rather large drop in numbers occurred in the 1960s. By the mid- to late sixties, annual counts fell to a few thousand, and the decade average was only 4,070. A gradual increase took place in the 1970s, raising the decade average to 6,497. This was followed by a considerably larger increase in the 1980s, to an average of 13,314 for the decade. Causes for these fluctuations are unclear, though perhaps the massive efforts to reduce populations in the middle 1900s (through shooting, poisoning, blasting, etc.) are reflected in the low 1960s totals. Breeding bird survey data also show a significant increase for the same period (1960s–1980s).

Seasonal migration of transient and resident crows in Michigan occurs from September to November and from mid-February to May. In autumn, most flocks have left the Upper Peninsula by early November, with thousands moving through southern Michigan until the end of the month. Northbound crows begin arriving in February or early March farther north. Passage in the southern counties concludes by late April, but at Whitefish Point and other migration corridors in the Upper Peninsula, transients are still on the move into the third week of May.

The breeding season for this large black bird commences around 1 April in southern Michigan, and three to four weeks later in the north. The bulky stick nest is placed high in a tree, preferably an evergreen located in a wooded area. Crows are secretive during nesting but resume their noisy ways when the young (usually 4–6) are older and calling from the nest. After leaving the nest in June or the first part of July, fledglings can be seen following their parents about, begging loudly for food.

Toward the end of the breeding season, crows begin to congregate in large communal roosts, to which they return each evening after the day's foray for food. In the late 1800s, Walter Barrows studied the crow's diet by examining more than 900 stomachs. Animal foods, including a diversity of insects, amphibians, crustaceans, eggs, birds, and small mammals, made up 67% of the summer diet. Vegetable matter was the larger proportion in winter, as crows consume large quantities of corn, wheat, and other agricultural grains plus acorns, beechnuts, and cultivated and wild fruits. The crow's "ingenuity" at obtaining foods is fascinating, whether it is dropping shellfish from the air to crack open the shell, feasting on drowned beetles in late spring, scavenging garbage and roadkill, or pulling up new sprouts of corn. Considering this bird's enormous numbers and food choices, it is no wonder many people, especially farmers, look upon this species as a pest. —Gail A. McPeek

# COMMON RAVEN
## (*Corvus corax*)

The Common Raven is Michigan's other large all-black bird, similar in appearance to the more familiar crow but considerably larger, with a body size five to six inches longer than that of its smaller relative. Accompanying its greater bulk is a heavy curved bill, giving it a powerful look. In flight the ravens wedge-shaped tail separates it from the smaller crow with its fan-shaped tail. At present, owing to a recovery of its population in the region, Michigan observers can find ravens over much of the northern Lower Peninsula and throughout the Upper Peninsula.

The Common Raven has an expansive distribution across the Northern Hemisphere. In North America, it occurs throughout Alaska, Canada, the western and northeastern United States (including the higher Appalachians), and Mexico. The habitats where it lives are quite varied but all somewhat remote, from tundra, seacoasts, and wooded marine islands to forest wilderness, mountains, and desert.

In Michigan, this species selects large tracts of mature forest with minimal disturbance for breeding, although recently some ravens are showing a greater tolerance of human activities. Large evergreens are most often used for nesting in this part of the bird's range, but cliff nests have also been reported, along with the occasional nest in a hardwood. Ravens construct a large stick nest which they fill with a thick lining of animal hair, mosses, and bark shreds. Nests appear much like those of a large raptor, measuring 2 to 4 feet in diameter, and are typically located 30 to 50 feet or more above ground.

The breeding season for the raven begins in the dead of winter, with nest building and egg laying in February or March and nestlings present between March and May. Northern Michigan is largely snowbound for much of the bird's breeding cycle, so it is no wonder that few nests are ever reported. Recent nests found in Alpena and Wexford counties fledged young on 12 and 21 May, though families have been seen in the state as early as late April.

During the summer months, ravens can be seen foraging about in their family groups. Like crows, they are opportunistic omnivores feeding on almost any kind of food, dead or alive. They are both resourceful and crafty whether scavenging roadkill or garbage at dumps, dropping shellfish onto rocks to get at the contents, or taking eggs from a nest while the owner is away fending off some other predator or distracted by human activity. Several authors have noted the strategic location of raven nests near winter deer yards, where starvation losses can provide sizable amounts of food.

Ravens are year-round residents, and yet there is also some migration or movement evident in the fall and spring along coastal areas in the Upper Peninsula. Similar observations are noted in Minnesota and Wisconsin, but it is not clear where these birds are headed or where they came from. A small number of ravens are reported south of known breeding areas in Michigan during fall and winter, but not enough to account for the movement seen in the north. Spring counts at Whitefish Point have exceeded 1,000 birds, with biggest flights occurring in April.

At the time settlers arrived in Michigan, it was the raven that was found throughout the state, not the crow. Forest clearing and persecution proceeded to quickly alter this status, with raven numbers decreasing and its range retreating farther northward into the remaining wilderness. By the early years of this century, the species was extirpated from Indiana, Illinois, Ohio, and lower Michigan as well as most of the Northeast. Ravens managed to hang on in the Upper Peninsula and, with laws protecting birds in place and forest regrowth beginning, populations started to recover around the 1940s.

Today, this species is common and found in good numbers throughout the Upper Peninsula, and is once again a regular, if not common, resident in the northern four tiers of Lower Peninsula counties. Nesting reports below the Straits have been increasing in frequency since the late 1970s, and at the conclusion of the Breeding Bird Atlas in 1988, the raven's range reached south to Lake and Clare counties. Associated with this expansion has been an increase in fall and winter sightings south to Huron, Tuscola, and Muskegon counties. Considering the forest regeneration which has occurred in parts of the southern Lower Peninsula, especially on public lands, the establishment of nesting ravens in this region is very possible in the near future. —Gail A. McPeek

# BLACK-CAPPED CHICKADEE

## (*Parus atricapillus*)

One bird that people often seem to fall in love with is the Black-capped Chickadee. No one can mistake this little bird in its formal attire of a black cap, black bow tie, and white cheeks. This common songbird is a resident of wooded areas throughout Michigan, including our neighborhoods, where it is a welcome visitor to feeders with sunflower seed.

There are several chickadee species in North America, but none are as widely distributed as the Black-cap. It is found throughout the northern half of the United States and all of southern Canada north to Alaska. This species is versatile in its habitat requirements, breeding in deciduous and coniferous forests, small woodlots, thickets, and orchards—practically anywhere there are some trees suitable for nesting. Like all members of the Paridae family, the Black-capped Chickadee nests in tree cavities, which is probably one of its most limiting requirements. Pairs may excavate a cavity in the decaying wood of a tree stump, or they may choose an old woodpecker hole or natural hollow. When they make their own cavities, they remove the wood shavings from their work and scatter them away from the nest.

This species readily accepts nesting boxes placed in appropriate habitat and made with an entrance hole of one and one-quarter inches. In winter these boxes or other cavities become important roosting sites for chickadees. You can also build special roost boxes with multiple perches inside and an entrance at the bottom to conserve heat.

Chickadee pairs are generally mated for life. Courtship begins as early as February in southern Michigan, a few weeks later in the north, and by May breeding is in full swing throughout the state. Probably everyone knows the "chick-a-dee-dee-dee" call, which is given year-round, but some may not recognize the whistled "fee-bee" song of males, heard most frequently in late winter and spring. Clutches average six to eight eggs which are incubated solely by the female for 12 days. Fledging of young occurs in about 16 days, and the juveniles remain with the parents for another one to two weeks.

Most chickadees remain near their breeding grounds for the entire year, but their habit of flocking makes them seem more abundant. A flock establishes a feeding territory, and birds may roam 40 to 80 acres. Studies have found that a hierarchy exists among flock members, which include a dominant pair, some juveniles, and some single adults. In areas where chickadee densities are high, the lowest-ranked individuals may not breed.

Joining the chickadee flocks in fall and winter are numerous other birds, both residents and migrants, including such species as titmice, nuthatches, woodpeckers, kinglets, and Brown Creepers. Benefits of this group action are access to food resources and detection of predators. The feisty chickadee is one of the first birds to respond to distress calls of other birds or to scold and mob a predator. Because of this behavior, the species is easily drawn to a tape-recording of a Screech-Owl or to a birder's pishing sounds.

We tend to think of this species as a permanent resident, but there is also evidence that some chickadees migrate. Transients are probably moving south from Canada. For example, at migration concentration points such as Whitefish Point, movements occur in September and October and again in April and May, with numbers fluctuating widely from year to year. Spring flights may be especially pronounced, with thousands recorded in a season and hundreds seen in a single day.

There is no question that the Black-capped Chickadee is one of Michigan's most common and widely distributed birds. During the Breeding Bird Atlas, it was sixth on the overall list of species reported in the most townships, and since the start of the breeding bird survey in 1966, chickadee numbers have increased significantly in the state. Winter data provide a similar picture of abundance, with Black-caps observed on 95% of the Michigan feeder counts and a doubling in numbers (per 10 party-hours) on Christmas bird counts since 1970. —Dick Schinkel

# CAROLINA CHICKADEE

## (*Parus carolinensis*)

The Carolina Chickadee is a nonmigratory resident of the eastern United States from central Indiana and Ohio south. It rarely appears north of this range, and the only Michigan record is documented by a specimen of an immature male collected on 17 July 1899 in Oakwood, Wayne County. There are no modern records, though observers and banders in our southernmost counties should be aware of the possibility of vagrants. While this species is nearly identical in appearance to the Black-capped Chickadee, the higher-pitched call notes and song of the Carolina can be used to differentiate the two. In the hand, banders should look for the Carolina's proportionately shorter tail and gray outer edges of the greater wing coverts. —Raymond J. Adams

# BOREAL CHICKADEE

## (*Parus hudsonicus*)

A rare to uncommon resident of Michigan's Upper Peninsula, this small bird has the familiar chickadee plumage scheme but with a brown cap instead of black like its more abundant relative. Other differences are the brown hues on its dorsal surface and flanks. The Boreal Chickadee's call is also a reliable distinguishing feature, being slower than the Black-cap's call and possessing a nasal quality, typically a "chick-a-daay" or "chick-a-dee-daay-daay."

The Boreal Chickadee is found in the boreal and mixed coniferous forests throughout Canada and central Alaska. Its range barely enters the United States in northern Montana, the Upper Midwest, and northern New England. In Michigan, its range is generally restricted to the Upper Peninsula, although sporadic fall and winter movements have resulted in some individuals wandering south of their normal range. According to Wood (1951), there is also one summer record for the Lower Peninsula, from 15 July 1933 in Cheboygan County, just below the Straits.

Spruce bogs and other spruce-dominated woodlands are the preferred habitats of this species. *The Atlas of Breeding Birds of Michigan* identified two seemingly disjunct populations in the Upper Peninsula. The first occurs primarily from western Chippewa to central Alger County, where spruce bogs at such places as Betchler Lake, Newberry, and Seney National Wildlife Refuge harbor good numbers of Boreal Chickadees. The second population is concentrated from western Marquette to eastern Gogebic County. In this region, breeding pairs were found to be especially common in white spruce habitats bordering the Peshekee River (Marquette County). After the breeding season, this species has also been found in other conifer habitats including jack-pine plains.

Boreal Chickadees nest in a natural cavity, an old woodpecker hole, or a cavity excavated by the pair in soft rotting wood. The bottom of the cavity is lined with moss, lichens, root fibers, and plant down. Clutches containing six to nine eggs are probably laid in late May or early June, though perhaps later. So few nests of this species have been found that our knowledge about its breeding cycle is poor. A recent nest record from Houghton County had eggs on 3 July and nestlings on 11 July. Other nest records are from 20 June 1954 in Chippewa County and 25 June 1956 in Baraga County.

During the fall and winter months, Boreal Chickadees congregate in feeding flocks with their own kind or with Black-capped Chickadees, woodpeckers, and nuthatches. Seasonal movements for this species are poorly understood but are probably related to available food supplies, as is the case for many boreal species. In some years, there is an influx of Boreal Chickadees from farther north, adding to our resident populations. These movements vary in magnitude and may be evident by an increase in sightings in the Upper Peninsula or by individuals wandering to the southern Lower Peninsula. At other times the influx is apparent only in the large numbers of spring transients seen at Whitefish Point as they make their way north.

Seasonal surveys along with data from Whitefish Point Bird Observatory and other sources provide some interesting information regarding movements and invasions. For example, a major winter invasion occurred in 1972–73, when more than 60 birds were reported in the Lower Peninsula, including 46 in the Detroit-area counties. A few individuals even lingered into spring, with late dates of 17 April in Genesee, 8 May in Kalamazoo, and 20 May in Presque Isle County. Good though not exceptional numbers were noted at Whitefish Point that spring. In sharp contrast, the following winter (1973–74) had no Boreal Chickadee occurrences in the Lower Peninsula and only a few reports in the Upper Peninsula, yet an average movement was still noted at Whitefish in spring.

Winter data from 1986–87, including 13 reports on Christmas bird counts, suggest an influx that year but not a particularly large one, but then the following spring, a record high of 1,463 Boreal Chickadees were tallied at Whitefish Point, leaving birders wondering "Where did they all come from?" Based on these highly variable records and the meager information on nesting, it is clear that we have much to learn about our other Michigan chickadee. —Dick Schinkel

# TUFTED TITMOUSE

## (*Parus bicolor*)

The Tufted Titmouse is a popular permanent resident in Michigan's Lower Peninsula, frequently seen at backyard feeding stations. This species is the largest member of the titmouse-chickadee family (Paridae) found in the state, and it is the only one with a crest. Sexes are identical with gray upperparts, a pale

*Black-capped Chickadee*
DAVID MOHRHARDT

Cyndy Callog

breast and belly, rufous flanks, and a black forehead patch. Large black eyes give it a mouse-like appearance, hence the name titmouse. The voice of this bird is disproportionately loud for its small size, often translated as "peter-peter-peter." Titmice also possess a variety of harsh scolding calls heard throughout the year.

The Tufted Titmouse occurs in the eastern portion of the continent north to southern Ontario and northern New England, west to the plains, and south to Florida, Texas, and Mexico. In Michigan, the species is presently limited to the Lower Peninsula, being most abundant in the southern half, particularly in the more wooded western counties. North of Midland and Lake counties, titmice are rare and locally distributed, though they appear to now be fairly regular residents in the Traverse City area. Habitat requirements are rather broad, encompassing most deciduous and mixed woodland communities in both bottomland and upland situations. This can also include the suburban environment of tree-lined streets and landscaped backyards.

The status of the Tufted Titmouse in Michigan has changed dramatically over the last one hundred years. Described by M. Gibbs in 1879 as a mere accidental visitor, this bird has experienced a major range expansion and growth in its population since then. Writings and records show that by the 1960s, titmice had reached counties in the northern Lower Peninsula and were abundant throughout the south. While we do not know for sure what caused this change, the common contributing factors mentioned are the general climatic warming trend which occurred during the early and middle decades of this century, the regrowth of woodlands in many areas, and enhanced food supplies due to the large increase in bird feeding. Results of the Breeding Bird Atlas indicate that further expansion northward has slowed in recent decades, although numbers continued to increase as was evident in both the state breeding bird surveys and Christmas bird counts.

Although titmice are not yet established in the Upper Peninsula, there are three recent records from the region, all in 1990. Included were one spring and one summer sighting in Delta County and one spring encounter in Menominee County. As with a few species (Cerulean Warbler and Henslow's Sparrow, for example) which have recently reached the Upper Peninsula, these counties which border Wisconsin are the first places we would expect the titmouse to appear.

The Tufted Titmouse is a cavity nester, selecting natural tree cavities, abandoned woodpecker holes, or bird boxes. The breeding season generally commences in April, with most egg laying occurring in May. Clutches contain five to seven creamy white eggs which hatch in about two weeks. Both parents attend to the young, which fledge the nest in a little more than two weeks. Like other cavity-nesting birds, the titmouse does not have

to contend with brood parasitism by the Brown-headed Cowbird.

During the nesting season, titmice generally prefer more wooded habitats, tending to shy away from residential areas. Once breeding is complete, though, family groups wandering in search of food will regularly visit neighborhoods and parks, especially where there are feeders. This species is quite an acrobat and can be seen hanging in many awkward positions as it forages.

In the fall and winter months, Tufted Titmice travel in loose flocks with other family groups. They also regularly join with chickadees, small woodpeckers, and nuthatches, forming some rather large feeding flocks. Adult birds usually remain close to their breeding range year-round, and titmouse flocks do not typically cover as much ground as Black-capped Chickadee flocks. Only first-year birds are thought to move large distances as they disperse from their natal territory. —Dick Schinkel

# RED-BREASTED NUTHATCH
## (*Sitta canadensis*)

This tiny bark-foraging bird is a common inhabitant of Michigan's evergreen forest. As a breeding species, the Red-breasted Nuthatch is primarily limited to the coniferous and mixed woodlands in the northern two-thirds of the state and is most abundant in the Upper Peninsula and on Isle Royale. Scattered nesting pairs have been found south to Kalamazoo and Oakland counties. During migration and winter, the species is generally distributed throughout the state, though winter populations fluctuate in accordance with food availability.

The Red-breasted Nuthatch resides in the northern coniferous and montane forests of North America. Distribution in the West extends from southern Alaska to southern California and Arizona, while in the East it can be found from Newfoundland to the Great Lakes and New England states and farther south in the Appalachians. There is a large gap in the central United States where the species does not breed. Wintering occurs within the breeding range and irregularly throughout the central and southern states, except for the Florida peninsula and extreme southern Texas.

The Red-breasted Nuthatch is only four and a half inches long and is easily identified by its bluish-gray color above, white eyebrow, and thick black eye stripe. Males have a black cap and rusty breast and belly, while females have a gray cap and fainter underparts. Its voice is similar to that of the more familiar White-breasted Nuthatch, but higher-pitched and more nasal in quality.

This nuthatch or "upside-down bird," as it is sometimes called, forages by inching downward headfirst on tree trunks, investigating crevices in the bark for insects, insect eggs, and other foods. Seeds of conifers, extracted from cones with its tiny bill, are also consumed, as are seeds of ash and maple. Red-breasted Nuthatches will readily come to bird feeders that offer sunflower seed, suet, and peanut butter mixtures. Much like a chickadee or titmouse, this species will retrieve a seed from the feeder and fly to a nearby branch, where it forces the seed into a crevice and proceeds to peck it open.

The extent of the southward migration of Red-breasted Nut-

*Blue-gray Gnatcatcher*
*Tufted Titmouse*
*Cedar Waxwing*
CYNDY CALLOG

hatches depends on food supplies in the north, particularly seed crops of pines and spruces. In years when food is plentiful, there is little migration from the breeding grounds, but when the seed crop is poor, large numbers head south in the fall. During these years, substantial numbers are seen in southern Michigan, some of which stay the winter while others continue farther south. Arrival usually begins in September, occasionally August, with birds traveling in family groups or small flocks.

The return northward occurs from April until mid- to late May. In fact, many resident nuthatches are already breeding when some of the last transients are still passing through the state. As with other cavity-nesting birds, nesting commences fairly early, marked by an increase in song in late winter, with egg laying in May. When courting a female, the male nuthatch performs a rather unusual-looking display, raising his head and stubby tail, dropping his wings, and then swinging his head back and forth with back feathers erected. Offering food to the female is also part of the ritual.

Red-breasted Nuthatches select a hole in a rotted tree, branch, or stump for nesting; on occasion they will excavate their own. The pair often smear pitch around the entrance, probably to discourage insects and predators. They gather this pitch from nearby conifers, applying it throughout the nesting period. The Red-cockaded Woodpecker practices the same technique. Red-breasted Nuthatches usually lay five to six eggs, which are incubated by the female for about 12 days. They raise only one brood per season, with young fledging 18 to 21 days after hatching.
—Dick Schinkel

# WHITE-BREASTED NUTHATCH

## (*Sitta carolinensis*)

The more familiar of the two nuthatch species found in Michigan, the White-breasted is a common permanent resident of wooded habitats throughout both peninsulas. Probably everyone at one time or another has seen this comical bird perched upside down on a tree trunk. The sexes have similar plumages but can be separated by the color of the cap, which is black in males and mostly gray in females. Nuthatches are small, stocky birds with short legs, a stubby tail, and long toes for clinging to the sides of trees. Their long, chisel-like bills are suited for probing and digging out insects from bark as well as opening seeds.

White-breasted Nuthatches are found throughout the United States and parts of southern Canada wherever deciduous forests are prevalent. In Michigan this species shows a preference for beech-maple woodlands, although any area with hardwoods is usually suitable, including farm woodlots, orchards, parks, and our more wooded suburbs. According to *The Atlas of Breeding Birds of Michigan*, its distribution becomes more diffuse in the conifer-dominated forests of the Upper Peninsula, habitat favored by the Red-breasted Nuthatch. Elsewhere in the north, where woodlands have a mixed composition, the two species coexist well.

Prior to lumbering of the extensive conifer forests in the northern Lower Peninsula, there was a marked decrease in White-breasted Nuthatches north of the state's midline. Today this difference is only minor, with slightly lower densities in the region. Breeding bird surveys show abundance in the Lower Peninsula to be greatest in the southwestern counties, moderate in most of the north, and lowest in the areas dominated by urban and suburban development and agricultural land uses.

Although the White-breasted Nuthatch is classified as a permanent resident, at least a portion of the population will undergo some southward migration in some years. These shifts in distribution have been noted in some eastern states, with numbers increasing for a short time in spring and autumn. People living in the more densely populated regions of the state are likely to see more nuthatches in the fall and winter months. These may be local birds which bred in nearby forested areas, dispersing immatures, or migrants from farther north.

During winter, White-breasted Nuthatches are frequent members of the mixed feeding flocks with chickadees and titmice. This species is widely reported on Michigan Christmas bird counts, with annual totals for the past several years ranging between 3,500 and 4,500. There has been a substantial increase in overall numbers reported since the 1960s, but when weighted against observer effort (party-hours), the increase is only slight. The standardized breeding bird surveys provide a better index and show a significant increase in Michigan's White-breasted Nuthatch population from the mid-1960s to 1991.

The breeding cycle starts in winter, beginning with a remarkable increase in the birds' distinctive nasal "yank, yank" calls. Although pairs typically remain together year-round, there is a period of courtship and pair bonding. You may witness this activity around your feeder. The male will display to the female, raising his crown feathers to an almost crest-like posture, spreading his wings and tail feathers, and bowing and singing. He will also court his mate with food, sometimes placing seed or bits of suet in crevices for the female to retrieve.

White-breasted Nuthatches prefer large hardwoods for their nesting cavity. Rarely a pair will excavate their own hole; in most instances they choose a rotted knothole or other natural cavity, or one left by a woodpecker. Pairs may also take advantage of nesting boxes in suitable habitat. Nuthatches line the cavity with soft bark, feathers, and animal hair, and you may see them taking hair from a road-killed rabbit or other mammal. According to A. C. Bent, this can cause the nest to "resemble a buzzard's domicile rather than a nuthatch home."

Egg laying generally occurs in April or May, with clutches ranging from five to nine eggs. Females are in charge of incubation, which takes about 12 days. The young fledge the cavity in about two weeks. Unlike the first plumage of many songbirds, that of a young nuthatch resembles the adult plumage, so juveniles will show black or gray caps. Thus, if you examine a nest box occu-

*White-breasted Nuthatch*
*Red-breasted Nuthatch*
*Brown Creeper*
DAVID MOHRHARDT

pied by this species, you can often determine the number of each sex within the brood.

The nuthatch spends the greater part of the day searching tree trunks and limbs for insects, including their pupae and eggs. They also take advantage of seeds and nuts and are common visitors to feeders, dining on sunflower seed, suet, and mixtures of peanut butter, rendered suet, and cornmeal. —Dick Schinkel

# BROWN CREEPER

## (*Certhia americana*)

One of the most easily overlooked species in the state, this dainty, secretive bird is named for its habit of creeping along tree trunks and branches. Measuring about five inches in length, the Brown Creeper is brown-streaked above and whitish below with a white eye stripe. This combination of characteristics makes it an exceptionally well camouflaged bird, able to blend into the bark of trees upon which it forages. Other helpful identification features are the slightly decurved bill and long, stiff tail, similar to that of a woodpecker.

Except during the breeding season, the common sound given by the creeper is a single, thin note repeated sporadically. This high-pitched "seep" can be easily confused with the calls of other woodland birds, especially kinglets and chickadees. The species' territorial song, usually heard for only a brief time in spring, is quite melodic and louder than its call, but it, too, can be difficult to recognize. Unless one is familiar with this breeding song, it often goes unidentified.

The Brown Creeper occurs over much of North America as either a permanent resident, summer resident, or winter resident. In the eastern United States, breeding is largely restricted to the northernmost states and Appalachian Mountains. Come winter, some remain on their breeding grounds, while many others vacate the higher latitudes and altitudes, migrating as far south as the Gulf coast and Florida. A profile of creepers in Michigan includes a mixture of permanent, breeding, and winter residents. Breeding occurs locally throughout the state but is more common in the northern two-thirds. In the southern counties, creepers are more familiar to us during migration and winter than in the breeding season.

Brown Creepers generally prefer wet forests such as those found in floodplains, bogs, and swamps, but drier woodlands may be used as well. The type of forest (coniferous or deciduous) is less important than the availability of food and nesting places. Preferred forage includes insects, insect eggs, and pupae, and other small invertebrates found on and in the crevices of bark. Fruits and nuts may form a small portion of their diet. Nest sites are quite specific and typically involve trees (dead or alive) that have loose or peeling bark, creating a small cavity where the nest can be placed.

For a long time the nesting habits of the Brown Creeper remained a mystery. Even ornithological "greats" such as Alexander Wilson and John James Audubon maintained that creepers nested in woodpecker cavities. Today we know that their nests are located behind pieces or plates of bark where they wedge masses of bark, moss, twigs, and needles. Nest building may take up to several weeks to complete.

The nesting season in Michigan extends from May to July. Those who have observed creepers at the onset of breeding may have been fortunate enough to see their courtship flight, which involves spiraling chases around tree trunks and aerial loops. Clutches contain five to six white eggs with sparse reddish-brown markings, which are incubated by the female while the male attends to her needs. Hatching occurs in about two weeks, and the young fledge in another two weeks, although once they become mobile they are able to creep around the nest tree. Groups of fledglings and adults roost at night in a tight circle on the side of a tree with their heads pointing inward, in contrast to some birds, such as Bobwhite Quail, which roost with their heads outward from the circle.

Brown Creepers are interesting to watch as they diligently search the bark and bark fissures for food. Foraging begins as a bird alights on the lower trunk of a tree and hops upward in a spiral fashion, inspecting the bark and probing with its thin bill. Upon reaching the upper trunk, it flies downward to the lower portion of another tree and repeats the procedure over again. Creepers will even follow this same pattern when approaching a suet feeder. It may take a year or more for birds to find and begin using a suet feeder, but once familiar with this food source they will remain faithful. Because of this steadfastness, it is wise to keep successful suet feeders placed in the same location year after year.

The autumn migration of creepers into southern Michigan is first noticed around the middle of September. Some continue farther south, while others remain for the winter. The reverse trip generally occurs in April to mid-May. Years of data for Berrien County identify 23 September as the date of average arrival and 10 May for departure in the south.

Although solitary most of the year, Brown Creepers may accompany small wintering flocks of chickadees, nuthatches, and titmice. Observers will notice, however, that the creeper generally keeps to itself within the flock, as if it has its own foraging agenda. Winter populations in the state vary from area to area, especially in the Upper Peninsula, where numbers are normally low. Christmas bird counts indicate a fair number of wintering creepers in the Lower Peninsula. Annual totals typically range from 200 to 350 individuals, with higher counts of 469 in 1982–83 and 425 in 1979–80. —Dick Schinkel

# ROCK WREN

## (*Salpinctes obsoletus*)

The Rock Wren provides an excellent example of the range of environmental conditions to which birds have adapted. This species occupies dry, desolate, rocky habitats such as cliffs, quarries, canyons, and talus slopes. It breeds across most of the western United States, north to southwestern Canada and south through Mexico to Middle America. Rock Wrens are partially migratory and have a tendency to wander far from their normal haunts. They are accidental to casual in the Midwest and have been found east to Massachusetts. There have been at least six published reports for

Michigan, including one specimen from Wayne County in October 1910. Records such as the one at the Detroit Railway station in 1937 or 1938 support the theory that a few strays travel by railroad boxcar.

Most midwestern observations have come in the last 30 years, with 60% of the reports in autumn. In 1979 a number of Rock Wrens wandered to the Midwest, including two birds in Michigan. One of these was an individual which remained from 8 to 10 May at Whitefish Point, where it was photographed and banded. The other was found on 29 October at Copper Harbor in Keweenaw County. In 1988 a singing male was discovered on 9 July at Centennial in Houghton County, where it remained around an abandoned mine until 4 August. The most recent report is from Whitefish Point, this time in the fall from 8 to 10 November 1992. There have probably been other Rock Wrens in the state, but their preferred habitat is mostly in areas where they are less likely to be discovered. —Raymond J. Adams

## CAROLINA WREN

### ( *Thryothorus ludovicianus* )

With Michigan located at the northern periphery of its range, the Carolina Wren occurs here as a rare permanent resident in the southernmost counties and a casual resident elsewhere in the Lower Peninsula. This species is our only representative of a large group of tropical American wrens. Although sensitive to cold climates, it shows no regular pattern of migration, remaining year-round throughout its range in the eastern United States, Mexico, and Central America. Consequently, populations in northern states such as Michigan fluctuate widely over time in accordance with winter severity.

The Carolina Wren is an inhabitant of thickets or woodlands with dense underbrush, often in association with streams or marshes. This species is slightly larger than the more familiar House Wren but is easily separated by its deep rufous plumage, buffy underparts, and prominent white eye line. Its explosive melodious song, often described as "tea-kettle, tea-kettle, tea-kettle," can be heard in any season, though it is sung most frequently during the breeding season. The fact that it will sometimes imitate songs of other bird species, such as the cardinal, bluebird, and meadowlark, accounts for the nickname "Mocking Wren."

You are much more likely to locate a Carolina Wren by song than by sight, and once detected you can often bring this curious bird into view with squeaking noises made by kissing the back of your hand. The bird-watcher's ever-famous "pishing" sound also works extraordinarily well, as it resembles the wren's scolding notes, which the bird then repeats back to you. Watch for the typical wren behavior of flitting in and out of the underbrush, all the while chattering and jerking its upturned tail.

In Michigan the Carolina Wren's distribution is primarily confined to the southern three tiers of counties. Our harsh winter climate, especially the amount of snowfall, greatly restricts its occurrence in the state. Consequently, it is found only in small numbers in the south, becoming extremely rare to absent in the central and northern regions of the Lower Peninsula. No breeding has ever been documented in the Upper Peninsula, where infrequent sightings are probably dispersing young whose survival this far north is doubtful and depends on the availability of food through the winter.

In southern Michigan, Carolina Wren pairs often produce two broods in a season. Breeding begins rather early, usually in mid-April, and can continue into July with second broods. Nests of the Carolina Wren, which are sometimes built with a dome and side entrance, are typically located near forest edges or clearings and are placed low in thick underbrush, in cavities, or within the roots of upturned trees. Like the House Wren, this species occasionally chooses peculiar sites such as cardboard containers, pipes, mailboxes, hanging flower baskets, and various nooks and crannies in buildings and bridges. A Kalamazoo bird-watcher even installed a special wren doorway in her garage, which was used readily by a nesting pair.

Throughout the twentieth century, Carolina Wrens have extended their range northward during periods of mild winters. At times they have been spotted as far north as southern Canada. It is usually not long, however, before a brutal winter or series of winters take their toll, decimating populations as far south as the Ohio River Valley. The worst crash in recent years came with the harsh winters of the late 1970s, when the entire Michigan population was evidently wiped out.

Records during the 1980s indicate a slow but steady comeback in the state. In *The Atlas of Breeding Birds of Michigan*, Carolina Wrens were reported in 33 Lower Peninsula townships, with probable or confirmed breeding in nearly a dozen southern counties and even an observation of nest building near Traverse City. The recovery is further demonstrated by the gradual increase in sightings on Christmas bird counts in recent years, with the total in 1992–93 reaching a record peak of 92 Carolinas.

For now we can count on the state supporting a small population of Carolina Wrens in the Lower Peninsula. In the winter season, most observations are of individuals visiting feeders where suet or peanut butter is offered. As long as winters remain average to relatively mild and snow cover is light or of short duration, this species will continue to persist and likely increase and expand its range in the state until the next hard winter comes. —Charles Nelson

## BEWICK'S WREN

### ( *Thryomanes bewickii* )

Distinguished from other wrens by its white outer tail feathers, the Bewick's Wren is a casual visitor to Michigan. Its current range includes the southern states, the Pacific coast, and northern Mexico. East of the Mississippi, populations have declined to a point where this species is now rare and only locally distributed. On a national scale, however, breeding bird surveys show that overall populations have remained fairly stable since counts started in 1966. Reduced numbers in the East were first noted in the 1950s, and the continued change in status has been due, in part, to the severe winters of the late 1970s. Increased competition with the House Wren is also a suspected factor, resulting in lower numbers in the eastern part of its range.

Like some other wrens, the Bewick's is a cavity nester. Nesting sites include holes in trees and fenceposts, birdhouses, mailboxes, crevices in stone walls, and numerous other natural or man-made cavities. This species is able to live in a variety of habitats such as thickets and brushy uplands, shrubby wetlands, orchards, and yards.

The Bewick's Wren was first recorded in Michigan in the late 1800s, and the first nest was documented in 1894 in Kent County. Between the end of the last century and 1970, this species was a rare but irregular migrant and summer resident. Most sightings occurred from April to June in the southern third of the state. The only other successful nesting record is from Washtenaw County.

After 1970, this wren essentially stopped appearing in the state. Exceptions include a lone male at the Fort Custer Recreation Area in Kalamazoo County on 4–6 June 1983, and an individual in Barry County which remained from the autumn of 1979 to February 1980 and was seen by many Michigan birders. This individual was using the orbit of a deer skull as its roost. Most recently, one was discovered in Bloomfield Hills, Oakland County on 12 May 1993. Given the Bewick Wren's present status in the East, it is doubtful that this species will return to Michigan, even on a rare basis, anytime soon. —Charles Nelson

# HOUSE WREN

## (*Troglodytes aedon*)

The House Wren is a common to abundant summer resident in Michigan, often observed around suburban and rural communities where its bubbly, chattering song is heard incessantly during the breeding season. Like other wrens, this species has a chunky body, slender downcurved beak, and stiff, usually upturned tail. Its plain appearance, near-lack of an eye line, and song are the best identifiers.

The House Wren is easily the most common wren in the East. It has an expansive breeding distribution which includes southern Canada, most of the United States, Mexico, and Central America. Wintering grounds extend from the southern United States to the tropics. On rare occasions individuals remain farther north, and there have been eight reports of House Wrens on Christmas bird counts since 1970.

This species is found in abundance in the southern two-thirds of the Lower Peninsula, becoming less numerous just below the Straits and in the more forested Upper Peninsula. In these northern regions it occurs most frequently in and around residential and rural areas where edge habitats are prevalent. The only areas where House Wrens are generally uncommon are those of heavy urban development, intensive agriculture, or dense forests.

The clearing of forests resulted in a substantial increase in Michigan's House Wren population over the last century, and in many areas (Kalamazoo, for example), numbers continue to rise. Breeding bird survey data for the period 1966–91 reveal a significant increase in House Wrens nationwide. Areas with mostly brushy vegetation, such as yards, gardens, parks, and woodland

edges, are preferred habitats for this wren. These sites support large quantities of insects, which constitute the major portion of its diet.

Male House Wrens generally begin arriving in southern Michigan in late April, and in the Upper Peninsula in early May. One exceptionally early return date was recorded in Kalamazoo County on 30 March 1962. Upon arrival, males immediately get down to the business of staking out territories, which they defend aggressively with their persistent chattering and chasing of intruder males. They also start construction of several partial stick nests in different cavities within the territory. When a female returns, she chooses one and finishes it, lining the nest with feathers, hair, or wool.

The male's behavior of building partial nests is one that can readily be observed around your yard, especially if you have several birdhouses. Many people think they have more than one wren, but if you watch closely you will note that it is one industrious individual placing nesting materials in each box or natural cavity. You will also notice that the male likes to leave one twig sticking out of the entryway, perhaps a way to advertise his handiwork to prospective females.

Typical nesting sites are birdhouses or small holes in trees. The House Wren also uses its share of unusual spots, including abandoned nests of paper wasps, flower pots, tin cans, pump nozzles, and pants on a clothesline. To encourage nesting, a wren house can be constructed and placed in or near shrubby vegetation. The box should be made of cedar or other durable wood, with an entrance hole no bigger than one inch in diameter.

House Wrens often raise two broods in a season, with clutches containing four to nine eggs. In Michigan, the first breeding cycle usually occurs between the middle of May and late June, although nest building can be observed in April. The female may then leave the young of the first brood in the male's care while she goes to a different territory to lay a second clutch. These second nestings typically occur between early July and early August.

In areas where there are large populations of small hole-nesting birds or a shortage of cavities, competition for nest sites can be severe, and the aggressive House Wren not only may visit sites occupied by other species, but may destroy their eggs or young. On occasion this nest predation may backfire, and the wren may become the victim if the nest occupant returns while the wren is still there. Competitors for nest sites include other birds, such as the Black-capped Chickadee, Eastern Bluebird, and Tree Swallow, as well as animals such as deer mice and wasps. If you want to attract a variety of hole-nesting birds, you will want to be cautious and selective in your placement of wren houses and boxes meant for other species in order to minimize conflicts and not cause any undue mortality. —Charles Nelson

*House Wren*
*Carolina Wren*
DAVID MOHRHARDT

# WINTER WREN
## (*Troglodytes troglodytes*)

Observers must be quick to spot the Winter Wren as it darts in and out among the dense underbrush of the coniferous forest. This tiny wren likes to stick close to thickets and tangles, and it takes a trained eye to recognize the stubby, upturned tail and pronounced barring on the flanks, two characteristics which help distinguish it from other members of the wren family. More often than not, I have identified Winter Wrens by their long, melodious song without ever actually seeing the birds themselves.

The Winter Wren is a common summer resident in Michigan, nesting throughout the Upper Peninsula and the northern one-third of the Lower Peninsula. It is the most common wren in the northern coniferous and mixed forests. Restricted breeding occurs in the middle third of the Lower Peninsula, and no nests have been reported south of Allegan County. Beyond Michigan, the Winter Wren can be found nesting in Canada, in the northern United States, and at high elevations throughout the western states and in the Appalachians. This is the only member of this large family (59 species) to extend its range into Eurasia, where it is simply known as the Wren.

Spring migration begins in late March, with numbers reaching their peak during April. The breeding season extends from May through July and occasionally into August. The male's song, which is often sung from a low perch, is a most impressive rendition lasting seven seconds and containing 108 to 113 rising and falling notes blended together into a melodious sequence. Upon first hearing a Winter Wren, I was amazed by the variety and number of notes, warbles, and trills contained in this little bird's song. In addition to its song, the more intent listener may catch its sharp, two-syllable warning call of "kip-kip."

The Winter Wren prefers small openings in cool northern conifer forests and swamps where rotting stumps, fallen trees, and abundant mosses provide perfect cover for nests. It may also hide its nest in entanglements of exposed roots at the edges of bogs or along stream banks. The male builds one to four bulky nests of moss, grass, twigs, rootlets, feathers, and animal hair. When the female arrives, she chooses one of these and lays four to seven white, brown-spotted eggs.

The fall migration commences in September, with the bulk of the movement taking place from late September to late October. Winter Wrens do not travel too far, with the central and southern United States being the primary wintering areas. Some individuals always hang a bit north in winter, and in most years small numbers are present in southern Michigan. Occasionally mild conditions entice more to remain, as happened in the winter of 1974–75, when a high total of 80 individuals were recorded on the Christmas bird counts.

High mortality during severe winters has caused wide fluctuations in Winter Wren populations. This was evident after the harsh winters of the late 1970s, when numbers dropped by 50% over much of the United States, according to data from the federal breeding bird survey. Such fluctuations are expected, however, and by 1985, numbers had recovered to earlier levels.

There is some concern that loss of suitable nesting habitat will lead to declines of Winter Wren populations. Human land-use practices, such as draining or filling northern wetlands, altering rivers and streams, and cutting conifer swamp forest, can be detrimental. Studies have found that this species tends to avoid narrow tracts of woodland and intensively managed conifer stands, and instead favors large expanses of mostly undisturbed forest. Maintaining continuous coniferous and mixed forest tracts with minimal disruption to bogs and other northern wetland communities is an important consideration for the conservation of Winter Wrens in Michigan. —Charles Nelson

# SEDGE WREN
## (*Cistothorus platensis*)

Of all our wrens, this one is probably the most elusive and most difficult to see. On more occasions than I care to recall, I have watched patiently from the edge of a grassy marsh with a chorus of Sedge Wrens before me without getting more than a fleeting glimpse. This fairly common summer resident of Michigan is best located by its abrupt, rapid-fire song, sometimes written as "chap-chap-chap-p-p-r-r." Otherwise, it can be distinguished from the similar Marsh Wren by its slightly smaller size, mostly brown body, streaked crown, and less conspicuous eyebrow.

The summer range of this wren includes portions of extreme southern Canada and the upper half of the eastern United States west to the Dakotas. It winters in more southerly latitudes along the Atlantic and Gulf coasts to Texas and Mexico. Other Sedge Wren populations reside year-round in Central and South America.

The name Sedge Wren is more fitting than the former designation of Short-billed Marsh Wren. This shy bird prefers the slightly drier areas associated with a wetland. In Michigan these areas are characterized by sedges or other grasses, cattails, and buttonbush. Sedge Wrens have also adopted our hayfields and pastures as breeding habitat. Toward the latter part of the summer, it is common to find them in fields of goldenrod and aster and brushy grasslands.

Sedge Wrens usually return to southern Michigan during the first two weeks of May, reaching the Upper Peninsula around the middle of the month. The reverse trip occurs in August and September, and by the end of September, most have left for the warmer South. There is but one Christmas bird count record to date, from 1970–71.

Nesting primarily occurs in June and July, although nests can occasionally be found as early as May and as late as August. The Sedge Wren's nest is a woven ball of grass with an entry hole on the side. The male often builds more than one nest within his

*Sedge Wren*
*Marsh Wren*
JOHN FELSING

territory; the female chooses one and lines it with cattail down, fur, feathers, and catkins. Most females produce two broods per season, but not necessarily with the same male.

Sedge Wrens are widely distributed in Michigan, but their occurrence is extremely local because of the patchiness of suitable habitat. This makes it difficult to assess the status of this species, which varies from locally abundant in some areas to rare or absent in others. In general, Sedge Wrens are more numerous in the Upper Peninsula, where there is greater availability of quality sedge marshes, bogs, and other wet grassy habitats. They are also common in some of the larger coastal and interior marshes in the Lower Peninsula. Regions from which they are largely absent include the heavily urbanized and intensively farmed areas in the southeast and south-central counties, and the more extensively forested lands in the north.

Difficulty in censusing this wren further complicates our ability to assess its status and monitor populations. Whereas singing males can be used as a measure of abundance for many birds, they are not always reliable for this species. Scientists are not sure whether male Sedge Wrens begin singing upon arrival at the breeding grounds or if they delay territorial activity. Also, individuals do not always breed at the same time each year, nor do they consistently return to the same nesting site year after year.

We do know, however, that Sedge Wrens have declined significantly in Michigan since at least 1966, when the breeding bird survey began, and that the biggest contributing factor has been the widespread loss of suitable wetland and grassland habitat, especially in the south. Recent observations and field work clearly reveal their rarity or absence from areas where formerly they were described as common or locally abundant. Human development and agricultural practices have greatly reduced the acreage of sedge marshes and other wet grassy habitats, and those that are left are dissected into a haphazard patchwork of small, isolated plots. In Ohio the Sedge Wren is now listed as endangered, while in Indiana it is considered threatened. In order to preserve this species in Michigan, we must continue to push for protection of the state's remaining wetlands and grasslands and increase efforts to restore others. —Charles Nelson

# MARSH WREN

## (*Cistothorus palustris*)

This common summer resident is named for the cattail marshes in which it lives. As long as you are in marshland terrain, it is possible to catch glimpses of this quick little bird. White streaks on its back, a solid brown cap, and a bold white eye line will confirm that this is the type of wren you have spotted. So too will the male's dry, rattling song, which you are likely to hear before seeing the bird.

The Marsh Wren (formerly Long-billed Marsh Wren) has a fairly extensive breeding range that includes parts of southern Canada and the United States and Mexico. People living along the Gulf, Atlantic, and Pacific coasts know this species as a year-round resident. Migratory populations which breed in the north winter in the southern states and Mexico.

The arrival of the Marsh Wren to Michigan's Lower Peninsula occurs in late April and early May, with appearance in the Upper Peninsula two to three weeks later. Thirty years of data identify 4 May as the average arrival time for Berrien County. Fall migration occurs more gradually, with adults retreating as early as late August and young of second broods leaving as late as mid-October. Nearly every year, a few birds remain into December in the larger marshes in the south, especially along Lake Erie. This species has been reported on 25 of the last 34 Christmas bird counts, dating back to 1960.

From April to October when Michigan is home, Marsh Wrens are found most frequently in the southern Lower Peninsula. They inhabit both inland and coastal marshes and are especially common in our wildlife preserves, game areas, and other public lands where large marshes have been maintained. Some examples of prime spots for observing this species are St. Clair Flats, Pte. Mouillee, Saginaw Bay, and the Allegan and Muskegon state game areas. North of Bay and Muskegon counties, the distribution of the Marsh Wren is much more limited. Breeding occurs only in widely scattered locales in the northern Lower and the Upper Peninsula. Throughout the state, its occurrence depends upon the location of quality wetland habitat.

Male Marsh Wrens typically return to the breeding grounds first to establish territories and build an average of six "courting nests" woven from, and attached to, cattails or other reeds in the marsh. When a female arrives on the scene, she selects one nest to complete or sometimes builds her own. The final product is an oblong, coconut-shaped nest lined with soft grass and cattail fluff. Nest records from the Lower Peninsula indicate that laying of the first clutch of five to six eggs begins around mid-May. Once the female is incubating, the male usually moves to the other side of his territory to repeat the courting rituals in hopes of attracting a second mate. With these later pairings and second broods, the breeding season extends well into August.

Both sexes have similar plumages and energetic, darting manners, but an observer is more likely to detect the more vocal and visible male. During the breeding period, male Marsh Wrens can be seen flying 5 to 15 feet in the air and fluttering down at an angle to advertise their territories. Owing to the patchiness of their habitat, it is not uncommon for males to become concentrated in an area, forming loose breeding colonies. The boardwalks at the Sarett Nature Center lead through some prime cattail habitat and provide great opportunities to see males put body and soul into furious flaps and flutters of their airborne display.

The all-too-common tale of habitat loss to development and human progress applies to the Marsh Wren. Declines are particularly evident in the southeast and south-central regions of Michigan, where development and agricultural pressures have been greatest. Although it is not yet a species of "special concern,"

*Golden-crowned Kinglet*
*Ruby-crowned Kinglet*
CYNDY CALLOG

Cyndy Callog

populations have suffered concurrently with the destruction of marshlands across the state. Today, observers can hardly find a Marsh Wren in some counties where Walter Barrows called them common less than one hundred years ago. —Charles Nelson

# GOLDEN-CROWNED KINGLET

## (*Regulus satrapa*)

The Golden-crowned Kinglet is one of our smallest songbirds, measuring only three and one-half to four inches in length. Both sexes are nearly identical in appearance, their most distinctive feature being the yellow crown stripe bordered by black. Rarely discernible in the field is the male's patch of orange feathers nestled within its yellow crown. When the bird is agitated or displaying, these crown feathers are erect, revealing the orange patch.

The breeding range of this kinglet is associated with the continent's cool coniferous forests in both the eastern and western regions. These habitats prevail in northern latitudes as well as in higher elevations in the mountains. In the East, its range extends from Newfoundland and the Hudson Bay south to the Upper Midwest, the northeastern states, and to North Carolina in the Appalachians. Populations spread out more in the winter, withdrawing from the northernmost regions and occurring throughout most of the United States and southernmost Canada.

The Golden-crowned Kinglet is best known in Michigan as a migrant and winter resident. Birds arrive in the Lower Peninsula as early as August, with the main migration in September and October. Some remain all winter, while others continue farther south. Christmas bird counts give some indication as to the variability in numbers remaining, with totals over the past five years ranging from 127 to 462. For their small size, kinglets are hardy birds, but severe weather has been known to cause significant declines in populations. This was especially evident following the bitter winters in the late 1970s, though numbers have since recovered.

During migration and winter, Golden-crowns broaden their habitat use and may be found in various woodland types as well as brushy vegetation. They do, however, still exhibit their preference for evergreens and during winter are found most frequently in areas with conifers, including plantations. As spring arrives, birds begin their journey north. Movements in southern Michigan are noted from late March until the end of April.

As a breeding species in Michigan, the Golden-crowned Kinglet is primarily found in the Upper Peninsula and the northern tip of the Lower Peninsula. Although it is a common nester in these parts, pairs are difficult to observe in their dense conifer haunts and are easily overlooked. Several authors have suggested that because coniferous forests were more widespread in northern Michigan prior to settlement, the species was a more common breeder historically. During the recent Breeding Bird Atlas, a few nesting pairs were found elsewhere in the Lower Peninsula south to Ottawa and Kalamazoo counties. These isolated breedings are associated with spruce or pine plantations or bog habitats.

Nesting records for this species in Michigan are scant, but data from other parts of its range indicate a preference for spruce, although other evergreens are also used. The Golden-crown's nest is probably one of the most intricate of any bird, sometimes taking nearly a month to construct. The female builds a hanging nest of mosses, lichens, and other materials attached to twigs of a horizontal branch. The opening is located at the top, and the inside is lined with fine strips of bark and feathers (often grouse) with quills pointed down and tips arching over the eggs. Oftentimes the walls of the nest are an inch or more thick, making it almost impermeable to cold and water.

Egg laying probably occurs sometime in June, with clutches averaging eight to nine eggs. Because of the small size of the nest, eggs are arranged in two layers. Wood (1951) provides information for a few records from the Upper Peninsula, including a nest with eggs on 13 July, nestlings on 2 July, and fledglings on 10 July. There is also one Isle Royale record of a nest with eggs on 21 July. —Dick Schinkel

# RUBY-CROWNED KINGLET

## (*Regulus calendula*)

The Ruby-crowned Kinglet averages a bit larger than the Golden-crowned and is easily identified by its broken white eye ring and plain crown. Actually, the male's crown has a scarlet patch, but this is rarely visible except when the bird is excited and the crown feathers are erect. This species shares with its cousin the charactertistic of flicking its wings as it moves about the foliage in search of food. This seemingly nervous behavior is thought to scare insects into flight.

The Ruby-crowned Kinglet is a common migrant throughout the state. Michigan lies between the main breeding and wintering grounds of this species. The breeding range includes most of Alaska, Canada, and the western mountain ranges, but in the East extends only as far south as the Upper Great Lakes and northern New England. Included in this distribution is extreme northern Michigan, where Ruby-crowns are local breeders. Wintering occurs along sections of the Pacific coast and in Mexico, and across the southern United States north to Maryland, with sporadic occurrence farther north.

Fall migrants usually begin arriving in Michigan in September, with birds reaching the southern counties by the second and third weeks. Migration is heaviest during October, and most Ruby-crowns are through the state by early November. These transients can be found in wooded and shrubby habitats and may join mixed foraging flocks composed of chickadees, titmice, nuthatches, and sometimes Golden-crowned Kinglets.

While most Ruby-crowned Kinglets vacate the state before winter, very small numbers remain, primarily in the southern counties. Participants on Michigan Christmas bird counts typically find a dozen or more. Since 1970, totals have varied from a low of 1 in 1991–92 to a high of 52 in 1974–75. The spring migration commences about two weeks later than that of the Golden-crowned, with good numbers first present around the middle of April. Passage northward continues through the middle of May, with average departure from Berrien County on 18 May. Late migrants have been encountered into late May and even early June in some southern counties.

During the breeding season, Ruby-crowned Kinglets are mostly confined to the Upper Peninsula and Isle Royale. The species is quite specific in its selection of habitat, nesting in lowland areas such as bogs or muskegs which contain spruce, fir, tamarack, or white cedar. During the Breeding Bird Atlas, Ruby-crowns were found most frequently in western Chippewa and Luce counties in the eastern Upper Peninsula as well as in most of the western region, with concentrations in the Marquette-Dickinson-Baraga County area, in Keweenaw County, and on Isle Royale. There was one report of breeding in Cheboygan County, just below the Straits, and a few scattered summer observations south to Clinton County.

Ruby-crowns have probably always been uncommon, local breeders in Michigan's northernmost regions, yet the first nest (containing six young) was not discovered until 6 July 1925 in Chippewa County. The pendant-shaped nest is very much like the Golden-crowned Kinglet's, and the eggs of the two species are indistinguishable. Observers must see which species is at the nest to identify its occupant. As with Golden-crowns, Ruby-crowns favor spruce trees for their nests.

The male's red crown, for which this species is named, is most noticeable during the spring courting season. In the presence of a potential mate, the male raises his crown feathers and bows his head for the female to see. Displays and singing occur regularly during migration, aiding in the detection of this bird in spring. The male's song is surprisingly loud, starting with a series of four or five high-pitched notes followed by an array of musical tones increasing in pitch and speed as if the bird were bubbling over with excitement. —Dick Schinkel

# BLUE-GRAY GNATCATCHER

## ( *Polioptila caerulea* )

The Blue-gray Gnatcatcher is a relatively common summer resident in the lower two-thirds of Michigan. This petite, energetic bird is easily recognized provided it sits still long enough for you to get a look at it. Males are blue-gray above and white below, and their long dark tail is bordered on both sides with white feathers. Females are similar but grayer, and lack the narrow black eye line of the male. The breeding range of this species includes most of the United States, north to the New England states, southern Ontario, and Oregon in the West and south into Mexico. Wintering occurs from the extreme southern states to Central America.

Michigan lies along the northern periphery of the gnatcatcher's breeding range, so the majority of the population is found in the southern Lower Peninsula. A similar distribution was described in earlier writings, with Zimmerman and Van Tyne (1959) emphasizing that reports from the northern Lower Peninsula required verification. Based on this statement and the recent findings of the Breeding Bird Atlas, it is clear that this species has

since expanded its known range in the state. While still most common in the southern counties, Blue-gray Gnatcatchers regularly nest throughout Midland County, and scattered pairs are now found north to Manistee and Alpena counties in the Lower Peninsula, and to southern Menominee and Dickinson in the Upper Peninsula. This expansion follows along with significant increases in the East from the mid-1960s through the 1970s. The gnatcatcher nests in a variety of wooded habitats but shows a preference for riverine and floodplain forests. The maturation of second-growth forests across parts of the state has probably contributed to its expansion.

The first gnatcatchers arrive in Michigan during the latter part of April, with migration complete by mid-May. Early recorded dates include 31 March in Kalamazoo County and 17 April at Whitefish Point in the Upper Peninsula. Nesting occurs primarily in May and June, but renesting following failures may extend the season into July. Departure from the state comes early, commencing in August and largely complete by September. Stragglers are occasionally reported, even into November. Exceptional is the appearance of an individual on 25 November at Whitefish Point.

The nest of this species is small, about two inches in diameter. It is usually built on a horizontal branch anywhere from 4 to 80 feet above ground, though most are between 15 and 30 feet. The cup-shaped nest is quite intricate, resembling that of a hummingbird, only larger. Both sexes help in construction, using various bits of plant fibers and plant down. In wet forested areas, favored sources for this down are willow catkins, sycamore fuzz, and cinnamon fern hair. The outside of the nest is covered with spider silk and lichens to match the bark of the limb upon which it is placed.

Gnatcatchers lay four to five pale blue eggs, generally marked with brownish spots. Hatching occurs in about 13 days, with both sexes incubating and sharing in the care of the young, which fledge in another 12 days. Like many open cup nesters, this species may serve as a host to eggs of the Brown-headed Cowbird.

Like kinglets, this species seems to be in constant motion from the time it arrives in spring until it departs in fall. Feeding primarily on insects, including larvae, pupae, and eggs, gnatcatchers can be seen restlessly flitting from branch to branch, their tails flicking as they go. The easiest way to locate these birds is by their persistent buzzy call, which sounds like "spee spee." They frequently call about the nest, which can help in its detection. —Dick Schinkel

# NORTHERN WHEATEAR

## ( *Oenanthe oenanthe* )

This ground-dwelling, bluebird-sized thrush, recognized best by its white rump and bold black and white tail pattern, is an accidental visitor to Michigan with four records, including one photograph. A widespread breeder in Eurasia, the Northern Wheatear also nests in the rocky tundra of Alaska and the Yukon territories. Vagrants have occasionally appeared in the United

States, mostly on the Atlantic coast, with only very rare occurrences in the interior. Michigan's records are all during the fall migration period. The first report came on 7–9 October 1943 at McMillan in Luce County (Payne 1983). It was 1980 before another Wheatear was seen, this one at St. Ignace, Mackinac County (Weir 1981). The third record, documented by a photograph, was of an individual which remained from 12 to 15 October 1981 in White Pine, Ontonagon County. The fourth and only Lower Peninsula record was of a bird discovered on 20 October 1989 at the Freemont Sewage Ponds in Newaygo County. This stray was seen by a large number of in- and out-of-state birders before its departure on 23 October. —Raymond J. Adams

# EASTERN BLUEBIRD

## (*Sialia sialis*)

Popularized in poem and song, the Eastern Bluebird is one of Michigan's most endearing year-round residents. Its cherry "tru-a-lly, tru-a-lly" song and distinctive "chir-wi" flight call are, to many, a welcome sign of spring. The summer range of this beautiful thrush encompasses the eastern half of the United States to the Rocky Mountain foothills and including the southerly portions of adjoining Canadian provinces. Bluebirds withdraw from the north to winter in the central and southern states and Mexico, while some remain closer to their breeding grounds northward to lower Michigan and New York.

While the bluebird's status has remained relatively unchanged over the past one hundred years, its abundance and distribution have varied substantially. First, the arrival of the English Sparrow (House Sparrow) in the 1870s proceeded to displace the bluebird from our cities and parks. Then in the winter of 1894–95, the Eastern Bluebird, the American Robin, and other semi-hardy species suffered massive mortality as a result of record cold and heavy snow. By the early 1900s, populations had recovered from these winter losses but not from the effects of House Sparrow competition. Still, Barrows (1912) found the bluebird universally distributed throughout the state in summer and "common during the larger part of the year."

The bluebird continued to be labeled as a common summer resident into the 1940s. In the interim, however, the European Starling reached Michigan in the 1920s, so that bluebird populations were contending for cavities with both the starling and the House Sparrow. By 1950, bluebirds were no longer common around human habitation, and overall numbers had declined. Exceptionally cold weather in the South in 1957–58 again caused

heavy mortality. In addition, habitat changes harmful to bluebirds were also taking place at that time. Modern farming practices reduced the availability of nesting cavities by removing wooden fenceposts and windbreaks, and affected foraging habitat through shifts to row crops and greater pesticide use. The result of these combined factors was a substantial decrease in bluebirds from areas where they had once been common. Human concern prompted action and a major increase in the placement of nesting boxes, dubbed "bluebird trails," in many parts of their range. Such efforts helped the species stage a major comeback in the 1970s and 1980s, although the harsh winters of the late 1970s caused a setback for a few years.

Breeding Bird Atlas results provide a fairly complete picture of this thrush's current distribution and status in Michigan. Bluebirds continue to breed statewide, although birds are somewhat more scattered in the extensively forested regions of the north. They remain noticeably scarce in metropolitan and agriculturally dominated areas, primarily in the southeast, Thumb, and Saginaw Bay regions. Breeding bird surveys show a dramatic increase in bluebird numbers in the past ten years, as do Christmas bird counts, with reported totals more than doubling since the mid-1980s. To monitor bluebird numbers and productivity, the DNR initiated the Michigan Nestbox Network program through contributions to the Nongame Wildlife Tax Check-off. This program, which is now coordinated at the Kalamazoo Nature Center, involves more than 400 state residents who reported 6,654 bluebird young fledged from 2,285 nesting attempts in 1991 and 5,779 fledglings from 2,226 attempts in 1992.

The breeding cycle of this hole nester commences in late February or early March as overwintering birds carve out territories and migrants return from the South. Nesting can begin as early as late March, but most egg laying does not occur until the third week of April in the south, and in May farther north. Clutches typically contain four to five light blue (occasionally white) eggs, which hatch in two weeks. Fledging takes 16 to 17 days, and after a short delay the female begins a second clutch. Rarely do Michigan pairs raise three broods, but they do regularly renest up to three or four times after failures. After the season ends, bluebirds gather in flocks prior to departing for the southern wintering grounds in October.

Proper habitat for the Eastern Bluebird includes open fields, uncultivated farmland, cutover woodlands, gardens, and orchards. Elevated perches are a necessary component for searching for prey items, primarily grasshoppers, crickets, beetles, and other insects in spring and summer. For birds that overwinter, their diet of honeysuckle, Virginia creeper, poison ivy, grape, pokeweed, holly, and sumac fruits can be supplemented by the offering of mealworms or a peanut butter-cornmeal mixture.

Bluebirds will investigate any potential cavity during their search for nest sites, which can lead to surprising and unfortunate encounters with people. Uncapped woodstove pipes, smokehouse pipes, and, in the South, tobacco-drying shed chimneys all present a possible cavity, but with disastrous results if there is not someone nearby to release the trapped bird from its sooty tomb. To prevent this from happening, be sure there are screens or cover guards over all outdoor piping large enough for birds to enter. —Raymond J. Adams and Stephen Allen

*Eastern Bluebird*

JOHN FELSING

## [MOUNTAIN BLUEBIRD]
### (*Sialia currucoides*)

There are as yet no specimens or photographs documenting the Mountain Bluebird's occurrence in Michigan, which leaves it to be categorized as "hypothetical" based on a small number of sight records. Like the Say's Phoebe, this western resident began appearing in new areas of the Midwest several decades ago, starting with Wisconsin in 1954, Ontario in 1962, and Illinois in 1969. By the 1970s, the Mountain Bluebird was even a regular but rare visitor in Minnesota. The first Michigan report came from Eau Claire in Berrien County in June 1979, although the month of this sighting contrasts with the December–May time period of occurrences from adjacent states. The second record, in October 1980, also came from Berrien County (St. Joseph). The third and best-documented of the three observations is of an adult male discovered in Kingston Plains, Alger County, on 6 November 1983 (Ilnicky 1984). —Raymond J. Adams

## TOWNSEND'S SOLITAIRE
### (*Myadestes townsendi*)

Indigenous to coniferous habitats in western North America, the Townsend's Solitaire is a casual transient and winter visitor to Michigan. A relative of the American Robin and Eastern Bluebird, this thrush was unknown in the state until the late 1950s, when a bird was discovered on 30 December 1956 on the Jackson Christmas bird count and subsequently collected on 4 January 1957. Since then 19 additional reports have occurred in the state, including 5 from Christmas bird counts.

Very few Townsend's Solitaire records exist for the Midwest prior to the 1950s. Writing about this species in the western Great Lakes, N. Cutright (1980) pointed to an increased incidence of reports from Illinois and Wisconsin (plus the one Michigan record) in the 1950s and 1960s. The upswing in Michigan observations began the following decade, as birders found five Townsend's in the 1970s, eight in the 1980s, and six so far in the 1990s.

Encounter dates for this species in the state range from 9 October through 24 April, plus one exceptional report from 15 June 1988 at Whitefish Point, Chippewa County. Six of the 20 reports originate in October–November, 11 from December–February, and 2 from April. Observations are about equally divided between the Upper and Lower peninsulas, although there is a small concentration of records from Chippewa County (6), with 4 from Whitefish Point.

Like the Varied Thrush, the Townsend's Solitaire feeds on fruit in fall and winter, including juniper, poison ivy, mountain ash, and ornamental crabapples. Once an individual finds a suitable food source, it may remain for several weeks. The bird's feeding behavior is intriguing, as it will frequently pick fruit from a branch while in flight. The Townsend's Solitaire, a mostly grayish bird, can be difficult to identify as it bears some resemblance to a Northern Mockingbird. The former has a more upright posture, prominent white eye ring, shorter bill, buff wing patch, and buffy-white outer tail feathers. —Raymond J. Adams

## VEERY
### (*Catharus fuscescens*)

The Veery is a common summer resident of Michigan's moist woodlands. This reddish-brown thrush has a finely streaked breast rather than the prominently spotted breast seen in its close relatives. The Veery sings a sweet song, likened to the descending notes of two flutes in a deep well. While this song is similar to that of other woodland thrushes, it has a quality all its own which makes it easy to recognize in the field.

The Veery's breeding range includes southernmost Canada and the northern tier of states, extending farther south in both the Rocky Mountain and Appalachian Mountain ranges. The rest of the year is spent in the tropical forests of Central and northern South America. Veeries can be found throughout Michigan during the breeding season, although they are more numerous and widespread across the northern half of the state and highest densities are found in the Upper Peninsula. Populations in the southern Lower Peninsula are limited by the availability of proper forest habitat, with Veeries being rare to absent where the landscape is dominated by extensive agriculture and urban and suburban sprawl.

This thrush nests in a fairly wide variety of deciduous and mixed woodlands, including partially forested areas. Swampy woodlands, river bottoms, streamside thickets, and other wet forest habitats are especially preferred. Veeries also do well in second-growth woods on recently cut or burned-over lands, characterized by a dense understory and tree species such as aspen and poplar. Open woodlands may be suitable as well, provided they have a good undergrowth of shrubs and brush.

Although Veeries normally arrive in Michigan during the first week of May, their peak spring flight occurs in the last three weeks of May. Occasionally, individuals arrive sooner. Among the earliest published dates are 8 April in Kalamazoo and 24 April in Delta County in the Upper Peninsula. After nesting in June and July, the fall migration begins as August progresses and is usually complete by the first week of October. Stragglers are seen into late October, but by then most Veeries are well on their way to the tropics. Unusual was a sighting on 16–18 November 1972 in Oakland County, and a lone individual found on the 1984–85 Christmas bird count, apparently the only winter record for this species in Michigan.

The nest of the Veery is among the largest of the thrushes, and is usually placed on the ground or low in a shrub. A damp to wet

*Veery*
*Swainson's Thrush*
*Hermit Thrush*
JOHN FELSING

forest floor is often chosen for its initial nesting attempt, and the nest is constructed on a pile of leaves to prevent moisture from penetrating inside. Clutches average four eggs, which are a typical thrush-blue color. The eggs hatch in about 12 days. The young are fed a diet of arthropods and leave the nest in approximately 10 days.

When foraging, the Veery often sits on a low perch and "hawks" for insects. At other times it flies down from the perch to snatch insects from the ground, much the way a bluebird does. These feeding behaviors may be one reason it prefers the multi-layered foliage typical of second-growth forests. The dense undergrowth provides nesting cover as well as a diversity of low foraging sites.

With its habitat choices, Veery populations have persisted well in Michigan and perhaps have even increased in the northern regions in response to the regrowth of forests over the past several decades. Statewide, however, no increasing trend is evident, probably because of offsetting declines in the south where continual fragmentation of woodlands has eliminated Veery habitat. Although this species will use fairly small woodlots, pairs and their nests are more susceptible to predation (by Blue Jays, raccoons, and squirrels, for example) and cowbird parasitism, to which the Veery can be a common host. —Dick Schinkel

# GRAY-CHEEKED THRUSH

## (*Catharus minimus*)

Early Michigan ornithologists and bird-watchers were not as familiar with the Gray-cheeked Thrush as we are today. Whether it is any more common, however, is not clear. Currently, this species is an uncommon spring migrant and fairly common fall migrant, although numbers are quite variable from one year to the next.

This thrush is difficult to get to know. Like other members of its genus, it is retiring and somewhat secretive, disdaining close approach. The Gray-cheeked Thrush spends considerable time foraging on or near the ground, frequently hidden from view by surrounding vegetation. It can be misidentified because of its similarities to the Veery, Hermit, and Swainson's Thrushes. The Gray-cheek lacks a distinct eye ring and has grayish cheeks, olive-brown to olive-gray upperparts, bold breast spots, and olive-gray shading on its sides.

In spring the Gray-cheeked Thrush regularly reaches Michigan in the first week of May, less frequently in the last week of April. Some earlier records are no doubt accurate; however, identification problems suggest caution when reviewing exceptionally early or late records. The spring migration window extends to the last week of May, although lingering birds have been found into June. During spring passage, this thrush is outnumbered by the Swainson's 5 to 1.

Migrant Gray-cheeked Thrushes are attracted to most wooded or shrubby habitats, from city park preserves and suburban yards to immature and mature woodlands, riparian sites, and swampy borders. Foods consumed in migration include beetles, ants, caterpillars, and other insects plus spiders and worms. Fruits such as dogwood, spicebush, wild grapes, and blackberries are important in fall.

Among the *Catharus* thrushes, the Gray-cheeked nests the farthest north. Its breeding range extends across northern Canada and Alaska to northeastern Siberia. In the East, the subspecies *bicknelli* nests south into the higher elevations in New England. To get to their tropical wintering grounds, from Costa Rica to northern Peru and Brazil, Gray-cheeks travel through the United States, mostly east of a line from North Dakota to Texas.

Fall migrants reach Michigan's Upper Peninsula in late August and the southern Lower Peninsula in the first week of September. Migration extends into October, with most birds gone by the end of the first week; rarely do any individuals linger past the third week. Numbers are greater in fall than spring, and large concentrations may be seen, such as the 302 on 14 September 1992 at Whitefish Point, Chippewa County. This nighttime migrant is susceptible to tower kills, and the numbers lost indicate that many Gray-cheeks do pass over the state in fall. L. Caldwell and G. Wallace reported 609 fatalities from the early 1960s, and I collected 180 from a tower kill the night of 16–17 September 1976.

Data from banding stations and tower kills provide information on the demography of the Gray-cheeked Thrushes which pass through Michigan in fall. For other thrushes in this group, calculated age ratios (young vs. adult) run approximately 75% young or higher, while Gray-cheeks consistently average 60% young or less. As far as abundance goes, Gray-cheeked Thrushes are usually more numerous than Veeries but are outnumbered by the Swainson's Thrush 4 to 1.

Late fall and winter observations of the Gray-cheeked Thrush are exceptional. Besides East Lansing records from 16 November 1974 and 17 November 1972, there have been three Christmas bird count reports, all from 1975. One bird at an East Lansing feeder that year remained from the second week of December to the end of the month. —Raymond J. Adams

# SWAINSON'S THRUSH

## (*Catharus ustulatus*)

An inhabitant of boreal and montane forests, the Swainson's Thrush is a common migrant in the state and a locally common summer resident in the northernmost regions. Most Michigan residents know this species only as a transient. There is a fairly narrow window of time during which it passes through, primarily the months of May and September. Because of this concentrated migration, numbers seen are large and generally outnumber those of all other *Catharus* thrushes.

The Swainson's Thrush subspecies found in this region of the continent is easily distinguished from its relatives. Key features are its buff-colored eye ring and buffy throat and breast marked with the characteristic thrush spots. The upperparts are a uniform olive-brown color. Typical of its group, this species has a pretty flute-like song described as an ascending spiral of varied whistles, heard mostly in the early morning and evening hours.

Except for a small area of the northern Great Lakes and the northeastern states, the Swainson's Thrush summers primarily in Alaska, Canada, and the western United States. Michigan's breeding population is generally limited to the coniferous and mixed forest habitats associated with cool northern climates. These are forests typically composed of canopy-level spruce, fir, cedar, or tamarack and a various mix of hardwoods. Such communities are, of course, found mainly in the Upper Peninsula. During the recent Breeding Bird Atlas, this species was reported from 35% of the townships in this region, compared to a mere 3% in the northern Lower Peninsula. In addition to Isle Royale and Keweenaw County, where Swainson's are especially common, breeding individuals were frequently encountered in Alger County and neighboring areas. Considerably fewer birds are found along the southern edge of the Upper Peninsula and in the counties just below the Straits. Most Atlas records for this region came from a narrow band extending from Benzie to Montmorency counties.

Whereas Swainson's Thrushes in the West seem to prefer shrubs for nesting, those found in the East select small trees. The nest is usually placed close to the trunk on a horizontal limb, 8 to 12 feet above the ground. There is little information on nests for Michigan, but spruce, balsam fir, or other evergreens are probably preferred, based on findings from other northeastern states. Clutches of three to four eggs are most common, and the blue eggs have brown spots. Incubation is reported to take about 12 days. Both parents supply the young with various insects and fruit, and fledging occurs in about two weeks.

As indicated, May is the primary month of spring migration in the state. April sightings are rare but do occur, and individuals have been noted in southern Michigan as early as mid-April. One record from 10 March 1977 in the Detroit area should be viewed with caution. Spring migrants are also known to linger into early June in the southern Lower Peninsula.

Their time on the breeding grounds is brief, as the fall migration begins in August in the Upper Peninsula. On occasion, individuals have even appeared in southern Michigan in late summer. One such bird was banded at the Kalamazoo Nature Center on 18 July 1978. It is unknown if these are Swainson's which have already completed nesting or perhaps failed and left early. By far the greatest numbers pass through the state during September, with the migration usually ending in the first week of October in the south. It seems there are always a few stragglers, resulting in occasional reports into November, and very rarely, a Swainson's Thrush is found on a Christmas bird count. Between 1970–71 and 1992–93, the species was recorded in five winters. The Swainson's normal winter home includes Mexico, Central America, and northern South America. —Dick Schinkel

# HERMIT THRUSH

## (*Catharus guttatus*)

This thrush is distinguished from its relatives by its rusty-red tail, which it frequently cocks. Otherwise it is similar in appearance, with the characteristic spotted breast and a grayish-brown back. It also possesses a beautiful flute-like song, which is regularly heard during the morning choruses of songbirds in our northern coniferous and mixed forests. The Hermit Thrush is a common migrant in the state and a common summer resident throughout the northern half.

This thrush's breeding range extends across Canada and Alaska and south into the western states, the Upper Midwest, and northern New England. The winter range includes the southern portions of the United States to northern Central America, with some birds remaining closer to the breeding grounds, as is evident in southern Michigan. The Hermit Thrush is the only member of its group that winters regularly in the States.

Nesting populations of the Hermit Thrush in Michigan are primarily limited to the northern two-thirds of the state, with highest densities found across the Upper Peninsula and in the north-central counties of the Lower Peninsula. Distribution diminishes rapidly south of Lake and Clare counties. Occasional summer sightings are reported in the southern Lower Peninsula, with localized breeding verified in St. Clair, Barry, Kalamazoo, and Allegan counties in recent decades. A variety of wooded habitats may be used for nesting, including conifer and mixed conifer-hardwood forests, woodland edges, and bogs. A survey of breeding habitat conducted during the Atlas project found a preference for dry coniferous forests, such as jack-pine plains and pine plantations, as well as mesic mixed forest types dominated by spruce and northern hardwoods.

The nest of the Hermit Thrush is usually built on the ground, and occasionally in a tree at heights of two to four feet. Nests are not easy to find, as they are well concealed by overhanging vegetation from a small tree, bush, or fern. Twigs, leaves, bark fibers, mosses, grasses, and sometimes mud are used to construct the bulky, compact nest. The inner lining is composed of softer materials and conifer needles. Eggs are pale blue and usually unmarked, with clutches averaging three to four eggs. Incubation and nestling periods are about 12 days each. Both sexes provide the young with insects, spiders, and some fruit.

Nesting data for Michigan are minimal at best. Nests with eggs are mostly found in June. Barrows (1912) mentions an early nest with three eggs on 20 May 1879 from Ottawa County, and Wood (1951) found a rather late nest with three eggs on 28 July in the Whitefish Point area. The fairly recent nesting documented in Kalamazoo County was even later, with a bird incubating two eggs on 4 August 1973.

Migration periods for this common thrush in Michigan are well known. First arrivals can be expected sometime between the last week of March and the first week of April in the southern counties. An individual has even appeared as early as 30 March at the Whitefish Point Bird Observatory in the Upper Peninsula. The bulk of the spring migration occurs during April and extends into early May in the north.

The onset of fall migration occurs in the latter part of September, with large numbers moving through the Lower Peninsula during October. By November birds are rare but still regularly found in the southern counties. Some remain well into December and occasionally overwinter. Hermit Thrushes are seen annually on Christmas bird counts in the state. Totals between 10 and 30 have been typical in most years since 1970, with the lowest count of 4 recorded in 1988–89 and the highest of 64 in 1978–79. —Dick Schinkel

# WOOD THRUSH
## (*Hylocichla mustelina*)

This common summer resident of our eastern temperate deciduous forests is easily recognized by its reddish-cinnamon upperparts, heavily spotted breast, and narrow eye ring. Also distinctive is its melodic, flute-like song ("eee-o-lay"), which is heard most often in the hours around sunrise and sunset, and even continuing into the evening. The Wood Thrush breeds throughout the eastern United States (except the Florida peninsula) west to the Great Plains and north into southern Ontario and Quebec. Wintering occurs in Mexico and Central America, with small numbers remaining in the southern states.

The Wood Thrush is found throughout Michigan in areas containing deciduous forest, with a preference given to wet and mesic types. Mixed forests are rarely used, and conifer forests seem to be avoided by this species. Wood Thrushes occur most frequently in the southern Lower Peninsula, where they were found in 85% of the townships during the Breeding Bird Atlas survey. Breeding pairs are also common and generally widespread in the northern Lower Peninsula, particularly in those counties adjacent to the Great Lakes, and become noticeably uncommon to rare in the conifer-dominated north-central counties. The same pattern is evident in many parts of the Upper Peninsula where conifer forests are prevalent. However, there are also sections in this region where the species is quite common, such as in Dickinson and Ontonagon counties.

Some Wood Thrush arrive in Michigan in mid- to late April, but the bulk of the spring migration occurs in the first half of May in the south and the latter part of the month in the north. Fall migration commences soon after nesting ends in August and is usually complete by the first week of October. On extremely rare occasions, individuals have been seen in November and into the winter period. There are four Christmas bird count records dating back to 1960, and one Wood Thrush was observed between 3 December 1974 and 5 January 1975 at the Fenner Arboretum in East Lansing.

Nest building begins soon after arrival in May, and nests with eggs are commonly reported by the fourth week of the month in southern Michigan. The nest is usually located on a horizontal tree branch, at heights averaging 8 to 12 feet, often in a dense, dark area of the forest. It is constructed in less than a week and appears much like a robin's nest, but smaller and generally less elaborate. The base is composed of leaves and large plant material, sometimes interspersed with bits of cloth and paper. The female incubates the three to four blue eggs for about 14 days. Fledging occurs in another 12 days, and it is very possible for birds in lower Michigan to have a second brood. Nests with eggs have been found as late as 28 July.

According to data from breeding bird surveys, the Wood Thrush population in Michigan declined an average of 5% per year from the mid-1960s to mid-1980s, and similar downward trends have been seen in other midwestern states. As with so many Neotropical migrants, concern over declining populations is of paramount importance, as species are being threatened by habitat loss on both the breeding and wintering grounds. While the Wood Thrush has actually expanded its range northward in Michigan since the turn of the century, these more recent declines are thought to be mostly associated with reduced habitat in the southern half of the state, caused by increasing development and fragmentation of remaining forests. Studies have shown that pairs nesting in smaller woodlots are more susceptible to predation and cowbird parasitism, leading to below-average productivity. Although Wood Thrush populations are by no means in serious trouble in Michigan, monitoring and research into the reasons for declines are warranted. We must also take a serious look at our land-use policies as they relate to the fragmentation of our forests.
—Dick Schinkel

# AMERICAN ROBIN
## (*Turdus migratorius*)

The "Robin Redbreast" is our most familiar thrush and songbird, seen regularly about our yards and gardens tugging earthworms from the ground. During the breeding season, this large thrush is distributed throughout the North American continent except for extreme northern Alaska and Canada. Its winter range includes nearly all of the United States south to Mexico, with only small numbers found in those states adjacent to Canada. Chosen to be Michigan's state bird, the robin is an abundant migrant and summer resident in all counties, as well as an uncommon winter resident in the south. During the recent Breeding Bird Atlas project, the robin was found in more survey blocks than any other bird.

Few birds have adapted as well to human-altered habitats as the American Robin. It is especially common in suburban yards, parks, golf courses, pastures, orchards, and other similar areas which offer grassy areas for foraging and scattered shrubs and trees for nesting and cover. In addition, breeding pairs will nest in a wide variety of brushy and woodland situations, even forests. Fall and winter habitat includes areas with large residual fruit and berry crops.

Fondly considered a harbinger of spring, the first robins begin arriving in Michigan in March, sometimes even late February. This early return makes them susceptible to late snowstorms, which can cover up worms when the berry crop has been exhausted. The results can be devastating, causing high mortality as occurred after the blizzard of 3 April 1982. The seasonal survey report for that period described "hundreds killed" from starvation or car collisions as birds huddled on roads for warmth. You can help robins through such storms by clearing an area on the ground and providing berries, chopped apples, raisins, moistened

*American Robin*
*Wood Thrush*
JOHN FELSING

dog food, and bits of hamburger or other raw meat.

The bulk of the spring migration occurs during April, with large flocks seen moving along lakeshore locations. One excellent spot to witness these masses is Berrien County, where observers counted an estimated 7,000 robins on 1 April 1974 and again on 8 April 1975. Major concentrations are also noted at Whitefish Point in the Upper Peninsula, with numbers peaking in mid- to late April.

Nesting occurs from April through July, with two broods commonly raised. Along with the traditional nest sites of trees and shrubs, robins also choose ledge surfaces provided by man-made structures, such as porches and outbuildings. Nests are made of various materials held together with a mud layer and then lined with soft grasses. An average clutch contains four blue eggs, incubated by the female for 12 to 14 days, with the young leaving the nest at about two weeks of age. The male often cares for the fledglings of the first brood while the female begins a second nest. Juveniles are easily recognized by their spotted breasts.

After breeding has concluded, robins behave much as blackbirds do, consorting in large flocks for foraging and roosting. At this time of the year, they can become a major pest to fruit and berry growers. By September the migration is underway, with large movements evident in the Lower Peninsula through October. In Berrien County, flocks containing hundreds of robins are regularly found where berries of multiflora rose, holly, mountain ash, crabapple, and autumn olive are prevalent.

Not all robins vacate Michigan for the winter. Christmas bird count participants find between 200 and 800 individuals in most years, with numbers occasionally being much higher. Examples include the 5,042 recorded in 1980–81 and 2,737 in 1984–85. Most wintering robins are concentrated in the southern two to three tiers of counties, but a few may be found farther north, and individuals have even been known to overwinter successfully in the Upper Peninsula.

American Robin populations incurred significant declines during the middle of this century, caused by the unrestricted use of DDT which accumulated in the soil and food chain. The robins' heavy consumption of earthworms made them especially vulnerable. Michigan researcher George Wallace played a major role in documenting massive die-offs and declines of robins, the findings of which were expounded in Rachel Carson's book *Silent Spring* in 1962. After the ban of DDT in the United States and Canada, populations rebounded quickly. According to the breeding bird survey, numbers in Michigan and over much of the continent have increased significantly since the mid-1960s. —Dick Schinkel

## VARIED THRUSH

### (*Ixoreus naevius*)

Why does a bird which nests in conifers somewhere near the West Coast of North America travel halfway across the continent to winter in Michigan? Whatever the reason, the Varied Thrush has been doing so with increasing frequency. This robin-like thrush was unknown in the state prior to 1936, when a male appeared on

3–4 April in Grand Rapids. It was February 1955 before another Varied Thrush made the trip. After three more in the 1950s, the mid-1960s had additional reportings, and by the 1970s the species had become a regular but very rare winter visitor and migrant in Michigan. Other Great Lakes states have experienced similar increases. In most winters one to three birds are seen in the state, although seven individuals were present in the winter of 1976–77, with six in 1980–81. Undoubtedly other Varied Thrushes go undiscovered or are not reported to the seasonal surveys.

Including the winter of 1992–93, there have been at least 69 published records from more than 30 counties. Those counties with multiple sightings are typically along the Great Lakes shoreline. Muskegon County has hosted birds in eight different winters, with presumably the same individual present three years in a row at the same location. Seldom is more than one Varied Thrush found at a site.

As a rule, birds first appear in November or December. The earliest fall record is 3 November in Keweenaw County. December is the best month to look for a Varied Thrush. About 50% of the individuals found in December remain into the following months. The longest recorded stay at any one site was a bird at Gull Lake, Kalamazoo County, from 16 December 1978 until 9 April 1979. A bird at Hillman, Montmorency County, remained from 7 January to 11 April in 1972. These winter visitors are typically associated with bird feeders, fruiting shrubs, and/or evergreens. Few Varied Thrushes have stayed past March, although the latest observation is from 12 May 1975 in Dickinson County. The one out-of-season report was a bird seen in Marquette County on 8 August 1973. —Raymond J. Adams

## GRAY CATBIRD

### (*Dumetella carolinensis*)

The Gray Catbird is a common to abundant summer resident throughout Michigan, becoming somewhat less common and more irregularly distributed in the heavily forested Upper Peninsula. This edge-loving species is one of a number of birds which have benefited greatly from the widespread landscape alterations associated with settlement and human land use.

The breeding range of this thrasher encompasses southern Canada, the eastern United States, and much of the western United States, excluding the far West and Southwest. It is a short- to medium-distance migrant, wintering in the southeastern states, in the Caribbean Islands, and into Central America. In late April and early May, Gray Catbirds migrate to Michigan in association with warm southerly air flows. Average date of first arrival

*Northern Mockingbird*
*Gray Catbird*
*Brown Thrasher*
HEINER HERTLING

H.C. Hertling

in Berrien County is 27–28 April. Any seen prior to mid-April may be individuals which overwintered successfully in the state.

Catbirds are fairly conspicuous upon arrival despite their preference for dense thickets and other shrubby vegetation. This species is sassy, aggressive, and ever-curious, responding readily to unusual activity anywhere in its territory. Like other mimids, it is especially protective around the nest. The pishing and squeaking sounds employed to draw birds closer work effectively on the catbird, as it quickly bounds into view with tail cocked, scolding in its raucous voice.

Kin to the Northern Mockingbird, the catbird is also an accomplished singer. The territorial song consists of a long series of melodious, raspy, and squeaky notes, broken up with catlike "mews" and short intervals of silence. An individual male may sing as many as 180 syllables within a period of five to eight minutes before most of his full repertoire has been given.

The catbird is a species of woodland edge and both upland and lowland shrub habitats, including shrub wetland. In areas where the vegetation is dense and the amount of edge is substantial, breeding densities can reach two or three pairs per acre. The continued spread of suburban habitats into the countryside with extensive ornamental landscaping has had a profound positive impact on populations, especially in the southern Lower Peninsula. Breeding bird survey data since 1966 reveal an increase of more than 1% per year south of the state's midline, and in Kalamazoo County local survey routes show an increase of more than 200% in 22 years. We have also seen a substantial increase in the north during this century, especially in the Upper Peninsula, where formerly this species was described as rare.

Catbirds nest in a wide variety of trees and bushes. In Walter Nickell's extensive study of more than 4,000 catbird nests in Michigan, a total of 116 plant species were used. Among these, gray dogwood, tartarian honeysuckle, hawthorn, wild grape, and common elder were used most frequently. The average height for nests was 5 feet, with most below 10 feet. Nests are built of twigs mixed with grapevines, leaves, weed stems, paper, and whatever else is available.

Most catbirds rear two broods per season in Michigan, with early clutches averaging four to five eggs and later clutches three to four. First nestings begin as early as mid-May in the south, two to three weeks later in the north. Renestings and second broods often carry the breeding season into August. Eggs take two weeks to hatch, and the nestlings leave the nest in 11 to 12 days. It is interesting to note that both hatching and fledging typically occur in the afternoon. Once on their own, immature catbirds disperse from the natal site until they encounter suitable habitat to occupy until the fall migration and to which they may return the following spring.

As seems to be common for many edge-dwelling species, predation pressures on nests and nestlings are high. Enemies of the catbird include red and gray squirrels, chipmunks, raccoons, garter snakes, and House Wrens, to name a few. On the other hand, parasitism by the Brown-headed Cowbird is seldom a factor. The blue-green eggs of the catbird contrast sharply with the mottled brown and white eggs of the cowbird, which are quickly removed by the host.

The food habits of this versatile species change as the season progresses. Insects, such as crickets, grasshoppers, beetles, and caterpillar larvae, give way to blackberries, honeysuckle, dog-

wood, and sumac as the summer gives way to autumn. The southward migration begins in late August, with movements of immatures peaking in mid-September, at least a week before adults. By the middle of October the vast majority of catbirds are gone. In most years, a few linger and overwinter in the southern part of the state, with Christmas bird count participants typically finding one to four individuals annually. —Raymond J. Adams

# NORTHERN MOCKINGBIRD
## (*Mimus polyglottos*)

The Northern Mockingbird is celebrated among birds for its superb musical renditions. Known as a masterful mimic, it would be well loved in any case for its abundance around homes, its dynamic personality, and its spring nighttime serenades. This representative of the mimic thrush family can be found over most of the lower 48 states, except for the northernmost regions and higher mountains, with the range extending to southern Mexico. It is an especially common resident in the South, while farther north populations are limited by harsh winter weather. The mockingbird is primarily a sedentary species, but birds along the northern fringe of the range migrate south.

In Michigan the Northern Mockingbird is a less familiar species, being generally rare and sparsely distributed as a breeding resident, and with most but not all individuals withdrawing from our borders for the winter. Field work for the Breeding Bird Atlas (1983–88) showed the population to be limited almost entirely to the southern and western counties of the Lower Peninsula. Specifically, north of the southern four tiers of counties, all but a few records were within 50 miles of Lake Michigan. A very small number of individuals were reported in the eastern half of the Upper Peninsula, but these are mostly single wandering birds, though breeding has occasionally been verified. Currently the species is locally common only in some of the southwestern counties such as Berrien, Van Buren, and Allegan.

There is a clear explanation for the mockingbird's distribution; concentrations in the western Lower Peninsula are largely associated with the major fruit-growing regions. While insects are a large part of the diet in spring and summer, fruits and berries are staples for autumn and winter. This includes wild and ornamental fruits, such as wild grape, raspberry, and multiflora rose, as well as residual fruits in orchards. Such sources are vigorously defended from robins and other fruit-eating birds, a testimony to their importance for mockingbird survival.

Edge habitats with both open ground and brushy shrubs are preferred by the mockingbird. Orchards or hedgerows which provide cover for nesting plus a good supply of fruit are ideal. When foraging for insects, this species either hops around on the ground in search of prey or sits on a perch, jumping to the ground when an insect is spotted.

Nonresident mockingbirds start returning to lower Michigan in late April and early May. The species is a regular late May visitor to the Whitefish Point area in the northeastern Upper Peninsula. Spring is the peak season of song for mockingbirds, allowing for easy detection. The singer often continues for minutes without a break. The most distinctive feature of its multifaceted song is that each phrase is repeated identically several times. Many of the phrases are imitations of other birds; a mockingbird in Emmet County was heard to include the calls and songs of more than 20 species.

Nesting in Michigan occurs primarily from June to August. The mockingbird's nest is a bulky, loose cup placed fairly low to the ground in a tree, shrub, or vine. It is built from various materials including thorny twigs, leaves, and bark and lined with fine grasses. A typical clutch size is four eggs, which are incubated by the female for nearly two weeks. This species is a notoriously bold defender of its nest. In response to an approaching cat, I have watched a mockingbird call loudly and fly excitedly from perch to perch, at times swooping so low as to nearly strike the intruder.

Most of Michigan's mockingbird population departs during October, while some overwinter annually. State Christmas bird counts provide a good index of the size of our winter population. In recent years totals have been quite low, usually less than 10. Numbers were larger in the past, peaking just prior to the harsh winters of the late 1970s. Maximum counts of 51 and 41 were recorded in 1975–76 and 1976–77, respectively.

The history of the mockingbird in Michigan shows a slow but steady increase in numbers during most of this century. Around 1900 the species was a rare visitor, not even recorded every year in the state. From this time until the 1970s, numbers increased, and the range spread northward, with the first Upper Peninsula sightings coming in the 1950s. After the middle 1970s, when numbers were at their peak, several severe winters resulted in a major decline in the population. The impact was perhaps stronger on the more sedentary birds of southern Michigan, where numbers are still comparatively low. —Jack Reinoehl

# SAGE THRASHER

## ( *Oreoscoptes montanus* )

This denizen of sagebrush plains in the western United States is the smallest of the thrashers. In the Midwest and along the East Coast, this species occurs as an accidental visitor during times of migration. The only Michigan record is from the Whitefish Point Bird Observatory on 16 May 1986, when a Sage Thrasher was discovered by four observers in jack-pine scrub habitat (Evers 1987). Photographs confirmed its identity. This individual typically remained on the ground under brush except when "forced" from hiding. Normally, Sage Thrashers move back and forth from the western breeding range to wintering grounds in the southwestern United States and Mexico. While many of the eastern vagrants have appeared in the fall, half of the records from the Great Lakes states are from May. Other regional records include one summer and two October reports from Minnesota and winter reports from Minnesota and Wisconsin. —Raymond J. Adams

# BROWN THRASHER

## ( *Toxostoma rufum* )

The Brown Thrasher is one of the finest songsters of the Michigan spring, and a regular visitor to yards, both in suburbs and in the countryside. It can readily be seen on the ground searching for food and on treetop perches when in song. Found throughout the state, this sleek bird is a common summer resident in most of the Lower Peninsula and generally uncommon in the Upper Peninsula, particularly in the heavily forested regions.

There are several species of thrashers in North America, nearly all of which have highly localized distributions in the West or Southwest. The Brown Thrasher is the only one which breeds in eastern North America, occurring from southern Canada to the Gulf coast. The western edge of its range parallels the Rocky Mountains from Colorado to Alberta. With the advent of winter, this species withdraws to the southeastern United States.

The Brown Thrasher makes use of a variety of brushy and shrubby habitats throughout our state. Hedgerows are one such habitat, especially in southern Michigan, as are old fields. These areas provide dense cover for nesting and nearby open ground for foraging. Even in some agricultural lands where brush remains, the thrasher is a common sight. A long-tailed rufous bird startled up from the road which dives into vegetation is surely this species. Other favored habitats are areas with small conifers; thrashers are frequent inhabitants of Christmas tree farms. Although generally scarce over the forested regions of the Upper Peninsula, they are one of the few birds found in cutover jack-pine barrens.

The thrasher is an omnivorous species whose diet varies with the season. In spring it consumes plant seeds in cool weather, switching to insects as they become available with warmer temperatures. Fruits and berries enter the diet later in the season. Hopping about on the ground with strong legs, this species uses its long, slightly curved bill to sweep through the litter as it forages.

Thrashers migrate into southern Michigan about mid-April. The first individuals are sometimes seen before 10 April, but this is the exception at any particular locality. Farther north, returning residents are not encountered until late April or early May. The first thrasher of the spring is typically detected by its song. Males will sing for much of the day after their arrival, with single bouts often lasting for minutes without a break. The song is distinctive, consisting of numerous short phrases each repeated twice (occasionally thrice). The double repetition differentiates the thrasher's song from the other Michigan mimids, the Gray Catbird and Northern Mockingbird, both of which also have long-continued songs. After May the song is seldom heard, but the bird's call note, a loud smacking sound, is given in all seasons.

The thrasher's nest, a bulky cup low in a shrub or small tree, is built in late April or the first half of May in southern Michigan, usually a week or two later in the north. Second broods are frequent, so nests with eggs may be found well into summer. Both sexes incubate and care for the young, with the whole nesting process taking about one month. The female may mate with the same male for her second nest or find another.

Thrashers depart the state mainly during September, but small numbers can always be found into early October in southern

Michigan. Their flexible diet permits a few to remain much later, sometimes with the aid of bird feeders. In recent years, the species has been recorded regularly but sparingly on Christmas bird counts, with totals always less than 10 and usually 3 or fewer.

In Michigan, Brown Thrasher numbers on breeding bird surveys declined significantly (about 30%) over the 1971–85 period. Some of this decrease may have been caused by several severe winters which affected much of the eastern United States. However, losses of this nature tend to be only temporary. Probably a greater factor in this long-term decline is the loss of brushy habitats to development, modern agriculture, and succession of old fields and young second-growth. —Jack Reinoehl

# WHITE/BLACK-BACKED WAGTAIL
## (*Motacilla* sp.)

The appearance of a wagtail (White or Black-backed) at the Muskegon Wastewater System from 14 to 24 April 1985 attracted birders from around the state and elsewhere in North America. During its 11-day stay, this accidental visitor could be found in an empty settling basin, around the edges of the ponds, or along the dikes. It was not easily approachable by either foot or car, but a few pictures were obtained. Separation of White and Black-backed Wagtails is difficult in the field, and positive identification of this stray could not be determined. The light gray coloration of its back suggests a White Wagtail but does not preclude a female Black-backed Wagtail hatched the previous summer. In addition to its pale gray back, this individual had a black cap and nape, black chin and throat, and dark wings (with little white in the primaries). The White Wagtail (*M. alba*) is a widespread Eurasian species whose origin could have been no closer than western Alaska or Greenland, while the similar Black-backed Wagtail (*M. lugens*) is a Siberian species which migrates through the western Aleutian Islands. Both species move south in the fall and are very rare vagrants along the West Coast of the United States. How this individual got inland to Michigan we'll never know, though one possibility is the strong weather front which passed through the Great Lakes on 6 April. —Raymond J. Adams

# AMERICAN PIPIT
## (*Anthus rubescens*)

This pipit is a rare to fairly common transient in the state, and a casual winter visitor. Its abundance and distribution vary considerably from season to season, year to year, and place to place, and nowhere is this variation more noticeable than in the timing of spring arrival. First reported dates can differ by as much as a month from one year to the next. For example, the first 1990 record was 17 March in the Allegan State Game Area, whereas the following year the first sighting was not until 21 April. In the Lower Peninsula, the spring migration window can range from late March to the middle of May. In the Upper Peninsula, birds

can be found regularly into late May and casually to 12 June at Whitefish Point.

Inland, the American Pipit can be quite rare in spring. In the Kalamazoo area, two or three springs may pass without a single report. Closer to the Great Lakes, the species is more consistent in its passage. From 1989 through 1993, spring counts at the Whitefish Point Bird Observatory ranged from 115 in 1992 to 620 in 1990. In 1984, up to 345 were seen at this locale in one day. Other large flocks have been recorded in spring, notably at Port Sheldon, Ottawa County, where 450 were present on 23 April 1988. These transient pipits are traveling north on the way to their breeding grounds in the arctic tundra. Nesting populations also occur south through the high mountains in the western United States and to Maine in the East.

During migration, American Pipits can be found on wet agricultural fields, mud flats, and beaches, where they feed on a variety of insects and small seeds. They are typically inconspicuous, often blending in with the background in large open settings. The slim body, tail-pumping habits, streaked buffy breast, and white outer tail feathers are clues to this pipit's identity. One of the best indicators is the diagnostic two-syllable call, a "pit pit," "wit wit," or "jee-eet," which is often given in flight.

There is at least one summer record for Michigan, that of a bird at Otsego Lake, Otsego County, on 18 July 1962. It is unknown if this was an early fall migrant or an oversummering individual. On its return trip through the state, the American Pipit is more widespread, being found with greater frequency inland compared to spring. Habitats used in fall include upland fields, such as pastures, in addition to plowed fields, mud flats, and beaches. Migration begins in mid-September and continues through late October and early November. Flocks of 100 or more individuals are fairly common and especially noticeable near the Great Lakes. In Berrien County, congregations as large as 300 have been seen until 12 November.

Occasional reports on Christmas bird counts indicate that pipits can occur into late December. One or more birds have been recorded on counts in 10 of the last 34 years (since 1960). Very rarely do American Pipits survive into January, but at least one individual managed from 30 January to 11 March in 1973.

Readers should be aware that in 1987 this pipit again underwent a name change, as this primarily Nearctic breeder was separated from its Palearctic relative the Water Pipit (*Anthus spinoletta*). Most field guides do not yet reflect this new classification. —Raymond J. Adams

# SPRAGUE'S PIPIT
## (*Anthus spragueii*)

The Sprague's Pipit is an accidental migrant and summer vagrant to Michigan. This species breeds from the Canadian Prairie Provinces south to North Dakota and Montana, and winters primarily from the southern Great Plains to Mexico. On the nesting grounds it prefers short-grass prairie, but in migration it can be found in a variety of habitats, including beaches, agricultural fields, and short-grass or weedy fields, usually drier habitat than that preferred by the related American Pipit. The Sprague's Pipit, which is sparrow-like in appearance, is difficult to both find and identify.

Addition of this species to the Michigan bird list was guaranteed on 26 June 1935 when a male was collected near Lovells in Crawford County. Discovered on 21 June, this bird had taken up residence in the jack-pine plains. The other report supported by physical evidence (photograph) is that of an individual present at the Muskegon Wastewater System from 12 May to 4 June 1979. A third record, well described by its observers, occurred on 25 May 1986 at Whitefish Point, Chippewa County. Other reports for the state are not as well documented. These are from 21 May 1960, Oakland County; 10 May 1983, Allegan County; and 29 September 1967, Ottawa County. Additionally, a report from 29 May 1989 at the Shiawassee State Game Area is plausible but not conclusive. —Raymond J. Adams

# BOHEMIAN WAXWING

## (*Bombycilla garrulus*)

The Bohemian Waxwing is a regular but erratic migrant and winter visitor in Michigan, being fairly common some years and quite scarce in others. This species nests in coniferous forest, deciduous forest, and muskeg habitats across the Northern Hemisphere. Its North American breeding range extends from northwestern Ontario to western Alaska and south to Washington, Idaho, and Montana. During the fall and early winter, large masses of waxwings leave their summer home in search of food. Like the Cedar Waxwing, the Bohemian relishes fruits and berries in winter, including those from mountain ash, ornamental crabapple, multiflora rose, and juniper.

Bohemian Waxwings reach Michigan in November or December, although there is little pattern evident in the length of their stay. Some years they remain all winter, while in other years these visitors are gone in January. Extreme arrival and departure dates recorded for the state extend from at least 9 November to 2 May.

Northern Michigan residents are more familiar with this nomad than those in the south, since in most winters, Bohemian Waxwings venture only as far south as our northern counties. Every few years, though, some spill over into the southern Lower Peninsula as scattered individuals mingle with lingering flocks of Cedar Waxwings. A Bohemian is fairly conspicuous within a flock of Cedars; in addition to its larger size, it has mostly gray plumage above and below, cinnamon undertail coverts, white wing patches, plus white and yellow spots on the wings. Most cities and towns in Michigan have played host to this species at some point in time. Only rarely do the larger flocks typical of the north appear in the southern part of the state. Probably the largest such occurrence came on 19 February 1920, when more than 1,000 Bohemians were seen near Waterloo in Jackson County.

This species has been present in Michigan annually for the past 34 years, and has been recorded on Christmas bird counts in 31 of those years. On the 1989–90 count, participants found a total of 3,291 Bohemians, more than triple the number for any previous year. Historically, the appearance of large numbers in the state exhibits no clear pattern or cycle. The species was fairly common immediately prior to 1900 and less so right afterwards. There were few reports in southern Michigan from 1923 to the early 1940s, and Bohemians were fairly scarce in the 1970s but more common again beginning in the 1980s. Regardless of the numbers present, observers always take pleasure in finding this waxwing in Michigan. —Raymond J. Adams

# CEDAR WAXWING

## (*Bombycilla cedrorum*)

One of the more elegantly plumaged songbirds, the Cedar Waxwing is a common Michigan resident, distributed throughout the state during the breeding season and wintering in irregular numbers in the Lower Peninsula. The waxwing is named for the red, wax-like tips of its secondary wing feathers. Other plumage features include a soft brown crest, sleek black mask, and yellow-tipped tail.

You can find the Cedar Waxwing almost anywhere in the continent at some time of the year. Breeding occurs in a wide band across southern Canada and the northern half of the United States, while populations winter throughout the lower 48 states and farther south through Mexico, Central America, and the West Indies. This species is considered a vagabond during migration and winter, wandering wherever berry crops are in good supply. Some birds may not even reach their wintering grounds in Central America until January or February.

According to the Michigan literature, the Cedar Waxwing has always been common in the southern region of the state and can now be described as common in the north as well. The increase in edge habitats, orchards, and ornamental plantings around residences has benefited this species over the years. Other nesting habitats include open woodlands, cedar and tamarack swamps, and streamside tangles. Breeding Bird Atlas and breeding bird survey data reveal a uniform distribution, with averages of 10 to 30 individuals per route reported over much of the state. Additionally, numbers of waxwings have increased significantly since the middle 1960s.

Because of their wandering tendencies, it is difficult to tell exactly when migration begins and ends. Records from Berrien County indicate that the onset of fall migration usually occurs in mid-September, and large movements have been documented along Lake Michigan during the month. The migration is apparently concluded by mid- to late October, with variable numbers remaining and/or moving through the state during winter. Annual Christmas bird count totals typically range from 4,000 to 8,000 birds, but the highest count on record is 14,701 in 1984–85.

The Cedar Waxwing feeds extensively on berries for much of the year, including cedar berries, from which the other half of its name is derived. This dependence makes habitats with fruit- and berry-producing trees and shrubs especially important. Waxwings are also adept at catching flying insects, and during the summer months they can usually be found along streams, rivers, and lakes, flying out over the water in search of insects.

The spring migration period, like that of fall, is difficult to discern. Large flocks may be noted in March, April, or May. Many authors tell of two major movements, one earlier in spring and one later. In Berrien County in 1980, an estimated 5,000 waxwings were observed in passage on 24 May, with another 1,000 to 1,500 seen on 26 May. At Whitefish Point in the Upper Peninsula, large flocks are still on the move into June.

Nesting does not take place until June, July, or even later, and is generally timed with peak berry crops. Pairing, however, begins in the winter and involves several rituals. One display that is easily recognized is a berry pass and side-hop. Those birds pairing will pass a berry to one another, hop to one side, then hop back again to have the berry returned. This ritual occurs frequently, and pairs may continue this behavior through the spring until incubation.

Three to five bluish eggs with dark spots are laid in a nest which has been built in an evergreen or deciduous tree or shrub. Cedar is a favorite nest site among conifers, and orchard trees are also frequently chosen. Hatching occurs in about two weeks, and the young fledge in about 16 days. Fledglings can be distinguished from their parents by their streaked underparts. One brood is most common in Michigan, although some pairs may produce two. Because nesting can sometimes be delayed, it is difficult to know if late summer nests are second broods, replacement clutches, or first nests. Even during the nesting season waxwings are gregarious, preferring to nest in loose "colonies," with adults foraging in groups as they obtain food for their young. —Dick Schinkel

# NORTHERN SHRIKE

(*Lanius excubitor*)

The Northern Shrike is an uncommon but regular member of Michigan's winter avifauna. This northern counterpart of the Loggerhead Shrike migrates south into our region in late autumn, stays for a few months, and then returns to its breeding grounds in the Far North. Its nesting haunts are the muskeg and open boreal forests found just south of the arctic tundra in northern Canada and Alaska (also Eurasia). Wintering occurs from southern Alaska and middle Canada south into the United States. The southern limit of its winter distribution is highly variable, including only the northernmost states in some years but stretching to the middle states in others, sometimes even reaching Texas and southern California.

The majority of Northern Shrikes in Michigan are seen between the months of November and February. Individuals occasionally arrive in October, with published records as early as 2 October at Whitefish Point (Chippewa County) and 7 October on Isle Royale. Departure from the state is mostly complete by the end of March, though some lingering into April may be observed, especially in larger invasion years. Seasonal surveys cite exceptionally late dates of 3 May 1987 (Saginaw County), 4 May 1982 (Chippewa County), and 8 May 1992 (Huron County), but there is no indication as to whether sufficient documentation was obtained to ensure they were not Loggerhead Shrikes.

Like many boreal species, the Northern Shrike has irruptive tendencies resulting in variable numbers and an irregular distribution in the state. During most winters, birds are concentrated in the Upper and northern Lower peninsulas, and reports typically range between 20 and 50 individuals. Then, about every fifth year, a substantial influx occurs and Northern Shrikes are more widespread, with birds seen in southern as well as northern counties. Christmas bird counts since 1970 identify large influxes in the winters of 1976–77 (103 reported), 1981–82 (122), 1986–87 (95), and 1990–91 (108). These major invasions are thought to be related to crashes in rodent populations farther north. Numerous specimens at the University of Michigan Museum of Zoology reveal most of our winter visitors to be immature birds.

The Northern Shrike belongs to a unique family of songbirds which make their living by preying on small birds, rodents, reptiles, amphibians, and insects. Shrikes are equipped with a stout, hooked beak for catching and killing prey, but they lack the large talons typical of other predatory species. To compensate, they have perfected the technique of impaling prey items on thorns or other pointed objects for handling and for caching. This behavior has earned the species the unflattering name of Butcher Bird (*Lanius* is Latin for butcher). Watching a small bird snatched from a feeder or finding impaled prey in a thorny tree may be disconcerting for some, but we should not think any less of the shrike because of its predatory lifestyle.

There are 74 species of shrikes worldwide, of which only 3 live in North America, and 2 of these (Northern and Loggerhead) occur in Michigan. Both are near lookalikes and possess similar habits, including a preference for open lands with scattered trees. What best separates the two are their continental ranges and the different times when they occur here. Due to the serious decline in Loggerhead populations, the Northern Shrike is now the species seen most frequently in the state. There is a potential for overlap during migration, but even this is minimal given their distributions and the highly endangered status of the Loggerhead. March–April and October–November are the time periods when both may be present. The Northern Shrike may be carefully identified by its slightly larger body size, a larger and more sharply hooked beak, and a narrower black mask that ends where the bill begins. —Gail A. McPeek

# LOGGERHEAD SHRIKE

(*Lanius ludovicianus*)

For reasons we do not fully understand, Loggerhead Shrike populations in the Northeast and Midwest have been on a downward spiral for the past 25 to 30 years. The species has disappeared from a few states and in others, including Michigan, Wisconsin, Indiana, and Ohio, it is listed as endangered. Early writings indicate

*Loggerhead Shrike*
HEINER HERTLING

H. C. Hertling

that the Loggerhead Shrike was once a fairly common summer resident in Michigan's Lower Peninsula, with nesting records from most counties. Reduced numbers were apparent in the 1960s and 1970s, but it was not until the Breeding Bird Atlas (1983–88), when fewer than 10 pairs were found, that the full extent of the decline was realized.

The Loggerhead Shrike is an open-country bird, favoring short-grass areas with scattered trees, utility wires, and other perches from which to hunt. Suitable habitats may include pastures, meadows, orchards, hayfields, and other cultivated lands plus lawns and golf courses. Prey items are varied, ranging from insects to amphibians and reptiles, small mammals, and small birds. Preferred nest sites are trees or shrubs with a dense or thorny structure such as red cedar, hawthorn, wild crabapple, and various orchard species.

I had the good fortune to observe a pair of shrikes in the summer of 1987 in Allegan County, the only site in the state where breeding occurred consistently through the 1980s. The territory contained some pasture and mowed grass plus row crops and nearby orchards. The nest was located about five feet up in a cedar within a fencerow of spruce and cedar trees separating lawn and house from adjacent cornfields. My first thought was that such habitat was seemingly available in many parts of Michigan, so why was the shrike so endangered?

This mid-summer nest was suspected to be a second brood or replacement clutch, as first nests are typically initiated in April, with four to six eggs laid. This nest contained three young about 10 to 12 days old and already showing the shrike's characteristic black mask. Both parents regularly brought insects for the nestlings. Some were captured from the lawn and pasture areas, while others were obtained from the bare soil among rows of corn. I did not observe any taking of small birds, mice, or other vertebrate prey, but caches discovered by others earlier in spring did include some of these larger items. Overall, the Loggerhead's diet is mostly insects, with less than 10% made up of vertebrates.

The impaling and caching behaviors exhibited by this species are fascinating. Those who have studied caching have found that the impaled prey may be more than just a larder. The fact that caching is done primarily by males and most frequently early in the breeding season suggests that this may be a way for males to advertise that they are holders of good territories and will be good providers. Experimental manipulations of cached items revealed that males with larger caches mated first and sired more offspring (Yosef and Pinshow 1989).

Migration times for this shrike are primarily in March and April in spring, and August, September, and occasionally into early October in fall. There is potential for overlap with the arrival (October) and departure (March–April) of the Northern Shrike, so observers should take special care in identifying any shrike during these months. Not all Loggerheads are migratory; those found throughout the southern United States and Mexico are permanent residents, while populations in the northern states and portions of southern Canada withdraw from their breeding territories to winter in the South.

The outlook for this species in Michigan is bleak. Breeding since the mid-1980s has been verified only at isolated locations in Allegan, Huron, Alcona, Benzie, and Grand Traverse counties, and pairs have not been consistently present at most of these lo-

cales. Biologists are unable to institute any specific management programs in the absence of information pinpointing the cause of their demise. Land-use changes which have reduced the amount of short-grass habitats and tree fencerows are one possible factor. So, too, is the widespread use of pesticides in areas where shrikes are likely to forage. Since most declines are associated with the migratory subspecies (*L. l. migrans*), a more recent hypothesis suggests that populations from the north are encountering problems on their wintering grounds due to limited habitat and competition with resident shrikes already occupying the available quality spaces. At present, conservation efforts in Michigan need to be directed toward research, surveys, monitoring, and protection for all remaining breeding pairs and their habitats.
—Gail A. McPeek

# EUROPEAN STARLING
## (*Sturnus vulgaris*)

It is almost unimaginable to think that the current European Starling population in North America, estimated at more than 200 million birds, could result from the liberation of one small flock in New York's Central Park in 1890. After several unsuccessful attempts at introduction, this one worked, and what followed was a phenomenal population explosion across the continent. Presumably, the notion was that this familiar Eurasian species, known for its voracious appetite for insects, would be good to have around. Another story is that someone was trying to introduce all species mentioned by Shakespeare. Regrettably, whatever the reason, the starling turned out to be a major pest to farmers and city dwellers, and a detrimental competitor with many native avifauna.

These robust, speckled birds first appeared in Michigan in 1924, with reports of individuals or small flocks from several different southern locales. Six years later the species was an established permanent resident over most of the Lower Peninsula and had moved into several towns in the Upper Peninsula. By the 1940s it ranked among the most numerous birds in the state, a status it still holds today.

There are several attributes which account for the starling's remarkable success. One is its adaptability to the many environmental changes associated with our cities, suburbs, farms, and the many edges and disrupted habitats in between. Others include an omnivorous diet, an ability to utilize a variety of cavities as nest sites, and an aggressive temperament allowing it to compete effectively with native species for both food and nesting resources. Add to this its highly gregarious nature and reproductive po-

*Brown-headed Cowbird*
*Common Grackle*
*European Starling*
*House Sparrow*
DAVID MOHRHARDT

tential, and you have a bird well suited for the human-modified environment. We saw the same success with the House Sparrow, introduced a few decades before.

Although the starling is seldom present in extensive forests, it can be found in some of the state's most remote places, including northern wilderness areas and islands such as Isle Royale. Numbers are minimal and distribution is spotty in these mostly forested regions, but as long as there are minor breaks created by roads, towns, logging, and small farms, starlings will take up residence.

Overall, their occurrence in Michigan is heavily skewed toward the south. As most people are well aware, starlings achieve their greatest abundance in and around our farmlands, cities, and towns. Annual breeding bird surveys show average densities in these areas to be three to four times higher than elsewhere in the state. Lawns, parks, pastures, and farm fields yield a generous supply of food, while buildings, bridges, barns, and large shade trees provide roosting sites.

Starlings will select almost any kind of tree cavity, building crevice, or box for their sloppy nest mass. Wherever this nonnative species occurs, it reduces the availability of cavities and takes over holes of many of our native birds. On more occasions than I care to recall, I have watched these pesky birds confiscate cavities of others for their own use. Northern Flickers, Red-headed and Red-bellied Woodpeckers, Great Crested Flycatchers, and Eastern Bluebirds are just some of the hole-nesting species whose cavities are regularly usurped. To exclude starlings from birdhouses, keep the entrance hole equal to or less than 1 ½ inches in diameter.

The starling's early start at breeding also gives it an upper hand over many native cavity nesters. Even those starlings which shifted south for winter are beginning to reappear in the Upper Peninsula in late March. First nests of starlings are built in April, sometimes even in the latter part of March, so many cavities are already taken by the time some species return. The young come off these first nests in May, and second broods are laid in June, with fledging in July. Clutches typically contain four to six eggs, so each pair has the potential to produce 8 to 12 young per year.

Starlings socialize in small flocks once the first young have fledged. Then, toward late summer, these smaller groups of adults and juveniles come together in progressively larger groups resulting in the flocks of hundreds, even tens of thousands, we see in fall and winter. Anyone who has spent time watching flocks forage over a field or descend upon a communal roost at dusk has probably recognized that there is some form of organization or structure within these congregations. The birds move in concert with one another, changing directions in midair and performing precise movements as if they were a single unit. Somehow there is a transfer of information among flock members which leads to this intriguing social lifestyle.

Many flocks from the northern part of the starling's range, including some from Michigan, migrate to the central and southern states, where people must contend with gigantic noisy and dirty roosts of starlings and other blackbirds. Other flocks remain all winter, and those that stay in the north are vulnerable to severe weather and food shortages. Starling totals on Michigan Christmas bird counts range from 60,000 to 100,000 when we experience harsh conditions early in the season. In milder years,

counts of 200,000 to 300,000 are more typical, the bulk of which occur at an incredibly large roost below the Ambassador Bridge in Detroit. —Gail A. McPeek

# WHITE-EYED VIREO
## (*Vireo griseus*)

The White-eyed Vireo is aptly named for the white iris surrounding a dark pupil, which develops as the bird matures. Its white eyes are made even more conspicuous by the yellow "spectacles" encircling them. This vireo sticks close to thickets and underbrush, being rather secretive until it bursts into a loud song sometimes described by the phrase "pick-up-the-beer-check-quick."

The primary breeding range of the White-eyed Vireo extends from the lower Great Lakes to Florida, Texas, and Mexico. With Michigan located at the northern periphery, its status here is that of a rare migrant and summer resident, and its distribution is mostly limited to the southernmost extremes of the Lower Peninsula. This vireo was first observed nesting in the state in Kalamazoo County in 1960, during an apparent range expansion which occurred during the 1960s and 1970s. Currently, a small population is established in the southern tier, with most individuals concentrated in Berrien and Hillsdale counties.

The number of White-eyed Vireos occurring in the state is highly variable, ranging from only a few local reports some years to numerous reports which are widely dispersed in others. Some of the formerly suitable habitat in southern Michigan has been modified by succession or lost to development, and the increases in White-eyed Vireos evident during the 1970s gave way to decreases in the latter years of the 1980s.

The White-eyed Vireo can be found in deciduous thickets and dense undergrowth around ponds and streams. These habitats provide its preferred nesting cover and plenty of insects—the primary food of vireos. It may also inhabit old fields where tangled brambles provide cover and a tasty treat.

Spring migration begins in April, with most arrivals to southern Michigan in May. An occasional White-eyed Vireo may fly well beyond its usual range and end up in the central or northern Lower Peninsula. There is even one spring record for the Upper Peninsula, at the Whitefish Point Bird Observatory in Chippewa County. These vagrants seldom remain for more than a few days, and breeding in Michigan has never been recorded north of St. Clair County.

Nesting occurs from late May through July. The deep cup nest is typically placed from one to eight feet above the ground in a

*White-eyed Vireo*
*Yellow-throated Vireo*
*Solitary Vireo*
JOHN FELSING

J Felsing

sapling or shrub near a woodland opening. Only one brood is raised in Michigan, but farther south two broods are common for this vireo.

Because the White-eyed Vireo prefers nest sites close to the ground and along a wooded or brushy edge, it often becomes a host for the Brown-headed Cowbird. The cowbird's brown-speckled eggs are almost identical to the White-eye's, and the 12- to 15 day incubation period means that the cowbird egg (or eggs), which require 11–12 days, will hatch first and give the cowbird young a head start.

The male White-eyed Vireo sings throughout the nesting period and even into September, just before departing for the wintering grounds along the Gulf coast south to Nicaragua. Each individual male has several songs and will sing one repeatedly before going on to another. This species is also a fairly proficient mimic, imitating songs of the House Wren, American Robin, and Song Sparrow, among others. —Charles Nelson

# BELL'S VIREO

## ( *Vireo bellii* )

The Bell's Vireo was named for John James Audubon's companion, John G. Bell, who first discovered the drab grayish-olive bird. This vireo breeds throughout the southwestern and central United States, coming as far east as Illinois and Ohio. As Michigan is immediately outside this songbird's range, it makes only rare appearances here. There is but one confirmed breeding record for the state: adults were seen feeding young in southwestern Berrien County on 28 June 1980. This makes the Bell's Vireo one of Michigan's rarest and most irregular nesting birds.

This species had been recorded in the state only three times prior to 1970, but it has been found every year since, with half of all sightings from Berrien County. Others have been reported north to Kent and Montcalm counties and in the southeast, to Livingston and Macomb counties. When a Bell's Vireo does make it to Michigan, it usually arrives in mid- to late May. Most individuals leave within a few days, except those in Berrien County, which tend to stay through July and sometimes August. It is doubtful that the Bell's Vireo will ever become a more regular summer resident in Michigan, as there are noted declines in its eastern population.

Scrubby vegetation and thickets of willow, brambles, and weedy ground cover, particularly along streams, are favored habitats of the Bell's Vireo. One day while I was working along a patch of brush at the Sarett Nature Center (Berrien County), an unfamiliar vocalization caught my attention. It was as if the bird I was hearing were both asking and answering its own question. Checking my field guide and bird tape later, I realized that this "Cheedely, cheedely, chee? Cheedely, cheedely, chew!" belonged to the Bell's Vireo and that I was enjoying one of its rare visits to our state. This male stayed around that brushy patch of sumac, blackberry, young cherry, and aspen all spring and half the summer, singing every day. He left suddenly one day and was never seen or heard again. —Charles Nelson

# SOLITARY VIREO

## ( *Vireo solitarius* )

Formerly called the Blue-headed Vireo, this species is distinguishable by its blue-gray head, white throat, and white "spectacles" encircling dark eyes. This common migrant and summer resident spends most of its time in the forest canopy, a habit which frustrates those hoping to see its attractive plumage.

The summer range of the Solitary Vireo stretches across Canada, encompasses the Great Lakes states, and then extends down the Appalachian Mountains to Georgia at altitudes up to 6,000 feet. It also occurs in the Rocky Mountain states west to the Pacific, at altitudes up to 9,000 feet, and south into Mexico. The winter range includes the southern United States, Mexico, and Central America south to Nicaragua.

The Solitary Vireo makes its home in coniferous and mixed coniferous-deciduous forests. It especially likes small openings or canopy gaps where thick undergrowth provides cover for nests, which are often placed in lower branches of conifer or hardwood trees within 10 feet of the ground. In some regions, this species will also breed in dry deciduous woods.

In Michigan the Solitary Vireo is most commonly found in the Upper Peninsula, where expanses of northern coniferous and mixed forests provide good nesting habitat. In the Lower Peninsula, it is widely distributed and generally common in the northeastern counties, uncommon in the northwest, and occurs only sporadically in the central and southern sections to Van Buren, Kalamazoo, and Livingston counties. There is one locale in southwestern Michigan—the Allegan State Game Area—where this vireo has become fairly common in recent decades.

Best detected by song, the Solitary Vireo sings a series of whistled phrases with short pauses, very similar to that of the Red-eyed Vireo but with two syllables (instead of three). The Solitary's song also tends to be higher-pitched. I first learned the song of this vireo while working as a naturalist at Mount Rainier National Park in Washington State. In the Northwest its song is lower and slurred compared to that of the Red-eyed, and I was surprised to find the same species in Michigan singing higher and sweeter.

Observations of migrating Solitaries in Berrien County occur between 29 April and 7 May, but in nearby counties where nesting occurs, as in Allegan and Kalamazoo, singing males can be heard earlier. The peak spring migration in southern Michigan is usually during the second week of May, just as early arrivals are reaching the Upper Peninsula. After a few months devoted to breeding, the southward migration commences in late August in the Upper Peninsula, with most individuals gone from the southern Lower Peninsula by mid-September. During migration Solitaries will search out thicket, scrub, and forest habitats to obtain the various insects and fruits which make up their diet.

Males return to their breeding grounds prior to females and immediately begin staking out territories. When a female arrives, the male fluffs his yellow flank feathers while bobbing and bowing toward her in courtship. If his displays are ignored, he will follow her about, serenading with a low song.

The breeding period in Michigan extends from May until August. Clutches average three to five eggs, which are incubated for about two weeks, with nestlings fledging in another 10 to 12 days. The parenting pair may raise more young than they bargained for, as this vireo tends to be one of the more common hosts of the Brown-headed Cowbird—a species notorious for laying its eggs in the nests of other birds. In areas where cowbirds are abundant, productivity of breeding Solitaries may be severely reduced.

Solitary Vireo populations have also been affected by heavy logging in Michigan. Both their abundance and distribution have changed noticeably in the past one hundred years. Early bird lists describe this species as merely a rare migrant in the state, suggesting that nesting populations may have been decimated around the turn of the century because of habitat loss. Gradually, through reforestation and establishment of pine plantations, the Solitary Vireo has become more widespread and common in Michigan. On the national level, breeding bird survey data indicate that it increased significantly in numbers between 1966 and 1991. —Charles Nelson

# YELLOW-THROATED VIREO

(*Vireo flavifrons*)

This common summer resident stands out from its relatives by its bright yellow throat and breast and the yellow "spectacles" around its eyes. Michigan lies at the northern edge of the Yellow-throated Vireo's breeding range, which encompasses the eastern states south to the Gulf and west to the Prairie states. Consequently, its distribution and numbers are concentrated in the southern region of the state, with recent expansion north to the Straits and southwestern Upper Peninsula, along the Wisconsin border.

This vireo spends the winter in the tropics, primarily from Central America to northern South America, with smaller numbers remaining north to Texas and Florida. Northbound migrants begin reaching Michigan in early May, or rarely in late April. County records for Berrien identify 2 May as the average arrival date, while first sightings at the Whitefish Point Bird Observatory in the Upper Peninsula range from 8 to 22 May. Generally, the spring migration is complete by the third week of May. Fall migration gets underway in August and proceeds fairly quickly, with most gone by mid-September. Average departure from Berrien County is 17 September, and only a few Yellow-throated Vireos have been reported in the state in October.

Preferred habitat of this species is the canopy of semi-open deciduous forest, either second-growth or mature. Oak-dominated forests are heavily used, as are riparian woodlands. Historically, the range of the Yellow-throated Vireo was largely confined to the southern Lower Peninsula, since conifer and mixed forests prevailed over the northern portions of the state. Settlement and logging practices altered both the landscape and forest composition in the north, creating more open forests and an increase in deciduous communities. These changes allowed the Yellow-throated Vireo population to increase and expand northward in the state during the 1900s. Breeding bird surveys for the state reveal a significant increase in numbers between 1966 and 1991.

The northward extension of this vireo's range and its increased presence are well documented by the Breeding Bird Atlas conducted during the 1980s. While the southern Lower Peninsula continues to be the mecca of its breeding population, it is now commonly found in more than half of the northern Lower Peninsula counties where deciduous forests occur. Even more incredible is the fact that this species was recorded in 40 Upper Peninsula townships, mostly Menominee, Dickinson, and Iron counties, which border Wisconsin. A local population has clearly become established in this region, something unheard of 50 years ago. Along with its northward expansion, the Yellow-throated Vireo continues to do well in the southern half of the state, where its numbers have increased significantly in recent decades, probably in response to maturation of second-growth woodlands in many areas.

The nesting season for this species in Michigan begins in late May, with most egg laying completed by mid-June and young fledging in late June or July, and occasionally as late as August if renesting has occurred. The woven cup nests hang from horizontal forked limbs at fairly substantial heights, typically 25 to 50 feet above the ground. Both sexes participate in the incubation of the four pinkish-brown splotched eggs. Like most if its kin, the Yellow-throated Vireo is known to be a frequent host to the Brown-headed Cowbird. The associated decline in productivity can be especially detrimental to small, isolated populations in fragmented habitats where cowbirds are more abundant.

It is rare for the Yellow-throated Vireo to be anywhere but high in the forest canopy, so in order to locate one you must keep your ears open and eyes looking up. The male's song is most similar to that of the Red-eyed and Solitary Vireos, but once you learn to recognize the harsh or husky quality to its abrupt phrases, separating the Yellow-throated is relatively easy. You may still find the species challenging to find in the tree foliage, but you will at least be aware of its presence through song, which persists over the course of the breeding season. —Charles Nelson

# WARBLING VIREO

(*Vireo gilvus*)

The Warbling Vireo's song is so distinct and the bird so nondescript that positive identification is most often done by voice. One interpretation of its rambling warble is, "If I see you out of season, I will seize you and I'll squeeze you till your squirt." I remember hearing this vireo as a young lad, and one day I skipped class and spent the morning chasing down this elusive bird. To my surprise and disappointment, it was the most colorless bird I had ever seen. The song, however, is delightful, and I always look forward to hearing it when the Warbling Vireos return in spring.

A common transient and summer resident, this species can be found throughout the state, with the greatest abundance in the southern Lower Peninsula and the lowest numbers in the eastern Upper Peninsula. Beyond Michigan the breeding range of the Warbling Vireo extends north to southern Alaska and central Canada and south to Alabama, California, and Mexico. Winters are spent in Mexico and Central America.

The Warbling Vireo inhabits a variety of deciduous and mixed deciduous-coniferous forests, often in association with water. A typical suitable community might include groves of cottonwood and aspen, or stands of alder, elm, maple, and sycamore. This species often selects isolated mature trees in open woodlands, and is therefore also common in orchards, parks, and treelines bordering lakes, fencerows, and roadsides. Occasionally it will nest in shrubby habitat.

Spring migration usually begins the first week of May, although Warbling Vireos have been seen in Michigan as early as mid-April. Autumn movements commence in late August, and the migration continues through September. A few reluctant stragglers have been spotted in Michigan as late as mid-October, with later dates being exceptional anywhere in the Great Lakes region.

Records for the state show that nesting occurs between May and July. Nests are of typical vireo design—a woven cup suspended in the fork of a horizontal branch. Unlike some of its relatives, the Warbling Vireo usually builds its nest quite high, often 30 to 50 feet above ground. Clutches typically contain four white eggs marked with sparse brown and black spots. These hatch in about two weeks, and it takes another 12 to 14 days for the young to fledge. Both parents incubate and care for the brood, with the male frequently singing while on the nest. When Blue Jays, Common Grackles, red squirrels, or other potential predators come near the nest tree, the strident alarm calls of the parents command your attention.

Since the Warbling Vireo prefers open woods, it was probably less common in Michigan prior to settlement, being confined more to forest openings bordering lakes, rivers, wetlands, and prairies. Additional suitable habitat was created through clearing of the land, and a population increase and range expansion noted by authors in the middle 1900s seemed to parallel further opening of the forest.

In recent decades, human changes to the landscape have not always benefited this species. Breeding bird survey data for Michigan indicate a significant downward trend in Warbling Vireo numbers from 1966 to 1991, in contrast to a general increase for the nation as a whole. On a more local level, survey routes in Kalamazoo County reveal a substantial decline in the population since 1970. Contributing factors for these decreases include urban and suburban development, which usually eliminates mature tree growth, and at the other end of the spectrum, the regrowth of forests in other areas, which benefits the Red-eyed Vireo but renders habitat less suitable for the Warbling Vireo. Cowbird parasitism may further contribute to local declines, and mortality from heavy pesticide use to control epidemics, such as Dutch elm disease, has also been reported. Past experience has shown that use of chemicals to rid humans of pests can also harm vireos and other insect-eating birds, our natural pest exterminators. —Charles Nelson

*Red-eyed Vireo*
*Warbling Vireo*
*Philadelphia Vireo*
JOHN FELSING

# PHILADELPHIA VIREO
(*Vireo philadelphicus*)

One of the lesser-known vireos in Michigan, this species is an uncommon spring and fairly common fall migrant, and a rare summer resident in the far north. Named for the place of first discovery in 1842, the Philadelphia Vireo is difficult to distinguish from some of its relatives and even some warblers. Species such as the Red-eyed and Warbling Vireos and Tennessee and Orange-crowned Warblers can easily be confused with the Philadelphia when individuals are flitting about in the canopy as they so often do. With its olive plumage above and yellow below, this species blends in well with the dense foliage in which it prefers to live. And, in addition to its mostly nondescript plumage, its song is exceedingly similar to that of the more common and familiar Red-eyed Vireo.

The breeding distribution of the Philadelphia Vireo, which is fairly limited, includes portions of central and eastern Canada and just barely enters the United States in the north-central and northeastern states. The southern edge of this range brushes extreme northern Michigan, with local breeding in the Upper Peninsula and northern tip of the Lower Peninsula. The other half of the year is spent in the tropics, with the bulk of the population wintering from Guatemala through Panama.

Most Philadelphia Vireos seen in Michigan are transients, passing through our region as they travel between their summer and winter homes. The numbers of this species in spring average 10 to 15% those of the abundant Red-eyed Vireo. Philadelphias have been recorded as early as 2 May in Kalamazoo County, but the more typical arrival time for the southern part of the state is the second week of May, with the migration continuing through the end of the month. At the Whitefish Point Bird Observatory in the Upper Peninsula, transient Philadelphia Vireos have been recorded as early as 11 May and as late as 8 June.

Banding records, tower kills, and seasonal survey data indicate that this species occurs more commonly in the state during the fall migration. Southbound transients are usually first reported in the latter part of August in the north, with movements through the Lower Peninsula during the month of September. During migration, which is the most likely time for observers in Michigan to see this vireo, individuals frequent edges of mature deciduous woodlands consisting of oaks, hickories, maples, and beech. They can also be found in willow and alder thickets along streams.

The Philadelphia Vireo was considered to be strictly a migrant in Michigan until the first breeding was confirmed 8 July 1966, when a fledgling was found in Charlevoix County. Shortly thereafter, a fledgling was collected on 20 July 1970 in Alger County, providing full documentation of nesting. Its status has since been modified to that of migrant and rare but regular breeder in the extreme northern regions of the state. *The Atlas of Breeding Birds of Michigan* reported this species in 48 northern townships, with confirmed breeding in Ontonagon, Baraga, Marquette, Chippewa, and Cheboygan counties.

The higher terrain in the western Upper Peninsula provides a large area of deciduous forest and good nesting habitat for Philadelphias. These forests contain aspen, sugar and red maple, red oak, and white and yellow birch. Woodland edges appear to be favored, and this species has probably benefited from mosaic clear-cutting, regeneration of forests on abandoned lands, and the addition of small forest roads.

The nest of this vireo is a rather large cup made of grass and bark strips (especially birch) and lined with thistledown and lichens. The only nest found in Michigan was located by Laurence C. Binford in Houghton County on 27 June 1990. It was suspended from a forked branch of a red maple about 35 feet above ground, and both male and female were observed incubating.

Because Philadelphia and Red-eyed Vireos can readily coexist in northern deciduous forests, and the latter is the more abundant and better known of the two, it is easy for even the more experienced birders to overlook the former. Patience, practice, and keen senses are needed to locate and identify the Philadelphia Vireo in Michigan. —Charles Nelson

## RED-EYED VIREO

(*Vireo olivaceus*)

The Red-eyed Vireo is a common transient and summer resident found in deciduous and mixed woods throughout the state. Its widespread distribution and abundance make it our most common vireo, both in Michigan and in North America. Only the most urban and nonwooded areas of the state are uninhabited by breeding Red-eyed Vireos.

An olive bird with no wing bars, this species' most distinguishable features are its red eyes, dark eye stripe below a white eyebrow, and gray cap. Song is even more useful for identification purposes than physical appearance. In fact, most of the time people recognize this vireo solely by its melodious song, for it is a laborious task to find this greenish bird when it is concealed in the trees.

The Red-eyed Vireo breeds over much of North America, north to British Columbia and Hudson Bay and excluding much of the West and arid Southwest. After wintering in northern South America, individuals may begin returning to Michigan as early as the last week of April. More typically, average arrival time in southern Michigan is the first week of May, with peak numbers coming in mid- to late May. You cannot miss this bird's return; listen for the questioning notes ("Who is it? Who did it? Is that you?") which are so characteristic of this species.

Breeding commences soon after arrival, starting with the male's establishment of a territory and courting of a female with chases, tail fanning, and swaying from side to side. After pairing, a suitable forked branch is chosen for the nest, usually 5 to 10 feet above ground but occasionally up to 60 feet. The female appears to do most of the construction work, making a cup-shaped nest from a variety of materials including grasses, roots, bark strips, webbing from tent caterpillars, spider silk, and lichens to decorate the outside. Incubation of the three to five eggs is also done solely or primarily by the female while the male continually sings, even on the hottest summer days. Its song is often so relentless that it becomes background noise for other woodland activities.

Although care is taken to protect the eggs when the parents are away from the nest, this species seems to be regularly parasitized by the Brown-headed Cowbird. Summarizing decades of records from the University of Michigan Biological Station near Pellston (Emmet-Cheboygan counties), William and Linda Southern reported at least one cowbird egg in 178 of 257 (69%) Red-eyed nests.

Studies have found that when foraging, male Red-eyed Vireos tend to search in the middle to upper canopy, while females work the lower canopy foliage. Foods include such delicacies as caterpillars, wasps, bees, flies, and ants; they have even been known to eat gypsy and brown-tailed moths. Their mostly insect diet is supplemented with blackberries, elderberries, sassafras, and other fruits, particularly later in the season.

By mid- to late July nesting has ended, although the male continues to sing well into August. Unlike many songbirds, adult Red-eyed Vireos wait to molt until they reach the tropics. Departure from the Upper Peninsula begins as early as late August, and migrants are mostly through by the first of October. In the Lower Peninsula they are still common through September, with a gradual decline during the first half of October. Stragglers in November are exceptional.

Despite human alteration of natural forest habitat, the Red-eyed Vireo has remained common and widespread in the state. In the northern regions, averages of 20 to 40 territorial males are typical on a 25-mile breeding bird survey route, far exceeding that of any other vireo. In addition to large tracts of forest, this species also readily uses small woodlots, fragmented forests, and wooded parks and suburbs. These latter habitats, however, may be less suited for breeding. Numerous studies have found that Red-eyed Vireos as well as other forest birds tend to have poor productivity in small, fragmented patches of woodland because of greater pressures from predation and cowbird parasitism. —Charles Nelson

## BLUE-WINGED WARBLER

(*Vermivora pinus*)

Trace the history of the Blue-winged Warbler in Michigan and you find a bird which has gone from being absent, to rare, to common across the southern half and moving northward. This species was first authoritatively listed for the state by M. Gibbs in Kalamazoo County in 1879. Other sporadic reports for a few southern counties followed in subsequent decades, and by the 1940s it was a rare summer resident north to Livingston County with four nesting records (Wood 1951). The increase seemed to accelerate thereafter, first in the southwest and then in the south-

*Golden-winged Warbler*
*Blue-winged Warbler*
JOHN FELSING

east, with expansion northward to Newaygo County in the 1950s and Midland and Isabella counties over the next two decades.

At present we can describe the Blue-winged Warbler as a common breeding bird in southern Michigan, a local breeder in the midsection (north to Lake and Gladwin counties), and a rare migrant and summer resident elsewhere in the Lower Peninsula. This characterization, too, may become obsolete before long if the population growth and expansion continue. Occasionally spring migrants reach the Upper Peninsula, but as yet there are no known nestings. The northernmost breeding confirmation during the 1980s was a Blue-wing–Brewster's pair in Benzie County.

This change in the Blue-wing's status has not been unique to Michigan. Other northern peripheral states have seen similar invasions and increases during this century. The current breeding range extends from northern Georgia and Arkansas to New England, southern Ontario, the Upper Great Lakes states, and as far west as Iowa and Nebraska. Most who have observed and studied this species relate its range expansion to the increased availability of early to mid-successional habitats created by human land uses.

Blue-winged Warblers nest in a variety of shrub-dominated habitats, including woodland clearings, stream borders, willow swamps, and abandoned fields with shrubs and saplings. Interestingly, some authors describe a preference for damp situations, while others note a more frequent use of dry upland sites. Rather than a contradiction, this reflects both local differences and the Blue-wing's flexibility in habitat selection. Many credit this broad tolerance for its population expansion and the frequently reported displacement of the Golden-winged Warbler, a close relative with similar but narrower requirements.

Blue-winged Warblers generally arrive in Michigan in early to mid-May, although records from Kalamazoo County on 19 April and Benzie County on 25 April remind us that individuals sometimes appear earlier. Males are easily detected by their "bee-buzzz" song, typically sung from a conspicuous perch atop a shrub or tree. Observers should enjoy such views of these tiny yellow and bluish warblers; otherwise they stay mostly hidden in the low, dense vegetation. Nests are placed on or slightly above ground and are skillfully concealed in thick herbaceous growth.

The nesting period for this species in Michigan extends from the latter part of May to July. Published records of nests with eggs (usually 4–5) are mostly from the first two weeks of June, with fledged young reported between mid-June and mid-July. Several records included the presence of cowbird eggs or young, and in some local areas, Blue-wings have been found to be a fairly frequent host.

The breeding period concludes quietly with little singing in July, and departure from the state is barely noticed. Fall banding stations, which provide the best data, indicate that migration occurs primarily from the end of August to mid-September. There are almost no incidences of stragglers beyond the third week of September. Wintering grounds of this warbler are in Mexico and Central America, with small numbers seen in the Caribbean.

Observers should be aware of the similarities in song of Blue-winged and Golden-winged Warblers, and that the former sometimes sings the primary song of the latter, while hybrids possess either song depending on parentage. There is now considerable overlap in the ranges of these two species in Michigan, and care should be taken to verify song identification with visual observation. —Gail A. McPeek

# GOLDEN-WINGED WARBLER

(*Vermivora chrysoptera*)

The Golden-winged Warbler is a fairly common summer resident found in early to mid-successional habitats in most counties of the state barring the southernmost tiers, where it is exceedingly rare to absent. After wintering in the tropics from the Yucatan to northern Venezuela, this tiny warbler with the prominent yellow wing bars arrives on its Michigan breeding grounds in May, rarely late April. By the third and fourth weeks of May, most have returned and pairing and nesting are underway.

Favored breeding habitats include moist woodlands with thickets of alder and willow, and overgrown fields in the shrub-sapling stage. Nest records in the Michigan literature often describe dense edge situations between second-growth woods and old fields, in either lowland or upland sites. Where habitat is suitable, it is not uncommon to find several territorial pairs sharing the area. The nest is a rather bulky structure built on or close to the ground, usually at the base of a weed stalk, brier clump, or sapling. The four to five eggs are laid in late May or June, with young hatching in about 10 days and fledging in another 8 to 10 days.

Migration south commences in August, and the birds evidently make a quick and quiet departure, unlike in spring, when the male's buzzy song marks their return. Records indicate that most Golden-wings are through the state by mid-September with periodic stragglers, including one as late as 11 October in Kalamazoo.

Like its close cousin the Blue-winged Warbler, the Golden-wing has undergone a rather dramatic distribution change in Michigan during this century, becoming increasingly common in the northern regions while decreasing in the south. When Barrows (1912) and Wood (1951) wrote, the species was almost exclusively found in the southern Lower Peninsula. A considerably different distribution is apparent today with the publishing of *The Atlas of Breeding Birds of Michigan* (1991). A greater proportion of the population now breeds in the northern Lower Peninsula, with lesser and nearly equal occurrence in both the Upper and southern Lower peninsulas.

This northward shift and southern withdrawal in the Golden-wing's distribution has been a rangewide phenomenon, with increases and expansion reported along the northern boundary from southern Manitoba and the northern Great Lakes east to southern New England. This expansion is mostly attributed to the large amounts of successional habitat created in the wake of logging. At the same time, declining populations have occurred in the southern and eastern regions, from Illinois to Pennsylvania and in the Appalachians to northern Georgia. Availability of appropriate successional habitat is one probable reason, but perhaps more compelling is the nearly simultaneous expansion of the Blue-winged Warbler, which seems to result in the displacement (and replacement) of the Golden-wing.

Observations in such states as New York and Ohio indicate

about a 50-year replacement rate from the time Blue-wings first move into an area to the time Golden-wings disappear. Michigan records suggest a similar pattern first evident in some southwestern counties, with Blue-wings already outnumbering Golden-wings by the 1950s. Two decades later the same was true for many southeastern counties. Based on habitat selection and behavioral observation, numerous authors give the Blue-winged Warbler the competitive edge. There are, however, a fair number of sites in southern Michigan, such as the Allegan State Game Area and George Reserve (Livingston County), where the two species have coexisted for numerous decades, apparently owing to a large, diverse supply of successional habitats.

One other factor which seems to contribute to the displacement of Golden-wings is cross-breeding between the two species, resulting in recognizable hybrid offspring, either first-generation Brewster's or second-generation Lawrence's. Since intermediates are genetically more like Blue-wings, hybridization proves more detrimental to Golden-wings.

It will be interesting to watch the continuing saga of these two warblers in the coming decades. There is much concern over the fate of the Golden-wing. According to the federal breeding bird survey, population declines have exceeded any increases from northward expansion, and Michigan data reveal a 2% annual decrease in numbers since 1966. As a result of these downward trends, this species received "management concern" designation in the United States in 1987. Conservation efforts in Michigan will be particularly important since our state lies within the Golden-wing's principal summer range. —Gail A. McPeek

# TENNESSEE WARBLER

## (*Vermivora peregrina*)

An uncommon and local breeder in the Upper Peninsula, this small songbird is usually seen in Michigan during times of migration. The Tennessee Warbler is a common transient in both spring and fall, though its numbers can vary considerably from one year to the next. At times, numbers passing through Michigan rival those of the Yellow-rumped, our most abundant migrant warbler, while in other years its numbers are much reduced. Long-term migration data at Kleinstuck Preserve, Kalamazoo County, illustrate this variability, with spring totals ranging from a low of 23 in 1992 to a high of 562 in 1982.

The spring weather pattern is one factor which greatly influences the magnitude of the Tennessee Warblers' migration through Michigan. Once they depart their tropical wintering areas in southern Mexico, Central America, and northern South America, they move north through Texas and up the Mississippi Valley to the breeding grounds across Canada and the extreme northern United States. During this journey strong frontal systems can carry flocks farther east or west than usual.

Migrant Tennessees begin arriving in Michigan during the first week of May, rarely sooner. Thirty years of data for Berrien County indicate an average arrival date of 3 May. An 18 April 1978 observation in Van Buren County is very early. Peak migration encompasses the middle two weeks of May in southern Michigan

and the latter two weeks in the north. Often an inhabitant of the canopy during spring migration, this warbler is difficult to detect and identify among newly emerging leaves. Fortunately male Tennessees fervently sing their three-part, staccato song in migration. In years of big movements, it seems nearly every large tree in the countryside or city contains a singing male or two.

Most Tennessee Warblers continue north through Michigan to the boreal forests of Canada. Some migrants dawdle into early June, and a small population remains in the Upper Peninsula to breed. Prior to 1950, summer records for the state were scarce. Lawrence Walkinshaw found the first Michigan nest on 23 June 1956, north of Seney in Schoolcraft County. This nest was situated in a sphagnum moss hummock under grasses and sedges in a bog of black spruce. Nearby in Alger County, the Cottrilles found six nests in similar habitat from 1981 to 1984. During the 1970s, Dave Baker located a group of breeding pairs and found 11 nests in a bog near Hulbert in Chippewa County. He noted that they were inhabiting "park-like stands of mature black spruce" in association with larch and aspen, and that the males sang throughout the breeding season, even when attending young. Based on these records, five-to-six-egg clutches are typical, nests with eggs occur from mid- to late June, and nests with young in late June and July.

During the Michigan Breeding Bird Atlas (1983–88), Tennessee Warblers were reported from 55 townships scattered across most of the Upper Peninsula, including Isle Royale. While this survey provided much improved information on breeding distribution of this species in the state, the population was likely underreported because of the reclusiveness and inaccessibility of bog habitats. Further complicating assessment of its status are natural fluctuations in response to cyclic spruce budworm outbreaks, a major prey item. Neither the Cottrilles nor Baker could find Tennessees in their respective areas in the late 1980s. No nesting is known for the Lower Peninsula, and summer observations in this region are late spring or early fall migrants.

Observations and banding records suggest that some adult Tennessee Warblers leave their breeding areas extremely early and prior to molting. On 8 July 1987 in Allegan County, I saw an unmolted female attending young only two weeks or so out of the nest. This family evidently emigrated considerable distance before their chance discovery. Also noteworthy is a record of a molting adult Tennessee banded by R. and B. Keith in Kalamazoo County on 1 August 1990, which was recaptured at the same location on 20 July 1991. Clearly this individual left its breeding grounds during or prior to molt two years in succession.

With the exception of such early adults, the typical fall migration begins with flocks of southbound immatures moving through Michigan in the latter half of August. Adults join the exodus in September, and most have left by 10 October. In fall, Tennessees frequently forage lower in the vegetation, affording better views compared to spring. During outbreaks of spruce budworms on the breeding grounds, the number of young produced increases, and large flocks of immatures are seen in fall. Two young banded in Kalamazoo and Tawas Point in the fall and recaptured in the Dakotas the following spring suggest that some of our fall migrants originate from parts of Canada northwest of Michigan. —Raymond J. Adams

# ORANGE-CROWNED WARBLER

*(Vermivora celata)*

This nondescript warbler is an uncommon to fairly common migrant in Michigan, casually remaining into the winter. Anyone who spends much time afield during the spring and fall seasons may see one; the trick is knowing where to look, when to look, and what to look for. You need to see this species extremely well for proper identification. Fortunately it spends very little time high in the tree canopy with some of its cohorts. Birds with which it can be confused (especially in fall) are Tennessee, Nashville, Wilson's, Yellow, and Pine Warblers and possibly Philadelphia and Bell's Vireos. Orange-crowns are drab olive above and dingy greenish-yellow below, with yellowish undertail coverts and blurred streaks on the breast and flanks. The orange crown is seldom visible and is nearly nonexistent on some individuals.

The geographic range of this warbler is quite substantial, especially in western North America. Breeding occurs from eastern Canada through Alaska and south through much of the western United States. Eastern birds tend to winter along the Gulf and southern Atlantic coasts, while the remainder of the population winters from California and Arizona south through Mexico to Guatemala.

The Orange-crowned Warbler has never been common in Michigan. Barrows (1912) called it a decidedly rare bird, and Wood (1951) labeled it uncommon. Banding and migration surveys over the past thirty years have improved our understanding of the Orange-crown's occurrence, and suggest that it may have been more common than early authors realized. One factor lending to underreporting is this species' tendency to sing less in migration relative to those warblers which remain to nest in the state. Its weak trill does not carry far and is quite similar to songs of other species. Furthermore, the timing of its migration can make it seem less common than is actually the case.

Compared to most warblers, this species is an early migrant. The first birds frequently appear before the end of April, with the flight peaking in southern Michigan during the first two weeks of May. Migration is a week to ten days later as you move into the Upper Peninsula. Numbers are generally low and variable from year to year. Long-term counts at Kleinstuck Preserve in Kalamazoo have ranged from 0 to 25 birds per spring, with an average of only 8. Large groups of Orange-crowns are rarely found, and occasionally individuals will travel in loose flocks of mixed warblers, often containing at least a few Tennessees.

The Orange-crowned Warbler can be found in a variety of habitats during migration. At the Kalamazoo Nature Center it is most often encountered in willow clumps along a stream. Other areas used are hedgerows, thickets, and overgrown fields as well as mature and second-growth woods. This warbler occupies similar habitats on the breeding grounds, including thickets, brushy open woodlands, and field and streamside borders.

While Orange-crowns may return to Michigan as early as late August, they are generally among the latest warblers to pass through the state. In the Upper Peninsula the migration window extends from late August to mid-October, while observers in the Lower Peninsula rarely see this warbler before mid-September, with numbers peaking in southern Michigan in the first two weeks of October. Even in fall, transients rarely travel in flocks of any size. No more than seven have been recorded at one time in Berrien County, and in over twenty years of fall banding at the Kalamazoo Nature Center, there are only a handful of dates when five or more Orange-crowns were netted in a single day.

This tiny warbler is reasonably hardy, with a number of reports from November, at least seven from December, and two from January, including a bird banded in Ann Arbor on 31 January 1932. Surprisingly, an Orange-crowned Warbler has not yet been reported on a Christmas bird count, although one was seen during the count period in 1979–80. —Raymond J. Adams

# NASHVILLE WARBLER

*(Vermivora ruficapilla)*

The Nashville Warbler is a common migrant in Michigan and a common summer resident in the northern Lower and the Upper peninsulas, where it ranks among the most abundant breeding warblers. South of the state's midline, however, it is irregular in summer, with scattered local breeding reported. This sharp contrast in its distribution stems from its affinity for northern coniferous and mixed forest habitats. These include both dry and wet types, ranging from jack-pine plains to spruce, tamarack, and cedar bogs, and encompassing a variety of other mostly damp woodland habitats with evergreens. Lowland sites typically support the highest breeding densities, but in the northern Lower Peninsula, largest numbers are found in the dry jack-pine areas shared by the Kirtland's Warbler. Nashvilles are encountered most frequently in the Upper Peninsula, where they were found in 75% of the townships during the Breeding Bird Atlas.

This species has one of the more unusual disjunct breeding ranges of the North American warblers. In the West, Nashvilles reside in a relatively restricted region from southern British Columbia and Saskatchewan south in the mountains to central California and Nevada. In the East, their distribution extends through the boreal forest from Manitoba to Nova Scotia and south to the Great Lakes and the northeastern states, and at higher elevations to West Virginia. During winter, they can be found from the extreme southern United States (California, Texas, and rarely Florida) through Mexico into Central America.

The Nashville is one of the earlier warblers to reach Michigan each spring, with first arrivals invariably seen by the last week of April or the first few days of May. Early published dates include 6 April for Washtenaw County and 11 April for the Capital Count area (Lansing). Peak movements through the state generally occur

*Tennessee Warbler*
*Bay-breasted Warbler*
DAVID MOHRHARDT

in the second and third weeks of May. The abundance of this species is readily apparent during spring migration. At Kleinstuck Preserve in Kalamazoo, the Nashville numbers third behind the Yellow-rumped and Tennessee Warblers in overall abundance. During migration, you can find Nashvilles in a wide range of habitats. They seem to be especially attracted to woodland edges, thickets, orchards, and large shade trees, and can often be spotted at midstory levels.

Courtship and nesting begin as early as late May in warm years, and nests with eggs have been reported anytime from late May to late July. Records indicate that young generally fledge between mid-June and late July. Clutches average four to five eggs, and the nests are placed on the ground in moss or a grass clump near the base of a shrub or sapling. Time required from incubation to fledging is about 23 days.

The summer status of this species in southern Michigan is not easily determined. It is rare and local at best, and those territorial or breeding Nashvilles which have been found are mostly associated with tamaracks, which tend to be present in inaccessible boggy areas. The male's song is a relatively weak, two-part trill but, more important, it is given less frequently if competition for territories with other Nashvilles is minimal to nonexistent. An adult male was captured in mid-June in two consecutive years near Vicksburg (Kalamazoo County), with no other indication that it was present at the site (R. and B. Keith, pers. comm.). Adults will occasionally reappear in July, most of which are probably early fall migrants.

The southbound flight generally gets underway in mid- to late August, beginning primarily with immatures. Adults begin moving in September, the month of peak fall migration. Passage continues into October, and by the middle of the month only stragglers remain. The latest Nashville encountered in Kalamazoo County occurred on 6 November 1972.

Although the Nashville Warbler continues to be one of the most common Michigan warblers, there has been a change in numbers of late. The breeding bird surveys detected a decline in the Great Lakes region from 1966 to 1979, and beginning in the 1980s, numbers in Michigan have decreased about 7% per year—a significant decline. Spring migration data for Kalamazoo also show a similar declining trend. —Raymond J. Adams

# VIRGINIA'S WARBLER

(*Vermivora virginiae*)

When J. Craves captured a second-year female Virginia's Warbler on 13 May 1993 on the University of Michigan's Dearborn campus,

*Northern Parula*
*Nashville Warbler*
DAVID MOHRHARDT

Wayne County, the species became an unlikely addition to our state bird list. This individual, the first and only Michigan record to date, was banded, photographed, and shown to other observers prior to its release. The Virginia's Warbler is seldom prone to vagrancy, especially this side of the Great Plains, yet it has been documented in Illinois, New Jersey, and now Michigan. This warbler breeds on mountain slopes and in ravines of the southwestern United States, and migrates to Mexico for the winter. It is quite similar in size, plumage, call, and behavior to the Nashville Warbler, but has a diagnostic yellowish rump and less yellow underneath. —Raymond J. Adams

# NORTHERN PARULA

(*Parula americana*)

The Northern Parula is a bird which has received little attention in Michigan, primarily because it is difficult to observe and very local in its distribution. This warbler is an uncommon migrant throughout the state, and an uncommon to fairly common summer resident in the Upper and northern Lower peninsulas. The Parula's overall breeding range extends from southeastern Canada through most of the eastern United States, with the exception of a large region in the southern Great Lakes states.

In Michigan's Upper Peninsula this species occurs in all counties, varying in status from locally common to uncommon and probably rare in most of Menominee, Delta, and eastern Chippewa counties. Breeding Bird Atlas data indicate general population centers in the western region east into Marquette County, and the northeastern region around Luce and eastern Alger counties. In the northern Lower Peninsula, Parulas were found in widely scattered locales representing 11 counties, all in the northern four tiers, with the only confirmed breeding in Iosco County.

The Northern Parula breeds primarily in coniferous or mixed coniferous-deciduous forests. Four nests discovered in Wilderness State Park in 1949 were built in balsam fir trees within clumps of the lichen *Usnea*. Elsewhere in Michigan, I have seen this species in mature eastern hemlock, white cedar swamps, and black spruce and tamarack bogs. Others have reported it in northern hardwood and mesic mixed forest communities. All indications are that breeding pairs in northern Michigan are dependent on the presence of *Usnea* (known to many as "old man's beard") for their nests. Research into this association is greatly needed, as this lichen is known to be sensitive to airborne pollution and acid rain.

Parulas lingering or oversummering in southern Michigan, such as in Berrien County, are invariably found in mature river-bottom forest with large sycamores and silver maples. Two singing males were present along the Kalamazoo River in the Allegan State Game Area in June of 1993; a single individual had been detected there the previous summer. It is not known if any of these southern territorial birds are breeding.

Early migrants reach the state in the first week of May or rarely the last week of April. The earliest date comes from northern Lower Michigan on 13 April 1968. Migration in the southern counties peaks from 9 to 16 May, and in the Upper Peninsula, transients are still moving through Whitefish Point at the end of May. Breeding occurs in June and July, with the autumn migration commencing in mid- to late August, peaking in September, and complete by the first few days of October or sooner.

Parulas are rarely found in large numbers on migration. From 1973 to 1993, a total of 132 (average of 6 per spring) were recorded at Kleinstuck Preserve in the city of Kalamazoo. At Whitefish Point from 1982 to 1987, 38 were observed during spring migration, also about 6 birds per season. Banding data and tower kills also provide evidence as to the general rarity of this species in the state on migration. Of approximately 160,000 birds banded in fall at the Kalamazoo Nature Center from 1973 through 1993, a mere 16 were Parulas. While some may no doubt avoid capture by remaining higher in the trees, the absence of visual records in fall indicates that the results are generally representative. A large tower kill on the night of 16–17 September 1976 in Barry County yielded no Parulas, while data from tower kills here and elsewhere from 1959 to 1964 produced only 6 out of 6,504 individuals (Caldwell and Wallace 1966).

One of the challenges in finding Northern Parulas in migration is their preference for the upper forest canopy in the company of Cerulean Warblers and other treetop-dwellers. Their small size and deliberate pattern of foraging make them difficult to locate. Occasionally they will forage with mixed flocks at a much lower level, providing opportunities for good looks at this attractive warbler. Both sexes are gray-blue above, with males having narrow red and blackish bands on a yellow breast. The same detection difficulties also occur on the nesting grounds. Not well represented on breeding bird survey routes, the Northern Parula is a strong candidate for periodic specialized surveys to get a better handle on its status and monitor its populations.
—Raymond J. Adams

# YELLOW WARBLER

## (*Dendroica petechia*)

The Summer Yellowbird, as it was once called, has long been one of our best-known wood warblers. Anyone who has visited a marsh or walked through a shrubby field has probably seen one and heard its cheerful song, a loud "tsee-tsee-tsee-tsee-titi-wee." Its plumage is mostly yellow, including the wing bars and yellow (instead of white) inner webs of the tail feathers, which are unique among other similar warblers. Males have prominent chestnut streaks on their breast and belly, while females show only faint streaks. People less familiar with birds may sometimes confuse the Yellow Warbler with its late summer counterpart the American Goldfinch, another bright yellow bird of marshlands and shrublands.

The Yellow Warbler has one of the largest breeding ranges of any North American warbler. Its summer distribution extends coast to coast and from northern Alaska and Canada through the lower 48 states to southern California, Oklahoma, and northern Georgia. Additionally, there are disjunct populations in the Florida Keys and West Indies, and resident populations from Mexico south. As summer wanes, birds withdraw to winter from the southwestern states through Mexico and Central America to Brazil and Peru.

In Michigan, the Yellow Warbler is a common summer resident and migrant with a statewide distribution. This versatile bird occupies a variety of habitats dominated by shrubs and small trees. It appears to respond to the habitat structure more than the moisture of the site (wet or dry), although wetlands tend to be preferred and typically support the highest breeding densities. Among the many habitats this warbler uses are shrub wetlands, shrub uplands, old fields, blueberry bogs, semi-open wet deciduous forest, gardens, even shrubby wildlife plantings. Given the abundance of these communities in the modern landscape, it is no wonder that populations in the state have increased significantly over the past few decades.

Although Yellow Warblers breed in all three major geographic regions in Michigan, they are most abundant in the southern Lower Peninsula. During the Breeding Bird Atlas, they were found in well over 90% of the townships in this region, compared to 76% in the northern Lower Peninsula and 51% in the Upper Peninsula. The urban and agriculturally dominated sections lacking wetlands do not attract Yellow Warblers as readily, nor do the heavily forested lands in the north. Particularly high numbers are centered around Barry, Calhoun, and Kalamazoo counties, where breeding bird surveys (1983–88) indicate averages between 16 and 32 birds per route.

Traditionally, the Yellow Warbler returns to southern Michigan sometime during the last week of April. Birds arrive as the first flush of insects appears, but well before most leaves have emerged. By the first week of May, males are plentiful and establishing territories throughout the southern counties, reaching the Upper Peninsula by mid-May. Females arrive a few days after males, and nesting begins shortly, unless delayed by unseasonably cold weather. The female builds a well-constructed compact nest within the crotch of a small tree, shrub, or vine. Commonly chosen sites include dogwood, willow, elderberry, hawthorn, multiflora rose, and grapevine.

There are numerous nest records and breeding studies on the Yellow Warbler in Michigan. Eggs have been found as early as mid-May and as late as early July for renestings. Clutches average four to five eggs (range three to six). Hatching occurs in 11 to 12 days, and the young remain in the nest for 10 to 12 days before fledging. The Yellow Warbler is known to be heavily parasitized by the Brown-headed Cowbird, but this is one species which often recognizes and responds to these intruder eggs. On some occasions, the female buries the cowbird egg in the nest lining and then builds over the original nest. At other times, a completely new nest will be made using materials from the original. Depending on the circumstances, nesting success can range from 28 to 80%.

*Yellow Warbler*
*Prothonotary Warbler*
CYNDY CALLOG

The Yellow Warbler is definitely an early fall migrant. Juveniles begin departure by late July, while adults require three to four weeks to molt before leaving in August. The male often remains on territory and may sing sporadically during this period. Most Yellow Warblers are gone by the first week of September, but each fall a small number of individuals linger. Besides a handful of October records, there is one November report and one Christmas bird count sighting from 18 December 1993 in Niles, Berrien County. —Raymond J. Adams

## CHESTNUT-SIDED WARBLER

### (*Dendroica pensylvanica*)

This common Michigan migrant and summer resident is a bird-watcher's delight. In migration, it is often tolerant of approach and usually remains well within view, choosing to flit about the understory thickets and lower subcanopy, while only occasionally roaming into the upper foliage. Males even tend to sing from a not-so-high perch, where you can admire their lemon-yellow crowns and chestnut-colored sides.

The overall breeding range for this handsome, energetic warbler is roughly triangular, extending from south-central and southeastern Canada to the Upper Midwest and Northeast states, and extending farther south in the Appalachians to Georgia. Chestnut-sideds prefer deciduous habitats with a fairly dense shrubby ground cover, often an area where tangles and thickets are interspersed with tall herbaceous plants. In Michigan, such habitats are frequently associated with regenerating clearcuts and other young forests, woodland edges, shrubby wetlands, old fields, and rights-of-way.

Many authors have commented on the more common status of this warbler in the modern era compared to the time of European settlement. As Michigan's forests were cleared in the early 1800s, the Chestnut-sided responded to the increased edge and early successional habitats created throughout the landscape. Areas unsuitable for farming reverted to old fields and thickets, while the extensive lumbering of old-growth forests provided a generous supply of regenerating woodlands. By 1900, Barrows (1912) described this warbler as abundant in all but the southern half of the state, where it was present but not as common.

The Chestnut-sided's current distribution, which was well documented by the 1980s Breeding Bird Atlas, continues to exhibit a north-to-south pattern of decreasing presence. Reports were received from 77% of the Upper Peninsula townships, 54% of the northern Lower Peninsula townships, and 29% of the southern Lower Peninsula townships. Abundance data from breeding bird surveys identify this as one of the most numerous breeding warblers in northern Michigan, with some of the highest densities found in the far western Upper Peninsula. Numbers are also known to be high on Isle Royale.

Although the Chestnut-sided Warbler is a species of regenerating or otherwise disturbed habitats, its distribution in southern Michigan is somewhat similar to that seen for area-sensitive woodland birds—those which need contiguous tracts of forest. The species is largely absent from the southeast corner, parts of the Thumb, and the tri-county areas around Lansing and Saginaw, with largest populations found mostly in the southwestern counties. In the Allegan State Game Area, for example, more than 100 singing males were detected during avian surveys in 1993. This overall pattern suggests that small, isolated patches of edge found in most residential or intensively farmed areas are generally not suitable. Given the fact that the Chestnut-sided is highly susceptible to cowbird parasitism, it is possible that the impact of nest parasitism could be shaping this distribution. The Yellow Warbler, which has similar habitat preferences but also adaptive behavioral responses to thwart cowbirds, is much more widespread in all southern counties.

Chestnut-sided Warblers first return from their wintering grounds in Mexico and Central America in early May, or occasionally the last week of April in southern Michigan. Unusually early were arrivals on 7 April 1896 and 16 April 1986. Farther north, residents have been known to return in the first week of May, but more typically in the second week. This is another species for which the peak migration occupies the middle two weeks of May.

Nesting occurs from late May to late July, with three to five eggs laid in a cup-shaped nest usually located one to four feet from the ground. Commonly chosen nest sites include blackberry, viburnum, and other small shrubs or saplings. Nests can be relatively easy to find if you do not mind the briers and brambles which are often part of the territory. Most young have fledged by mid-July but renesting may result in later hatching and fledging dates.

By late August, Chestnut-sided Warblers have begun their southward journey, with migration peaking during September. Their numbers are not as large as in spring, and at times they can be downright uncommon. Reasons for this seasonal difference are not clear. For the most part, birds do not linger for long periods, and most are gone by the last week of September. There is one exceptional winter report from a Christmas bird count in Cass County on 1 January 1963. —Raymond J. Adams

## MAGNOLIA WARBLER

### (*Dendroica magnolia*)

This beautiful wood warbler was named by Alexander Wilson for the trees in which he first saw this species (Terres 1980). However, the breeding grounds of the Magnolia Warbler are associated with the continent's northern coniferous woodlands, particularly areas with a spruce-fir component. Breeding occurs throughout most of Canada west to British Columbia and in the northeastern

*Chestnut-sided Warbler*
*Magnolia Warbler*
*Cape May Warbler*
JOHN FELSING

United States from Minnesota to New England, with a southward extension into the Appalachians to West Virginia.

In Michigan, the Magnolia Warbler is a common migrant and an uncommon to common summer resident in the northern half. The need for cool coniferous or mixed coniferous-deciduous woodlands limits its occurrence once you travel south of the Straits. Most of the state's breeding population is concentrated on Isle Royale and in the western and eastern counties of the Upper Peninsula. Breeding Bird Atlas results indicate a rather sparse distribution in the central counties, including Dickinson, Menominee, and Delta. Numbers drop off appreciably in the northern Lower Peninsula, although local pockets of breeding occur in such counties as Benzie, Emmet, Cheboygan, Crawford, Montmorency, Alpena, and Iosco. Every year a few Magnolias remain and establish territories in the southern two-thirds of the Lower Peninsula, invariably along the Lake Michigan shoreline. While some of these birds probably fail to attract mates, a small proportion may breed successfully, as evidenced by a nest found in Berrien County in 1975.

Magnolia Warblers can be found in mesic to wet coniferous and coniferous-deciduous woodlands, either young or mature. According to various habitat studies, an important common denominator of breeding territories is the presence of regenerating conifers. Spruce, balsam fir, eastern hemlock, and cedar are the frequently chosen nest trees, and placement of the nest is relatively low, often from 3 to 15 feet. A characteristic lining of black rootlets is almost always present in the loosely made cup nest. As is common of most warblers, incubation of the three to four eggs requires 11 to 13 days, with fledging in 8 to 10 days. Michigan data indicate nests with eggs in June and early July.

For birders who do not frequent the north woods, there are vast opportunities to see this warbler during the spring and fall migrations. Magnolias spend much of the time foraging in the shrub to middle canopy layers, well within viewing range. This is one of several warblers which are predominantly yellow underneath. A distinct white band crossing most of the middle of its black tail is unique.

Rarely do individuals appear before May; exceptional were sightings on 17 April in the Capital Count area (Lansing) and 18 April in Van Buren County. Average arrival is typically around 6 May in southern Michigan and about a week later in the north. Numbers peak in the middle two weeks of May, often in synchrony with movements of American Redstarts and Chestnut-sided Warblers. Male Magnolias typically reach the breeding grounds a few days before females.

Reports suggest the fall migration brings even more Magnolias through Michigan than the spring. Numbers present, coupled with a protracted period of migration, make this one of the three or four most abundant warblers of the season. Departure begins about the first of September in the north and continues through the month and into October in the south. Small numbers in the second week of October are not uncommon, but few remain thereafter. Late dates for several southern counties are from the last week of October. The only published winter record is of a bird found dead in Oakland County on 5 December 1979. The Magnolia Warbler's wintering grounds are in Mexico, Central America, and the West Indies. —Raymond J. Adams

# CAPE MAY WARBLER
## (*Dendroica tigrina*)

The Cape May Warbler is an uncommon and local summer resident in northern Michigan, and a fairly common migrant throughout the state. This warbler is well known as a spruce budworm specialist, whose distribution and abundance vary substantially from one year to another in response to food availability. Its breeding range is associated with spruce forests in Canada, from British Columbia to Nova Scotia, and the extreme northern United States from North Dakota east.

The Michigan literature indicates that the status of this species in the state has changed within the past 70 years. Barrows (1912) described it as "less uncommon than generally supposed," but "no instance of its nesting has come to our notice." A few decades later, Wood (1951) called it a regular transient with summer reports in Luce County. His comments were based on the discovery in 1941 of 19 Cape May Warblers in a spruce bog northwest of Newberry. In the 1980s, Breeding Bird Atlas results provided a rather different picture, showing that this species was now a widespread summer resident in the Upper Peninsula, and rare and irregular in the northern Lower Peninsula. While the exact chronology of its expansion as a summer resident is unknown, it appears that much of the change took place in the 1970s.

Concentrations of Cape Mays in the Upper Peninsula correspond well to the distribution of large bogs dominated by medium-aged to mature black spruce in association with other wetland conifers. They are currently found in all 15 counties in the region, having local population centers on Isle Royale; in Ontonagon-Gogebic counties; in Marquette County; and in Schoolcraft, Alger, Luce, and Chippewa counties in the east. In contrast, they seem to be absent from much of Iron, Menominee, Delta, and Mackinac counties—across the southern edge of the peninsula. In the northern Lower Peninsula, breeding was confirmed in Crawford and Alpena counties, with scattered reports from eight additional counties south to Roscommon and Iosco. Altogether, the Cape May Warbler was detected as a summer resident in 137 townships during the Atlas.

Identification of this species can be a challenge, both visually and vocally. Few birders will have trouble with the tiger-striped male and his chestnut ear patch, but they can be more easily confused by the female, especially in migration. Many one-year-old females show very little yellow in the rump or underparts during their first spring, and instead are mostly gray and nondescript. The Cape May's song, a "seet, seet, seet, seet" all on the same high pitch, can be confused with similar songs of the Bay-breasted, Blackburnian, and Black-and-white Warblers and the American Redstart. Furthermore, the male favors the uppermost center of the tree for his singing.

Records indicate that Cape May Warblers generally pass through southern Michigan during the second and third weeks of May, and through the north in the third and fourth weeks. First arrivals are typically noted around 6 to 8 May, though occasionally individuals appear in late April, once on 21 April in Kalamazoo County. When migrating, this warbler is more flexible in its habitat choice. It can be found in areas with large oaks and pines, and is especially fond of flowering trees from which it can glean insects attracted to the nectar. Sizable flocks are seldom seen, especially away from the lakeshores.

There are few actual breeding records for Michigan. The Cape May's nest is usually well hidden high in the center of a dense black spruce or balsam fir. Nesting may begin in late May, but most egg laying probably occurs in June. Clutches average six to seven eggs, and young are present in the latter part of June and into July.

Writing in *The Atlas of Breeding Birds of Michigan* (1991), L. Binford described observations of dispersing or wandering individuals as early as 19 July in the Upper Peninsula, but early August is more typical. Migrants reach southern Michigan by the last week of August, with the peak movement during the month of September. Most have left for the West Indies by the beginning of October. The magnitude of the migration is highly erratic, with large numbers of young present in years corresponding to spruce budworm outbreaks. During fall you can look for this species in various habitats, including thickets, brushy or wooded roadsides, even old fields. Larger concentrations are seen along the Great Lakes shorelines than inland.

The Cape May is a semi-hardy warbler, and a few sometimes linger into late fall and winter given adequate food and milder weather. These stragglers are usually associated with large spruce or fir trees in the southern counties. At least three individuals have been seen into December, and singles have been reported on four Christmas bird counts since 1970. Two of these four birds were known to have survived into the first week of January. —Raymond J. Adams

# BLACK-THROATED BLUE WARBLER

## (*Dendroica caerulescens*)

This is a bird for which the male and female are so dissimilar in plumage that early ornithologists John James Audubon and Alexander Wilson thought them to be different species and named the female Pine Swamp Warbler. Of all the warblers, none is as sexually dimorphic in appearance as this one. The Black-throated Blue Warbler has a fairly small North American breeding range centered in the Northeast. The northern limits are southeastern Manitoba, Quebec, and Nova Scotia, with the southern boundaries around central Minnesota and Michigan in the Midwest and Connecticut in the East, but extending considerably farther south in the Appalachians to northern Georgia.

The Black-throated Blue Warbler is a common migrant throughout Michigan and a fairly common summer resident in the northernmost regions, where it inhabits extensive deciduous and mixed woodlands. Highest densities are typically associated with the northern hardwoods (beech-birch-maple) forest type. Alger County in the north-central Upper Peninsula is a particularly prime spot to observe good numbers of Black-throated Blues. While hiking one stretch of trail at Pictured Rocks, I encountered more than 25 males singing their buzzy, ascending "zwee zwee zwee" song.

In the Lower Peninsula this warbler's breeding range is almost exclusively limited to the upper three tiers of counties. Populations are widely scattered and generally sparse in this region except for northwest counties such as Benzie and Emmet, where it is locally common. Black-throated Blues are largely absent as a breeding species in the central and southern Lower Peninsula. Formerly, nesting had been documented south to Ottawa (1878) and Kalamazoo (1891) counties. In recent decades there have been a small number of regular summer reports (with documented breeding in Muskegon) in counties along both lakeshores south to Ottawa and St. Clair. It remains to be seen if additional regrowth of forests will result in an increase in breeding Black-throated Blues in the south, as has occurred for some other warblers.

Pockets of dense undergrowth within a forest appear to be favored by this warbler for nesting. Such pockets are generally available in undisturbed forest as well as some regenerating stands. Of the nests described in the Michigan literature, two were in berry bushes, two in small maples, two in fallen birch tops, two in bracken fern, and one in a small hemlock. Common to all was that they were well shaded and well hidden, and were located within two feet of the ground. Lawrence Walkinshaw and William Dyer are responsible for finding four of these nests, which they said were well made yet rather loosely constructed, the exteriors being mostly birch bark and dead wood with cobwebs woven into the outside. Egg dates range from 29 May to 20 July, and adults with fledged young have been reported as late as 3 August in the Upper Peninsula.

Spring migration brings this species to southern Michigan in the first week of May, although earlier arrivals have been noted on occasion, including a male on 25 April in Kalamazoo. The spring flight peaks in the second and third weeks of May in the south and a week later in the Upper Peninsula. Flocks of migrant Black-throated Blues tend to be small (2–10 birds), with males preceding females by about seven days. In an analysis of Michigan specimens, John Hubbard found the average collection date for adult males to be 9 May, while for first-year males and females it was 16 and 17 May, respectively.

The autumn Black-throated Blue migration commences in late August, peaking in September, and most have departed by early October. There are some rather surprising exceptions, however, including an individual visiting a suet feeder on 7–8 November 1976 in the Upper Peninsula (Marquette County). Another bird was observed at a feeder on 17–21 November 1980 in Mason County, and there are four December records (three in Berrien and one in Kalamazoo).

Like many warblers, this one is a Neotropical migrant. The large majority of Black-throated Blues spend our winter months in the Caribbean. Although they have been found to use the understory of coffee plantations or other disturbed forest situations, there is concern for this species over the effects of habitat loss. To date, federal breeding bird surveys indicate that populations overall have generally remained steady over the past few decades. —Gail A. McPeek

# YELLOW-RUMPED WARBLER
## (*Dendroica coronata*)

One of the more familiar members of the wood warbler family, this songbird is usually first recognized by its conspicuous yellow rump patch, which is readily visible as it flits and forages about. This species can be found in Michigan year-round—as a common breeder in the north, an uncommon winter resident in the south, and an abundant spring and fall migrant statewide.

The Yellow-rumped Warbler has an expansive North American distribution comprising two distinct forms—the Myrtle and Audubon's Warblers. Myrtles breed from the northeastern United States and Canada west to northern British Columbia and Alaska, while the latter form nests throughout the West from British Columbia to Mexico. For years these two were considered separate species, but documentation of regular interbreeding in the northern Rockies led to reclassification under a single name. Use of their former names is still common, as the two are easily distinguished by throat color (white in Myrtle, yellow in Audubon's).

Unlike most warblers, Yellow-rumps have a relatively abbreviated migration, with large numbers wintering in the southern United States, along the East and West coasts and on islands in the Caribbean. Berries are a major food item in fall and winter, and it was the Myrtle's fondness for wax myrtle and bayberry which gave rise to its name.

Return to the breeding grounds comes early. First waves of migrant Yellow-rumps generally reach the state around the middle of April, with numbers peaking in southern Michigan in early May and a week later in the Upper Peninsula. It is not uncommon for some migrants to appear in the south in early April, even late March in mild years. It was unusual, though, for an individual to show up on 26 March at the Whitefish Point Bird Observatory in the Upper Peninsula.

Numbers of migrating Yellow-rumps far surpass those of any other warbler seen in the state. Daily counts taken during peak flights frequently total hundreds, even thousands, of individuals. Examples include counts of 300 to 800 on three mid-May dates in 1974 in Delta County, and 4,000 on 9 May 1975 in Berrien County.

The Myrtle's breeding range in the state is largely restricted to the coniferous and mixed forests of the Upper Peninsula and northern Lower Peninsula south to Manistee and Iosco counties. Modern-day records clearly indicate that this warbler is a common nester in northern Michigan; apparently this is a change in status from what Barrows (1912) described as an irregular and somewhat scarce summer resident in our northern parts. Perhaps his account reflects a low point in the Myrtle's occurrence in the state following widespread lumbering of the virgin northern forests.

Nesting is typically associated with evergreen trees in mixed or pure coniferous woods. An occasional nest is found in a hardwood, but most often they are located on a horizontal branch of a hemlock, spruce, pine, cedar, or tamarack, close to the trunk and at heights around 20 feet. Males typically return to the breeding grounds a few days before females. Their territorial song is a variable trill which can sound very similar to that of either a Chipping Sparrow or a Dark-eyed Junco. Nests with eggs in Michigan have been found mostly in June, with young fledging in July. The earliest record is a nest with four fledging young on 20 June 1932, which translates into a late May start.

Southbound migration may begin as early as August, but the main push across the Upper Peninsula occurs around mid-September, with large flocks moving through the Lower Peninsula during October and mostly departed by early November. A small contingency of Myrtles stay the winter, with numbers varying from year to year. During the 1980s, Christmas bird count totals ranged from a low of 4 in 1988–89 to highs of 195 in 1989–90 and 192 in 1984–85. Nearly all overwintering individuals occur in the southern tiers of counties, so it was exceptional when a Myrtle remained through the winter of 1980–81 at Escanaba in the Upper Peninsula. This species may become a regular visitor at feeders which offer suet, peanut butter, or oranges. —Gail A. McPeek

# BLACK-THROATED GRAY WARBLER
## (*Dendroica nigrescens*)

This western wood warbler is an accidental visitor to the eastern United States, with four reported occurrences in Michigan to date. A yellow lore spot and bold black and white head pattern contrasting with a gray back make this species easy to recognize when it does wander. Records for Michigan and elsewhere show that Black-throated Gray Warblers appear in the East during times of migration, either April–May or September to November–December.

The first three state reports are from the southeast, beginning with a male discovered at the Ann Arbor arboretum on 30 April 1958 (Ford 1958). This individual was relocated and collected on 1 May, with the specimen housed at the University of Michigan Museum of Zoology. The next record was an immature male found dead in a yard in Northville (Wayne County) on 25 November 1962 (Kelley 1963). The third was a male observed on 29–30 April 1975, in woods near the River Rouge in Wayne County. The fourth and most recent record was of a female Black-throated Gray Warbler discovered on 21 April 1991 in Kleinstuck Preserve in Kalamazoo during my daily spring migration counts. This individual (documented by a photograph) remained through 26 April, allowing many observers the opportunity to add this vagrant to their state bird list. —Raymond J. Adams

*Yellow-rumped Warbler*
*Black-throated Blue Warbler*
David Mohrhardt

## TOWNSEND'S WARBLER

*(Dendroica townsendii)*

This warbler inhabits the conifer forests of the Pacific Northwest, from northern Wyoming to central Alaska. Occasionally individuals stray from their usual range, and records show this species to be an accidental visitor to the Great Lakes, with one lone sight record for Michigan. Townsend's Warblers wander east mostly in spring (late April–May) as migrants return from their wintering grounds in Mexico and Central America. There are at least a half-dozen records from Ontario, two from the Chicago area, and one from Minnesota. The single Michigan report is from the Dearborn Nature Study Area at the University of Michigan on 1 May 1988. Although no photograph was obtained, the observers' description of an unmistakable male Townsend's in its brilliant yellow and black breeding plumage provided acceptable documentation to add this species to the state list. The Townsend's Warbler is one of a group of five related *Dendroica* species thought to have evolved from a common ancestor during the Pleistocene ice ages. Others in this strongly patterned group include the Black-throated Green, Black-throated Gray, Hermit, and Golden-cheeked Warblers. —Raymond J. Adams

## BLACK-THROATED GREEN WARBLER

*(Dendroica virens)*

The Black-throated Green Warbler is a common migrant throughout the state and a common summer resident in the northern regions with local breeding in the south. No doubt this forest inhabitant is now absent from some parts of the middle and southern Lower Peninsula where formerly it occurred, but overall its status today is much like that described by Walter Barrows in 1912.

The breeding range of this eastern *Dendroica* extends from central and eastern Canada to the northern Great Lakes and northeastern states, and continues south in the mountains to northern Georgia and Alabama. Distribution in Michigan has always been skewed toward the north because of its decided preference for mature woods with an evergreen component, either hemlock, spruce, fir, pine, tamarack, or cedar. By far the greatest numbers are found in the Upper Peninsula and on Isle Royale, where mixed forests are widespread. In the northern Lower Peninsula, it nests commonly in most areas south to Manistee and Roscommon counties. Black-throated Greens will also use pure hardwood and pure conifer stands, but at a much lower frequency. In a study of bird communities on Beaver Island, this species was found to be four times more abundant in mixed deciduous-coniferous forest compared to adjacent beech-maple stands.

Suitable habitat becomes increasingly scarce further south, particularly in the more heavily settled central and eastern regions. Modern-day records of breeding or summering are mostly from Oakland, St. Clair, Tuscola, and Huron counties in the southeast and Muskegon, Ottawa, Allegan, Kalamazoo, Van Buren, and Berrien counties in the southwest. Observations generally involve a small number of pairs per county except for the Muskegon-Ottawa-Allegan region, where Black-throated Green Warblers are locally common.

The nest of this warbler is invariably built in an evergreen, and although the height is usually within 10 to 20 feet of the ground, placement in thick foliage makes locating one extremely challenging. In some instances, curls of white birch bark which are often woven into the outside layer may help one spot the nest amid the evergreen needles. Nests with eggs have been found mostly in June or early July in Michigan, with young typically fledging in July. Early and late published dates include adults feeding fledglings on 27 June and 30 September. Late nestings most likely result from second attempts, but second broods are possible as well.

During migration Black-throated Green Warblers can be seen throughout the state and in a greater array of wooded and shrubby habitats. The first spring transients generally reach southern Michigan the first week of May. Warm fronts may bring a few in late April, but reports of individuals on 6 April in Kalamazoo and 11 April in southeast Michigan are unusually early. By the second and third weeks of May, numbers have reached their peak, and by the fourth week the migration wanes.

The return flight south occurs primarily in September, with some departure from the north in August and the migration largely concluded by the first week of October in southern Michigan. The latest record published in the seasonal surveys is 25 November 1981, when an individual visited a feeder in Oceana County and evidently lingered through the end of the month. The winter range of this warbler extends from the southern tip of Florida to the West Indies and from southern Texas through Mexico to Panama, with largest numbers reported in Central America.

Surely the Black-throated Green is one of our more familiar warblers. Its yellow face, greenish upperparts, double white wing bars, and prominent black throat are unmistakable, and the male's lazy song of "zee zee zee zoo zee" and "zoo zee zoo zoo zee" are among the easiest to learn. As a result of these characteristics and its general commonness, this species is well represented in field surveys and has been the subject of numerous studies on habitat selection and foraging behavior. —Gail A. McPeek

*Blackburnian Warbler*
*Black-throated Green Warbler*
CYNDY CALLOG

Cyndy Callog

# BLACKBURNIAN WARBLER

## (*Dendroica fusca*)

The Blackburnian Warbler is a common migrant throughout the state, but its breeding distribution is primarily northern, where it nests in hemlock, spruce, or other conifers. Observers will find this species common in summer in the Upper Peninsula, fairly common in the northern third of the Lower Peninsula, and rare and locally distributed elsewhere. This wood warbler's association with mature evergreens in either coniferous or mixed forests is evident across its range, from Saskatchewan to Nova Scotia and south to the northern Great Lakes and New England states and in the Appalachians to northern Georgia.

The Blackburnian is a Neotropical migrant with southern Central America and northern South America providing its winter home. Arrival to its breeding grounds in Michigan occasionally begins in the last few days of April, but more typically in early May. Among the earliest recorded arrival dates are 21 April in Kalamazoo and 25 April in Kent County. Numbers reach their peak during the second and third weeks of May in the southern counties, and in the third and fourth weeks in the Upper Peninsula. Migration counts indicate that males arrive, on average, a week before females.

Although the male has an unmistakable flame-orange head, throat, and upper breast, it is his wiry, high-pitched song that usually results in first detection. A scan of the upper canopy will hopefully yield a view of this striking warbler. During migration you may find Blackburnians in deciduous as well as coniferous woods. This wood warbler is most definitely a canopy bird. Both sexes flit about in the upper branches of tall trees, with males tending to forage slightly higher than females. Their diet includes an assortment of insects gleaned from the foliage or hawked from the air.

Nesting also takes place high in the canopy (20–80 feet), either in a small fork near the top of an evergreen or saddled on a horizontal branch away from the trunk. Needless to say, this positioning in a dense conifer renders the nest nearly impossible to spot from the ground. Patient observation of females during nest building or of adults carrying food for nestlings may reveal its location.

Based on the small number of published records for Michigan, nests with eggs are found in June, with young fledging in July. Females, which do the nest building, have a similar plumage pattern to that of the males, but with yellow on the face and throat instead of orange. Incubation of the four, or occasionally five, eggs takes 11 to 12 days, and both parents share in the feeding of the young.

By summer's end, the migration south is underway. Some Blackburnians begin leaving the northern breeding grounds in early to mid-August, with the main push through the state during September. Average departure from Berrien County is 20 September. Small numbers may still be seen in early October, but an individual found in southeastern Michigan on 15 November 1981 is exceptionally late.

Because of the strong association the Blackburnian has with mature conifer woodlands, its populations were no doubt affected by the changes to Michigan's forests following widespread lumbering. Early writings describe a bird that was common in the northern two-thirds of the state and present in suitable habitat in the south. Today, the Blackburnian's occurrence in the Upper Peninsula is probably similar to that historically, but its distribution and numbers are somewhat less in the northern Lower Peninsula, where the white pine and hemlock components of the forests have been greatly reduced. During the Breeding Bird Atlas it was found to be common in those counties just below the Straits, but was generally rare and irregular south of Benzie, Crawford, and Alcona counties. It clearly does not nest in as many southern locales as it once did, although recent forest regeneration has improved habitat for Blackburnians in a few areas. Records for Michigan beginning in the 1970s reveal some increase in observations in the south in conjunction with maturing pine plantations or mixed forests, usually with hemlock or cedar near the lakeshore. Territorial males are now regularly reported from St. Clair and Tuscola counties in the southeast, and in locales in Ottawa, Allegan, Barry, Kalamazoo, and Berrien counties in the southwest. —Gail A. McPeek

# YELLOW-THROATED WARBLER

## (*Dendroica dominica*)

Following a prolonged absence of more than half a century, the Yellow-throated Warbler recently returned to southern Michigan as a rare and extremely local summer resident. Estimates place the population in the range of 15 to 25 pairs, most of which occur in a narrow corridor of bottomland forest along the southern Galien River in Berrien County. With its reestablishment in the state, the status of "threatened" was accorded to provide for its protection under the state Endangered Species Act.

The range of the Yellow-throated Warbler is centered in the southeastern United States, particularly in the southern Atlantic and Gulf states, where it is a year-round resident. Breeding distribution wanes around Missouri, Ohio, and Maryland, but migrants and scattered local populations may be found north to the southern Great Lakes and southern New Jersey. Within this range, it occupies two dissimilar habitats: pine and pine-oak woodlands typical of coastal plains and dry uplands, and bottomland and floodplain forests. In coastal regions, nesting is closely associated with large trees draped in Spanish moss, while in the Mississippi Valley preference is for towering sycamores. It is this latter form (*D. d. albilora*), fittingly referred to as Sycamore Warbler, which occurs in Michigan.

We know from ornithological writings in the late 1800s that the

*Yellow-throated Warbler*
*Cerulean Warbler*
JOHN FELSING

Yellow-throated Warbler was a local summer resident in the Raisin, Huron, and Kalamazoo river valleys of southern Michigan. Nesting was reported in Monroe and Kalamazoo counties, but the extreme heights prevented any collection of nests or eggs. Then, just prior to the turn of the century, reports diminished rapidly and the species disappeared from all three areas, marked by the last summer observation in Washtenaw County in 1906. Populations also disappeared from most of Ohio during this period, indicating a regionwide decline. The cause remains a mystery; some speculate a weather-related incident of high mortality on the wintering grounds or during migration.

For the next 60 years there were only three records for the state, each a migrant seen in early spring. The first signs of an increase came in the 1970s, and as before, this change paralleled events south of our borders in Ohio and Indiana. Perhaps the vagrant which visited Escanaba (the only Upper Peninsula record) from 20 to 31 May 1969 was an omen of things to come. Since then Yellow-throated Warblers have been recorded on a nearly annual basis, with appearance concentrated in the southern two tiers of counties, most consistently in Berrien.

It was during surveys in 1988 that a local breeding population (14–21 pairs) was confirmed along the southern Galien River in Berrien. Whether this was an increase in numbers from the one to four singing males reported in years previous or was the result of intensive effort is unknown. Most likely it was a combination of the two. I had the opportunity to join fellow birders in this survey, covering areas by foot while others canoed suitable sections of the Galien and its tributaries. Canoeing proved the best method, providing the most access to the banks where sycamores remained. All Yellow-throated Warblers were detected vocally first, then visually if the dense canopy allowed, and none were singing or foraging in trees other than sycamore.

This site in Berrien County is presently the only locale in the state with regular breeding. During the early 1980s, sycamore habitat along the Black River in St. Clair County apparently harbored a few pairs, with a nest reported on 29 June 1982. Other southern counties where possible breeding has been noted of late are St. Joseph, Branch, Hillsdale, and Livingston. Whether small populations will become established at other sites in Michigan remains to be seen. Riparian habitats are not what they used to be, so for the most part, recolonization of other areas seems doubtful.

Spring observations continue to make up the bulk of the records in the state. This warbler is an early migrant, with first arrivals usually noted in Berrien County in mid- to late April. A returnee to the Galien River on 6 April 1991 set a new state record. There is almost no information to report on nesting, owing to the often difficult access of floodplain habitats and height of nests (30–80+ feet). May is probably the main period of nest building and egg laying, with nearly a month required for incubation and fledging of young.

Since Yellow-throated Warblers become quiet by July, there are also few data about their time of departure. Most are likely gone by late September if not sooner. When breeding occurred in Monroe County back in the 1800s, they were occasionally seen into early October. There were no winter records for this species until recently, when an individual lingered in Jackson County through the fall of 1987 and was reported on the area Christmas bird count. —Gail A. McPeek

## PINE WARBLER
### (*Dendroica pinus*)

True to its name, the Pine Warbler is rarely found nesting or foraging in any trees other than pines. Although its niche is not as narrowly defined as that of the endangered Kirtland's, also a "pine" warbler, this species' absence from nonpine forests throughout its eastern North American range leaves no doubt as to its habitat connection. In Michigan, breeding is associated with three species in the genus *Pinus*, either white, red, or jack pine.

Since the state's pine forests occur primarily in the north and have an irregular distribution, so, too, does the Pine Warbler. Breeding populations are clustered in regions with extensive tracts of mature pine timber, mostly on public or privately managed forest lands. Occupied habitats include pine and mixed pine-hardwood forests, sandy ridges bordering bogs, lakes, and streams, open stands with large pines, and even single-species plantations. In fact, this is one of the few birds found in these intensively managed plots.

Summer records and breeding surveys identify two main areas of concentration in the Upper Peninsula, one from Schoolcraft County eastward and the other in Dickinson and central Marquette counties. Elsewhere in the region, breeding occurs in widely scattered local pockets of appropriate habitat. The Pine Warbler is well distributed in the northern Lower Peninsula south to Roscommon and Iosco counties, and is especially common in the Mackinac and AuSable state forests and Huron National Forest. One of the most frequently recommended places to observe this species, as well as a number of other conifer-associated warblers, is Hartwick Pines State Park in Crawford County.

Across the southern two-thirds of Michigan, the Pine Warbler is known primarily as a migrant, except for a small number of areas with suitable pinelands. The tip of the Thumb, in Huron County, harbors a local breeding population, just as it did earlier this century when the species was described as locally abundant there. Other summer and breeding records come from about a dozen widely scattered sites, mostly on lands where pines were planted back in the 1930s under government work programs.

The maturation of pine forests in the south has allowed this warbler to become established in an increasing number of locales. At a pine plantation near Ann Arbor, for example, several pairs were first noted in 1973, with 4 to 6 pairs the following year, and a reported 10 pairs nesting there in 1975. Similar observations of new colonization have been made in other counties, including forests and game areas in Newaygo, Muskegon, Allegan, Barry, and St. Clair counties. The Allegan site harbors a substantial population. Whereas breeding residents in the north can relocate to other

*Palm Warbler*
*Pine Warbler*
David Mohrhardt

suitable habitat, these locally isolated populations in the south are vulnerable to clearcutting and elimination of pine species from forest rotations. Maintenance of Pine Warbler populations at these isolated locales will require careful management.

Data on nests and breeding chronology for the state are scant, as nests are extremely difficult to find. Pine Warblers favor large pine trees, building a cup nest saddled on a branch that is often 30 to 50 feet or higher above ground and hidden from below by a cluster of pine needles. Among the small number of published records are reports of nest building in late May and June, and nests with eggs or young in June and July. I consider myself fortunate to have found not only a Pine Warbler nest, but one that was easily visible from an elevated dune which put me at eye level with the jack pine in which it was located. Coastal habitats, with their windswept dunes and stunted jack pines, can be good sites to observe this species. Positioning yourself atop fire towers and even rooftops in pine stands is another way to enhance your view of both nesting and foraging behaviors.

The Pine Warbler is one of the few warblers with an abbreviated migration, wintering primarily in the southern Atlantic and Gulf states and nearby islands, where it resides year-round. During the breeding season, its range expands northward to Maine, southern Quebec, the Great Lakes region, and southeastern Manitoba. Since travel distance for those which migrate is relatively short, individuals return early in spring and depart later in fall. First arrivals are usually observed around 15 April, with the main flight from the last week of April to the middle of May, ending about the time most other warblers are starting to peak. The reverse trip begins in the second half of August in the north and continues into mid-October in the south. Extreme records to date include an early returnee to Crawford County on 7 April 1991, a late migrant at Whitefish Point on 11 November 1991, and one at a feeder in Bay County on 27 November 1987.

On rare occasions this hardy warbler is recorded during the winter in southern Michigan. Singles were located during Christmas bird counts in 1979–80, 1980–81, 1981–82, and 1985–86, with two on the Hudsonville count in 1986–87. Another rarity was an individual found on 11 February 1970 in Kalamazoo County.

The Pine Warbler is among the more misidentified or unfamiliar warblers in the state. This can be attributed to its generally plain appearance; a trilly song easily confused with that of a few other species, especially the more familiar and abundant Chipping Sparrow; and a propensity for foraging, nesting, and singing in the pine canopy. Fall is a particularly trying time for birders since song is absent, plumage is even more nondescript, and individuals flock with other similar warblers which also have become duller. —Gail A. McPeek

# KIRTLAND'S WARBLER

(*Dendroica kirtlandii*)

Most people in Michigan have never seen a Kirtland's Warbler, yet they are probably aware of its existence and uniqueness to the state. This rare songbird breeds nowhere else in the world except Michigan's northern Lower Peninsula. Almost equally restricted is its winter home on the Bahama Islands. Although the Kirtland's has never been an abundant bird because of some very specific habitat requirements, an alarming drop in the population a few decades ago led to its immediate listing as a federally endangered species, and marked the beginning of an intensive cooperative effort to save it from extinction.

The first specimen from which the Kirtland's was described and named was collected near Cleveland, Ohio, on 13 May 1851, but it would be another fifty years before the breeding range was discovered. While on a fishing trip, E. H. Frothingham and T. G. Gale found and collected an unfamiliar bird in western Oscoda County on 13 June 1903. It was identified at the University of Michigan by N. A. Wood, who then traveled to the area and after much searching found the first Kirtland's Warbler nest in early July.

Today, information about this species is abundant. There have been hundreds of articles written plus a few books. Habitat preferences have been a major topic of study, identifying such particulars as stand age, stem density, tree height, ground cover, and so forth. Basically, Kirtland's favor young, dense pine stands (jack pine and occasionally red pine) with trees between 5 and 23 years of age, or about 6 to 18 feet tall. Their ground nests are built near the base of a pine and hidden by grasses, sweet fern, blueberries, or other cover. Ideal conditions occur in regenerating stands after a wildfire, though some similar habitat has been created through dense plantings. The significance of fire-created stands was made none too obvious just recently, when large numbers of pairs moved to the Mack Lake area as trees came of age following the 1980 fire which burned more than 24,000 acres. Associated with this has been the first major increase in the population, up to 347 males in 1991, 397 in 1992, and an incredible 485 in 1993.

To review a bit of recent history, the first full Kirtland's Warbler census was conducted in 1951, during which 432 singing males were detected. The next count, in 1961, found 502 males spread over nine counties, but ten years later, in 1971, the total dropped to 201 males in only six counties. Although a reduction in habitat probably had some effect, Brown-headed Cowbirds were considered the primary cause, as studies by L. Walkinshaw were uncovering parasitism rates of 69% and productivity less than one fledgling per pair. As a result of the fear that this could completely wipe out the species, control of cowbirds in the Kirtland's breeding areas began in earnest in 1972.

For many years after that, the Kirtland's population remained fairly stable, somewhere around 200 males (and thus about 200 pairs), fluctuating from a low of 167 in 1974 to a high of 242 in 1980. While management efforts were creating habitat to replace stands as they surpassed suitable age and cowbird removal successfully improved productivity to 3.1 fledglings per pair, the population was not increasing. Researchers now believe that the unburned jack-pine stands in use from the 1970s to the middle

*Kirtland's Warbler*
CYNDY CALLOG

1980s had regenerated marginally after timber harvest, and that high-quality habitat was still in shortage. The population growth which has since occured in association with the increased habitat of the Mack Lake burn supports this theory.

Historic records show that in the years around the turn of the century, the Kirtland's distribution was somewhat more extensive, reaching north to Presque Isle, south to Clare, west to Wexford, and east to Alpena and Iosco counties. H. Mayfield has speculated that there was probably a surge in the population in the 1880s and 1890s in the aftermath of lumbering and burning of lands in the northern Lower Peninsula. At the same time, several specimens were obtained in various nearby states during spring and fall migration, and collectors found the species with relative ease in the Bahamas.

The current distribution of the Kirtland's Warbler is centered in Crawford and Oscoda counties, extending west to Kalkaska, south to Roscommon and Ogemaw, and east to Alcona. Dispersing birds have occasionally been reported outside this range, from the Upper Peninsula to Wisconsin, Ontario, and Quebec. Except for one observation of an adult feeding fledglings in Ontario in 1948, there have been no other confirmed breedings beyond the northern Lower Peninsula. Arrival in spring generally occurs from 5 to 20 May or slightly later, with nesting primarily in June and July. Departure in fall is fairly early, mostly in the first part of September. Recent post-breeding banding programs noted one adult as late as 1 October. The remainder of the year (October–April) is spent in similar barren habitats on the Bahama Islands.

The boost in the Kirtland's population since 1988 is a welcome sign to so many who have worked hard to preserve this rare "bird of fire." The large natural fires which occurred in 1988 and 1990 should further improve the habitat situation. The goal of 1,000 breeding pairs established by the Kirtland's Warbler Recovery Team now seems more attainable, although the species is by no means out of the woods. Those who have never seen this special Michigan bird are encouraged to take one of the guided tours offered by the U.S. Fish and Wildlife Service or the U.S. Forest Service. —Gail A. McPeek

# PRAIRIE WARBLER

## (*Dendroica discolor*)

The Prairie Warbler may be the most "endangered" bird on Michigan's list of threatened species. At best it is an uncommon migrant and an uncommon to rare summer resident. Reasons for its decline are puzzling, though habitat loss is probably one factor, and similar trends have been noted in other states. The breeding range of this warbler is centered in the southern two-thirds of the eastern United States, with populations occurring irregularly north to New England, New York, Ontario, and Michigan. Wintering occurs in a geographically restricted area, primarily from the Florida peninsula to the West Indies and Bahamas.

The Prairie Warbler is reasonably easy to identify. Its characteristic song is a long series of rising buzzy "zee" notes. The combination of yellow underparts, black side stripes, two black facial marks, chestnut streaks on the male's back, and tail-wagging habits are features used to eliminate similar warblers. Its name is certainly misleading, as the species occurs more frequently in upland shrub habitat than prairie grasslands.

In *The Atlas of Breeding Birds of Michigan* (1991), Lawrence Walkinshaw recognized three shrubby habitats in which this species is found in the state. All are associated with dry, sandy soils and are successional in nature, causing the Prairie Warbler to have an erratic, spotty distribution. Young jack-pine plains, such as those used by the Kirtland's Warbler, are one such habitat. Since the mid-1980s, however, the species has apparently disappeared from these sites. Other burned lands (former pineries) regenerated to deciduous shrubs and trees are a second type, but the availability of these areas is much reduced. Currently, most of the state's Prairie Warblers occupy the third option listed by Walkinshaw—the early successional communities of the Great Lakes dunes. Young pine plantations and brushy old fields are additional habitats where I have encountered individuals in migration or on territory.

The Prairie Warbler has been present in Michigan since at least the time of the first state bird list (Sager 1839). During the late 1800s, Gibbs found it locally common in Ottawa and Montcalm counties. Other scattered records from Huron County and the Detroit area suggest that it was not very plentiful and its distribution was poorly known. The renaissance of the Prairie Warbler in Michigan did not begin until the 1930s, a time when our knowledge of the Kirtland's improved as well. From 1932 through the 1950s, considerable information was collected on the Prairie's distribution and breeding status, and records indicate its numbers probably peaked during the latter part of this era. The majority of the population occurred in Crawford, Oscoda, Montmorency, and numerous other counties in the northern Lower Peninsula, but birds were also found in Marquette, Alger, and Schoolcraft counties in the Upper Peninsula and in Berrien, Ottawa, Muskegon, and Huron counties in the southern Lower Peninsula.

Sometime after the middle 1960s, numbers apparently declined, and by 1981 the Prairie Warbler had been added to Michigan's bird watch list. During the Breeding Bird Atlas the species was found in a mere 28 townships, all in the Lower Peninsula except for two Delta County observations. Also of concern was the fact that many of the reports seemed to involve unmated males, which sang for a while on territory but then moved on. Records were about equally split between the northern and southern Lower Peninsula, with breeding confirmations from Livingston and Benzie counties. In 1993 at least 28 singing males were located in the Sleeping Bear Dunes area, possibly the only truly viable population left in the state. Studies are greatly needed for this species, which was assigned a threatened status in 1990.

*Prairie Warbler*
JOHN FELSING

Prairie Warblers typically return to Michigan in May, with most migrants reaching the southern counties in the second week. A few may appear in late April, but one on 17 April 1982 at Kensington Metropark in Oakland County was unusually early. Nest building probably begins in late May, with egg laying between early June and early July. The small, compact nest, usually located one to four feet above ground, is well constructed and contains three to five eggs. Incubation takes 12 to 13 days, with a nestling phase of 10 days. The Prairie Warbler is among those species prone to cowbird parasitism, and Walkinshaw discovered cowbird eggs in 6 of the 26 nests (23%) he found.

Fall migration commences in August, usually about the middle of the month, and few Prairie Warblers linger past mid-September. Late departures include a bird in St. Clair County on 4 October 1987 and a female at Whitefish Point on 1–2 November 1990. One winter record exists, for 12 December 1971 in Ann Arbor. —Raymond J. Adams

# PALM WARBLER

(*Dendroica palmarum*)

The ground-dwelling Palm Warbler is a common migrant in the state and an uncommon to rare summer resident, with small numbers breeding locally in our northernmost counties, primarily in the Upper Peninsula. This is one of the more distinctive members of the genus *Dendroica*. While it can sometimes be seen up in the trees with its woodland relatives, it is far more likely to be found on or near the ground. During migration it frequents weedy fields, forest edge, and wooded roadsides and fencerows— places where you might typically find a sparrow.

A useful characteristic for identifying the Palm Warbler is its nearly perpetual tail wagging. This up-and-down pumping of the tail is pronounced both when the bird is perched on a fence wire or when it is hopping across the ground. In spring and summer, key plumage features are a rufous cap, yellow eyebrows, yellow throat and streaked underparts, and yellow undertail coverts.

Michigan lies at the southern periphery of the Palm Warbler's breeding range, which includes most of eastern and central Canada as far as the western mountains, and extends south into the United States only in the Upper Great Lakes and northern New England. There are two recognized races, with those occurring in Michigan being mostly of the western form (*D. p. palmarum*). The eastern race (*D. p. hypochrysea*) is at best casual in the state, as documented by a record (banded and photographed) of a transient in October 1990 in Kalamazoo County. Palm Warblers winter along the south Atlantic and Gulf coasts, including all of Florida, and in the West Indies, Mexico, and parts of Central America.

The Palm is among the earliest warblers to return to Michigan each spring. Thirty years of data in Berrien County indicate an average arrival date of 23 April. Kalamazoo County has one extremely early record from 6 April 1947. The best time to see Palm Warblers is during the first two weeks of May in the Lower Peninsula, the middle two weeks in the Upper Peninsula.

The return flight in fall commences in late August in northern Michigan and continues through mid-October in most years. Peak numbers are present from mid-September through the first week of October. Movements can be especially large along the Great Lakes. For example, Wood (1911) reported "thousands" between 13 and 18 September and 5 and 11 October during an expedition to Charity Island (Huron County). Palm Warblers may occasionally linger into December, with at least four recorded on Christmas bird counts since 1970, and one seen on 5 January 1975 in Iosco County.

As a breeding bird, this warbler has been recorded in a small number of locales in the Upper and northern Lower peninsulas. During searches for Kirtland's Warblers in 1931, Walkinshaw and others discovered a small population of Palm Warblers in jack-pine habitat near Lovells in Crawford County. They observed 15 adults and 6 fledged young, and collected a few for specimens. Years later, in 1955, the first nest was found in the jack-pine plains near Oscoda in Iosco County (Walkinshaw and Wolf 1957). In nearly all cases, nests or recently fledged young were discovered by the birds' agitated behavior in response to human intrusion. Most recently (1989–90), breeding pairs were reported in Oscoda County, also in the same dry pine habitat.

Data indicate that the majority of the state's resident Palm Warblers breed in the open spruce-tamarack bogs in the eastern Upper Peninsula. Territories are associated with bog edges or open pockets within a bog, where sphagnum moss, sedges, leatherleaf, Labrador tea, and swamp laurel are the dominant ground plants. Two nests found in Schoolcraft County, near Seney National Wildlife Refuge, were sunken in sphagnum at the base of a tree, while a third was on the ground along a jack-pine ridge adjacent to a bog (Walkinshaw and Wolf 1957). Based on the seven published nest records for Michigan, the breeding season begins in late May and extends into July.

In *The Atlas of Breeding Birds of Michigan*, D. Evers noted that the extensive peatlands of Lake Superior State Forest and Tahquamenon Falls State Park (Luce and Chippewa counties) "contain the greatest numbers of summering Palm Warblers known in Michigan." The Atlas survey also documented summering in a few sites in the western Upper Peninsula, including confirmed breeding in southern Houghton County. These northern boreal habitats are a unique part of Michigan's natural heritage. More attention and protection needs to be paid to these communities, particularly the spruce-tamarack bogs scattered across the Upper Peninsula, to ensure the continued existence of rarities such as the Palm Warbler in Michigan. —Raymond J. Adams

# BAY-BREASTED WARBLER

(*Dendroica castanea*)

The Bay-breasted Warbler is best known in Michigan as a common spring and fall migrant. We can claim it as a summer resident as well, but its distribution is extremely local and limited to cool boreal habitats in the northern regions of the state, primarily in the Upper Peninsula. This warbler, like the Cape May, is a spruce budworm specialist with a breeding range that corresponds to the continent's spruce-fir forests, found primarily in a narrow zone across central and eastern Canada. Michigan is located at the southernmost edge of this range, which barely enters the United States in the Upper Great Lakes and northern New England.

Breeding records for the state are scant. Reports include an adult with fledged young on 1 August 1933 at Burt Lake, Cheboygan County; an adult with a fledgling on 1 July 1949 at Gratiot Lake, Keweenaw County; a nest on 27 June with young fledging on 13 July 1974 in Grand Marais, Alger County; and a nest on 16 June 1982 at Tahquamenon Falls State Park, Chippewa County. Adding to these records are two confirmations obtained during the Breeding Bird Atlas: one of a pair feeding nestlings on 3 July 1987 at Rabbit Bay, Keweenaw County, and the second of a pair feeding fledglings on 2 July 1988 near Betsy, also in Keweenaw County.

These records as well as those involving singing males link the Bay-breasted Warbler to cool mesic conifer-dominated forests of white spruce and balsam fir, along with other species such as white pine, birch, and aspen. The Atlas survey provides a good illustration of this species' rarity. After six years of intensive effort, Bay-breasteds were reported from only 41 townships, all but 3 of which were located in the Upper Peninsula. Most encounters occurred in the eastern counties, on the Keweenaw Peninsula, and on Isle Royale. The individuals detected in the three northern Lower Peninsula townships were in all likelihood nonbreeders, although the possibility of breeding does exist, as was proven by the 1933 record from Cheboygan County.

The handful of breeding records indicate a June–July nesting period, with courtship probably beginning in late May. Of the three Michigan nests, two were in balsam fir, while the third was in white spruce. These nests ranged in height from about 14 to 30 feet above ground. Clutches typically contain four to five eggs, but six or seven may be present in years corresponding with outbreaks of this species' primary food, the spruce budworm. Incubation is strictly by the female, with both parents feeding the young.

Like other species which respond to particular insect infestations, the abundance of Bay-breasted Warblers varies greatly from year to year and place to place. Because the state is but a minor breeding area, Michigan birders are apt to notice such fluctuations during migration. In Kalamazoo County, for example, long-term spring counts have been as high as 120 birds and as low as 13 (average 50), while fall banding totals have ranged from as many as 231 to a low of 4 (average 52).

The Bay-breasted is among the later warblers to pass through Michigan each spring. Average first arrival dates are 9 May in Kalamazoo, 10 May in Berrien, and 13 May in the Detroit area. Two aberrant records are from Hillsdale (1984) and Kalamazoo (1985) counties, both on 26 April. Peak migration in the southern half of the state usually occurs between 12 and 25 May, slightly later in the north, and late migrants have been noted into the first part of June. When available, conifer woods are favored during spring migration just as they are for breeding. Detection of this species among the foliage is challenging, and its song, a "seetzy, seetzy, seetzy, see," is weak and high-pitched. With persistent searching, you will hopefully be rewarded with the sight of the male's beautiful chestnut and black breeding plumage.

The return flight in fall gets underway in northern Michigan by the second or third week of August, with transients reaching the southern counties by the end of the month. Migration continues through September, with stragglers seen until mid-October. Easily the greatest concentration of Bay-breasted Warblers mentioned in the literature would have to be the "thousands" reported on Charity Island (Huron County) on 3 September by Wood (1911). There are four published November records, the latest from 22 November 1990 at Muskegon State Park. Observation opportunities are better during the fall passage as Bay-breasteds utilize a range of habitats, including shrubby wetlands, thickets, shade trees, and almost any forest type (deciduous or coniferous). They also forage at lower levels in the vegetation, a helpful behavior since the birds are in their duller fall plumages and the Bay-breasted, Pine, and Blackpoll Warblers are now quite similar in appearance. —Raymond J. Adams

# BLACKPOLL WARBLER
## (*Dendroica striata*)

Strictly a migrant in Michigan, the Blackpoll Warbler is one of the more abundant wood warblers in North America. It breeds in spruce, fir, and alder-scrub woodlands throughout most of Alaska and northern Canada, with local nesting in the higher mountains of the extreme northeastern United States. In Michigan, this species is generally uncommon in spring but common in fall, largely a consequence of differential migration patterns. During the northbound flight, Blackpolls migrate over land, with a pronounced movement up the Mississippi Valley. In autumn, much of the breeding population heads east or southeast to the Maritime Provinces and the New England coast, a route that brings greater numbers through Michigan. Once they reach the coast, Blackpoll Warblers embark on a long journey over water to northern South America, with scattered islands providing the only potential stopover sites.

Despite its distinctive breeding plumage, this warbler is difficult to observe in spring, as it usually forages high in the canopy and the vast majority pass through subsequent to leaf-out. Roughly 70% of the spring transient Blackpolls are found between 15 and 25 May in southern Michigan. Some early dates include 28 and 29 April in Berrien County and 30 April in Kalamazoo, while examples of late dates are 6 June in Berrien and 15 June at Whitefish Point in the Upper Peninsula. Numbers tend to be small in spring, although I recall one exceptional total of at least 256 Blackpolls during a Kalamazoo County "Big Day" bird count on 19 May 1984. Late-night rains had grounded large numbers of migrants, and the floodplain forests of the Kalamazoo River were bustling with warbler activity.

This boreal breeder is extremely rare in summer in Michigan. Published reports are from Mackinac Island in late June–July 1906, from Kalkaska County in July 1971, and a singing male at Wilderness State Park in the summers of 1977 and 1978. These individuals are either oversummering nonbreeders or extremely early migrants. The bulk of the fall migration occurs from the last week of August through September, with some arriving in early August in the Upper Peninsula and others lingering into the second week of October in southern Michigan. The latest fall date on record is 5 November 1975 in Berrien County.

At times this warbler is quite common in fall, as evidenced by banding records and casualty data. Banders in Oakland County captured 150 Blackpolls on 13 September 1964. Across the state at the Kalamazoo Nature Center, an average of 30 are banded each fall. Sadly, the real extent of the migration in Michigan is best demonstrated through mortalities noted at television towers and other tall artificial structures. From 1959 to 1964, Larry Caldwell and George Wallace reported 1,063 dead Blackpolls out of 6,504 birds killed at towers in three Lower Peninsula counties, and on 17 September 1976, at some of the same towers, a tragic kill of 2,255 birds, including 194 Blackpolls, occurred.

The recovery of an individual of unknown age and sex banded by Lawrence H. Walkinshaw in Muskegon County on 19 September 1974 provides clear indication as to the direction of the autumn migration. After its banding in Michigan, it was captured six days later in Stamford, Connecticut—a trip of 700 miles in an easterly direction.

While the Blackpoll Warbler is a more consistent and numerous migrant in the fall than in the spring, it is harder to identify. The adult male loses the contrasting black, gray, and white plumage in the post-breeding molt, becoming just another greenish-yellow bird with streaks and wing bars. At this time it looks very similar to those two other confusing fall warblers, the Bay-breasted and Pine. —Raymond J. Adams

# CERULEAN WARBLER

## (*Dendroica cerulea*)

The Cerulean Warbler is an uncommon migrant and summer resident in Michigan, confined mostly to the southern Lower Peninsula. This elegantly colored bird is known intimately by very few people because of its habits and habitat. A denizen of mature hardwood forests, the Cerulean spends most of its time in the upper canopy, with males often singing from treetops 80 to 120 feet high. Finding one usually requires much persistent searching, and only rarely are you likely to catch it in the right lighting to observe its porcelain-blue dorsal surface. They will, at least, forage quite frequently in the subcanopy and occasionally venture down into the understory for food, nesting material, and water.

The breeding range of the Cerulean Warbler is restricted to the eastern United States and parts of Ontario and southwestern Quebec. Populations are distributed as far west as Nebraska and Texas and east to North Carolina, the mid-Atlantic states, and northeastern Vermont. Throughout this range, mature floodplain and swamp forests are primary habitats, with smaller numbers found in large stands of mature deciduous woodlands on upland sites.

Information on Ceruleans in Michigan is largely anecdotal, but the writings and records which are available indicate a long-term decline in numbers in the state. Both Barrows (1912) and Wood (1951) describe substantial populations in southeastern Michigan 80 to 100 years ago. Observers in Wayne, Monroe, Washtenaw, Macomb, and St. Clair counties regularly reported 10 to 20 birds per outing, with some totals as high as 40. Even as recently as 1960, the species nested in moderate numbers in Oakland, Macomb, and St. Clair counties. Except for a few remnant populations in some of these counties (mostly on public lands), the Cerulean is now mostly absent from the southeast.

Declines are also apparent in southwestern Michigan, but this region currently contains the bulk of the state's resident population. During the Breeding Bird Atlas, Ceruleans were reported in 155 townships, 143 of which were in the southern Lower Peninsula. A handful of Upper Peninsula records (including one confirmed breeding) are of recent origin, probably coming from populations in northeastern Wisconsin.

The pattern of distribution across southern Michigan shows a correlation with areas of large contiguous forested lands, suggesting that this warbler is area-sensitive and does not tolerate small isolated patches of woods. Atlas data and additional surveys also document highest densities in riparian habitats with mature silver maple, elm, ash, and other floodplain species. Census work in 1992 found 46 Ceruleans along the Kalamazoo River in the Allegan State Game Area and 32 along the Galien River in Berrien County (Kalamazoo Nature Center, unpublished data). Other occupied habitats include red maple–oak swamps and mature beech-maple forests.

Most of the state's nest records are from the period prior to World War I, when the Cerulean was still common in the Detroit area. The nesting period usually extends from the last week of May to early July. Nest heights can range from 15 to 70 or 80 feet, with the compact nest saddled on a horizontal limb or in an upright fork of a deciduous tree. Clutches include three to five eggs, which are incubated by the female.

In those years when the spring is well advanced, Cerulean Warblers reach Michigan in the first week of May, rarely late April. A late spring and leaf emergence results in a delayed arrival, typically during the second week of May. The time of fall departure is not so clearly defined. Exodus from the state occurs mostly in late July and August. A few birds remain into September, and a sighting on 2 October 1962 in Kalamazoo County is exceedingly late. Wintering grounds for this Neotropical migrant are in South America, from Colombia and Venezuela to eastern Peru and northern Bolivia.

With the recent documentation of declines in Michigan and many other states, concern has been expressed over the status and long-term viability of the Cerulean Warbler. In 1987 it was added to the Fish and Wildlife Service's list of species of management concern for the north-central region of the United States. More recently, in the 1990s, members of the "Partners in Flight" initiative for conservation of Neotropical migrant land birds placed the Cerulean first on their priority list for the Northeast, and third for the Midwest (including Michigan), behind the Kirtland's and Golden-winged Warblers. Concern for this species stems from habitat degradation on both the breeding and wintering grounds. —Raymond J. Adams

# BLACK-AND-WHITE WARBLER

## ( *Mniotilta varia* )

This distinctive black and white striped warbler is a common migrant and summer resident over most of the state, nesting only rarely in some areas of the south. A bird of mostly mixed woodlands, this species has an extensive breeding range that includes nearly all of the eastern United States and Canada west to the Northwest Territories. Its wintering range is also large and includes the extreme southeastern states, Mexico, Central America, and northern South America.

A number of authors have noted the negative impact of forest fragmentation on the Black-and-white Warbler (for example, Whitcomb et al. 1981 and Terborgh 1989). Based on its current Michigan distribution, as mapped by the Breeding Bird Atlas, fragmentation of woodlands appears to have a substantial negative influence on its occurrence. This species is almost entirely absent from the southern two tiers of counties, as well as most of the southeastern and south-central sections of the Lower Peninsula. The landscape in these regions is dominated by residential and industrial development and agriculture, leaving only small isolated woodlots, which are evidently avoided by this wood warbler. A pattern of rare and irregular occurrence is also apparent across the heavily farmed middle counties of the Lower Peninsula.

Among the few locations in southern Michigan where Black-and-white Warblers are regular breeders are the large tracts of forested public lands in Allegan and Barry counties. During a 1993 survey in the Allegan State Forest, 24 singing males were detected. Scattered pairs are also found in the forested dunes along Lake Michigan. In the southeast, similar isolated nesting populations occur in St. Clair and Tuscola counties. Once you reach the northern Lower Peninsula, around Mason and Arenac counties, Black-and-white Warblers become more common and widespread. Largest densities are found across the heavily forested Upper Peninsula, with especially high numbers in the western end.

This warbler seems equally at home in large tracts of both mature and second-growth woodlands. Habitats most frequently associated with breeding territories during the Atlas were mesic mixed forest, wet mixed forest, and wet coniferous forest. About 50% of the observations came from a mixed hardwood-evergreen forest type. In southern Michigan, birds also occur in dry deciduous or dry mixed woods as long as the topography is varied. In Allegan County, singing males are encountered most often along the steep slopes of the Swan Creek valley and the bluffs bordering the Kalamazoo River floodplain. Many of these sites have a well-developed understory.

The Black-and-white Warbler can be an easily overlooked bird. Its weak sibilant song, usually written as "wee-see, wee-see" in couplets of six to eight, carries poorly over any distance. The natty male is a born ventriloquist, its song seeming to come from one direction after another. Coupled with its tree-creeping habits and its striped plumage, this bird has a knack for staying out of sight. Although males and females appear similar on first glance, they can be distinguished, as males have the stronger head pattern with black cheeks and a black throat.

Black-and-white Warblers have a rather extended migration period, arriving in the southern Lower Peninsula the last week of April, and with passage continuing into late May in the Upper Peninsula. They are among the first warblers to reach Michigan, and there are at least two exceptionally early dates of 28 March in Kalamazoo County and 31 March in Berrien County. During migration the species is most frequently found in small intraspecific groups which have joined mixed flocks of other warblers. The Black-and-white's distinctive behavior of foraging for insects on bark surfaces, much like a nuthatch or creeper, reduces competition with most of its traveling companions. A variety of wooded areas will be visited on migration, with birds remaining longer where there is an abundance of food.

Black-and-white Warblers nest on the ground, often on hillsides or slopes of ravines. The nest is usually placed at the base of a tree, shrub, stump, or large rock and is quite difficult to find. Nesting chronology and other aspects of breeding have not been well documented in Michigan. One early nest mentioned in the literature from Oakland County had young three to four days old on 28 May. Based on general sources, nests with eggs (usually five) should occur from mid-May to early July, with young fledging into late July from replacement clutches.

Like the spring flight, the fall migration period is also fairly lengthy, with some birds moving southward beginning in August and others continuing through the state until early October. Because this warbler is not known to linger into the late fall or overwinter, the report of an individual on 21 February 1978 in Okemos, Ingham County, is most intriguing. —Raymond J. Adams

# AMERICAN REDSTART

## ( *Setophaga ruticilla* )

Known in French as "Paruline Flamboyante," the American Redstart is an energetic and flashy warbler. Common in Michigan as a migrant and summer resident, this warbler is seemingly always on the go as it flits from perch to perch when foraging, often behaving like a flycatcher. The male's contrasting black and orange plumage is unmistakable, while the female's gray and yellow colors are less showy but distinctive nonetheless, following closely the pattern seen in the male.

The American Redstart has one of the largest breeding ranges of the North American warblers. It can be found over most of the eastern United States, across a significant portion of Canada to southern Alaska, and in the northwestern states south to Utah. The principal wintering grounds are from central Mexico to northern South America and the West Indies.

In Michigan, the redstart has a statewide distribution. Nearly 100 years ago, Barrows (1912) thought the species bred "more freely" in southern and central Michigan than farther north. Whether or not his assessment was correct, this description is not true today, as numbers are greatest in the northern half of the state. During the 1980s Breeding Bird Atlas, reports were received from 47% of the southern Lower Peninsula townships, compared to 80% in the northern Lower Peninsula and 74% in the Upper Peninsula. The American Redstart is known to be an area-

sensitive species, requiring larger-sized woodlands for breeding (Robbins et al. 1989). The vast majority of the population inhabiting the state's southern counties persists in extensive, contiguous forested tracts, with few to no birds found in the more heavily urbanized and agricultural areas. Within this southern region, redstarts can also be found along the wooded dunes of Lake Michigan and Lake Huron in the Thumb.

Northward in Michigan, the species is found more frequently and in larger numbers, achieving highest densities in the Upper Peninsula. In the eastern and western regions of the Upper Peninsula, breeding bird surveys conducted during the Atlas years (1983–88) averaged up to 18 and 24 birds per route, respectively.

The redstart's general abundance and widespread distribution can be attributed to the range of wooded habitats selected for breeding. In southern Michigan, it is found most commonly in forested river bottoms. For example, in one stretch along the Kalamazoo River in the Allegan State Game Area, 115 singing males were recorded during a recent census—a total more than double the combined counts from other forest types in the game area (Kalamazoo Nature Center, unpublished data). Elsewhere, beech-maple forest or other mesic woodland types with an adequate sapling component are used. In northern Michigan, young deciduous and mixed forests with dense understories of regenerating saplings are preferred. Pure conifer stands are typically not a habitat of choice, but in some areas, such as Drummond Island, redstarts can be found in white cedar and even stands with spruce.

In migration this warbler may be seen in most wooded habitats, including thickets, orchards, shrub swamps, woodland borders, and deciduous and coniferous forest. Arrival in spring usually occurs in the first week of May, although strong south winds may bring individuals earlier. Three unusual records for Kalamazoo County are from 18 March 1942, 5 April 1903, and 12 April 1908. Peak migration occurs in the middle two weeks in the south, and a week later in the north. A high count in Berrien County of 127 redstarts was recorded on 20 May 1984.

Nesting begins in the latter part of May, with eggs present in some years as early as the last week of the month. The female constructs a firm cup nest, usually situated in the pronged fork of a young tree or shrub, 5 to 30 feet above ground. The four eggs (average) hatch in about 12 days, and the young fledge in another 8 to 9 days. Replacement clutches can extend the breeding season well into July, with broods being raised into mid-August.

The fall migration may commence in late July or early August, but the first dependable movements start in mid-August as immatures begin to pass through the Upper Peninsula. The migration reaches southern Michigan in the last week of August and continues through September. Few stragglers are seen past 10 October. Noteworthy was an individual seen on 19 November 1980 in Kalamazoo County. —Raymond J. Adams

*American Redstart*
*Black-and-white Warbler*
CYNDY CALLOG

# PROTHONOTARY WARBLER

*(Protonotaria citrea)*

Among all the warblers found in Michigan, this is the only one which utilizes tree cavities for its nest. The best way to find a Prothonotary Warbler, an inhabitant of wooded swamps and riverine forests, is often by canoe. It is not a plentiful Michigan bird, but rather an uncommon summer resident and migrant with a distribution restricted to the southern Lower Peninsula. When searching for this species, observers should look for a resplendent golden-yellow warbler with blue-gray wings, and listen for a loud, ringing song consisting of five to nine "zweet" notes.

Except for a small area of Ontario, the Prothonotary's breeding range is limited to the eastern United States, with highest densities found in the bottomland forests of the South. Northward its distribution ends in Michigan and Pennsylvania, and excludes the Appalachians. Although it has never been a common species here, records suggest a decline in some areas due to loss of suitable wooded riparian habitat. None were found along sections of the Grand River in the 1980s, in areas where they were formerly abundant. After being reported from only 74 townships during the Breeding Bird Atlas, the Prothonotary Warbler was designated a species of special concern in Michigan. Most of the current population is concentrated in the southwestern counties, with breeding confirmed north to Muskegon County.

Despite their disappearance in some areas, Prothonotaries appear to be doing well in others. Rivers such as the Kalamazoo, St. Joseph, Paw Paw, and Battle Creek all harbor populations. Surveys targeting species of special concern in 1992 turned up 103 singing males along the Kalamazoo River, 19 along the St. Joseph River, and 15 along the Paw Paw River (Kalamazoo Nature Center, unpublished data). Protection of these riparian habitats is essential for maintaining healthy populations in Michigan.

Prothonotary Warblers are seldom found far from flowing or standing bodies of water. Besides heavily wooded river bottoms, they also inhabit streamsides, shrubby wetlands (with buttonbush), swamp forest, and occasionally pond or lake edges. One of the best sites anywhere in the state is the large Ottawa Marsh unit of the Allegan State Game Area, where at least 54 territorial males were present in 1993.

After wintering in the tropics from southern Mexico to northern South America, the Prothonotary returns to Michigan in late April to early May. The average arrival date for the Battle Creek River, Calhoun County, was 4 May but varied from 26 April to 14 May over a 12-year period. The earliest record is that of a bird on 14 April 1974 in Berrien County. Most individuals reach the state between 10 and 24 May, and few migrants are noted away from areas where resident populations do not already exist.

Our knowledge of the Prothonotary's breeding biology in Michigan comes from the exhaustive work of Lawrence Walkinshaw from 1937 to 1948 along the Battle Creek River. Among his many findings was the fact that females returned a few days after males had established their territories, and that males often selected a nesting cavity prior to the females' arrival. Nest building ensued shortly after pairing, and first eggs were laid between 8 and 25 May (average 18 May). Clutches averaged five eggs, which were incubated by the female for 12 to 14 days, with young fledging 8 to 10 days later. Prothonotaries will use cavities or nest boxes located near or above water, and about half of the cavities selected were old Downy Woodpecker holes.

During Walkinshaw's study, productivity was found to be low, with only 50 of the 178 nests (28%) having at least one offspring which survived to fledging. House Wrens caused the loss of more than 100 eggs, as did mammal and bird predators combined. Nest box placement to benefit the Prothonotary had also attracted wrens to the area, as they were uncommon along other parts of the river. The high mammal predation was possibly a response to the human activity during the study. Other nest failures in some years were attributed to high water levels. Such low productivity would be insufficient to maintain an existing population without recruitment from other areas.

After the young fledge, family groups can be found together foraging along the river or swamp. Fall migration begins possibly as early as late July and continues through most of August. Prothonotaries remain into September in some years, with one present in Kalamazoo County as late as 2 October 1962. —Raymond J. Adams

## WORM-EATING WARBLER
### (*Helmitheros vermivorus*)

This warbler, a relatively recent addition or re-addition to Michigan's bird list, is a rare migrant and casual summer resident in the state. Typically, the Worm-eating Warbler resides in the eastern United States from Iowa, northern Ohio, and New York south to the Gulf states. Walter Barrows (1912) included this species in *Michigan Bird Life* on the basis of two undocumented reports (June 1868 and 21 May 1878) and its presence on the lists of G. Stockwell (1877) and A. J. Cook (1893). Although evidence for its inclusion was weak at the time, this bird does and no doubt did stray north of its normal breeding grounds.

The recent history of the Worm-eating Warbler shows a dramatic increase in Michigan beginning around 1960. Following visual reports in May 1956 on the campus of Michigan State University and on 23 May 1959 on Garden Island (Charlevoix County), an individual was captured, banded, and photographed on 20 May 1961 at the Cranbrook Institute of Science in Oakland County. Within another five years there were 11 separate reports, including two specimens and additional photographs.

During the late 1960s and early 1970s, one or more Worm-eating Warblers remained into the summer around Grand Mere, Berrien County. Although nesting was never confirmed, birds stayed into June and July in three of four years. It was not until 4 July 1985 in Ottawa County that evidence of breeding was obtained when a Worm-eating Warbler was seen carrying food into cover, presumably to feed young. Territorial birds were present at this site from 1983 to at least 1989. Throughout the 1970s and 1980s, this species was reported fairly regularly in the state in very small numbers, with others probably being overlooked.

There are a number of sites along the western side of the state where suitable habitat for this warbler exists. These sand dune forests are scattered all along the lakeshore, but much of it is private property and therefore inaccessible. Nearly all of the summer reports come from these sites. One exception is the mixed deciduous-coniferous forest covering the hillsides at Kellogg Forest, Kalamazoo County. Most intriguing was the discovery in 1993 of eight Worm-eating Warblers, including seven singing males, in the Allegan State Game Area on heavily wooded bluffs.

The challenge with this warbler has to do with finding it rather than identification, as its buffy head with prominent dark stripes is distinctive. This is a bird of the understory, often associated with steep ravines, where it spends much of its time on the ground or foraging in the low, dense vegetation. The best clue to its presence is a rapid, buzzy trill, reminiscent of a Chipping Sparrow but drier.

Information from Berrien and Kalamazoo counties indicates that the Worm-eating Warbler arrives in the state from late April through the third week of May. The earliest published report is 20 April, with an average arrival time of 12 May. During migration, individuals also appear in southeastern Michigan but with less reliability. Based on data from Ohio (Peterjohn 1989), nesting should begin in late May or early June, with young fledging in late June or early July. The nest is placed on the forest floor, typically on a steep hillside or ravine. The usual complement of four to five eggs requires nearly two weeks to incubate and about ten days for the young to grow and leave the nest.

Precisely when this species departs for its wintering grounds in Mexico and Central America is not well known, particularly since it is so rare in the state. In Berrien County, birds were not detected after mid-July, and a territorial bird at Kellogg Forest remained until at least 31 July in 1984. There are two banding records from the Kalamazoo Nature Center, one on 27 August 1984 and one on 24 August 1992. In Ohio, the fall migration period is thought to extend from around 20 August to the middle of September. Most bizarre was the appearance of a Worm-eating Warbler in Escanaba, Delta County, in December 1987, the first and only Upper Peninsula record to date. —Raymond J. Adams

## OVENBIRD
### (*Seiurus aurocapillus*)

For over a century and probably much longer, the Ovenbird has been a common Michigan migrant and summer resident. Its statewide distribution and substantial population make it accessible to anyone who cares to see and hear one. Uncertain, however, is whether this warbler will continue to be so common in the future. Like many other Neotropical migrants, the Ovenbird faces

*Hooded Warbler*
*Worm-eating Warbler*
*Kentucky Warbler*
DAVID MOHRHARDT

threats of habitat loss on both the wintering and breeding grounds. In the winter it has to cope with the rapid rate of tropical deforestation in Mexico to northern South America, while in parts of its North American breeding range, fragmentation of forests is affecting populations.

In southern Michigan, Ovenbirds were found to be absent from about 40% of the townships during the recent Breeding Bird Atlas. The distribution of these townships correlates with areas dominated by intensive agriculture and industrial and residential development, where only isolated small woodlots persist. Despite such known losses in southern Michigan, the twenty-five-year trend statewide shows a statistically significant increase in Ovenbird numbers, probably a response to forest maturation across other regions of the state.

Provided woodlands are of sufficient size, this warbler breeds in a wide variety of forested habitats, including those of deciduous, mixed, and coniferous composition. Habitat data collected during the Breeding Bird Atlas indicate some preference for dry mixed forest and dry and mesic deciduous forests. Both mature and immature stands may be used, as long as suitable nesting cover is available in the understory. Ovenbirds spend most of their time on or near the ground. They forage methodically on the forest floor, searching in and around leaves and other litter for insects, spiders, snails, slugs, earthworms, and occasional small seeds. Within these surroundings, the bird's dull brownish-olive back and streaked underparts allow it to blend right in.

Among the forest-interior species in Michigan, the Ovenbird and Red-eyed Vireo usually vie for honors as most abundant. From 1982 through 1991, an average of 14.7 Ovenbirds were recorded on each breeding bird survey route in the state. In high-quality habitat it is not uncommon to hear four to six males singing at the same time. Densities are generally greatest in the eastern half of the Upper Peninsula, the north-central Lower Peninsula, and the Allegan State Game Area in southwestern Michigan.

While Ovenbirds are secretive by nature, they are readily detectable, especially the extremely vocal territorial males. During bouts of song, males are usually found perched on a branch 5 to 20 feet above the forest floor. A person unfamiliar with the owner of the resounding "teacher, teacher, TEACHER" song would expect to encounter a bird at least twice as big. The Ovenbird also seems innately curious. An observer's squeaking or pishing sounds are usually rewarded by one or both members of the pair flying up to a small branch and walking back and forth in a decidedly agitated manner.

The first Ovenbirds reach Michigan in late April or early May, occasionally earlier. Peak numbers can be expected to pass through southern Michigan during mid-May, and a week later farther north. Birds can be easily overlooked during migration;

on annual counts at Kleinstuck Preserve in Kalamazoo, Ovenbirds make up roughly 7% (about 100/spring) of the total warbler migration. Given their abundance on the breeding grounds, they are likely underrepresented in these counts.

Nest building may already be underway in mid-May in the southern counties, while northern migrants are still passing through. The female builds a nest resembling an old dutch oven—a domed depression under an arch of dead leaves. The clutch of three to six eggs is incubated by the female for about two weeks, with the young fledging in eight to ten days. Records for Michigan nests indicate fledging may occur between early June and late July.

After breeding, adult Ovenbirds undergo a complete feather molt in late July and August, either on their territories or in a new location. They leave for their winter quarters in September, with immatures departing anytime from mid-August into October. There are at least five exceptional records of birds lingering into late autumn and winter. Among these are four December–January observations, all from southern Michigan, three of which involved birds appearing at feeders. —Raymond J. Adams

# NORTHERN WATERTHRUSH

*(Seiurus noveboracensis)*

This fairly common spring and fall migrant is also a widespread, common breeding resident over the northern two-thirds of the state. Michigan lies at the southern limit of this warbler's breeding range, which extends north to the treeline across Alaska and Canada and south into the United States in the Northeast and Northwest. In migration it can be found over much of the lower 48 states but is especially numerous along the Atlantic coast and Mississippi Valley. The winter range stretches from southern Florida and the West Indies through Central and northern South America.

Male Northern Waterthrushes are easily identified by their exuberant song, which has an accelerated down-slurred ending. However, both the Louisiana and Northern Waterthrushes produce similar emphatic chip notes, and it takes an experienced, well-trained ear to distinguish the lower tone of the Northern. Similarities in plumage also cause confusion in identification of these two close relatives. Reliable characteristics used to distinguish this species include eyebrows which do not widen behind the eye, the presence of streaks or small spots on the throat, uniformly yellowish or whitish flanks and underparts, and streaked undertail coverts which can be seen during frequent tail-bobbing.

This wood warbler is partial to wetlands, including bogs, swamps, lakes, and ponds, bordered by low shrubs or herbaceous growth, with moss and evergreens often included within its territory. While running water is not essential as it generally is for the Louisiana, the Northern Waterthrush frequently associates itself with streams or rivers. These habitats are usually not easily accessible, nor are the birds easily observed, as they spend much of their time on or close to the ground.

Nesting for this species is poorly documented in Michigan be-

*Louisiana Waterthrush*
*Ovenbird*
*Northern Waterthrush*
JOHN FELSING

cause of its use of secluded habitats, its secretive nature, and its well-concealed nest. More information is available from the southern part of the state, where it breeds locally in smaller numbers. Nests found in Macomb County were placed in upturned roots of fallen trees or in a stump cavity along a river bank. Other Michigan nests have been found in exposed banks along streams or concealed within vegetation on the ground.

Nest building begins around mid-May in the south and a little later in the north. Clutches of this single-brooded species contain three to five white eggs with brown and gray blotches. Egg dates in southeastern Michigan extend through June. Incubation and fledging times are poorly known but should be similar to those of the Louisiana Waterthrush—about 13 days for incubation and 10 days for fledging.

It seems likely that the Northern Waterthrush would have been a somewhat common summer resident in Michigan at the time of European settlement, and that the extensive logging which took place during the 1800s would have had a profound impact on its distribution and population. Early authors such as Maurice Gibbs (1879) believed it to be a common summer resident, but corroborating evidence was scarce. If its range did retract north with the clearing of the forests, then there appears to have been a southward expansion starting about 60 years ago, when nesting was first confirmed in Livingston County in 1931. By the 1950s, a small population of Northern Waterthrushes occupied parts of Macomb and Oakland counties as well.

At present, this is one of the few warblers that breed farther south on the east side of the Lower Peninsula (to Livingston and Oakland counties) than the west (to Montcalm and northern Kent counties). Northward in the Lower Peninsula and Upper Peninsula, this waterthrush is much more common and widely distributed.

Northern Waterthrushes first arrive in the state in late April, with occasional exceptions such as those of 13 April 1931 in Huron County and 16 April 1974 in Kalamazoo County. The spring migration peaks during the second week of May in southern Michigan and 7 to 10 days later in the Upper Peninsula. Fall migration begins the first two weeks of August, with many adults moving through at this time. Immatures follow in late August and September, with stragglers seen into the first two weeks of October. The latest recorded date is 11 December 1948. Bird-watchers should be aware that waterthrushes present in Michigan after August are almost invariably Northerns.

The numbers of migrant Northern Waterthrushes in the state can vary widely from year to year, particularly in spring. Counts at the Kleinstuck Preserve in Kalamazoo during the 1970s and 1980s ranged from 2 to 31 per spring (average 12.5). Fall banding data show a greater consistency in numbers, with about 70% of the migrants being young of the year. —Raymond J. Adams

# LOUISIANA WATERTHRUSH

(*Seiurus motacilla*)

To those birders who know this species well, its ethereal song often evokes visions of mature forest, fast-flowing streams, and secluded vistas. For many Michiganians, however, the Louisiana Waterthrush is an unfamiliar bird. This wood warbler is an uncommon summer resident and transient at the northern edge of its range in Michigan. It nests irregularly in the western Lower Peninsula from Berrien north to Wexford and Manistee counties and is largely absent elsewhere in the state except for a few scattered locales in the southeast north to Tuscola County.

The Louisiana Waterthrush shows a decided preference for hilly terrain with mature forest and ravines or valleys cut by running water. These sites are generally uncommon in the state but do occur in areas with river valleys or higher relief in the Lower Peninsula. Males typically return to southern Michigan in mid-April, with females arriving several days later toward the end of April. Rarely, birds return earlier in association with spring warm fronts. A record on 30 March 1977 in Berrien County is exceptional. The only Upper Peninsula record from the spring period is an individual captured and banded by Tom Allan on 28 April 1990 at Vermilion Point, Chippewa County.

Immediately upon their return, males commence singing to claim territories and attract mates. This waterthrush has a unique song characterized by three to four slurred introductory whistles followed by a descending series of twittering notes fading into obscurity. The song is usually given from a horizontal branch averaging nearly 20 feet above ground. In Warren Woods in Berrien County, I have frequently observed this species singing in subcanopy trees. Both frequency and duration of song for this early-morning singer decline as the nesting cycle progresses, making it one of the more difficult warblers to census.

Nest building commences in May, although a nest already containing six eggs was found on 3 May 1892 in Isabella County. Only one brood is raised per year, but second nesting attempts ensue following early failures. The four to six eggs require 12 to 14 days to hatch, with most nests fledging young in June or early July, and young from second attempts fledging as late as the third week of July. Some studies have found the Louisiana to be a common host of cowbird eggs, which could be a significant problem in areas where waterthrush populations are small.

The relatively large, bulky nest with a leafy base can be found in three distinct situations. In areas of old-growth forest, as in Warren Woods, this waterthrush may place its nest in the exposed roots of a large windthrown tree. Another common location is an exposed bank or root mass created by the erosive powers of a stream or river. Occasionally nests have been found in crevices in exposed rock faces adjacent to flowing water. Louisianas also nest in conjunction with still water, as occurs in swamps and bogs, though some of these sites have a short duration of use, which may relate to the greater exposure of nests.

Fall migration begins in July, shortly after the nesting cycle concludes. Adult males linger on the breeding grounds during the molt, and recrudescence of song is not uncommon. Most have departed by the end of August for the wintering grounds in Mexico, Central America, and northern South America. The latest fall date is 18 October 1948, and one intrepid individual remained at the Botanical Garden in Ann Arbor until 22 December 1974, where it was discovered on a Christmas bird count.

Population trends for the Louisiana Waterthrush are poorly documented. Monitoring programs, such as the national breeding bird survey, include relatively few individuals because of the remoteness of its habitat. Results of the Michigan Breeding Bird Atlas indicate evidence of nesting in only 68 townships, and based on information in Barrows (1912) and Wood (1951), there is a strong indication that many historical nesting sites, especially in the southeast, are no longer active.

Protection of existing breeding habitat is essential for the preservation of the Louisiana Waterthrush in Michigan, now a state species of special concern because of the small and local distribution of the population. Noteworthy sites to visit to enjoy this warbler are the Galien River in Berrien County, the Kalamazoo River and Swan Creek as they pass through the Allegan State Forest, the Pere Marquette River in Lake and Mason counties, and the Pine River in Lake and Wexford counties. —Raymond J. Adams

## KENTUCKY WARBLER

### (*Oporornis formosus*)

If you look at a map in almost any field guide, you will notice that the summer range of the Kentucky Warbler covers most of the southeastern United States, ends in Ohio and Indiana, and does not include Michigan. What these maps show, however, are usual or normal areas of occurrence, and readers must realize that a general boundary line drawn for our purposes is not so well defined from a bird's point of view. We know from experience and the record books that the Kentucky Warbler does occur in Michigan, both as a rare spring visitor and as a casual summer resident in the southern one-third of the state.

Every spring in recent years, observers in the state encounter one or more of these forest-loving warblers. Males are detected by their loud "tur-dle, tur-dle" song. Some who hear this two-syllable song may write it off as a Carolina Wren or Ovenbird and not pursue the individual to confirm its identity. But those who recognize the difference and search for its source will find that it is indeed a Kentucky Warbler. This shy species will do its best not to be seen, but your efforts will be rewarded if you get a look at its bright yellow belly, black forehead and sideburns, and yellow "spectacles."

May is the month when Kentucky Warblers usually show up in Michigan. We can characterize most of these individuals as ones which have overflown their "normal" breeding range. It seems that males are more prone to these overflights than females, but this observation may be heavily biased by our ability to better detect males because of their song. These overambitious migrants tend to linger for a few days, sing persistently, and then disappear, after failing to attract a mate or encounter others of their own kind. Sometimes, however, an individual stays for several weeks and presumably establishes a territory. Whether or not it actually breeds is another question. Reports seldom involve a pair of Kentucky Warblers or other evidence of potential breeding. Observers have even discovered males returning to the same territory in consecutive years, but were never able to determine if the bird was nesting or had found a mate.

There is one documented nest record for the state, on 28 June 1982 in eastern Jackson County (Baker 1984). A male had been seen at this site every summer since 1979, and that year a female was also found. After an exhaustive search, a nest was finally discovered beneath a clump of ferns, and there were four young in the process of fledging. This was a remarkable find because Kentucky Warblers hide their nests extremely well, and the adults are extremely secretive near the nest. The nest was at the base of an oak tree in a fairly moist woodland immediately adjacent to a tamarack bog. Although this was somewhat atypical habitat for a Kentucky Warbler (primarily a forest-interior bird with a fondness for shaded ravines), Baker noted that other common forest associates, such as Hooded Warbler and Acadian Flycatcher, had also nested here.

The second breeding confirmation for the state came just recently, in 1992, when a pair attending young was found on 27 June at the Ottawa Nature Preserve in Ottawa County. Given the regularity with which this species appears in southern Michigan, it would be reasonable to presume that a few other pairs have probably nested within our borders. Lost Nations State Game Area in Hillsdale County is one likely site, as singing males and pairs have been seen on a fairly consistent basis.

Most reports of Kentucky Warblers come from our southern two to three tiers of counties. Berrien, Kalamazoo, Hillsdale, and Wayne counties, for example, have had almost annual sightings for the past 10 to 20 years. There are a few records of exceptional vagrants, like the ones banded in Presque Isle County (18 May 1970) and North Manitou Island, Leelanau County (11 May 1985), and a singing male in Clare County (28 May 1970). There is even one Upper Peninsula record from Schoolcraft County (28 May 1977).

Michigan also has a small number of fall reports, mostly from the month of September. Recent dates range from 16 August 1980 in Kent County to 27 September 1986 in Kalamazoo County. In 1981 and 1982, fall migrants or post-breeding dispersers were found in Lake County, one each on 20 and 11 September, respectively.

Numerous writings from our southern neighbors point to a northern expansion of the Kentucky's breeding range during this century. A comparison of Michigan's historic and recent published records also reflects this trend, with a noticeable increase in the frequency of spring and summer sightings beginning in the 1960s. Perhaps this forest songbird has been responding to the maturation of woodlands across the northern part of its range. Elsewhere, observers have noted declines due to forest clearing and fragmentation, and there is concern over habitat loss on the wintering grounds of this Neotropical migrant. Only time will tell if Kentucky Warblers will become more regular in Michigan, or more rare should population declines in some regions continue. —Gail A. McPeek

## CONNECTICUT WARBLER

### (*Oporornis agilis*)

With all our books, journals, and years of observations devoted to birds, it seems as if we know so much about avian life. But then we come to a species such as the Connecticut Warbler and find we know so little. Here is a bird which is a regular summer resident in upper Michigan, and yet our volumes of records contain only one documented nest. We obviously still have much to learn.

Cyndy Callog

The breeding range of the Connecticut Warbler is relatively small and almost entirely in central Canada. It enters the United States only in the western Great Lakes, in northern Minnesota, Wisconsin, and Michigan. This range does not include the state for which it was named, but Connecticut was where Alexander Wilson first discovered this species in 1812, during its migration.

The limited information we do have indicates that northern woodlands, either wet or dry, are used for breeding, and that probably the most important habitat characteristic is a well-developed understory. Most of Michigan's summer reports come from tamarack-spruce bogs, open poplar woods, and jack-pine barrens, all of which provide thick undergrowth for its nesting and foraging requirements. The Connecticut is not one of those neck-breaking, canopy-flitting warblers; you have to search on or near the ground for this one.

Even if you know where to look, finding and observing this skulker is a real challenge. It has a naturally spotty distribution, even in suitable habitat; and if you do locate one, usually by the male's loud song ("beecher-beecher-beecher-beecher"), there is still the task of actually seeing it amid the dense tangles and brush. Many observers tell of the male's reluctance to flush from his perch. With persistence and luck, you may get a look at this attractive bird with its slate-gray hood, white eye ring, olive back, and pale yellow underparts. Females are similar but with a fainter, brownish hood.

As if these traits were not enough to test a birder's patience, finding its well-concealed ground nest is close to impossible, judging from the scant records in the literature. The parent birds have an annoying habit of landing 30 to 40 feet from the nest and walking to it, so even if you do happen upon an adult carrying food, you are likely to lose sight of it long before it gets close to the nest.

Walkinshaw and Dyer (1961) describe regular summer observations of several singing males at a site in Ontonagon County in 1954, 1956, 1957, and 1960. It was during the latter year, on 1 July, that they found the state's first and only Connecticut Warbler nest, which contained five ready-to-fledge young, suggesting a starting date around 5 June. It was a rather bulky nest made of dead leaves and other debris piled in a mass, which is apparently typical for dry areas. In wet habitats they choose hummocks of sphagnum moss for nesting, similar to another locally occurring and less known relative, the Palm Warbler.

Although no nests for this species were discovered during the Breeding Bird Atlas, the intensive effort from 1983 to 1988 greatly advanced our information on distribution and status. While it is by no means a common summer resident, it is also not as uncommon as past records led us to believe. Connecticuts were found during the breeding season in all Upper Peninsula counties plus four counties at the northern tip of the Lower Peninsula,

mostly in the Mackinaw State Forest. Luce County, with its many bogs, is one of the better places to go and search for this species. A few individuals have summered south to Crawford and Oscoda counties, but this is clearly the edge of its breeding range. The occasional summertime sightings in southern Michigan are late spring or early fall migrants.

The Connecticut Warbler has a long flight from its winter grounds in northern South America, and typically does not begin reaching Michigan until mid-May. There are some earlier spring records, such as that of 29 April in Kalamazoo, but most pass through in the latter half of May and the first few days of June. Fall migration extends from late August to early October, with most reports during September.

For most people, the opportunity to see this warbler is best during the migration when it occurs statewide. In mid-May, Kleinstuck Preserve in Kalamazoo County is a prime spot. You still have to search the underbrush, but individuals tend to frequent more accessible areas, including brushy roadsides and damp thickets. Also, males are fairly active singers as they make their way north in spring. All of my observations have been migrants, mostly ones caught in mist nets during banding operations in the fall at the Kalamazoo Nature Center. I always savored seeing in the hand birds such as the Connecticut which are so elusive in the field. —Gail A. McPeek

# MOURNING WARBLER
### ( *Oporornis philadelphia* )

The Mourning Warbler is a common migrant and summer resident in Michigan. It and the Connecticut are of the same genus, *Oporornis*—a group of wood warblers with fairly robust bodies, long pinkish legs, and a hooded appearance. For breeding males this hood is a slate-gray, contrasting with an olive back and yellowish belly. For females, immatures, and post-breeding males it is more of a faded brown. Identification between and within species is a real challenge.

Observers can take some comfort in knowing that almost anywhere they go in the state, they are far more likely to encounter a Mourning than a Connecticut. Throughout their summer ranges, which show considerable overlap, the former is more common and evenly distributed. Breeding Bird Atlas participants found Mournings in nearly 800 townships, Connecticuts in 65.

One should also know that neither of these brush-loving species is easy to see, and that learning their respective songs is your best option. Should you spot a breeding male, the Mourning Warbler has a crescent-shaped black bib and lacks the white eye ring characteristic of the Connecticut. Female and immature Mournings may have a faint, incomplete eye circle but not the conspicuous eye ring seen in their close relative. There is also a slight size difference, with Mournings slightly smaller, but this is usually helpful only if you can compare the two in hand.

After wintering in the tropical climes of Central and northern South America, Mourning Warblers embark on a long journey to their breeding grounds, which includes the northeastern United States west to Minnesota and Canada west through Alberta. They

*Connecticut Warbler*
*Mourning Warbler*
Cyndy Callog

return later than many species, a timing which allows for sufficient growth of understory vegetation—their favored habitat. Most reach Michigan in the latter half of May, with a few sometimes seen in early May and small numbers still passing through in early June. The average first arrival date in Berrien County from 1962 to 1991 was 15 May. Singing males heard prior to 15 June in our southern counties, where the Mourning is an uncommon breeder, could still be migrants, and observers should revisit the site a week or two later to see if a territory has been established.

Mourning Warblers can be found in a variety of woodland situations as long as there is ample thick undergrowth. Imagine places choked with tangles of blackberries and briers and the ground covered with jewelweed, ferns, and nettles, and that is what Mourning Warblers like. Burnt and cutover lands in the shrub-sapling stage of succession make for ideal habitat, as do aspen-birch stands, shrubby woodland edges, and swampy thickets. Low, dense vegetation is important for concealing their nests, which are located on or close to the ground.

The breeding season for this species is amazingly short. Nesting commences soon after arrival, eggs (usually 4) hatch in only 12 days, and the young are out of the nest in 7 to 9 days, before they can even fly. This quick maturation and fledging is probably a necessary adaptation for birds which nest on or near the ground where predators have easy access to eggs, young, and incubating females. Records for Michigan indicate that most nests are initiated in the first three weeks of June, and that young are usually fledging in the first part of July. Adults are easily agitated when attending young, so if you want to observe this species, this is a good time to be out searching the thick underbrush of our state's second-growth woodlands.

By early August, sometimes even late July, Mourning Warblers are heading south. Immatures have been found all the way to Texas in August. Most depart in late August and early September, and nearly all are gone from our parts by late September. They go quickly and quietly, which makes them seem more rare in fall compared to spring.

Although the Mourning Warbler's summer range includes all of Michigan, it is considerably more common in the northern two-thirds and attains its greatest abundance in the Upper Peninsula, especially in the western half. Once you get below Saginaw Bay, breeding pairs tend to be widely scattered and uncommon except for a few localized areas where they are fairly common, such as in Tuscola County in the east and Montcalm, Muskegon, and Allegan counties in the west. Nesting has been confirmed as far south as Kalamazoo and Livingston counties.

Like most bird-watchers, I have heard many more Mourning Warblers than I have seen. The male's cheerful song is a giveaway but, as with the Connecticut, finding it in the dense undergrowth is another matter. Males are known to sing from somewhat higher and more visible perches, and they can be rather responsive to recorded calls. Anxious to see my first nonmigrant Mourning Warbler when I moved to Michigan, I turned to my trusty Peterson tape after hearing a male during field work in Alpena County. Much to my delight, both the male and female quickly popped into view, and two nearby territorial males burst into song.
—Gail A. McPeek

# COMMON YELLOWTHROAT
## (*Geothlypis trichas*)

This small thicket bird is a common summer resident and migrant in all parts of Michigan, and a casual winter resident in the south. Its widespread occurrence together with its lively "witchity-witchity-witchity" song makes it one of our most familiar warblers. The Common Yellowthroat has an expansive North American breeding range which extends from Alaska and Canada to Mexico and includes all of the United States. Populations in the south are permanent residents while those in the north are migratory, wintering from the southern United States to Central America and extreme northern South America.

Common Yellowthroat habitat includes a vast array of marshy borders, swampy thickets, brushy roadsides, overgrown fields, and regenerating clearcuts. Basically, any area of lush undergrowth is suitable. Wet areas are frequently selected, and breeding densities will be especially high along streams, ponds, marshes, and bogs, even roadside ditches. These habitats offer plenty of insects for food and thick, often impenetrable cover for nests.

The Yellowthroat's spring return to Michigan commences in late April and early May in the southern counties and a week to 10 days later in the north. Migrants are occasionally recorded in the first week or two of April, but those seen any earlier are probably overwintering birds. The black-masked males arrive first, and their perpetual singing makes for easy detection. When a female appears on the scene, song diminishes briefly as the male's attention turns to pairing and mating.

The breeding season for this warbler in Michigan extends from early May to early August. Studies conducted in Washtenaw County found second broods to be a generally uncommon occurrence this far north in its range, and renestings probably account for the majority of late broods. This species is a frequent host of cowbird eggs, so such later nestings have a much better chance of being parasite-free. Females construct the bulky, layered nest, which is located on or close to the ground. The three to four eggs hatch in about 12 days, and the young have a short nestling phase of 8 to 9 days. Observers in the vicinity of a Yellowthroat nest will receive a harsh scolding by the female or both parents.

The southward movement extends from late August to mid-October. An occasional bird may linger well into December, and during most winters in recent decades between one and a half-dozen Yellowthroats have been found on Michigan Christmas bird counts. The highest total was nine, recorded on the 1969–70 count. There are few data on whether such individuals remain and survive the winter or eventually move farther south when weather conditions worsen.

*Common Yellowthroat*
*Yellow-breasted Chat*
David Mohrhardt

The Common Yellowthroat is clearly a bird which has fared well in the modern human-modified landscape characterized by an abundance of early-successional vegetation. The loss of much wetland acreage has apparently been more than compensated for by the copious supply of other suitable habitats. No other warbler was recorded in more blocks during the Michigan Breeding Bird Atlas, and according to state breeding bird surveys, populations have increased significantly over the past few decades. —Gail A. McPeek

## HOODED WARBLER

### ( *Wilsonia citrina* )

The Hooded Warbler breeds in mature deciduous forests in the eastern United States, from Florida and Texas to southern New England and the southern Great Lakes. Accustomed to the male's flirtatious "weeta-weeta-wee-tee-o" song in eastern Kentucky, in the heart of its range, I sorely missed this bird after moving to Michigan and found myself searching for woodlands which harbored this familiar friend.

Here at the northern fringe of its range the Hooded Warbler is an uncommon migrant and summer resident. It occurs in forested habitat in the state's lower half, mostly in the southwest corner. It needs fairly large tracts of deciduous woodland and is especially partial to damp areas with lush undergrowth, as is common along ravines and stream bottoms. It is apparent from comparisons of past and current information that populations have declined in Michigan and some other parts of its range, probably because of reductions in forest habitat.

The handsome black-hooded male is hard to confuse with any other. Both sexes have yellow faces and are bright yellow below and olive-green above. Females have partial hoods or none at all, though there have been a few documented cases in which an adult female has had an almost male-like hood. Another useful identification feature is its habit of flicking open its tail, exposing conspicuous white spots.

Most Hooded Warbler sightings in Michigan occur between late April and July. This includes a mixture of migrants, which have flown past their usual range, and breeding residents, which are here for the season. Reports are concentrated in the southern two to three tiers of counties, and are heavily biased toward males because of their loud and persistent singing. Occasionally individuals wander farther north, particularly along the lakeshore. Vagrants have been recorded in Benzie, Alpena, and Cheboygan counties in the northern Lower Peninsula, and on 5 June 1992 a Hooded was found in the northern Upper Peninsula, on Grand Island just north of Munising.

For those which establish breeding territories, the main arrival time is early to mid-May. The small sample of nest records for the state indicate that females are usually on eggs by late May or early June, with young fledging three to four weeks later. For unsuccessful pairs, however, the nesting season can be prolonged to July. Such was apparently the case with nests found in a small 15-acre woodlot in Jackson County in 1985 (Cottrille 1986). At least two territorial pairs were present in May, one of which had its nest destroyed on 25 May. Return visits in mid-July led to the discovery of nests for both pairs from which young fledged on 24 and 28 July.

While it is not known how many attempts were made by these pairs or what caused their earlier failures, this record provides a good example of a problem facing many other forest species as well. Numerous studies have been finding that many birds adapted to life in large-sized woodlands do not do as well in small fragmented patches. These "area-sensitive" species may avoid these smaller patches altogether or fail to sustain populations in a situation to which they are less suited. For a forest-interior bird such as the Hooded Warbler, a nest in a small woodlot is more vulnerable to cowbird parasitism and various predators which concentrate their activities in and around woodland edges.

The effects of land clearing are obvious in maps of the current distribution of this species, which is extremely spotty in southeastern Michigan, where woodlands are highly fragmented. Only sporadic sightings and nestings are recorded in this region. The bulk of the state's breeding population occurs in the southwest, from Berrien and Cass counties north to Barry and Ottawa. Deciduous forest acreage is more contiguous in this region, particularly on some of our public lands in Allegan and Barry counties. Should these areas in the southwest become overly fragmented, the Hooded Warbler might disappear from the state.

Once breeding finishes, Hoodeds slip away quietly in August and September to winter in tropical forests in Mexico, Belize, Guatemala, and other parts of Central America. Here, too, they must cope with habitat loss, as forests are being rapidly cut and carved into a patchwork. Researchers have found that males and females hold separate territories, which may compound the effects of this loss.

Weighing together information on population status, declines, and habitat conditions on the breeding and wintering grounds, the Hooded Warbler was added to Michigan's list of special concern species in 1990. We need to keep a close watch over this and other forest birds and make sure we are doing all we can to provide adequate habitat for maintaining healthy, viable populations. —Gail A. McPeek

## WILSON'S WARBLER

### ( *Wilsonia pusilla* )

This petite, lemon-yellow warbler is a common migrant in Michigan, but as far as breeding goes, it is one of our rarest birds. The Wilson's Warbler is a widespread summer resident in Canada and most of western North America, but in the East, its breeding range barely enters the States, which is why we know this species primarily as a migrant.

*Wilson's Warbler*
*Canada Warbler*
JOHN FELSING

Back in the early 1900s, Walter Barrows believed it possible that this species nested within our boundaries, even though records at the time were all from the migration period. It was not until 1980, when two singing males were found on Isle Royale in July, that we had our first evidence of summering and possible nesting. Since 1980 there have been a number of summer observations in the Upper Peninsula, including two breeding confirmations, allowing us to add the Wilson's Warbler, rare though it may be, to our list of breeding residents.

The best time to search for this warbler is in late spring and early fall, as it travels to and from its breeding grounds. Damp areas consisting of willows, alders, or other shrubby growth are its preferred habitat, and its active behavior and low foraging height make detection relatively easy. This species regularly twitches its tail while feeding and is adept at flycatching. In fact, it was the sharp snap of what I thought was a flycatcher's bill which led to my first life observation. What a surprise to find that the sound was made by a yellow, black-capped warbler which I quickly recognized as a male Wilson's.

This is one of our later spring migrants. A few arrive in early May, but the main flight does not reach the southern counties until mid-May and the Upper Peninsula toward the end of the month. At the Whitefish Point Bird Observatory, an exceptionally early Wilson's was seen on 25 April 1982. With its rather late passage, it is not uncommon for lingerers to be seen into early June, even in southern Michigan. These sightings can be misleading, so return visits later in June are important to determine the status of these individuals and whether or not summer residency has been established.

Migrants heading back south begin to appear in mid-August and peak from the end of the month through the first half of September. They are scarce by late September, with only stragglers seen into October. A sighting on Belle Isle, Wayne County, on 10 November 1972 is exceptional.

Our information on breeding in Michigan is still scant and of recent origin. Records throughout the Northeast suggest an increase and range expansion along the southern periphery of the Wilson's range in the 1970s and 1980s. Wisconsin had its first confirmed breeding in 1977, followed by New York in 1978 and Minnesota in 1980. The first major influx into upper Michigan came in 1985, when field workers for the Breeding Bird Atlas discovered singing males in nine blocks. These were from Seney National Wildlife Refuge, three locales in Luce County, and the Tahquamenon River area in Chippewa County. Of particular significance were a territorial male and agitated female at the Dollarville Flooding in Luce County, the first strong evidence of breeding. Unfortunately, follow-up searches for a nest came up short.

Additional summer observations followed in 1986, 1987, and 1988. These were mostly from the same three eastern Upper Peninsula counties and from Isle Royale. Then in 1988, five males were heard around the mouth of the Tahquamenon River, and toward the end of June, a female carrying food into the brush, presumably to feed young, was suggestive of breeding. Again, though, no nest was found. The most recent evidence came in the summer of 1992, when a female with an obvious brood patch was caught and banded at the Seney Refuge (D. Evers, pers. comm.).

Each of these summer records has been associated with alder and/or willow thickets in a wet, boggy setting. Other common components were tamarack and spruce and a ground cover of sphagnum moss and sedge. This is typical habitat reported elsewhere in its range. Nests are sunken into moss or other ground plants, so it is no wonder that the few searches in Michigan have been unsuccessful. As long as this boreal warbler continues its rare but regular summer residency here, discovery of the first nest is only a matter of time. —Gail A. McPeek

# CANADA WARBLER
## (*Wilsonia canadensis*)

The Canada Warbler is by no means limited to Canada; rather, its name refers to the place of first discovery. Its breeding range includes much of Canada, from the Rockies eastward, as well as the northeastern United States west to Minnesota and south to Georgia in the Appalachians. This mountain extension makes it one of the most southerly nesting boreal warblers.

Canadas are fairly common spring and fall migrants in Michigan and common summer residents in the Upper Peninsula and northern third of the Lower. Pairs also breed locally in suitable forest expanses in the southern two-thirds of the state, particularly on the west side. Among places where they are regular in the south are the Allegan State Game Area and the wooded dunes along Lake Michigan south to Berrien County.

For most of the year, Canada Warblers live in forests in northern South America, and time spent on the breeding grounds is brief. They migrate north in May, nest in June and July, and then head back to the tropics in August. State records indicate that the bulk of spring migration occurs from mid- to late May, with some seen earlier in the south and others lagging into early June.

Nesting commences soon after arrival; apparently claims to territories, courtship, and nest building all happen fairly quickly. Information from a little more than a dozen records for Michigan indicates that females are usually on eggs by the first part of June. Nests with young or sightings of adults with fledglings have been reported between the latter half of June and the end of July. An early record is that of a nest with three young found in Macomb County on 15 June 1959. Nests are invariably located on the ground and carefully built into mossy hummocks, exposed banks, or rotted stumps.

By August the southbound flight is already well underway, and few Canadas are seen beyond the middle of September. There is little mention of this species in our fall seasonal surveys, probably because of its early departure. During 1981, when a high of 104 were banded at the Kalamazoo Nature Center, movement occurred between 18 August and 19 September and peaked on 1 and 3 September. Late dates include an individual on 16 September 1989 at Whitefish Point in the Upper Peninsula, and 8 October 1988 at the Kalamazoo Nature Center.

The Canada Warbler has one of those hard-to-describe songs, which causes underreporting and confusion with other species. Even with several years of birding experience, I still have difficulty recognizing its rapid, jerky warble and occasionally have to track down the source for verification. Once found, though, it is easily identified by its bluish-gray upperparts, yellow underparts and "spectacles," white undertail coverts, and, in the male, a bold "necklace" of black spots and blotches. The female is similar but has a dusky, less distinct necklace and grayish cheeks instead of black.

Cool, moist forest with heavy undergrowth is where this warbler likes to breed. Either deciduous or mixed woodlands are used; the main feature is usually a stream bank, ravine, or spring. These damp, dark places are filled with mosquitos, flies, and other insects upon which they feast. Like the Hooded and Wilson's Warblers, also in the genus *Wilsonia*, the Canada is adept at catching insects on the wing. It also gleans them from twigs and leaves, and confines most of its activity to within a few feet of the ground. Large supplies of insect repellent are recommended when seeking out this species.

Something interesting has been happening to the Canada Warbler in the past 20 to 30 years. Reports of summering and breeding in some areas of southern Michigan have become more frequent. Back around the turn of the century, its range was restricted to the northern half of the state following the widespread lumbering in the south. Apparently, this forest bird is now reoccupying areas where habitat is again suitable. —Gail A. McPeek

## PAINTED REDSTART
### (*Myioborus pictus*)

Michigan has but one documented record of this flashy warbler, which is an accidental visitor almost anywhere in the United States, since its range includes only a small portion of southern Arizona, New Mexico, and southwestern Texas. It is an inhabitant of mountain canyons with various pine and oak species, with most of its breeding grounds in the highlands of Mexico south to Nicaragua. How one came to be in our parts is unknown, but on 12–13 November 1983, a bird in adult plumage appeared in Delta County (photographed by C. Taylor). There was no question as to its identity; adult Painted Redstarts are most distinctive with their jet-black upperparts, scarlet belly, white wing patches, and white outer tail feathers. —Gail A. McPeek

## YELLOW-BREASTED CHAT
### (*Icteria virens*)

This large, yellow-breasted warbler is probably unfamiliar to most people in Michigan because of its restricted distribution and uncommon to rare status. The chat is another one of those peripheral species whose breeding range wanes as it reaches the lower Great Lakes. Summer residency in the state is confined to the southern half, with most reports concentrated in the bottom two rows of counties. Spring and summer records from the 1980s identify Berrien, Van Buren, Cass, Kalamazoo, Branch, and Hillsdale counties as among the most reliable locales to observe this bird.

Like most of our warblers, Yellow-breasted Chats return to Michigan in May. A few individuals often show up in the first week, but most arrive in the middle of the month unless lingering cold weather delays their return a week or so. In Berrien County, where chats are reported most frequently in the state, the average arrival date is 10 May. Migrants occasionally overshoot their usual range and end up in northern Michigan, though breeding has been documented only to Kent and Oakland counties. On occasion, an individual even makes it to the Upper Peninsula, such as the one found on 17 June 1987 along the Manistique River in Schoolcraft County and the 26 June 1988 record in Baraga County, an aberrant summer of hot, dry weather.

The Yellow-breasted Chat inhabits early successional communities typical of abandoned fields, woodland clearings, and some riparian areas. Places thick with rose tangles, briers, red cedar, and other brushy growth are ideal, but only if it covers a fairly large area. Chats do not take to narrow shrubby corridors and isolated patches of thicket as are common along fencerows and ditches.

This oversized warbler builds a large, bulky nest in low, dense cover. There are only a handful of nest records for Michigan, which is not unexpected given this bird's uncommon status and the impenetrable structure of its habitat. Its secretive nature around the site also hinders nest-finding, although female Brownheaded Cowbirds seem to have no trouble. Writings in the literature identify the chat as a fairly regular cowbird host.

Nests typically are initiated between the last week of May and the first two weeks of June, with young fledging in mid-June to July. Double-brooding is common in much of its range, but there are few data to suggest this to hold true this far north, although two broods were confirmed for a pair in Kalamazoo County (J. Granlund, pers. comm.). Late-season nests are more likely to be retries of failed attempts rather than second broods.

The time of departure for chats is poorly known. Fall reports are few compared to those in spring, since they leave quietly. Their trip south seems to occur mostly in August, with only scattered reports in September and the first week of October. Most unusual was an individual banded on 15 October 1992 at the Whitefish Point Bird Observatory in the Upper Peninsula. Some chats winter in the southern states, but most migrate to Mexico and Central America.

As wood warblers go, this one is most atypical. Its olive-green and yellow plumage is warbler-like, but that is where the similarity ends. The chat averages two inches larger than its relatives; it has a heavier bill, a long tail, and a bizarre raucous chatter reminiscent of a thrasher or mockingbird. After years of wondering if this bird got misclassified, it seems our doubts can be put to rest. Recent DNA analysis indicates that it is a wood warbler with no genetic ties to any nonwarbler group.

Some describe the chat as a skulker and difficult to see even though its song is clearly audible. My experience has been mostly the opposite; the males not only burst into song at my presence but did so from an exposed perch atop a shrub. Perhaps females were skulking nearby, but the males were all quite conspicuous. These observations have all come early in the breeding season, which probably explains my good fortune. No doubt they become much harder to find once nesting is well underway.

The distribution and abundance of the chat are dictated by the dynamics of its habitat and the availability of new areas to occupy once others succeed beyond the shrub-sapling stage. Local populations tend to fluctuate, as breeding pairs use a site for a few years and then move on to find a more suitable one. Before urban sprawl took over most of southeastern Michigan, chats were regularly reported in counties such as Monroe, Wayne, and Washtenaw. In fact, most nest records for the state came from this region. —Gail A. McPeek

## SUMMER TANAGER

### (*Piranga rubra*)

Michigan lies north of the Summer Tanager's breeding range, which includes the southeastern United States north into Illinois, Indiana, and Ohio, as well as the far southwestern states and Mexico. Currently, this species is a rare spring migrant and a casual summer and fall visitant to Michigan. Its presence in the state is of recent occurrence, as Barrows (1912) listed this tanager only as hypothetical, based on two unsubstantiated reports. The first fully documented record occurred in 1948 when an immature female was collected on 6 November near Pinckney in Livingston County. This was followed in 1958 by the discovery of a male and female on 27 April at Portage Lake in Jackson County. The male was photographed and the female collected for a specimen. A Summer Tanager observation on 11 July 1960 north of Rudyard in Chippewa County was followed by 4 more records in the 1960s, 24 in the 1970s, and 41 in the 1980s.

The vast majority of Summer Tanager encounters are from spring, as individuals overshoot their traditional breeding range. These birds arrive most often in late April and the first two weeks of May, with the earliest published report on 21 April 1973 in Berrien County. Occasionally, a few appear in late May and June. Not surprisingly, the majority of sightings involve males— conspicuous and unmistakable in their all-red plumage, lacking the black wings of male Scarlet Tanagers. The male Summer Tanager will often announce his presence with a song that is more robin-like and not nearly as hoarse in quality as that of the Scarlet Tanager. How frequently females occur in Michigan is less clear because their plumage is nearly identical to that of female Scarlet Tanagers.

Summer Tanagers can be found in a variety of wooded habitats, from mature deciduous stands with an open or closed canopy to mixed deciduous-coniferous woods. These birds have an appetite for bees, wasps, caterpillars, beetles, and, later in the season, small wild fruits. To the best of our knowledge, nesting has never occurred in Michigan, although it seems plausible that breeding may have occurred at some point in the past 40 years. There are 13 observations from June, 7 from July, and 2 from August. Records suggestive of potential breeding include a territorial male present from 8 July to 5 August 1987 in Hillsdale County; a pair seen on 25 June 1989 in Van Buren County; and in at least one instance in Berrien County, a bird was present in the same area for two consecutive years.

More than half of the state's records have come from three counties: Berrien and Kalamazoo in the southwest corner and Wayne in the southeast. Additionally, there are five observations from the northern Lower Peninsula and six from the Upper Peninsula. Post-breeding dispersal and autumn wandering also bring Summer Tanagers northward, and there are a handful of fall records for Michigan extending from 24 October to 1 December. —Raymond J. Adams

## SCARLET TANAGER

### (*Piranga olivacea*)

The Scarlet Tanager is a common summer resident of the eastern temperate forest, and you should be able to find this species in almost any woods you visit in Michigan. It occurs most frequently in the larger tracts of deciduous and coniferous forest, though numbers drop off somewhat in the more boreal habitats of the Upper Peninsula, at the northern edge of this species' range.

Tanagers are least common in some of the southern counties where woodlands have been cut and fragmented into small, isolated parcels. Their distribution is especially sparse in the highly urbanized and agriculturally dominated sections of the southeast. Tanagers occasionally nest in parks or wooded suburbs with large groves of mature shade trees, and after the nesting season, they can sometimes be seen foraging in orchards or along wooded roadsides.

I became quite familiar with this species while conducting bird surveys here in Michigan and in other parts of the East, and have always found densities to be highest where oak and pine are the dominant tree species. The tanager's penchant for foraging in oaks is well documented in the literature. Data from the various state surveys and breeding census plots show centers of abundance in upland deciduous and mixed woodlands, which prevail in parts of the southwest, north-central, and northeast Lower Peninsula. Tanager hot spots include such counties as Allegan, Van Buren, Muskegon, Iosco, Ogemaw, and Alcona.

If you think spotting this brilliant scarlet bird in the forest is easy, think again. Even with a contrasting backdrop of green foliage, the red and black male tanager can blend right in with the dense canopy, where it spends most of its time. If you hear its hoarse, robin-like song and nasal "chip-burrr" calls high up in the canopy, it may take minutes of patient searching just to see one. Tanagers do not flit about with the same nervous energy as warblers or even vireos; instead they forage in a slow, deliberate manner, looking over individual leaves and stems for caterpillars and other insect prey. Some feeding occurs in the subcanopy, and then you can usually get a better view of the showy scarlet male or dull, olive-green female.

*Scarlet Tanager*
*Rose-breasted Grosbeak*
DAVID MOHRHARDT

Fortunately, male tanagers are quite vocal during the breeding season, making them easy to detect and census. This species first returns to Michigan in late April and early May, with an average arrival of 2 May in Berrien County. The main migration comes after 10 May, even in the south. Nesting in the state occurs from the latter part of May to July. Their nests have eluded many people, though that is no surprise since they are placed well out on a limb at heights of 30 to 60 feet or more. The female is the sole nest builder and incubator. Both parents bring food for the nestlings, which grow incredibly fast and leave the nest after only 9 or 10 days.

Once nesting is complete, usually by midsummer, tanagers can be more conspicuous as family groups forage about, sometimes joining mixed flocks with grosbeaks, vireos, and other forest species. This is when I have had my best luck observing this species and have even found a few males during the post-breeding molt, when their plumage is a patchwork of red, yellow, and green feathers. By the time of fall migration, in September and October, males, females, and young of the year are all similar in appearance, though you can still separate adult males by their brighter green plumage and black (instead of brown) wings.

The Scarlet Tanager is a member of a large subfamily (Thraupinae) of tropical birds with heavy, curved beaks and brightly colored males. Of the four species which occur north of Mexico, the Scarlet Tanager makes the longest migration, from its breeding grounds in the eastern United States to its winter home in Central and South America. Like other Neotropical migrants, there is concern for this species over the impacts of winter habitat loss. Montane forests, which are their principal wintering habitats, are being rapidly cut in many areas of the tropics.

While this forest bird is also susceptible to habitat loss and fragmentation on its breeding grounds, surveys over the past decades have not detected any significant decreases in their populations. In Michigan, Scarlet Tanager numbers increased significantly from 1966 to 1991, a trend attributable to regrowth of forests over much of the state. However, if the current pace of deforestation on the wintering grounds continues along with further fragmentation here on the breeding grounds, noticeable declines of this tropical beauty are likely to occur before too long. —Gail A. McPeek

# WESTERN TANAGER
## (*Piranga ludoviciana*)

The Western Tanager is an accidental spring migrant and late summer visitor to Michigan. Since 1965 there have been at least nine reported observations, two of which have good supporting details to clearly justify this tanager's inclusion on the state bird list. Documentation for the remainder of these reports is lacking or inadequate. Specifically, most lack any mention of the two wing bars, an essential element for identification. Females are rather plain, while breeding males have a bright yellow body with black wings, upper back, and tail, and a gaudy red face.

Both of the state's well-documented reports are from spring, the first occurring on 23 May 1989, when a female Western Tana-

ger was captured at the Vermilion Research Station, Chippewa County. The second was on 31 May 1992, when members of an Oakland Audubon Society field trip discovered a male at Tawas Point State Park, Iosco County. Spring reports which lack complete descriptions are from 27 April 1965, Kensington Metropark, Oakland County; 27 May 1974, Ross Township, Kalamazoo County; 3 June 1981, near Newberry, Luce County; and 6 May 1990, Marquette, Marquette County. Three August reports include a female banded on 29 August 1971 at North Point, Alpena County, now thought to have been an aberrant Scarlet Tanager; a bird on 3 August 1973 at Little Girl's Point, Gogebic County; and one on 31 August 1977 at Hoffmaster State Park, Muskegon County. Documented reports from other Great Lakes states indicate that May and August are appropriate times to find this tanager in Michigan. —Raymond J. Adams

# NORTHERN CARDINAL
## (*Cardinalis cardinalis*)

Surely it is the beauty and familiarity of birds such as the cardinal which lure people into the addictive hobbies of bird-watching and bird-feeding. Now a common resident in lower Michigan, this species has found habitats to its liking in our neighborhoods, gardens, parks, brushy roadsides, and woodland margins. Long-time state residents will remember when the "Red-bird" was a rare bird in the south and was not seen at all in the north.

The current range of the Northern Cardinal encompasses all of the eastern United States, west into the Central Plains and north to upper Michigan, Maine, and extreme southern Canada. It also occurs locally in the southwestern states and Mexico. This is an expanded distribution from a century ago, as our landscape changes have provided more habitat opportunities for this bird.

The cardinal is a permanent resident throughout its range, even where the winters are cold and long as they are in northern Michigan. Individuals are mostly sedentary, and pairs are seen together during the course of the year. As winter approaches, the residents of an area often associate together in loose flocks and settle in shrubby lowlands or neighborhoods where food is plentiful. In our more southerly counties, gatherings as large as 50 to 100 cardinals may be found foraging in swales with dogwood, sumac, and other fruit-persistent plants.

Flocks usually disband by early March as pairs move into their breeding territories. The start of the nesting season is marked by renewed singing, sometimes as early as February, and mate-feeding to strengthen the marriage between the pair. This courting can often be witnessed at feeders in late winter and early

**Northern Cardinal**
CYNDY CALLOG

Cyndy Callog

spring. This is also the time when a cardinal may respond to its reflection in a window, displaying and attempting to fight with a bird it thinks is an intruder.

Another unifying behavior is countersinging between the pair. Female cardinals are very capable singers, and the two will engage in a form of coordinated song in which one repeats the clear whistled notes of the other. This exchange of song also occurs between neighboring males during territorial defenses.

Most cardinal pairs raise two broods in Michigan, with three or four attempts often required for success. Records indicate that nesting generally takes place between the latter half of April and early August, with the bulk in May, June, and July. There are exceptions, though, including an active nest on 28 March 1981 reported for southeastern Michigan, and some nesting well into September, as evidenced in banding records from the Kalamazoo Nature Center.

Look for a basket-like nest in dense evergreens or bushes, somewhere in the range of 5 to 10 feet above ground. Clutches usually contain three to four bluish or greenish eggs with spots of browns and purples. Females do the building and are fed by their mates during the 12-to-13-day incubation. Both parents care for the young, feeding them a diet of protein-rich insects. Noises and heads of begging nestlings can usually be detected around day seven.

Because the cardinal resides in habitats close to our own and is a popular, easily recognized bird, its occurrence and improved status are well documented in records and writings. Maurice Gibbs called it an "accidental visitor" in one of the state's earliest checklists (1879), and shortly thereafter, A. J. Cook (1893) reported the first nest, from Monroe County in 1881. A decade later the "Red-bird" was rare but fairly widespread in the southern counties. In his 1912 book, Walter Barrows commented on its expansion into the state and that winter observations outnumbered those of summer.

By the time Norman Wood wrote and published in 1951, a substantial change had occurred and the cardinal was common in the southern third, rare into the Upper Peninsula, and was continuing its northward spread. There were a number of sightings from the north in the 1920s to 1940s, but no definite nest records beyond Saginaw Bay. Within the next ten years, local populations became established in several northern counties and breeding was confirmed for the Upper Peninsula.

This brings us to the cardinal's present status of an abundant resident in the southern Lower Peninsula, locally common in the northern Lower, and rare in the Upper Peninsula. This bird's strong affinity for shrubby foliage will probably always limit its occurrence in the largely forested northern regions. Michigan is only one of many northern states which have experienced such an increase. No doubt favorable habitat changes were a major contributing factor. Others believe winter bird-feeding and a period of somewhat milder temperatures in the early to middle 1900s also helped stimulate expansion.

Breeding bird surveys for Michigan show that cardinal numbers continued their increasing trend from the 1960s through 1992, though its invasion of our northern regions may have slowed. Data from Kalamazoo County, in the south, show a doubling in the numbers of breeding cardinals in the past 20 years. Trends from Christmas bird counts are less clear. Statewide totals

from the 1980s do average a few thousand more cardinals compared to the 1960s, but when counts are weighed against effort by participants (party-hours), the totals for the two decades are quite similar. The Christmas counts do reflect the temporary drop in numbers which followed the severe winters of the late 1970s. I wonder what the cardinal's status will be in another 25 years.
—Gail A. McPeek

# ROSE-BREASTED GROSBEAK
## (Pheucticus ludovicianus)

This handsome songbird, which is both a common migrant and a summer resident in Michigan, is likely to be encountered in almost any deciduous woodland, especially along the edges. In fact, the Rose-breasted Grosbeak is probably more common than most people realize. The key is knowing where to look and how to recognize its metallic-sounding "chink" notes and robin-like song.

The Rose-breasted Grosbeak opts for habitats with layers of foliage provided by a mix of trees, saplings, and shrubs as is typical of woodland borders and corridors. Second-growth vegetation along streams, lakes, or marshes is ideal. Also suitable are orchards, parks, and wooded suburbs. In northern regions of the state, mesic mixed woodlands are used as well as deciduous.

With its occupation of edge situations, it is no wonder that this species has fared well in the current landscape. It is widely distributed in Michigan, being uncommon only on Isle Royale and in the most industrial and urbanized areas. Though a woodland bird, it is also not as common in large continuous stands of mature forest where the amount of edge is less. *The Atlas of Breeding Birds of Michigan* reported Rose-breasted Grosbeaks in 83% of the state's townships, with highest densities in parts of the northern and western Lower Peninsula.

According to the breeding bird survey, a positive but nonsignificant increase in numbers occurred in Michigan from the mid-1960s to the early 1980s. Similar increases have been documented in many northeastern states and provinces. More recently, however, the trend in the state has reversed, with significant declines in numbers of grosbeaks evident from about the middle 1980s to the present. Such fluctuations are generally expected for birds which occupy mostly successional, and therefore changing, communities.

The Rose-breasted Grosbeak has quite an extensive breeding range, which includes the northeastern and north-central United States and a good portion of Canada west to the Rockies. The Appalachian Mountains provide nesting south to Georgia; otherwise its range in the East ends around southern Ohio and Maryland. In the Great Plains, it occurs to Kansas, Nebraska, and the Dakotas, where it meets up with its western cousin, the Black-headed Grosbeak. Studies have found occasional interbreeding in the zone of overlap.

Tropical habitats from northern South America to Mexico are the Rose-breasted Grosbeak's other home. Here, too, it occupies mostly second-growth woodlands. Occasionally stragglers remain in the States, and at least one turns up on a Michigan Christmas bird count in most winters. A maximum total of eight were found on the 1985–86 count.

The grosbeak's return to southern Michigan generally begins in the last few days of April, with numbers of migrants peaking through the second week of May. Arrival in the north lags 10 to 14 days behind. This is a good time to observe the radiant plumage of adult males, before full leaf-out obscures the view. Their spring migration coincides with the flowering of many plants, including cherries and other orchard species, of which grosbeaks can sometimes take more than their fair share of blossoms and new buds. Later their appetite for potato bugs and other insects is a benefit.

When male grosbeaks return, they proclaim their territories with song from the treetops. During courtship the pair exchange song and "chink" calls and males advertise their white wing and tail spots. The breeding season begins in mid-May and extends into July. The nesting duties are shared, and both sexes, particularly the male, sing while sitting on the nest. This seems like a good way to attract unwanted attention, but perhaps it does just the opposite and warns other grosbeaks and enemies to stay away.

The flimsy twig nest, which is similar to a cardinal's, is not difficult to locate. The regular vocal activity helps reveal its whereabouts, and the nest is often placed within 10 feet of the ground near the edge of an opening. Young grosbeaks are as noisy as their parents and seem to beg constantly as nestlings and fledglings. There is a period in late summer when molting keeps individuals out of sight, but the species is again conspicuous in September and early October, when it departs the state.

The gross size and shape of this finch's beak are an obvious clue to its diet of mostly seeds and fruits. Its bill is as powerful as it looks. I have had my fingers and hands pinched and bitten numerous times while banding them. I also learned that if you catch one grosbeak, others are bound to follow, as their loud, persistent alarm calls may draw the entire family or flock into the net, plus orioles, robins, and assorted other species.

Despite the pain inflicted, banding is a great way to observe differences in males, females, adults, and immatures. Breeding males are gorgeous in their glossy black and white plumage and rose-colored bib and underwings. In the fall, adult males retain the rich black primaries (lacking in young males), but their heads are brown and the reds have faded. Females are mostly brown and white with broad crown and eye stripes and yellow underwings. Juveniles resemble females but have buffier tones and less streaking underneath, and young males can be separated from young females by their respective pinkish or yellowish wing linings. —Gail A. McPeek

# BLACK-HEADED GROSBEAK

(*Pheucticus melanocephalus*)

A casual visitor to Michigan, this species breeds in woodland habitats from western Canada south through the western United States to northern Mexico, and withdraws completely into Mexico for the winter. The Black-headed Grosbeak is the western counterpart of the closely allied Rose-breasted Grosbeak, with which it sometimes hybridizes in the narrow band of range over-lap in the Great Plains. Identification of adult males of both species comes with ease, but not so with the similar-looking female and immature birds, and observers need to be extremely careful and consult good field guides plus get confirmation from other knowledgeable birders (or a sharp photograph) when claiming a possible Black-headed Grosbeak.

There are no reports of this grosbeak in Michigan prior to 1963 (Barrows discounted writings in the 1800s which included this species). The first record came that year from Ann Arbor, where a male, observed on 17 and 24 March, was netted and collected on 25 March (the only state specimen to date). The following winter a female became a regular visitor at a feeder in Flint from 20 November 1963 to mid-January 1964 (Payne 1983). The third documented state report came ten years later, in 1973, when a male appeared at a Grand Rapids feeder on 26 November and was later banded and photographed.

There are 10 additional reports subsequent to 1973, totaling 11 individuals in six years (1978, 1981, 1982, 1983, 1984, and 1990). Calendar dates for 8 of these observations range from 28 April to 30 May, while the other 2 are winter records from 25 November to 3 December and from 21 December to 4 January. The validity of each of these reports, however, is uncertain because of limited written documentation and the potential for misidentification with the common Rose-breasted Grosbeak. The scarcity of records in the Great Lakes region prior to the 1960s is followed by a spate of observations throughout the region over the next two decades. There is little correlation among states as to the years of occurrence, but there is a consistent pattern to the seasonal distribution of reports, with most between late April and late May or during the winter months when this species finds its way to feeders. —Raymond J. Adams

# BLUE GROSBEAK

(*Guiraca caerulea*)

An accidental visitor in Michigan, this grosbeak nests in the southern two-thirds of the contiguous United States and winters in Mexico and Central America. Occasional wanderers reach the northern states, usually during the spring migration period but also at other times of the year. While there have been at least a dozen published reports of the Blue Grosbeak in Michigan, there are no photographs or specimens, and thus there is little in the way of substantive documentation. To date, two thoroughly written reports have been accepted by the Michigan Bird Records Committee. Neighboring Wisconsin and Ontario have numerous acceptable records, suggesting that other Michigan records are probably valid. The primary concern with undocumented reports is the strong possibility of misidentification with the common Indigo Bunting pair, which the male and female Blue Grosbeak resemble.

Barrows (1912) discounted two records from the late 1800s, and Wood (1951) makes no mention of Blue Grosbeaks in his extensive writing which includes reports up through the early 1940s. E. M. Brigham, Jr. (1941), in a *Jack-Pine Warbler* article, summarizes four observations from 10 May 1927 in Berrien County, 20 May 1928 in Kalamazoo County, 4 August 1929 in Calhoun County, and 26

May 1940 in Ottawa County. Unfortunately, none of these reports has supporting evidence, although the descriptions are rather detailed. Zimmerman and Van Tyne (1959) list these reports in their state checklist but give the species only hypothetical status.

The next report of a Blue Grosbeak in the state came in 1972, followed by four reports over the next seven years, although again complete documentation was lacking. Payne (1983) maintained the hypothetical status on our next state checklist, stating that "some sight records may apply to Indigo Buntings with buffy wing bars." The increase in observations during the 1970s does, however, correspond to a period of increased extralimital sightings in the Great Lakes region. In fact, breeding bird surveys indicate a significant growth in populations nationwide since 1966.

The most recent Michigan reports are of a female in Newaygo County on 9 June 1990, seen by four observers; a second-year male discovered in Berrien County on 18 May 1991 by three observers; a female/immature male at Whitefish Point (Chippewa County) on 20 September 1992, witnessed by two observers; and an individual in Leelanau County on 20 May 1993. The Berrien and Chippewa counties reports have been approved by the Bird Records Committee. With continuing increases being reported in the Blue Grosbeak's breeding range, this species will likely become a more frequent visitor to the state, particularly the southernmost counties. Currently, the closest nesting populations to Michigan are in southern Ohio, Indiana, Illinois, and southwestern Minnesota. —Raymond J. Adams

# INDIGO BUNTING

## (*Passerina cyanea*)

This is the other "blue" bird of Michigan and the eastern United States. A common inhabitant of old fields, brushy roadsides, and woodland borders, this species can be easily found throughout the state, and yet many people seem never to have seen one. In the words of Walter Barrows, "It is surprising how abundant the bird can be without attracting the attention of the average resident." Barrows wrote this back in 1912, but it is equally appropriate today.

Only adult males have the turquoise plumage—a color created by the diffraction of light through the feathers rather than by pigments. In the right setting, our eyes feast upon a gorgeous iridescent blue bird, but in poor lighting or from a distance, we see only a dark bird on a wire. It is this latter image of a nonblue silhouette that is seen more often when gazing up at a male on his high perch. Shift your position to change the angle of the sun and the Indigo's remarkable color shines through.

Indigo Buntings return to Michigan primarily in May after wintering in the tropics, from the Gulf coast and the tip of Florida to Mexico and Panama. Average first arrival in Berrien County is 4 May. A few individuals may be seen in late April, especially if we have an early warm spell. Males precede females and older males precede first-year males, which are distinguishable by lingering brown feathers amidst their blue plumage.

The sexes are indeed opposite, in both appearance and behavior. Except for faint blue highlights in the wings and tail,

females are a plain brown; and, unlike males, which regularly expose themselves from a perch, females rarely present themselves for viewing. Their return is barely noticed, since they spend most of their time in the dense brush. My observations of females have come largely by chance after wandering into a nesting territory. When this happens you are invariably scolded by the male and female as they hop from branch to branch, flicking their tails. It is also possible to catch a glimpse of a female when she is gathering food for her hungry brood.

Nest records from the state indicate an extended breeding season from mid-May to August, sometimes even September, with most pairs having two broods. That is not to say that both are successful; there are many predators roaming the edge habitats where Indigos nest, not to mention the challenges imposed by cowbird parasitism. Numerous authors report the Indigo to be a common host, and I have regularly observed adults caring for cowbird fledglings during my years of birding.

The compact woven nest is low to the ground, well concealed, and extremely difficult to find. A typical clutch contains three to four eggs, and is incubated nearly two weeks, with the young fledging in about 10 days. There is a definite division of labor between the sexes, with females handling most of the nesting and rearing duties, while males devote their time to singing and guarding the territory. Indigo males are consistent singers, and their excited finch-like song is one of the few heard in midafternoon on those 95-degree-day scorchers. Only after the young leave the nest does the male join in the parenting, and he is often left in charge of the first family so the female can start a second.

We mostly see these birds in singles, pairs, or families, but in the fall they assemble into fairly large flocks, visiting fields with weed seeds and grain. If you take time to observe these flocks, you will see that the post-breeding molt has produced mottled males with arbitrary patches of brown on blue, like an old pair of jeans. These flocks are maintained through the winter, and hundreds are reported along the roadsides in the Yucatan.

The autumn migration in Michigan occurs primarily in September, with more remaining into the first half of October than most people realize. An Indigo at the Whitefish Point Bird Observatory on 2 November 1991 is exceptionally late, and there are a handful of winter observations, including one on the 1971–72 Christmas bird count and a mid-January record from Berrien County.

The Indigo Bunting has been nothing less than common in Michigan, and as with many "edge" occupants, its populations have increased over the years. Breeding bird surveys reveal a significant jump in numbers from 1966 to 1991. Locally, in southwestern Michigan, Indigo numbers peaked during the 1980s and declined slightly in the early 1990s. The main habitat requirement appears to be the combination of thick cover for nesting and tall

*Indigo Bunting*
CYNDY CALLOG

Cyndy Callog

trees or wires for perching, and since these are widely available, Indigos find plenty of places to live. They have also become more frequent in the Upper Peninsula, even though their distribution is local because of the contiguous forested lands.

Extensive studies of this finch's habitat, song, and life history have been conducted here in Michigan (Cass and Livingston counties) by Dr. Robert Payne. Among his many findings are an extremely high degree of dispersal from natal areas by first-year birds; a fairly good return rate to breeding territories held the previous year; and a tendency for breeding males to settle near other males, creating Indigo "neighborhoods" where individuals become well acquainted with their neighbors and sing similar songs. —Gail A. McPeek

# PAINTED BUNTING
## (*Passerina ciris*)

An adult male of this small finch species truly does appear painted with its blue head, green back, red rump, and complete red underside. Females, on the other hand, are plain green above and yellowish-green below. Normally found in the south-central and far southeastern states, individuals occasionally stray north, and the half-dozen or so Michigan records give the Painted Bunting the status of accidental visitor. The first documented occurrence (photograph) was that of an adult male present at a feeder from 5 to 7 May 1968 in Marquette. Prior to this, an adult male had been reported on 30 April 1966 in Benton Harbor, Berrien County, and Rapp (1931) claimed to have seen a Painted Bunting on 9 May 1920. Other reports include a male on 24 June 1969 in Berrien County; a male on 2 May 1973 at a feeder in Port Huron, St. Clair County; and a male at a feeder in Kalamazoo County from 28 April to 4 May 1983, seen by a large number of people. These records suggest a pattern of spring vagrancy by males, although one cannot ignore the possibility that some of these colorful finches may be escaped cage birds. There is also a single report of a female on 25 September 1973 in Grand Mere, Berrien County, which should be considered with caution. —Gail A. McPeek

# DICKCISSEL
## (*Spiza americana*)

"Erratic" and "unpredictable" are words often used to describe the distribution of this unique American finch. Throughout its range and especially in peripheral states such as Michigan, the Dickcissel can be common one year and scarce to absent the next. Evidently what happens here is determined by habitat conditions and population size to the south and west of us, in the heart of its breeding range.

The variable nature of the Dickcissel's abundance and distribution makes for an interesting case. We know from historic accounts that its range once included the farming districts in the East, but this changed toward the end of the 1800s, as populations disappeared from the region. Since the turn of the century, the Midwest has been its primary summer home. At the present time, breeding occurs chiefly in an area from the Great Lakes and Montana south to the central Gulf states and Texas.

Dickcissel occurrence in Michigan has always been one of ups and downs and, beginning with the earliest writings, the regularity of its irregularity is noted in the literature. The decades of the 1870s and 1890s, for example, included years of abundance and scarcity. From the 1930s to the 1960s, records indicate a general increase of Dickcissels in Michigan as well as a northward extension of their range. The invasion of 1934 was the first of several which led to scattered observations beyond the southern four tiers of counties.

Major influxes of late occurred in the 1972–74 period, with a peak in 1973, and in several summers from 1984 to 1989, culminating in the "big" invasion of 1988. This is, by far, the best-documented invasion for the state, since it came during the last field season of the Breeding Bird Atlas. Dickcissels were both common and widely distributed that summer, with reports from more than 200 locations and breeding confirmed north to Delta, Menominee, and Houghton counties in the Upper Peninsula. Large increases along the eastern periphery coincided with decreases in numbers in the center of its range, which in all likelihood were triggered by the harsh drought conditions that year.

When Dickcissels do come our way to breed, they settle in old fields, hayfields, pastures, and wet meadows. People often think of these birds as "little meadowlarks" because of the likeness in appearance and similarity in habitat. From the back the Dickcissel looks like a large sparrow, but from the front it shows several distinctive features including a thick bill, white chin, yellow breast, and, in the male, a black triangular bib. You should have no problem recognizing males as they frequently perch atop fenceposts, wires, and shrubs.

Mid- to late May is the main arrival time, although numbers can increase into June depending on the year and conditions to the south. Dickcissels typically nest in loose aggregations, and in the most suitable habitats—those with large volumes of ground vegetation—colonies are often large and males practice polygamy. During the summer of 1988, many fields across the state were buzzing with the "dick, dick, cissel-cissel-cissel" song.

Most nests are reported during June and early July, but sometimes breeding extends into August. This, too, varies from year to year and place to place, often in response to changes in habitat brought on by mowing, grazing, plowing, or other factors. Local movements are frequent as individuals or whole colonies relocate to renest if first attempts fail or to raise second broods. Losses from predation, disturbance, and cowbird parasitism are notoriously high, as is the case for many grassland species which nest on the ground.

*Henslow's Sparrow*
*Dickcissel*
Cyndy Callog

Cyndy Callog

There are few fall reports of the Dickcissels, suggesting an early departure. A stay by six birds at an Ann Arbor feeder for most of October 1971 is unusual, as are singles on 9 and 22 October 1989 at the Whitefish Point Bird Observatory. It is improbable that these late birds complete the migration to the tropics, where the rest of the Dickcissels have gone. Some strays seem to remain every winter and are usually spotted in the Northeast with flocks of House Sparrows. Michigan has a few winter records, such as the one found on a 1974–75 Christmas bird count and visitors coming to feeders in Lansing (1979) and St. Clair County (1980).

People have been keeping an eye on this species because of the fairly steady decline in numbers since about the mid-1960s. Reduction in farmland and changes in agricultural practices on the breeding grounds are suspect, as are habitat losses and pest damage control on its winter range in the Llanos (native grasslands) and rice fields of northern South America. Recently, sizable numbers have been found in nontraditional wintering areas in Central America. It seems that the key to survival for the Dickcissel lies in its ability to change its distribution. —Gail A. McPeek

## GREEN-TAILED TOWHEE

### (*Pipilo chlorurus*)

The chance discovery of a Green-tailed Towhee on 23 December 1974, during the Allegan Christmas bird count, remains one of my favorite birding memories. A photograph was obtained, providing the first physical evidence for this species in the state and the second reported observation. There have been four sightings since then. Other state records are from the following dates and places: 1 November 1955 in Port Inland, Schoolcraft County; 20 May 1979 in West Olive, Ottawa County; mid-January through 23 February 1985 in Euclid, Bay County (later found dead and converted to a specimen housed at the Jennison Nature Center); mid-October 1985 to 28 February 1986 at a feeder at Sylvan Lake, Oakland County; and 14 May 1988 at Consumers Power Karn Plant, Bay County. The Green-tailed Towhee breeds in mountainous country in the interior western United States, withdrawing to lower elevations and the extreme southwestern states and Mexico for the winter. During times of migration, a few wander east as far as the Atlantic coast. This towhee is unmistakable when seen well, having a rust-colored crown, white throat bordered by black and white stripes, and an olive back and tail. —Raymond J. Adams

## RUFOUS-SIDED TOWHEE

### (*Pipilo erythrophthalmus*)

The Rufous-sided Towhee is a common summer resident and migrant found in a variety of brushy and wooded situations in Michigan. The forest margins, shrubby uplands, and second-growth woodlands prevalent in today's landscape provide ample habitat for this sparrow relative. Most of its time is spent on or near the ground, except when males ascend to a perch to sing

"drink-your-TEA." This diagnostic song and the slurred "to-whee" and "chewink" calls given by both sexes makes this species easy to locate and identify.

Another good clue to its whereabouts is the loud rustling of leaves made when foraging. Towhees use a backward hopping and scratching technique to find insects, seeds, and other foods in the accumulated ground litter. This behavior produces considerable noise suggesting a much larger bird or mammal, not an eight-inch towhee. Observing this long-tailed, rufous-sided bird is usually quite easy, especially when an individual or pair are pre-occupied with mealtime.

Of the four towhee species found in North America, the Rufous-sided has the largest distribution, extending from the southern edge of Canada to Florida, California, and Guatemala. Within this range there are three recognized forms: a "spotted" race in the West, a "red-eyed" race in the East, and a "white-eyed" race in the Southeast. Plumage-wise the three are not that different, but there is a wide degree of geographic variation in their voices, particularly those of the eastern and western races. Had researchers not discovered that these two interbreed where their ranges overlap, we would probably still classify them separately and use the name Red-eyed Towhee in Michigan.

Although the breeding range of the Rufous-sided Towhee encompasses the state, it is not uniformly distributed or common throughout. It does nest in abundance in most counties of the Lower Peninsula, except for areas where extensive urbanization and agriculture severely limit the habitat it needs. Once you reach the Straits and beyond, the towhees become less common and local in occurrence. They do breed regularly in the south-central Upper Peninsula but are uncommon to rare elsewhere in the region and are nearly absent from the Keweenaw Peninsula and Isle Royale.

According to *The Atlas of Breeding Birds of Michigan*, greatest densities tend to be associated with sandy or other well-drained soils where there is plenty of ground litter, as is typical of oak or oak-pine woodlands and jack-pine plains. One such locale with large numbers of breeding towhees is the Allegan State Game Area. These habitats meet both their foraging and nesting requirements. Towhees build a sturdy open cup nest of leaves, bark strips, weed stems, and grasses. Ground nests are far more common, though occasionally females will choose a shrub. Most mated pairs raise two broods in a season, and selection of an above-ground site tends to occur more with second nests.

Towhees are relatively early spring migrants, with arrival in lower Michigan beginning in late March and continuing through April. Published records reveal a delayed return farther north, probably dependent on the extent of snow cover. There are some towhee sightings in April in the Upper Peninsula, but most do not arrive until May. As females return and courting begins, you

*Chipping Sparrow*
*Clay-colored Sparrow*
**Rufous-sided Towhee**
CYNDY CALLOG

Cyndy Callog

can witness both sexes spreading their wings and tails to reveal their prominent white patches.

Breeding data for the state, mostly from the Lower Peninsula, show that females are usually incubating first clutches by the end of May, with young fledging in June. There is then another period of nestings in July, either second broods or second attempts, with family groups again seen toward the end of summer. With clutches averaging four to five eggs and the ability to double-brood, towhees have a high reproductive potential. This capacity is hampered, however, by the vulnerability of nests to a variety of predators and to parasitism by the Brown-headed Cowbird, of which the towhee is a favorite host. It is not uncommon to find a nest with one or several cowbird eggs, nor to see an adult towhee feeding a fledgling cowbird along with, or instead of, one of its own.

Some people suspect that the greater abundance of cowbirds and certain predators, such as raccoons and cats, have contributed to a decrease in towhees in the East during recent decades (though no such trend is evident in Michigan). Urbanization and forest maturation are also mentioned as possible causes. Although the information on populations appears reliable, it is important to emphasize the need to develop better measurements for documenting long-term changes for towhees and other species which live in transitional habitats and are subject to natural fluctuations simply due to succession.

Although most Rufous-sided Towhees migrate from Michigan in the fall, with peaks from late September to early October, small numbers are found in some southern counties through the winter. Christmas bird counts since 1970 have totals numbering mostly in the teens and twenties. Extremes are a single individual in 1987–88 and a maximum of 43 in 1976–77. Those that do stay consort in small flocks with other remaining towhees, or with cardinals or sparrows. —Gail A. McPeek

# BACHMAN'S SPARROW

(*Aimophila aestivalis*)

This secretive resident of the southeastern United States experienced a northward expansion of its breeding range into Ohio and West Virginia in the late 1800s, reaching as far north as western Pennsylvania in the early 1900s. This led the way for spring migrants to occasionally appear even farther north, and for a time (1940s–1960s) the Bachman's Sparrow was an accidental visitant to Michigan. There are five records from this period, the first two documented by specimens at the University of Michigan Museum of Zoology: a male collected on 29 April 1944 in Monroe County and a male taken on 13 May 1946 in Wayne County. The next two occurrences were singing males detected on 23–24 April 1948 in Washtenaw County and 27 July 1954 in Livingston County. The fifth and most recent sighting was an individual seen on 26 April 1964 at Metrobeach in Macomb County. The absence of records since then probably reflects the retraction of its range following a brief northern invasion. Bachman's Sparrows vacated Pennsylvania around 1937, and none were reported in Ohio during that state's breeding bird atlas in the 1980s. Significant declines have been noted elsewhere along the northern edge of the breeding range since the 1960s. These trends make the recurrence of Bachman's Sparrows in Michigan highly unlikely. —Gail A. McPeek

# CASSIN'S SPARROW

(*Aimophila cassinii*)

The Cassin's Sparrow holds the distinction of being the single species on the Michigan bird list which is known only from a specimen, having never actually been seen alive in the state. On 16 September 1985, a road-killed bird was found along U.S. 41 near Central in Keweenaw County. This "unknown" small grayish sparrow was sent to the Kalamazoo Nature Center, where it was identified as a Cassin's Sparrow—the first and only record of this species in Michigan. The specimen is now housed at the University of Michigan Museum of Zoology. The Cassin's Sparrow is native to the arid grasslands of the Southwest, breeding from southeastern Colorado and southwestern Kansas to northern Mexico and southern Arizona, and wintering in the southern portions of this range to central Mexico. It is known to wander on migration and has been recorded several times in the Great Lakes region, including six times in Ontario (three at Pte. Pelee). This suggests that the Cassin's may have occurred in the state more times than the single specimen indicates. —James Granlund

# AMERICAN TREE SPARROW

(*Spizella arborea*)

The American Tree Sparrow ranks right up there with the Dark-eyed Junco as one of our most abundant winter sparrows. This hardy bird breeds in the arctic and subarctic zones of North America in dense stands of stunted spruce and brushy margins of pools and grassy bogs. For the winter, it migrates to the northern and central United States, where the wheat and corn belts harbor the greatest densities. Considerable numbers will stay farther north during mild winters.

The Tree Sparrow is a common widespread migrant in Michigan. Arrival in the fall generally commences in early October in the north and around 15 October in the south. Some years bring an earlier start, with first migrants seen in the latter part of September but rarely sooner. Exceptional is a Kalamazoo record from 1 September. By late October, Tree Sparrows are common throughout the state, and numbers continue to build into November. Come December the migration is mostly complete, and those remaining make up our winter population.

The return flight north becomes apparent on the first warm days in March. The weather change even inspires some males to sing their clear, sweet song. The migration in southern Michigan is usually in full swing by late March, with numbers diminishing in the second week of April. Farther north, transients peak in mid- to late April, and most are gone by early May, except for the occasional straggler. Alice Kelley reported a remarkably late spring date of 28 May 1979 for southeast Michigan.

As a winter resident, the Tree Sparrow is common to abundant in the southern half of the state and uncommon to rare in the north. Winter occurrence early in the season is well documented by the Christmas bird counts. Numbers can vary widely from year to year depending on food supply, temperature, and snow cover. A good example of this variation occurred in two consecutive, contrasting winters in the 1980s, when the low total of 7,511 in 1984–85 was followed by a record high count of 28,296 in 1985–86. Even though Tree Sparrows were reported from the same number of stations (52) around the state in both years, numbers in 1985–86 were nearly four times higher. In the first of the two winters, December temperatures were mild (3–8°F above normal), snow cover was sparse, wild foods were plentiful, and species such as the Tree Sparrow were widely dispersed. The following year was just the opposite; December temperatures were well below average (5–12°), deep snow covered the ground over much of the state, and many songbirds flocked to feeders in large numbers. The 28,296 Tree Sparrows tallied that winter was the third-highest species total, outdone only by the starling and House Sparrow.

In addition to millet and other seed offered at feeders, Tree Sparrows consume large quantities of weed and grass seeds, and watching a large flock forage in a field is always an enjoyable part of winter birding. Flock members will dangle from the tops of weed stalks, causing the seeds to scatter on the ground below, where they become a meal. It is easy to see why, when the snow becomes deep, they make greater use of bird feeding stations.

The Tree Sparrow is not a "tree" bird at all, but was given the name because of its similar appearance to the European Tree Sparrow. The American species favors open country and spends most of its time on the ground in fields or in brushy cover of a hedgerow, thicket, or marsh. With its chestnut cap, the Tree Sparrow resembles two of our common breeding sparrows, the Chipping and Field, and those unfamiliar with their individual characteristics may confuse the three. Only the Tree Sparrow has a central black breast spot. Other distinguishing features are a dark bill (the Field Sparrow's is pink) and faint brownish eye line (the Chipping Sparrow's is more pronounced and black). —Gail A. McPeek

# CHIPPING SPARROW

(*Spizella passerina*)

The rapid, monotone trill of the Chipping Sparrow is one of the most common bird songs heard about our yards, gardens, and parks during the spring and summer months. This abundant Michigan bird is found nearly everywhere you travel in the state. When the Breeding Bird Atlas project was complete, only the American Robin and Song Sparrow were reported in more townships.

The breeding range of the Chipping Sparrow encompasses most of North America, from the treeline in southeast Alaska and Canada south to northern Florida, Mexico, and Central America. Clearly this species must be adapted to a diversity of habitats to have such a large distribution. Most observers in Michigan tend to first associate the "Chippy" with towns, suburbs, and other residential areas landscaped with shrubs and trees ideal for nesting and manicured lawns for foraging. This sparrow does, however, find many other habitats to its liking, including orchards, open woodlands, forest edge, stream and lake margins, spruce bogs, and Christmas tree and other conifer plantations.

Arrival of Chipping Sparrows from the wintering grounds typically begins in the first few days of April, and by the middle of the month, birds are widespread across the south and making their way into the Upper Peninsula. Earlier returns, such as those recorded on 16 March in Kalamazoo and 25 March in Battle Creek, are rare occurrences. Males favor high perches for singing to proclaim their territories. Both males and females, which are identical in appearance, will defend the nest tree and chase off intruders.

There is no shortage of information on nesting for this common backyard bird. The small cup nest is made of dried grasses and weeds and is lined with animal hair, a habit which gave rise to the nickname "Hair-bird." Popular nest sites include spruce, cedar, juniper, and pine, as well as dense, non-evergreen plants such as orchard trees, rose bushes, and vine tangles. Ground nests are quite rare for this sparrow; instead placement is typically 3 to 10 feet above ground, with late-season nests often higher than earlier ones. In coniferous woodlands, however, it is not uncommon for nests to be at considerably greater heights (10–40 feet), located on the outer end of a limb in a large pine or the top of a black spruce.

Chipping Sparrows regularly attempt two broods in a season, with first nests in Michigan found chiefly in the middle of May and second nests around 1 July. The male feeds the female as she incubates the eggs for about two weeks. Clutches average three to four eggs, which are a blue-green color with brown spots wreathed about the larger end.

By late summer, family groups can be seen foraging about in weedy fields, fencerows, and woodland edges. Insects are the primary food during nesting, but thereafter a variety of grass seeds, grains, and weed seeds are consumed. The fall migration occurs primarily during September and the first half of October. Stragglers in November are expected in southern Michigan, but reports of individuals on 14 and 21 November in the Upper Peninsula are exceptional. Most Chipping Sparrows winter from the southern United States to Nicaragua, but small numbers remain farther north, and Christmas bird count participants in Michigan have turned up one or a few in most recent winters.

Since the time of the earliest writings, this sparrow has been an abundant migrant and summer resident throughout the state. There are some references to declines around the turn of the century in association with House Sparrow competition, and Walter Barrows (1912) commented that it would be even more common if not for the House Sparrow and cat. In the absence of any measures of numbers at the time, the extent of any decline cannot be determined.

Modern data indicate the Chipping Sparrow to be generally abundant throughout the state, with averages of 14 to 40 birds on most breeding bird surveys from 1983 to 1988. Densities tend to be particularly high in the north-central region of the Lower Peninsula where dry, conifer-dominated woodlands are prevalent. Findings from these surveys over the long term (since 1966) also reveal a significant increase in Chipping Sparrow populations in Michigan and throughout the Great Lakes region. —Gail A. McPeek

## CLAY-COLORED SPARROW

(*Spizella pallida*)

Spreading eastward from its breeding range in the northern Great Plains, the Clay-colored Sparrow has emerged as a fairly recent addition to Michigan's avifauna. Around the turn of the century, this western sparrow was described as a straggler to the state but nothing more. Today it is a locally common summer resident in the Upper and northern Lower peninsulas, with occasional breeding farther south.

Lumbering of forests in the Great Lakes region cleared the way for the Clay-colored Sparrow's expansion beyond its traditional breeding grounds from British Columbia and Alberta to Iowa and Illinois. Today its range extends east to Michigan, Ontario, and, rarely, New York, although the majority of the population still occurs west of the Mississippi. Expansion into Michigan first became apparent in the early decades of the 1900s, with an increase in reports and the first documented breeding in 1924. By the late 1950s, the species was a local summer resident in parts of northern Michigan, and its population growth has continued to the present.

Whenever I think of this sparrow, my mind flashes back to a young Christmas tree plantation in northern Michigan where I encountered Clay-colors for the first time. A chorus of low-pitched buzzes caught my attention, and after patient observation I located at least four territorial males among the small conifers. This is just one of the low shrub communities where this species may breed. Other habitats include regenerating burned-over lands, old fields overgrown to weeds and shrubs, woodland edges, and streamside thickets. Many, but not all, of these habitats are characterized by poor, sandy soils.

Current distribution centers in the state are the western Upper Peninsula and north-central Lower Peninsula, where it occupies burns with the Kirtland's Warbler. Other notable pockets of breeding occur in eastern Chippewa county (south of the "Soo"), and in parts of Cheboygan, Alpena, Iosco, Antrim, and Manistee counties in the northern Lower Peninsula. Away from these areas, Clay-colored Sparrows are widely scattered and generally rare to absent. Breeding has been documented in a few southern locales in the Thumb region, including Sanilac, Genesee, and St. Clair counties. In fact, it is reputed to be fairly common at the Minden State Game Area in Sanilac.

After departing their winter home in Mexico and extreme southern Texas, Clay-colored Sparrows arrive in Michigan in late April or early May, with numbers peaking in the second and third weeks of May. A few individuals have even reached the Upper Peninsula as early as 21 and 24 April. The small number of spring reports in the southern counties suggests that many migrants bypass this region on their flight north. Periodic June and July sightings in the southern region (other than those at known nesting sites) are most likely late spring or early fall migrants, but observers should be on the lookout for possible breeders as well.

The breeding season for this sparrow commences in late May and often lasts into August with second broods. Nests with eggs have been found as early as 1 June and as late as 1 August. Our best information comes from Lawrence Walkinshaw, who located 40 nests in a dry, brushy prairie near Lovells, Crawford County, during the late 1930s and early 1940s. He noted that the female builds the nest but is often accompanied by the male on her trips for materials, and that first nests tend to be closer to the ground than later ones; he also proved through color-banding that some pairs raise two broods in a season.

Clay-colored Sparrow nests are frequently placed at the base of a grass tuft, weed stem, fern, or bush and raised slightly off the ground. Others may be placed on a low branch of a conifer or dense deciduous shrub. These latter nests resemble those of its more familiar cousin, the Chipping Sparrow, but are less compact. The three to four brown-spotted, blue eggs of the two species are indistinguishable.

In August, Clay-colored Sparrows begin to gather in small flocks for the migration south. Departure from the state occurs during September and the first part of October. Transients can be found in weedy fields and scrubby edge habitats where they commonly associate with other *Spizella*s, particularly Chipping Sparrows. One can easily overlook Clay-colors at this time of year because of the plumage similarities of these two species. —Gail A. McPeek

## FIELD SPARROW

(*Spizella pusilla*)

This pink-billed, rusty-capped sparrow is a common migrant and summer resident in Michigan, though its range is confined mostly to the Lower Peninsula. Once you approach the Straits, numbers diminish rapidly, and the Field Sparrow is only rare and locally distributed in the Upper Peninsula.

The North American range of this bird includes nearly all of the eastern United States west to the Plains. Breeding occurs north to Maine, southern Ontario, the Upper Great Lakes, and southern Quebec, and south to northern Florida and Texas. The Field Sparrow resides year-round over much of its range, retreating only from the northern states for the winter and extending its distribution slightly farther south into southern Florida, southern Texas, and northeastern Mexico.

This sparrow does occupy field habitats as its name implies. More specifically, it prefers early successional fields which are overgrown with weeds, shrubs, and young trees. In Michigan, such habitats are most typical on abandoned farmland, rights-

*Song Sparrow*
*Field Sparrow*
*Vesper Sparrow*
DAVID MOHRHARDT

of-way, cutover or burned-over lands, and young pine plantations. Males are strongly territorial, requiring an area of two to three acres or larger in size depending on the quality of the habitat. Unlike Chipping, Song, and House Sparrows, the Field Sparrow seems to keep its distance from residential areas, rarely nesting near houses.

Observers in southern Michigan frequently note the first returning Field Sparrows during the last ten days of March. Average arrival in Berrien County is reported to be 22 March. By the first week of April the migration is in full swing, with birds reaching the more northern counties in the second and third weeks. Noteworthy is the particularly early sighting of a Field Sparrow in the Upper Peninsula (Dickinson County) on 30 March 1976.

Breeding commences soon after arrival, resulting in many first nests in May. Active nests have been recorded as early as 6 May in southern Michigan. With this early start there is time for many second broods, and a resurgence in nesting is evident in late June or early July. Hatching and fledging of young is mostly complete by early to mid-August. Exceptionally late was a nest with fledging young found in Calhoun County on 10 September, perhaps a third brood for the season, which is not uncommon in the southern states.

Nests of this species are located on the ground or at low heights, usually below four feet. During many years of observation of Field Sparrow nests in Michigan, Lawrence Walkinshaw found that the large majority of early nests were placed on the ground, whereas later nests (July) were all in small bushes or trees. The Field Sparrow is known to be a common host to cowbird eggs in many areas. For his sample of more than 600 nests, Walkinshaw reported a 27% parasitism rate, with May nests being most susceptible and regularly deserted. Later nests are generally free of cowbird eggs since females are no longer laying.

Loose flocks of migrating Field Sparrows make their way south in September and early October, and are mostly gone from the state by mid-October. Small numbers linger in the southern counties, with some overwintering reported. From 1970 to the present, Christmas bird count totals for Field Sparrows have varied from a low of 18 in 1991–92 to a high of 196 in 1973–74, when many appeared at feeders.

The Field Sparrow's status and distribution in Michigan have clearly changed over time. Historically, it was believed to be somewhat uncommon and locally distributed until settlement began to open up the landscape. By the late 1800s and early 1900s, the species was described as common, even plentiful, in the south but with only minor presence in the north. A few decades later, in the 1940s and 1950s, the status of common summer resident applied to the entire Lower Peninsula, as populations benefited from the large supply of field habitats created after logging and burning. There were also a handful of reliable reports for the Upper Peninsula by this time.

The Field Sparrow's current status is not much different from that of several decades ago, when acreage of old field and other early successional habitats was probably at a peak. It continues to be a common, widespread breeder in the Lower Peninsula, although numbers have been on a downward slide since the mid-1960s. Similar declines have been documented in numerous other eastern and central states. As before, this trend is suspected to be habitat-related but in the opposite direction, as old fields have become less available through a combination of natural succession, urban and suburban sprawl, and modern farming practices. Meanwhile, the Field Sparrow has continued to increase its presence in the Upper Peninsula, though it remains generally rare. Atlas participants in the 1980s confirmed breeding in five Upper Peninsula townships spanning five counties (Mackinac, Delta, Menominee, Dickinson, Marquette), and reported probable breeding in another nine townships. —Gail A. McPeek

# VESPER SPARROW

## (*Pooecetes gramineus*)

The Vesper Sparrow is a common breeding bird in Michigan often found in some rather barren lands with sparse vegetation, including cultivated fields showing mostly bare soil early in the season. It is also frequently seen along dirt roads between fields, either foraging for insects and seeds or taking dust baths, a seemingly daily activity in this bird's life. Upon approach, the species will flush from the road, revealing its white outer tail feathers. While this is a distinguishing characteristic, one should not assume a Vesper simply by the tail, since the Horned Lark shares this feature as well as the habitat.

The breeding range of the Vesper Sparrow primarily covers the southern half of Canada and the northern half of the United States. Distribution is somewhat more extensive in the West, stretching north to Alberta and south to Arizona and Texas. Populations depart most of the range for the winter, occurring from the southern edge of the breeding grounds to southern Mexico.

Vesper Sparrows are early migrants, arriving in southern Michigan beginning sometime during the last ten days of March. By early April the migration is well underway, and flocks of a dozen or more birds are a common sight in the better-drained fields and pastures. Arrival in the Upper Peninsula is often two to three weeks later, depending on the progress of snow melt; usually they are common by late April or early May.

Nesting pairs are found in various habitats, though dry fields with sparse vegetation are reported to be the most favored. Uncultivated and cultivated fields are used, as are orchards, shrubby uplands, cutover lands, and dry, open forest. In the north-central counties of the Lower Peninsula, recently burned jack-pine plains are a suitable option. Several researchers have noted the importance of elevated song perches in Vesper Sparrow habitat, either fenceposts, wires, shrubs, or trees. While most of their time is spent on the ground, territorial males prefer the highest point available from which to sing.

Nests are typically located in a sparsely vegetated area, placed in a hollow at the base of a grass tussock, weed stem, or dirt clod. Some are concealed at the time of egg laying, but others are exposed, becoming hidden only after the surrounding vegetation grows. Published records for Michigan indicate nests with eggs as early as 25 April and as late as 26 July. Double broods can be common, and the male may take over care of the fledglings while the female starts a second nest. Frequent renestings are also reported for this species, as disking, mowing, and predation destroy many attempts.

The migration south usually commences in September, with some movement noted in the latter part of August in the Upper Peninsula. Most Vesper Sparrows have left the state by mid-October, with a few lingering into November and December. Between the winters of 1970–71 and 1992–93, numbers ranging from one to ten were reported on Christmas bird counts during most years, while others had none. On occasion a Vesper (or two) is seen well beyond the count period, confirming that at least some stay through the winter.

The Breeding Bird Atlas and other current information show this sparrow to be common and generally distributed throughout the Lower Peninsula and to a lesser extent across the Upper Peninsula, where large regions of unbroken forest offer less habitat. Older farming methods were probably more in the Vesper's favor, whereas modern practices disrupt more nests and reduce fencerows, perches, and even foods via chemical applications. The significant drop in numbers measured by breeding bird surveys over the past few decades probably reflects these changes. Increased land development and regrowth of woodlands where once there were fields are also considered contributing factors. Similar declines have been documented all over the East, and while the Vesper Sparrow is still a common Michigan bird today, a similar status a few decades from now is not assured. —Gail A. McPeek

# LARK SPARROW

## (*Chondestes grammacus*)

Formerly a local summer resident in southern Michigan, the Lark Sparrow today is a casual visitor seen primarily during times of migration. As a breeding bird, it was officially placed on the state's extirpated list in 1990 after three decades lapsed without any signs of nesting.

The Lark Sparrow is believed to be an original member of Michigan's avifauna, nesting in the dry prairies and oak savannas which were present in the southwestern Lower Peninsula and also possibly in the western Upper Peninsula. It was included on Sager's 1839 list, the earliest published account for the state. Writings which followed indicated an increase in the late 1800s to the point where the species became locally common in a number of southern counties.

The improved status of the Lark Sparrow came on the heels of settlement and the replacement of woods with pasture and cultivated land. These changes even allowed for expansion into Pennsylvania, New York, and Maryland—states east of its traditional range. In the end, however, such increases proved to be short-lived. Local populations in Michigan did persist fairly well into the 1940s, as Wood (1951) considered it a summer resident north to St. Clair, Livingston, and Kent counties.

Exactly when the species began to disappear from the state is unclear, but records indicate a dramatic decline in the 1950s. In 1959, Zimmerman and Van Tyne characterized it as a very local summer resident and much less numerous than formerly reported. Lark Sparrows vacated the George Reserve in Livingston County after being common breeders there from 1933 to 1950. The last published nest records came from Muskegon County in 1953 and from Kalamazoo County in 1952 and 1959.

During the 1950s and 1960s, declines in Lark Sparrow populations were also evident in many neighboring states, including Ohio, Indiana, and Illinois. This trend has evidently continued, affecting its status continentwide. Breeding bird survey data since 1966 reveal a significant reduction in numbers in many central states, and the species is now rare and irregular east of the Mississippi. Its current breeding range falls primarily between the Mississippi and the Pacific coast, north to Washington and extreme southern Canada in the Plains. Wintering takes place from southern California and Texas to Central America.

When this species did breed in Michigan, it selected sparsely vegetated areas dotted with shrubs and saplings as are typical of poorer, sandy soils. Nests were a simple depression in the ground, often where it was bare but shaded by a clump of grass or weeds. If these habits sound somewhat familiar, it is because they are much like those of the common Vesper Sparrow.

Today, Michigan observers encounter the Lark Sparrow only on an irregular basis, with most reports occurring during spring migration. Interestingly, records published in the seasonal surveys during the past few decades indicate that individuals are just as likely to appear in northern Michigan as in the south, and that the Whitefish Point Bird Observatory, of all places, has become the most reliable spot for observation.

Since 1970, there have been at least 30 reports in the state, spanning the dates of 11 April and 27 October. The majority of records are from the late April–May migration period, with only a handful from the summer and fall. One sighting per year has been the norm, but occasionally observers have found more than one Lark Sparrow in a year. In 1992, singles were reported on 23 April at Whitefish Point (Chippewa County), on 24 April at Seney (Schoolcraft County), and on 19 May in Lake County. In 1990, sightings included a bird on 21–24 April at Grand Mere (Berrien County), one on 3 May at Whitefish Point, one on 24 May at Shelldrake Dam (Chippewa County), and one on 7 October at Copper Harbor (Keweenaw County).

Given the current status of the Lark Sparrow elsewhere in its range, a return to Michigan as a breeding species is doubtful. To see this species in the state today, birders will have to rely on luck and word of mouth. —Gail A. McPeek

# BLACK-THROATED SPARROW

## (*Amphispiza bilineata*)

An inhabitant of desert scrub, sagebrush, and arid mountain regions in the Southwest, this sparrow has occasionally wandered eastward, and to date there are three reports for Michigan. The first came on 7 December 1982 when an individual was discovered at a feeder in Muskegon County. This record is documented by a photograph, and many birders traveled from near and far to see this sparrow with the diagnostic black chin, throat, and breast bib which remained until 23 February. The next record lacks physical evidence, but the written description of a bird seen on 20 November 1989 in Barry County matches that of a Black-throated

Sparrow and was accepted by the Michigan Bird Records Committee. The third and most recent sighting occurred on 13 November 1992, when a Black-throated Sparrow was found under a juniper at Whitefish Point in the Upper Peninsula. It remained there for three days and was seen by several observers. Ontario, Wisconsin, and Minnesota also had reports of vagrant Black-throated Sparrows in the fall of 1992. Occurrences in the Great Lakes region seem to indicate an increase in wanderings of this sparrow over the last few decades. —Gail A. McPeek

## LARK BUNTING

(*Calamospiza melanocorys*)

The Lark Bunting is a casual Michigan visitor in the spring and summer seasons, with a few accidental fall and winter appearances. A resident of grassland and sagebrush habitats, this species breeds from south-central Canada to northern Texas, and winters from Texas to Mexico. Regular occurrences beyond this range reflect the Lark Bunting's propensity to wander during migration. Gregarious by nature, those that do stray typically join flocks of sparrows or other similar species.

Although there are a few historical reports, the first satisfactory sight record for Michigan did not come until 26 June 1942 at Douglas Lake, Cheboygan County. This was followed on 23–25 July 1964 by the first record with physical evidence, that of an individual photographed in Schoolcraft County. There have since been at least 17 sightings in the state through 1992. Most are from scattered locales in the Upper Peninsula during the Lark Bunting's extended spring migration period (April to June). Early and late dates are 9 April and 17 June, with the bulk of the spring records between mid-May and the first week of June.

Autumn and winter visits are much more unusual. The two autumn records are from the Whitefish Point Bird Observatory, Chippewa County. Both are recent sightings, the first on 16 September 1989 and the second from 18 October through November 1991. The only two winter records come from Berrien County on 13–19 January 1982 and the Whitefish Point Bird Observatory on 18 December 1991 (the same individual reported that fall). Identification of the jet-black breeding males with their large white wing patches comes with ease, while females and winter males are more of a challenge; observers should carefully consult field guides. —Gail A. McPeek

## SAVANNAH SPARROW

(*Passerculus sandwichensis*)

The widely distributed Savannah Sparrow has more than a dozen recognized subspecies, which vary geographically in body size, color, bill size, and extent of streaking. Those found in Michigan are heavily streaked above and below, with yellowish eyebrows (in most) and dark "whisker" stripes. For some birds the breast

streaking may merge to form a central spot, similar to that of the Song Sparrow.

The combined breeding range for all subspecies encompasses Alaska, Canada, and much of the United States, south to Maryland and Ohio in the East and to New Mexico and California in the West. Most forms are migratory, wintering from the southern states through Mexico, with some populations staying farther north along both coasts. In Michigan, the Savannah Sparrow is a common migrant and summer resident, with the occasional winter visitant.

A variety of grassy habitats are utilized by this species throughout its range, practically anything from tundra and mountain meadows to fresh and saltwater marshes and grassy dunes. Damp areas are favored in most regions, and dense ground cover is selected over sparse. In Michigan, hayfields have become one of the habitats of choice. Data collected during the Breeding Bird Atlas ranked the Savannah Sparrow at the top of the list among species most frequently reported in hayfields (the meadowlark ranked second). Other habitats include pastures, old fields with dense growth, row crops, shoreland, and grassy or shrubby wetlands.

Michigan observers generally note the arrival of this sparrow in early April in the south and somewhere around 15 April in the Upper Peninsula. A few have been encountered in late March, with an early date of 13 March 1990 for Hillsdale County. By the third and fourth weeks of April, fields across the state are full of Savannahs, although the male's thin, lispy song may be drowned out among a chorus of blackbirds, meadowlarks, bobolinks, and others. Some say their feeble song makes the species easily overlooked, but if you know what to listen for and when, I have found that they can be readily detected.

Except when singing from a perch, this sparrow keeps close to the ground, where it nests and forages for seeds and insects. Running is a common means of escape; otherwise when flushed it flies rapidly ahead and drops quickly out of sight in the dense cover. This bird's ground nest is extremely hard to find, placed in a natural depression or scrape and concealed from above by the surrounding vegetation. Nests with eggs are generally reported from the second week of May to 1 August. Double-brooding is not uncommon, although many later nests are as likely to be second or third attempts from failed first nests, considering the hazards of mowing or other agricultural activity in chosen fields.

Fall records are not as comprehensive as those marking spring arrival. The main flight from the Upper Peninsula occurs chiefly in the first half of September, with numbers peaking in the south during the third and fourth weeks. Passage from the state is largely complete by mid-October, but with stragglers regular through November and even into December. Lingering is virtually nonexistent in the Upper Peninsula, making the Savannah

*Grasshopper Sparrow*
*Savannah Sparrow*
Cyndy Callog

Cyndy Callog

Sparrow at Whitefish Point on 26 November 1989 a record-setter. The occasional winter reports come primarily from Christmas bird counts, with one to four birds seen in about half of the years since 1970.

Michigan records and writings dating back to the 1800s suggest an increase in Savannah Sparrows as more lands were converted from forest to field, pasture, and cropland. Although this bird was clearly an abundant migrant around the turn of the century, nesting reports were so scarce that Barrows (1912) had a difficult time describing breeding status. Wood (1951) later characterized the species as a common resident in the north but concluded it to be uncommon and local in the south because of the lack of nest records from several well-studied areas.

Today, the Savannah Sparrow is common throughout the state, and it seems nearly every suitable field has at least one pair. During the Breeding Bird Atlas it was found in a greater percentage of southern Lower Peninsula townships compared to either the northern Lower or the Upper Peninsula. These data suggest a greater presence in the south than 50 years ago, probably due in part to an increase in hayfields (alfalfa).

Breeding densities for this species are highly variable across the state. Savannahs averaged 15 singing males per route during the Atlas years, yet some routes yielded much higher numbers, such as the one in eastern Chippewa County (the "Soo" area) which averaged 120. More recently, long-term data from breeding bird surveys indicate a downward trend in numbers since 1976. Declines may be related to habitat loss in some areas due to reforestation or suburban sprawl, and to lower productivity caused by changes in haying practices and mowing now common at the height of the nesting season. —Gail A. McPeek

# GRASSHOPPER SPARROW

## (*Ammodramus savannarum*)

This obscure grassland bird is an uncommon migrant and summer resident in Michigan found mainly in the Lower Peninsula. Meadows, hayfields, and weedy fields are among the best places to search for the Grasshopper Sparrow, which, by the way, is a fitting name because of both its buzzy, insect-like song and its appetite for grasshoppers. Glimpses of this "little brown bird" are rare; individuals would much rather run across the ground than fly, and males spend relatively brief amounts of time singing from an exposed perch.

The breeding range of the Grasshopper Sparrow encompasses most of the United States and extreme southern Canada, though it is concentrated primarily in lands east of the Rockies. Inherent throughout this range is a spotty distribution dictated by the patchy nature of suitable habitat. Such a localized occurrence can make the species seem less common than is actually the case. You can visit numerous fields along a country road in Michigan during June and not locate a single Grasshopper Sparrow, then follow a similar route a few miles away and find one or more meadows each containing several singing males.

After wintering in Mexico and the southern tier of states, Grasshopper Sparrows arrive on their Michigan breeding grounds beginning in late April, rarely in mid-April. The main migration occurs in May, and many pairs in the southern counties are already mated and building nests by the end of the month. The first few weeks following their return is the best time to listen and look for territorial males.

Grasshopper Sparrow nests are skillfully hidden at the base of a clump of alfalfa, clover, grass, or other ground cover, and several walkways lead to and from the nest. Two nests found in Livingston County on 30 and 31 May, each containing small young, are among the earliest published records for the state. The 11-to-12-day incubation places egg laying for these nests sometime around 15–18 May, possibly sooner. June is a more typical time to find nests. Late records, such as a nest with eggs on 19 July and fledglings on 24 August, are products of renestings or second broods. To satisfy food and cover requirements, birds may shift to a different locale for their second nests.

The scant data from the fall season indicate migration from the state primarily in September, with nearly all individuals departed by early October. Observations much beyond that, such as an early November record from Berrien County, are highly unusual.

The Grasshopper Sparrow's distribution in Michigan has changed rather dramatically over the past one hundred years. As with several other grassland species there has been an increasing presence in the north in response to more open land, and a decreasing presence in the south as urban and suburban sprawl and modern agricultural practices have eliminated habitat. At the time when Barrows (1912) wrote, distribution was virtually limited to the southern Lower Peninsula. In the mid-1900s, a spread into the northern Lower Peninsula was apparent, though the species was only rare and the southern half was clearly the main breeding area. Individuals were also oversummering in Luce County in the Upper Peninsula by that time.

Results of the 1980s Breeding Bird Atlas revealed an even bigger change in distribution. First, Grasshopper Sparrows are found in nearly equal frequency in the northern and southern Lower Peninsula. Second, the abundance as reported on breeding bird surveys in the northern Lower Peninsula now averages twice that of the south. And third, breeding populations are established in some areas of the Upper Peninsula, most notably in the south-central counties of Menominee and Delta. Despite this greater presence northward, long-term data from breeding bird surveys indicate a significant decline in Grasshopper Sparrows in Michigan since 1966, attributable to the substantial decreases in many southern counties. Whereas settlement and early farming practices in the south first benefited this and other grassland species, the more recent land-use patterns have not been in their favor. —Gail A. McPeek

# HENSLOW'S SPARROW

## (*Ammodramus henslowii*)

There has been much concern of late over this tiny, reclusive bird because of a significant downward trend in numbers over the last few decades. As with a number of grassland species, the ups and downs of the Henslow's Sparrow are tied to human land uses, with forest clearing and farms of early settlement creating more habitat, while the more recent changes and trends have done just the opposite. The result has been widespread declines, severe enough in some parts of its range that several states (including some of our neighbors) have added the Henslow's to their threatened or special concern lists. Although it is not yet so listed in Michigan, significant declines have been documented here as well.

The Henslow's Sparrow breeds from the plains in eastern Kansas and South Dakota east to the New England area and North Carolina. Its current status in Michigan is that of a local and generally uncommon summer resident. During the 1980s Breeding Bird Atlas, this sparrow was reported in a fraction (11%) of the total number of townships in the state. Breeding is largely confined to the southern two-thirds of the Lower Peninsula. There is also a small, disjunct population in the south-central Upper Peninsula, centered in Menominee County, where breeding was first documented in 1985.

Grasslands of a particular kind are the key to the Henslow's distribution and abundance. Choice habitats are neglected grassy or weedy fields with scattered shrubs. These are frequently located in damp situations, although drier upland fields are also used. The feature of primary importance, as determined by numerous studies, is the presence of dense ground cover with a substantial component of dead stems along with new growth.

Because the suitability of such grasslands may change during the course of the season and from year to year, the local population of this bird changes as well. A field hosting a colony of 20 to 30 territorial males one year may not have any the next, just as a field with a colony in early June may be vacant in July if the habitat has been altered in some way. Factors which may make an area unsuitable include natural succession, plowing, mowing, development, or some other disturbance. Studies have found that unmowed timothy-clover hayfields, which are widely accepted by this species, are readily abandoned after cutting, and that many first nests may be lost if haying occurs at the height of the nesting season.

Henslow's Sparrows generally arrive in southern Michigan during the latter part of April and are present in numbers by the second week of May. Exceptionally early records include individuals seen on 30 March (Kalamazoo) and 2 April (Detroit area), both in 1977. Nesting commences in late May and may continue into late August with second broods or renestings. Males sing a weak, cricket-like "tsi-lick" song, barely audible amid the chorus of Red-winged Blackbirds, Eastern Meadowlarks, Bobolinks, and other songbirds typically residing in the area. The fact that Henslow's breed in loose colonies is some help in that there are usually several males singing in the same field, and sometimes as many as 30 or 40.

Nests are well concealed and extremely difficult to find, since adults spend most of their time on the ground, especially around the nest. Jerome Robins (1971) located nine nests in a brome–alfalfa–red clover hayfield in Kalamazoo County, and all were located at the base of clumps of vegetation and made of old growth (no green stems). A typical clutch contains four to five eggs, and the young leave the nest about 10 days after hatching. Foraging occurs on or near the ground, with insects, such as crickets, grasshoppers, weevils, caterpillars, and ants, forming the bulk of the diet.

An examination of records shows that Henslow's Sparrows are rarely noted in Michigan after mid-August, even though they generally remain on their breeding grounds through September and into October. Late observation dates include a bird killed by a cat in the Detroit area on 27 October 1980, and an individual seen on 10 November 1979, also in the Detroit area. This sparrow is a short-distance migrant, wintering in the southeastern states from South Carolina and Florida west to Texas. —Gail A. McPeek

# LECONTE'S SPARROW
## (*Ammodramus leconteii*)

Familiarity with this species does not come easily. Between its elusive nature and the usual remoteness of the wet, grassy habitats where it lives, the LeConte's is an inconspicuous and little-known sparrow. As a matter of fact, its range and distribution remained largely uncharted for many years. While it is true we have more information about this species today, our knowledge is far from adequate.

The LeConte's Sparrow has a fairly small breeding range nestled within the northern plains and bogs, from Ontario to Alberta and south to the Upper Great Lakes, North Dakota, and Montana. Throughout this area, which includes Michigan's Upper Peninsula, distribution is highly localized and semicolonial in accordance with suitable sedge meadows and other grassy wetlands. For the winter months, populations migrate to similar habitats in the southern United States, west to Texas and Kansas and east to South Carolina and Florida.

In Michigan, this sparrow is considered an uncommon migrant and uncommon local summer resident in the Upper Peninsula. To many the term "rare" probably seems more fitting, but one must take into account the bird's reclusive ways, and for every one found there are no doubt others which go undetected. Even the male's weak, insect-like song is of little help. It is sung at unpredictable times at dawn, at dusk, and after dark.

According to Wood (1951), the first authoritative record of a LeConte's Sparrow in Michigan did not come until 1934, at Munuscong Bay. The following year (1935), Lawrence Walkinshaw and a few colleagues paid several visits to the site, finding a nest on 4 June and 10 singing males on 6 June. The nest contained five eggs which hatched on 16–17 June. Birds were inhabiting the drier borders of a rush-grown marsh, where new stalks grew amid the old and small willows were interspersed throughout. Nests are skillfully concealed beneath the dead cover and woven to live stems. Although they are raised slightly above ground, flooding of nests can cause failure, as Walkinshaw noted at Munuscong. This area was reportedly abandoned following a season of continually high water five years later.

Over time, we have slowly accumulated other summer reports for the LeConte's Sparrow, mostly from Chippewa, Mackinac, Luce, and Schoolcraft counties. The 1980s Breeding Bird Atlas provided a big boost to our information on distribution and

Cyndy Callog

status, with observations from 37 blocks scattered across most of the Upper Peninsula, but still concentrated in the east where open bogs and damp grasslands are most prevalent. The Munuscong Bay site is evidently still deserted. Michigan's largest (and most accessible) breeding population resides at Seney National Wildlife Refuge, Schoolcraft County, where vast sedge meadows provide optimal habitat. Farther west, Marquette and Ontonagon counties had a handful of probable breeding reports, while Keweenaw County had a single confirmation.

The meager number of spring records suggests a migration period of late April to late May. Dates at the Whitefish Point Bird Observatory, Chippewa County, range from 24 April to 20 May. Data from Seney indicate first arrival in early May, with the migration largely complete by the end of the third week. In 1990 as many as 20 males were already present on territory at Seney by 25 May. Early and late spring migration dates for Michigan are 18 April in Berrien County and 2 June on Isle Royale.

In contrast to spring, in which the species seems to largely bypass the Lower Peninsula, there are a fair number of fall reports from the region, mostly in our southern counties. Transients are primarily encountered in September and October, with a peak from late September to early October, based on several records from the 1930–1940 period at the Portage Lake marshes, Jackson County. The earliest and latest fall dates are mid-August and 27 October, both from Berrien County. —Gail A. McPeek

spring observations occurred between 23 April (Allegan County) and 19 May (Delta County). Nearly all reports of this sparrow involve one or two birds, so the observation of at least 28 on 18 May 1984 and 8 the following day at the south end of Stonington Peninsula, Delta County, is especially noteworthy. The two June records are both from the Whitefish Point Bird Observatory, in 1982 on the 4th and in 1989 on the 24th.

Fall migrants are primarily seen in the state in September and October, the earliest published date being from Whitefish Point on 6–8 September 1989. Unusual is the one winter record of an individual found at Pte. Mouillee, Monroe County, on 27 December 1975 by several observers participating in a Christmas bird count. Observations of Sharp-tailed Sparrows in Michigan typically occur in coastal areas, including beaches and wetland habitats, or occasionally in interior marshes. Many of the state's specimens came from a marsh in Jackson County, although in recent decades there have been no reports from this locale.

Care must be taken in identifying this species as it prefers to remain hidden in the vegetation and resembles the LeConte's Sparrow, a close relative which occurs regularly in the state. The Sharp-tail's rich, sulfur-yellow eye line and breast contrast with its gray crown, nape, and cheek patch and make a striking pattern. The LeConte's has a similar appearance but lacks the gray nape and has a white stripe in the middle of its grayish crown. —Gail A. McPeek

# SHARP-TAILED SPARROW

## (*Ammodramus caudacutus*)

This small, stubby-tailed sparrow is a casual spring and fall migrant in Michigan, with one or more individuals reported in most years. There are three recognized subspecies of the Sharp-tailed Sparrow, two of which breed in salt marshes along the East Coast and a third which nests locally in wet meadows and marshes from central Canada to North Dakota and winters along the Gulf coast. Specimens indicate that it is this latter form (*A. c. nelsoni*) which primarily occurs in Michigan.

The first documented record of the Sharp-tailed Sparrow in the state occurred when two specimens were taken in Kalamazoo County on 5 October 1878. Past writings report this species to be more regular in the fall season compared to the spring. Zimmerman and Van Tyne (1959), for example, knew of 22 fall records but only 3 spring. While this is probably still true, it is interesting to note that among the 10 records published in the state seasonal surveys from 1980 to 1992, 6 were from the spring migration period, 2 were from June, and the remaining 2 were from fall. The

*Swamp Sparrow*
*LeConte's Sparrow*
*Lincoln's Sparrow*
CYNDY CALLOG

# FOX SPARROW

## (*Passerella iliaca*)

This large, ground-dwelling sparrow is a common to uncommon migrant and occasional winter visitor in Michigan. Transients seen here are members of the eastern race which breeds in northeastern Canada and winters in the eastern United States, primarily south of the Potomac and Ohio rivers. Another 17 subspecies inhabit Alaska, western Canada, and the western United States.

Fox Sparrows in the East are recognized by their rufous-red tail, rusty highlights on the wings, back, and head, and heavily streaked underparts. By appearance, this seven-inch bird is more likely to be confused with a Hermit Thrush than with any sparrow. And as habits go, it behaves much like a towhee, often remaining hidden in dense undergrowth and using a double-scratch technique to search the litter for food.

Fox Sparrows are early spring migrants. The first individuals arrive in Michigan in March, typically toward the end of the month but occasionally earlier. In 1973, for example, migrants were generally reported in the state after 6 March. Published records identify late March to mid-April as the main passage time in the south, the last two weeks of April in the north. Most Fox Sparrows are through the state by the first week of May. Late dates include stragglers on 12 May in Kalamazoo and Luce counties and one on 28 May in Ontonagon County.

The fall migration occurs primarily during October and early November. Some transients arrive in the latter part of September, particularly in northern counties, and most are south of Michigan by early November. In Berrien County, 30 years of data identify 2 October and 19 November as the average arrival and departure dates. Individuals have been noted as late as 11 and 18 November in the Upper Peninsula.

The number of migrant Fox Sparrows present in Michigan fluctuates from year to year. Flocks of 20 to 40 birds may be common and widespread one spring but rare the next. These fluctuations are probably attributable to weather patterns affecting movements along the Mississippi Valley and Atlantic coastal states, its two principal flyways. When the 3 April blizzard in 1982 grounded scores of birds, Fox Sparrows were noted in large numbers, making it one of the biggest migrations in recent memory.

Swampy tangles, stream borders, and woodlands are among the various habitats used by migrant Fox Sparrows. In fall, flocks also frequent hedgerows, more open fields, and weedy grain fields. They are common associates of juncos and other sparrows, and will come to feeders for millet and other seed.

Winter sightings of this species are rare but seem to have become more regular in recent decades, perhaps as a result of the food provided at bird feeders. Wood (1951) gives only two December records, both in Monroe County, and Zimmerman and Van Tyne (1959) listed three more, two in the south and one of a bird which overwintered in Manistique in the Upper Peninsula. Christmas bird counts dating back to 1970 now indicate that Fox Sparrows are nearly annual winter visitors, though tallies are usually very small (1–5 birds per year). High counts include 11 in 1975–76 and 13 in 1988–89. —Gail A. McPeek

# SONG SPARROW

## (*Melospiza melodia*)

This streaky-brown sparrow with the sweet song is one of our most familiar birds, and rightly so; only the American Robin was reported more frequently during the Michigan Breeding Bird Atlas. The Song Sparrow's ability to use a wide range of habitats, many of which are closely associated with our own, results in ubiquitous distribution few birds can match. In the southern half of the state, it is a common resident year-round, although numbers are considerably lower in winter. Northward, it is a common summer resident and migrant and casual winter bird.

The breeding range of the Song Sparrow stretches from the Aleutians in Alaska east across Canada to the Atlantic and south to northern Georgia, Kansas, and northern Mexico. Within this large range are 31 subspecies which show regional variation in body size, bill shape, coloration, and streaking. Shared characteristics include broad grayish eyebrows, distinctive dark "whiskers" bordering a white throat, and a long, rounded tail. The winter range is similar but shifted slightly to the south, with populations vacating most of Canada (except along the Pacific coast to Alaska) and extending as far south as Florida, the Gulf coast, and northern Mexico.

Almost any habitat you can think of can provide a home for the Song Sparrow. "A bird of edge" is a good description of this species, which has a fondness for places near water. Shrub wetlands and shrub uplands topped the list of habitats reported for this sparrow during the Breeding Bird Atlas. Others include woodland edge, pond and stream margins, and a variety of brushy habitats associated with towns, suburbs, farms, roadsides, and rights-of-way. Feeding takes place either on the ground or in bushes and trees. Weed and grass seeds are the main winter foods, while large quantities of insects are important during the nesting season.

Although some Song Sparrows overwinter in the state, most migrate south of our borders, and their return is first apparent in early March or sometimes even late February if weather conditions have been mild. The main flight is underway by mid-March and concludes around the first or second week of April. Arrival of adult males precedes that of females and first-year males. The migration south in fall generally does not commence until October and continues through November in the southern counties.

With its lengthy or permanent residency on the breeding grounds, the reproductive potential of this species is high, with two and even three broods raised, each containing three to five eggs. In southern Michigan, nests with eggs have been found as early as 2 April and as late as 19 August. Dry years will bring the season to a close sooner than those with ample precipitation.

The Song Sparrow nest, built primarily by the female, is a rather bulky structure (5 to 9 inches across) of grass, weed stems, bark fibers, and leaves. Early-season nests are usually placed on the ground or sometimes in an evergreen, whereas later nests tend to be several feet up in a dense bush or tree. Males sing consistently and are aggressive defenders of territories, mates, and nest sites. Intruders and curious bird-watchers will receive a good scolding if too close to the nest.

The common, widely distributed Song Sparrow is also one of the most common hosts for the parasitic Brown-headed Cowbird and its similar, heavily spotted eggs. In the Song Sparrow's favor is its ability to often rear one or two of its own young along with the cowbird, something most other host species, particularly smaller birds, are unable to do. Nests in April and May are most susceptible, while later ones are usually spared as female cowbirds conclude their egg laying.

Numbers of wintering Song Sparrows in Michigan vary from year to year depending on weather severity. Christmas bird counts provide a good index as to the extent of winter residency. Totals since 1980 have mostly been in the 600 to 1,000 range, with a distribution mostly confined to the southern Lower Peninsula, although occasionally a few individuals are reported farther north. —Gail A. McPeek

# LINCOLN'S SPARROW

## (*Melospiza lincolnii*)

This sparrow is probably more common in Michigan than we realize, but its retiring nature and local distribution make it an easy bird to overlook. The breeding range of the Lincoln's Sparrow extends across Alaska and most of Canada south in the East to northern New England and the northern Great Lakes, and in the western mountains to southern California, Arizona, and New Mexico. In Michigan, it is an uncommon to locally common summer resident, confined primarily to the northern Lower and the Upper peninsulas. During migration this species can be found throughout the state, with fall reports outnumbering those in spring.

One of the first steps in tracking down a Lincoln's Sparrow is knowing the particulars about its habitat. In the Upper Peninsula, breeding is most often associated with cool northern bogs composed of sphagnum moss and leatherleaf plus added ground cover from grasses and sedges. According to Lawrence Walkinshaw, who has found several Michigan nests of this species, those in bogs are usually sunken into hummocks of mosses or lichens over water and concealed by surrounding vegetation.

The other primary habitats used by this sparrow, especially in the north-central Lower Peninsula, are the dry jack-pine plains. The regenerating low growth and debris left after fires and logging apparently provide nesting sites to its liking, and the Lincoln's Sparrow has been a beneficiary of management efforts to increase Kirtland's Warbler habitat. In these situations, Walkinshaw found nests diligently hidden beneath dead bracken fern and grasses. Other habitats which may harbor this species are wet alder thickets and brushy wet meadows.

The arrival of Lincoln's Sparrows in spring is barely noticed owing to their skulking habits and lack of song by males. Records for the state indicate a concentrated passage during the last three weeks of May. Migrants are rarely seen earlier, though there are exceptions, including observations on 12 April 1979 in southeast Michigan and 15 April at Whitefish Point in the Upper Peninsula. Once males reach the breeding grounds, their song becomes the best means of detection, even though they are not persistent singers, nor do they favor singing from an exposed perch. The Lincoln's song is often described as having the similar bubbly notes of a House Wren's and the musical qualities of a Purple Finch's.

Based on the small pool of breeding records for the state, nest building and egg laying begin in the last few days of May or the first part of June, with young fledging between mid-June and mid-July. Incubation of the four-to-five-egg clutch takes about 13 days, and the fast-growing young leave the nest in 9 to 10 days.

It is during fall migration, from late August to mid-October, that most Michigan observers encounter the Lincoln's Sparrow. At this time of year a variety of brushy habitats are used, such as weed fields, farm hedgerows, stream borders, marshes, and even bird feeders. Its shy habits are still apparent, but individuals will often respond to squeaking noises used by birders to entice birds from their concealing cover. Only rarely do Lincoln's linger into November or later, but there are occasional winter sightings, including reports on seven Christmas bird counts between 1960 and 1990.

A comparison of current and past information for Michigan suggests that this sparrow has become more common since the early 1900s. Breeding evidence was first reported in Schoolcraft County in 1932, in Luce County in 1940, and in Crawford County in 1941. By the 1950s, Zimmerman and Van Tyne (1959) upgraded its status to fairly common summer resident in the eastern Upper Peninsula and locally present in summer in Crawford, Oscoda, Missaukee, and Clare counties. Then in 1970, an isolated but rather large population was discovered at a leatherleaf-blueberry bog in the Minden City State Game Area, Sanilac County, in the state's Thumb.

Lawrence Walkinshaw (1983) believed that this increase in records was the result of a real increase in Lincoln's Sparrows rather than simply more effort by observers. Most recently, during the Breeding Bird Atlas, this species was found to be locally common in both the western and eastern Upper Peninsula; locally common in Crawford, Oscoda, and some surrounding counties in the north-central Lower Peninsula; and still present in good numbers at the Minden site in southern Michigan. There also seems to have been an increase in summer reports, including some singing males, in other southern counties such as Allegan, Kalamazoo, and Oakland, suggesting that further southward expansion is a possibility. —Gail A. McPeek

# SWAMP SPARROW
## (*Melospiza georgiana*)

Although not as familiar as its neighbors the Common Yellowthroat, Song Sparrow, and Red-winged Blackbird, the Swamp Sparrow is also a common bird of cattail and sedge marshes, shrubby wetlands, and other similar habitats. Observers cognizant of its metallic, even-pitched song should have no problem finding this common summer resident and migrant in Michigan. Close study, however, requires a bit more effort, not to mention wading boots and a small boat, to gain better access to breeding territories and nests.

The summer range of the Swamp Sparrow includes the eastern half of the northern United States south to Missouri, Ohio, and Maryland, and a large portion of Canada from Newfoundland west to the Rockies. For the winter, populations concentrate in the eastern United States from Texas, the Gulf coast, and Florida north to Iowa, the southern Great Lakes, and Massachusetts. Here in Michigan, Swamp Sparrows are distributed throughout the state during the breeding season, and while most depart in the fall, small numbers stay to overwinter in our southern counties.

Northbound migrants begin arriving in late March, with the main flight commencing in mid-April and continuing into the last week of May in the Upper Peninsula. Michigan's resident Swamp Sparrows are usually on territory by early to mid-May, so movements thereafter are mostly transients on their way to Canada. Nests are generally found between mid-May and the second or third week of July, but earlier initiation is not uncommon for pairs in the south. Among the earliest published dates for nests with eggs are 21 and 30 April. Those found into July may be second broods or renestings.

Though common, this sparrow has a fairly narrow range of habitats acceptable for breeding. Open wetlands, either sedgegrass or cattail, were found to be the habitat of choice during the Breeding Bird Atlas. These are typically large expanses of wetland, but occasionally lake and streamside marshes are suitable. Brushy wetlands and bogs are also widely used, but only if the vegetative growth is not too dense. In large areas of particularly suitable habitat, densities can be quite high as pairs occur in a loose colony of sorts.

The Swamp Sparrow nest is a bulky structure with a base of dead marsh grass and an inner cup of newer grass stems. It is often located a foot or so above water among reeds or in a small bush or tree. Except for times when males sing from their perches, both sexes keep low in the vegetation when foraging and when entering and exiting the nest. Much of their food (mostly insects during breeding) is even obtained from the water's surface. Because nests are usually situated over water that is two feet deep or more, fluctuations in water levels which lead to flooding can be a primary cause of nest failure. Likewise, a drop in level could improve access to nests for mammalian predators.

After the breeding season ends, Swamp Sparrows broaden their habitat use to include a variety of fields, brushlands, and open woodlands, and their diet now includes many weed seeds. Migration south is a gradual process lasting from August to November, with the main flight between late September and late October. Wintering is reported primarily in the two southernmost tiers of counties and occasionally north to Saginaw Bay. Christmas bird counts indicate a fair degree of annual variation in numbers remaining. Since 1970, totals have typically ranged from 50 to 300, with a maximum count of 450 in 1976–77.

Past and present writings generally concur on the Swamp Sparrow's common status and widespread occurrence in Michigan. It continues to be a generally distributed species, though there have been some changes, particularly in the highly developed areas in the south where the impact from wetland degradation is evident in the rareness or absence of breeding pairs. The same is true in some of our agriculturally dominated sectors where drainage and filling of wetlands has long been a common practice. Thus it is surprising that since the breeding bird surveys began in 1966, the average number of Swamp Sparrows detected has increased significantly in Michigan. This result should be interpreted with caution, however, because the sampling of wetlands and other less accessible habitats has reportedly improved over the years. It does appear, at least, that Swamp Sparrow populations are holding their own, which is much more than can be said for most bird species reliant on wetlands. —Gail A. McPeek

# WHITE-THROATED SPARROW

## (*Zonotrichia albicollis*)

Anyone who has spent time outdoors in Michigan's north country has surely heard the sweet song of the White-throated Sparrow, sometimes written as "Old Sam Peabody, Peabody, Peabody." This summer resident is quite abundant throughout the forested habitats of the Upper and northern Lower peninsulas. It is one of the more easily recognized sparrows, by both its song and its striking head pattern, which includes a white throat patch, black and white striped crown, and yellow spots (lores) in front of the eyes. A second color morph with brown and tan crown stripes is also seen in the state.

The White-throated Sparrow has a northern breeding distribution encompassing most of Canada (west to the Rockies), the Upper Midwest, and the northeastern states. Wintering occurs primarily in the middle and southern states of the East, casually farther north, and locally in California, the Southwest, and northern Mexico. Most White-throats migrate from Michigan for the winter, but every year small numbers remain in low-lying brushy areas or neighborhoods with shrubs and feeders, mostly in the southernmost counties. Totals seen on Christmas bird counts for the past several years varied between 53 and 281 birds, and the maximum ever recorded was 390 in 1983–84.

It is during times of migration that the White-throated Sparrow is abundant throughout the state. The spring flight commences in the Lower Peninsula around mid-April with numbers peaking from late April to early May. When movements are their heaviest, virtually every thicket and woodlot has migrating White-throats. The same is true in fall throughout much of September and October. A flock of 20 to 30 individuals scratching in the litter in search of food can make quite a racket. Data from banding stations in Michigan indicate that nearly two-thirds of the birds passing through in October are young of the year.

Breeding populations of White-throats are largely restricted to the northern half of the state where dense coniferous and mixed forests, young or mature, are plentiful. Bogs, muskeg, and other lowland habitats are especially favored and typically support the highest densities of nesting pairs. During the Breeding Bird Atlas this sparrow was among the most common birds reported in the Upper Peninsula, and it is especially abundant on Isle Royale. White-throats are also common breeders throughout the northern four tiers of counties in the Lower Peninsula, but they quickly become scarce south of Roscommon County. Their exact breeding status from Midland County southward is difficult to ascertain because of occasional summer reports, believed to be mostly late migrants or nonbreeders. The species does, however, appear to be a possible breeder in parts of Tuscola and Sanilac counties. In the past, nesting was verified south to Lapeer County.

White-throated Sparrows nest on or close to the ground in dense undergrowth at the edge of a clearing. These sites may be associated with natural openings, such as the edge of a bog, lake, or burned area, or they may be the consequence of logging or clearings adjacent to roads. The nest is well concealed in grassy cover, in a slash pile, or under a low-hanging branch. Clutches usually contain four to five eggs, which are incubated by the female alone for about two weeks. The nesting season in Michigan extends from May to August, with two broods possible but considered to be rare. By late summer, birds which have completed breeding begin to gather in loose flocks in preparation for the southward migration. Juveniles can be recognized by their heavily streaked breasts and sides.

The White-throated Sparrow is extremely common at bird feeders, both during migration and on the breeding grounds. The best way to attract this species is to spread millet and oil sunflower mixes on the ground in an area that is near shrubs or other protective cover. Wild foods include many weed seeds plus some fruits (such as dogwood, elder, and spicebush), buds, and insects. —Dick Schinkel

*Dark-eyed Junco*
*White-throated Sparrow*
CYNDY CALLOG

Cyndy Callog

# GOLDEN-CROWNED SPARROW

## (*Zonotrichia atricapilla*)

The Golden-crowned Sparrow is an accidental visitor to Michigan, recorded two, and possibly three, times in the state. The normal range of this sparrow is in far western North America from Alaska to California. Vagrants to the East have been confirmed on exceedingly rare occasions. The first documented Michigan record came on 12 January 1978, when an immature bird was captured during banding operations in Barry County (Wykoff 1979). This individual was photographed, banded, and released and for the next few months (until 3 April) was seen by many observers at the feeding station where it was captured. Based on measurements taken during banding, there is also the possibility that this bird was a Golden-crowned/White-throated Sparrow hybrid (Payne 1979). The second record is of an unmistakable Golden-crowned Sparrow in breeding plumage found on 1 May 1991 near Hickory Corners, Barry County, confirmed by photographs and seen by several observers. This individual, which remained for four days, was seen at a feeder with flocks of White-throated and White-crowned Sparrows, its close kin. In addition to these two documented records, there is an uncorroborated report in the autumn seasonal survey of a Golden-crowned Sparrow sighted on 14 October 1976 in East Lansing, Ingham County. —Gail A. McPeek

# WHITE-CROWNED SPARROW

## (*Zonotrichia leucophrys*)

This large sparrow with the boldly striped black and white cap is a common transient and rare winter resident in Michigan. Those who live in rural or suburban areas and feed birds are probably most acquainted with this species, which is often seen in the company of its more abundant eastern cousin, the White-throated Sparrow. Seed scattered on the ground with plenty of brushy cover close by offers the most hospitable situation for White-crowns.

Both the breeding and wintering ranges of this species are quite expansive, particularly in western North America. Nesting populations in the East are limited to subarctic Canada, while those in the West occur throughout Alaska and Canada and south in the mountains to California and northern New Mexico. In winter, White-crowned Sparrows are distributed over most of the central and southern United States, with highest densities in the Southwest. Of the five recognized races, *Z. l. leucophrys* (black-lored) is the primary form found in Michigan, with an occasional *gambelii* (white-lored) reported.

Southbound migrants generally reach northern Michigan in the second and third weeks of September. Earlier arrivals are occasionally noted, but none have surpassed the 8 August 1919 record of a White-crown at Douglas Lake in Cheboygan County. By the last week of September the species is also common in southern Michigan. In Berrien County, the date of arrival averaged over 30 years was 26 September. Passage through the state is largely complete by late October, with stragglers and/or potential overwintering birds seen into November, even in the Upper Peninsula.

White-crowned Sparrows generally travel in small flocks of 5 to 20 birds in the fall. The difference in abundance between this species and the White-throated Sparrow is well illustrated in data collected at various stations around the state. At the Whitefish Point Bird Observatory, for example, 20 White-crowns were banded in 1991 compared to 269 White-throats.

The spring season brings larger numbers of White-crowned Sparrows through Michigan. During the height of the migration, it is not uncommon for observers to record up to 100 or more in a day. Concentrations are especially pronounced at Whitefish Point, where in 1987, 951 individuals were banded in spring, with a peak of 600 on 17 May.

This species seems to be in no hurry to return to its subarctic summer home. Transients rarely reach Michigan until the latter half of April, with the majority en route in the second and third weeks of May and a fair number lingering into early June, mostly in the northern counties. Particularly late records include an individual present from 14 to 21 June 1982 in Kent County, two males singing as if on territory from 11 June to 5 July at Whitefish Point, one on 1 July 1978 in Jackson County, and a male singing on 12 and 13 July 1990 in Presque Isle County. Even though some of these behave like territorial birds, there is no evidence that breeding has ever occurred this far south of its normal range.

The winter status of this sparrow in Michigan has changed quite markedly in recent decades—a trend evident in other northern states as well. There are only two published reports in the literature up through Zimmerman and Van Tyne's 1959 checklist, and yet White-crowns have been observed regularly on Christmas bird counts since the 1960s, with totals typically ranging between 50 and 80 birds. The heavily supplemented food supply provided by bird feeders has probably played the major role in this status change. Count totals in the 1980s ranged from 23 in 1981–82 to 178 in 1985–86. The majority of individuals occur in Berrien County, but during years of larger numbers such as 1985–86, White-crowns are also found scattered across southern Michigan. There was even a sighting in the Upper Peninsula (Marquette) that winter. —Gail A. McPeek

# HARRIS' SPARROW

## (*Zonotrichia querula*)

With its pink bill and black facial mask, an adult Harris' Sparrow is easy to recognize when one appears in Michigan. This species is an uncommon to rare migrant and rare winter visitor in the state. Its breeding grounds are in a small zone of subarctic habitat in north-central Canada, and winters are spent primarily in states along the eastern border of the Great Plains.

A review of state records shows that the majority of migrant Harris' Sparrows occur in the western Upper Peninsula, with fall sightings usually outnumbering spring. Among those counties where individuals are regularly seen are Ontonagon, Houghton,

Keweenaw, and Marquette. There are also a fair number of reports from those Lower Peninsula counties bordering Lake Michigan. Occasionally birds wander to the far eastern side of the state, appearing in such places as Whitefish Point, Chippewa County, and Port Huron, St. Clair County.

Spring dates for the Harris' Sparrow range from the latter part of April to the end of May, though by far the majority of reports come during the middle two weeks of May. Nearly all spring records are of singles present at a site for only one to a few days. Fall transients, which are more prone to linger, are seen primarily in October, but records span the period from mid-September through November. Published reports in the seasonal surveys indicate that in addition to singles, small flocks of 2 to 10 birds are sometimes observed in the fall.

Every once in a while Michigan experiences an influx of migrant Harris' Sparrows in the fall. Sometimes these incursions are only local, as happened in 1983 when "hundreds" passed through White Pine, Ontonagon County, between 21 September and 5 October, with more than 10 seen on 2 October. At other times the influxes are more widespread, as was the case in 1987. Reports that fall included 1 seen from 19 September to 5 October in St. Clair County, 2 on 23 September in Keweenaw County, 1 on 26 September in Leelanau County, 1 from 29 September to 12 October in Houghton County, 1 from 14 to 17 October in Kalamazoo County, and 1 in November in Berrien County.

Rarely, a Harris' Sparrow or two are seen in Michigan during the winter. Including those from Christmas bird counts, there are published reports from 12 winters between 1959–60 and 1991–92. These are mostly singles which appear at feeders and remain for much of the season. Unlike those during migration, winter records are not concentrated in the western part of the state but are widely scattered throughout.

Hedgerows bordering fields in rural country as well as bird feeders are the best places to search for this species in Michigan. Individuals are often seen in the company of White-crowned Sparrows, a close relative. In the fall and winter months, Harris' Sparrows are more variable in plumage owing to the presence of molting (or molted) adults and immatures. Winter adults, for example, may show only a black chin and throat rather than the full mask. Immatures resemble winter adults but lack the bold facial features, although their brownish head and dark whisker marks hint of the pattern to come. —Gail A. McPeek

# DARK-EYED JUNCO

## (*Junco hyemalis*)

This common and popular feeder bird is more familiar as a migrant and winter resident in Michigan than as a breeding species. During times of spring and fall migration, Dark-eyed Juncos are found in sizable numbers throughout the state, and in winter they flock to feeders for the generous portions of millet and other seed we provide. Indeed, for many people, it is the arrival of this "snowbird" that signals the beginning of winter.

Like many members of the sparrow family, this species has several distinct races. The breeding range for all races or forms,

known collectively as the Dark-eyed Junco, is associated with the boreal and mountainous evergreen forests of North America. The Slate-colored race has the largest distribution, nesting throughout most of Alaska and Canada south to the Upper Great Lakes (including northern Michigan), the northeastern states, and extreme northern Georgia in the Appalachians. The other four races (White-winged, Oregon, Pink-sided, and Gray-headed) have more limited, westerly distributions.

The winter range of the Dark-eyed Junco includes southern Canada, the United States (except for the southern tips of Florida and Texas), and northern Mexico, with Slate-colors residing primarily in the East. Nearly all juncos in Michigan are of this form, but occasionally, in times of migration or winter, individuals of the black-hooded Oregon form are seen. Additionally, there are some apparent records of the White-winged race, such as a November specimen from Alpena County and another banded on 18 September in Presque Isle County in 1972 (Payne 1983).

During the autumn and winter months juncos are social birds, consorting in flocks which are readily visible as they forage about in fields, fencerows, and woodland edges. The fall migration in northern Michigan occurs from late August to mid-October, with the main flight in the south from late September to early November. Largest numbers move through during October, as evidenced by the high count of 3,000 recorded on 12 October 1974 in Berrien County. By mid-November those still present make up the state's winter population.

Winter flocks tend to be small, typically 15 to 25 individuals. It is not uncommon for these flocks to associate with those of the American Tree Sparrow, and the two are frequently seen together foraging at bird feeders or in snow-covered fields. Juncos are common winter residents in the southern Lower Peninsula, and uncommon to rare in the north. Records show that a few remain even in such far northern counties as Houghton in the Upper Peninsula. Christmas bird count totals for the state vary widely from year to year, depending on weather conditions. From 1980 to the present, counts ranged from a low of 8,640 in 1991–92 to a record high of 22,636 in 1985–86.

Spring migration begins in March and occurs primarily in April, with only a few juncos lingering in southern Michigan past the second or third week of May. Breeding in the north begins in May, with most nesting during the month of June. Early records include a nest with five eggs found 30 May in the Upper Peninsula, and adults feeding already fledged young on 15 June in Oscoda County. Pairs with such early successful first nests are likely to attempt a second brood.

Breeding habitat of the Slate-colored Junco includes mixed and coniferous woods, with birds exhibiting a decided preference for edge situations, such as those created by small clearings, streams, or small roads. Their ground nests are usually located on a bank or slope, or against an exposed tree root or fallen log. Occasionally, nests are placed several feet up in a tree. Incubation takes nearly two weeks, and the young fledge in 11 to 12 days, or sooner if disturbed.

During the breeding season, juncos are generally distributed across the Upper Peninsula and the northern third of the Lower Peninsula. Abundance tends to be higher in the Upper Peninsula, but pairs are also locally common in a few Lower Peninsula counties, particularly those in the north-central region where jack-pine forests are the predominant habitat. About one hundred years ago, nesting was documented for a few southern counties, but in modern times no breeding has been confirmed south of Missaukee and Arenac counties. Present-day records do indicate, however, that occasional summer sightings in the south are not unexpected. —Gail A. McPeek

## MCCOWN'S LONGSPUR

### (*Calcarius mccownii*)

Certainly the rarest longspur to occur in the northern Great Lakes region, the McCown's has been recorded only once in Michigan. This species breeds from southern Alberta east to North Dakota and south to Colorado, and winters from Arizona and southwestern Oklahoma south to northern Mexico. It is considered uncommon even in the center of its range, breeding in remnant short-grass prairies and similar dry habitats. The McCown's is not known to wander, making the appearance of a male on 27–29 May 1981 at Whitefish Point in Chippewa County even more extraordinary. This individual remained near the beach and was easily seen and photographed by many birders. To gauge the rarity of this sighting, one must only consider that at the time of this writing Ontario, whose bird list exceeds Michigan's by nearly 50 species, has no record of a McCown's Longspur. —James Granlund

## LAPLAND LONGSPUR

### (*Calcarius lapponicus*)

The Lapland Longspur is a common migrant and uncommon to rare wintering species in Michigan. Often the only evidence of this skulking bird is a dry rattle heard when it is flushed from beneath your feet. Lapland Longspurs are typically found on migration along the Great Lakes shoreline or wintering in open fields with Snow Buntings and Horned Larks.

Both Walter Barrows (1912) and Norman Wood (1951) characterized this species as a transient and winter visitant. However, they also indicated that the exact status was uncertain because of the highly irregular nature of its encounter. This description remains true today as the Lapland Longspur is irruptive, being common some years and difficult to find in others. Still, during both spring and fall migration, a considerable number of individuals are encountered each year.

The first spring migrants begin arriving in late February, with the movement peaking in mid-March in the Lower Peninsula and in mid-April in the Upper Peninsula. Most have departed by mid-May, although a few individuals linger into the last week of May in northern locales such as Whitefish Point, Chippewa County. Here, Laplands have been recorded as late as 29 May in both 1977 and 1979. Spring transients are often encountered in sizable flocks numbering 50 to 100 individuals, sometimes even larger. An extraordinary concentration of more than 3,000 was seen on

16 March 1986 at a sod farm in southern Clinton County.

Fall migrants may begin appearing as early as the first week in September; however, the migration begins in earnest in mid-September and quickly reaches a peak in late September and early October. Numbers dwindle quickly in the Upper Peninsula by late November and early December, although each year a few birds overwinter in flocks of Snow Buntings. In the Lower Peninsula numbers may remain high into late December, but by January most Lapland Longspurs have passed through the state. As in spring, most flocks encountered are of 50 to 100 birds. Exceptional concentrations include 400 on 7 October 1989 at the Muskegon Wastewater System and 250 on 5 October 1991 in Manistee County.

In some milder winters, this species can be quite common in the southern half of the Lower Peninsula throughout the period. On Christmas bird counts from 1970 to 1991, approximately 1,500 individuals were recorded, with a high total of 428 in 1973–74, of which 414 were seen on the New Buffalo count in Berrien County. Other good years were in 1977–78 with 194 and 1987–88 with 249, and in each case, 140 were reported on the South Kalamazoo count. More typically, however, only a small number of individuals are encountered in locales with ample agricultural fields, particularly in the southwestern part of the state.

The Lapland Longspur is Holarctic in distribution, being one of the commonest breeding birds on the tundras of the Northern Hemisphere. In North America individuals winter from southern Canada to central Texas, with largest numbers found in the southern Great Plains. —James Granlund

## SMITH'S LONGSPUR

### (*Calcarius pictus*)

Of the four longspur species, this one shows the greatest amount of white in the outer tail feathers. Although this may be a useful field mark, it is likely one would notice a Smith's Longspur because of its strong face pattern and rich buffy underparts. There are three records for this species in Michigan, all documented with photographs. The first record was of a male molting into breeding plumage which lingered in Midland from 25 April to 2 May 1971. The second was a male seen on 20 October 1981 in Ontonagon County. Most recently a basic-plumaged female was present from 17 to 20 September 1993 at Whitefish Point, Chippewa County.

Smith's Longspurs breed locally near the treeline from central Alaska east to Hudson Bay and winter mainly in the central Great Plains. The eastern edge of their migration route appears to bring them up the west side of Lake Michigan, since birds are annually found in good numbers in northern Illinois and Indiana. However, the species is rare to casual in Wisconsin and only accidental in Michigan. This situation has perplexed birders in both states. Some hypothesize that if observers could find the preferred stopover habitat and gain knowledge of the migration chronology, the Smith's Longspur could be found regularly in Wisconsin and Michigan. So far such efforts in both states have met with failure. An equally likely explanation is that birds fly directly from staging areas in Illinois and Indiana to their breeding grounds without stopping for significant periods of time. —James Granlund

## CHESTNUT-COLLARED LONGSPUR

### (*Calcarius ornatus*)

The bright chestnut nape for which this bird is named is found only on the male, being most obvious in the very elaborate alternate or breeding plumage. The female Chestnut-collared Longspur is the least marked of all the longspurs, particularly in basic or winter plumage. Michigan has four records of this species to date, all in spring and including both of the above plumages. Three of the four records come from Whitefish Point, Chippewa County, with a breeding-plumaged male on 31 May 1980, and another on 28 April 1985, and a basic-plumaged female on 18 May 1988. The first and last records were each documented by a photograph. The fourth record was of a female from Brockway Mountain, Keweenaw County, on 9 May 1982; however, detailed documentation for this observation is unavailable. The Chestnut-collared Longspur nests in the northern Great Plains from southeastern Alberta and Manitoba south to northeastern Colorado and northern Nebraska. It winters primarily in the southern Great Plains from Arizona east to Texas and south to Mexico. This species often wanders during migration and has been recorded in several of the Great Lakes states as well as on the Atlantic coast. Based on this, it is a likely candidate to be found in the state again, particularly at Whitefish Point. —James Granlund

## SNOW BUNTING

### (*Plectrophenax nivalis*)

The spectacle of a flock of Snow Buntings swirling over a wintry field is best likened to a snow flurry; it is no wonder that its local name is Snow Bird or Snow Flake. This species is Holarctic in distribution, nesting on the high tundra, farther north than any other passerine. In North America it winters from central Alaska east to Labrador and south to northern California and the Carolinas. In Michigan, the Snow Bunting is a common migrant and winter resident, although its abundance is quite erratic.

The first Snow Buntings may appear as early as late September, but the main migration begins in early October in the Upper Peninsula and about two weeks later in the Lower Peninsula, with numbers peaking in November. Snow Buntings are sometimes encountered in very large flocks in autumn. Examples include 3,000 on 6 November 1976 and 2,500 on 21 November 1981 at the Muskegon Wastewater System, and 2,000 on 20 October 1981 in Marquette County. More typically, though, flocks range from just a few birds to a couple hundred individuals.

Snow Buntings have mostly moved south of the Upper Peninsula by late December, although each year some flocks remain through the winter. Good locations include the fields in the Rud-

yard area, Chippewa County, and the shorelines of Lakes Michigan and Superior. In the Lower Peninsula, Snow Buntings remain through the winter in varying numbers, depending on habitat and weather. Some years flocks can build to incredible sizes. Examples include 4,000+ on 24 January 1963 in Clare County, and estimated flocks of 5,000 in late February 1978 in Kalamazoo County, 13 January 1980 in St. Clair County, and 14 February 1988 in Lenawee County. Whether these are overwintering birds or migrants returning north is difficult to judge. On Christmas bird counts since 1970, numbers of this winter resident ranged from 2,058 in 1974–75 to 13,841 in 1989–90, with most individuals being found in the northern Lower Peninsula.

The northward migration of Snow Buntings certainly starts in earnest by early March and continues en masse through March and into early April. By mid-April only a scattering of birds are found in the Lower Peninsula, and by mid-May nearly all are gone from the Upper Peninsula. A straggler or two are typically seen into late May along the Lake Superior shoreline, particularly at Whitefish Point, Chippewa County. The latest published date is of an individual collected in Midland on 31 May 1961, farther south than expected. As in fall, large flocks with thousands of buntings can be encountered. Exceptional totals include 5,000 in late March 1981 and 3,000 on 28 March 1986 at Fish Point, Tuscola County.

The Snow Bunting is most often encountered in open fields and along the beaches of the Great Lakes. It is easily recognized in flight by the large white wing patches and distinctive whistled "teer" or "tew" notes. One of the best ways to find Snow Buntings in any season is to visit large fields, particularly ones which offer an ample supply of weed seeds or other forage. They can often be spotted from a great distance as flocks "roll" along feeding. —James Granlund

## BOBOLINK

### (*Dolichonyx oryzivorus*)

The Bobolink is a characteristic breeding resident of large grassy meadows, where the male attracts attention with his unusual plumage and delightful song. In Michigan, this species is common and widely distributed throughout the Lower Peninsula, being somewhat less common in parts of the Upper Peninsula. Numbers are greatest where large fields are allowed to lay fallow or are cultivated for hay. Bobolinks are found in abundance in many such areas in the northern Lower Peninsula, as well as the northeastern Thumb and sections of the Upper Peninsula, particularly near Sault Ste. Marie. Populations are smaller and more scattered in the urbanized and intensively farmed areas of the southern counties and the extensive forested areas in the north.

The rather unusual name refers to the Bobolink's song. Any transcription in words is vastly inadequate to express this rapid jumble of sounds. The reedy, musical notes pass by ebulliently, almost too fast for the ear to distinguish, in a pattern of ascending pitch. Equally distinctive, though not so memorable, is the call note—a single metallic "pink," often heard overhead in the early morning during the fall migration.

The Bobolink's song, along with the accompanying songs of Savannah Sparrows and Eastern Meadowlarks, makes up a typical morning chorus in our grassy meadows. A single large field may host 8 to 10 male Bobolinks, and a like number of much less conspicuous females. Flying with fluttering wingtips, the males deliver their song from the air, often several at once in different quarters of the field. The area bustles with activity as energetic males spend much of their time chasing females or each other. Though most of Michigan's Bobolinks nest in hayfields, pastures, or old fields, they also can be found in some grassy marshes in the Upper Peninsula where other field habitats are relatively scarce.

The Bobolink's entire summer range forms a somewhat narrow band across the northern United States and southern Canada from the Atlantic coast to British Columbia. A long-distance migrant, this species travels to the grasslands of Argentina, where it winters in huge flocks. In fall the whole population heads toward the East Coast, then south through Florida across the Caribbean and on to South America. The return flight retraces these steps but crosses the Gulf of Mexico in a broad front.

Departing Argentina in March, Bobolinks reach southern Michigan about 1 May, with a few usually seen in late April. Females come a few days after males, and in the Upper Peninsula arrival is about ten days later than in the southern part of the state. Nests are built during the latter half of May, with eggs laid in late May or early June, although renestings may extend the breeding season into July. Failures can be especially high in hayfields, where modern harvesting practices are often carried out during peak nesting time for this species. With the decrease in fallow fields and a greater dependency on hayfields, numerous authors attribute local and regional declines in Bobolinks to such nesting losses.

The nest is a frail cup hidden in dense tall grass or other herbaceous cover. The nest was regarded by A. C. Bent as among the most difficult to find. Like many grassland species, Bobolinks do not take flight from or land near the nest but instead walk a substantial distance on the ground before leaving or arriving. Trusting to their near-invisibility on the nest, incubating females will allow themselves to be approached within a foot or less without flushing.

Bobolink clutches contain four to seven eggs, and the young are able to leave the nest in about three weeks after laying. Once nesting duties are complete, these sociable birds gather in flocks. Where abundant, I have seen groups of 10 to 15 males loafing together in nesting areas as early as mid-June after their mating activities were through. By late July, male Bobolinks have molted into their duller winter plumage. Large flocks of males, females, and immatures reside quietly in damp, weedy areas before heading south. Fall departure for most of our population occurs in

August, with individuals remaining into October once in a while. Arrival in Argentina is mostly in November. —Jack Reinoehl

# RED-WINGED BLACKBIRD

(*Agelaius phoeniceus*)

The Red-winged Blackbird is the most typical of Michigan's roadside birds. During spring and summer, on a fencepost, bare tree, or other exposed perch, one is likely to see a territorial male Redwing anywhere in the state. This black bird with the bright red wing patch readily attracts attention, and if you walk near an active nest the male becomes even more conspicuous. Hovering low overhead and diving noisily toward the intruder, he dramatically does his best to protect nest and young.

This blackbird ranges from Alaska and Canada south to Costa Rica, being absent only where excluded by tundra, desert, or unbroken forest. In winter it withdraws generally from Canada and the northern states, concentrating in massive numbers in the southern part of its range. The species is found throughout Michigan during migration and in summer, but in only a few locales in winter.

In my home county of Hillsdale, Red-winged Blackbirds are entirely absent for most of the winter. Their arrival varies with the weather in late winter and early spring. During the last 11 years, the first birds were seen before 15 February three times and after 5 March three times. Soon after first sighting, males are on territory everywhere in the county, posing with their bright red epaulets on display as they sing their gurgling "ong-ka-ree."

Females do not arrive until a week or two after males, and with them arrive many Red-wings which will establish territories farther north. When bad weather delays their northward migration, these transients gather in huge noisy flocks with other species of blackbirds, roosting at dusk in the vicinity of lakes and swamps. Adverse weather will also bring this species to bird feeders in numbers. Spring can be very slow to arrive in the Upper Peninsula, and Red-wings may not reach this region until early April.

First nests are built in April or May by the female, and the four eggs are laid soon after. The situation of the nest varies with the habitat used. The woven cup nest may be on or near the ground in a grassy meadow, suspended over water among cattails, or placed in a willow or other bush near the water. Second broods are not infrequent, and the breeding season may extend into August.

Large numbers of blackbirds will frequently nest together in a field or marsh of moderate size. Within these colonies males are regularly polygynous, with two or more females nesting in the territory of a single male. Individual pairs are also observed where a very small amount of habitat is available. A hawk, crow, or other potential predator near nesting Red-wings will be vigorously chased, often by several males together or in succession. Despite this diligent protection, nests often suffer predation from mammals and snakes as well as several types of birds.

In the fall Red-winged Blackbirds, often joined by other blackbirds, gather in large flocks for the migration south. Flocks of hundreds or thousands will visit farm fields, where they consume

*Eastern Meadowlark*
*Bobolink*
*Western Meadowlark*
JOHN FELSING

both grain and insects. The main departure is during October, but birds regularly linger into December in the southern part of the state. They are annually recorded on about 20 Christmas bird counts in the late December–early January period, with numbers statewide usually between 100 and 1,000. However, relatively few birds stay the entire winter except in the extreme southeast or southwest.

Though the male is easily recognized by everyone, the female Red-wing is a confusing bird, especially when not associating with males. The female is a dark brown bird, lighter below and heavily streaked. The larger size and longer, thinner bill help to distinguish it from the many other streaked brown birds, mostly sparrows. In fall, young males closely resemble females but have a hint of red in the wing. —Jack Reinoehl

## EASTERN MEADOWLARK

### (*Sturnella magna*)

The song of the Eastern Meadowlark is one of the typical spring sounds of field and meadow throughout the state. Delivered from a telephone wire, fencepost, or low bush, the whistled song could be transcribed as "tee-yah, tee-yair," with the last note lower and longer. This species also frequently makes an unmusical chatter and other brief call notes.

The Eastern Meadowlark breeds from the Atlantic coast west to Minnesota and Nebraska, and from southern Canada to the Gulf coast. Within this part of its range, populations withdraw from Canada and the northern states for the winter. This meadowlark is also a resident in the southwestern grasslands and throughout Mexico and Central America into northern South America.

The Eastern Meadowlark is a common migrant and summer resident throughout Michigan. Results of the 1980s Breeding Bird Atlas show this species to be widely distributed in every county in the Lower Peninsula. Northward into the Upper Peninsula its distribution is more localized, mostly because of lack of habitat in areas of extensive unbroken forest. Preferred nesting habitat in Michigan is grasslands of different sorts, with hayfields particularly favored. A few bushes or trees scattered around the area make useful song perches.

Although common in the state, Eastern Meadowlarks seem to have decreased somewhat in the last few decades, based on data from breeding bird surveys. Changing patterns of land use are judged to have caused this decrease, which has affected many grasslands species. More intensive farming eliminates nesting habitat by leaving fewer fallow fields; this species is also clearly vulnerable to early mowing of hayfields. Abandonment of farm-

*Red-winged Blackbird*
*Yellow-headed Blackbird*
JOHN FELSING

land conversely leads to brushland unsuitable for meadowlarks.

The average arrival date of this species in southern Michigan is mid-March. A few individuals usually appear earlier, even in late February if the weather is unseasonably warm. Very cold weather may cause these early arrivals to resume their winter habits, gathering in flocks of 10 to 20 in grain fields. Their winter and early spring food consists of vegetable matter, mostly seeds of grasses and other plants. Come spring and summer a large variety of insects is consumed.

Nest building generally begins in April. The nest, a cup constructed of grasses, is often built in a slight depression in a grassy field. Plants surrounding the nest are woven together to form a matted roof which makes the nest nearly invisible from above and also protects its contents from sun and rain. Eggs (usually five) are typically laid in late April or May and hatch after about 14 days. The young leave the nest in 11 to 12 days, though they are fed by the adults for another two weeks. During this time, the female may be building a nest and laying eggs for a second brood.

Meadowlarks remain in their fields in flocks and family groups through October. By early November most are gone from the state. Each year, however, a few remain into December, and the species is found on Christmas bird counts in southern Michigan. In recent years an average of 10 have been found among the 60 or so counts conducted across the state.

The plumage of the Eastern Meadowlark, common to both sexes, is an interesting example of a number of different types of protective coloration. The back is brown and streaked, blending perfectly into its surroundings. A meadowlark on the ground facing away from an observer is nearly invisible. The contrasting front is bright yellow with a black "V" on the breast, a pattern seen in other birds of open country around the world. This black mark is an example of disruptive patterning, which diverts a predator's eye from noticing the shape of the bird. Finally, the white on the outer tail feathers is an example of flash patterning, which confuses a pursuer by attracting attention while the bird is in flight and then disappearing when it lands. —Jack Reinoehl

## WESTERN MEADOWLARK

### (*Sturnella neglecta*)

The Western Meadowlark, an uncommon bird in Michigan, is virtually identical in plumage to the more abundant Eastern Meadowlark. Although there are subtle differences in appearance, the two species cannot be reliably differentiated by sight alone, and identification should be based on voice. The song of the Western Meadowlark has a rich, flute-like quality, and when compared to the relaxed, slurred whistles of the Eastern Meadowlark, its notes fly by rapidly. This species also has a large number of other vocalizations, including a distinctive soft "chuck" which does sometimes permit individuals to be distinguished from their eastern counterparts in winter.

The range of this meadowlark is western North America. Breeding occurs north in the Prairie Provinces to central Alberta and Saskatchewan and east through Illinois and Wisconsin, where it is fairly common, to northwestern Ohio and southeastern Ontario, where it is rare. In winter Western Meadowlarks withdraw from the northern part of their range, being found then from Washington and Colorado south to Mexico. Small numbers winter along the western Gulf coast.

According to accounts from the previous century, this western species did not occur historically in Michigan. It was first recorded here in Marquette County in 1894, having spread east as settlement continued west, opening up the forests. By the 1930s, nesting had been verified in both peninsulas, though it was still regarded as rare. Numbers increased through the 1950s and 1960s but dropped rapidly thereafter. On breeding bird survey routes in Michigan, only 3% as many Western Meadowlarks were detected in 1981–85 as were detected in 1966–70. The timing suggests that the severe winters of the late 1970s may have played a part in this decline. Also responsible are changes in land use; in fact, most grassland species have experienced population declines in Michigan over the same period, though none so severely.

Currently, this species is spread very thinly across the state. During the 1980s Breeding Bird Atlas it was found in a large majority of counties, but at only one to three sites in most of these. No other land bird whose range covers the entire state is so scarce throughout. In the Lower Peninsula, it was found most frequently in Berrien County in the southwest and in a group of counties in the Traverse Bay area, most notably Antrim County.

The Western Meadowlark inhabits open country. An individual may share its field with an Eastern Meadowlark, but these species have somewhat different preferences. Over the continent as a whole, the Western Meadowlark is dominant where rainfall is less than 24 inches, and the Eastern Meadowlark where rainfall exceeds that total. In Wisconsin, Robbins (1991) noted that the latter species is more likely to be found in untilled pasture, while the former is more fond of grain fields. In Michigan, the most stable populations of Western Meadowlarks seem to be on sandy, well-drained soils. In most other areas they typically occupy the same territory for only a year or two. In areas where both meadowlarks are common, hybridization (detectable in specimens but usually not in the field) was found to be very rare. The difference in songs is apparently sufficient to prevent most interbreeding between these species, in spite of their nearly identical appearances.

Spring and fall migration periods for the Western Meadowlark are the same as for its eastern relative. The nesting habits and appearance of the nest and eggs are very similar as well. The Western Meadowlark has not been detected on any recent Christmas bird counts, but has been recorded during the winter in Berrien County in the past. This would be the most likely place to discover a wintering individual at some future date. —Jack Reinoehl

# YELLOW-HEADED BLACKBIRD

(*Xanthocephalus xanthocephalus*)

The Yellow-headed Blackbird is a highly localized nester in Michigan. This is a result of its specialized habitat requirements and its recent spread into Michigan. Though it is seldom encountered over most of the state, birders can be assured of seeing this blackbird in the spring and summer at Fish Point in Tuscola County or Nayanquing Point in Bay County. The breeding male is a splendid sight—a black bird about the size of a robin with a bright yellow head and breast.

The breeding range of the Yellow-headed Blackbird encompasses western North America, north to central Alberta and Manitoba and south to Oklahoma and southern California. This range extends east along the Canadian border, where the species is common in Minnesota but quite uncommon in Wisconsin. The easternmost breeding locations are sparsely scattered in Michigan, western Ohio, and southern Ontario. Wintering takes place in the southwestern United States and Mexico.

In Michigan, this blackbird is a rare summer resident, being most numerous in the Saginaw Bay area, where it nests in several localities. Among the 13 townships in which breeding was confirmed during the Atlas project (1983–88), 6 were on or near Saginaw Bay. Three more were in Muskegon County, and the rest were widely scattered around the Upper Peninsula. While most sites were near the Great Lakes, breeding was noted at inland marshes in Kalamazoo, Schoolcraft, and Ontonagon counties. Prior to the 1980s, nesting was observed in a few other counties including Cheboygan and Gratiot. Away from nesting areas, this species is a casual migrant and winter visitor.

This western blackbird only recently spread into Michigan. Although the first state record was in 1890 in the western Upper Peninsula, the species was but a visitor seen only in the Upper Peninsula. The first nesting was not observed until the 1950s in Gogebic County, and about the same time Yellow-headed Blackbirds also appeared in the Lower Peninsula at Saginaw Bay.

For breeding, marshes with permanent standing water are required. Cattails or other reeds in two to four feet of water are typical habitat for a colony. Out West these colonies can have 50 or more nests, but in Michigan the largest colony, at Nayanquing Point, is usually about 15 pairs, with a maximum of 20 pairs in 1979. The nest is a bulky structure suspended from reeds one to two feet over the water.

On the basis of records from Saginaw Bay, the average spring arrival of Michigan's Yellow-headed Blackbirds is mid-April, with the earliest sighting in this area on 2 April. Spring migrants are casual away from nesting areas, seen most often in May but sometimes recorded in late April. Upon arrival, males establish territories at a site within the colony. They use both song and display to attract a mate. Their unmusical song is a raspy crackling sound with a pattern slightly reminiscent of a Red-winged Blackbird. The female builds the nest in May, with egg laying in late May and early June. Within three to four weeks after eggs are laid, the young are able to leave the nest. By the end of July, juveniles molt into the plumage they will wear the first winter—dusky brown with a yellowish face and breast resembling the female.

Fall departure is during September, and most of Michigan's small population has left by October. A few are occasionally found in December, and single individuals have been recorded on Christmas bird counts in about one-third of the years since 1975. A high total of four were seen in 1983 on the Anchor Bay count in St. Clair County. —Jack Reinoehl

# RUSTY BLACKBIRD
## (*Euphagus carolinus*)

The Rusty Blackbird has been found nesting in Michigan on only a very few occasions. The spruce bogs of our state rarely host this species, though it nests regularly just north of Lake Superior. Breeding coincides with the north woods from northern New England and the Maritimes west to central Alaska. Its winter range includes the eastern United States north to the southern Great Lakes. This is one of a number of essentially eastern species whose summer range extends far to the west in the boreal forest. In Michigan, the Rusty's primary status is as a fairly common migrant and secondarily a rare summer resident and winter visitor.

The name of this bird refers to the fall plumage, which for both sexes is dull rufous on the head, back, and breast with dark gray wings and tail—an appearance different from that of any other blackbird. By spring males are all black with limited iridescence, while females are uniformly gray. The light eye of the female distinguishes it from the female Brewer's Blackbird, which is otherwise similar in spring.

The easiest way to detect and identify a Rusty Blackbird is by song, which could be transcribed in simplified form as "chu-keeee," with the first note short and scratchy and the second note about an octave higher. The Common Grackle's familiar song is somewhat similar to the ear, but more rattling and without such a long, clear tone at the end. Migrants give the song regularly in spring, often while in flight. It is heard in fall as well, sometimes in a fuzzy version only vaguely reminiscent of the song in spring.

The Rusty Blackbird is present in Michigan for extended periods in the spring and fall as a migrant. The earliest individuals to arrive are seen a week or two after the earliest grackles and Red-wings, often joining in with huge mixed flocks of blackbirds in mid-March. This species remains after these massive congregations have dispersed, and small flocks of Rusty Blackbirds can be found in favored river swamps into early May, even in southern Michigan. In the Upper Peninsula they remain longer; the latest spring record at Whitefish Point is 21 May.

Fall passage through Michigan is even more prolonged. The first southbound individuals return in early September, and the bulk of the migration occurs from late September to early November. Wooded wetlands are again the favored migration habitat, but Rustys also join flocks of other blackbirds in fields and visit feeders for grain late in the season. Lingering birds are found through November and into December, and some are recorded each year on Christmas bird counts in Michigan. Numbers observed vary greatly, from as few as 1 to 10 statewide in some years to more than 1,000 in 1990–91, most on the Rockport count in southeastern Michigan. In 1992, one was even reported on an Upper Peninsula count in Sault Ste. Marie.

There are very few observations in Michigan that verify breeding of Rusty Blackbirds, and actual nests have been discovered only once. These were located in willows along the Paint River in Iron County in June 1943. In the 1980s, an adult attending young in Delta County was reported by an observer for the Breeding Bird Atlas. Also during the Atlas, breeding was confirmed near Betsy Lake in Luce County, an area well known for its rich variety of nesting boreal species. There, adults were observed carrying food into a stand of coniferous trees. The remote area was searched but no nest could be found. Though the species no doubt nests in the Upper Peninsula more often than suggested by this meager number of records, populations are likely small, impermanent, and inaccessible to observers. —Jack Reinoehl

# BREWER'S BLACKBIRD
## (*Euphagus cyanocephalus*)

The Brewer's Blackbird is one of the typical birds of the sagebrush plains in the western United States, where it has adapted well to human presence. There, it is a familiar bird in parks and around residences. In Michigan, to which it has spread only during this century, it is not a well-known bird. The areas around human habitation which it might have occupied were already used by the large, bold Common Grackle. The Brewer's is found in towns and other residential areas sparingly here, mostly in the western Upper Peninsula.

The northern edge of this blackbird's range is in Canada from the Pacific east to central Manitoba. The southern edge stretches from northern Baja California to north Texas. During the 1900s the range has extended east from Minnesota to Michigan and central Ontario, north of Lakes Superior and Huron. In winter the species remains sparingly in the colder parts of its range, while migrants reach the southeastern United States and southern Mexico.

Currently, the Brewer's Blackbird breeds throughout Michigan but is very local and rare in the south. Within the southern Lower Peninsula, large open fields with hedgerows are used, and sod farms are especially favored. It becomes a fairly common summer resident as you reach the northern one-third of the Lower Peninsula and the Upper Peninsula. Many Michigan birders probably saw their first Brewer's Blackbird in the jack-pine plains, a habitat it shares with the Kirtland's Warbler when trees are young. They are also widespread in grassy and brushy areas, including burnt-over lands and borders of marshes and bogs in the north. In Otsego County, I regularly see this species foraging in the I-75 median.

Spring arrival is typically in late March in southern Michigan and mid-April in the Upper Peninsula. This blackbird usually nests in small colonies, but solitary nests have been recorded as well. The cup nest is constructed of twigs and grasses, often strengthened with mud. Michigan nests are usually on the ground in thick cover. Reported egg dates range from May to July.

The fall migration of this species occurs from September to November. Brewer's Blackbirds occasionally linger into December in very small numbers, and in some years are seen on state Christmas bird counts. When found, they are almost as likely to be in northern Michigan as in the south.

The range expansion of the Brewer's Blackbird east across Minnesota and Wisconsin occurred during the first quarter of this century. Moving into Michigan between the early 1930s and mid-1950s, the species spread across the Upper Peninsula and into the northern Lower Peninsula. About this same time it appeared

in the southwestern counties as well, but has never become widely established in this area. At present, Brewer's are essentially absent in the south outside of Allegan County, except for an occasional transient pair or colony. They have never been found nesting in Ohio. In contrast, their spread across the north has continued, and today the Brewer's range extends 250 miles east of Sault Ste. Marie, Ontario.

This is one of three entirely black birds with light eyes. The male Common Grackle and male Rusty Blackbird could both be mistaken for a Brewer's. The familiar grackle is larger, with a creased tail that is wedge-shaped rather than square. The male Rusty is even more similar in appearance to the male Brewer's, and in migration the two are most easily separated by the former's preference for wooded swamps. The female Brewer's is gray with a distinctive dark eye. In Michigan, most Brewer's Blackbirds are seen on territory with both male and female present, so the dark-eyed female provides definite identification. —Jack Reinoehl

## COMMON GRACKLE
### (*Quiscalus quiscula*)

The Common Grackle is the familiar all-black bird, larger than a robin, with a long creased tail. In southern Michigan, it was found in more townships than any other species except the American Robin and Mourning Dove during the recent Breeding Bird Atlas. The grackle readily uses the habitats that people create for themselves, especially well-watered yards with ornamental pine trees for nesting. Its early spring arrival, habit of feeding on lawns, and frequent attendance at feeders combine to make it one of the best-known birds in the state.

The breeding range of the Common Grackle is eastern and central North America west to New Mexico, Montana, and northwestern British Columbia. Northern populations are migratory, and in winter this species is found north to the southern Great Lakes. It is a very common summer resident throughout Michigan but is not quite so abundant in the north as in the rest of the state.

The grackle is found in many different habitats. This bird, which is very content in suburban tracts, may also be seen in large woodlands. There it forages either in trees or on the forest floor, as well as along ponds, where it feeds on various insects and even fish. Grackles are fond of many sorts of wetland; willows and other dense brushy vegetation near water are among their favorite locales for nesting, but the choice of a site is highly variable. The nest is a sturdy structure, often built with a heavy mud base and lined with fine grasses, hair, and other soft materials. Isolated nests are seen, but this species often nests in loose colo-

nies with as many as 20 to 30 nests in a small area.

Along with the Red-winged Blackbird, this is among the earliest species to arrive in southern Michigan in the spring. The arrival may fall any time between 20 February and 10 March, depending on the weather. In the Upper Peninsula, arrival averages a month later. Soon after their return, males use song and display to attract a mate. The male puffs out his feathers, spreads his wings and tail, and throws back his head while delivering his song. Such a display shows off the male's green, purple, and bronze iridescence, which makes these birds very attractive in good light. The loud, two-syllable song is not so appealing to human ears, being sometimes likened to a rusty gate.

Eggs are laid mainly during May, with the young fledging during June. Insects are the main fare of both young and adults in summer. The grackle's diet is extremely varied through the year, including grain and berries in autumn. This species also has the unsavory habit of robbing eggs and young from other birds' nests. After nesting is complete, adults and young gather in large groups. Flocks of grackles flying to their roosts each evening are a sign of the advancing summer throughout the state.

Grackles molt mainly in August and September, and the occasional completely tailless individual may be an identification problem even for an experienced birder. Fall migration takes place in October and early November, and by December few grackles are left over most of the state. In the southwest and southeast corners good numbers may sometimes remain, particularly in the river bottoms of Berrien County, where grackles often overwinter. More than 3,000 have been seen on the Berrien County Christmas bird counts, but the number is more usually in the hundreds. —Jack Reinoehl

## BROWN-HEADED COWBIRD
### (*Molothrus ater*)

The Brown-headed Cowbird, now ubiquitous in Michigan, was certainly rare or absent in presettlement days. The eastward spread of this species from the Great Plains as the primeval forests of eastern North America were cleared for farming is well documented. Cowbirds were already common in New York by 1790 and reached southern Michigan by 1850—the early days of settlement here.

Today, this species ranges over most of North America to southern Mexico, excluding northern Canada and Alaska. In winter it withdraws mostly south of the Canadian border. In Michigan, the Breeding Bird Atlas recently documented that there are no regions of any size where the cowbird is absent, although it is considerably less abundant across most of the Upper Peninsula.

The cowbird is a brood parasite. It never builds its own nest; instead females lay their eggs in the nests of other birds. Usually only open nests are chosen; there is almost no evidence of parasitism on cavity-nesting birds. Most species equal to or smaller than a robin have been parasitized on occasion. Studies have shown that various warblers, vireos, flycatchers, and small finches such as the Field Sparrow and Indigo Bunting are the most frequently chosen hosts of cowbird eggs.

*Rusty Blackbird*
*Brewer's Blackbird*
JOHN FELSING

Female cowbirds find nests of other species by watching for building activity. They generally prefer to deposit their eggs during the time when the owner of the nest is laying. Cowbird eggs are laid mostly in May and June, although activity has been recorded between April and July. The number of eggs laid by a single cowbird in the wild is difficult to determine, but a captive female once laid 13 eggs. Cowbird eggs hatch in 10 to 12 days, an incubation period as short as that of the smallest passerines.

The young cowbird grows rapidly in size and strength and regularly pushes rival eggs and/or nestlings out of the nest. A small songbird feeding a loudly begging young cowbird is an all-too-familiar sight in early summer. Eventually the young cowbird departs, instinctively seeking out pastures and feedlots where it joins birds of its own kind, which it has never before seen.

The cowbird may have a significant effect on the reproductive success of woodland birds in Michigan. For the already small, endemic population of the Kirtland's Warbler, the effect was catastrophic. Woodland species show less response to parasitism than edge and open-country birds, which have contended with the cowbird for millennia. The latter respond in such ways as removing cowbird eggs or abandoning the nest to start another. Since the cowbird operates primarily in early summer, species that raise more than one brood often complete a second nesting without disturbance.

The first migrant cowbirds arrive in southern Michigan sometime between late February and mid-March, reaching the Upper Peninsula in late March or early April. The males soon gather in small groups and display to females. Assuming various postures, they give their gurgling song, which has something of the quality of water quickly escaping a jug. Also heard often in spring is the flight call, consisting of two thin-whistled notes, the first even in pitch and the second downslurred.

In late summer and fall cowbirds become less conspicuous, departing the suburbs and woodlots to gather in pastures. There they feed on insects disturbed by cattle or share the cattle's grain. During the late summer molt, young males assume adult feathers, and their dull brown-gray plumage shows irregular dark patches for a time. Females retain this dull plumage throughout their lives; their most distinctive feature for identification is perhaps their conical bills.

Most cowbirds have left the state by late October. When the weather turns bad late in the season, remaining birds begin to visit feeders regularly. A flock will sometimes overwinter at a suburban feeder in southern Michigan. Largest numbers in winter are found in with the multitude of starlings around cattle barns. Cowbirds are found on state Christmas bird counts throughout the south and occasionally well to the north. In recent years totals have ranged from about 2,000 to more than 6,000. —Jack Reinoehl

your attention. The rich, warbled song, loud and elaborate, has a slightly brassy quality. The singer is not easy to find; it moves relatively infrequently and is hidden by the fresh new foliage. Finally, you see a bird which from beneath is yellow with a black throat, smaller than the familiar Northern Oriole but too large for a warbler. For a Michigan birder, this is a likely description of a first encounter with an Orchard Oriole. The individual you have found is a first-year male.

Adult males are quite different in appearance, with head and back black and rump and underparts a deep chestnut color, appearing completely dark in poor light. Females are dull yellow below and green above with two white wing bars. They are distinguished from the female Northern Oriole by their smaller size and lack of any orange color beneath.

The overall summer range of this oriole encompasses most of the eastern and central United States, west to the base of the Rockies, north in the Great Plains to the Canadian border, and south to northern Florida and into Mexico. In Michigan, this species is an uncommon summer resident in the southern Lower Peninsula, found most commonly in the southern three tiers of counties. It is rare but regular north to Clare and Mason counties, and the northernmost documented breeding is from Leelanau County. Breeding habitat consists of open country with scattered trees. Many Orchard Orioles seen in Michigan are young males, which often sing for a few days in one location, then disappear.

Orchard Orioles arrive in Michigan during the first half of May, with an occasional April sighting. Individuals will sometimes appear north of the usual breeding range during spring migration, often at such spots as Tawas Point in Iosco County. They have even been recorded in the Upper Peninsula but are very rare this far north. Like many other insectivorous birds, this species is drawn to flowering trees to feed on insects attracted to the blossoms.

Nesting occurs from mid-May to mid-July in Michigan. The nest is a woven deep cup suspended from a forked branch, similar to that of a Northern Oriole but not nearly so pendulous. It is usually placed 6 to 20 feet up in a tree or shrub. The four to five eggs hatch within 14 days, and in another two weeks the young are ready to leave the nest. Throughout its range this species is a regular host of the parasitic cowbird. In New Orleans, I once observed an Orchard Oriole feeding juveniles of both Brown-headed and Bronzed Cowbirds. In fact, this oriole was extirpated in the New Orleans area shortly after the latter cowbird species arrived there from the Southwest.

Along with the Yellow Warbler and Louisiana Waterthrush, this oriole is one of the first species to depart Michigan for the south. Although there are a few records for August and September, it is seldom seen past the end of July. Wintering birds are found from

# ORCHARD ORIOLE

### (*Icterus spurius*)

While you are birding in southern Michigan in mid-May, perhaps near a lake or along a tree-lined road, an unfamiliar song attracts

*Orchard Oriole*
*Northern Oriole*
DAVID MOHRHARDT

southern Mexico to northern South America, where large flocks feed on flowering trees.

This species appears to be declining in much of its range. During the last 25 years, a significant decrease in numbers was detected in the nationwide breeding bird survey. In Michigan an expansion of the range northward has been observed, and good numbers were found in many southern counties during work on the Breeding Bird Atlas (1983–88). Increases in range and numbers have also been noticed in Ohio during the last few decades, so this oriole appears to be faring better in the Midwest than in other parts of the country. As already pointed out, however, the species is quite vulnerable to cowbirds, which may be part of the reason for its overall decline. Another suspected factor is the heavy use of pesticides in orchards, on both breeding and winter grounds. —Jack Reinoehl

# NORTHERN ORIOLE

## (*Icterus galbula*)

A familiar wintertime sight along country roads is a finely woven cup nest suspended from the tip of a slender branch of a large tree. This intricate nest, the lower end of the deep cup somewhat globular in shape, belongs to the Northern Oriole. The strength of the nest is evident from its survival into the winter; hanging from twigs, it is safe from larger predators. It is a structure of both utility and beauty.

When the leaves are gone and the nests are visible, the orioles are also gone from the state. Small numbers winter in the southeastern United States, but most retreat to Central America and northern South America. The summer range covers most of the United States, excluding Florida and the Gulf Coast region, and extends north to southern Canada and south to Mexico.

Prior to 1983, eastern representatives of this species were known as the Baltimore Oriole, and those west of the Great Plains were called the Bullock's Oriole. Male western birds, with their orange cheek and large white wing patch, look quite different from eastern males with their all-black head and mostly dark wings. Both share the brilliant orange underparts, which grow more vivid as the bird ages. Since these two varieties are known to hybridize extensively in the central part of the continent, they were combined into a single species by the American Ornithologists' Union.

In Michigan, the Northern Oriole is a common summer resident, especially in the Lower Peninsula. There it can be found in every township. In the Upper Peninsula, it is absent from extensive areas of coniferous forest and most common in the southwestern region adjoining Wisconsin. Near Lake Superior it is particularly scarce, although individuals have been found even on Isle Royale.

This oriole's habitat is deciduous woodlands of different types. It is perhaps most familiar as an inhabitant of mature shade trees, being a typical nesting species in the groves of trees around houses in farm country and in parks and towns. Orioles also enjoy lakesides, streamsides, and swamps with willows and occupy less open habitats as well, both edges and interiors of deciduous forest.

Average spring arrival of the Northern Oriole is around 1 May in southern Michigan and about ten days later in the Upper Peninsula. As with many songbirds, males arrive first to establish a territory. Their song and bright colors proclaim the territory and attract a female. The song is a rich melodic whistle, the pattern of which is extremely variable from one male to the next. Both sexes give a harsh scolding chatter when excited and whistled call notes that resemble the male's song in quality.

Nesting in Michigan is primarily from late May to late June. The birds' diet consists mainly of insects but also fruit and nectar from flowers. If an oriole lives near your home, it can be attracted to close range by a feeder with sliced oranges. They will also visit hummingbird feeders. Around mid-July young birds leave the nesting area, although the family group often remains together for the next month. At this season, orioles are quiet and may easily escape detection.

Orioles depart the state mostly during the last half of August and are rare after 1 September throughout the state. With the advent of feeders and ornamental plantings, this species has expanded its winter range northward, but it is still astounding that this usually Neotropical migrant would attempt to winter in Michigan. Yet it has happened a few times, most recently in the winter of 1992–93, during which an oriole survived the winter at a feeder in Bath, Michigan. This was possible only because the bird had a steady supply of suet and other high-energy food. —Jack Reinoehl

# BRAMBLING

## (*Fringilla montifringilla*)

This small finch, native to Eurasia, is an uncommon migrant to the Aleutian Islands of Alaska, but it is certainly not a species one would expect to see in Michigan. Yet on 25 November 1991, a Brambling appeared at a feeder in Cooper Township, Kalamazoo County, where it remained through 29 November, allowing people from all over Michigan and the Midwest to add this bird to their life list. Excellent photographs were obtained to document the sighting. Bramblings are known to wander and have been seen in many inland locations in North America, including Ontario and Minnesota. Nearly all sightings of this distinctively colored black and orange finch have occurred in late fall or winter at bird feeders. Based on its vagrancy pattern, it would not be at all surprising for a Brambling to appear in Michigan again. —James Granlund

# GRAY-CROWNED ROSY FINCH

## (*Leucosticte tephrocotis*)

The Gray-crowned Rosy Finch is a member of a complex of species which were at one time separated into five species and then "lumped" into one, only to be resplit into four. Regardless, all have the rosy belly and flanks from which they derive their name.

Rosy Finches inhabit the high altitudes of the Rocky Mountains from Alaska to California, where they nest in cracks of cliff faces and tumbled rocks of talus slopes. In winter they withdraw far from home and have been recorded as far east as Maine. Michigan has two records, both documented by photographs. The first was an individual seen on 26 February 1984 at a feeder in Romeo, Oakland County, which remained through March. The more recent record was from 24–27 February 1991 at a feeder in Pigeon, Huron County. —James Granlund

# PINE GROSBEAK

## (*Pinicola enucleator*)

There is no finer sight in a northern Michigan winter than a brilliant red male Pine Grosbeak delicately extracting seeds from cones of a snow-covered spruce tree. This large finch resides throughout the Northern Hemisphere, breeding in North America in the northern coniferous forests from Alaska through Canada and at the higher altitudes of the western mountain ranges south to California, Arizona, and New Mexico. Populations remain in their breeding range in some winters, while in others they withdraw south, sometimes reaching the southern United States.

The Pine Grosbeak is an annual migrant and winter visitor to Michigan, yet the number of individuals present is highly erratic. First migrants may appear as early as mid-October, though more typically they arrive in mid-November, with numbers peaking by mid-December. They are often seen in flocks ranging from 10 to 50 birds, and occasionally larger flocks are encountered such as the 150 seen feeding on Michigan holly on 13 December 1987 south of Paradise, Chippewa County.

Pine Grosbeaks normally winter in the northern part of the state, being found annually in the Upper Peninsula and in most years in the extreme northern Lower Peninsula. Numbers vary drastically from just a few, as in the winter of 1992–93, to extremely abundant, as in the winter of 1985–86. It is during these irruption or invasion years that Pine Grosbeaks can be found wintering throughout the state. Since 1960, records show that noteworthy statewide incursions occurred in the winters of 1961–62, 1965–66, 1971–72, 1977–78, 1980–81, 1985–86, and 1989–90. Fluctuations are readily apparent from Christmas bird count data, which varied from a low of 2 birds in 1970–71 to 2,384 birds in 1985–86 during the 1970–92 period. However, these data are not always representative of winter occurrence, since in some years birds arrive and depart prior to the count period, while in others they may arrive after.

Most Pine Grosbeaks have departed the state by late March. Occasionally an individual or pair may remain well into May. Examples include individuals on 25 May 1988 and 26 May 1991 at Whitefish Point Bird Observatory, Chippewa County.

In even rarer situations, Pine Grosbeaks have been found in Michigan during the summer. There are five published records between 1958 and 1992, including two reports from June and three from July. The June observations are, in all likelihood, lingering migrants, particularly the individual seen on 21 June 1982 in Barry

County. The July records, however, suggest the possibility that this species occasionally breeds in the state, with pairs reported on 12 July 1965 and 2 July 1967 in Melstrand, Alger County, and a female seen in appropriate habitat on 9 July 1986 in Keweenaw County. Not surprisingly, these records and the availability of suitable nesting habitat in the Upper Peninsula have prompted some authors to hypothesize that Pine Grosbeaks breed in Michigan. The fact that nesting pairs occur on the north shores of Lake Superior, as close as Sault Ste. Marie, Ontario, lends credence to this viewpoint. Regardless, there is no direct evidence of nesting. The closest indication of breeding occurred in August 1965, when a female with nearly full-grown fledged young was found on Isle Royale. However, the tendency of this species to disperse immediately after fledging leaves this evidence equivocal.

Pine Grosbeaks breed in open coniferous or mixed deciduous-coniferous habitat, with the nest well concealed in a spruce or fir tree located from 6 to 30 feet high. They sing softly and for a very short duration while on territory, and pairs are extremely secretive during nesting. Perhaps someday a sharp birder will overcome these obstacles and finally locate a nesting pair in Michigan. —James Granlund

# PURPLE FINCH

## (*Carpodacus purpureus*)

The elaborate, musical song of the Purple Finch can be heard in the coniferous forests of much of the northern portion of Michigan. It is a common breeding species in the northern two-thirds of the state and a common migrant throughout, although numbers vary widely from year to year. Purple Finch nest from British Columbia to Labrador, south to the Upper Midwest and Northeast, and down the western mountains to California and the Appalachians to Virginia. In winter they withdraw from this range, some years migrating as far south as the Gulf coast and Mexico.

The Purple Finch's breeding range is strongly associated with conifers, particularly moist habitats with cedar, hemlock, balsam fir, or white pine. As a result of this preference, the majority of breeding in Michigan occurs in the Upper and northern Lower peninsulas, with only sporadic breeding in the southern Lower Peninsula. Historically, Walter Barrows (1912) placed the southern limit of breeding slightly farther north, at the Grand and Saginaw rivers. Norman Wood (1951) noted breeding reports as far south as Kalamazoo, St. Clair, and Ingham counties; however, he discounted them and went on to describe a range similar to that of Barrows. In the late 1960s observers began to report oversummering pairs south of this range, and by 1985 nesting was confirmed in a number of counties south of the original limit. It seems likely that Purple Finch have always nested in the southern portions of the state where proper habitat existed, but in very small numbers and at erratic intervals.

On its main breeding range, the Purple Finch is not uncommon in proper habitat. It is typically found in wet bogs, near waterways and the Great Lakes shoreline, and less commonly in drier habitats such as jack pines, hedgerows, pine plantations, and

Cyndy Callog

ornamental evergreen plantings. Its nest is built of grasses and roots woven together with hair, and is typically placed in a conifer tree, from 15 to 20 feet high, although sometimes much higher. A clutch usually contains four to five light green to bluish eggs which are laid between mid-May and June. Incubation lasts about 13 days, and young are attended by both parents and fledge in about 14 days. Purple Finch are primarily seed and fruit eaters, relying heavily on the former in winter and the latter in summer, while taking insects and other forage when available.

Soon after breeding, Purple Finch form loose flocks which move from one foraging area to another. Although it is difficult to ascertain when migration truly begins, the first flocks appear in southern Michigan by late August to early September. In the Upper Peninsula there is a small peak of migration from October to early November, with most individuals gone by early December, although some may overwinter. In the Lower Peninsula, Purple Finch are common by late October and remain through the winter in areas where forage is abundant. On Michigan Christmas bird counts from 1970 to 1993, the high total was 1,420 reported in 1982–83, and the low was 150 in 1979–80. Typically birds are most abundant in the northern and southwestern portions of the Lower Peninsula.

The northward migration probably begins in late February and continues through March and April, with most migrants gone by May. Sometimes large numbers of Purple Finch are encountered during spring migration, particularly along the lakeshore. Exceptional were the 2,000 counted on 11 May 1982 at Whitefish Point, Chippewa County. —James Granlund

# HOUSE FINCH
## (*Carpodacus mexicanus*)

The House Finch is a recent addition to Michigan's avifauna. This species' original range was from southern British Columbia east to Wyoming and south to central Mexico. In the late 1930s bird dealers in New York City began importing House Finches for sale as "Hollywood finches," but in 1940 authorities were alerted to the illegal sale, resulting in termination of the practice. In that year a dealer released his now unsalable birds, which by the 1950s became established in the wild. By the 1960s House Finches spread throughout the Northeast, and in the 1970s and 1980s the species literally exploded across the eastern United States.

In Michigan the first House Finch was recorded on 13 February 1972 in Berrien Springs, Berrien County. The expansion proceeded slowly in the 1970s, then rapidly during the 1980s. The first

*Purple Finch*
*House Finch*
CYNDY CALLOG

nest was recorded in Southfield, Oakland County, on 17 July 1981. By 1982 reports were received from 11 counties, primarily in the southeastern portion of the state. By 1984 the number of counties grew to 18, with numbers increasing across the southern portion of the Lower Peninsula. In 1986 the species was becoming common as far north as Midland County, and on 2 January 1988 the Upper Peninsula had its first documented record near Cornell, Delta County. The first nest record for the Upper Peninsula occurred on 17 May 1991 in Marquette. By 1992 House Finches had essentially overtaken the entire state, with reports in 44 Lower Peninsula counties and 5 Upper Peninsula counties.

Meanwhile its westward march continued, reaching Minnesota in the 1980s. Amazingly, as the eastern population expanded, so did the western population, steadily moving across the Great Plains. In the mid-1980s it likely reached Minnesota from the west. Certainly by the end of this century the species will have spread from coast to coast.

At present the House Finch is a common resident in the southern two-thirds of the Lower Peninsula and a locally common resident in the northern third. It is still uncommon to rare in the Upper Peninsula, being found only in larger towns or at migration points such as Whitefish Point Bird Observatory. The success of the House Finch is attributed to its ability to use the altered landscapes provided by man. The real centers of abundance are in cities and towns, where it nests in a wide variety of situations. From these centers the species then expands into the countryside, nesting near dwellings or in close proximity to man. It also benefits tremendously from bird feeders for sustenance during the long Michigan winters. In some locations it can displace the normal feeder birds such as Purple Finch, and has even competed for nest sites and food with the nearly irrepressible House Sparrow.

The seasonal occurrence of the House Finch is complicated and poorly understood. Banding data indicate some migration, perhaps along the route taken to reach the state. Additionally, banding indicates a propensity for the birds to disperse after breeding, often hundreds of miles. Regardless, the species is present throughout the year in much of the southern two-thirds of the Lower Peninsula; whether the same birds remain in the same locations is difficult to ascertain. In the northern reaches of the range, most birds seem to withdraw. On Michigan Christmas bird counts, there has been a steady increase in individuals from 1 in 1978–79 to 15,220 in 1992–93.

Nesting commences in late March in the southern portions of the state (later farther north) and may continue into August. The nest is fairly well built of twigs, roots, string, and other materials and is placed in an amazing variety of locations, including conifer trees and ledges on buildings—in fact, any location which affords some protection from the elements. A typical clutch consists of four to five eggs, with incubation lasting between 12 and 15 days and fledging occurring in an additional 11 to 19 days.

The House Finch has an interesting history in that, unlike many other introduced species, it is native to North America. Yet as with the House Sparrow, European Starling, and others, its success is predicated on its ability to coexist with man. Also like these species, it will certainly have an effect on the local birds which may compete for the same resources. Luckily there seems

to be little impact so far. However, the expansion is fairly recent, and only time will tell if the House Finch, with its colorful red plumage and pleasing song, will be a welcome introduction.
—James Granlund

# RED CROSSBILL
## (*Loxia curvirostra*)

Few birds have a name as descriptive as the Red Crossbill—the adult males are truly red, and the bills are bizarrely crossed. The crossed bill is an ingenious adaptation for extracting seeds from conifer cones; this explains the close association between this species and these trees. The Red Crossbill breeds in the coniferous forests of the Northern Hemisphere, being found in North America from southern Alaska east to Newfoundland, south to northern New England and the Upper Great Lakes, and farther south in the Appalachians to North Carolina, and in the Rockies to Central America. It is an uncommon permanent resident in Michigan and an irruptive, sometimes abundant, winter resident and migrant.

This species shows a great deal of variability, and various authors have split it into several species at different times. The debate continues, and it is likely that splits will occur in the future. There are specimens of at least three subspecies in Michigan, including *L. c. pusilla*, *L. c. minor*, and *L. c. benti*, the latter two having been known to breed in the state.

The exact status of the Red Crossbill in Michigan varies from year to year. In most years it breeds sparingly in the state, being locally common in the northern Lower and Upper peninsulas in suitable habitat. Each season it appears that some birds migrate into the state to winter, occurring most commonly in the northern counties, but how many of these birds are local breeders is simply impossible to tell. In some years a major invasion occurs. The reason for these irruptions is not known, although they are likely due to a scarcity of food in the birds' main breeding or wintering grounds.

A good index for these events is the Michigan Christmas bird counts. From 1970 to 1992, the highest total occurred in 1976–77 with 304 individuals, while none were recorded in some other years. Significant invasions outside that period include 1960–61 and 1967–68, when the amazing observation of several thousand Red Crossbills was made on 24 February 1968 along a 25-mile stretch from Seney to Grand Marais (Alger County). I witnessed a similar migration on 3 March 1985 on the road from Paradise to Whitefish Point in Chippewa County.

Many of these incursions are initiated in late summer, with increased sightings as early as late July, but the main migration occurs in November and December, when flocks of several hundred birds are encountered. Examples include 400 on 26 November 1960 in Schoolcraft County and on 28 November 1967 at Naubinway, Mackinac County. During winters of irruptions, birds travel around in groups, decimating cone crops, and then moving on to new areas. In these years they will often reach the southernmost reaches of the Lower Peninsula. Most Red Crossbills begin departing in late January through March; however, good numbers may remain as late as May.

After major incursions, some birds may remain and breed south of their normal range. Examples include a report of an adult attending young on 17 May 1968 in Holland, Ottawa County. But the great majority of breeding occurs in the northern portions of the state, particularly in the Upper Peninsula. Here in Michigan, Red Crossbills seem to prefer red pine for breeding, although nests are not uncommon in jack pine and spruce. The breeding cycle of this species is erratic and may be initiated by the presence of a good cone crop. Typically nesting commences in late winter, extending from February through June, although it could possibly occur in any month.

The Red Crossbill's nest is placed well away from the trunk of a conifer at a height ranging from 5 to 80 feet, with most being between 10 and 40 feet. It is a bulky structure of twigs and rootlets which is well lined with mosses, feathers, or other soft materials. A typical clutch consists of three to four pale bluish or greenish-white eggs, which are spotted with browns or purple. Incubation lasts for 12 to 18 days, with fledging occurring in an additional 15 to 20 days. Once nesting is complete, the young and adults form loose flocks and congregate in areas with suitable cones or other forage. —James Granlund

# WHITE-WINGED CROSSBILL
## (*Loxia leucoptera*)

The prominent white wing bars for which this finch is named are a sure way to distinguish it from the similar Red Crossbill, yet the careful observer will see other differences as well. The bill of the White-winged Crossbill is somewhat slimmer, allowing it to take seeds from spruce and tamarack cones, something the Red Crossbill has trouble doing. This explains why the White-wing is more prevalent in bogs and other habitats which have these trees as their principal component.

Like its close relative, the White-winged Crossbill breeds throughout the Northern Hemisphere, being known as the Two-barred Crossbill in Eurasia. In North America it breeds in the coniferous forest from Alaska east to Newfoundland and south to the northern Great Lakes and the extreme northern portions of the American Rockies and Cascades. This species winters on its breeding grounds and irrupts irregularly as far south as the central Great Plains and Middle Atlantic states.

In Michigan, the White-winged Crossbill is a regular winter visitor to the Upper Peninsula and northern portions of the Lower Peninsula, and an irregular visitor farther south. As with other winter finches, its occurrence is irruptive in nature; it is absent

*Red Crossbill*
*White-winged Crossbill*
CYNDY CALLOG

Cyndy Callog

from nearly the entire state in some years and in others winters abundantly in even the southernmost portions. A good gauge of the White-wing's abundance is the Michigan Christmas bird counts. From 1970 to 1992, the number of White-winged Crossbills varied from a high of 1,491 in 1989–90 to none seen in 1970–71, 1983–84, 1990–91, and 1991–92. Other years of exceptional numbers include 995 in 1992–93 and 713 in 1984–85. During years of increased numbers, it is possible that food supplies on their main breeding grounds have failed, resulting in birds moving south.

During both spring and fall migrations, small numbers of White-winged Crossbills are encountered in northern Michigan. Prior to and after major winter irruptions, large flocks may be encountered, particularly at concentration points such as Whitefish Point, Chippewa County. For example, in the fall prior to the 1989–90 invasion, 777 individuals were counted at Whitefish, including a peak of 127 on 11 November. The following spring at that location, 1,820 were sighted, including a peak of 181 on 27 March. As might be suggested from the preceding data, numbers peak in the fall from November through early December, while in spring numbers swell in late February through March. Even in years of scarcity, lone birds can often be found on migration in the southernmost reaches of the state, some of which may linger through the winter and even through the summer.

In summer, the White-winged Crossbill must be considered a rare breeding species in our state. During the recent Breeding Bird Atlas, only 40 reports were submitted, and only 2 of confirmed breeding, 1 each in Houghton and Marquette counties. Most reports came from the western Upper Peninsula; because of the remoteness of this region, it is quite possible the species is more common than known. Norman Wood (1951) gave a very similar account of this bird's historical status in the state. He could cite but one definite nest record from Delta County, but postulated that the bird may be more abundant in the Upper Peninsula.

The species is an irruptive breeder. Apparently when a suitable cone crop is available, good numbers of White-winged Crossbills will remain within the state and breed. An excellent example of such an event occurred in the summer of 1992 in southwestern Chippewa County, where more than 50 singing males were recorded along two 25-mile breeding bird survey routes. Later visits to the area turned up numerous family groups with dozens of individuals, indicating a sizable number of successful nestings.

White-winged Crossbills may initiate breeding nearly anytime during the year. Certainly the availability of food is important in the onset of breeding. Nests are placed in spruce trees from 8 to 15 feet above ground. The structure is a deep cup of twigs, rootlets, and other materials and is lined with fine grasses, feathers, or bark. A typical clutch consists of three to four eggs which are pale blue to greenish-white with spots, scrawls, or blotches of browns or purples. Much remains to be learned about the breeding biology of this species. —James Granlund

# COMMON REDPOLL
## (*Carduelis flammea*)

The term "poll," meaning top of the head, is unfamiliar to many in Michigan; the Common Redpoll, however, is no stranger. This name refers to the red patch on the front of the crown of this arctic finch. The Common Redpoll breeds throughout the Northern Hemisphere on the margin between the taiga and tundra, and at higher elevations. In North America it is limited to northern Canada and Alaska. There are at least four recognized subspecies, of which *C. f. flammea* or Mealy Redpoll and *C. f. rostrata* or Greater Redpoll have been recorded in Michigan. The former subspecies is far more common and breeds throughout the Northern Hemisphere, while the latter is quite rare and breeds on Greenland and adjacent islands. The Greater Redpoll can be recognized by its darker coloration and larger size.

The Common Redpoll can best be described as an irruptive migrant and winter resident in Michigan, in some years being abundant and in others nearly absent. The causes for these invasions must be tied to food supplies on its main breeding and wintering grounds. Christmas bird count data are a good demonstration of this erratic nature. From 1970 to 1992, the number of Common Redpolls varied from a high total of 10,439 in 1985–86 to a low of 22 in 1990–91.

In noninvasion years the first Common Redpolls begin arriving in November and peak in numbers in December. In invasion years birds begin arriving a month earlier. In the period from 1960 to 1992, the earliest arrival date was 1 October 1989 at Whitefish Point, Chippewa County. During normal seasons, flocks of 20 to 30 birds are typically encountered, whereas during invasions the flocks are often very large, numbering into the hundreds and even thousands. Examples include a flock of 1,000 individuals on 16 November 1968 near Traverse City and a staggering total of 3,000 birds seen on 30 November 1980 in Newaygo County.

In most winters redpolls remain in the Upper Peninsula and northern Lower Peninsula, where they are often found at feeders, in weedy fields, or feeding on catkins of trees and shrubs, particularly alders. During invasion years birds may exhaust food supplies in the north and continue into the southern portion of the state, in some years passing completely through.

Redpolls begin returning north in February through March, when again very large flocks may be encountered. Most individuals have departed the Lower Peninsula by late March, although some may linger; exceptional were 15 on 11 May 1978 in Ottawa County. Common Redpolls are often present through April in the Upper Peninsula, with fewer birds lingering into May. The latest published record since 1960 is that of 14 May 1989 at Whitefish Point, Chippewa County. To date there are no documented summer records for this species.

During invasion years it is easy to find Common Redpolls throughout the state, particularly along the coasts. In most years, though, redpolls are scarce and may be difficult to locate. Perhaps the best locations in these years are in the eastern Upper Peninsula in the Sault Ste. Marie area, and the western Upper Peninsula in the Marquette area. Additionally, birds can often be found on migration at Whitefish Point during November and again from late February into March. —James Granlund

# HOARY REDPOLL
### (*Carduelis hornemanni*)

The term "hoary" means white or grayish-white, a good description of this redpoll, a much paler rendition of the more abundant Common Redpoll. Like the Common Redpoll, the Hoary Redpoll is a bird of the high arctic, breeding throughout the Northern Hemisphere on the tundra. There are two recognized subspecies of the Hoary Redpoll, the Greenland Redpoll (*C. h. hornemanni*) and the Hoary Redpoll (*C. h. exilipes*); both have been recorded in Michigan, although the latter constitutes the bulk of the records.

Unlike its sibling species, the Hoary Redpoll is a rare to uncommon visitor to our state, typically appearing only in years of invasions with the Common Redpoll. To fully comprehend its abundance (or lack thereof), one must only consider that in the period from 1970 to 1993, 87 Hoary Redpolls were reported on Michigan Christmas bird counts, compared to 44,013 Common Redpolls. The Hoary's true status in Michigan is complicated by the complex task of separating the redpoll species. So difficult is this task that many ornithologists treat the Hoary and Common not as separate species but rather as color morphs of the same species, much like the Blue and Snow Goose.

Records indicate that Hoary Redpolls arrive in the state about the same time as Common Redpolls, in November and early December. Exceptional was an individual on 10 October 1991 at Whitefish Point, Chippewa County. They are never present in large numbers; most encounters are of single birds, although groups as large as four have been reported. Hoarys winter primarily in the northern portion of the state, with most records coming from the Marquette and Sault Ste. Marie areas, where they can often be found at feeders or feeding on alder catkins. Many times individuals can be found, with great care, in large flocks of Common Redpolls. In spring, they migrate back north with Commons, most departing the state by late March, although several have lingered into April.

Identification of a Hoary Redpoll is not a trivial matter. The larger subspecies, the Greenland Redpoll, is the easiest to separate from a Common Redpoll, as it is very large and pale. The rump is all white, as are the undertail coverts. There is little streaking on the sides, and the upperparts and the face are relatively unmarked. Most noticeable is the bill, which is very short and broad, giving it a squashed look. The other, more common subspecies (*exilipes*) is much more difficult to separate from the Mealy form of the Common Redpoll (*C. f. flammea*). Many characters overlap between these two species, including coloration of the rump and undertail coverts, the most often used field marks. To exacerbate the situation, redpolls pale with age so that older Commons will resemble younger Hoarys. All in all, observers must take great care when claiming this species in the state. —James Granlund

# PINE SISKIN
### (*Carduelis pinus*)

The Pine Siskin is a highly mobile, gregarious finch which is often seen moving about in large flocks. This drab, densely streaked little bird is most easily identified by its wheezy, nasal call, which it seems to incessantly chatter. The Pine Siskin breeds in the coniferous forest from the panhandle of Alaska east to Newfoundland and south through New England, the Upper Midwest, and the western mountains to southern California and Mexico. It winters erratically within and south of its breeding range, throughout the United States (except southern Florida) to central Mexico. In Michigan, it is a fairly common summer resident in the Upper and northern Lower peninsulas, a rare and local summer resident in the south, and an erratic migrant and winter resident throughout the state.

Ascertaining the migration chronology of the Pine Siskin, like that of other erratic species, is difficult. Data collected at Whitefish Point, Chippewa County, seem to indicate that fall migrants begin arriving in mid-September through October, oftentimes in tremendous flocks such as the 5,058 recorded on 25 October 1992. More typically, flocks range from a few to a hundred birds. The arriving siskins either remain to winter in the Upper Peninsula or slowly filter into the Lower Peninsula, reaching peak numbers in the southern portions of the state in late October and November.

In some years Pine Siskins pass completely through the state, while in others they remain and winter in good numbers throughout. A good index to these fluctuations is the Christmas bird counts. In the period from 1970 to 1992, siskin numbers fluctuated from a high of 5,837 in 1987–88 to a low of 4 in 1970–71. Often siskins become rather scarce from January to mid-February, but numbers begin building again by late February and March in the southern portions of the state and by late March to mid-April in the north. The spring migration continues well into May, with northbound migrants passing through as resident birds are already well into their breeding cycle.

As the name suggests, the Pine Siskin shows a great affinity to conifers, its primary breeding habitat, but will occasionally occur in other types. Siskins typically nest in loose colonies, although at times they nest as isolated pairs. In Michigan nesting occurs from mid-March through May. While birds become territorial during this period, they remain gregarious and continue to feed in flocks.

Nests are typically located in a conifer on a horizontal branch, well out from the trunk and from 6 to 35 feet above ground. The nest is a large shallow cup constructed of twigs, grasses, and similar materials and is lined with mosses, hair, or other soft substances. A typical clutch consists of three to four eggs, which are pale greenish-blue, spotted or dotted with browns and blacks. The female incubates the eggs, with hatching in 13 days and the young fledging in an additional 14 to 15 days.

In Michigan, the Pine Siskin breeds most commonly in the Upper Peninsula, becoming less common though still regular in the northern three to four tiers of counties in the Lower Peninsula, and breeding only sporadically southward. This pattern

was verified during the Breeding Bird Atlas when siskins were reported from 319 townships, of which 217 were in the Upper Peninsula, 68 in the northern Lower, and 34 in the southern Lower Peninsula. During the Atlas, nesting was confirmed as far south as the Indiana border in St. Joseph County, as well as in Kalamazoo and Oakland counties.

Certainly the overall distribution and abundance pattern seen in the state stems from habitat availability, with conifers being much more abundant in the northern portions of the state. Some have hypothesized that frequency of breeding in the south increases following a large winter invasion. Historically, siskins have always had this same general status, although early researchers had a difficult time confirming breeding. —James Granlund

# AMERICAN GOLDFINCH
## (*Carduelis tristis*)

This common Michigan resident is more often called the wild canary than its true name, the American Goldfinch. In summer, the bright yellow males are a familiar sight throughout the state, and in winter the duller males and much drabber females are one of the most common visitors to bird feeders. The American Goldfinch breeds from coast to coast and from southern Canada to the Gulf states, and winters over most of its breeding range south to Mexico.

It is difficult to ascertain whether birds seen in Michigan in winter are the same birds that breed here in summer. Banding records have shown that goldfinch have a highly erratic migration. Some Michigan birds travel considerable distances, while others move little. It seems likely that birds migrate and disperse in response to food supplies (primarily seeds of composite plants), making it difficult to detect when migrations begin and end. Data from migration points such as Whitefish Point, Chippewa County, suggest that spring migrants begin arriving in the north in late April and peak in mid- to late May. During this period large numbers of goldfinch may be encountered throughout the state. Examples include 400 on 6 May 1969 and 600 on 14 May 1971, both in Berrien County.

Birds become very vocal in May, with courtship and pair-bonding prevalent during late spring and early summer, although breeding is not initiated until July through mid-September, when seeds and other foods become available. During the Breeding Bird Atlas, American Goldfinch were found nesting throughout the state, being slightly more abundant in the southern and central Lower Peninsula in areas of extensive fields, and somewhat less abundant in the more forested areas of the northern Lower and Upper peninsulas.

*Pine Siskin*
*Evening Grosbeak*
DAVID MOHRHARDT

Nesting occurs in open country with ample weedy growth for forage and scattered trees and shrubs. The nest is a durable woven cup of plant fibers and is placed on a horizontal limb or fork, usually 3 to 10 feet from the ground (range 1–33 feet). A typical clutch consists of five pale bluish-white eggs which are incubated for 10 to 12 days, with fledging in an additional 11 to 17 days.

Toward late summer, goldfinch begin to aggregate into large foraging flocks, sometimes reaching several hundred individuals. By mid-October through November the migration is underway, at which time tremendous numbers may be encountered, particularly along the lakeshore. Exceptional concentrations include 5,500 on 3 October 1971 and 5,000 on 9 November 1972, both in Berrien County, and 1,000 on 5 November 1964 at Tawas Point, Iosco County.

Many goldfinch remain in Michigan during the winter, their numbers varying greatly from year to year. A good index to these fluctuations is the Christmas bird counts. During the 1970–92 period, numbers ranged from a high of 22,817 in 1988–89 to a low of 3,050 in 1970–71. As on migration, they are often encountered in large flocks, being found in weedy uncut fields that provide plentiful seeds. Excellent examples include 1,000 on 30 December 1973 at the Muskegon Wastewater System and 2,000 on 13 to 20 January near Port Huron, St. Clair County.

The American Goldfinch's status has changed little since the state's earliest writings. Walter Barrows (1912) indicated that it was one of the most common and familiar birds in the state. If anything, the species became more abundant in the 1800s as forests were cleared and lands converted to agricultural uses and later to grassy and shrubby fields. —James Granlund

# EVENING GROSBEAK
## (*Coccothraustes vespertinus*)

Michigan has the esteemed honor of being the location in which the Evening Grosbeak was first revealed to science. To be more specific, the type specimen was collected by Henry Schoolcraft in Sault Ste. Marie on 7 April 1823. The name was derived from the mistaken idea that the species sang only just before twilight, something we now know is untrue. Today, this stocky yellowish finch is one of the most recognizable species in the state, being a fairly regular resident in the Upper and northern Lower peninsulas, and an irruptive migrant and winter visitor in the remainder of the state.

The Evening Grosbeak breeds in the continent's coniferous forests from Newfoundland, northern New England, and the northern Great Lakes west to the central Canadian Rockies and south in the mountains to southern California and central Mexico. It winters within its breeding range and irrupts periodically farther south to the central United States. This species has extended its range eastward over the past 150 years, an expansion which apparently began in the mid-1850s with birds being found east of the Great Lakes, in Ontario. They had reached the Atlantic coast of Massachusetts by 1890 and finally to the Maritime Provinces in the 1960s. Reasons for this expansion are unclear, although some have postulated that the expanded range of the box-elder, a favorite food source of the Evening Grosbeak, drew the bird eastward. Also, the availability of sunflower seeds at winter feeding stations has helped to increase its numbers.

Even though the first specimen of this species came from Michigan, it is doubtful that the Evening Grosbeak was a very common resident prior to the 1850s. In fact, the next observation after Schoolcraft's original description did not occur until 1869, although Native Americans appeared familiar with the species, indicating it has always been an irruptive winter visitant. It became increasingly regular from the 1870s through the early 1900s and finally was quite abundant by 1910, when large flocks were seen everywhere. In 1951, Norman Wood described the species as an irregular winter visitant to the Lower Peninsula and a fairly regular winter visitant and uncommon local summer resident in the Upper Peninsula, yet he could list only two breeding records (28 July 1922 at Whitefish Point, Chippewa County, and 19 June 1930 in Baraga County).

Through the 1950s, 1960s, and 1970s there were increasing numbers of breeding records throughout the Upper Peninsula and into the northern Lower Peninsula. Most recently, during the 1980s Breeding Bird Atlas, there were reports from 350 townships in the Upper Peninsula, of which 37 involved confirmed breeding, including all counties except Menominee. In the northern Lower Peninsula, observations came from 91 townships with 14 breeding confirmations, the southernmost in Arenac County. In some years birds have lingered as late as June farther south, but no breeding records have been substantiated from the southern Lower Peninsula.

The Evening Grosbeak nests in coniferous forests, particularly in spruce and fir, although it may also occur in mixed forests and occasionally in hardwood stands. The nest is normally placed in a conifer from 20 to 60 feet above the ground, and is a loosely constructed elliptical cup of twigs interwoven with mosses or lichens. A typical clutch consists of three to four eggs which are incubated for 11 to 14 days, with fledging occurring in about two weeks. Detecting nests is extremely difficult, and most breeding confirmations are of family groups visiting feeders.

During invasion years, birds begin appearing as early as late August in the southern part of the state, although the main migration is from late October to November. During such years large concentrations can be seen; examples include 1,000+ on 30 October 1983 in Berrien County and 1,000 on 19 October 1985 in Allegan County. As with many other irruptive species, numbers seem to build along the Great Lakes coasts. In some years most individuals pass through the state, and banding records indicate that many travel as far as the eastern seaboard. In other years many remain and overwinter statewide. On Christmas bird counts from 1970 to 1992, numbers varied from a high of 9,080 in 1977–78 to a low of 923 in 1984–85. There was a general trend of increasing numbers in the late 1970s to mid-1980s, followed by a decrease through the remainder of the period. In most years individuals winter in the Upper Peninsula, particularly in the western portions, while in other years they may be quite scarce.

In spring numbers begin to increase in late February in the Lower Peninsula, and the migration continues through May in the Upper Peninsula. At concentration points such as Whitefish Point, large numbers may be recorded, as on 11 May 1979 when 1,217 were seen in a single day. —James Granlund

# HOUSE SPARROW
## (*Passer domesticus*)

Although its habits and habitats are a bit repugnant, the male House Sparrow is really a rather stunning bird, having brown upperparts boldly streaked with black and a black throat and gray crown. Yet much of the species' reputation and disdain are well earned. The House Sparrow, or English Sparrow, was introduced to North America in 1850 primarily to help control cankerworms. Societies diligently worked to establish the bird, even to the extent of dispatching with competing native birds. Today this widely introduced species can be found on all continents, aside from Antarctica.

Michigan received its first House Sparrows between 1874 and 1876, when birds were released in Jackson. These Old World birds, being well suited to live in close proximity to man, prospered throughout the late 1800s and early 1900s. Additionally, they benefited by the extensive use of horses for transportation, as they found bountiful food in their excrement. By the late 1800s it was becoming apparent that this introduction was a mistake—a bird which was brought in to control cankerworms ate more grain than worms. There was also concern that the House Sparrow could be the vector of diseases to livestock, including hog cholera.

Both the State of Michigan and the United States Department of Agriculture initiated programs to eradicate the species. The state enacted a bounty of one cent per sparrow in 1887, which was repealed in 1901 only to be reenacted in 1903 at two cents per bird. The USDA took a different approach, releasing pamphlets which promoted the eradication of this pest; included were tips on how to trap, shoot, and even cook the little sparrow. Neither technique had much effect, and the House Sparrow continued to spread. By the 1920s, however, populations began a decline which has continued to this day. There are many likely causes for the decline, including the reduction of food as horses were replaced by automobiles, a series of severe winters in the 1970s, the lack of nesting crevices on modern buildings, and competition with the European Starling and House Finch for food and nesting places.

Today, the House Sparrow is still abundant in urban and suburban areas as well as around farms and other rural structures. During the recent Breeding Bird Atlas, the species was found in all counties, with the greatest concentration in the southern two-thirds of the Lower Peninsula, being rather sparsely distributed across the Upper Peninsula. This distribution is probably a function of land-use practices and severity of winters.

House Sparrows breed in a variety of habitats, with their large woven nests built in a crevice, a cavity, or even a dense bush or

*American Goldfinch*
JOHN FELSING

Felsing

shrub. The nest is composed of grasses, feathers, or almost any material including paper, string, or other litter. These materials are woven into a large ball that normally fills the cavity or crevice it occupies. A typical clutch consists of five eggs, which are white and spotted with grays or browns. Pairs normally double-clutch, and in some cases raise three broods a season. Incubation requires 10 to 13 days, with both sexes participating. The young fledge in an additional 14 to 17 days. Although House Sparrows are said to be nonmigratory, there does appear to be some post-breeding dispersal, as birds occasionally appear at migration points such as Whitefish Point Bird Observatory.

Aside from its habits of pilfering grains and leaving its acidic guano everywhere, the House Sparrow has an even more serious impact on native birds. It actively competes with other species for nesting cavities, and the most pronounced impact has been on birds such as the Tree Swallow and Eastern Bluebird, for which humans have provided housing in the form of boxes. Unfortunately for the native species, the pugnacious House Sparrow commandeers these structures, and its populations are therefore benefited unintentionally. Even more disturbing is the House Sparrow's habit of killing native inhabitants of boxes and cavities, both hatchlings and adults. It is thus important when monitoring a nest-box trail to control House Sparrows by actively removing their nests and discouraging their presence. —James Granlund

# BIBLIOGRAPHY

Adams, R., V. Janson, J. Lerg, and D. McWhirter. 1981. Michigan bird watch list. Jack-Pine Warbler 59:123–129.

Adams, R. J., Jr. 1978. A Ferruginous Hawk in Michigan. Jack-Pine Warbler 56:51–52.

Adams, R. J., Jr. 1979. Seasonal distribution and abundance of birds in the Kalamazoo, Michigan, area. Jack-Pine Warbler 57:91–105.

Adams, R. J., G. A. McPeek, and D. C. Evers. 1988. Bird population changes in Michigan, 1966–1985. Jack-Pine Warbler 66:71–86.

Adkisson, C. S. 1966. The nesting and behavior of mockingbirds in northern lower Michigan. Jack-Pine Warbler 44:102–116.

Albert, D. A., S. R. Denton, and B. V. Barnes. 1986. Regional landscape ecosystems of Michigan. Ann Arbor: University of Michigan, School of Natural Resources.

Allan, T. A. 1977. Winter food of the Snowy Owl in northwestern Lower Michigan. Jack-Pine Warbler 55:42.

American Ornithologists' Union. 1957. Check-list of North American birds. 5th edition.

American Ornithologists' Union. 1983. Check-list of North American birds. 6th edition.

American Ornithologists' Union. 1985. Thirty-fifth supplement to the American Ornithologists' Union check-list of North American birds. Auk 102:680–686.

American Ornithologists' Union. 1989. Thirty-seventh supplement to the American Ornithologists' Union check-list of North American birds. Auk 106:532–538.

American Ornithologists' Union. 1991. Thirty-eighth supplement to the American Ornithologists' Union check-list of North American birds. Auk 108:750–754.

American Ornithologists' Union. 1993. Thirty-ninth supplement to the American Ornithologists' Union check-list of North American birds. American Birds 47:384–386.

Ammann, G. A. 1963. Status of Spruce Grouse in Michigan. Journal of Wildlife Management 27:591–593.

Ammann, G. A. 1963. Status and management of Sharp-tailed Grouse in Michigan. Journal of Wildlife Management 27:802–809.

Andrle, R. F., and J. F. Carroll. 1988. The atlas of breeding birds in New York State. Ithaca: Cornell University Press.

Anonymous. 1989. Proceedings of the Kirtland's Warbler Symposium: at the crossroads—extinction or survival. USDA Forest Service, Huron-Manistee National Forests.

Armstrong, W. H. 1958. Nesting and food habits of the Long-eared Owl in Michigan. East Lansing: Michigan State University Museum Publications Biological Series 1:61–96.

Austin, O. L., Jr. (Ed.). 1968. Life histories of the North American cardinals, grosbeaks, buntings, towhees, finches, sparrows, and their allies. 3 volumes. U.S. National Museum Bulletin No. 237.

Baker, D. E. 1978. Observations of Cape May Warblers in Michigan. Jack-Pine Warbler 56:94–96.

Baker, D. E. 1979. Tennessee Warblers nesting in Chippewa County, Michigan. Jack-Pine Warbler 57:24–25.

Baker, D. E. 1984. Kentucky Warbler nesting in Michigan. Jack-Pine Warbler 62:26.

Barlow, J. C. 1987. Review of "The Birds of Canada." Auk 104:800–801.

Barnes, B. V., and W. H. Wagner. 1981. Michigan trees: a guide to the trees of Michigan and the Great Lakes region. Ann Arbor: University of Michigan Press.

Barrows, W. B. 1912. Michigan bird life. East Lansing: Michigan Agricultural College Special Bulletin.

Batts, H. L., Jr. 1957. A preliminary report on seasonal distribution of birds in Kalamazoo County, Michigan. Jack-Pine Warbler 35:9–13.

Bazuin, C. W. 1938. Arkansas Kingbird nesting in Michigan. Auk 55:125.

Bellrose, F. C. 1980. Ducks, geese, and swans of North America. 3rd edition. Harrisburg, Pennsylvania: Stackpole Books.

Bent, A. C. 1919–1958. The complete life history series of North American birds. U.S. National Museum Bulletins.

Berger, A. J. 1951. The cowbird and certain host species in Michigan. Wilson Bulletin 63:28.

Berger, A. J. 1951. Notes on the nesting season of the Catbird. Jack-Pine Warbler 29:115–118.

Berger, A. J. 1957. Population density of Alder Flycatchers and Common Goldfinches in *Crataegus* habitats of southeastern Michigan. Wilson Bulletin 69:317–322.

Berger, A. J. 1958. The Golden-winged–Blue-winged Warbler complex in Michigan and the Great Lakes area. Jack-Pine Warbler 36:37–73.

Berger, A. J., and D. F. Parmelee. 1952. The Alder Flycatcher in Washtenaw County, Michigan: breeding distribution and cowbird parasitism. Wilson Bulletin 64:33–38.

Berger, D. D., and H. C. Mueller. 1969. Nesting Peregrine Falcons in Wisconsin and adjacent areas. Pp. 115–122 *in* Peregrine Falcon populations: their biology and decline (J. J. Hickey, Ed.). Madison: University of Wisconsin Press.

Binford, L. C. 1993. First Illinois record of the Sandwich Tern. Meadowlark 2:13–14.

Blake, J. G., and J. R. Karr. 1987. Breeding birds of isolated woodlots: area and habitat relationships. Ecology 68:1724–1734.

Blokpoel, H., and G. D. Tessier. 1986. The Ring-billed Gull in Ontario: a review of a new problem species. Ottawa, Ontario: Canadian Wildlife Service Occasional Paper No. 57.

Bohlen, H. D. 1989. The birds of Illinois. Bloomington: Indiana University Press.

Booth, W. M. 1971. Migration of Blue Jays in southwestern Michigan. Jack-Pine Warbler 49:82–86.

Bourgeois, A. 1977. Quantitative analysis of American Woodcock nest and brood habitat. Proceedings of the Woodcock symposium 6:109–118.

Brauning, D. W. (Ed.). 1992. Atlas of breeding birds in Pennsylvania. Pittsburgh: University of Pittsburgh Press.

Brewer, R., G. A. McPeek, and R. J. Adams (Eds.). 1991. The atlas of breeding birds of Michigan. East Lansing: Michigan State University Press.

Brewer, R., and A. Raim. 1965. Summer observations of Nashville and Black-throated Green Warblers in Kalamazoo County, Michigan. Jack-Pine Warbler 43:169.

Brigham, E. M., Jr. 1941. Some sight records of the Blue Grosbeak in Michigan. Jack-Pine Warbler 19:19–20.

Brittingham, M. C., and S. A. Temple. 1983. Have cowbirds caused forest songbirds to decline? BioScience 33:31–35.

Butler, A. W. 1898. A catalogue of the birds of Indiana. Report of the state geologist of Indiana for 1897. Pp. 515–1187.

Cade, B. S. 1966. Habitat suitability index models: Brown Thrasher. Washington, D.C.: U.S. Fish and Wildlife Service Biological Report No. 82.

Cadman, M. D., P. F. J. Eagles, and F. M. Helleiner. 1987. Atlas of the breeding birds of Ontario. Waterloo, Ontario: University of Waterloo Press.

Caldwell, L., and G. Wallace. 1966. Collection of migrating birds at Michigan television towers. Jack-Pine Warbler 44:117–123.

Campbell, L. W. 1968. Birds of the Toledo area. Toledo: The Blade.

Carpenter, T. 1975. Sighting of a Black Vulture in Michigan. Jack-Pine Warbler 53:114.

Carson, R. 1962. Silent Spring. Boston: Houghton Mifflin Co.

Chamberlin, M. L. 1977. Observations on the Red-necked Grebe nesting in Michigan. Wilson Bulletin 89:33–46.

Choate, E. A. 1985. The dictionary of American bird names. Boston: Harvard Common Press.

Clark, W. S. 1987. A field guide to hawks of North America. Boston: Houghton Mifflin Co.

Coady, G. 1988. Ontario bird records committee report for 1987. Ontario Birds 6:42–50.

Collins, S. L., F. C. James, and P. G. Risser. 1982. Habitat relationships of wood warblers (Parulidae) in north central Minnesota. Oikos 39:50–58.

Colvin, B. A. 1986. Barn Owls: their secrets and habits. Illinois Audubon 216:9–13.

Confer, J. L., and K. Knapp. 1981. Golden-winged Warblers and Blue-winged Warblers: the relative success of a habitat specialist and a generalist. Auk 98:108–114.

Cook, A. J. 1893. Birds of Michigan. 2nd edition. East Lansing: Michigan Agricultural Experiment Station Bulletin No. 94.

Cottrille, B. D. 1975. Bay-breasted Warbler in Michigan. Jack-Pine Warbler 53:33–34.

Cottrille, B. D. 1986. Hooded Warblers nesting in Jackson County. Jack-Pine Warbler 64:19–20.

Coues, E. 1903. Key to North American birds. 5th edition. Boston: Page Company Publishers.

Covert, A. B. 1876. Birds of lower Michigan. Forest and Stream, volumes 6 and 7.

Cox, G. W. 1960. A life history of the Mourning Warbler. Wilson Bulletin 72:5–28.

Craig, R. J. 1985. Comparative habitat use by Louisiana and Northern Waterthrushes. Wilson Bulletin 97:347–355.

Craig, R. J. 1987. Divergent prey selection in two species of waterthrushes. Auk 104:180–187.

Craighead, J. J., and F. C. Craighead, Jr. 1956. Hawks, owls, and wildlife. Harrisburg, Pennsylvania: Stackpole Company and the Wildlife Management Institute (Repr. 1969 Dover Publications).

Cramp, S. (Ed.). 1985. Handbook of the birds of Europe, the Middle East, and North Africa: the birds of the western Palearctic. Volume 4: Terns–woodpeckers. Oxford: Oxford University Press.

Cramp, S., and K. E. L. Simmons (Eds.). 1977. Handbook of the birds of Europe, the Middle East, and North Africa: the birds of the western Palearctic. Volume 1: Ostriches–ducks. Oxford: Oxford University Press.

Cramp, S., and K. E. L. Simmons (Eds.). 1980. Handbook of the birds of Europe, the Middle East, and North Africa: the birds of the western Palearctic. Volume 2: Hawks–bustards. Oxford: Oxford University Press.

Cramp, S., and K. E. L. Simmons (Eds.). 1983. Handbook of the birds of Europe, the Middle East, and North Africa: the birds of the western Palearctic. Volume 3: Waders–gulls. Oxford: Oxford University Press.

Cuthbert, N. L. 1954. A nesting study of the Black Tern in Michigan. Auk 71:36–63.

Cuthbert, N. L. 1962. The Michigan Audubon Society Phoebe study (part II). Jack-Pine Warbler 40:68–83.

Cuthbert, N. L. 1963. The birds of Isabella County, Michigan. Ann Arbor: Edwards Brothers.

Cutright, N. 1980. Townsend's Solitaire in the western Great Lakes region. Jack-Pine Warbler 58:93–94.

DeGraaf, R. M., and K. E. Evans (Eds.). 1979. Management of North Central and Northeastern forests for nongame birds. USDA Forest Service General Technical Report NC-51.

del Hoyo, J., A. Elliot, and J. Sargatal (Eds.). 1992. Handbook of the birds of the world. Volume 1. Barcelona, Spain: Lynx Edicions.

DellaSala, D. A. 1985. The Yellow Warbler in southeastern Michigan: factors affecting its productivity. Jack-Pine Warbler 63:52–60.

DeSante, D., and P. Pyle. 1986. Distributional checklist of North American birds. Lee Vining, California: Artemesia Press.

Dodge, P. 1961. Birds of the Huron Mountains, Marquette County, Michigan. Jack-Pine Warbler 39:3–33.

Dorr, J. A., and D. F. Eschman. 1970. Geology of Michigan. Ann Arbor: University of Michigan Press.

Douglass, D. W. 1942. A Prairie Chicken booming grounds survey in central Michigan. Wilson Bulletin 54:171–172.

Drury, W. H. 1973. Population changes in New England seabirds. Bird-banding 44:267–313.

Dunn, E. H. 1979. Nesting biology and development of young in Ontario Black Terns. Canadian Field-Naturalist 93:276–281.

Dunne, P., D. Sibley, and C. Sutton. 1988. Hawks in flight. Boston: Houghton Mifflin Co.

Dutcher, W. 1888. Bird notes from Long Island, N.Y. Auk 5:169–183.

Dwight, J. 1917. The status of *Larus thayeri,* Thayer's Gull. Auk 34:413–414.

Eastman, J. 1976. First breeding record of Hermit Thrush in Barry County, Michigan. Jack-Pine Warbler 54:91.

Eaton, R. J. 1931. Great Black-backed Gull (*Larus marinus*) breeding in Essex County, Massachusetts. Auk 48:588–589.

Eaton, S. W. 1958. A life history of the Louisiana Waterthrush. Wilson Bulletin 70:211–236.

Eckert, K. R. 1984. Minnesota's first Lesser Black-backed Gull: October birding, part II. Loon 56:240–243.

Edwards, J. L. 1935. The Lesser Black-backed Gull in New Jersey. Auk 52:85.

Ehrlich, P. R., D. S. Dobkin, and D. Wheye. 1988. The birder's handbook: a field guide to the natural history of North American birds. New York: Simon and Schuster.

Eichenlaub, V. L., J. R. Harman, F. V. Nurnberger, and H. J. Stolle. 1990. The climatic atlas of Michigan. Notre Dame, Indiana: University of Notre Dame Press.

Einsweiler, S. S. 1988. Black Tern nesting biology in Cheboygan County, Michigan. M.S. Thesis, Central Michigan University.

Ellarson, R. S. 1956. A study of the Oldsquaw duck on Lake Michigan. Ph.D. Dissertation, University of Wisconsin.

Erdman, T. C. 1976. The first documented nesting of Little Gulls in USA. Passenger Pigeon 38:86–87.

Eustis, O. B. 1978. Common Raven nesting in Alpena County. Jack-Pine Warbler 56:45.

Evers, D., and J. Granlund. 1991. The checklist of the birds of Whitefish Point Bird Observatory. Paradise, Whitefish Point Bird Observatory.

Evers, D. C. 1987. First state record: Sage Thrasher. Jack-Pine Warbler 65:37–38.

Evers, D. C. 1989. White-winged Dove: first Michigan record. Jack-Pine Warbler 67:29.

Evers, D. C. 1992. A guide to Michigan's endangered wildlife. Ann Arbor: University of Michigan Press.

Ewert, D. N. 1980. Notes on some bird species observed during the breeding season in Isabella and Clare counties, Michigan. Jack-Pine Warbler 58:104–110.

Ewert, D. N. 1981. The occurrence of closely related species-pairs in central Michigan: Willow and Alder Flycatchers and Golden-winged and Blue-winged Warblers. Jack-Pine Warbler 59:95–98.

Farrand, J., Jr. (Ed.). 1983. The Audubon Society master guide to birding. 3 volumes. New York: Alfred A. Knopf.

Farrand, W. R., and D. F. Eschman. 1974. Glaciation of the southern peninsula of Michigan. Michigan Academy of Science 7:31–56.

Feare, C. 1984. The Starling. Oxford: Oxford University Press.

Ficken, M. S., and R. W. Ficken. 1968. Ecology of Blue-winged Warblers, Golden-winged Warblers, and some other Vermivora. American Midland Naturalist 79:311–319.

Fisher, D., J. Hubbard, and P. DeBenedictis. 1966. First Michigan specimens of the Little Gull and Franklin's Gull. Jack-Pine Warbler 44:50.

Fisher, L. W. 1939. Studies of the Eastern Ruffed Grouse in Michigan. Michigan State College Agricultural Experiment Station Technical Bulletin No. 166.

Fisher, W. 1971. Yellow-crowned Night-Heron nests in Michigan. Jack-Pine Warbler 49:86.

Fleming, R. C. 1979. A late Cape May Warbler in Michigan. Jack-Pine Warbler 57:167.

Forbush, E. H., and J. B. May. 1939. A natural history of American birds of eastern and central North America. Boston: Houghton Mifflin Co.

Ford, N. 1958. Black-throated Gray Warbler in Michigan. Wilson Bulletin 70:382.

Francis, C. M., and F. Cooke. 1986. Differential timing of spring migration in wood warblers (Parulinae). Auk 103:548–556.

Francke, C. 1984. White Ibis sighted in Saginaw County. Jack-Pine Warbler 62:56.

Francke, C., R. Grefe, and E. Kenaga. 1988. New Michigan nesting record: Cattle Egret. Jack-Pine Warbler 66:20–21.

Freer, M. F. 1958. Observations on a nesting of the Black-throated Blue Warbler. Jack-Pine Warbler 36:12–16.

Friedmann, H. 1963. Host relations of the parasitic cowbirds. Washington, D.C.: U.S. National Museum Bulletin No. 233.

Gaige, F. M. 1914. The birds of Dickinson County, Michigan. Report of the Michigan Academy of Science 16:74–91.

Gaston, A. J., and R. Decker. 1985. Interbreeding of Thayer's Gull, Larus thayeri, and Kumlien's Gull, Larus glaucoides kumlieni, on Southampton Island, Northwest Territories. Canadian Field-Naturalist 99:257–259.

Getz, L. L. 1961. Hunting areas of the Long-eared Owl. Wilson Bulletin 73:79–82.

Gibbs, M. 1879. Annotated list of the birds of Michigan. Bulletin of the U.S. Geological and Geographical Survey of the Territories 5:481–497.

Gibbs, M. 1885. A catalogue of the birds of Kalamazoo County, Michigan. Ornithologist and Oologist, volume 10.

Gibbs, M. 1898. Additions to the avifauna of Kalamazoo County, Michigan. Bulletin of the Michigan Ornithological Club 2:7.

Godfrey, W. E. 1986. The birds of Canada. Revised edition. Ottawa, Ontario: National Museums of Canada.

Goodwin, C. E. 1976. Ontario region. American Birds 30:948–952.

Gosselin, M., and N. David. 1975. Field identification of Thayer's Gull (Larus thayeri) in eastern North America. American Birds 29:1059–1066.

Green, J. C., and R. B. Janssen. 1975. Minnesota birds—where, when, and how many. Minneapolis: University of Minnesota Press.

Greenhouse, J. A., and J. P. Kleiman. 1972. Second nesting of Yellow-crowned Night-Herons in Michigan. Jack-Pine Warbler 50:29.

Hamas, M. J. 1979. Groove-billed Ani in northern Michigan. Jack-Pine Warbler 57:218–219.

Harrison, C. 1978. A field guide to nests, eggs, and nestlings of North American birds. New York: William Collins Sons and Co.

Harrison, H. H. 1975. A field guide to birds' nests in the United States east of the Mississippi River. Boston: Houghton Mifflin Co.

Harrison, H. H. 1984. Wood warblers' world. New York: Simon and Schuster.

Hayman, P., J. Marchant, and T. Prater. 1986. Shorebirds: an identification guide to the waders of the world. Boston: Houghton Mifflin Co.

Hespenheide, H. A. 1971. Flycatcher habitat selection in the eastern deciduous forest. Auk 88:61–74.

Hoffman, R. H. 1989. Status of the Sandhill Crane population in Michigan's Lower Peninsula, 1986–87. Jack-Pine Warbler 67:18–28.

Howell, S. N. G. 1990. Identification of White and Black-backed Wagtails in alternate plumage. Western Birds 21:41–49.

Hubbard, J. P. 1965. Migration of the Black-throated Blue Warbler in southern Michigan. Jack-Pine Warbler 43:162–163.

Hull, C. N., M. Wercinski, E. D. Lake, S. Lake, and B. Wilson. 1989. First and second documented records of Rufous Hummingbird in Michigan. Jack-Pine Warbler 67:94–96.

Hume, R. A. 1993. Common, Arctic, and Roseate Terns: an identification in review. British Birds 86:210–217.

Hussell, D. J. T. 1981. Migrations of the Least Flycatcher in southern Ontario. Journal of Field Ornithology 52:97–111.

Hussell, D. J. T. 1982. The timing of fall migration in Yellow-bellied Flycatchers. Journal of Field Ornithology 53:1–6.

Hyde, A. S. 1939. The life history of Henslow's Sparrow, Passerherbulus henslowii (Audubon). Ann Arbor: University of Michigan Museum of Zoology Miscellaneous Publication No. 41.

Ilnicky, N. J. 1984. Mountain Bluebird in Upper Michigan. Jack-Pine Warbler 62:50.

Jansen, V. S. 1964. Wood Ibis sighting near Lansing. Jack-Pine Warbler 42:229.

Janssen, R. B. 1987. Birds in Minnesota. Minneapolis: University of Minnesota Press.

Jensen, W. F., W. L. Robinson, and N. L. Heitman. 1982. Breeding of the Great Gray Owl on Neebish Island, Michigan. Jack-Pine Warbler 60:27–28.

Johnsgard, P. A. 1973. Grouse and quails of North America. Lincoln: University of Nebraska Press.

Johnsgard, P. A. 1981. The plovers, sandpipers, and snipes of the world. Lincoln: University of Nebraska Press.

Johnsgard, P. A. 1988. North American owls. Washington, D.C.: Smithsonian Institution Press.

Johnsgard, P. A. 1990. Hawks, eagles, and falcons of North America. Washington, D.C.: Smithsonian Institution Press.

Johnsson, R. G., and P. C. Shelton. 1982. (Rev. by P. A. Jordan.) Wildlife of Isle Royale. Isle Royale Natural History Association.

Kammeraad, J. W. 1964. Nesting habits and survival of Yellow Warblers. Jack-Pine Warbler 42:243–248.

Kammeraad, J. W. 1966. Further notes on nesting and survival of Yellow Warblers. Jack-Pine Warbler 44:124–129.

Kaufman, K. 1990. A field guide to advanced birding. Boston: Houghton Mifflin Co.

Keller, C. E., S. A. Keller, and T. C. Keller. 1979. Indiana birds and their haunts: a checklist and finding guide. Bloomington: Indiana University Press.

Kelley, A. H. 1963. Second Michigan record of Black-throated Gray Warbler. Jack-Pine Warbler 41:91.

Kelley, A. H. 1966. Changes in bird-life of the Detroit-Windsor area 1955–1965. Bloomfield Hills, Michigan: Cranbrook Institute of Science Bulletin No. 50.

Kelley, A. H. 1968. Michigan bird survey, summer 1968. Jack-Pine Warbler 46:131–136.

Kelley, A. H. 1978. Birds of southeastern Michigan and southwestern Ontario. Bloomfield Hills, Michigan: Cranbrook Institute of Science.

Kelley, A. H. 1983. Birds of S.E. Michigan and S.W. Ontario—notes on the years 1975–1981. Jack-Pine Warbler 61:3–12.

Kelley, A. H., D. S. Middleton, and W. P. Nickell. 1963. Birds of the Detroit-Windsor area, a ten-year survey. Bloomfield Hills, Michigan: Cranbrook Institute of Science Bulletin No. 45.

Kenaga, E. E. 1956. Birding in the Saginaw Bay area. Jack-Pine Warbler 34:39–56.

Kenaga, E. E. 1983. Birds, birders, and birding in the Saginaw Bay area. Midland, Michigan: Chippewa Nature Center.

Kendeigh, S. C. 1948. Bird populations and biotic communities in northern lower Michigan. Ecology 29:101–114.

Kielb, M. A. 1990. Nesting Falconiformes in Michigan and the Great Lakes region. Northwind 5:6.

Kielb, M. A., J. M. Swales, and R. A. Wolinski. 1992. The birds of Washtenaw County, Michigan. Ann Arbor: University of Michigan Press.

Kienholz, D., and P. Backstrom. 1986. A Sandwich Tern in Duluth. Loon 58:103–104.

Kilham, L. 1983. Life history studies of woodpeckers in eastern North America. Cambridge: Publication of the Nuttall Ornithological Club No. 20.

Kleen, V. M. 1977. Middlewestern prairie region. American Birds 31:336–339.

Kleen, V. M. 1980. Middlewestern prairie region. American Birds 34:781–785.

Kneeland, S. 1857. On the birds of Keweenaw Point, Lake Superior. Proceedings of the Boston Society of Natural History 6:231–241.

Knox, A. G. 1988. The taxonomy of redpolls. Ardea 76:1–26.

Kroodsma, R. L. 1984. Effect of edge on breeding forest bird species. Wilson Bulletin 96:426–436.

Langille, J. H. 1884. Our birds in their haunts. Boston: S. E. Cassino.

Laughlin, S. B., and D. P. Kibbe. 1985. The atlas of breeding birds of Vermont. Hanover, New Hampshire: University Press of New England.

Lawrence, L. deK. 1967. A comparative life-history study of four species of woodpeckers. Lawrence, Kansas: American Ornithologists' Union, Ornithological Monographs No. 5.

Lerg, J. M. 1984. Status of the Common Barn-Owl in Michigan. Jack-Pine Warbler 62:39–48.

Ludwig, F. E. 1943. Ring-billed Gulls of the Great Lakes. Wilson Bulletin 55:234–244.

Ludwig, J. P. 1962. A survey of the gull and tern populations of Lakes Huron, Michigan, and Superior. Jack-Pine Warbler 40:104–119.

Ludwig, J. P. 1974. Recent changes in the Ring-billed Gull population and biology in the Laurentian Great Lakes. Auk 91:575–594.

Ludwig, J. P. 1984. Decline, resurgence, and population dynamics of Michigan and Great Lakes Double-crested Cormorants. Jack-Pine Warbler 62:91–102.

Lumsden, H. G. 1984. The pre-settlement breeding distribution of Trumpeter (*Cygnus buccinator*) and Tundra Swans (*C. columbianes*) in eastern Canada. Canadian Field-Naturalist 98:415–424.

Lynch, J. M. 1981. Status of the Cerulean Warbler in the Roanoke River Basin of North Carolina. Chat 45:29–35.

MacArthur, R. H. 1958. Population ecology of some warblers of northeastern coniferous forests. Ecology 39:599–619.

MacQueen, P. M. 1950. Territory and song in the Least Flycatcher. Wilson Bulletin 62:194–205.

Martin, A. C., H. S. Zim, and A. L. Nelson. 1951. American wildlife and plants: a guide to wildlife food habits. New York: McGraw-Hill Book Co.

Martin, C. J. 1989. Additions to the bird fauna of Isle Royale National Park, Keweenaw County, Michigan. Jack-Pine Warbler 67:67–69.

Mayfield, H. F. 1960. The Kirtland's Warbler. Bloomfield Hills, Michigan: Cranbrook Institute of Science Bulletin No. 40.

Mayfield, H. F. 1977. Brown-headed Cowbird: agent of extermination? American Birds 31:107–113.

McWhirter, D. W. 1979. Michigan bird survey, spring 1979. Jack-Pine Warbler 57:148–161.

McWhirter, D. W., and D. L. Beaver. 1977. Birds of the Capital Count area of Michigan with seasonal and historical analysis. East Lansing: Michigan State University Museum Publication Biological Series No. 5.

Mearns, B., and R. Mearns. 1992. Audubon to Xántus. New York: Academic Press.

Medley, M. 1964. Observations of Laughing Gulls and Franklin's Gulls at St. Joseph, Michigan. Jack-Pine Warbler 42:231.

Mershon, W. B. 1907. The Passenger Pigeon. New York: Outing Publishing Company.

Messner, C. J., and H. W. Messner. 1953. Notes on the Raven in the Upper Peninsula of Michigan in 1949. Jack-Pine Warbler 31:54.

Michigan Loon Recovery Committee. 1990. A plan for the recovery of the Common Loon in Michigan. Lansing: Michigan Department of Natural Resources.

Michigan Piping Plover Recovery Team. 1988. Piping Plover—Michigan Recovery Plan. Lansing: Michigan Department of Natural Resources.

Middleton, D. S., and B. J. Johnston. 1956. The Michigan Audubon Society Phoebe study (part I). Jack-Pine Warbler 34:63–66.

Mitts, R., and D. McWhirter. 1978. Three-year summary of the Capital Count area phoebe census. Jack-Pine Warbler 56:49–50.

Mlodinow, S. 1984. Chicago area birds. Chicago: Chicago Review Press.

Morden, J. A., and W. E. Saunders. 1883. The ornithology of western Ontario. Canadian Sportsman and Naturalist 3:243.

Morehouse, E. L., and R. Brewer. 1968. Feeding of nestling and fledgling Eastern Kingbirds. Auk 85:44–54.

Morlan, J. 1981. Status and identification of forms of White Wagtail in western North America. Continental Birdlife 2:37–50.

Morse, D. H. 1989. American warblers. Cambridge: Harvard University Press.

Mumford, R. E. 1964. The breeding biology of the Acadian Flycatcher. Ann Arbor: University of Michigan Museum of Zoology Miscellaneous Publication No. 175.

Mumford, R. E., and C. E. Keller. 1984. The birds of Indiana. Bloomington: Indiana University Press.

Murray, B. G., Jr. 1966. Blackpoll Warbler migration in Michigan. Jack-Pine Warbler 44:23–29.

Murray, B. G., and F. B. Gill. 1976. Behavioral interactions of Blue-winged and Golden-winged Warblers. Wilson Bulletin 88:231–253.

National Geographic Society. 1987. Field guide to the birds of North America. 2nd edition. Washington, D.C.: National Geographic Society.

Nero, R. W. 1980. The Great Gray Owl: phantom of the northern forest. Washington, D.C.: Smithsonian Institution Press.

Nero, R. W., R. J. Clark, R. J. Knapton, and R. H. Hamre (Eds.). 1987. Biology and conservation of northern forest owls. USDA Forest Service General Technical Report RM-142.

Nickell, W. P. 1965. Habitats, territory, and nesting of the Catbird. American Midland Naturalist 73:433–478.

Nolan, V., Jr. 1978. Ecology and behavior of the Prairie Warbler Dendroica discolor. American Ornithologists' Union, Ornithological Monographs No. 26.

Oldfield, W. A. 1891. [Breeding of Rose-breasted Grosbeak and Red-backed Sandpiper in Sanilac County, Michigan]. Ornithologist and Oologist 16:144.

Palmer, R. S. (Ed.). 1962. Handbook of North American birds. Volume 1. New Haven, Connecticut: Yale University Press.

Parmelee, D. F. 1988. Some observations on nest dates and site fidelity of Gray Jays and Ravens in Dickinson County, Michigan. Jack-Pine Warbler 66:158–159.

Parmelee, D. F., and J. A. Johnson. 1955. Nesting of the Raven in Dickinson County, Michigan. Jack-Pine Warbler 33:137–138.

Paterson, R. L., Jr. 1982. Passerine community structure at the beech-maple coniferous forest interface. Jack-Pine Warbler 60:15–21.

Paulson, D. 1993. Shorebirds of the Pacific Northwest. Seattle: University of Washington Press.

Payne, R. B. 1979. Two apparent hybrid Zonotrichia sparrows. Auk 96:595–599.

Payne, R. B. 1983. A distributional checklist of the birds of Michigan. Ann Arbor: University of Michigan Museum of Zoology Miscellaneous Publication No. 164.

Payne, R. B., and L. L. Payne. 1993. Breeding dispersal in Indigo Buntings: circumstances and consequences for breeding success and population structure. Condor 95:1–24.

Peck, G. K., and R. D. James. 1983. Breeding birds of Ontario: nidology and distribution. Volume 1: Nonpasserines. Toronto: Royal Ontario Museum, Life Sciences Miscellaneous Publications.

Peck, G. K., and R. D. James. 1987. Breeding birds of Ontario: nidology and distribution. Volume 2: Passerines. Toronto: Royal Ontario Museum, Life Sciences Miscellaneous Publications.

Peterjohn, B. G. 1987. Middlewestern prairie region. American Birds 41:286–290.

Peterjohn, B. G. 1989. The birds of Ohio. Bloomington: Indiana University Press.

Peterjohn, B. G., and D. L. Rice. 1991. The Ohio breeding bird atlas. Columbus, Ohio: Department of Natural Resources.

Petersen, P. C., Jr. 1964. Middlewestern prairie region. Audubon Field Notes 18:359–360.

Peterson, R. T. 1980. A field guide to the birds east of the Rockies. 4th edition. Boston: Houghton Mifflin Co.

Peterson, R. T. 1990. A field guide to western birds. 3rd edition. Boston: Houghton Mifflin Co.

Petrides, G. A. 1938. A life history study of the Yellow-breasted Chat. Wilson Bulletin 50:184–189.

Pettingill, O. S., Jr. 1959. Yellow-bellied Flycatchers nesting in lower Michigan. Jack-Pine Warbler 37:111.

Pettingill, O. S., Jr. 1971. Cape May Warbler nesting in Michigan. Jack-Pine Warbler 49:125–126.

Pettingill, O. S., Jr. 1974. Ornithology at the University of Michigan Biological Station and the birds of the region. Kalamazoo, Michigan: Kalamazoo Nature Center.

Pettingill, O. S., Jr., R. R. Graber, and J. W. Graber. 1957. The summer birds of Wilderness State Park, Michigan. Jack-Pine Warbler 35:43–63.

Pinkowski, B. C. 1977. Notes on effects of fire and logging on birds inhabiting jack pine stands. Jack-Pine Warbler 55:92–94.

Pinkowski, B. C. 1979. Effects of a severe winter on a breeding population of Eastern Bluebird. Jack-Pine Warbler 57:8–12.

Pitelka, F. A. 1950. Geographic variation and the species problem in the shore-bird genus Limnodromus. University of California Publications in Zoology 50:1–108.

Pitelka, F. A. 1959. Numbers, breeding schedule, and territoriality in Pectoral Sandpipers in northern Alaska. Condor 61:233–264.

Pogacnik, J. 1980. Ohio's first Heerman's Gull. Cleveland Bird Calendar 76:6–7.

Post, P. W., and E. J. Restivo. 1961. A midsummer visit to Canarsie Pol. Linnaean News-letter 14(9).

Potter, E. F., J. F. Parnell, and R. P. Teulings. 1980. Birds of the Carolinas. Chapel Hill: University of North Carolina Press.

Powell, D. J. 1985. Great Lakes region (White/Black-backed Wagtail). American Birds 39:302–305.

Rabe, D. 1977. Structural analysis of woodcock diurnal habitat in northern Michigan. Proceedings of the Woodcock Symposium 6:125–134.

Raim, A. J. 1975. Territory and mating system in the Bobolink, Dolichonyx oryzivorus. M.A. Thesis, Western Michigan University.

Rapp, F. W. 1931. Bird list of Vicksburg, Michigan. Privately published.

Rapp, F. W. 1966. Supplement to my 1931 bird list of Vicksburg, Michigan. Privately published.

Reed, M. L. 1980. Yellow Warblers nesting in junipers. Jack-Pine Warbler 58:150.

Reed, S. A. 1959. An analysis of 111 pellets from the Short-eared Owl. Jack-Pine Warbler 37:19–23.

Robbins, C. S., D. Bystrak, and P. H. Geissler. 1986. The breeding bird survey: its first fifteen years, 1965–1979. Washington, D.C.: U.S. Fish and Wildlife Service Resource Publication No. 157.

Robbins, C. S., D. K. Dawson, and B. A. Dowell. 1989. Habitat area requirements of breeding forest birds of the Middle Atlantic states. Wildlife Monograph No. 103.

Robbins, S. D., Jr. 1991. Wisconsin birdlife. Madison: University of Wisconsin Press.

Roberts, T. S. 1932. The birds of Minnesota. 2 volumes. Minneapolis: University of Minnesota Press.

Robins, J. D. 1971. A study of the Henslow's Sparrow in Michigan. Wilson Bulletin 83:39–48.

Robinson, W. L. 1980. Fool Hen: the Spruce Grouse on the Yellow Dog Plains. Madison: University of Wisconsin Press.

Robinson, W. L. (Ed.). 1984. Ruffed Grouse management: state of the art in the 1980s. St. Louis: North Central Section of The Wildlife Society and Ruffed Grouse Society.

Root, T. 1988. Atlas of wintering North American birds: an analysis of Christmas bird count data. Chicago: University of Chicago Press.

Rowher, S. A. 1972. A multivariate assessment of interbreeding between the meadowlarks, *Sturnella*. Systematic Zoology 21:313–338.

Ryel, L. A. 1979. On the population dynamics of the Kirtland's Warbler. Jack-Pine Warbler 57:76–83.

Ryel, L. A. 1981. Population change in the Kirtland's Warbler. Jack-Pine Warbler 59:77–90.

Ryel, L. A., and V. S. Janson. 1971. Lincoln's Sparrows in jack pine stands. Jack-Pine Warbler 49:96–97.

Sager, A. 1839. Report of Doctor Abraham Sager, Zoologist of Geological Survey. Lansing: House Documents of the State of Michigan. Pp. 410–421.

Salomonsen, F. 1950. The birds of Greenland. Copenhagen: Ejnar Munksgaard.

Sauer, J. R., and S. Droege. 1990. Recent population trends of the Eastern Bluebird. Wilson Bulletin 102:239–252.

Scharf, W. C. 1983. New Caspian Tern colonies in Lake Huron. Jack-Pine Warbler 61:13–14.

Scharf, W. C. 1989. Coastal Great Blue Heron and Great Egret colonies of the Michigan Great Lakes. Jack-Pine Warbler 67:52–65.

Scharf, W. C., and G. W. Shugart. 1981. Recent increases in Double-crested Cormorants in the United States Great Lakes. American Birds 35:910–911.

Scharf, W. C., and G. W. Shugart. 1984. Distribution and phenology of nesting Forster's Terns in eastern Lake Huron and Lake St. Clair. Wilson Bulletin 96:306–309.

Scharf, W. C., G. W. Shugart, and M. L. Chamberlin. 1978. Colonial birds nesting on man-made and natural sites in the U.S. Great Lakes. Vicksburg, Mississippi: U.S. Army Engineer Waterways Experimental Station Technical Report D-78-10.

Schorger, A. W. 1966. The Wild Turkey: its history and domestication. Norman: University of Oklahoma.

Schumacher, C. M. 1986. Common Raven nest in Wexford County. Jack-Pine Warbler 64:20.

Scott, G. A. 1963. First nesting of the Little Gull (*Larus minutus*) in Ontario and in the New World. Auk 80:548–549.

Sherry, T. W. 1979. Competitive interactions and adaptive strategies of American Redstarts and Least Flycatchers in northern hardwood forests. Auk 96:265–275.

Simcox, R. 1970. White-faced Ibis in Cass County. Jack-Pine Warbler 48:33.

Skutch, A. F. 1985. Life of a woodpecker. Santa Monica, California: Ibis Publishing Co.

Slater, E. 1974. A Western Tanager in Michigan. Jack-Pine Warbler 52:46.

Sloan, N. 1975. New state record—Say's Phoebe. Jack-Pine Warbler 53:76.

Smith, N. G. 1966. Evolution of some Arctic gulls (*Larus*): an experimental study of isolating mechanisms. Ornithological Monographs No. 4.

Smith, R. 1983. 1983 field notes. Goldeneye 22:1–7.

Smith, R., W. Booth, and C. Witkoske. 1993. The birds of Berrien County Michigan: 30 year summary (1962–1991). Berrien Springs: Berrien Audubon Society.

Smith, W. J. 1959. Movements of Michigan Herring Gulls. Bird-Banding 30:69–104.

Snell, R. R. 1989. Status of Larus gulls at Home Bay, Baffin Island. Colonial Waterbirds 12:12–23.

Southern, W. E. 1968. Dispersal patterns of subadult Herring Gulls from Rogers City, Michigan. Jack-Pine Warbler 46:2–6.

Southern, W. E. 1974. Seasonal distribution of Great Lakes region Ring-billed Gulls. Jack-Pine Warbler 52:154–179.

Southern, W. E., and L. K. Southern. 1980. A summary of the incidence of cowbird parasitism in northern Michigan from 1911–1978. Jack-Pine Warbler 58:77–84.

Stalmaster, M. V. 1987. The Bald Eagle. New York: Universe Books.

Stewart, R. E. 1953. A life history study of the Yellow-throat. Wilson Bulletin 65:99–115.

Stoddard, H. L. 1931. The Bobwhite Quail: its habits, preservation, and increase. New York: Charles Scribner's Sons.

Stokes, D. W. 1979. A guide to bird behavior. Volume 1. Boston: Little, Brown and Co.

Stokes, D. W., and L. Q. Stokes. 1983. A guide to bird behavior. Volume 2. Boston: Little, Brown and Co.

Swales, B. H. 1903–1904. A list of the land birds of southeastern Michigan. Bulletin of the Michigan Ornithological Club 4:14–17; 5:37–43.

Swales, B. H. 1913. A critique of Barrows' "Michigan Bird Life." Wilson Bulletin 25:3–12.

Temple, S. A., and J. R. Cary. 1987. Wisconsin birds: a seasonal and geographical guide. Madison: University of Wisconsin Press.

Terborgh, J. 1989. Where have all the birds gone? Princeton, New Jersey: Princeton University Press.

Terres, J. 1980. The Audubon encyclopedia of North American birds. New York: Alfred A. Knopf.

Tessen, D. 1976. Western Great Lakes region. American Birds 30:957–961.

Tessen, D. 1985. Lesser Black-backed Gull at Kewaunee. Passenger Pigeon 47:39.

Thompson, M. C. 1965. Report of a Western Kingbird's nest. Jack-Pine Warbler 63:147–148.

Thompson, W. L. 1982. A Burrowing Owl specimen from the Lower Peninsula of Michigan. Jack-Pine Warbler 60:118.

Torodoff, H. B. 1966. Additions to the birds of Michigan. Jack-Pine Warbler 44:2–7.

Tramer, E. J., and L. W. Campbell. 1986. Laughing Gull nesting attempt on Lake Erie. Wilson Bulletin 98:170–171.

Trapp, J. 1967. Observations at a Cerulean Warbler nest during early incubation. Jack-Pine Warbler 45:42–49.

Trautman, M. B., and J. Van Tyne. 1935. The occurrence of Sprague's Pipit in Michigan. Auk 52:457–458.

Twiest, A., and M. Twiest. 1976. Say's Phoebe in Muskegon, Michigan. Jack-Pine Warbler 54:93.

Udvardy, M. D. F. 1977. The Audubon Society field guide to North American birds—western region. New York: Alfred A. Knopf.

U.S. Fish and Wildlife Service. 1987. Migratory nongame birds of management concern in the United States: the 1987 list. Laurel, Maryland: Office of Migratory Bird Management.

Van Orman, J. B. 1976. Avian succession on Lake Michigan sand dunes. M.S. Thesis, Western Michigan University.

Van't Hof, T. J., G. P. Waldbauer, and H. M. Van't Hof. 1983. Summer records of Northern Three-toed Woodpecker and Gray-cheeked Thrush in northern Michigan. Jack-Pine Warbler 61:82.

Van Tyne, J. 1938. Check list of the birds of Michigan. Ann Arbor: University of Michigan Museum of Zoology Occasional Paper No. 379.

Veit, R. R., and L. Jonsson. 1984. Field identification of smaller sandpipers within the genus *Calidris*. American Birds 38:853–876.

Waite, T. A. 1988. A field-test of density-dependent survival of simulated Gray Jay caches. Condor 90:247–249.

Walkinshaw, L. H. 1935. Studies of the Short-billed Marsh Wren (*Cistothorus stellaris*) in Michigan. Auk 52:361–368.

Walkinshaw, L. H. 1937. LeConte's Sparrow breeding in Michigan and South Dakota. Auk 54:309–320.

Walkinshaw, L. H. 1937. The Virginia Rail in Michigan. Auk 54:464–475.

Walkinshaw, L. H. 1939. Additional information on the Prothonotary Warbler. Jack-Pine Warbler 17:64–71.

Walkinshaw, L. H. 1939. The Yellow Rail in Michigan. Auk 56:227–237.

Walkinshaw, L. H. 1940. Summer life of the Sora Rail. Auk 57:153–168.

Walkinshaw, L. H. 1941. The Prothonotary Warbler, a comparison of nesting conditions in Tennessee and Michigan. Wilson Bulletin 53:3–21.

Walkinshaw, L. H. 1944. The Eastern Chipping Sparrow in Michigan. Wilson Bulletin 56:50–59.

Walkinshaw, L. H. 1949. Birds along the Tahquamenon. Jack-Pine Warbler 27:91–98.

Walkinshaw, L. H. 1949. The Sandhill Cranes. Bloomfield Hills, Michigan: Cranbrook Institute of Science Bulletin No. 29.

Walkinshaw, L. H. 1949. Twenty-five eggs apparently laid by a cowbird. Wilson Bulletin 61:82–85.

Walkinshaw, L. H. 1952. Observations on the Pine Warbler in Michigan. Jack-Pine Warbler 30:94–99.

Walkinshaw, L. H. 1953. Life history of the Prothonotary Warbler. Wilson Bulletin 65:152–168.

Walkinshaw, L. H. 1955. Nesting of the Olive-sided Flycatcher in Schoolcraft County, Michigan. Jack-Pine Warbler 33:134–136.

Walkinshaw, L. H. 1957. Tennessee Warbler nesting in Michigan. Jack-Pine Warbler 35:97–98.

Walkinshaw, L. H. 1959. The Prairie Warbler in Michigan. Jack-Pine Warbler 37:54–63.

Walkinshaw, L. H. 1961. The effect of parasitism by the Brown-headed Cowbird on *Empidonax* flycatchers in Michigan. Auk 78:266–268.

Walkinshaw, L. H. 1966. Studies of the Acadian Flycatcher in Michigan. Bird-Banding 37:227–257.

Walkinshaw, L. H. 1966. Summer biology of Traill's Flycatcher. Wilson Bulletin 78:31–46.

Walkinshaw, L. H. 1966. Summer observations of the Least Flycatcher in Michigan. Jack-Pine Warbler 44:150–168.

Walkinshaw, L. H. 1967. The Yellow-bellied Flycatcher in Michigan. Jack-Pine Warbler 45:2–9.

Walkinshaw, L. H. 1968. Observations of summering and migrating wood warblers in Muskegon County. Jack-Pine Warbler 46:42–56.

Walkinshaw, L. H. 1973. Cranes of the world. New York: Winchester Press.

Walkinshaw, L. H. 1978. Birds of the Battle Creek, Calhoun, Michigan area. Ann Arbor, Michigan: University Microfilms International.

Walkinshaw, L. H. 1978. Life history of the Eastern Field Sparrow in Calhoun County, Michigan. Ann Arbor, Michigan: University Microfilms International.

Walkinshaw, L. H. 1983. Kirtland's Warbler: the natural history of an endangered species. Bloomfield Hills, Michigan: Cranbrook Institute of Science Bulletin No. 58.

Walkinshaw, L. H. 1983. The Lincoln's Sparrow in Michigan. Jack-Pine Warbler 61:75–81.

Walkinshaw, L. H. 1984. Changes in winter bird life in Michigan: sixty years of Christmas bird counts in the Battle Creek, Michigan, area. Jack-Pine Warbler 62:63–69.

Walkinshaw, L. H., and W. A. Dyer. 1953. Nesting of the Black-throated Blue Warbler in Michigan. Jack-Pine Warbler 31:2–9.

Walkinshaw, L. H., and W. A. Dyer. 1954. Brown-capped Chickadee nesting in Michigan. Jack-Pine Warbler 32:106–109.

Walkinshaw, L. H., and W. A. Dyer. 1961. The Connecticut Warbler in Michigan. Auk 78:379–388.

Walkinshaw, L. H., and C. J. Henry. 1957. Yellow-bellied Flycatcher nesting in Michigan. Auk 74:293–304.

Walkinshaw, L. H., and C. J. Henry. 1957. Incubation and nestling periods in the Olive-sided Flycatcher. Auk 74:389–390.

Walkinshaw, L. H., and R. H. Hoffman. 1974. Southern Michigan Sandhill Crane survey, 1971–1973. Jack-Pine Warbler 52:102–114.

Walkinshaw, L. H., and M. A. Wolf. 1957. Distribution of the Palm Warbler and its status in Michigan. Wilson Bulletin 69:338–351.

Wallace, G. J. 1948. The Barn Owl in Michigan: its distribution, natural history, and food habits. East Lansing: Michigan State College Agricultural Experiment Station Bulletin No. 208.

Wallace, G. J. 1959. The plight of the Bluebird in Michigan. Wilson Bulletin 71:192–193.

Wallace, G. J. 1969. Endangered and declining species of Michigan birds. Jack-Pine Warbler 47:70–75.

Wallace, G. J., W. P. Nickell, and R. F. Bernard. 1961. Bird mortality in the Dutch elm disease control program. Bloomfield Hills, Michigan: Cranbrook Institute of Science Bulletin No. 41.

Weir, A. S. 1981. Wheatear sighting at St. Ignace, Mackinac County. Jack-Pine Warbler 59:66.

Whitcomb, B. L., R. F. Whitcomb, and D. Bystrak. 1977. Island biogeography and "habitat islands" of eastern forests. III. Long-term turnover and effects of selective logging on the avifauna of forest fragments. American Birds 31:17–23.

Whitcomb, R. F., C. S. Robbins, J. F. Lynch, B. L. Whitcomb, M. K. Klimkiewicz, and D. Bystrak. 1981. Effects of forest fragmentation on avifauna of the eastern deciduous forests. Pp. 125–205 *in* Ecological studies 41: forest island dynamics in man-dominated landscapes (R. L. Burgess and D. M. Sharpe, Eds.). New York: Springer-Verlag.

Wilcove, D. S. 1985. Nest predation in forest tracts and the decline of migratory songbirds. Ecology 66:1211–1214.

Wilds, C. 1993. The identification and aging of Forster's and Common Terns. Birding 25:94–108.

Wilds, C., and M. Newlon. 1983. The identification of dowitchers. Birding 15:151–166.

Wolinski, R. A. 1973. Review of the nesting status of the Ruddy Duck (*Oxyura jamaicensis*) in Michigan. Jack-Pine Warbler 41:141–142.

Wolinski, R. A. 1988. Some bird population changes in Michigan: 1900–1965. Jack-Pine Warbler 66:55–69.

Wolinski, R. A. 1988. Status of the Yellow-crowned Night-Heron in Michigan. Jack-Pine Warbler 66:117–119.

Wood, N. A. 1904. Discovery of the breeding area of the Kirtland's Warbler. Bulletin of the Michigan Ornithological Club 5:3–13.

Wood, N. A. 1911. The results of the Mershon Expedition to the Charity Islands, Lake Huron. Wilson Bulletin 23:78–112.

Wood, N. A. 1912. The breeding birds of the Charity Islands with additional notes on the migrants. Report of the Michigan Academy of Science 14:178–188.

Wood, N. A. 1951. The birds of Michigan. Ann Arbor: University of Michigan Museum of Zoology Miscellaneous Publication No. 75.

Wood, N. A., and A. D. Tinker. 1934. Fifty years of bird migration in the Ann Arbor region of Michigan. Ann Arbor: University of Michigan Museum of Zoology Occasional Paper No. 280.

Wykoff, J. N. 1979. First record of Golden-crowned Sparrow in Michigan. Jack-Pine Warbler 57:109.

Yosef, R., and B. Pinshow. 1989. Cache size in shrikes influences female mate choice and reproductive success. Auk 106:418–421.

Zimmer, K. J. 1990. The Thayer's Gull complex. Pp. 114–130 *in* Kaufman, K., A field guide to advanced birding. Boston: Houghton Mifflin Co.

Zimmer, K. J. 1991. Plumage variation in "Kumlien's" Iceland Gull. Birding 23:254–269.

Zimmerman, D. A. 1956. Cape May Warbler summering in lower Michigan. Wilson Bulletin 68:245–246.

Zimmerman, D. A. 1959. Recent changes in the Michigan avifauna as reflected by the new state check-list. Jack-Pine Warbler 37:120–126.

Zimmerman, D. A., and J. Van Tyne. 1959. A distributional check-list of the birds of Michigan. Ann Arbor: University of Michigan Museum of Zoology Occasional Paper No. 608.

Zink, R. M., and B. A. Fall. 1981. Breeding distribution, song, and habitat of the Alder Flycatcher and Willow Flycatcher in Minnesota. Loon 53:208–214.

# LIST OF SPONSORS

## FIRST OF AMERICA.

*The publisher and authors gratefully acknowledge the significant financial contributions to this project from the First of America Bank Corporation. Publication of this lovely book would not have been possible without First of America's indispensable support.*

*In addition, the following individuals and organizations helped to sponsor the book by purchasing original paintings or limited-edition prints.*

**LEAST BITTERN**
Mr. and Mrs. Dean R. Kelly, Original
Mr. and Mrs. Charles W. Allen, Print

**RUBY-THROATED HUMMINGBIRD**
Ludlow Travel Service/Carlson Travel Network, Original
Rosenele Zack, Wild Birds Unlimited, Print

**PURPLE MARTIN AND TREE SWALLOW**
David and Mary Anne Marvin, Original
Paul J. and Marie V. Callog, in honor of Jason Biddigs, Print

**GOLDEN-CROWNED KINGLET AND RUBY-CROWNED KINGLET**
Susan E. Hoover and Willard L. Sakeriska, Original
Wightman and Associates, Print

**BLUE-GRAY GNATCATCHER, CEDAR WAXWING, TUFTED TITMOUSE**
Alice Schinkel, Original
John and Lucy Vanden Heede, in memory of Elmer Lepel, Print

**YELLOW WARBLER AND PROTHONOTARY WARBLER**
Ann M. Biek, Original
Susan Rohdy, Print

**BLACK-THROATED GREEN WARBLER AND BLACKBURNIAN WARBLER**
Iola L. Dunsmore, Original
Robert, Terri, Katie, and Robert K. Doepker, Print

**KIRTLAND'S WARBLER**
Grace B. Loewe, in honor of Berrien Audubon Society, Berrien County, Michigan, Original
Lou Ann and Ralph Stahlberg, Print

**AMERICAN REDSTART AND BLACK-AND-WHITE WARBLER**
Dorothy Kohtala, in memory of Ray Kohtala, Original
Paul J. and Marie V. Callog, in memory of Frank and Stella Krejci, Print

**CONNECTICUT WARBLER AND MOURNING WARBLER**
Elizabeth Owen Case, Original

Paul J. and Marie V. Callog, in honor of Christopher Biddigs, Print

INDIGO BUNTING
Paul and Lucy Bridgham, Original
Christopher and Joanne Carlin, in memory of Myrtle E. McNally, Print

NORTHERN CARDINAL
Michael Godfrey, Original
Janet and Bob Helman, Print

DICKCISSEL AND HENSLOW'S SPARROW
Richard Schinkel, in honor of Jennifer Schinkel, Original
Mr. and Mrs. David Shannon, Print

CHIPPING SPARROW, CLAY-COLORED SPARROW, RUFOUS-SIDED TOWHEE
James and Frances Kochensparger, Original
Dona and Wilbur Wolske, Print

SAVANNAH SPARROW AND GRASSHOPPER SPARROW
Dr. Norman R. Wilhelmsen, Original
Jean and Chuck Wallin, Print

LECONTE'S SPARROW, LINCOLN'S SPARROW, SWAMP SPARROW
Emily Joy Craig, Original

DARK-EYED JUNCO AND WHITE-THROATED SPARROW
Phyllis Barents, Original
Glenna and Joe Collins, Print

PURPLE FINCH AND HOUSE FINCH
Mary and Edwin Meader, Original
Wild Birds Unlimited Nature Shop, Kalamazoo-Portage, Michigan, Print

RED CROSSBILL AND WHITE-WINGED CROSSBILL
Thomas Hardy, Original
Paul J. and Marie V. Callog, in memory of Frank and Stella Krejci, Print

GREEN HERON AND AMERICAN BITTERN
Terry and Liz Allen, Original

GREAT BLUE HERON
Jon and Kathleen Stryker, Original
Don and Marilyn Henkel, Print

MUTE SWAN AND CANADA GOOSE
Joseph and Judith Bilodeau, Original
Mr. and Mrs. Paul A. Taglia, Print

MALLARD AND AMERICAN BLACK DUCK
Aimee and Ted Chester, Original
William H. Bright and Mary E. Kurz Bright, Print

CANVASBACK AND REDHEAD
Consumers Power Company, Original
William H. Bright and Mary E. Kurz Bright, Print

RING-NECKED DUCK AND RUDDY DUCK
Loretta A. Gold, Original
William H. Bright and Mary E. Kurz Bright, Print

BROAD-WINGED HAWK AND NORTHERN GOSHAWK
Whirlpool Corporation Training and Education Center, Original
Elizabeth S. Fernandez, Print

RED-SHOULDERED HAWK
Robert K. and Dolores Sykora, Original
Lawrence H. Merritt, Print

RED-TAILED HAWK AND AMERICAN KESTREL
Kaye and William Centers, Original
Jon D. Hamelink, Print

RING-NECKED PHEASANT AND NORTHERN BOBWHITE
Joanne Muldoon, Original
Dennis and Barbara Shouse, in memory of Mark Strand, Print

EASTERN SCREECH-OWL AND GREAT HORNED OWL
Milt and Linda Stibal, Original
Teresa A. Peterson, Print

BARRED OWL AND NORTHERN SAW-WHET OWL
Jim, Julie, Chris, Catey, and Liz Bradford, Original
Jan Osborn, Print

LONG-EARED OWL
Anonymous, in honor of Steve Allen and Andrea Trautman, Print

DOUBLE-CRESTED CORMORANT
Eugene E. Kenaga, in memory of Mark A. Wolf and Nicholas L. Cuthbert, Print

GREAT EGRET AND CATTLE EGRET
Mr. and Mrs. Forest Durham, Print

WOOD DUCK
First of America Bank Corporation, Original
Robert D. Brown, Print

GREEN-WINGED TEAL AND BLUE-WINGED TEAL
Paul T. Mountjoy and Ingeborg B. Markus, Original
Bill and Jane Marohn, Print

NORTHERN PINTAIL AND NORTHERN SHOVELER
In memory of Leland F. Wagener, Senior Partner, Easton LTD. Gallery, Maumee, Ohio, by Mary Lou, David, and Deborah Wagener, Original
William H. Bright and Mary E. Kurz Bright, Print

GADWALL AND AMERICAN WIGEON
Dedicated to Heiner and Diane Hertling, FRIENDS FOREVER
David and Debbie Wagener, Monclova, Ohio, Original
Allan Puplis Family, in memory of Joseph P. Puplis Jr., Print

RED-BREASTED MERGANSER AND COMMON GOLDENEYE
Preston S. and Barbara J. Parish, Original
William H. Bright and Mary E. Kurz Bright, Print

HOODED MERGANSER AND COMMON MERGANSER
Mr. and Mrs. Jim Northrup, Original
Jean and Chuck Wallin, Okemos, Michigan, Print

TURKEY VULTURE AND NORTHERN HARRIER
> Whirlpool Corporation Training and Education Center, Original

TRUMPETER SWAN
> W. K. Kellogg Bird Sanctuary, Kellogg Biological Station; commemorating the swan's restoration to Michigan, Original
>
> Ray and Pat Adams, in memory of Marion Minckler and Robert Adams, Print

OSPREY
> Kaye and William Centers, Original
> Mr. and Mrs. Jim Northrup, Print

BALD EAGLE
> First of America Bank Corporation, Original
> D. Wayne and Phyllis Root, Print

SHARP-SHINNED HAWK AND COOPER'S HAWK
> Thomas E. and Carolyn Owen, Original
> Emma Bickham Pitcher, in memory of Martin and Edith Bickham, Print

MERLIN
> Sarah and Martha Todd, Original
> Toni and Wally Larson, Print

PEREGRINE FALCON
> Sarah and Martha Todd, Original
> Lawrence H. Merritt, Print

SPRUCE GROUSE AND RUFFED GROUSE
> R. C. Merson, Original
> Joseph Floyd Barnes, Print

SHARP-TAILED GROUSE AND UPLAND SANDPIPER
> Christian J. and Claire K. Martin, Print

WILD TURKEY
> Joseph L. Maggini, Original
> Jean and Chuck Wallin, Print

COMMON SNIPE AND AMERICAN WOODCOCK
> R. C. Merson, Print

GREAT GRAY OWL
> Richard Schinkel, in honor of Cara Schinkel, Original

NORTHERN FLICKER AND PILEATED WOODPECKER
> Noble, Jane, and Mary Lewallen, Original
> Mr. and Mrs. S. Eugene Hubbard, Print

AMERICAN CROW, COMMON RAVEN, BLUE JAY
> Glen and Gail Smith, Original

GRAY CATBIRD, NORTHERN MOCKINGBIRD, BROWN THRASHER
> Joseph Floyd Barnes, Original
> Mr. and Mrs. Jim Northrup, Print

COMMON LOON
> Jon and Kathleen Stryker, Original
> Sarah and William Reding, Print

VIRGINIA RAIL AND SORA RAIL
> Ed and Linda Ketterer, Original
> Fred and Mary Siegwart, Print

PIPING PLOVER
> James and Carolyn Henning, Original

KILLDEER AND SPOTTED SANDPIPER
> In memory of Foster Mohrhardt, Original
> George and Kathleen Borden, Print

BARN OWL
> David and Stephanie Merling, Original
> Raymond Keith in honor of Richard and Brenda Keith, Print

RED-HEADED WOODPECKER AND RED-BELLIED WOODPECKER
> Chet and Thelma Krause, in memory of Ed and Edna Toney, Original
> Mr. and Mrs. Jim Northrup, Print

HORNED LARK, CLIFF SWALLOW, BARN SWALLOW
> In memory of Otto and Olympia Stegeman, Original
> Mr. and Mrs. Jim Northrup, Print

GRAY JAY, BOREAL CHICKADEE, WINTER WREN
> John and Liz Simpson, Original

BLACK-CAPPED CHICKADEE
> Phyllis J. Barents, Original
> Dr. and Mrs. D. E. Drucker, Print

RED-BREASTED NUTHATCH, WHITE-BREASTED NUTHATCH, BROWN CREEPER
> Nancy and Gene Heth, Original
> Deborah Ralston Sparbel and Gary Sparbel, Print

CAROLINA WREN AND HOUSE WREN
> Paul L. and Phyllis D. Griffeth, Print

NASHVILLE WARBLER AND NORTHERN PARULA
> Phyllis J. Barents, Original
> David G. Dvorak, M. D., Print

BLACK-THROATED BLUE WARBLER AND YELLOW-RUMPED WARBLER
> Deborah Ralston Sparbel and Gary Sparbel, Print

KENTUCKY WARBLER, WORM-EATING WARBLER, AND HOODED WARBLER
> Stephen D. Minard, Original
> Betsy and Don Whitehead, Print

COMMON YELLOWTHROAT, YELLOW-BREASTED CHAT
> Chuck and Kathy Nelson, Original
> Roberta Woodruff, in honor of Sarett Nature Center, Print

ROSE-BREASTED GROSBEAK AND SCARLET TANAGER
> Mr. and Mrs. Leonard J. Smit, Original
> Sharon and Lonnie Kuntzman, Print

FIELD SPARROW, VESPER SPARROW, SONG SPARROW
> Jennifer Evelyn Craig, Original

PINE SISKIN, EVENING GROSBEAK
  Bill Sisson, Original

ORCHARD ORIOLE, NORTHERN ORIOLE
  In memory of Foster Mohrhardt, Original
  Mary Greiner, Print

BLACK-BILLED CUCKOO AND YELLOW-BILLED CUCKOO
  Sarett Nature Center in honor of Rob Venner, Original

YELLOW-BELLIED SAPSUCKER AND BLACK-BACKED WOOD-PECKER
  In memory of Chester B. and Enid R. Campbell, Original
  Marge Johns, Print

DOWNY WOODPECKER AND HAIRY WOODPECKER
  Mr. and Mrs. S. Eugene Hubbard, Original
  Gail and Mark McPeek, Print

ACADIAN FLYCATCHER, WILLOW FLYCATCHER, LEAST FLY-CATCHER, EASTERN WOOD-PEWEE
  Mr. and Mrs. Jim Northrup, Print

EASTERN PHOEBE AND GREAT-CRESTED FLYCATCHER
  John and Liz Simpson, Original

NORTHERN ROUGH-WINGED SWALLOW, BANK SWALLOW, BELTED KINGFISHER
  Sarett Nature Center in honor of Ed Lewis, Original
  Maureen Lannon and Steve Leuty, in memory of Redus Leuty, Print

EASTERN BLUEBIRD
  Marian and Carl Haussman, Original
  Lisa and Owen Daly in memory of Elisabeth F. Hudnutt, Print

VEERY, SWAINSON'S THRUSH, HERMIT THRUSH
  Sarett Nature Center in honor of Richard and Patricia Schinkel, Original

Peggy and Fred McAllister, in memory of Edna Clauer, Print

WHITE-EYED VIREO, SOLITARY VIREO, YELLOW-THROATED VIREO
  James R. Hewitt, Print

WARBLING VIREO, PHILADELPHIA VIREO, RED-EYED VIREO
  Richard and Brenda Keith, Print

AMERICAN ROBIN
  Anonymous, Original

MAGNOLIA WARBLER, CAPE MAY WARBLER, CHESTNUT-SIDED WARBLER
  Roger and Molly Williams, Original
  Cecil C. Kersting, Print

OVENBIRD, NORTHERN WATERTHRUSH, LOUISIANA WATERTHRUSH
  Richard Schinkel, in honor of Marna Schinkel, Original

WILSON'S WARBLER, CANADA WARBLER
  Robert M. Kemp, Print

RED-WINGED BLACKBIRD, YELLOW-HEADED BLACKBIRD
  Mr. and Mrs. Jim Northrup, Original
  Dianne Braybrook and Rob Venner, Print

EASTERN MEADOWLARK, WESTERN MEADOWLARK, BOBOLINK
  Marian and Carl Haussman, Original
  Kenneth H. Heathcock, Print

AMERICAN GOLDFINCH
  H. Lewis Batts, Jr., Original
  Robert and Vickie Wagner, Print

LOGGERHEAD SHRIKE
  Richard L. Campbell, in memory of Chester B. and Enid R. Campbell, Original

*Indiana University Press gratefully acknowledges the generous
support of the following individuals and organizations whose
gifts have helped underwrite the manufacturing cost of* The Birds
of Michigan.

*Phyllis J. Barents, Portage*
*Consumers Power Company, Kalamazoo*
*Marian and Carl Haussman, Lansing*

*Bill and Jane Marohn, St. Joseph*
*Mary and Edwin Meader, Parchment*
*Dick Merson, South Haven*

# CONTRIBUTORS

## ARTISTS

CYNDY CALLOG graduated from Adrian College with majors in art and elementary education. Her watercolor paintings can be seen in many state and national shows, and her work has been chosen by several companies for use on their products. Among these are the National Wildlife Federation (cards, calendars), the Bradford Exchange (collector plates), the Pimpernel Company, Sunrise Greeting Cards, and Field Crafts Apparel. She is a recipient of the People's Choice Award and top seller at the Michigan Wildlife Art Festival.

JOHN FELSING, a graduate of Michigan State University, has received many awards for his artwork, including Michigan Wildlife Artist of the Year and the first Owen J. Gromme Grant from the American Museum of Wildlife Art. His paintings have been selected numerous times for the prestigious Leigh Yawkey Woodson Museum "Birds in Art" exhibition, and have been a part of exclusive exhibitions which have traveled the world to such places as Russia, Japan, and China. He has also illustrated two bird books for Dr. Paul Johnsgard.

HEINER HERTLING immigrated to the United States from Hamburg, Germany, in 1965. Trained as a commercial artist, he entered the wildlife art field in 1981 and has since won many competitions and awards. Among these are the Florida Duck Stamp, Kentucky Trout Stamp, and Michigan Trout and Salmon Stamp contests, Michigan Ducks Unlimited Artist of the Year, and the Eagle Artist Award. He has also been the featured artist at the Michigan Wildlife Festival and has had paintings chosen for the Leigh Yawkey Woodson Museum "Birds in Art" exhibition.

DAVID MOHRHARDT earned his degree at Michigan State University and has more than 20 years of art experience. He illustrated two Michigan DNR books, *Coat Pocket Bird Book* and *Kitchen Table Bird Book* (published by Reader's Digest, Time-Life, McGraw-Hill, and National Geographic). He has also worked as an artist-preparer for the Kalamazoo Nature Center and Kellogg Bird Sanctuary. His paintings have won awards in the Michigan Duck and Trout Stamp contests and the Ducks Unlimited contest, and he was selected Waterfowl Artist of the Year by *Michigan Out-of-Doors*.

GIJSBERT VAN FRANKENHUYZEN received his training at the Royal Academy of Arts in Arnhem, Holland. He has had several paintings in the renowned Leigh Yawkey Woodson Museum, and was recently honored as "Artist in Residence" by Isle Royale National Park. Michigan Wildlife Artist of the Year and Award of Merit from the Roger Tory Peterson Institute are just a few of his many awards. He served as art director for the *Michigan Natural Resources Magazine* for 17 years, and currently operates his own gallery and teaching workshops for adults and children.

## AUTHORS

RAYMOND J. ADAMS, a graduate of Kalamazoo College, is an avian biologist and research director at the Kalamazoo Nature Center, where he began working in the mid-1960s under the guidance of H. Lewis Batts, Jr. He feels especially lucky that his vocation and avocation are one and the same. His work has focused on long-term monitoring of birds through such programs as breeding bird surveys, Christmas bird counts, nestbox trails, and bird banding. He is also involved in land conservation. He coordinated and was co-editor of *The Atlas of Breeding Birds of Michigan*.

STEPHEN ALLEN has long been interested in the out-of-doors, especially birds. He received a B.S. in biology from Western Michigan University and has worked as a research biologist and educator at the Kalamazoo Nature Center since 1991. He has also had seasonal positions in research and education at the Whitefish Point Bird Observatory. He has served on the Board of Directors and was vice president of the Michigan Audubon Society, as well as past president of the Audubon Society of Kalamazoo.

PHILIP C. CHU has a Ph.D. in biology from the University of Michigan, where he is currently working as a visiting research investigator in the bird division of the Museum of Zoology. Gull systematics and evolution of plumage coloration are his primary interests. He was a contributor to *The Atlas of Breeding Birds of Michigan* and the *Jack-Pine Warbler*, and is now on the editorial board of the new state journal, *Michigan Birds and Natural History*. He is also the current chairman of the Michigan Bird Records Committee.

**JAMES GRANLUND** is a graduate (B.S.) of Northern Michigan University with majors in chemistry and biology. He has been involved in Michigan ornithology for the past decade. His major activities include serving as compiler for the state seasonal bird survey, the Christmas bird count, and the western Great Lakes region for *American Birds*. He has served on the Board of Directors of both the Michigan Audubon Society and the Whitefish Point Bird Observatory. He was a contributor to *The Atlas of Breeding Birds of Michigan* and is managing editor of *Michigan Birds and Natural History*.

**MICHAEL KIELB** has a graduate degree (M.S.) in biology from Wayne State University, and is a research associate at the University of Michigan. He has been studying birds in Michigan for nearly 20 years, with raptors a primary interest. He co-authored *The Birds of Washtenaw County*, currently serves on the Michigan Audubon Society board, and is editor-in-chief of the new state journal, *Michigan Birds and Natural History*.

**GAIL A. MCPEEK** is a wildlife biologist with degrees from Cook College, Rutgers University (B.S.), and the University of Kentucky (M.S.). She has been involved in bird research and wildlife conservation for 10 years. She worked at the Kalamazoo Nature Center from 1985 to 1991, where she helped coordinate and write *The Atlas of Breeding Birds of Michigan*. Now residing in Vermont, she is a board member of the North American Loon Fund and works as a freelance writer and consultant.

**CHARLES NELSON** has degrees in forestry (B.S.) and wildlife ecology (M.S.) from the University of Wisconsin in Madison. For more than 20 years, he has been the Director/Naturalist of the Sarett Nature Center in Benton Harbor, a wildlife sanctuary and environmental education facility of the Michigan Audubon Society. He teaches graduate courses in environmental education at Western Michigan University and also conducts an annual bird identification class at Sarett Nature Center.

**JACK REINOEHL** is on the faculty of Hillsdale College, where he teaches mathematics and computer science. He has a Ph.D. in mathematics from the University of California at Berkeley. Having a keen interest in birds, he participated in both the Michigan and Indiana breeding bird atlas projects and was a contributor to *The Atlas of Breeding Birds of Michigan*. He is a current member of the Michigan Bird Records Committee and serves on the editorial board of the new state journal, *Michigan Birds and Natural History*.

**RICHARD SCHINKEL** has an Associate Arts degree from Lake Michigan College and Bachelor and Master of Science degrees from Western Michigan University. He was the chief naturalist and development administrator at Sarett Nature Center for many years. He is now president of his own business, the Ol' Sam Peabody Company, a wholesaler of wild bird supplies and merchandise.

**ANDREA TRAUTMAN** became interested in birds after meeting her husband, Stephen Allen, and helping band birds at the Kalamazoo Nature Center. She has a liberal arts degree from Western Michigan University and has been a teacher for more than 20 years. She currently works at Delton-Kellogg High School as an English teacher, with classes in honors and advanced placement composition. She and her husband co-authored several accounts for this book.

# INDEX

Boldface indicates illustration.

# THE BIRDS OF MICHIGAN

*Editor:* Jane Lyle
*Book and Jacket designer:* Matt Williamson
*Production coordinator:* Tarry Curry
*Typeface:* Minion
*Compositor:* Books International
*Printer and Binder:* Tien Wah Press